REPORTING AT
WIT'S END

REPORTING AT WIT'S END

Tales from *The New Yorker*

St. Clair McKelway

Introduction by Adam Gopnik

New York   Berlin   London

Published by Bloomsbury USA, New York

The pieces in this collection were originally published, sometimes in somewhat different form, in *The New Yorker*, and in the books *Gossip: The Life and Times of Walter Winchell*, *True Tales from the Annals of Crime and Rascality*, *The Edinburgh Caper*, and *The Big Little Man from Brooklyn*.

All papers used by Bloomsbury USA are natural, recyclable products made from wood grown in well-managed forests. The manufacturing processes conform to the environmental regulations of the country of origin.

Library of Congress Cataloging-in-Publication Data

McKelway, St. Clair.
    Reporting at wit's end : tales from the New Yorker / St. Clair McKelway; introduction by Adam Gopnik.—1st U.S. ed.
        p. cm.
    ISBN 978-1-60819-034-8 (pbk.)
    I. Gopnik, Adam.   II. New Yorker (New York, N.Y. : 1925)
III. Title.
    PS3525.C54R48 2010
    814'.52—dc22
2009028891

First U.S. Edition 2010

1   3   5   7   9   10   8   6   4   2

Typeset by Westchester Book Group
Printed in the United States of America by Worldcolor Fairfield

CONTENTS

Note on the Text   vii

Introduction by Adam Gopnik   ix

The 1930s

Firebug-Catcher   3

Place and Leave With   27

The Innocent Man at Sing Sing   43

Average Cop   70

Who Is This King of Glory? (*with A. J. Liebling*)   80

The 1940s

Some Fun with the F.B.I.   125

Mister 880   134

The Cigar, the Three Wings, and the Low-Level Attacks   173

The Wily Wilby   197

Gossip Writer   235

The 1950s

The Blowing of the Top of Peter Roger Oboe   255

The Cockatoo   305

A Case of Felony Murder   329

This Is It, Honey   353

The Perils of Pearl and Olga   371

The Rich Recluse of Herald Square   392

The 1960s

The Edinburgh Caper   413

The Big Little Man from Brooklyn   524

NOTE ON THE TEXT

The pieces in this book all appeared originally in *The New Yorker*, and appear here arranged by the decade of their first publication. "The Cigar, the Three Wings, and the Low-Level Attacks" was the third of a four-part series of articles that appeared in the New Yorker in 1945 under the heading "A Reporter with the B-29s." "Gossip Writer," St. Clair McKelway's six-part profile of Walter Winchell (the first part of which appears here), and "The Edinburgh Caper" were later revised and expanded into the books *Gossip: The Life and Times of Walter Winchell* (1940) and *The Edinburgh Caper: A One-Man International Plot* (1962). McKelway also revised and updated many pieces for publication in two collections of his work, *True Tales from the Annals of Crime and Rascality* (1951) and *The Big Little Man from Brooklyn* (1969). *Reporting at Wit's End* preserves, as far as possible, the original spelling, punctuation, and style of all the pieces; those that appeared in the 1951 and 1969 collections reflect McKelway's own revisions. Minor changes were made only where necessary for consistency within pieces and the sake of clarity.

The title *Reporting at Wit's End* derives from the *New Yorker* heading under which "The Blowing of the Top of Peter Roger Oboe" appeared in 1958: "That Was a Reporter at Wit's End."

INTRODUCTION
REDISCOVERED SAINT

ADAM GOPNIK

St. Clair McKelway is a *New Yorker* author of the Golden Age—okay, *one* of the Golden Ages—whose work, out of print for a long time, is now mostly unknown and overlooked (the temporary condition of most good writing, so no big deal there.) He was a standby on the magazine from the mid-thirties to the mid-sixties, with a significant break in the forties when he worked as a public relations officer in the Air Force, rising to the rank of lieutenant colonel, in the Pacific. Through all that time, he was as well known to *New Yorker* subscribers as any of the writers whose names are more familiar now, as well known and as keenly relished by readers as Liebling and Mitchell and White and those few others whose reputations have been rehabilitated, as they liked to say in the old Soviet Union, by the suffrage of readers and the backward looking hopes of publishers.

McKelway could do it all—comment, stories, profiles. He was especially skilled as a rewriter of other people's troubled stuff, a gift that helped save *The New Yorker* career of the great A.J. Liebling. But he was most famous for his pieces about odd crimes and strange criminals: imposters, rascals, embezzlers, con men, counterfeiters, and the like. In those saner days, publishers were willing to put out barely veneered collections of magazine pieces without a pretense of more than minimal thematic unity, and so McKelway's pieces could be found in books as well as in the magazine. That's where I found him first, actually, in an old edition of his 1951 collection *True Tales from the Annals of Crime and Rascality*, which Mark Singer, the master "Talk of the Town" hand of the time, loaned me when I was a young pup reporter beginning to write "Talk," too.

There were so many of these that a "McKelway crime story" was as much a signature item as a Trillin murder piece is now. What made McKelway's pieces so startling, and so much better than, say, Herbert Asbury's romantic crime books, was the solidity of their reporting, their reliance on assembled fact, and the charm of their tone. They are thorough without being dull, and funny without feeling forced; crime reporting drained of melodrama and sensation, those tabloid things replaced with sly irony, wit, a love of detail, and a feeling for the sad realities of human character. McKelway's are fact-based pieces that have, as reviewers like to say, the excitement and surprise of fiction—only not of big fiction, but of exquisitely shaped small fiction, of an O'Hara story. All set in New York, and all bending toward some odd edge of character revelation, they render the outer edges of experience as the normal shape of life.

McKelway wrote about process servers and insurance men and embezzlers and imposters with a clear hard edge that allowed for a curious kind of compassion. Firebugs are dangerous and have to be suppressed, but they are otherwise normal men who just happen to be in love with the look of flaming warehouses. "He was an admirable man except for that one quirk," the embezzler's wife says about McKelway's embezzler, the Wily Wilby, and the reader accepts the judgment. Quirks of the higher and odder kind are McKelway's real subject—with the understanding that a quirk of distinction is simply a quiddity, and life is made up of those.

McKelway's is a New York still largely middle class and lower middle class in make-up, where the cops and process servers and fire inspectors came from essentially the same immigrant pool of Irishmen and Italians and Jews as the small time crooks and insurance defrauders and firebugs. It's the prose reality of Damon Runyon's poetic dream world. McKelway's stories are not exactly "three dimensional"—their cartoonish clarity and stenographic elegance are part of their charm—but they bear the same relationship to Runyon, or to tabloid newspaper reporting, that Peter Arno's cartooning does to a newspaper comic strip. They are deceptively simple, not simply deceptive.

Where the great Joe Mitchell's gift was for urban fable, McKelway's was for the short, significant parable. His stories aren't illustrative of trends or tendencies in modern crime or modern manners. He takes it for granted that there will always be more or less the same number of firebugs and coiners and for that matter crazy generals, and that, apart from their vocational oddities, they will always be in other respects like the rest of us. The typical magazine "trend" piece says, almost always falsely, "More and more people are acting this way!" The classic McKelway piece says, accurately, "Very, very few people act this way, which is what makes the ones who do so interesting." This belief in the thing for its own sake, which was shared by his generation of *New Yorker* craftsmen, creates the equanimity that distinguished their work, and still sets it apart from most other journalism: All of them assumed universals of eccentricity, duplicity, and political corruption, and other universals of good fellowship, comradeship, and ironic appreciation as counter-weights. The reformer's rage was as alien to the style as the reactionary's revulsion.

"Mister 880," which became a (pretty good) movie, is perhaps the best known of all these crime pieces and is a perfect example of the McKelway style. The subject is a counterfeiter of almost absurdly small ambitions and extravagantly crude capacities: He makes fake one dollar bills, and makes them badly, with Washington's name misspelled as "Wahsington." The Secret Service embarks on a twenty-year search for him, and, maddeningly, can't find him because of his smallness, the deliberate inconsequence of his crimes. Along the way, McKelway broods on the loneliness of old men, the history of bad money (and of good), and ends his tale with a beautiful irony, almost too neat to believe.

(Let me add right here, in a paragraph-long parenthesis, that that dollar may, just may, be what Huck Finn calls a stretcher. McKelway, in his lovely confessional story called "The Cockatoo," admits that his first published newspaper article was more or less made up, though harmlessly so, and there are often in McKelway's writing bits of shapely storytelling and sprightly dialogue that belie their factual surface. The truth, politely held in a vault on West Forty-third Street, is that writers of his generation worked with a general understanding that a story could be kneaded into shape as long as the kneading was done gently and with good purpose; the well-wishing tone of their work is due in part to its being gently held in hostage to the good will of the subjects. Character can only be revealed, in the shortish span even of a long magazine piece, by a certain element of caricature; the license of cartoonists to draw a black outline and exaggerate an eyebrow was the license they claimed, with the understanding that it wouldn't be used maliciously—when, in later years by other writers, it began to be, the license was revoked.)

The strongest, and longest of these "rascality" pieces is McKelway's profile of the Harlem holy man (and gentle fraud) called Father Divine. That's the one in which he rescued Liebling's career, with terrific long-term effects for the magazine, and, really, for American literature. Liebling, as he later admitted, had a hard time adapting his wiseguy newspaper feature style, all short punchy paragraphs and local-color jokes, to the pages of the magazine, and in the mid-thirties he seemed likely to leave, or be pushed out. Reporting the Father Divine story practically to death, he ended with what he admitted ruefully was essentially a thesis on comparative religion. (It is, though, typical of what separated Liebling from the pack that he was capable of writing such a thing.) McKelway took it over, recast it as a narrative, and made it into a terrific piece, salvaging Liebling's career at the magazine and giving him a template of how erudition and detail could be sublimated into storytelling-style rather than left dangling in bunches. To be sure, Father Divine looks a lot more plausible as a figure to us now, since we understand what Libeling and McKelway only imply—that if there was a lot of con man in him there was also a lot of dignity and quiet resistance to white rule. And no one who has read contemporary literary criticism will fail to respond to Father Divine's language, so much like it, and which shows how far pure word power can take a man: "God is not only personified and materialized. He is *re*personified and *re*materialized. He *re*materializes and *re*material*ates*. He *re*material*ates* and He is *re*material*izable*. He *re*personificates and He *re*personifi*tizes*."

M c K E L W A Y ' S C H O I C E O F subjects and heroes, whether Mr. Eight-Eighty or Father Divine, was always just right. But, as with all writers worth reading, what matters is the quality of his line, the standard of his sentences. His prose style is a beautiful instance of the Old *New Yorker* faux naïf: sly and sober-faced, with a lot more reading and intelligence just beneath the surface than the writer feels is quite mannerly or classy to let on. The gently ironic edging unto the disbelieving sardonic, a strong edge of mockery made generous-seeming by the curiosity and complicity of the mocker—we are all just this quirky, the prose says, and yet only some of our quirks are allowed. Condescension and a too easily amused tone is the risk; wry wisdom and a sense of classical proportion, the reward. This passage, again from "Mister 880," is typical in its details and delights:

> Counterfeiting is a prehistoric form of gainful skullduggery. The idea of money was conceived somewhere on the other side of antiquity, and so was the idea of counterfeit money.

The idea of money is older than the idea of counterfeit money, but older, perhaps, by no more than a few minutes. There is evidence of the use of both the genuine article and the counterfeit article in the earliest recorded civilizations, and it has been established that primitive tribes had both good money and bad money before there were any civilizations to record. It seems that immediately after certain people realized that they could easily make tokens to represent cumbersome property, such as collections of animal skins and stores of food-stuffs, certain other people awoke to the fact that they could just as easily make tokens to represent the tokens that repre-sented the cumbersome property. The two ideas are so closely related that they are practically twins, and, like the products of the ideas, they are hard to tell apart. If it were not for counter-feit money, the story of money might be simply beautiful. As it is, the pattern formed by the fateful entwinement of money and counterfeit money is intricately grotesque.

This lovely intertwining—or fateful entwinement, as he would have written—of research and plain relation, is, in its carefully gauged mock-simplicity, the classic *New Yorker* sound at its best. It's all said as lucidly as can be, but the fun lies in the choice to turn an encyclopedia entry into an entertainment: Let's take something that everyone makes solemn, or lurid, and treat it lightly. This is a simple idea—a *modest* idea—of prose, but it's a potent one. It infu-riated some people then, and it still infuriates some people now, who feel threatened by a craft they experience as condescension and by a surface of delight they imagine as highhanded and insuf-ficiently crabby, inadequately malicious. But its satisfactions are real, too. In a sentence such as that one on counterfeiting a lot of reading, economic theory, and anthropological history has been neatly compressed for the reader's benefit not just into the simplest possible language, but into the most pregnant possible language.

INTRODUCTION

You couldn't possibly say it more neatly than *that*: An alarming anthropological complexity has been reduced to a sequence of aphorisms. Or take this description of the dubious dance of bonding your employee-boss relations, from "The Wily Wilby":

> When the first news stories appeared in the New York papers about Ralph Marshall Wilby's embezzlement of $386,921.29 from the Knott Company, he was described as a "trusted employee" over and over again. All the stories made a point of rubbing that in. In Wilby's case, as in the cases of most embezzlers in these times, the cliché was inaccurate and its use indicates an old-fashioned and romantic idea of the relationship between bookkeepers and the people who employ them. The ugly truth is that the higher a bookkeeper climbs in the accounting department of a firm, the lower the estimate of his trustworthiness becomes in the minds and hearts of his employers . . . One of Wilby's best friends at the Knott corporation, and seemingly one of his greatest admirers, was the company's treasurer, Mr. Casey. It was Casey who had encouraged and aided Wilby's progress from the position of traveling auditor to that of chief accountant and assistant treasurer. Yet this same Mr. Casey, acting for the corporation in what a romanticist would have to consider an abominably gelid manner, had bet the Travelers Insurance Company (which insures all kinds of people besides travelers) that Wilby would someday steal of the corporation's funds. The Travelers Insurance Company had bet that Wilby wouldn't. This wager was represented by a bond of three hundred thousand dollars, the terms of which were that the Knott corporation would pay the Travelers Insurance Company an annual premium of a good many thousands of dollars as long as its chief accountant and assistant treasurer didn't steal any money from the corporation.

In a passage like that, classic McKelway, a lot of information has to be conveyed, in detail, and at the same time something has to happen somewhere in the sentence to assure the reader that the crate hasn't just been packed tight for the sake of packing. The minutiae are there, down to the last twenty-nine cents. But the thing explodes with McKelway's cynical-cunning explanation of the real meaning of bonds for employees, and nothing could be wittier than his explanation of that practice of bonding as a series of bets placed by the corporation against its employees, and by the insurance company on them. "The Travelers Insurance Company had bet that Wilby wouldn't" is the comic payoff to all the patient, coaxing explanation that has come before. Classic *New Yorker* style is a method of turning argument into ornament, and reporting into wit. (Bad *New Yorker* style, involved just that kind of dutiful packing, which had the look of good writing without actually being any good, made by writers who had learned the sober assembly of the body parts but forgot the twist in the tail.) It strives for the simplicity of the man in a worn monogrammed shirt and a pair of old plaid shorts on the beach on Fire Island, not the simplicity of a guy who has moved to Vermont and put on overalls. (And when E.B. White did move to Maine and put on overalls, his style became folksier and less brittle-lucid.) McKelway's personal history is more vexed than his style. In an extended try at self-revelation, in the confessional story "The Cockatoo," McKelway gives us a picture of his early years, as the restless son of an upper-middle-class household in Washington D.C. with a father who died too soon, leaving his son permanently unhappy with school and dreaming of a life as a newspaperman, a romantic occupation in those days. Later, we learn a lot about his life in the army, working for the "mad bomber," General Curtis Lemay, still an admired figure in those days when his attention was on beating Japan rather than on ending the world. (McKelway's complacency at Lemay's plan to drop jellied gasoline on hundreds of thousands of Japanese civilians, though entirely of its time, may make us more than uneasy now.)

Yet deeper inlets of unhappiness run below the jaunty surface. Married five times—make up your own joke—and often, it's related, sparring with mental disturbances, McKelway had such a happy style that it is easy to miss the current of misery that runs just beneath it. His work floats on a sea of liquor. The hard edges of heavy drinking in those years were so nicely upholstered that the reality—of men and women in the grip of an addiction as soul- and life-destroying as meth addiction is now—tends to float away from our consciousness, as it was designed to do. Realizing how much hard and disastrous drinking is going on in some of McKelway's writing is as startling as it might be to have discovered our actual fathers at five o'clock with rubber tourniquets around their arms, cheerfully injecting heroin into their veins.

The charming "The Edinburgh Caper," for instance, is on the surface a kind of Cary Grant-Hitchcock thriller with a shaggy-dog story structure. Yet the whole point of the beautifully rendered intrigue is its ultimate inconsequence: The "caper" turns out to exist only in the tipsy mind of McKelway. But beneath that is the realization that one is also dealing—as one scotch after another goes down the drain and one charming warm Scottish bar after another is visited—with a drunk at the inner edge of paranoia. (One of the things about writing alcoholics is that they convince themselves that social drinking is all they're doing until they suddenly find themselves all alone and raving, wondering what happened to the pals.)

The competition in self-destruction between McKelway and one of those wives, the beautiful and doomed writer Maeve Brennan, who wed him in the mid-fifties, are still part of the magazine's saddest legend. Brennan, whose "Long-Winded Lady" pieces for the "Comment" section of the magazine remain a model of plaintive urban haiku, has had a revival lately, and gotten a biography. Her descent from a Holly Golightly high-heartedness into madness and isolation is one of the more heartbreaking of literary stories. Yet there is no better picture of New York life during the mid century than her work and McKelway's superimposed: Brennan's poignant, lyrical, and a little pixilated, all midtown Italian restaurants and pigeons taking flight at twilight; McKelway's comic and low-life obsessed, all penny arcades and Times Square kids.

Drinking this way is the Celtic Curse, of course, and when McKelway's Scots drinking met Brennan's Irish kind, some records were set which people still talk about; records only for sadness, of course, since hard drinking ends no other way. (John Updike, a few months before his death, remarked to a friend that the industry and accomplishment that set his work, and that of his great Tweedledee, Phillip Roth, apart was simply the consequence of not drinking, and not even having to take the time to dry out.) Yet McKelway manages to use even his drinking to good effect, making us sense in "The Edinburgh Caper" that the line between paranoid fantasy and intelligent work is so fine as to be nonexistent even in the minds of those engaged in it. (James "Jesus" Angleton would have been a perfect McKelway subject.) You also have to envy McKelway the license he enjoyed. No one now would publish "The Edinburgh Caper"; where all the fun (and in a way the deeper point) is that *nothing actually happens.* The joy is in the space between the expertly paced narration, potentially sinister and significant, and the balloon-popping deflations that wait around every period and paragraph break.

In a queer way, "major" figures, even minor major figures, like Liebling and Mitchell and White and Thurber, are hard writers to use as models, because what they do depends so entirely on who they are and what they've been through that you have to become them to write like them. To write a Liebling sentence, with its baroque braiding of high literature and low life, Parisian suave and race-track savvy, you have to have lived a bit like Liebling, and have a mind like his. But McKelway, like his other unduly forgotten

New Yorker contemporary, Wolcott Gibbs, offers a real model for all writers, as he supplies pleasure to all readers, because what works in his stuff is all there in his stuff. Though his style can't be reduced to rules, it can be summed up as recommendations: find weird data, funny facts, and align them nicely; listen to strange people and give them space to talk; keep a cartoonist's license but not a caricaturist's smugness; rely on the force of simple words, but don't be afraid of big ideas, or of the stuff of history, if you can make it sound like learning casually attained. Above all, keep your voice hovering just above your material, neither below it "subversively" nor alongside it chummily, but above it, a few light and happy inches over the page. If McKelway's love of quirks and mastery of the light style still sound to some like a recipe for what is called whimsy—well, as Nabokov said emphatically to Edmund Wilson, *all* good writing is whimsical in the end, and the best is never lost for long.

The 1930s

FIREBUG-CATCHER

ONE NIGHT IN August, 1912, when Thomas Patrick Brophy was the Fire Marshal of Brooklyn, four men were getting ready to build a fire in a stable far out on Johnson Avenue, in one of the more desolate sections of the borough. That day the men had removed from the stable seven sound horses, which had been insured for two hundred dollars apiece, and had led into the stalls seven old, decrepit horses, all of them lame and one blind, which they had bought at auction sales for three and four dollars apiece. The men laid the fire carefully. They piled straw against the wooden walls of the stable and around and under the horses in the stalls. They poured kerosene oil over the straw and with sponges rubbed kerosene into the coats of the seven horses. There were no houses near the stable, which stood in the middle of a wide meadow, but to be on the safe side the men made another big pile of hay in the doorway so that anybody who might happen along would have to go through flames to get to the horses. They poured kerosene over that, and then they got out their matches. But this arson plot didn't succeed, because Brophy had found out about it in advance. He was hiding in the tall grass outside the stable, with seven assistant fire marshals, four firemen carrying fire extinguishers, and a couple of police detectives. Two blocks away, Engine Company No. 237 waited in an alley ready to rush to the stable. As soon as the first flicker of flame could be seen, Brophy fired his revolver twice into the air, which was the signal for the engine company to come on, and with his men closed in on the stable. The fire was put out, the horses were saved, and the four men went to Sing Sing.

Brophy was able to be there, hiding in the meadow, because of nothing more complicated than his habit of going for long walks by himself, talking to people, trying to keep track of everything that was going on in Brooklyn. He had known that about a third of the stable fires in the city that year had been of undetermined origin, which is the fireman's way of saying that they may have been incendiary. So on his customary walks, on which he systematically covered the whole borough of Brooklyn, he had been making the acquaintance, among hundreds of other people, of horse auctioneers. He knew that among the myriad forms of fire-insurance fraud was the system of burning up worthless horses which had been substituted for valuable ones, adequately insured. Worrying about this, he went about asking auctioneers for the names of men who were buying up worthless horses. He got the names of dozens of people who bought that kind of horse, and his deputies investigated them all. Some of them were representatives of firms that shipped horses to France to be eaten by the French, or were otherwise in legitimate, if curious, trades. But after many such horse-buyers had been investigated, one was found who seemed to have no legitimate business. Yet he owned seven sound horses, which he kept idle in a stable out on Johnson Avenue. His name was Louis Evansky and he was clearly not a racing man or a polo player. The rest was a comparatively simple matter of watching the stable and shadowing Evansky.

This *coup* of Brophy's received wide publicity at the time, and editorials appeared in most of the papers calling attention to the hideous cruelty of the firebugs who had tried to burn up horses. The notice it attracted probably was an important factor in Brophy's eventual elevation to the post of Chief Fire Marshal and the establishment of the Bureau of Fire Investigation of the New York Fire Department, which he directed until his retirement in 1948. The public interest in that case has always puzzled Brophy, because it seemed a minor one to him, since only horses were involved. He had saved the lives of dozens of people before that by the same general method of painstaking detective work, and the public had shown hardly any interest at all.

In December, 1911, for instance, a citizen of Brooklyn had taken out an insurance policy on his furniture in a flat on Cleveland Street and had hired two professional firebugs to set fire to the place. When the firebugs arrived at the apartment house on the afternoon appointed for the fire, they looked up and down the street to make sure they were not being watched. All they saw were two peddlers with a vegetable wagon down at one end of the block and a couple of street-cleaners sitting on the curb in front of the corner saloon, drinking beer from a growler. They went up to the flat, started the fire, and came down to the street again. Brophy, who had been hiding in the areaway, grabbed them both, and when they resisted knocked them down with two efficient blows of his fist. The street-cleaners at the end of the block fished fire extinguishers out of their wagons and came running. The peddlers produced three hundred feet of hose from the vegetable wagon, connected it at a fireplug, and rushed into the flat with it. The fire was put out before it spread to adjoining flats, in which, among the other tenants, were two invalids and several babies.

Brophy kept on engineering feats of this kind until the day of his retirement. The Plaza Hotel at Rockaway Beach would probably have been burned down in 1932 if Brophy had not been there to intercept the professional firebugs before they lit the fire. Only two or three years ago he caught a professional firebug and put out the fire he had started in a Bronx tenement house in which fifty-four families were sleeping.

Just where Brophy fits into the scheme of civic evolution is a little uncertain. He might be catalogued as a sort of municipal freak, part fireman, part detective. The distinguishing characteristics of both the Police and Fire Departments may be observed in Brophy, which suggests that firemen and policemen do not represent two distinct species, as might be supposed, but must have sprung from some common source. When he was a fire marshal, he had a fire-alarm signal in his home, but wore neither boots nor helmet, and carried a gun. He went to fires in a red automobile, with bell clanging, but never touched hose or ladder, and usually turned his back to the blaze and watched the crowd.

The New York Bureau of Fire Investigation itself is an anomaly, originally built around Brophy. When Brophy took a civil-service examination and entered the Fire Department in 1907 as a young assistant fire marshal in Brooklyn, arson was a crime that usually fell halfway between the Police and Fire Departments, and lay there indefinitely, unsolved. The function of fire marshals was to inspect all fires and to find out which ones were incendiary. They traveled about on streetcar or afoot, and usually did not get around to the scene of a fire until hours after it had been put out. If a dwelling or a store appeared to have been saturated with kerosene and eye-witnesses had seen a man run from the place before the fire broke out, the chances were that the fire marshal would report that the fire was "suspicious," but the task of catching the firebugs was usually left to the Police Department. After the Fire Department had thus dropped a case, and before the Police Department had picked it up, a good deal of time and enthusiasm was lost, and incendiarists, as a result, were seldom caught.

Brophy had been a district reporter on Bennett's *Herald* before he became an assistant deputy fire marshal, and the idea of going to a fire after it was out seemed to him too ridiculous to be considered. There was no provision in the Fire Department budget for the rapid transportation of fire marshals, so Brophy bought a motorcycle with his own money. He used to rush to fires as soon as an alarm was turned in and often got there before the engines. The fact that he did not have explicit powers of arrest did not bother him; he would follow up clues until he was sure of his man and then call in a policeman. He solved a number of cases of professional arson in his first few months on the job, and his work began to attract attention at Fire Headquarters. After three years he was appointed Fire Marshal of Brooklyn. In a few more years it had become clear that something extraordinary would have to be done with the Brooklyn Fire Marshal. He had begun, by then, to arrive at fires not only before the engines but before the alarm had been turned in, and several times he had nabbed incendiarists at the moment they applied the match, as in the case of the stable fire. Brophy had also begun to study intelligently that singular type of city dweller known as the pyromaniac—the lunatic who sets fire to things for fun. He had installed a cross-index system in his Brooklyn office in which were filed the names and peculiarities of all known pyromaniacs and people he suspected of being pyromaniacs. He had learned more about their habits than had been known before, and had caught a number of them. In 1915, Fire Commissioner Adamson decided that Brophy was the man to deal with the problem of incendiarism for the whole city. He abolished the fire marshals' offices in the various boroughs and set up the Bureau of Fire Investigation, with headquarters in the Municipal Building. Brophy was given the new title of Chief Fire Marshal and a staff of twenty-eight deputies to assist him. He could subpoena witnesses and take legal testimony, but when he decided that he had a prima-facie case against somebody, he would call in a policeman to make the formal arrest. In every other way, Chief Fire Marshal Brophy acted like a detective rather than a fireman, and the Bureau of Fire Investigation still seems like a branch of the Police Department rather than a branch of the Fire Department.

The idea of searching for potential firebugs and embryonic pyromaniacs in a city of this many million people makes a needle-in-haystack hunt seem about as simple as a two-handed game of who's-got-the-button. No other type of criminal is as hard to catch as a professional firebug who burns up buildings in order to collect insurance. If he is an expert and does his job well, all of what might be evidence against him is destroyed by the blaze he sets off. He does not have to be in the building when the fire breaks out. He can light a candle and fix it so that he will be blocks away by the time it burns down and ignites a bundle of oiled rags. He can use a piece of Chinese punk and a little gunpowder, and be in Philadelphia when the blaze starts. Or, having wired the doorbell of the place so that it will start the fire, he can call up Western Union and get a boy to go there and ring it. The pyromaniac is even harder to catch than the professional firebug. No rational motive is involved, only an insane whim. Yet the pyromaniac is cunning, and often his intelligence has been polished by good breeding and higher education. These are the two types of townspeople that Brophy had to keep ahead of.

Brophy was a practical man rather than an imaginative one, and his outlook was prosaic in the extreme. To begin with, he treated the largest metropolis in the world as if it were a village. He worried about New York. Street by street and section by section, the city troubled him, and sometimes he grew anxious about all five boroughs at the same time. He went about his work not so much with enthusiasm as with a grim, almost morbid determination. He had what would have been called, a generation ago, a sense of moral responsibility. He was shocked and outraged by a crime which endangers, and often takes, human life. When a case of professional arson was discovered, he would be genuinely indignant. He is a Catholic, and a devout one. He is one of those Irishmen whose eyes glisten perceptibly when they say "mother" or "little child." When he was Chief Fire Marshal, he never slept well or with any regularity. He was always getting up and going out at night to make sure everything was all right. He would ride to the district that was bothering him, leave his car at a firehouse, and walk around by himself for hours at a time, seeing how things looked, making a note now and then in a little book he carried in his vest pocket, talking to people— storekeepers, bartenders, taxi-drivers, the policeman on the beat. Sometimes on these informal excursions he was following a tip, some bit of information he or his deputies had picked up somewhere, but usually when he left his home in Brooklyn after a few hours' rest and went riding to some distant neighborhood in Manhattan or the Bronx or Queens, it was merely because that neighborhood had been on his mind and he wanted to look it over.

Brophy walked up and down nearly every sidewalk in New York at one time or another. He carried in his mind a picture of the whole city as graphic and full of detail as the picture most New Yorkers have of the block they live in. In his fire-alarm signal books (one at his office and another at home), he wrote down the names and tele- phone numbers of at least one resident for every fire-alarm box in the hazardous districts of the city, so that when an alarm came in he could call up that person and get quick first-hand information about the nature of the fire, often before the fire engines got there. He maintained a speaking acquaintance with hundreds of people besides—two or three, perhaps, in every square mile of the city— and through them kept abreast of a great deal of what was going on in all the hundreds of neighborhoods. If there had been a suspicious-looking fire in the garment district, Brophy was extremely likely to know whether the firm whose stock was destroyed had been doing well, or whether it was in such bad shape that its propri- etors were desperate. He knew a good deal about business condi- tions in general—how things were going with manufacturers of women's hats, for instance, and which of the warehouses down on the waterfront were packed with perishable goods that owners would never be able to sell. His cross-index of pyromaniacs covered all five boroughs, and filed away in it are case histories of some four hundred known pyromaniacs, and the names and peculiarities of several hundred other people who he suspected were pyromaniacs who had never been caught in the act.

Brophy and his deputies checked up on all these people discreetly and systematically, and when suspicious fires broke out in Brooklyn or Queens or the Bronx or on Manhattan Island, the search for the person who applied the torch became a great deal easier. And there was always the possibility that Brophy might find out that a professional firebug had been hired to set fire to the clothing store or the hat factory or the warehouse, and be waiting there to grab him; there was always the chance that Brophy would catch a wild-eyed lunatic sneaking into a tenement hallway with a bundle of excelsior under his arm. That kind of thing happened just often enough to keep Brophy from relaxing very much or sleeping more than three or four hours at a time.

Brophy had practically no personal life as Chief Fire Marshal and did not seem to care about anything very much but his work. He had no hobbies and indulged in no luxuries to speak of. He would forget even the necessities when he was preoccupied with an important case. Brophy's deputies often had to lead him into a restaurant, order something for him, and hand him a knife and fork. It was not unusual for him to work on a case for thirty-six hours without going to sleep at all. After a stretch like that, he would go home and go to bed, but never for more than six or seven hours. Then he would reappear at his office in the Municipal Building, look over the record of fire alarms, and, if there was nothing much doing, go out for one of his walks. He lived in a brownstone house on Park Place in Brooklyn, not far from where he was born. His mother and two sisters lived with him. He never married and had only a few intimate friends, mostly men he had known all his life. When he went to their houses for dinner he nearly always brought along a box of candy for their wives and a present of some kind for their children. When he used to work late, and couldn't go home for dinner, he usually dined at the Schrafft's across the park from the Municipal Building. He had never been fond of drinking, and until recent years an occasional shot of straight rye at the home of a friend was all he ever cared for. Toward the end of his career as Chief Fire Marshal he usually had a couple of drinks before meals and sometimes a couple afterwards. His friends used to accuse him of being behind the times. A few years before his retirement, he was having lunch with one of them at Luchow's and they happened to sit near a young mother who was lunching with her small son and daughter. The mother had a cocktail or two and, between courses, smoked a cigarette. "Now, look at that!" said Brophy. "A mother oughtn't to set an example like that for those little kids." He was sincerely troubled about it. This incident occurred in 1947.

The building of the Williamsburg Bridge was partly responsible for Brophy's choice of career. As soon as the bridge was opened, in 1903, there began a great exodus from Manhattan's lower East Side. Thousands of families gathered up their belongings and crossed the bridge to settle in the new Williamsburg and East New York tenement districts. For a while the bridge was actually crowded during the day with caravans of movers, and was called "the fire escape." The term proved to be inappropriate. Within a year the Williamsburg and East New York sections of Brooklyn had become the worst fire areas in the city. The tenements were like tinder boxes, they were overcrowded, and the hallways were usually piled with rubbish. There were scores of bad fires, and some were plainly incendiary. Too many small merchants had moved into those neighborhoods, and some of them used the torch to save themselves from ruin. The tenements seemed to invite pyromaniacs. The big news stories in Brooklyn for the next few years were about the fires of Williamsburg and East New York. As a district reporter for the *Herald,* Brophy covered all of them.

He was the kind of reporter that has been almost entirely

stamped out by schools of journalism and the literary blight which has infected newspapers in the past thirty years. He did not know anything about fine writing, or care about it, and he could face a dozen spectacles without having a literary impression enter his head to obscure the facts. He just went around asking "How?" and "Why?" and when he telephoned his city desk he was full of information. His father was a police lieutenant, and Brophy knew most of the Brooklyn police and fire officials by their first names. He was accepted as one of them—an honor few reporters achieve today. The doom of the fact-gathering reporter was approaching, however, even as early as 1905. The *Herald* and the *Sun* were filled with *feuilletons,* the up-the-dark-stairs or delayed-lead era of the *World* was almost at hand, and Pulitzer had announced his plans for founding the Columbia School of Journalism. Brophy began to look around for something with some future in it, and decided to try the fire marshal's office.

When Brophy was trying to prevent arson by catching professional firebugs before they had started a fire, he had little assistance except from his own deputies. As soon as an important case of arson had been discovered, however, he could be sure that the New York Board of Fire Underwriters, which represents all the great fire-insurance companies, would investigate the fire whether their assistance was needed or not. Fire-insurance companies have traditionally maintained a somewhat ambiguous attitude toward the crime of arson. Practically the only motive for professional arson is furnished by fire insurance. What tempts the professional firebug and the people who employ him is that merchandise and household effects can without any difficulty be insured for more than they are worth. When a person is applying for a fire-insurance policy, the insurance companies seem to play the role of innocent, unsuspecting institutions which will take anybody's word for anything. The goods to be insured are not, in most cases, inspected before the policy is issued. But as soon as a fire occurs in a dwelling or a place of business that has been insured, the fire-insurance companies become openly suspicious and demand documentary proof that the property destroyed was worth as much as the policy-holder claimed it was when he paid his premium and got the policy. And if there is any evidence of incendiarism, the Board of Fire Underwriters assigns a firm of lawyers to help the district attorney. The fire commissioners of New York have urged for years that the insurance companies be made to inspect the property of all prospective policyholders at the time the policy is issued, but the insurance companies claim that this would cost so much it would ruin them.

It is undoubtedly true that the question of just how far to go with fire prevention is one that the insurance companies have to consider with care. Life-insurance men do not have to fear that institutional advertising of the sort that urges the public to be careful crossing streets and to button up its overcoat will eliminate the hazard of death, but too much fire prevention might, in time, very nearly eliminate the hazard of fire. If professional arson were eliminated, for instance, the fire hazard would be materially cut down and the demand for fire insurance would not be so great as it is now. It is difficult to tell exactly how many of New York's fires are incendiary, and Brophy, knowing more than anybody else about it, does not try to guess. What he considers important and indisputable is that between a hundred and a hundred and fifty persons are arrested every year for setting fires, and that most of them are convicted. Investigators for the Board of Fire Underwriters are more willing to guess, and their guess is that between fifty and seventy-five percent of the city's destructive fires are of incendiary origin. Yet the fire-insurance companies for years have appeared to show more interest in convicting professional firebugs after the fires have occurred than in making it harder for them to obtain the policies in the first place. The manager of the Scottish Union & National Fire Insurance Company of Edinburgh once made an illuminating speech on the general subject of fire prevention in which he said, "I say we cannot make profits for our shareholders without fires; within certain well-defined limits, we welcome fires." In his retirement, Brophy thinks and talks about this side of the situation sometimes but he would rather think and talk about the firebugs he has caught.

PROFESSIONAL FIREBUGS REGARD themselves as upright citizens and their calling as one that is made necessary by the exigencies of competition in the business world. They are at least as arrogant as bootleggers were during Prohibition, and as a rule enjoy a considerable amount of respect among the merchants who employ them. Charles Carmen, who went to jail in 1927 for a long term, was known as the Professor among the merchants he served. He was a snob at heart, and if he had followed his natural snobbish instincts, he might still be at liberty. When he was first asked by one Socrates Moscahlades to set fire to Bishop's Warehouse on Greenwich Street, he said, "I don't want to do any business with Greeks." But he finally took the job, and on June 24th, 1927, did set fire to the warehouse, which burned to the ground and destroyed merchandise which Moscahlades and some associates had insured for a million dollars. Carmen was so highly thought of by one local group, made up of merchants who either had hired him in the past or had thought they might hire him some day, that after his arrest and conviction they organized a benefit performance for him at a Yiddish theatre on lower Second Avenue. The benefit performance was duly held in December, 1929. In the course of keeping up with current events about town, Brophy learned of this benefit and attended it, but there was nothing he could do about it. It just gave him something more to ponder over.

Carmen made the mistake of leaving a gasoline tin behind him when he set fire to Bishop's Warehouse. He would never have left such a damaging piece of evidence if everything had gone smoothly. He had arranged on the second floor of the warehouse a fire-making apparatus consisting of a large candle placed on top of gasoline-soaked rags in such a way that the rags would catch fire when the candle burned down. The fire was supposed to start some four hours after he left the warehouse. As it happened, Carmen lit a match, and was bending over to light the candle when a black cat walked out from behind a packing case. Carmen jumped and the match dropped from his hand. It fell into the gasoline-soaked rags. The flames leaped up and Carmen had to run, leaving inside the gasoline tin he had intended to take away with him after he had lighted the candle.

The gasoline tin formed the basis of a painstaking investigation by Brophy which led to the arrest of the Greek merchants two months after the fire. They confessed and in their confessions named one Joseph Kwit as the person who had carried on the negotiations with the firebug, who was known to them only as the Professor. Kwit, however, maintained his innocence. He said he had been a stakeholder of the sum of five hundred dollars left with him by the merchants for payment to the Professor for some job the nature of which he had never known.

Kwit was ostensibly a merchant, dealing in furs, and had a shop on West Twenty-seventh Street. Not knowing exactly what he was looking for, Brophy went to the shop and examined all the papers in Kwit's desk. He came to a portion of an envelope on which appeared the name "Cormin," laid it aside, and looked at all the other papers in the desk. When he had finished, all he had that seemed even vaguely helpful was the envelope with the name Cormin on it. Something about that name had caused Brophy, almost unconsciously, to lay the envelope aside when he first came to it; now he thought about it some more and remembered that, ten years before, in 1917, he had sent to Sing Sing a professional firebug whose name was Carmen. Brophy went to Police Headquarters and picked up a rogues'-gallery photograph of Carmen. He also ascertained that Carmen had been released from Sing Sing a year or so before, and that he now lived on Pitkin Avenue, in Brooklyn. Brophy showed Kwit the photograph of Carmen, and Kwit admitted that this was the Professor. Brophy then got a uniformed policeman and went to Carmen's flat in Brooklyn. He thought Carmen would be on the alert, so he had the policeman ring the bell and say that a man named Carmen had been in an accident down the street and had given this address when he was taken to the hospital. "It couldn't be my husband," said Carmen's wife, "because he is here in bed, asleep." Brophy, who was hiding in the hallway, then rushed into the flat, followed by the policeman, and Carmen woke up with handcuffs on.

After Carmen had been arrested, Kwit admitted that his real business was that of acting as go-between for the Professor. As soon as Carmen had got out of Sing Sing, he had made Kwit his partner and, by way of demonstrating his skill as a firebug, had set fire to a small store Kwit owned at that time on the lower West Side. Kwit collected $12,500 insurance on this fire, and was able thereafter to recommend Carmen to other merchants with an enthusiasm based on personal experience.

Joe Eisenstein, another firebug who was convicted and sent to prison in 1930, prided himself especially on his knowledge of chemistry. He claimed to have worked out a secret formula for a highly inflammable fluid which left no suspicious trace or odor after it had been used. He wore tortoiseshell glasses and called himself *Dr.* Eisenstein. He was also proud of his timing. When he was finally arrested for setting off a blaze in the Dachis Fur Company building on West Twenty-seventh Street, he asked what time the alarm had been turned in. He said he had timed it to start three hours and a half after he had left the place. It turned out that he had been wrong by only twelve minutes.

Eisenstein lived like any respectable citizen. He had a wife and two boys, the elder of whom, it developed after his father's arrest, was specializing in chemistry. Eisenstein had been a clothing merchant in Pleasantville, New Jersey, at one time, but for five years before his arrest had been a professional firebug. He usually charged from eight hundred up for a fire, with a stipulation that he was to receive a bonus of one hundred dollars if he achieved "complete destruction." In going over his past record, Brophy found that in Philadelphia Eisenstein had once sued a merchant who had just had a fire, and had obtained an attachment on the insurance money the merchant was to receive. When he had contracted to set this merchant's store on fire, Eisenstein had accepted a part payment in cash, and had made the merchant give him conventional promissory notes for the balance. The merchant had tried to default, Eisenstein had hired a lawyer, and a Philadelphia court had made the merchant pay him out of the insurance money.

The Dachis fur store occupied the ground floor and the front half of the second floor of the building on Twenty-seventh Street. Months before the fire the fur merchant had partitioned off a section of the second floor and installed there a small perfumery shop. He hired a man named Leavitt, who, it turned out later, knew nothing about perfume, and made him the dummy proprietor of the shop. Dachis confessed later that this shop was set up simply to furnish an explanation for the inflammable liquids which would be used by the firebug. When Eisenstein was placed in charge, the first thing he did was to make several gallons of inflammable fluid, using his secret formula. Then he cut a hole about two feet square in the floor of the fake perfumery shop and a similar hole in the floor of the Dachis store, leading into the cellar. This was to insure a draught. To make the draught even better, he pulled up two or three floorboards in the store. Eisenstein then set up the fire-making apparatus. He had brought with him a grooved board, a piece of punk, some non-safety matches, some tissue paper, and several large bundles of absorbent cotton. All through these preparations he was chewing a large wad of chewing gum. He laid the punk along the groove in the board (which was nailed to the floor of the fur shop) and at one end of the board placed the chewing gum. The matches were stuck in the chewing gum so that their heads touched one end of the punk. The tissue paper was then laid over the matches, loosely fluffed. Leading from the tissue paper to the two rooms on the second floor, and to the four corners of the downstairs room, like streamers at a gala, were ropes of absorbent cotton which had been soaked in the inflammable fluid. An open container of the fluid stood at the end of each streamer. Eisenstein then lit the end of the punk, and left. When the inflammable fluid was ignited a little more than three hours later, the explosion was so terrific that it blew out the front wall of the building and hurled an iron gate across the street. It was after midnight on a Sunday, and the street was not crowded. The gate hit a passing Greek, who had to be treated for cuts and bruises at St. Vincent's Hospital, but no one else was injured by the explosion. Eisenstein achieved "complete destruction" on this job. It was a two-alarm fire.

Both Doc Eisenstein and Professor Carmen were family men who did not consort with professionals in other types of crime. This seems to be typical of firebugs. Brophy has found that most of them have been respectable married men, and while their wives knew what business their husbands were in, the ladies did not appear to consider it criminal. Some years ago a notorious firebug named Horowitz, who had been operating in the metropolitan area for some time without being caught, was killed in an explosive fire which went off before he expected it to in a store in Paterson, New Jersey. It was found that he lived in lower Manhattan, and had a family. When his wife was informed of his sudden death, she exclaimed in an aggrieved tone, "For three years I have been expecting something like this to happen!" Firebugs sometimes exhibit civilized feelings and a highly developed sense of decorum. Brophy once was hot on the trail of a gang of firebugs, and had learned of their plan to set fire to an East Side building on a certain day. Mysteriously, the setting of the blaze was postponed, and Brophy failed to catch them that time. Brophy did not find out why the postponement had been made until he arrested the firebugs some months later: somebody had died in the tenement next door to the store that was to be burned, and the firebugs had not wished to upset the funeral services by having a fire. So they had put off the fire for three days.

Professional arson seems to be a man's job, on the whole. Only a dozen or so women have been convicted of the crime in the past thirty years in New York. Several of these burned up outmoded clothes with the idea of making insurance companies buy new ones. Three were rooming-house keepers. Another, a widow, burned up her apartment in order to collect the insurance on her furniture. She was betrayed by an urn containing the ashes of her husband, who had been legally cremated some years before. Not wishing her husband's ashes to be mingled with the ashes of the furniture, she placed the urn in the oven of the kitchen range. Brophy always looks into everything when he investigates a fire. He investigated this one, looked into the oven, found the urn, and asked the widow about it. "It's nothing," she said vaguely. Brophy remarked that it must be something and started ostentatiously to pour some of the ashes into his hand, as if to examine them. "Oh, my poor husband!" the widow moaned. Brophy suggested gently that she would not have put the urn in the oven if she had not been expecting a fire, and she admitted that she had set fire to the place herself.

With only ten or twelve hours of steady work a day in and out of his office at the Municipal Building, Brophy was able to protect the city about as adequately as it could be protected from professional firebugs. What kept him working longer than that, and made him get out of bed when he ought to have stayed there, was the knowledge that every now and then some apparently normal, law-abiding citizen among the city's millions suddenly and inexplicably comes to the conclusion that what he has to do to be happy is to set fire to a building and see the fire engines come. Professional firebugs, and the dishonest merchants who employ them, are cunning, but they are rational individuals. They confide in their friends, get drunk and talk too much to strangers, are inclined to be too greedy in making claims against insurance companies, and otherwise leave clues lying around. Pyromaniacs go about satisfying their strange desires without telling even their best friends or the members of their own families. There is usually no concrete clue which will connect the pyromaniac with the particular building he chooses to see in flames. One building is as good as another for his purpose, and he may very well never have seen it before he applies the torch. Any neighborhood will do for him, although he usually chooses one far from where he lives and most frequently selects the tenement districts, where the buildings burn well and where hallways are full of inflammable refuse.

Psychiatrists have various explanations for the causes and the nature of pyromania, none of which has been of much help to Brophy. It is generally agreed among the experts that pyromaniacs are neurotic, frustrated, and crave the sight of flames or the satisfaction of being able to look at something as spectacular as a fire and say to themselves, "I did that." It is supposed to be a rather sexy and perverted mania on the whole; and it is one that used to give old-fashioned psychoanalysts immense satisfaction, because the symbolism of both fire and water could be worked in. Fascinated by this, some of them evolved elaborate theories, laying great emphasis on the traditional relationship, in all known languages, of desire and words like "fire," "burn," "hot," and "scorching." Modern psychiatrists believe that professional firebugs are borderline pyromaniacs who nurse a flame psychosis and happen to have been able to combine business with pleasure. They like to point to the case of a local firebug-pyromaniac who was, according to this theory, madly in love with a West Side warehouse. The firebug was employed by an importer to set fire to this commodious building, and during the negotiations which preceded the fire he wrote notes to his employer and used such euphemisms as "bride" and "sweetheart" when referring to the warehouse and "wedding" when referring to the night the fire was to take place.

From a practical point of view, Brophy knows more about the ways of pyromaniacs than anybody else in the country, but he doesn't theorize about them. "They are a strange bunch," he says, and lets it go at that. Some of them, he has found, look like lunatics, and others do not.

Brophy usually caught pyromaniacs simply by getting to fires while they were still burning. At most fires in the tenement districts, Brophy and some of his trained deputies were likely to be standing somewhere in the crowd, keeping an eye on the faces of the people who were watching, and taking note of what they said and how they acted. Brophy's mind accommodated an enormous gallery of faces, divided up into neat and clearly defined categories. There was a large section devoted to pyromaniacs he had sent to prison or to institutions and those he had arrested and released for lack of evidence at some time or other during the last four decades. These he could identify in the filing system at his office, with names and addresses and certain remembered peculiarities. Then there was an extensive section in which he could find the faces of men he had suspected, at one time or another, of being pyromaniacs—vague faces with no names to them, faces that he saw once weeks or months or years before and which for some reason, perhaps forgotten, aroused his suspicion. The face of a man who had once talked just a shade too excitedly about the fire he was watching would probably be in this group, or that of a man who had once been questioned at the scene of a fire but not arrested, because there was no real evidence against him. These faces did not, somehow, get mixed up with the faces of the hundreds of people in all the neighborhoods of New York with whom Brophy kept up a slight acquaintance and who were in no way suspicious characters. Those faces were in still another section of his mind. It was all part of the Brophy intellect.

Brophy always made it a point to go to practically all hospital fires. No other variety of fire creates as much excitement as a hospital fire, and for this reason a pyromaniac may easily be tempted to have a try at one. And if there is any chance that a pyromaniac has set fire to a hospital, Brophy wants to catch him before he does it again. When the nurses' home and dining hall of the Methodist Episcopal Hospital in Brooklyn was destroyed by fire in October, 1927, there was plenty of excitement. The fire threatened the hospital building, where three hundred patients were in bed. While smoke was billowing through the halls, an expectant mother gave birth to a baby, and two major operations which had been begun had to be completed. The most excited person in the whole place was one of the hospital porters. He had turned in the alarm, given advice to the firemen, and had finally run into the burning building yelling that he wanted to save the nurses. He had collapsed on a stairway, overcome by smoke, and when Brophy saw him was in the infirmary. The doctors and nurses were making a fuss over him and calling him a hero. But the porter's face was one of the faces in Brophy's memory. Brophy had had him arrested ten years before and charged him with having set a series of fires in the Park Slope section of Brooklyn. A sympathetic jury, unable to understand why he should set fires without any conceivable motive, had acquitted him. He confessed that he had started the hospital fire by stuffing a pile of gauze under a bureau and lighting it with a match. This man seemed a good-natured, slow-witted, rather likable chap to everybody who knew him. He admitted he had gone to work at the hospital with the express intention of setting fire to it.

Bellevue Hospital had a pyromaniac among its employees at one time, an Irishman who worked there as a plumber's helper. He succeeded twice in creating excitement by setting fire to newspapers he had stored in linen closets. He tried a third time, got caught, and was transferred to the psychopathic ward as a patient. Large institutions of all kinds attract the pyromaniac. In 1929, a guard who worked in the House of Refuge on Randall's Island confessed that he had started three fires there, and that earlier in the year, when he was working at the New Jersey State Hospital in Morris Plains, he had set fire to that institution, causing the destruction of a million dollars' worth of property.

Schools and hotels are also favored by the pyromaniac. Brophy has caught as many as three dozen public-school boys in the last thirty years who have tried to set fire to the schools they were attending. Pyromania usually develops in the adolescent period, and sometimes can be cured by modern psychiatric therapy. Not infrequently, however, it seizes a man of middle age. Brophy hurried over to the Hotel St. George in Brooklyn one day in the fall of 1929 when he received reports that four fires had broken out in the hotel between midnight and dawn. Brophy had five of his assistants disguise themselves as porters and waiters, and started watching the guests as they came and went. Brophy suspected a pyromaniac was loose in the hotel, because all the fires had started in vacant rooms or hall closets, where fires would not be likely to start by accident. The house detective, who had been up all night and had been commended by the management for discovering two of the fires himself, roved about from floor to floor and reported every fifteen minutes or so that all was well. Three more fires occurred in empty rooms and hall closets during the morning, and five more followed in rapid succession as the day wore on. Brophy's men were unnerved and the house detective was beside himself with excitement, rushing about from floor to floor, exclaiming about the mystery of it all. Brophy finally began to concentrate his attention on the house detective, and discovered that every now and then the man was going to his room in the hotel and taking a swig from a bottle of rye. Brophy thought there was something inconsistent about a man who pretended to be so interested in catching the pyromaniac and at the same time was getting royally drunk. The house detective was questioned and finally accused of setting the fires himself. He began to weep and readily confessed. He was a man of forty, and until this time, apparently, had never felt any conscious urge to set anything on fire. He had been grabbed by the impulse the day before, he said, and he had not been able to control it. "It's the greatest excitement in the world," he told Brophy. A good many pyromaniacs, both young and old, Brophy has found, start setting fire to things only when they start drinking.

BROPHY WAS ALWAYS gentle with pyromaniacs. While he does not subscribe to all the theories of the psychiatrists, he believes that pyromaniacs should be sent to asylums rather than prisons, and usually made this recommendation to judge and jury.

He talked to pyromaniacs kindly, pretended to admire their cunning, and led them painlessly into detailed confessions of all the fires they had set off. Every now and then the confessions of a pyromaniac seem to dovetail nicely with the theories of the psychiatrist. A young man who was an evening student at the Morris High School in the Bronx admitted, when he was caught, that he had set fire to twenty dwellings in Brooklyn and five in Manhattan. Brophy was convinced that he was not just bragging, because the youth was able to describe each fire in a way that checked with the Fire Department records. This pyromaniac worked during the day as a clerk in a Manhattan department store. In the Christmas season of 1934, a friend of his had taken his girl away from him and he had set fire to her house on West Fourth Street, down in the Village. He took up with another young lady, and when she moved away from her rooming house in Brooklyn, leaving no forwarding address, he set fire to that house, After that, he told Brophy, he set fire to a house every time he thought about either girl. The store clerk was arrested at the scene of a fire on Dean Street, Brooklyn. Brophy recognized him as a youth he had questioned, and let go, some months before at the scene of another fire. Brophy used to have various ways of verifying his suspicions when he asked an excited fire-watcher to go along to his office and talk to him. An innocent person, he has found, usually protests violently at the effrontery of such a request, while the guilty one almost invariably says, "Why sure. I have nothing to hide; take me along." Brophy once casually asked a suspect for a match, and the man replied indignantly, "I never carry matches." Brophy persuaded him without difficulty to come to his office and answer a few questions. At the office, he had the man searched. A box of matches was found in his pocket, and, confronted with the evidence that he had lied about carrying matches, the man broke down and confessed to having set off a string of fires.

Most pyromaniacs do not consider whether or not the building is occupied when they set fire to it. One that Brophy caught in 1924 burned unoccupied buildings only. He was a lawyer's son, in his late twenties, and was working as a bank clerk when Brophy arrested him. He had set fire to fifty empty buildings in Harlem and the Bronx in six months. When Brophy saw him standing in the crowd watching a fire in a vacant house on Amsterdam Avenue, he knew that he had seen him before. Brophy talked to him for a while and then remembered that this was a young man who had been sent to a mental institution three years before as a pyromaniac. He had been discharged as cured.

With all these cases, and hundred of others, in the back of his head, Brophy has no room in his mind for anything but the practical point of view. He knows that most psychiatrists no longer believe that the moon has anything to do with lunacy, but he knows, too, that statistics of his Bureau of Fire Investigation show that through the years more incendiary fires have occurred when the moon is full than at any other time. He does not know or care much why this is, but on bright moonlight nights, when he was still Chief Fire Marshal, he and his deputies were more alert than ever, and often didn't wait for the fire alarms to come in but tried to be nearby when a fire was started. They usually picked a certain neighborhood, or two or three neighborhoods, and stood watch on such nights. They knew that pyromaniacs usually return to the same neighborhood for a second or third try after having set off a successful blaze or two, and one of the functions of the Bureau was and is to keep track of unsolved incendiary fires by means of red pins stuck in maps of the five boroughs. With Brophy's knowledge of what all neighborhoods of the city look like, what sort of buildings are in them, and his habit of walking systematically around the city and talking to people, he seemed to be able to tell every now and then just about where to look for trouble. His deputies used to accuse him of being subject to a rheumatic twinge in the legs which told him when to expect an outbreak of pyromania or professional arson in a neighborhood that had been worrying him. Brophy denies this gravely, saying, "No, I have never been troubled by rheumatism." Undoubtedly he worked on hunches a good part of the time in hunting both pyromaniacs and professional firebugs, but they were the knowledgeable hunches of a man who had been working for over forty years on the problem of incendiarism, and thinking, during most of that time, about hardly anything else. In his retirement, Brophy lives a quiet life in Brooklyn these days and, although he still has an alarm box in his home, rarely goes to fires. He is chairman of the Arson Committee of the International Association of Chiefs of Police and is frequently called in as a consultant by fire-insurance companies who want an expert's opinion on the origin of certain fires. "I'm taking it easy," he says, "and I'm enjoying it."

PLACE AND LEAVE WITH

IN A LITTLE frame house near the intersection of Rogers and Flatbush Avenues in Brooklyn there lived until a few years ago an old lady named Mrs. Katherina Schnible. She was seventy-two and a little lame. She owned the house and rented out the first two floors as apartments, but there were mortgages and she had not met the payments. She knew the bank that held the mortgages was about to foreclose and she knew that it could do nothing until a process-server placed the papers in her hands. Her son, who lived with her, went out to work at eight in the morning and did not return until six, so from eight till six every day, except Sunday, Mrs. Schnible stayed in her room on the third floor and refused to open the door, no matter who knocked. Came a day when she heard a heavy footfall on the first landing, heard somebody running frantically up the first flight of stairs, heard a man's voice shouting something. Then the footsteps came closer, up the second flight of stairs, and right outside her door she heard yelled the word "Fire!" Mrs. Schnible opened her door and hobbled into the hall. "Hello, Mrs. Schnible," said a man standing there. "Here's a summons for you." He handed her the papers, and the proceedings were begun which eventually put Mrs. Schnible out of her house.

Harry Grossman, who was the man in the hall, is regarded by those who employed him as the champion process-server of all time.

A process-server is an instrument of justice and his profession is a cornerstone of civil law, but not many of the people he serves appreciate that. Their attitude is not entirely logical. The practice of process-serving is based on the premise that a defendant ought to be informed as soon as a suit against him is instituted. Early in the history of English law, process-serving was inaugurated to supplement a system called outlawry, under which a plaintiff often was able to seize the property of a defendant before the defendant even knew that he was being sued. As soon as defendants learned that they could not be outlawed, however, they conceived the idea of hiding, and they have always regarded process-servers not as friends coming to tell them what they ought to know, but as enemies coming to force them into court. When process-servers find them, defendants usually are irate, often violent. Grossman, in his time, was cursed by hundreds of defendants, many of them distinguished citizens. Defendants threw him down flights of stairs and shoved him off porches. He was pinched, slapped, and punched; and he was beaten up all over one time by a family of seven.

The inconsistency of all this embittered Grossman, but it never discouraged him. He was a refinement of metropolitan civilization, and was several jumps ahead of the ordinary city dweller, who regards his neighbors merely with indifference. Grossman's customary attitude toward strangers was one of frank animosity. Outside of an extremely small circle of friends, employers, and relatives, the city of New York, in his estimation, was composed of some seven million suspicious characters, most of them stupid, a few of them clever, and all of them capable of vicious and dishonest behavior. He talked in a shout, but his most acrimonious remarks were in the form of an interrogation, which is more conciliatory than a declarative sentence. "Who are you to talk to me like that?" he asked hundreds of defendants. "Who's being sued—you or me?" Many of them have had no answer for that but to put the summons in their pocket and slam the door in Grossman's face. Grossman was not pugnacious; he loathed physical violence of all kinds. His face, even in repose, was a masterpiece of boiling but controlled indignation. His livelihood for thirty years depended upon his ability to outwit people who were trying to outwit him.

"Place and leave with" is the legal phrase for what a process-server must do with a summons when he goes out to serve papers on a defendant, but the courts never have explained precisely what that means. Where the process-server must place the papers is still a nice legal question. A process-server once threw a summons and complaint at James Gordon Bennett and hit him in the chest with it, but the courts held that this was not a proper service. Another famous case in the lawbooks tells of a defendant named Martin, who in 1893 hid himself under his wife's petticoats and refused to receive the papers. The process-server saw him crouching there, so he put the papers on what seemed to be the defendant's shoulder, and went away. The Supreme Court rendered a decision which held that "where a person, to avoid service of summons, shelters himself in his wife's petticoats, the laying of the papers on his shoulder will be a sufficient service." In a case in which the defendant was handcuffed and therefore could not conveniently take hold of the papers, the courts held that it was proper for the process-server to place the papers in the man's pocket. But in another case the ruling was that it was not proper to shove the papers under the defendant's front door and ring the door bell even if the process-server knew the defendant was standing on the other side.

Grossman never bothered to look up legal precedents for his actions; he simply placed the papers in the hands of the defendant and left them there. On innumerable occasions he had to use ingenuity in order to get close enough to the defendant to do this, and only once was he forced to depart from a literal interpretation of the legal phrase. That was in the case of an elderly lady, who, like Mrs. Schnible, was trying to hide from him. This woman, whose name was Mrs. Mahoney, refused to leave her apartment in the East Side tenement she owned, and Grossman's routine tricks, such as shouting "Fire!" outside her door, failed to budge her. He knew she was there, because he had talked his way into a flat across the court from her and had seen her sitting at her kitchen table in front of an open window, peeling potatoes. Grossman went home to his own apartment in Brooklyn and thought for a while, and then began to practice throwing the summons. He put rubber bands around the paper to make it compact, placed a salad bowl on the dining-room table, and practiced all that afternoon, throwing the subpoena into the bowl from the middle of the living room. He went back next morning to the flat across the court from Mrs. Mahoney's kitchen. She came into the kitchen a little before noon, puttered around for a while, and then sat down at the table with a bowl of potatoes in front of her and began placidly to peel them. Grossman leaned out of his window and tossed the subpoena. The papers landed in the bowl just as the old lady reached into it. "There you are, Mrs. Mahoney!" Grossman shouted. "There's a foreclosure paper for you!" The courts never questioned his method of placing these papers, and Mrs. Mahoney lost her property.

Tens of thousands of papers have to be served in the course of a year in New York City, and the majority of them are handled for the law firms by process-serving agencies, which rely for their profits on quantity and quick turnover. These agencies take care of the routine cases—civil suits in which defendants make no great effort to avoid being served, and divorces in which husbands are frequently only too glad to meet the process-server halfway. Cases involving expert dodgers or stubborn hug-the-hearths usually are turned over to private detective agencies, and the detective agencies for many years usually hired Grossman to serve the papers. When the Electrical Research Products Institute sued the Fox Film Corporation for $15,000,000 in 1930, the lawyers for the plaintiff, naturally, surmised that it would be difficult to "place and leave with" William Fox, Winfield Sheehan, and other defendants the papers summoning them to come to court. Grossman received the assignment through a detective agency. He got in to see Fox by having a telegram sent from Boston saying that Mr. Grossman had "closed the theatre deal" and would call on Fox at eleven o'clock the next morning. When Grossman reached Fox's office, the film executive's secretary told him Mr. Fox had received the wire but was not sure what deal it was that had been closed. "My God," said Grossman, "the theatre deal—that's what deal! If this is the way I am to be received, never mind—to hell with it!" He started out, and the secretary called him back. "Just wait one moment," she said. "I'll tell Mr. Fox." She opened a door marked "Private" and went into an inner office, Grossman followed her and handed Fox the subpoena. Fox started up from his desk indignantly, but Grossman's indignation expressed itself first. "You, multimillion-aire!" Grossman shouted. "Is it decent, is it nice, for a multimil-lionaire who can be sued for fifteen million dollars to hide from me? Why don't you take the papers like a man?" This so flabber-gasted Fox that he sank back in his chair, and Grossman went through the corporation's offices unimpeded and served papers on Sheehan, two vice-presidents, the secretary, and the treasurer.

Grossman had all the attributes of character needed in his pro-fession. He chose process-serving as his lifework before he was old enough to qualify for the job. It is not a profession that has been re-stricted by difficult entrance requirements. Anybody who is a cit-izen and who has not been declared of unsound mind can serve summonses for a living, but he must be at least eighteen years old. At sixteen, Grossman went to work in a private detective agency, and he was ready to serve summonses months before he could meet that last requirement. On his eighteenth birthday, in 1915, he served his first paper, and he went right along serving them. The average private detective does not excel at process-serving, which is why the detective agencies usually called in Grossman on difficult cases. Grossman's eminence in his field suggests that private detectives are shy, sensitive creatures, dominated by their emotions. They expose chiseling employees, unmask struggling noblemen, and play an important role in the domestic unhappiness of the community, but when they are called upon to place a paper in somebody's hands, they are overwhelmed by bashfulness.

Grossman was brought up in an environment which might have produced a criminal instead of a boy who was to enlist on the side of justice. He was born in the Bushwick section of Brooklyn. It was a tough section, and young Harry was introduced to petty thievery, and had a knowledge of crime, criminals, and run-of-the-mill rascals before he was ten years old. With his playmates, many of whom are now, or have been, in prison, Harry shot craps on the sidewalks, pilfered merchandise from the neighborhood stores, and paid little attention to his studies. In his home, however, he gained a perspective on the subject of crime that influenced him strongly. His father had a small real-estate business on Graham Avenue; some of the best people of the neighborhood were his father's friends. One of these leading citizens of Bushwick was a lieutenant of detectives in the Police Department who used to stop in frequently at the Grossman home to have a bite of Mrs. Grossman's fruit cake and chat with the elder Grossman. His talk was mostly about detective work, and it fascinated Harry. The boy made friends with the lieutenant and got in the habit of going to the station house after school and hanging around. He would listen to the talk of the detectives, and sometimes they would let him go with them when they went on a case. By the time he was fourteen or so he knew a good deal about detective methods. He cherished, years later, a clipping from a Brooklyn newspaper that told how, at fifteen, he "furnished detectives with valuable information which led to the arrest of a neighborhood youth who had stolen some jewelry." When he was sixteen. Harry quit school and, aided by the friendly police lieutenant, went to work for Nicholas Brooks, a former police officer who had gone into the private detective business.

Harry had at that time completed his first year at the Alexander Hamilton High School. He went back to the school only one time afterward. That was three years later, on the day his class was to graduate. He learned that the class was to pose on the school steps for a group photograph and he waited inside the building until the photographer was ready to shoot, then stepped out on the steps and joined his former classmates. He bought a copy of the photograph and kept it on a wall at his home. It was inscribed "Graduating class, Alexander Hamilton High School, June, 1916." The early Grossman face was clearly discernible in the back row.

Working for Brooks, Harry established a reputation as an adroit private detective before he was old enough to serve subpoenas. Sent out to trail a salesman for an employer who suspected the man was not attending to business, Grossman furnished information which resulted in the salesman's dismissal, and at the same time gathered evidence on which the salesman's wife subsequently was able to get a divorce. But after he had passed his eighteenth birthday and had begun to serve summonses and subpoenas, it was evident to his employer, and to everybody else who knew him, that he had found a vocation in which he might expect to excel. During the first year he served Maude Adams by posing as a youthful adorer. When she came out of the stage entrance at the Empire Theatre after a performance one evening, Grossman stepped in front of her, holding in his left hand a bouquet of jonquils. "Are you Maude Adams?" he asked. "Oh, those aren't really for me!" she exclaimed, reaching for the flowers. "No, but this is," said Grossman, jerking back the bouquet. With his right hand he served her with a summons. He used to recall that he had paid fifty cents for the jonquils and that he had been able to sell them back to the florist for twenty.

His ability to become more indignant at the attitude of defendants than defendants were at his actions saved Grossman from bodily injury on many occasions. One of his early triumphs involved

Gutzon Borglum. The sculptor was at that time modeling life-size figures in a studio in the Gramercy Park section. Grossman entered by means of what he calls the rush act. A maid opened the door and Grossman rushed past her, saying perfunctorily, "Is Mr. Borglum in?" Borglum was chipping stone on a nearly completed nude. "Here's a summons for you, Mr. Borglum," said Grossman. "Of all the effrontery!" began the sculptor. "You—you—you ought to be . . ." Then Grossman began to shout. "How about you?" he asked. "Shouldn't you maybe be ashamed of yourself? You and your naked women!" He went out spluttering with indignation, leaving Borglum speechless, clutching the summons in his hand.

When, some years ago, Grossman served a summons on Max Block, a glazier, who lived on Atlantic Avenue in Brooklyn, he flew into his customary rage at Block's denunciation of his tactics, but Block had the moral and physical support of Mrs. Block, three grown sons, a daughter of high-school age, and a mother-in-law. The family dragged him from the vestibule into their living room and beat him up. The sons punched him, the father kicked him, the mother and daughter pinched him, and the mother-in-law hit him over the head with her cane. Grossman stayed in a hospital two days, and on the third day reappeared at the house, accompanied by a policeman. He served each member of the family with a warrant charging assault and battery. The next week Magistrate O'Neill found them guilty and fined them fifteen dollars apiece. Grossman had started a suit against them that day for damages, and as they left the courtroom he served them with summonses for that. The case was settled out of court for two hundred dollars, plus doctors' and hospital bills.

Grossman earned a straight salary of twenty-five dollars a week in the employ of Brooks. He knew that a good free-lance process-server, working on a daily basis, could make sixty or seventy dollars a week handling difficult cases for detective agencies and law firms. He had about decided to break away from Brooks and go out on his own when his career was interrupted by World War I. For Grossman, the conflict raged forty-three days. He was drafted on October 25th, 1918, and honorably discharged on December 7th of the same memorable year.

HIS PERIOD OF service in the United States Army was a profitable interlude. He was drafted seventeen days before the Armistice and discharged twenty-six days after it, and in those weeks, besides his pay and a sixty-dollar cash bonus he received later on, he cleared twenty-five hundred dollars. He had saved a few hundred dollars from his salary as a process-server before he went to war, and with this money he entered the company crap games at Fort Wadsworth and later at Camp Eustis, in Virginia. There was a man like Grossman in nearly every big crap game at the training camps in those days. He had more capital than any other player and he was able to cover everybody else's money; he bet consistently against the dice and never rolled them himself. According to the law of averages, this system made his chances of winning not quite even, but Grossman was sure it gave him an advantage and what happened was that he always came out ahead. Grossman hoarded his winnings and, when he returned to New York, decided to start out for himself as a free-lance process-server. During the first three months of his independent career, he made a record for serving papers on inaccessible defendants which has never been surpassed, not even by Grossman himself. He built up a reputation that established him as the leading process-server of the day, and when the three months were over he had a clientele among law firms and private detective agencies which kept him steadily at work in his chosen profession.

Grossman's success during that three-month period may be attributed entirely to his own ingenuity. He had returned to New York from Camp Eustis with his private's uniform and an overseas cap, and, like all ex-soldiers, he had the privilege of wearing them for three months. The first regiments of the A.E.F. were getting back from Europe about that time, and the government wished to give the men plenty of time to provide themselves with civilian outfits. Wearing his army clothes, Grossman served papers on defendants who had successfully evaded other subpoena-servers for months. His procedure was so simple he was unable to understand why nobody besides himself ever thought of using the army uniform in that way during that period. Foreclosure papers for elderly ladies were his specialty, but almost anybody was vulnerable. Doormen, elevator operators, secretaries, and house servants (who are usually stumbling blocks in the way of the process-server) would nod knowingly and grin when the khaki Grossman said, "Don't announce me—it's a surprise."

Grossman did not attempt to use his army uniform longer than the law allowed him to. Nowhere in his character was the spirit of recklessness which permits so many of his countrymen to break laws or at least to protest against them. He would gamble, if he was able to minimize the element of chance as he did in the army crap games, but he would never have thought of operating a gambling establishment himself, because that is against the law. He was one of the few motorists in New York history who observed meticulously all the traffic regulations, even the speed laws. When he drove home across the Brooklyn Bridge after a day's work in Manhattan, he kept his speedometer down to fifteen miles an hour, and if other motorists blew their horns and glared at him when they passed him, he glared back and shouted indignant interrogations. "Can't you read?" he would yell. "What you think I am—looking for a police court and a fine, maybe?" Grossman was comforted at all times by the majesty and the dignity of the social institution of which he was an important instrument. When he was working, he knew that the law stood firmly behind him and, at work and at play, he exhibited an enormous respect for it.

Grossman's success in khaki made him appreciate the value of a uniform in his kind of work. When he finally laid aside his army clothes early in 1919, he had a special outfit made that has deceived hundreds of other defendants in all sections of the city. It was blue, with brass buttons, and over the visor of the cap was the legend "Special Messenger." He wore it most of the time when he was working, and every couple of years or so bought a new one. He didn't have to have it made to order, because, except for the lettering on the cap, which he had sewed on by a tailor, the outfit really was just a bus driver's uniform, and he could get those ready-made from the firm that supplies the employees of the big bus companies. As a special messenger, Grossman was able to lure a great many people out of hiding. Sometimes he carried with him a long cardboard box of the sort florists use, or an empty candy box, done up elaborately with silk ribbon. He used these for inaccessible ladies. They peeped at him through keyholes, or looked at him from windows, and then opened their doors to him. For gentlemen, he often wrapped up an empty bottle in tissue paper and tied it with red ribbon in a way that made the shape unmistakable. These methods were most successful around Christmas, but they were pretty effective any time of the year.

A woman who lived on a secluded seaside estate at East Quogue, Long Island, failed to rise either to the flower box or the candy box, and this gave Grossman one of his best opportunities to demonstrate the versatility that was responsible for his success. He had walked up to her front door from the station three times on successive days—first as a man in civilian clothes, then as a special messenger bringing flowers, then as a special messenger bringing candy. The servants chased him away each time. As he was leaving the place the third day, Grossman saw the mistress of the house having tea in the back garden. Beyond the garden was a private beach. The only way to get into the garden, he decided, was to swim into the private beach. He went back to Brooklyn and returned to East Quogue the next day, carrying a pair of trunks, a bathing cap, and a pair of field glasses. From a tree a quarter of a mile away, on the other side of an inlet, he watched the lady's garden until the lady came out to have her tea. Then he changed into his trunks, put the summons in his bathing cap, and swam over. Grossman found it necessary to speak harshly to this lady. "This is an outrage," she said when he laid the damp paper in her lap. "An outrage, is it?" he shouted back irately. "Suppose I get cramps? Suppose I get drowned? Would that be an outrage or wouldn't it?" He swam back across the inlet, full of righteous indignation.

Women figure more prominently than men in the memoirs of Grossman. The courts have held that a process-server cannot enter a dwelling forcibly, but that he may enter through an open door or window. The hardest cases for a process-server are those in which a person simply closes all the doors and all the windows and stays inside the house. Men are only infrequently able to do this because they usually have to leave their homes in order to go to their offices. Grossman sometimes had to contend with women, though, who appeared to be perfectly contented to stay indoors the rest of their lives.

He served so many people in his time that it is not so surprising that in one of his most memorable cases he was called upon by a lawyer named Grossman to serve a foreclosure paper on a lady named Grossman. This Mrs. Grossman lived at Eighty-fourth Street and Third Avenue, in Brooklyn. She was alone in the house except for one servant, who did the marketing, and she sat all day at her parlor window and shook her fist at anybody who came to her front door. Grossman called at the house on three different days, wearing his special messenger's uniform. The first day he carried his flower box, the second day his candy box, and the third day he appeared with an intriguing bundle made of three sofa pillows wrapped in tissue paper and tied up with blue ribbon. Mrs. Grossman just sat and shook her fist at him. The process-server saw then that this case of Grossman vs. Grossman was to be a real test. He surmised that while the old lady was highly suspicious of her fellow-humans, she must be curious about them or she would not sit looking out of her window all day. He waited a week to give her a chance to forget about the special messenger and then went back to the neighborhood wearing an ordinary suit and, as a further disguise, dark glasses. About fifteen yards down the street from Mrs. Grossman's window, he found a lamp post to lean against. He stayed there all day, leaving the place only to go to the corner drugstore for some lunch. Early next morning he was back at the lamp post again. He thought it would be another day or so before Mrs. Grossman sent her servant to ask what he was doing there, but he had underestimated his adversary's curiosity. That afternoon a policeman came up to Grossman and asked him what he was up to. "The old lady down there called up the precinct," the officer explained. Grossman told the policeman he was trying to serve her with a summons and offered to pay him five dollars if he would tell her that the man standing by the lamp post was a detective from Newark who was on the trail of a counterfeiter, and was watching the house across the street. "Suppose she complains to the precinct when she finds out I'm lying?" objected the policeman. "Listen," Grossman said, "this is a foreclosure paper. She won't be on your beat very long." The policeman agreed, and a half an hour later the old lady opened her window and beckoned to Grossman. "Wouldn't you like to watch the house from my window?" she said. "Who is it you're going to arrest in that house?" The servant opened the door. Grossman walked into the parlor and served Mrs. Grossman with his summons.

Grossman was at home in any borough of the city. He served papers on residents of Manhattan, Brooklyn, Queens, Staten Island, and the Bronx. He once served a stay-at-home in an East Side tenement by squatting in the dumb-waiter and hauling himself up to her kitchen. He handed her the paper when she reached for the garbage pail. He served a paper one time in the Bronx by posing as

a laundry man. Standing outside a cottage in Queens one evening, he poured ketchup on his head, collapsed on the sidewalk,
and served the papers on the houseowner after he had been carried
inside. When a Mrs. Maude Waterbury refused to see him at her
apartment on Riverside Drive, he made a deal with an expressman
who had just delivered a trunk to somebody else in the building.
The two men took another trunk to Mrs. Waterbury's apartment
and walked in with it when the maid opened the door. "There is
some mistake," said Mrs. Waterbury when they entered the living
room, carrying the trunk. "I am Mrs. Waterbury and I am not expecting any luggage." Grossman put down his end of the trunk and
handed her the paper. "I shall report you to the express company,"
she said as they started out. Grossman didn't want to get the expressman in trouble. "Don't bother, lady," he told Mrs. Waterbury.
"Can't you see we're phonies?"

With some men Grossman had his little difficulties and his little
triumphs. When the firm of Rogers Peet was involved in litiga-
tion with the Amalgamated Clothing Workers of America, it was
necessary for Grossman to serve papers on Sidney Hillman, Joseph
Schlossberg, Jacob Potofsky, and other labor leaders. "Radicals,"
Grossman said later, "are harder than anybody else because they
don't usually have permanent addresses." He finally cornered the
labor men at one of their own mass meetings in Cooper Union.
The men he wanted were on the speakers' stand, and Grossman
spotted each one as he was introduced by the chairman. An Irish
police sergeant was on duty at the door, and Grossman showed him
the papers and asked the officer to protect him when he served
them. Most policemen, he had found, are awed by the sight of legal papers. This one studied the summonses for a while, examined
the handsome notary seals, and then accompanied Grossman to the
speakers' platform. "Go ahead and do your duty," he told Grossman.

A Mr. George Henderson, a manufacturer who lived on Seneca
Avenue in Queens some years ago, was a man who went to consid-

erable lengths to keep away from Grossman. Henderson was protected at home by two grown sons and at the office by a staff of
wide-awake secretaries. Grossman had been unable to get by the
secretaries, and when he had gone to the house, posing as a messenger with a bottle of champagne, the sons had grabbed the package, discovered that the bottle was empty, and thrown Grossman
over the porch railing. Grossman decided that the only way to
serve Henderson was to catch him between home and office, but
although he watched the front door of the house for three mornings he never saw Henderson leave it. Grossman watched the back
door the next day and found out how Henderson was going to his
office each day. The manufacturer entered the basement of a house
across a back alley, ascended to the roof, walked along the roof-
tops to the end of the block, and came down to the street through
another house. The next morning Grossman told the policeman
on the beat that something funny was going on in the neighborhood. "Come with me," said Grossman, "and I'll show you a guy
going up to the roof over there and coming down through the house
at the end of the block." Grossman and the policeman watched Henderson from the alley, and then from the street, and were waiting for
him when he came down again a few minutes later. "I'm George
Henderson," the manufacturer explained to the policeman, "and that
is the only way I can get away from those damned process-servers."
"Oh, so you're Mr. Henderson!" said Grossman with heavy sar-
casm, and handed him the paper.

Grossman's income was never more than sixty or seventy dollars a week, but it was seldom less. He lived with his wife in a furnished room on Union Street in Brooklyn. They preferred not to
spend much on mere shelter; they bought a new car every year
and had a good deal of pocket money all the time. Sometimes they
rented a furnished apartment for two or three months if they heard
of a good bargain, but they would just as soon, they said, have a double room somewhere, with a bath at the end of the hall. "What the

hell?" Grossman used to say on this subject. "It's just a place to sleep in, wherever it is, isn't it?"

Grossman always worked alone. He kept in touch with the lawyers' offices and private detective agencies regularly, and they assigned him to the hard cases of process-serving. On a case that required several days' work, he charged a flat rate of ten dollars per day. He wouldn't serve any paper for less than five dollars. His employers never had reason to suspect that he loafed on the job or tried to charge for more time than he really took. As soon as he had served a paper, he would hurry back to his client and tell how he did it. "Boy," he would say, "I knocked them cold!" or "They thought they were smart, but did I show them!" Grossman had no dangerous rivals in the profession. There are some good process-servers in New York, but none who has achieved the Grossman finesse. He was somewhat upset one time over something he found out about one of his colleagues. This process-server, Grossman learned, sometimes drafted his own mother to serve papers for him. She was a lady of sixty-eight, and her son had found that she could approach some people he could not. Grossman considered such tactics highly reprehensible. "That's no way to treat an old lady," he said, "even if she *is* his mother, is it?"

Grossman was reading a newspaper after supper one night in 1948 when his furiously active career was brought to a sudden conclusion by a heart attack. He had scarcely ever been ill in his life and there had never been any indication that there was anything wrong with his heart. He slumped down in his chair and the newspaper dropped to the floor. Nobody will ever know whether he was really reading the newspaper or was thinking indignantly about some incident in his past when his heart stopped beating.

THE INNOCENT MAN
AT SING SING

EARLY IN THE evening of December 8, 1938, a young man named Philip Caruso went outdoors for the first time in two weeks. He had gone to bed with the grippe on Thanksgiving Day and had stayed there for twelve days before the family doctor told him he could get up and move about the house. He had stayed indoors for two more days, reading magazines and listening to the radio. He lived with his father and mother, five of his seven brothers and a sister in a one-family house at 1957 Seventy-ninth Street, Brooklyn. He had a fever blister on the right side of his upper lip and he felt shaky from being in bed so long, but he was glad to get out of the house at last. He went straight to a cafeteria on Twentieth Avenue and Eighty-sixth Street, where he thought he might find some of his friends—clerks, office boys, and such, who lived in the neighborhood. He found three of them at the cafeteria, as he had hoped, and sat down with them. He drank some coffee and they talked about the hockey matches then going on at Madison Square Garden. He remembers all this distinctly, for it was while he was sitting there in the cafeteria, talking with his friends, that two police detectives came in and arrested him on a charge of first-degree robbery, accusing him of having taken part in a holdup in July, four months before. He remembers the fever blister particularly;

it was a singularly unfortunate blemish as things turned out. Although Caruso was innocent, he was tried, convicted, and sent to Sing Sing to serve a sentence of from ten to twenty years.

The police, the prosecuting authorities, and the judge who had sentenced Caruso found out that he was innocent after he had spent eight months in prison. After another month, during which considerably more time and effort were put forth to make sure of his innocence than had been expended at his trial in establishing his guilt, he was set free. Caruso's trial attracted no public attention whatever. It was one of fifty-odd trials during that month in New York City in which a defendant was convicted of a felony. When it was found that Caruso was innocent, a good many stories about the case appeared in Brooklyn and New York newspapers, and there were more stories when he was released from prison. These stories concerned themselves entirely with the circumstance which brought about Caruso's discharge from prison, this being simply that two young men from the Bronx confessed to the crime of which Caruso had been accused and were able to convince an understandably reluctant judge that they were telling the truth. The Brooklyn *Eagle* attempted to improve on the story by publishing a romantic article to the effect that Caruso's girl, named Mary Senatore, had hunted down the guilty parties singlehanded and, by an emotional appeal, had shamed them into confessing, thus setting free the boy she loved. This story was later proved in court to have been a complete fake. None of the papers showed any interest in the circumstances which brought about Caruso's arrest and conviction in the first place, although the stenographic transcript of Caruso's hearing before a City Magistrate, his indictment, his trial, and the subsequent hearing which established his innocence are matters of public record.

The most remarkable thing about the Caruso case is that it appears to be an ordinary, run-of-the-mill felony case, and an examination of the records leaves one with a feeling, not that Caruso was unluckier than any other young man similarly accused might be, but that his case may easily be typical of hundreds of other obscure cases which are tried hurriedly, without publicity. Caruso was arrested on what the police euphemistically call "information." This means that a stool pigeon told them that Caruso had participated in a certain holdup. There is nothing unusual about that; police make arrests every day on just such evidence, and if the injured party is able to identify the prisoner, the chances are he will be convicted. Stool pigeons are sometimes paid by the police, but more often exchange their "information" for favors. They are usually petty criminals who are given immunity from prosecution when they turn informer. There is a frank admission in the record of the Caruso case that the police helped to make the identification of Caruso appear to be more positive than it really was, and there is a suggestion that the District Attorney's office may have been cognizant of this. The defense attorney failed to take advantage of several opportunities to help his client's case, which he now may realize with regret. There is evidence that the magistrate who held the prisoner for the grand jury prevented the defense attorney from inquiring as deeply as he could have into the one phase of the case which might have cast doubt on the identification of the prisoner by the man who had been held up. The trial judge appears to have made up his mind that the defendant was guilty and to have conducted the trial accordingly. At one point during the trial the judge called into his chambers the prosecutor, the defense attorney, and the defendant, told Caruso he was a liar when he said he had nothing to do with the holdup, and urged him to plead guilty. This is not in the record, but I state it as a fact because the defendant says it did happen and I believe him. The defense attorney, when I asked him about this, refused to confirm Caruso's statement, saying that what happened in the judge's chambers was a private matter; then he gave me an instructive talk as to why such an act should not be criticized. It was an act which might have caused a mistrial, nevertheless, and probably would have done so had the defense attorney not been disinclined to violate legal etiquette by bringing such a matter into open court. I am told by people who ought to know that all this is a not unusual procedure in such cases and, in fact, that the whole trial was not unusual. In order to emphasize the impression that the personalities involved are significant only in that they seem to be typical of the kind of people who handle many such cases, I have chosen not to mention their names.

The case of the People of the State of New York against Philip Caruso, as this case is appropriately called, opens with some testimony taken in the office of an Assistant District Attorney in Brooklyn on December 9, 1938. The first witness was one Eugene Scaramellino, who on July 28, 1938, was held up by three men and robbed of $1,400. Scaramellino is a bookmaker's clerk working out of Jersey City for one of the big betting syndicates which operate there. He was driving around Brooklyn that morning in his car, making collections from small fry who accept bets for the syndicate. He stopped in front of a cigar store at 412 Forty-fifth Street and a man named Lefty, who runs the store, came out and gave him $112 of the $112.40 that had been taken in at the cigar store. Scaramellino didn't have change for a dollar, so Lefty went back into the store to get the forty cents. Scaramellino was sitting behind the wheel of his car waiting for the change when a man came up, pulled open the door on his right, and got in, pointing a revolver at his ribs and saying, "Not a sound, not a word. Otherwise I will let you have it." Scaramellino repeated this precise quotation at the subsequent hearings and at the trial. At almost the same moment a second man opened the front door on Scaramellino's left and got in, saying, "Move over." This man took the wheel. A third man got in the back and the car was driven away, with Scaramellino between the two men in front. The man on his right took all of Scaramellino's money, including, as the witness said, "my personal money," and kept telling him to look straight ahead. A few blocks away they gave the money to the man in back and let him out; then, further on, they let Scaramellino out and told him they would leave his car somewhere in the neighborhood where he could find it. The holdup was smoothly, almost politely, carried out. All through his testimony, Scaramellino referred to the holdup men as "the gentleman on my right," "the gentleman on my left," and "the gentleman in back." It developed that Scaramellino had been held up once before and on that occasion had chased the bandits, captured them, and held onto them until the police got there. He was badly injured in his fight with the bandits and spent several weeks in a hospital afterward.

Scaramellino was unable to describe to the Assistant District Attorney the gun which he said the gentleman on his right had pointed at him. He did not know whether it was an automatic or a revolver. A police detective at this point obligingly took out his own gun and Scaramellino was asked, "Did the gun look like that?" He said it did.

Scaramellino then described the holdup men. He said he hardly saw the man in back, "but at a glance I seen he was a heavy man." His description of the man on his right was confused. He said this man had on a polo shirt, but he didn't know what kind of coat. The Assistant District Attorney asked if he meant a sport shirt. "The collar went over the coat," said the witness. "That's why I can't tell, because he had a coat. But the coat must have been towards blue or brown."

Scaramellino said he had never seen any of the men before the holdup but that he had seen one of them since.

Philip Caruso was brought in then and the Assistant District Attorney said to Scaramellino, "Is this the man that you identified last night as one of the three men who committed the crime you already told me about?"

"Yes."

"And you are positive that he is the man?"

"Yes."

A statement from Caruso was then taken, in which he said that his nickname was Phil the Ghost, that he lived with his family, that he was out of work, that he was in the habit of staying up late and sleeping until past noon, that he had not had anything to do with this holdup, and that he had never been arrested before, either.

No further description of the man on Scaramellino's right appears in the record of the testimony taken in the Assistant District Attorney's office and it is not even made clear which of the three men Scaramellino claimed Caruso was. This is important in view of the fact that Caruso's subsequent conviction rests entirely on Scaramellino's identification of him as the man on his right, that there was no other evidence of any kind against Caruso, and that Scaramellino's identification was made more than four months after the holdup occurred.

THE CASE NOW moved to a City Magistrate's Court presided over by a magistrate who was in a hurry to get rid of it. Caruso was represented by an attorney whom his father hired for $25 and was being prosecuted by another Assistant District Attorney, representing the People of the State of New York.

At this sort of hearing the prisoner may be released if the magistrate decides there is not a prima-facie case against him or held for the grand jury if the magistrate thinks there is. Scaramellino repeated his story and this time made it clear that he identified Caruso as being the man on his right in the car, the man with the gun. He said that this man had told him to keep looking straight ahead but that he had replied, "I am in the habit of looking in the direction to whom I am speaking to," and that, having thus put the man in his place, he had been able to get a good look at him.

"And this is the man who was in the car?" asked the Assistant District Attorney, pointing to Caruso.

"This is the man."

"You are sure?"

"Positive."

Cross-examining Scaramellino, the defense attorney tried to find out more about his duties as a bookmaker's clerk and the magistrate grew impatient. "Step down," the magistrate said to the witness. "That's the end of the cross-examination," he went on, speaking to the attorney somewhat incoherently. "Did you have any particular point in questioning you want to ask, I will let you ask, but if you are going to ask these kind of questions—that's the end of the cross-examination."

"I believe I have a right to inquire what took place on that particular morning," said the attorney.

"If you tell me there is any point to this general line of inquiry, I will let you," replied the magistrate, while the witness evidently stepped up again, "but if you take minute by minute—that doesn't mean anything. Go back, and if there is any point in these questions I will let you go on with it indefinitely. Up to now there are generalities. Ask the next question."

The attorney gave up trying to find out what Scaramellino's job was like and fairly rapidly got down to the inadequacy of Scaramellino's description of the man on his right in the car.

"Well," said the witness defensively, "if anybody is scared, he ain't going to look at the suit he had on or the tie."

"Did you at any time see a full view of the defendant in the car?"

"What is that?"

"A full view of his face?"

"Well, about a three-fourths view."

"What kind of hat did he have on?"

"I couldn't say my attention was called to the hat. I don't believe I seen any hat because I noticed the hat on the fellow who was driving. I would have noticed a hat if he had worn a hat."

"You don't know whether he had a hat on or not?"

"Exclude it," interrupted the magistrate. "Don't keep talking about the same thing. Talk about something else—don't repeat."

The defense attorney then moved to dismiss the case on the ground that the People of the State of New York had failed to prove a prima-facie case against Caruso, but the magistrate denied the motion and held Caruso for the grand jury in $10,000 bail. Caruso could not furnish bail, so he was taken to the Raymond Street Jail, in Brooklyn. His brothers and sister and father and mother were permitted to see him for the first time since his arrest, and his girl brought him some cigarettes.

The grand jury then indicted Caruso on four counts, charging robbery in the first degree, grand larceny in the first degree, assault in the second degree (pointing the revolver at Scaramellino), and kidnapping—"wilfully seized, confined, inveigled and kidnapped the complainant with intent to cause him, without authority of law, to be confined and imprisoned within this state and to be kept and detained against his will." The fourth count was later dropped, possibly on the ground of overenthusiasm. Recorded in the indictment are a few more facts about Caruso: his age is twenty-four, his last occupation was that of a clerk in a fruit store, his religion is Catholic, his religious instruction is irregular, and he does not use drugs.

THE TRIAL OF Caruso began before a judge and a jury in the Kings County Court, in Brooklyn, on March 8, 1939, a little over seven months after the holdup and three months after Caruso's arrest. Caruso had stayed in jail since the arrest. He was represented by a new lawyer and the People of the State of New York were represented by the Assistant District Attorney in whose office the preliminary testimony had been taken the day after Caruso's arrest. Caruso's father paid this new lawyer $400 as a fee and $30 extra, with which the lawyer bought the stenographic record of Caruso's hearing before the City Magistrate.

Scaramellino was the first witness and he told his tale once more. It went along about as before but in greater detail, and throughout the story of the holdup itself he referred to "the fellow on my right," "the fellow driving," and "the fellow in back." He mentioned no names, which was proper. Then he got to his description of what happened after they let him out of the car.

"No sooner I got out they went ahead," Scaramellino said.

"Who went ahead?" asked the prosecutor.

"The car and all."

"The car and who else went ahead?"

"The man Caruso I believe his name is and the man at the wheel."

This was the first time Caruso's name was mentioned in testimony at the trial and it was brought in, probably inadvertently, in a way that must have left the distinct impression in the minds of the jury that Caruso was known to be one of the holdup men. This is not in accordance with the rules of court procedure and could have been objected to by the defense or ordered stricken from the record by the judge. Neither the judge nor the defense attorney took any notice of it and Scaramellino went on with his story. He called the man on his right Caruso so often that before it developed that the only evidence against Caruso was Scaramellino's identification of him four months after the holdup, the prosecutor was able to ask such questions as "Which part of the car did the defendant sit in?" and "What did this defendant say before you got out of the car?" and "Tell us what he said—we are talking about Caruso now." At one point Scaramellino was about to testify blithely as to what one of the detectives had told him about information he had gathered on Caruso when the judge interrupted him. The judge said to the defense attorney, "Why don't you object?" and then to the stenographer, "Strike it out." It was one of the few objections raised in behalf of Caruso at the trial. Although it was properly stricken out because it was hearsay testimony, the detective's story might have given the jury its only opportunity to hear that Caruso was arrested simply on the strength of a tale told to the detectives by a stool pigeon.

Scaramellino at one point contradicted his earlier testimony at the hearing before the City Magistrate.

"Did you ever get a full view of this defendant's face?" he was asked.

"I did," he answered.

The defense attorney picked this up and made a point of it. "You didn't say that at the examination," he remarked.

The prosecutor objected to this and the objection was sustained.

The testimony was enlivened, at least for a reader who knows the man convicted was innocent and that he had a fever blister the day he was arrested, when, under cross-examination, the defense attorney went into the circumstances of Scaramellino's identification of Caruso at the station house that night.

"Did you notice anything about his face which caused you to form the conclusion that he was the man that held you up or one of the men that held you up?" he asked the witness.

"Just I recognized him," said Scaramellino.

"You made no statement whatever?"

"I did not."

"Do you remember making this statement to the police officer in the station house: 'I recognize this man because of the mole on his lip'?"

"I didn't say that. I said at the time I was stuck up he had a mark on the lip which could have happened by a scratch which dries up or a mole or something of the kind."

"Did he have that mark in the station house on his lip?"

"He did not."

"You are positive of that?"

"I am positive."

"Did you make this statement to the District Attorney: 'Well, if it isn't he, it must be his twin brother'?"

"I did make that statement, I think. I meant to say that I was pretty positive."

What the judge now said at this point unquestionably aided the prosecution of Caruso, coming on top of Scaramellino's admission that he meant to say that he was "pretty positive" in his identification. The defense attorney called attention to the witness's using the phrase "I meant to say," and the judge interrupted, remarking, "Yes, he said he made that statement, if it was not he it was his twin brother, and he added he meant he was positive. Now he says that he said it meaning that he was positive this was the man."

"I move to strike it out," said the defense attorney.

"Motion denied."

This was the end of the cross-examination.

The judge thus effectively erased from the jury's mind the most significant adjective used in the trial—the adjective "pretty," which in the sense the witness had used it clearly indicated that he was only moderately certain of his identification of Caruso.

There was but one other witness for the prosecution. This was the detective. He merely testified that he had made the arrest and was present at the station house when Scaramellino identified Caruso. Four men, including Caruso, were lined up against a wall, he said, and Scaramellino picked Caruso as the man who had sat on his right in the car. That, with Scaramellino's testimony, was all there was to the case of the People of New York against Philip Caruso.

The defense was not much more impressive. Benjamin Cohen, a fruit merchant for whom Caruso had worked for several years, established beyond much question that Caruso was left-handed. Scaramellino had testified that the man on his right held the revolver in his right hand. The defense attorney himself did not seem to think as much of this revelation as he must have when he first plotted his strategy. In any event, he made very little of it.

Caruso's father was the next witness. He has worked for many years as a shoe-shine man on the Staten Island ferries and earned enough at it to raise his family and partially pay for the house in which all the Carusos live. He testified that Philip was home in bed at the hour the holdup occurred, but his story was weakened under cross-examination when the prosecutor made much of the size of the Caruso family and the difficulty the father would have in remembering what this particular son was doing on a day seven months before when he had had no reason for paying especial attention to him.

Philip Caruso then took the stand. He also said he was home in bed when the holdup took place. It was at this point, Caruso says, that the judge called the conference in his chambers and urged him to plead guilty. When Caruso returned to the stand he was asked what the detectives said to him after they came up to him that night in the cafeteria. He said, "They said, 'Is your name Phil?'" He was taken to the station house and, after they questioned him, was told to stand against a wall with three other fellows. "They all wore camel's-hair coats," Caruso testified. Scaramellino then identified him. Later, he said, the police lieutenant tried to persuade him to confess, saying, "Phil, I want you to help me out. This means a very big case to us."

The uncertainty of both the police and the Assistant District Attorney at this early stage is indicated by the rest of Caruso's testimony.

"The D.A. asked me, he said, 'Phil, I know you are a good kid. You come from a good family. Tell me who those other two fellows are and I will guarantee you will never go to jail.' I said, 'I don't know the other two fellows.' Then he called in the complainant, 'Are you sure this is the fellow?' The complainant says, 'If it ain't him it is his twin brother.'

"The D.A. then asked me if I had any brothers. I said, 'Yes, I have seven brothers.'

" 'Any like you?'

"I said, 'Yes.' I said, 'Yes, there is two that look like me, but they wouldn't do a thing like that neither.' "

Caruso's testimony then reverted to the scene at the police station when Scaramellino picked him out of the lineup.

"And the complainant came in and pointed directly at me and said, 'That's the fellow. He had a gray suit and he wore a gray hat and he had a mole on his lip.' I turned to the detective and I said, 'That isn't a mole, it is a fever blister. I just got out of bed.' "

Nothing was made of this point. The questions drifted off to the defense attorney's forlorn strategy about the left-handedness of his client.

There was some rebuttal from the police lieutenant who had wanted Phil to help him out. He said he had never said any such thing. The defense did not take the opportunity to follow up the matter of the mole and the fever blister. Then the stenographer who took down the statements of Scaramellino and Caruso in the Assistant District Attorney's office was called and swore to the accuracy of the work by which he earns his living, and the case was ready to go to the jury.

As is customary, there is no record of the addresses of the prosecutor or of the defense attorney to the jury. There is one of the judge's charge. The second paragraph of this seems favorable to the prosecution. The judge said to the jury, "You have got a very simple issue in this case, very simple. Was there a robbery or wasn't there? That is the only question to be submitted to you. Was there a robbery committed by this defendant? If there was, and you are satisfied according to the law which I will define to you as we go along, then your duty is to convict. If there was not, then acquit. The only question here is, 'Was there a robbery?' "

Not until several hundred words later did the judge make it

entirely clear that while there might have been a robbery the defendant might not have been one of the robbers. Then he said, "Was there a robbery committed at that point and, if there was, was this defendant one of the robbers?" and told the jury that this was for them to decide. In other respects the charge was conventional—the usual tiresome explanations of reasonable doubt and the rules of evidence, running on for some six thousand words.

The jury retired and some time later returned, having sent a note to the judge asking a question.

"Gentlemen," said the judge when the jury came back to the courtroom, "you ask if you can make a recommendation for clemency?"

"Yes," said the foreman.

"Yes, you can," the judge said, "and the Court will take cognizance of your recommendation and give it due consideration. If you are satisfied beyond a reasonable doubt that the defendant is guilty, then your duty is to say so, and if you feel you want to make a recommendation for clemency you have a perfect right to do so, and, as I say, the Court will give it full consideration. Is there anything else you want to know? Is there any doubt as to the testimony of any witness? You want to have any testimony read?"

The jury appears at this point to have had some notion of what was wrong with this trial, for the foreman answered, "Identification at the time the robbery was committed."

"The jury asked the Court for information," the judge said. "I will have to send them back to their room until the stenographer who took the minutes yesterday arrives. He is at home ill and we will notify him to come here. If you gentlemen can find your way clear to gain information you wish from members of the jury, all right. If there is any serious doubt as to the point involved and you must have the testimony of this witness read to you, you will have to wait a little while until the stenographer comes here. If, however, the testimony you want to have read, the point you have in mind can be solved among yourselves from your own recollection, then you may continue on with your deliberations and may arrive at some agreement, but if you cannot, if you find it necessary to have some particular testimony read to you, then stay in your room and we will have the stenographer come up here from his home and read it to you."

There is a chance, but not much of a one, that had the judge been able to summon the stenographer without any delay, the jury might have found Caruso not guilty. The jury seems to have been on the right track, but they did not want to wait for the stenographer.

The jury retired and soon returned with its verdict. "We find the defendant guilty as charged in the indictment, with a recommendation for clemency," said the foreman.

The defense attorney, as is customary, moved to set aside the verdict on the ground that it was contrary to the weight of evidence, and the judge denied the motion.

"The Court finds," said the judge, "upon the evidence that at the time this defendant committed the crime charged, of which he was found guilty, he was armed with a dangerous weapon, to wit, a revolver. I will accept the jury's recommendation for clemency and save this fellow five years. It will take about five years off his sentence."

Caruso was then remanded to the Raymond Street Jail, in Brooklyn, to await sentence. His family and his girl went to see him again at the jail and they talked, without much hope, of appealing the case. Almost a month later he was brought before the judge again.

"This is the case," said the defense attorney, refreshing the judge's recollection, "where the jury brought in a verdict of guilty of robbery and recommended clemency."

"Yes," said the judge, "robbery in the first degree, armed, and the jury recommended clemency. I said then that I would respect the recommendation as far as I could do, and I will consider it as robbery in the first degree unarmed, thereby saving him five years.

The rest of the sentence is mandatory. I think the verdict was a very fair verdict. Two or three of the boys got in and held up a man in his automobile and took $1,400 from him, rode around for a while and chased him out of the car and got away with the car for a while. The car was later recovered, but not the money. This is the man who had the gun according to the testimony.

"The sentence of the Court is that he be confined in Sing Sing Prison for a term not less than ten years and no more than twenty years."

So Caruso went to Sing Sing. If he did not break any rules or try to escape, he would have been summoned before the Parole Board on September 22, 1945, but if he did not then say he had been guilty all along and did not name the accomplices in the crime he had not committed, the Parole Board might not have paroled him. He did not break any rules and he did not try to escape. Aside from the ordinary discomforts of life in Sing Sing, he would not have minded being there as much as he did except that he slept little. "You see," he has said since, "when you are guilty and in Sing Sing you are O.K. You can get a good night's sleep. But I was innocent, and I kept thinking about that and I didn't sleep good."

He had been in the Raymond Street Jail, in Brooklyn, for four months and now he stayed at Sing Sing for four more months. Then he was transferred to the Great Meadow Prison at Comstock, New York. He was there three weeks. Then, nearly nine months after he was arrested, which is to say thirty-seven weeks, or 259 days, or 6,216 hours, he was taken back to Sing Sing and from there brought back to New York to appear at a hearing on a motion for a new trial before the judge who had accepted the jury's verdict of guilty and had sentenced him to Sing Sing.

CARUSO'S ENCOUNTER WITH the People of the State of New York was started toward its relatively happy denouement on the night of Friday, July 28, 1939, which happened to be exactly a year to the day after the holdup of Scaramellino. On that evening one Morris Gottlieb and one Jack Jacobson, who lived in the Bronx, were picked up by Bronx detectives and questioned. They were picked up on information given the detectives by a stool pigeon, just as Caruso himself had been picked up in December of the year before. It happened that this time the stool pigeon was well informed. The detectives convinced Gottlieb and Jacobson that they could be convicted of taking part in a number of holdups. They then decided to plead guilty and confessed to a number of holdups, including the holdup of Scaramellino.

The detectives believed that Gottlieb and Jacobson were telling the truth and they gave the story to the newspapers on Sunday for the Monday-morning editions. It was a story worth some space in the New York papers, because it is not often that a man serving a sentence at Sing Sing is proved to be innocent. The Brooklyn papers played up the story on the front pages. District Attorney Geoghan of Brooklyn, who, because of the unimportance of the case, had never paid any attention to it before, saw the story and determined to get Caruso out of prison as soon as possible. He announced his intention to the newspapers, and this was played up, too. He assigned the case to Assistant District Attorney Hyman Barshay, who had not been connected with it before, and Barshay made strenuous efforts to get Caruso out of prison. Since Caruso had been duly convicted and sentenced, he could not just be turned loose; first a hearing had to be held and the judge who had accepted the verdict of guilty had to be convinced that a new trial should be granted. Then, if he granted the motion for the new trial, the judge could decide that a new trial was really unnecessary and could entertain a motion to dismiss the indictment. It was considerably harder to get Caruso out of prison than it was to get him in.

The hearing opened on August 28, a month after Gottlieb and Jacobson had confessed. This was just a routine delay, similar to the four months which Caruso had spent in the Raymond Street Jail waiting to be tried and convicted. Once the hearing started, the judge went into the case with meticulous thoroughness. There is a stenographic record of the proceedings. Gottlieb and Jacobson testified first and told all about the holdup and their plans to carry it out with a third man. This third man had planned the holdup of Scaramellino some weeks before it took place but had run into bad luck. Before he could carry out his plan, he had been arrested. A Brooklyn policeman, acting entirely on a hunch, picked him up as a suspicious character when he was driving around Brooklyn, and a gun was found in the car. He was tried on a charge of carrying a dangerous weapon and later acquitted by a jury, but this interruption prevented him from taking an active part in the holdup he had planned with Gottlieb and Jacobson. They therefore brought in a fourth man, for whom the police are still looking.

Gottlieb, who testified that he was the man on Scaramellino's right, had a conspicuous mole on his upper right lip. After he had testified, the judge said ungrammatically but with apparently sincere surprise, "There is as much difference between Caruso and this man as the man in the moon. No resemblance at all. This man has a long nose, almost aquiline, a birthmark, a black mole, on his right upper lip, near the end of his mouth, dark complexion." When Jacobson testified, however, the judge was still suspicious. He tried to test the truth of Jacobson's statements by implying that Scaramellino had said that Jacobson sat on Caruso's right in the car. Jacobson did not fall into the trap. From this point on the judge indicated he was convinced that Caruso was innocent.

The detective who had testified at the trial of Caruso was then called, and it was brought out that in Scaramellino's original description of the man on his right he had said that the man had a mole on his upper lip. The detective admitted that this evidence, which cast doubt on the identification of Caruso by Scaramellino in court, had not been brought out at the trial.

The police lieutenant who had testified at the trial was then called, and for the first time in the Caruso case the question of how Caruso had ever come to be arrested in the first place was gone into. The lieutenant testified that a stool pigeon had said that Caruso "was implicated in a holdup of a bookmaker in the Bay Ridge section some time previous." From the lieutenant's testimony it is apparent that the stool pigeon's story was extremely vague and that he did not even know the name of the bookmaker or the date of the holdup. The lieutenant said he then looked up the records of holdups that summer, found the Scaramellino case, and then made inquiries as to where Caruso might be picked up. They did not find out where Caruso lived, evidently, but only that he sometimes frequented a cafeteria on Twentieth Avenue and Eighty-sixth Street. The detectives who arrested him were instructed to pick him up there, which they did.

Scaramellino then testified, and it now becomes clear that he was never really certain that Caruso was the man and that he expressed this doubt both to the police and to the Assistant District Attorney who prosecuted Caruso. He said he was positive that the man on his right had a mole on his lip and that when he had first seen Caruso in the lineup at the station house he had noticed that Caruso had a fever blister, not a mole. "I even passed the remark to the detective, 'That don't seem to be the right mark that I seen on his upper lip,'" he said. This was, of course, in direct contradiction of his testimony at Caruso's trial. There he had said that he had seen no mark on Caruso's lip at the station house.

The judge evidently began to feel some indignation at this point, although he perhaps did not remember that at the trial he himself had amended Scaramellino's statement that he was "pretty positive" and had made it "positive," thus preventing further inquiry into the doubt the witness had then quite clearly expressed.

A tragi-comic dialogue took place between the man who had either mistakenly or falsely identified Caruso and the man who had accepted the verdict of guilty and sentenced the innocent man to Sing Sing for from ten to twenty years. Scaramellino had just testified that as soon as he saw Gottlieb he knew that Caruso was innocent, that Gottlieb was the man beyond all question.

"As soon as you saw Gottlieb and you saw that mole you said, 'That is the man'?" asked the judge.

"That is positive. Then I was positive when I seen the right man."

"Weren't you positive before?"

"I was positive at the time until I seen Gottlieb. Until the last minute I still thought it was Caruso until I seen Gottlieb. Then that made me positive and I said so."

"Was there any resemblance between Caruso and Gottlieb?"

"There is."

"There is, is there? Have you seen Gottlieb's nose?"

"Well—still—Mr. . . ."

"Just answer my question. Have you seen Gottlieb's nose?"

"Yes, pointed nose."

"Very characteristic of a Jewish nose, isn't it? It is almost aquiline. Almost with a hook and pointed in, isn't it?"

"To my best judgment I gave the right description."

"How about Caruso's nose? Hasn't he got sort of a round nose?"

"He was sharp, too, Your Honor."

"You know you have done this boy a serious injury?"

"I am sorry. I don't mean to."

"I don't believe you."

"I never knew Mr. Caruso before he was arrested and I did not know Gottlieb. What interest would I have?"

"You were very neglectful and careless, grossly negligent, and you had no regard for his rights."

"I am awfully sorry."

"There is only one conclusion I can draw from your testimony: either you lied then or you were very, very careless in picking him out."

"I had no reason to lie, Your Honor."

"That is up to you, it is up to your conscience."

"I had no reason to lie, Your Honor."

The judge then called Caruso before him and questioned him at great length about his personal life, finding out that he often shot pool with his friends and sometimes even shot crap. Then the judge made this remarkable address to the man who had been in prison for the past nine months and who had been there as a result of the trial over which the judge himself had presided: "Well, Caruso, you have been in jail now for about five months. (The judge did not count the months Caruso was in jail before he was tried.) It is really sad that somebody made a mistake. I am convinced that this was a very sad experience that you had to go through. I am sorry. There is only one thing I want to ask you: Do not feel bitter against the administration of justice. There has been a wrong done to you, but it was an honest mistake. Neither the complaining witness nor the police have any grudge against you. It just happened that way. There was a mistake made and there it is. I want to give you a piece of advice, Phil. You live down around my old neighborhood in Bath Beach. Keep away from those poolrooms. That is not the place for you nor for any decent fellow. You have not been working for a year. You have been going around crapshooting. You have made money shooting crap. You are slipping and let this be a good lesson to you. Raymond Street Jail is no place for a person to live. Sing Sing is not a very good place either, and you have experienced that for the five months you were up there. Let this mistake be a good lesson. Keep away from that crowd. Go straight. Do you hear?"

"Yes, sir," said Caruso.

Caruso's father had hired another attorney to appeal his son's conviction—the third he had had to hire since Caruso was arrested. He paid this lawyer $400 to handle the appeal and agreed to pay him $200 more as soon as he could raise the money. The lawyer also got $40 extra in cash at this time to pay for the stenographic record of Caruso's trial. The lawyer filed notice of appeal and, under the regulations for such cases, he was supposed to complete his briefs and argue the case before an Appellate Court within three months. It happens, however, that the Justices of the Appellate Divisions of the Supreme Court of New York, who would have heard Caruso's appeal, close up their court and take at least two months off every summer; during July, August, and sometimes most of September, these justices will not listen to such cases as Caruso's or any other cases. So the justices, following their accustomed routine, were to hear Caruso's appeal on September 25 and not a day earlier. As it turned out, they could have taken all of September off, as far as this particular case was concerned, because the guilty men confessed in July, Caruso had been proved innocent, and the judge who had presided at the hearing for a new trial had finished telling the innocent man to keep out of poolrooms and was about to set him free.

The lawyer who would have handled the appeal and who was representing Caruso at the final hearing now made a pretty speech. He complimented the judge for his decision to free Caruso and he complimented the District Attorney for having been so co-operative. "And I just want to say in closing," he said, "that as far as this boy is concerned it is just like a dream come true. On May 24, 1939, he wrote a letter to me from Sing Sing and in the postscript he said, 'I was dreaming the other night that you had won my appeal and you have proved my innocence. I hope it comes true.' "

The judge made an appropriate reply to this, saying that it certainly was correct that the District Attorney had been very fair in the matter. He talked along for some little time. Then, as if it were an afterthought, he said, "All right, Phil, you can go home now."

So Phil went home. Under the laws of the Commonwealth of New York and other states, a man mistakenly convicted of a crime cannot sue the State unless the State gives the man permission to sue it, and this may be granted only by a special act of the legislature. Without such an act, the innocent man cannot even recover what he had to spend on lawyers to defend him. When a prisoner leaves Sing Sing after serving his sentence, he is given twenty dollars by the State to help him along. Caruso did not get the twenty dollars when he left Sing Sing, because he had not served his sentence. Caruso could sue Scaramellino, but unless he could prove malice, which he could not, he would have no chance of collecting damages. He could sue the police officers, the prosecutor, and perhaps even the judge as individuals, but he would also have to prove malice on their part in order to collect damages.

Caruso is a nice-looking young man, twenty-five years old, and although he still shoots pool occasionally with his friends and probably even shoots crap now and then, he seems to have taken at least some of the judge's advice. The last time I saw him—some months after he was set free—he seemed to hold no grudge against the administration of justice and he was not particularly indignant about what happened to him. Pretty soon, he said, the police are going to return to him the records of his fingerprints, and he is grateful for this. "They are going to wipe out the record here and even in Washington, where the G-men have got them," he said with awe. Mary Senatore was still his girl and they say they want to get married if Philip finds a job. He has never applied for relief. "I want a steady job," he said. He wishes they had let him out of Sing Sing as soon as the guilty men confessed because the *Daily Mirror* and *True Story Magazine* wanted him to write his own story for them, and Paramount wanted to make a short based on his case. He would have got some money from all three if he could have accepted their offers then. By the time he was released, six weeks later, none of them were any longer interested in his case. It had ceased to be news. He did make $250 for appearing on a radio program called "We, the People." The lawyer who started to prepare the appeal and who represented him at the final hearing charged him $50 for representing him in his negotiations with the radio station, but Caruso hasn't paid him that yet, nor has Caruso's father paid the $200 still owing the lawyer for starting the appeal. The lawyer recently sent Caruso a bill for $2,500, which he said included a fee for handling the motion for a new trial which resulted in Caruso's release from prison. This was a surprise to the Carusos, and they don't know what to do about it. If by any chance the People of the State of New York, through their legislature, should see fit to pay his father the $895 which he has actually given the three lawyers who handled his case, Caruso thinks that would be fine. Nobody has thus far suggested that the legislature do so.

THE PERSONALITIES OF the men involved with the arrest, prosecution, and trial of Caruso are, as I have said, significant only in that they are probably typical of the sort of people who conduct such cases every day. I have tried to support with evidence and quotations from the record my impression that Caruso was not extraordinarily unlucky in being arrested, convicted, and sent to prison. I am sure this impression is valid. Caruso did not just happen to run into detectives who kept silent about the evident uncertainty of his identification, an Assistant District Attorney who was probably conscious of the uncertainty but said nothing about it, defense attorneys who on the whole do not appear to have been outstandingly courageous or ingenious, and a judge who was more partial than he might have been and who committed at least one act, that of calling the defendant into his chambers and urging him to plead guilty, which by the laws of decency, if not of court procedure, made him unfit to preside over the remainder of the trial.

If there is any point to the Caruso case, it is that it is not an unusual one. The police make a practice of arresting people, especially of Caruso's class, on information furnished by stool pigeons who have reason to curry favor with the police. If the identification by the plaintiff is as uncertain as Scaramellino's was, both the police and the prosecuting authorities are in the habit of trying to make it appear to be positive. City magistrates invariably rush these cases to the grand jury. Men who have suffered at the hands of criminals are naturally anxious to see somebody pay a penalty, and their identifications of suspects are notoriously untrustworthy, although they may think even with more conviction than Scaramellino had that they are telling the truth. Defense attorneys in such cases often do not contribute as much time or ingenuity as they should, because the cases are unaccompanied by publicity and the fees, usually collected in advance, are small. They are also disinclined to annoy either judges or prosecutors by violating the customs of the bar. Judges continually make up their minds about the guilt or innocence of a defendant, although under the rules of jurisprudence the weighing of the facts of the case is no business of the judge; and judges continually convey their prejudice to the jury. It is also common practice for judges, particularly in minor cases, to call a defendant into his chambers in the middle of a trial and urge him to save the court time by pleading guilty, pointing out to him that he is certain to be convicted. There is what is improperly called a gentleman's agreement between judges and lawyers in such cases. If the defendant refuses to plead guilty, as Caruso did, the defense attorney is not supposed to make a motion for a mistrial. This system, of course, not only saves the time of the District Attorney's office and the judge but also saves the time of defense attorneys. Lawyers will tell you that quite often an innocent man is thus persuaded to plead guilty by a threatening judge and an indifferent defense attorney.

The attitude of the third attorney who represented Caruso supports the impression that the Caruso case was run-of-the-mill. This lawyer, who was handling Caruso's appeal before it was found that an appeal would not be necessary, has said since that he did not think there was much chance of an appeal's being successful, which indicates that he saw nothing extraordinary in the conduct of Caruso's trial. He also found nothing in it to cause him any indignation toward the police, the prosecuting authorities, or the judge. He was just mighty glad the boy's dream came true, that's all.

The mistaken or false identification of Caruso by Scaramellino is not unusual, but is an example of what happens in many such cases in which the only obtainable evidence is an identification by the injured party. This is recognized by progressive lawyers and has been written about a great deal, but in vain. In a book called *Convicting the Innocent*, which is a collection of sixty-five cases not unlike Caruso's, Professor Edwin M. Borchard of Yale has this to say:

> Perhaps the major source of these tragic errors is an identification of the accused by the victim of a crime of violence. Juries seem disposed more readily to credit the veracity and reliability of the victims of an outrage than any amount of contrary evidence by or on behalf of the accused, whether by way of alibi, character witnesses, or other testimony. These cases illustrate the fact that the emotional balance of the victim or eyewitness is so disturbed by his extraordinary experience that his powers of perception become distorted and his identification is frequently most untrustworthy. Into the identification enter other motives, not necessarily stimulated originally by the accused personally—the desire to requite a crime, to exact vengeance upon the person believed to be guilty, to find a scapegoat, to support, consciously or unconsciously, an identification already made by another. Thus doubts are resolved against the accused. How valueless are these identifications by the victim of a crime is indicated by the fact that in eight of these cases the wrongfully accused person and the really guilty criminal bore not the slightest resemblance to each other, whereas in twelve other cases, the resemblance, while fair, was still not at all close. In only two cases can the resemblance be called striking.

Caruso was not unlucky. He was lucky. A stool pigeon in the Bronx happened to have the right information about Gottlieb and Jacobson, two men Caruso had never seen or heard of. They were arrested and they confessed convincingly to the crime for which Caruso had been sent to prison.

In the dossier on the Caruso case, which contains also the record of the disposition of the charges of first-degree robbery against Gottlieb and Jacobson, is a letter addressed to the District Attorney's office. The letter is, as the judge in this case might say, irrelevant and immaterial. It is from Jacobson's wife and it says, in part. "After all, my husband is only twenty-two years now and this happened a year ago. For the sake of our baby coming to us in such a short time couldn't you please help him to at least a lighter sentence? Every day and at night all I can hear is ten years to twenty years and the thought of such a long time is driving me crazy. I have no place and no one to turn to except you. You see we are poor but we were happy. Make us so again please because I love him so."

The District Attorney's office could do nothing about this, since the sentence of ten to twenty years is the least a man can get for first-degree robbery. Jacobson was accordingly sent to prison for that length of time, and Gottlieb, who had carried the gun, got ten years more. This may be quite as it should be; they had held up a man and had pleaded guilty. But just as Caruso's case may be said to be typical, so is Mrs. Jacobson's letter. The same simple sentiments might very well have been expressed by the wife of a man who had not held up anybody and, as these things go, they would have been as ineffective and as easily forgotten as Mrs. Jacobson's letter.

AVERAGE COP

B Y ALL ORDINARY standards, Albert Moran Williams is something of an eccentric. He takes long walks six days a week,
sometimes strolling for eight hours with scarcely a rest. He is often
lonely during these jaunts through the city streets, yet when he
speaks to a fellow-man, it is almost always to upbraid him. He is
constantly getting himself embroiled in other people's affairs. If he
passes a store at night, he tries the door to see if it is unlocked, but
if he finds anybody else doing this, he chases him. He sleeps irregularly, and often has breakfast at 3 P.M. and lunch at midnight. Because of a sense of duty inordinately strong for a man of his years
and upbringing, he hardly ever relaxes as other men do. He is young
and healthy-looking, yet he clothes himself in a bag and, in winter,
a benny as well; he always carries with him, among other things, a
roscoe, a potsie, and a biscuit, and he is constantly on the lookout
for shoo-flies. He is rather deeply preoccupied with death and he
is more religious than any of the boys he grew up with on the
West Side, except the one who became a Catholic priest. He has
acquired a realistic, almost cynical conception of the human species,
and he, in turn, is regarded with a certain animosity by the average
citizen. Most of his friends are men of his own calling, and shop
talk dominates his conversation at work and at play. He has been

on the force four and a half years now; soon he will be a first-grade patrolman.

You would be puzzled by many of the words he uses. What most of us call his beat he refers to as his post, and when he is on it, he is working his tour, not his shift. His uniform is his bag and his winter overcoat his benny. A complaint against a law-breaker he calls a diddo. If he has an influential friend—a politician, a prominent banker, a big lawyer—this friend is his rabbi. His shield is his potsie and his gun is his roscoe. His watch, of course, is his biscuit. Bullets, to him, are liver pills. The sergeant is the boss, the captain is the skipper, and the lieutenants who supervise patrols and spy on patrolmen are shoo-flies. The telephone he uses to call his station house is the box. His wife, even to her face, is usually the cook.

Williams, at the moment, is a second-grade patrolman. Behind him is his work as third- and fourth-grade patrolman and probationary patrolman, or rookie. His first day on a regular tour is far in the past, and the rookie of twenty-five who stepped out of the detail for the first time and watched the squad of broad, blue backs go marching down the street away from him, leaving him alone to keep the peace on East Fifty-third Street, seems almost unrecognizable to him now. But the memory of that first day is vivid. He had had the uniform on before at home. While his wife was in the kitchen, he had looked at it appreciatively in the mirror in their bedroom. That first day on tour he thought that everybody must be looking at him, and felt desperately uncomfortable. As he walked along, his temples throbbing, he underwent the most devastating emotional experience of his life. All of his thoughts had been thrown inward and he had been seeing only himself in his blue uniform; and all at once he thought of bandits, of women stabbed in the throat and children kidnapped, of collisions and ambulances and fires, and of thieves dodging into areaways; he thought of crime and catastrophe and realized, all in a flash, what he was and what he was there for. He felt giddy and hysterical, and he remembers now that he stopped suddenly in his tracks, like a thoroughbred setter, and looked about him searchingly. That was all. In a few moments he was all right again. "It was the Goddamn'est thing ever happened to me," he says. "You know what? I almost fainted—would you believe it?"

Before his probationary period began, Williams had spent two years of part-time study at Delehanty's police preparatory school on East Fifteenth Street, where he had listened to one lecture a week and learned enough to pass the preliminary examination which made him eligible for the Police Academy of the Department. There followed a six months' intensive course, during which his mind was introduced to the intricacies of the penal code and his body subjected to scientific building and strengthening exercises. He learned, for instance, that garbage cans must be covered when placed on the sidewalk and that known pickpockets may be arrested for jostling if proof of a specific theft is lacking. He also learned to shoot 85 per cent accurately at life-size targets. Long before the course was ended, he had begun inevitably to think of professional criminals as his personal adversaries rather than as mere foes of society. The lectures on the sanitary code, traffic regulations, simple and felonious assault, forgery, larceny, and juvenile delinquency produced in him a similarly specialized attitude toward the public at large. He became intimately acquainted in theory with all manner of crimes and misdemeanors of profit and passion. The average citizen began to appear to Williams as a potential criminal, holding within him the capabilities of arson, thievery, sexual degeneracy, homicide, and a thousand variations of unsocial conduct. As he rode home to his flat in the Bronx in those days of preparation, he found himself scrutinizing the straphangers on the subway with a frank and uninhibited suspicion.

"That fellow there," he would say to himself cheerfully, "looks like a cheap forger to me."

His encounters with ordinary citizens since he began to patrol a post have made him aware of the citizen's grave misunderstanding of the patrolman's problems. He remembers with a sense of injury one of the first emergencies with which he was confronted while on his tour in the East Fifties. The hood of a taxicab occupied by two well-dressed businessmen burst into flames and the driver pulled up at the curb. Williams, still a bit overzealous, perhaps, dashed to a fire-box and turned in an alarm. But before the engines had time to get there, the fire was out, the motor running again, and the occupants of the cab were urging the driver to proceed.

"You got to wait," Williams told the driver, placing a restraining hand on the steering wheel. "The fire engines are coming."

"That's absurd," said one of the businessmen, leaning out of the window. "We are in a hurry; the fire is out. Go ahead, driver."

"No you don't," repeated Williams tensely.

In about five long minutes, the engines arrived; the firemen inspected the taxi, threw away some charred bits of cotton waste, got back in their engines, and departed, bells clamoring. Only then did Williams permit the cab to proceed on its way with its impatient occupants.

"Did they think I was going to let the damn cab go, and me standing there with nothing to show the firemen?" Williams demanded after relating this incident to his wife. "You'd think they'da seen that. But all they thought about was how they had to get wherever the hell they were going."

"Of course, dear," said Mrs. Williams.

The gulf is widened by other elements as well. From time to time he runs across references in the newspaper editorials to the "stupidity of the police force" and "graft in the police force." Once in his favorite popular magazine he was reading an entertaining story and enjoying it very much until he came to a terse simile: "as dumb as a cop." This infuriated him, and he has never bought that magazine again.

Then one afternoon, a couple of years ago, Williams shouldered his way through a crowd on Third Avenue in the Fifties and dragged the broken body of a young boy from under the wheels of a truck. A hysterical woman grabbed the policeman's arm as the ambulance was about to depart, and he had to show her the body; it was her son. The woman did not collapse, but she seemed so frail and helpless and forlorn that Williams walked with her to the tenement across the street, where she lived. He answered her distracted questions about having the body removed to an undertaker's. He promised to attend to this for her and so accompanied her into the little parlor of the flat, getting out his fountain pen and memorandum pad. Just then the father, who ran a bakery shop down the block, came through the front door and into the parlor—an anxious little Serbian immigrant with an apron around his waist and a dusty derby on his head.

"He's dead," the woman told her husband.

The baker uttered no word but stood there a moment and slowly sank into a chair with his hat still on his head. Then he became aware of the presence of Williams. He took off his derby hurriedly, and, looking up at the tall figure in uniform, he said, "Excuse me, Officer, I didn't see you."

Williams finds it difficult to explain his reactions to this incident.

"It sounds goofy, telling about it like that," he says. "But it made me feel kind of—well, lonely as hell, if you know what I mean."

As he grows older, Williams's outlook grows almost mellow; he approaches thirty with a more kindly feeling for the citizens who are his wards, but he retires deeper and deeper into the separate sphere of city life which is the Police Department. Having served four and a half years, he will become a first-grade patrolman in another six months and his salary, already increased three times, will be raised to four thousand, one hundred and fifty dollars a year. He knows he possesses a pecuniary security not enjoyed by most of the boys he used to play with on the western extremity of Twenty-third Street. He has even gone so far as to count off a group of ten of these boys on his fingers. One, as has been mentioned, became a priest. One is a taxi-driver; two progressed from petty thievery to gangdom, and one of these died in a gang fight two years ago; one is a doctor, overworked, poor, but cheerful; two studied law at night, and one of these is climbing rapidly—the other died in a Saranac sanitarium last winter of tuberculosis; another is a petty officer in the Navy; another is a saloon keeper; and the tenth is Williams, who feels he is doing pretty well.

He has a six-room flat in the Bronx and two kids thus far, both boys, one six and the other four. He thinks probably one more child would be sufficient and he hopes it will be a girl. He owns a Chevrolet and, although there is a Department regulation against it, he drives it to work and parks it on the street all day. He is buying a shack, as he calls it, up in Westchester. Next door on one side is a patrolman who went through the Police Academy with Williams. William's credit is automatically good at real-estate and automobile agencies and at department stores; they know policemen can be removed from the force for credit delinquency, and they know most of them are responsible fellows anyway.

His hours of work are trying: six eight-hour days of from 8 A.M. to 4 P.M., then thirty-two hours off; then six days of from 12 midnight to 8 A.M., then thirty-two hours off; then six days of from 4 P.M. to midnight, then thirty-two hours off, and the cycle commences again.

He has not fired his gun at any person yet. He has not been shot at yet, either, but he knows that a score of patrolmen are killed or maimed by bullets every year and, while he does not brood over this, it has given him an unnatural awareness of death. He is a Catholic. He swears conventionally and uses the names of God, the Saviour, and some of the saints in vain, but he goes to Mass fairly regularly and has shadowy convictions concerning a personal God whom he sometimes pictures patting him on the back. If ever he has to chase a brace of killers into a dark alleyway, he will in all probability risk a sudden ending without a second's hesitation, with his potsie—an excellent target—shining on his breast.

He has been called into innumerable family squabbles, has warned hundreds of householders about garbage cans, has discovered, by trying all the store doors at night, numerous burglaries after the loot has been taken. A glance at the statistics piled up by Williams and his comrades of the police force for an average year shows that the vast majority of arrests are for violations of the sanitary laws, the traffic laws, the gambling laws, and other unexciting statutes. Williams actually chased a burglar once and caught him merely by grabbing him, and he has stopped many street fights between toughs who needed firm handling. On the whole, however, he has had few dealing with professional criminals and gangsters, and often doesn't know the most notorious of the latter when he sees them. He has accepted, in all, perhaps three hundred dollars of what he calls honest graft from persons who have insisted on paying him not to do something that he probably wouldn't have done anyway, and Christmas presents from merchants amount sometimes to fifty dollars a year all together, but he has never viciously extorted any money from anybody. He knows the risk of detection is great and, besides, he is no greedier than any other wage earner and he has more personal pride, perhaps, than most. He has contributed to poor people on his post and to organized charities at least as much as he has accepted in graft and gratuities.

When he is on an evening tour, drunks become one of his chief concerns; he has sent some of these home in taxicabs, consoled others with philosophical reflections, complied with the insistent conversational demands of many, and arrested still others and taken them to Night Court. He likes his liquor himself, but he doesn't often get tipsy while on duty and never gets really drunk even when off duty.

Walking the tour isn't so bad, he thinks, except on muggy days, and then it is downright terrible. He's not supposed to smoke, and so he has to duck into a store or someplace to get a few puffs every now and then. He has to watch the time closely, though, for his periodic calls from the street boxes to the sergeant at the station house must be made on the minute, or else the sergeant grows irate and tells him to have his biscuit overhauled. His feet never bother him any more, but they did at first. The thick soles he affects are sensible—the pavements are broiling in summer and icy in winter. He gets a soft assignment once in a while, a prize fight or a political meeting. The Department parades bore him—just another long walk, he says.

During his first year on the force—he had been married then about three years—he got in pretty deep with a dumb Italian girl on his tour, and later on he had quite an affair with a rather swell lady, but he couldn't talk to either of them and finally gave up that sort of thing as too troublesome, too risky, and unsatisfactory all round. His wife seems to understand him and his boys are young enough to worship him. Every now and then, he takes his wife to Broadway, and they go to a show and maybe a chop-suey joint afterward, to give her a vacation from the kitchen. He has to carry his roscoe and his potsie even on these occasions, but when he is out with the cook like that, he wouldn't think of hitting anybody up for free grub or free drinks. He takes off his benny and his bag, of course, when his tour is over, and dresses in civilian clothes when off duty.

Williams's father was half Scotch and half English—a foreman in a lumber yard when he died four years ago. His mother was all Irish. Williams went through one year of high school and quit to go to work in the lumber yard where his father was foreman. He had a trivial tiff with his father there and left home for a while, traveling as far west as Newark and as far north as Yonkers, working as a bus boy in a lunchroom, as a timekeeper for a building contractor, and in lumber yards where his father was not the foreman. After a year and a half of this, he came home, got to going around with the girl he later married, and with the help of her father, who was a clerk in a big dairy company, obtained a steady job as a driver of a milk wagon. He made friends with one of the other drivers, whose brother was a cop—and that was how Williams happened to decide to become a cop himself.

He has no particular bent for deduction, though he sometimes imagines he has, and consequently he is unlikely to be chosen for the detective branch, where the pay is higher. The four thousand, one hundred and fifty dollars a year which he will achieve soon is the most he can make unless he becomes a sergeant, in which case he would receive about five hundred more dollars a year. He cannot get this promotion through influence alone, but his rabbi has been able to have some of the routine complaints of shoo-flies erased, thus making his next step up a little less difficult. Williams's rabbi is the boyhood friend who is now a rising lawyer and a Tammany worker. If Williams becomes a sergeant, he may rise later on to be a lieutenant, and he may even become a captain some day. But even if he remains a patrolman, as the great majority of patrolmen do, he will be eligible for retirement on half pay after twenty-five years' service. He has no desire to get in the traffic division because he thinks the traffic man has a solitary job, harder and more confining than his, and the pay is the same.

Williams is five feet, nine and one-half inches in height and he weighs one hundred and sixty-five pounds, which is the precise average for a New York patrolman. He possesses that comforting conviction most of us have: he thinks he is not quite like anybody else, or even quite like any other policeman. The New York police force includes seventeen thousand-odd patrolmen, who are variously slimmer, fatter, taller, shorter, and more or less greedy, intelligent, and ambitious than he is. But as these things go, Williams is the average patrolman whom one may see on the streets of New York any day one chooses to look for him.

WHO IS THIS KING OF GLORY?

FATHER DIVINE HAS said on more than one occasion that he is God. On the walls of his various Heavens here and in other cities there used to hang banners that said,

FATHER DIVINE
IS GOD ALMIGHTY

and on the buses that took his followers on joyous excursions from the Harlem Heavens to the Heavens of Newark and Jersey City was the invariable, red-lettered inscription:

FATHER DIVINE
(GOD)

The effect of this bold claim, on the press and government of New York City was remarkable. The newspapers, on the whole, appeared to regard his works as miraculous. The city government was for many years singularly deferential in its attitude toward him. The two principal candidates for Mayor of New York in 1933 called on him at one of the nightly meetings in his Harlem Heaven. "I came here tonight," said Mr. LaGuardia, "to ask Father Divine's help and counsel. Whatever he wants, I'll do it for him." Mr. O'Brien, appearing before the meeting a little earlier, had said, "Peace! Come what may, adversity, joy, or sorrow, you can meet it by reason of your leadership under Father Divine. Peace!" It looks sometimes as if a good many people besides Father Divine's followers think maybe he *is* God.

Father Divine would like everybody to believe that he was born mature, and only a few years ago, in Providence, which is neither in Rhode Island nor in the sky, but right here (or over there), like the pantheistic Deity or the Buddhists' eternal life. "Except a man be born again," Jesus told Nicodemus, "he cannot see the Kingdom of God." Father Divine not only sees the Kingdom of God every day, but leases it and lives in one of the main apartments himself. Naturally, he says, he had to be born again before that could be. He insists that he can't remember who he was or what he was like before that happened. "Can you remember back to before you were born?" he has asked skeptics who have questioned him on this point.

If you bear firmly in mind the fact that the Father is a short, dignified colored man with a bald head, the true story of his life is more impressive than his story of divine rebirth. It is a story of arduous struggle, onward and upward, from obscurity to prominence, from rags to riches. In a mere forty years, he rose from hedge-clipper and grass-cutter to evangelist, from evangelist to The Messenger, from The Messenger to Major J. Devine, from Major J. Devine to the Rev. J. Divine, and from the Rev. J. Divine to Father Divine (God). This tribute to him was written in 1936, and he is still going pretty strong, although the newspapers have got rather tired of trying to figure him out.

He was around sixty in 1936, and the earliest records of his life were obscure. People who knew him when he was in his twenties think he came from Georgia, or Florida, or Virginia. They are not sure which. But in 1899, beyond all question, he was a man named George Baker and was earning an honest living in Baltimore, mostly by clipping hedges and mowing lawns. He had a scythe and a pair of pruning shears, and he would canvass the white residential districts in spring and summer, offering his services for fifty cents a day. He was frugal, and when winter came he had usually saved up enough money to loaf for a while. If his store of coins began to get too low, he would find odd jobs on the docks. He did not seem to be very ambitious.

On Sundays he taught in the Sunday school of the Rev. Mr. Henderson's Baptist Church on Eden Street. He was a serious-minded young fellow and worried a lot about God. He didn't feel, or claim to be, closer to God than any of the other members of the Rev. Mr. Henderson's colored congregation. He just taught his Sunday-school class, read his Bible, and went about his work during the week with his head full of large words and sounding phrases. At Wednesday-night prayer meetings in the church he sometimes made little speeches, as any member of the congregation had a right to do, and in these he almost always would get tangled up with some tremendous thought, such as "God is personified and materialized." He would grasp the thought firmly and wrestle with it. "God," he would say, "is not only personified and materialized. He is *re*personified and *re*materialized. He *re*materializes and He *re*materi*ates*. He *re*materi*ates* and He is *re*materi*alizable*. He *re*personificates and He *re*personifi*tizes*." He would go on like that for a while, sweating, his eyes bulging a little, and then he would stop abruptly and resume his seat. People liked to hear him talk even then. There would be cries of "Amen, brother!" and "Brother, ain't it so!" between his words and sometimes between the syllables of his words. But he wasn't the superb orator then that he was later on, and he never seemed to be quite sure what it was he was driving at.

It was an almost white mulatto named Samuel Morris who, in time, showed Baker the way. Morris, like Baker, was deeply religious, utterly fascinated by the words of the Bible. In Allegheny City, Pennsylvania, where Morris lived and worked in the steel mills around the turn of the century, he occasionally spoke from the pulpits of Negro churches as a guest preacher. He gave the congregations mild, conventional sermons, full of Biblical and near-Biblical references, and is remembered as having been dull. He had read his Bible through more than once and, like any inspired reader, had sometimes permitted his own thoughts to lift him up and skip him over whole paragraphs, the sense of which he would miss entirely. While Baker was proceeding with his modest work in Baltimore, Morris was reading and rereading his Bible in Allegheny City, and one night Morris came upon a verse in the third chapter of First Corinthians that he had never found there before. It leaped out of the book and slapped him on the head, as he remembered it later on. It was "Know ye not that ye are the temple of God, and that the spirit of God dwelleth in you?" Morris took this remark to be addressed expressly to himself. There it was. If the spirit of God dwelleth in me, he reasoned, and if God, the Spirit, and the Word are all one, as the Bible says, then God himself dwelleth in me. And if God dwelleth in me, my body is His body, and *I* am *God*. Morris went to sleep that night full of excitement. He dreamed that he saw some men drowning and that a voice said to him, "Go to Baltimore and save them." He remembered the dream and the voice in the morning and figured that, while he himself had become God the day before, there seemed to be enough of God left over to order him around. He had no money, so he started off for Baltimore on foot.

Morris was then, and still is, too shrewd a man to be absolutely consistent in his beliefs. On the walk to Baltimore, knowing he was God, he nevertheless earned his food and lodging along the way by preaching his old, conservative sermons to his own people, never hinting that he was anybody but Samuel Morris. But when he got to the Negro churches of Baltimore he let loose. He would start his sermon quietly, and talk for a while with considerable restraint. Then the significance of that verse in Corinthians would overcome him and he would spread his arms suddenly, bring them together on his chest with a thud, spread them again, and shout, "I am the Father Eternal!" Every time he did this a Baltimore congregation would lift him up bodily and throw him out. He never spoke more than once in any one church.

When Morris preached his sermon in the Rev. Mr. Henderson's Baptist Church in Baltimore the only member of the congregation who was not enraged was George Baker. When Morris said, "I am the Father Eternal," Baker was impressed, and when Morris landed on the pavement outside the church, Baker went to him, helped him to his feet, and invited him to come home with him. Baker lived in a frame cottage then, on Fairmount Avenue, in East Baltimore, where a lady evangelist named Anna Snowden conducted a boarding house. She welcomed Morris and became, like Baker, a disciple. Morris got a job driving a horse and wagon for a trucking company, and once or twice a week in the evenings the three used to hold meetings in the little house. Not more than ten or twenty people ever attended these meetings, but those who did enjoyed them immensely. Morris was the principal preacher. He would give one of his routine sermons, then read his text from Corinthians, spread his arms, and shout, "I am the Father Eternal!" For the people who attended the meetings that was always a moment of joy. They did not precisely believe that Morris was God. They knew he drove a wagon for a living, they knew how gratefully he accepted their offerings of nickels and dimes, but it was thrilling, nevertheless, to hear him shout what he did, and there was always in the back of their heads the notion that if Morris *wasn't* the Father Eternal, the Father Eternal would surely strike Morris dead.

Morris usually said nothing more after he had made his awesome declaration. He would sit down, a little apprehensive, and Baker would take charge of the meeting, and talk about God. Baker never openly identified God with Morris, but the fact that his words always followed immediately upon Morris's declaration made it seem as if he were actually talking about the man who had just sat down, and the effect was powerful. Baker was learning to pick up a big phrase, worry it a little, and put it down again without letting it get the better of him. He learned to take a whole paragraph and do that with it, lengthening all the principal words with prefixes and suffixes, and ending up with something that brought ejaculations of rapture from the followers. He was getting better at it all the time. His talks never made much sense, but they were thrilling. For instance, he would say, much as Father Divine said later on, "The individual is the personification of that which expresses personification. Therefore he becomes to be personally the expression of that which was *im*personal, and he *is* the personal expression of it and the personification of the *pre*personification of God Almighty! Peace! It's wonderful! I repeat, it is *indeed* wonderful!" The followers made a refrain of that, a sort of ecstatic ritual. "It's wonderful," they used to chorus. "Peace! It is *indeed* wonderful!"

By 1907 Morris had been born again and was calling himself Father Jehovia, having added a syllable to the name "Jehovah." Baker, still rather modest, had announced that he had been born again, too, and that his new name was The Messenger. Morris accepted this without rancor and defined the title of his disciple as "God in the Sonship Degree." Morris's own title was defined as "God in the Fathership Degree." In the meantime, Baker continued to clip hedges and mow lawns and Morris continued to drive his wagon. Their meetings remained modest affairs. It was around 1908 that they were joined by an important disciple named St. John Divine Bishop. This St. John Divine Bishop had once been known in the flesh as John A. Hickerson and was a weather-beaten free-booter of the religious seas. He had been a clergyman in his native Alexandria (Virginia), had dabbled in Pentecostal Holiness, Holy Rolling, and other esoteric sects, and for a time had been a sort of assistant in one Elder Robertson's Live Ever, Die Never Church in Boston. He drifted into one of the Morris-Baker meetings one night and was deeply impressed with Morris's concept of

Christianity. He stayed on in Baltimore, finding odd jobs to do, and took a leading part in the meetings at Baker's house. Even in the late 1930's St. John Divine Bishop was a great preacher. You could hear him occasionally in Harlem on Sunday nights, usually at the Tabernacle of God, on 110th Street. He would begin slowly, in a soft mumble, and as he talked he walked around the lectern in a preoccupied manner. As his voice began to rise, he would break into a run, head low and haunches high. Then he would mount perpendicularly into the air, stiff-legged like a bucking horse, and land shouting. St. John Divine Bishop brought a few more followers to Baker's house, but not many. Baltimoreans, on the whole, were still not ready to accept Morris's declaration that he was the Father Eternal.

St. John Divine Bishop was a faithful disciple of Morris for four years, but after a while he began interpreting the text from Corinthians as applying to himself and the human species at large. He did not attempt to take the Fathership Degree away from Morris. His contention was simply that if the Bible said that the spirit of God "dwelleth in you," the "you" applies to anybody who reads the verse. Neither Morris nor Baker had thought of it just this way before. Morris definitely didn't like that interpretation and Baker was doubtful, but did not express himself. St. John Divine Bishop even went further into the New Testament and dug up other Scriptural supports for his argument that anybody and everybody is God. " 'God is love,' " he quoted, " 'and he that dwelleth in love dwelleth in God, and God in him,' " and " 'Whosoever shall confess that Jesus is the Son of God, God dwelleth in him and he is God.' " This last one was even more explicit than Morris's original text from Corinthians. The discussion dragged on, however, for several years more. Finally, in 1912, after thorough reflection, St. John Divine Bishop set out for New York to found the Church of the Living God. Baker decided then to go out on his own, too, and started south without telling anybody exactly what he planned to do.

Morris, who had begun to equivocate a little when St. John Divine Bishop sprang his doctrine of the indwelling God, clung to his title of Jehovia after Baker left him, but he never attempted to exploit it. He became the caretaker of some rural property near Hackettstown, New Jersey, acquired some years ago by a Harlem corporation called the De Soto Development Company, which sold lots to Negroes. He still likes to be called Jehovia, but his chief ambition now is merely to live forever where he is. He is almost certain he will do that. He has found a comforting text on the subject of everlasting life. " 'I say unto you,' " he quotes, " 'that if a man keep my saying, he shall never see death.' " He has a formula for keeping death away in case God forgets for a moment that he, Morris, is keeping His saying. Whenever he feels sick, he jumps into the air, clicks his heels together, and, as he says, kicks off whatever it is that is ailing him. He knows, he says, it must be just a passing sickness, not really meant for him. He is a sweet, mild old man, and he watched with an ironical eye the rise and gradual decline of St. John Divine Bishop, and the later success of his old disciple, Baker, The Messenger—now Father Divine.

The only documentary evidence of the progress of The Messenger through the Southland is the record of his trial for lunacy in Valdosta, Georgia, in February, 1914. He was still calling himself The Messenger when he was arrested at the instigation of a group of colored residents of the town, who thought he was a public menace. When the police officers asked one of The Messenger's followers what The Messenger's name was, however, the follower answered, "He ain't nobody but God." So the writ upon which he was brought to trial identifies him simply as "John Doe, alias God." During the trial he referred to himself as The Messenger and said he had no other name.

In Valdosta, The Messenger was declared to be of unsound mind. It was a gentle, informal sort of trial, full of mild crosscurrents of Scotch-Irish wit arising from attorneys, judge, and jurors, and no

student of the human mind would consider the verdict a thoughtful one. One of the two chief accusers of The Messenger was a
Dr. Stafford, a colored man of medicine who was also pastor of the
Holy Roller Church at Valdosta. Dr. Stafford's contention was that
the followers of The Messenger, who numbered thirty or forty
members of the community, thought that The Messenger was God,
and that since The Messenger had encouraged them in this belief
he was, *ipso facto*, crazy. The other chief accuser was a colored
Methodist pastor named White, whose opinion also was that The
Messenger was mad. The Messenger's attorney was J. B. Copeland,
a white man. Mr. Copeland, examining Dr. Stafford, asked him if
he could conceive of a person of sound mind believing the
Methodist interpretation of certain passages of the Scriptures, and
Dr. Stafford said he could not. Mr. Copeland then asked Pastor
White if he considered a Holy Roller sane, and Pastor White said
he certainly did not. "Gentlemen," Mr. Copeland said to the jury,
"the two principal witnesses against the defendant have testified that
they consider each other to be of unsound mind, because of the same
religious prejudice which is the basis of the present complaint."

This made the jurors laugh, but after they had heard a number
of colored men of the community testify that their wives had gone
crazy over The Messenger and had shouted to everybody they met
on the street that God had come to Valdosta, the jurors retired, de-
liberated, and rendered their judgment that The Messenger was of
"unsound mind." They gave as their opinion, however, that he was
not so crazy that he should be sent to the State Sanitarium, and
recommended that he be set free on the understanding that he would
leave Georgia immediately. The Court accepted both the verdict
and the recommendation.

Before The Messenger left Valdosta, his personal effects were returned to him. They included a small roll of money and two newspaper clippings. One clipping told of his having served sixty days

on a chain gang in Savannah (on what charge the clipping did not say) and the other clipping told of the wreck of a car full of prison inspectors. On the margin of the second clipping, The Messenger had written, "Be sure your sins will find you out."

Mr. Copeland, the attorney, talked to The Messenger after the trial. In recalling the details of the case a few years ago, he wrote, "I remember that there was about the man an unmistakable quiet power that manifested itself to anyone who came in contact with him. He told me that he tried to do God's will and that he was not conscious of doing anything contrary to God's will, and that he thought that to the extent that he could identify himself with God, he was God."

The Messenger came north from Valdosta by easy stages, holding meetings for a time in one town and then moving on to another. He did not travel alone. Three or four men and women had left their homes in Valdosta and had become faithful disciples. They would stop in a town for a month or so, and while The Messenger preached on street corners, and sometimes from the pulpits in the sections lived in by colored people, the disciples would find jobs and pool their wages to provide food and room rent and railroad fare for the journey to the next town. Other disciples joined the group on the way north. When The Messenger arrived in New York, in 1915, he had seven or eight devoted followers.

The Messenger found St. John Divine Bishop's Church of the Living God flourishing on West Forty-first Street, then a part of the city populated largely by colored people. St. John Divine Bishop had succeeded with his cult of the indwelling God. He still held, as he had in Baltimore, that the New Testament said that God dwells in us all, and that therefore everybody is God. This doctrine had been ecstatically received as soon as he began to preach it in New York. Now Gods were stomping all up and down the West Forties between Seventh Avenue and Ninth. At the Church of the

Living God, the immortals held meetings every afternoon and every evening. Male members of the congregation, or Temples of God, as they called themselves and each other, wore yellow turbans festooned with silver tinsel, and females wore a kind of hood over their heads and a shawl over their shoulders. The hoods were pink, the shawls purple. "God lives in this temple, and I'm so glad!" the Temples of God would shout. They sang, "So glad, so *glad*, so glad!" to the tune of "My Country 'tis of Thee." They would shout, "Going to live forever! Can't never die!" There was a chant that went:

> *God in you,*
> *God in me.*
> *You God,*
> *I God,*
> *Everybody* be *God.*

As Bishop Obey, an acquiescent pillar of the church, phrased the general spirit of the thing at the time, "I is the Eternal Am. I been everywhere. I come back from there. Yet I'm still there—and here. I ain't *bothered.*"

The Messenger took a flat on West Fortieth Street and lived there for a few weeks with his disciples. They believed not that they and everybody else were God but that The Messenger and nobody else was God. The Messenger guarded them jealously. He saw a good deal of St. John Divine Bishop, but he did not join the revelry at the Church of the Living God. He just looked on. He was interested, as a member of the evangelistic guild, in what St. John Divine Bishop had done, and he sometimes invited his old friend to come to his flat around the corner, eat a meal, and talk about his organization. But he never brought his own disciples to St. John Divine Bishop's church. The Messenger's disciples got jobs in Manhattan as cooks and waiters and laundresses and chambermaids, and, while The Messenger himself did not work, he was provided with food and clothes and rent money and even a little cash to carry in his pocket because his followers, believing him to be God, turned over to him every cent they made. He had grown rather secretive and did not talk much with St. John Divine Bishop about the Bible. He talked to him mostly about the financial side of the Church of the Living God.

Within a few months after The Messenger's arrival, the Church of the Living God began to disintegrate—not because of anything The Messenger did or said but because of the impractical doctrine on which the church had been founded. There was no discipline. To St. John Divine Bishop's adjurations to behave, the congregation, each member of which was just as much God as the pastor was, paid no heed. Being omnipotent, the members of the congregation took a high tone with their neighbors. A Temple of God would accost a passerby and shout at him, "Brute beastie! I going to kill you with fire and brimstone! I going to put out your light!" There were a good many street fights, and, according to the records of the West Forty-seventh Street police station, some stabbings. As St. John Divine Bishop should have known, there was a sect much like the Church of the Living God in twelfth-century Germany, based also on the doctrine of immanence, known as the Brethren of the Free Spirit. Each Brother was God, and they all got to going around naked, burned their neighbors' cottages, robbed, raped, and killed, and were finally stamped out by an inquisition with public sentiment behind it.

The Messenger sensed that the Church of the Living God was on its way to sure destruction. He moved his disciples to the Negro quarter on Myrtle Avenue in Brooklyn and there set up a sort of combination meeting house and employment agency. He rented a flat of four rooms and lived in it with his disciples, holding meetings every night during and after dinner. Every now and then a new disciple would be gathered into the fold. If the new disciple didn't have a job, The Messenger would get him one.

Sometimes he inserted "Situation Wanted" ads in the Brooklyn papers and found jobs for his followers that way. Sometimes The Messenger himself answered "Help Wanted" ads and recommended his people for the jobs. The thing grew—slowly, but fast enough to convince The Messenger that he had an idea there that was very valuable.

The followers of The Messenger were happier, perhaps, than they had ever been before. The community flat was congested; they slept three or four in a room sometimes. But every place they had ever lived in before had been at least that crowded. The food was excellent and plentiful. With a dozen people working at regular jobs and handing over their earnings to The Messenger, there was plenty of money for everything. Any one of the disciples who happened to be unemployed served as cook. And all day, as the disciples worked, they were conscious of the fact that they were living in the house of God. Unlike the earlier disciples of Morris, in Baltimore, these disciples really believed their leader *was* God. The Messenger didn't work and yet he was never in want. It seemed miraculous to his disciples. There was a fine dinner every evening, and The Messenger always had a roll of bills in his pocket. When the disciples wondered at these things, and asked The Messenger to explain them, he would say, "God will provide," and smile on them from the head of the table. They earned better wages than they had in the South, but the difference could not account entirely for the standard of living they now enjoyed. It was, as they often chanted in the evenings, wonderful. From The Messenger's point of view, it was, as he was accustomed to remark, *indeed* wonderful. His disciples earned $10 or $12 a week apiece. That meant a total income of around $130 a week, and he paid out of that only $40 a month for rent and perhaps $150 a month for food. Often the food bill was less than that, for his followers were Southerners and those who were cooks remained faithful to a custom followed by many Southern Negro cooks, known as "toting." Every evening, when they left their employers' kitchens, they would take modest helpings of flour, sugar, milk, salt, vegetables, and meat, and tote them to the house of God.

The disciples wanted for nothing. There was no drinking, because The Messenger frowned on that and preached against it. They never spent money foolishly, because, in the first place, they wanted nothing in the way of entertainment outside the house of God, and in the second place the only money they ever got from The Messenger, after they had turned over their wages, was carfare. He bought clothes for them when they needed them—cheap clothes, from second-hand shops, and had suits and dresses altered to fit by one of the disciples, who was a seamstress. The Messenger had discovered that the living expenses of twelve people are not twelve times what they are for one person. He had carried to a highly successful extreme the principle of the English mess or the American boarding house. Or you might call it a kind of communism. Whatever it was, it seemed to work splendidly.

Nobody was ever lonely in the house of God. The Messenger presided every night at dinner, and everybody sang and partook of much good cheer. There was nothing immoral about it. If there was any exchange of passion during the evening meetings, when the songs sometimes reached the frenzied state that they do at a Holy Roller meeting, the pleasure was vicarious. The sexes were segregated. Women slept in one room, men in another. There were, no doubt, occasional lapses in individual cases, some clandestine meetings and secret love affairs. But all the disciples were at least more continent than they had been in the past and some of them were beyond question celibate. The Messenger preached against sexual expression. His gospel was candid and practical. He demanded renunciation of all kinds of love among his disciples except the love of God.

In the fall of 1919, The Messenger left Brooklyn and moved his disciples to a house in Sayville, Long Island. A kind of providence seems to have guided him to the place that was to raise him to the status of a national phenomenon. His disciples numbered around sixteen or seventeen now and he wanted room to expand. Moreover, he wanted to keep them away from the contaminating influences of neighbors of their own color. They could keep their jobs in New York and come to Sayville for week-ends or he could find jobs for them in Sayville itself. They would not be influenced one way or another by their white employers. And in the evening or on Sunday they would be as glad as ever to come home to God—and there would be room in a real house to accommodate more of them.

It happened that in Sayville, a year or so after America entered World War I, a German-American named Edward Felgenhauer, who owned the town paint store and a house on Macon Street, changed his name to Fellows. Fellows's next-door neighbor, named Schaefer, did not change his name, and he twitted Fellows for his timidity. Fellows and Schaefer quarreled over that finally and Fellows decided to move away, and in moving to have the last word in his dispute with his next-door neighbor. He advertised his house for sale in the New York newspapers and inserted in the ad the word "colored." The Messenger saw the advertisement and went to see the house. It was a long, rambling two-story house with ten or twelve rooms and a sixty-foot lot. It was just what The Messenger wanted. He had been frugal and he had some cash on hand. It is possible that the savings of a colored woman from Newark named Pinninah, who had become one of his chief disciples and who was to achieve prominence later on as Mother Divine, made up part of the $700 which he paid down in cash to Mr. Fellows. A deed was drawn up, with mortgages for the remainder of the purchase price of some $2,500. One of the two signatures on the deed is Pinninah's. The other is that of Major J. Devine. The Messenger had evaporated and, amid the plenitude of military titles that year, Major J. Devine had come into being. George Baker had been born a third time. The regeneration seems to have taken place on the Long Island Railroad.

A CERTAIN AMOUNT of rapid recapitulation, or a pause for breath, seems to be rewarding in a tale as complicated as this one. Here we go: George Baker, the grass-cutter of Baltimore, who by a process of multiple birth had become The Messenger and then Major J. Devine, was born a fourth time, and then a fifth time, almost as soon as he established himself in Sayville, Long Island, in 1919. He became Rev. J. Divine, dropping the military title and substituting one vowel for another, thus giving his name a supernatural significance. Then almost immediately afterward he became Father Divine (God). He has been God ever since. On one occasion in 1936, his disciples in Harlem stretched a streamer of black-and-gold silk across the throne of Heaven, the headquarters of the cult, on West 115th Street, with the blaring legend:

Father Divine Is Dean
of the Universe

But that is rank hyperbole. The promotion to Dean of the Universe is simply a gratuitous expression of the enthusiasm of his followers and does not represent a formal rebirth. Neither in the early years in Sayville nor in the later years in Harlem or anywhere else has Father Divine ever hinted that he considers himself to be anything more than God.

As God, after he had settled down in Sayville, he was modest and almost entirely without affectation. His white neighbors on Macon Street were never exactly friendly with him, but they didn't particularly object to him. It was not a pretentious street. The houses, set back from the curbs in comfortable, shady yards, were occupied mostly by people who worked in the village the year round. The summer colony was on the other side of the Merrick Road and the hotels and great estates were still further away. To his neighbors, Father Divine was known not as Major J. Devine, the name signed to the deed when he bought his house, but as the Rev. J. Divine, and he told them he was operating an employment agency. He seemed to be an exceptionally clean, upright, and dignified colored man, with soft eyes and gentle manners. The neighbors did not know until some years later that he was supposed to be God. They used to see him doing odd jobs around his yard in his spare time, pruning the shrubbery, cutting the grass and tidying up the places where the former owner had allowed rubbish to accumulate. He was alone all day except for a cook. The twenty-odd men and women who lived with him were workers. Some of them were in New York except on Sundays; others left the house in the morning and returned in the evening. They were decent, orderly colored folk, and bothered nobody. They sang a good deal at night, especially on Sunday, but the singing was never strident and they hardly ever kept it up much later than nine o'clock. Inside the house George Baker was called Father Divine, and all his followers were sure that he was God.

Once each week Father Divine strolled down to the office of the *Suffolk County News*, near the Oystermen's Bank & Trust Company, and placed a classified advertisement offering reliable colored help for all work. Whenever a householder answered the advertisement, Father Divine would call in person, bearing a business card marked "Rev. J. Divine." He would remove his hat and, standing on the doorstep, would say, "I can guarantee and reguarantee the character and probity and uprighteousness of all my clients." The Sayville residents liked him, and within a year or so, working at a leisurely pace, he got jobs in and near Sayville for all of the early disciples. This relieved the communal purse of the cost of commuting, which had been a considerable strain.

These early followers of Father Divine had never had much to give him but their wages, and their wages were never high. They were poor people who labored on the outer fringe of domestic service. None of them was expert as cook or laundress. They worked mostly for families of three or four who could afford one servant and who paid not more than $10 or $12 a week. But now Father Divine began to attract from the kitchens and butlers' pantries of the summer hotels and big houses of Nassau and Suffolk Counties a new kind of disciple—colored people of some means, who earned sometimes as much as $100 a month, slept and ate in their employers' houses, and had bank accounts and insurance policies. To these people Father Divine seemed to be God in an even more wonderful degree than he had been to the early followers. As he became acquainted with the better class of colored folk in Sayville and neighboring towns, he commenced to invite them to Sunday dinners at his house; he preached to them after dinner, and never took up a collection. When the guests asked him candidly how he managed to give them free dinners, he would say cheerfully, "Father will provide," and his disciples would say, "It's wonderful! Ain't it wonderful? Sweet Father is God Almighty!" He enjoyed no sudden popularity. He attracted people to his house only by two's and three's. Some Sundays there were no outside guests at all; on others there might be three or four. For several years Father Divine's progress was slow. It was not until the late 1920's that things began to boom.

The experiences of a butler-and-cook couple named Thomas and Verinda Brown, who worked for a substantial white family in Forest Hills and earned a joint salary of $150 a month, plus board and room, are typical of the experiences of scores of disciples who joined the cult of Father Divine about this time. Thomas and Verinda occupied prominent places in Father Divine's Heaven from 1930 until 1933. They were what Father Divine calls Angels, a title conferred upon any person who assigns all his property to Father Divine, hands over all the money he earns, and takes a new name. Verinda was called Rebecca Grace, and throughout Sunday dinner in 1931 sat at the right hand of God. Thomas was called Onward Universe and for a while was one of God's favorite Angels. Now the two are Thomas and Verinda again and are back in Forest Hills, working for the same family they were with when they first met Father Divine. They no longer believe that he is God.

Verinda is a very tall, very healthy-looking middle-aged woman, the color of a fine mink coat. Her features are large and frank—a great nose, an enormous jaw, a mouth that opens and shuts decisively. Her natural expression is an expansive grin. Thomas is shorter, darker, less vivacious, a sort of understatement of Verinda. His eyes are drowsy and slow-moving. He is deliberate, methodical, and thoughtful by nature. Verinda comes from Barbados, Thomas from the Bahamas. Both have been in this country thirty years or more and they had been married ten. Both are excessively neat; Thomas is even something of a dude, and at one time owned sixteen suits of clothes, all of them in fair condition. Verinda is a fine cook and a capable children's nurse; as a butler and house man, Thomas is efficient and has a soothing manner. They are decent, honest people. They estimate that during the time they were Angels in Sayville they gave Father Divine, freely and of their own accord, something over $5,000, itemized as follows:

Savings withdrawn from the Railroad Co-operative
    Building & Loan Association . . . . $ 700
Verinda's salary of $75 a month from April, 1930,
    to October, 1933 3,225
Gold coins 100
Seven Florida lots (estimated value) 350
Thomas's salary, averaging $75 a month, for
    six months in 1930 450
Thomas's earnings at odd jobs in Sayville during
    eighteen months of 1931–32 750
Fifteen suits of clothes relinquished by Thomas
    (estimated value) 85
        Total $5,660

The manner in which Verinda and Thomas became acquainted with Father Divine seemed to them for a long time afterward to be clearly miraculous. One day in the spring of 1929, after Father Divine's Sunday dinners had become quite an event for the colored population in and near Sayville, without attracting attention in other quarters, a laundryman in Forest Hills made a mistake and left some strange clean clothes at the home in which Thomas and Verinda worked. Thomas knew that another family down the street patronized the same laundry, so he took the bundle to the servants' entrance of that house and introduced himself to the cook. He asked if by any chance the laundry bundles for the two houses had been transposed, and found that was just what had happened. The cook was a happy colored woman who said her name was Priscilla Paul. "After the Apostle," she explained. Thomas himself was a constant reader of the Bible and he and Priscilla exchanged, along with laundry bundles, a few Biblical texts. They parted friends. "Peace! It's wonderful!" Priscilla said as Thomas started off, and Thomas still remembers how pleasant and reassuring it sounded. ("It's a catching phrase," he says now, in the depths of his agnosticism.)

That night Priscilla Paul came to see Verinda and Thomas in their kitchen. "Peace!" she said as she entered. "It's wonderful!" She invited them to come to the evening meal at her father's house in Sayville the next Sunday. She explained that she went to Sayville every Sunday herself and suggested they go with her on the bus. They accepted, and on Sunday were surprised, but not displeased, to find themselves at a sort of religious meeting. The dinner was very good. The fact that each plate, before it was passed to the eater, was blessed by the man Priscilla and all the other diners called "Father" rather appealed to Verinda and Thomas. Father Divine said nothing memorable in his sermon after dinner. He did not say he was God, or even intimate that he was, but his phrase-making was glorious, and Thomas especially liked the Biblical sound of the things Father Divine said. Verinda thought Father Divine had the loveliest, softest eyes she had ever seen.

Verinda and Thomas had Sundays off after midday dinner, and they became regular visitors at Father Divine's house. They asked him if they shouldn't pay for the meals they had every Sunday—told him they'd be more than glad to, because they enjoyed themselves so much. But he would always wave them away with a cheerful smile and say, "Father will provide." It was wonderful. As they got to know the other disciples—a preoccupied and prim old fellow named Gabriel; an elderly woman named Susanna, who sang beautifully; and others named Ruth Rachel, Hozanna Love, Faith Sweetness, Frank Incense, Blessed Charity, and so on—they began to learn how much more wonderful it was than they had thought. Not only did the Father provide a dinner every week that must have cost $15 or $20; he worked other miracles besides. The loaves-and-fishes trick, to him, was just routine. He was a healer, too. Everybody there, it seemed, had been cured of some physical or spiritual disorder. After dinner in the evenings, between songs like:

> *Father Divine is the Perfect God*
> *Perfect God,*
> *Perfect God . . .*

and

> *I love to sing the praise of thee,*
> *Sweet Father Divine.*
> *I love to sing the praise of thee,*
> *Be practical all the time . . .*

testimonials would be given by the Angels. This phase of the meeting was a sort of burnt-cork Buchmanism, which was a Nordic

fad of those days. Verinda and Thomas were perfectly healthy physically, but both had stern consciences and they managed to join in
by telling things they had done wrong, and explaining that, since
they had come to know the Father, they didn't do wrong any more.

In the Father's sermons there ran a refrain which had to do
with "conscious mentality." He would say, "*Re*laxation of the conscious men*tal*ity is the *super*-mental *re*lax*ativ*eness of mankind."
The Angels, who sat nearest to him at the big dinner table, had
achieved this sublime state, it seemed. They had relaxed their conscious mentalities until they had been born again as Angels, they
had got fine new names, and they didn't remember anything that
had ever happened to them in the past. Verinda and Thomas thought
the Angels, and everything about them, were enviable, and they
began to try to relax their conscious mentalities. The way to do
this, they were told, was to love the Father and think about him all
the time.

The employers of Verinda and Thomas were puzzled, and
somewhat unnerved, when, during this period, their splendid servants seemed to be going to pieces. Upon being reprimanded for
breaking dishes or being slow with the cocktail things, Verinda and
Thomas would explain mournfully that they were trying to relax
their conscious mentalities. They seemed preoccupied, sad, and
solemn, and they probably would have lost their jobs had they not
been good and faithful servants for nine years past. Besides the
worry over their conscious mentalities, they had anxieties which
their employers did not understand. Thomas and Verinda had
grown to love Father Divine. He had been so kind to them during those first months, and he had seemed to know everything, to
feel everything, to be so confident when he said, over and over
at the dinners, "Your Father is rich in all your needs and all your
wants shall be supplied." Those ecstatic shouts of "Yes, Father, you
are *so* wonderful!" and "*Thank* you, Father!" which came from
the Angels were impressive and contagious. There was something

keenly satisfying and delightful about the idea of putting one's trust in somebody as the Angels put their trust in Father Divine. Verinda and Thomas had begun to think of him as God. And now, just when they were loving him so, and were trying so hard to please him, he seemed not to notice them at all. They found themselves seated further and further away from him every Sunday. When he looked at them at all, it was as if he despised them. He was always talking these days about sacrifice and self-denial and consecration, building the words up till they seemed four times as big as they really were. "He who would enter into the Kingdom of God must have nothing he can call his own," he would say sometimes, candidly. He preached against life insurance, against all forms of insurance, and said that anybody who stood to benefit by an insurance policy was a murderer or an incendiarist at heart. "Look," he would say, "at the Snyder-Gray case," a sensational murder case of that period. "If Albert Snyder hadn't been insured, he would never have been killed. He was putting temptation in the way of the iniquitous. Live right and keep my commandments and you shall never die. It is so written. He who insures his life or his property is a man of little faith." He did not tell his followers that he had insured his house against fire with the Firemen's Insurance Company, the Glens Falls Insurance Company, and the National Liberty Insurance Company, but he had.

When Verinda and Thomas heard the speech against insurance, they were delighted. It seemed to be addressed directly to them. They had small insurance policies of the kind that may be cashed in, and they applied for the money that Monday. When they got the cash the next week, Verinda bought a trunk for Thomas and Thomas bought a diamond ring for Verinda. Then they made a special night trip to Sayville to tell the Father about it, feeling sure that he would be pleased.

"Why didn't you ask me what to do with the money?" he demanded bluntly, and added in a more Godlike tone, "He that loveth father or mother, son or daughter, husband or wife, more than me is not worthy to enter the kingdom of God." They were abashed. Verinda, quicker of tongue than Thomas, said she was so sorry and asked the Father's forgiveness. They had, she said after a silence, a joint account in the Railroad Cooperative Building & Loan Association that contained about $700. They would do anything Father wished with that, she said. Father Divine said, "Draw it out. Lay not up treasures on earth where moth and thief and mouse break in and steal, but lay it up in Heaven with your Father."

This they did. Father Divine got the $700 that Friday.

Then, for a while, Thomas and Verinda dwelt in a state of beatitude. They were told that they had achieved the rank of Angels and were permitted to choose new names for themselves. Verinda chose Rebecca Grace, after some advice from the other Angels. Thomas had already thought up Onward Universe for himself, and he adopted it forthwith. They remained Thomas and Verinda to their employers, but they explained one day that their old names were really just nicknames, that their real names now were Rebecca Grace and Onward Universe. "But you just keep calling us Thomas and Verinda," Thomas said to his employer. "That will be perfectly all right."

Thomas and Verinda were happy now. They were moved back nearer the head of the table, and Father Divine beamed on them with heart-warming affection. As a matter of course, without being invited to do so by the Father, they began at once to turn over their wages to him every week, as all the other Angels did. Thomas took the deeds to his Florida lots out of his trunk and signed them over to the Father. When Verinda's employers, the following year, gave her a bonus of $100 in gold, Verinda turned that over to the Father. For one Sunday, Verinda sat on the right hand of God, and Thomas, only a few seats away, found himself talking intimately with God during dinner. They never talked with the other Angels about the money they were giving to Father Divine because part of the gospel taught at Heaven was that true believers "relaxed all recollection of material transactions." This was a phrase which, with prefixes and suffixes, Father Divine built into something of impressive proportions.

Father Divine was a keen-eyed God. He noticed that Thomas had on a different suit nearly every time he came to Heaven, and one day he asked Thomas about that and learned that Thomas had sixteen suits. "Bring me fifteen of those suits," he told Thomas. "Look how the lilies of the field are clothed, and they spin not."

He was a jealous God, too. In Brooklyn he had always preached the gospel of celibacy to the followers who lived in the flat with him, and now, in Sayville, with about twenty Angels living with him and forty living with their employers, he preached the same gospel with even more determination. When the conscious mentality is really relaxed, he argued, all love except for the Father has to relax, too. Verinda and Thomas were a devoted couple and they slept at night in a double bed. They took the Father's preaching literally and seriously, and Thomas faced the same hardships as those third-century monks who used to exorcise themselves by inviting attractive women to come to the monastery and tempt them. As Gibbon said of the monks, in *The Decline and Fall of the Roman Empire*, outraged nature sometimes vindicated herself. Whenever that happened, Verinda and Thomas would appear before the Father ill at ease and heavy of conscience, and he, looking at them, would say, "I see you have sinned. You cannot hide from God. I am everywhere. I see all. I know all." And they would moan and cry, "Oh, Father! Yes, Father! Forgive us, Father! You are *so* wonderful, Father!"

A man of Thomas's abilities was needed in Heaven, and six months after Thomas became Onward Universe, he left his job and his Verinda, and came to live in the house on Macon Street. He was one of the principal Angels, and for a while used to hold long Biblical discussions with the Father on weekday evenings. He was handy with tools, and by day he worked around Heaven, putting up partitions where the Father wanted them, repairing the roof, and doing other useful chores. Evidently it was worth the loss of Thomas's salary to Father Divine to have Thomas around. When there was nothing for Thomas to do, he found odd jobs in the village and earned a little cash from time to time, which he turned over to the Father. Verinda kept her job in Forest Hills and came to Heaven only on Sundays, and when they spoke to one another it was just to say, "Peace! It's wonderful!" For a long time it seemed to them that they were happier than they had ever been before. Verinda remained a faithful follower of Father Divine until the fall of 1933. By that time she had become just one of sixty-odd Angels, she was beginning to have her doubts about the divinity of the Father, and she was tired of not having any spending money. Her employers in Forest Hills, who were fond of her, advised her to quit going to Father Divine's meetings, and finally she took their advice. Thomas stayed with Father Divine a year longer, by which time he had been demoted to furnace man in the Harlem Heaven. Then one day he walked out, got his old job back and his Verinda, and never returned.

A good many other Angel couples became estranged in the same way during the Sayville period. Some of them lived separately in Heaven itself and some lived separately outside, and all of them were lonely, their hearts were full of affection, and they didn't love anybody but God. He looked after everything. As he had done in Brooklyn with his early disciples, he now provided second-hand clothes for his Angels, skillfully altered and made over by Angel seamstresses. The Angels had no outside expenses to speak of. They had no doctors' bills to pay. Father Divine preached against doctors and dentists. "Father is the Doctor" became the refrain of one of the Heavenly songs. If a disciple was in the habit of going to a clinic for treatment of some disease, even a most contagious one, Father Divine frowned upon him and told him not to be of little faith. Death, he said, could not come to a true believer. If it did come, it was a proof that the dead Angel had not been a true believer. At least one Angel died at the Sayville Heaven. This was a woman named Bowman. It was recorded at the time that she was a pauper, with no relatives to pay for her funeral, and she was buried in Sayville's potter's field.

How much money Father Divine was taking in during the winter of 1929–30 is anybody's guess. Figuring that sixty skilled and unskilled disciples earned an average of $15 a week apiece (some of them in those years were making $40 and $50), the total, aside from insurance policies and savings accounts which he took over, would have been $900 a week.

The Sunday dinners had become large affairs by the spring of 1930. Word of the strange preacher who seemed to be God, who gave free Sunday dinners, and who never took up a collection, had got back to Harlem. People began to go out to Sayville from Harlem to see for themselves and to eat the miraculous dinners. But they, like the new disciples, were not riff-raff. The round-trip ticket from New York to Sayville cost $2.40 and it was cheaper for people who had to count the pennies to eat at home. Only the well-to-do class of Negroes came to Father Divine's Sunday dinners. Some of them became Angels. A few newspaper stories appeared, all of them marveling at the hospitality of Father Divine, and, after the publicity, white people began to go to the Sunday dinners in Sayville. There was a Mrs. Withers, of Long Island City, for instance, who went through the customary initiation and eventually became an Angel named Sister Everjoy. She had been a Christian Scientist, had lost a child, and was vulnerable to any kind of new faith that came along. There was J. Maynard Matthews, an automobile dealer of Brookline, Massachusetts, who had tried Divine Science, Unity, and a number of swamis and yogis without having found what he wanted. He presented Father Divine with a Cadillac, abandoned his business, and became the Father's secretary. His name was changed to John Lamb and he got to be one of the most important Angels in the movement. Other white followers arrived from all over the country, not in great numbers, but singly— a widow from Charlotte, North Carolina; a doctor from Chicago; a young accountant from Kansas City. They were solitaries, marked by that peculiar, agonized look which profound faith seems to bring to people's eyes, and they were all looking for some new kind of life on earth.

By midsummer that year, the Sayville police on Sundays had to put no-parking signs up and down the block in which Heaven stood to prevent hopeless traffic jams. Trucks and buses were bringing scores of Negroes out from Harlem every week. Father Divine's neighbors rented parking space in their front yards, thus combatting the nascent depression. Not more than seventy-five persons could be seated in Father Divine's dining room, and he served the Sunday dinners to hundreds, in shifts, all day long and into the evening. A new technique of serving these meals was introduced about that time. The hungry visitors would sit down around the table and Father Divine would bless, first of all, the coffee and tea, and then those beverages would be served. There would be an interval of thirty minutes or so, during which everybody was urged to have four or five cups apiece. Then, when the diners had reached a bloated condition, great platters of spaghetti, potatoes, lima beans, and other starches would be blessed and served. Another half hour would go by before the impressive hams, roasts, chickens, and turkeys would appear. Usually these dishes, having been blessed and offered to everybody, would leave the table almost intact, to be blessed and served again at successive meals for the rest of the day and to turn up again on quiet week nights when the Angels sat down to dinner. Father Divine himself found the Heavenly meals unsatisfactory. He used to call on Verinda a little before noon on Sundays in her kitchen, in Forest Hills, and she would invite him to have a bite to eat. "I can't do that," he would say, drawing himself up to the table. "My Angels are waiting on me in Sayville, to bless their food," he would protest. Verinda would cook up some scrambled eggs, pancakes, sausage, fried potatoes, and coffee, and the Father would fall to, re-marking that he might have a snack, at that, to strengthen him on his drive back to Sayville. "When I scrambled eggs for him," Verinda said later on, "I always scrambled six."

As Father Divine's fame increased, so did the suspicions of many people outside his cult. Letters were sent to him containing cash, money orders, and checks, by investigators in the pay of the Sayville police authorities, who thought he might be open to prosecution on a federal charge of using the mails to defraud. In every case the enclosure was returned with a note that said, "Father will provide." The Suffolk County District Attorney planted two colored women from Harlem in Father Divine's Heaven in an effort to find out where his money came from, but at the end of two weeks they told him they hadn't been able to find out anything. This procedure was doomed from the start, for the reason that the two colored women were Harlem followers of Father Divine and were well on the way toward becoming Angels themselves. In the end, the Suffolk County authorities ceased trying to work up a criminal case against Father Divine. Nobody could with authority challenge his claim that his money came to him out of the sky. "Everything comes to him au-tomatically because he's God," the Angels used to say, and it seemed to be the only possible explanation.

By fall of that year, there were so many Angels in Heaven that Father Divine had to expand. Property in his block had declined in value somewhat since the big meetings had begun, and he bought the house next door, at No. 64 Macon Street. It was a smaller house than the other one, and was used as a dormitory for female Angels. This left room in Heaven for an extra dining room to ac-commodate the guests who came each Sunday in increasing num-bers. Father Divine had by this time about a hundred and fifty Angels living with him. In the summer of 1931, he leased a house across the street for white Angels exclusively. About the same time he established what he called an Extension Heaven in Harlem, a flat of five or six rooms on Fifth Avenue at 128th Street. Some twenty Angels who worked in New York lived in the Extension Heaven just as the suburban Angels lived in the one at Sayville. The sexes were segregated, and one of Father Divine's principal Angels looked after the marketing, directed the household work, and collected the wages of all the Angels every payday.

By the fall of 1931, the police authorities in Sayville and the Suffolk County District Attorney had decided that Father Divine was a public nuisance, and he was arrested on that charge on November 16th of that year. After a change of venue had been obtained, he was brought to trial in Nassau County, before Justice Lewis J. Smith, who turned out to be the man who contributed as much as anybody to the subsequent greatness of Father Divine. The Justice, according to the opinion of the higher court which subsequently overruled him, permitted prejudice to enter into the trial and charged the jury in a manner that virtually demanded a verdict of guilty. Father Divine was convicted and Justice Smith fined him $500 and sentenced him to one year in jail. Four days after Justice Smith pronounced this sentence, he died. He had been a robust man and was only fifty-five years old. His physicians said his death was caused by heart failure. It was obvious to all of Father Divine's followers, and to thousands of people, both white and colored, all over the country who read about it in the newspapers, that Father Divine had struck down the Justice. The appeal was handled brilliantly by James C. Thomas, a Negro attorney who is a former Assistant United States District Attorney. He donated his services because he believed the issue to be one of racial prejudice. When the Appellate Division reversed the conviction in January, 1933, it was accepted as further evidence of the divinity of Father Divine. The Angels gave Mr. Thomas no credit at all for the victory.

During the five weeks Father Divine had been held in jail without bail, scores of new followers joined his cult. The Heavens in

Sayville and the branch in Harlem had been efficiently maintained by a few trusted Angels, who came to him often at the Nassau County Jail for instruction and advice. He was ready now to expand still further, and he selected Harlem as his new headquarters. Leaving a few elderly Angels to look after his property in Sayville, he moved to New York. By this time not fewer than three hundred Angels were turning over to him everything they earned.

WHEN, AROUND 1936, Father Divine used to address his followers, he did it in Heaven, a roomy, five-story structure at 20 West 115th Street, and his demeanor was marked by an alertness which suggested that he was an extremely nervous man. One of his favorite routines was that of leading a chant which started like this:

> One million blessings,
> Blessings flowing free,
> Blessings flowing free.
> There are so many blessings,
> Blessings flowing free for you.

Then it went:

> One billion blessings,
> Blessings flowing free,
> Blessings flowing free,
> There are so many blessings,
> Blessings flowing free for you.

and so on—trillion, quadrillion, quintillion, and on up to what he called septdecillion. He would shout the catch line of each verse and then, as he hummed the chorus and the followers sang, his soft eyes would begin to wander. They would shift rapidly over the audience, glance for an instant at the entrance door, at the exits, and once or twice during the singing of a verse he would turn half about and look sharply behind him. He seemed agitated and apprehensive, and it was clear that there was more on his mind than the task of conducting a religious meeting. He had the detached, preoccupied manner of a bartender in the early days of Prohibition who, while mixing a highball, was always wondering when the police would come in.

That particular Heaven used to be the headquarters of a Negro fraternal organization and was owned by the Union Square Savings Bank. Downstairs is a large hall, in the center of which is a dining table at which about a hundred and fifty persons may be seated. Smaller tables, seating six or eight apiece, are set close to the walls around the room. Father Divine served free meals then only to Angels and a few privileged guests—people who were considered worthy of special treatment and who had been introduced and recommended by Angels. All other visitors were charged fifteen cents for a meal, baldly and without apology. Soup was a nickel extra and so was dessert. "Thank you, Father!" the waiters and waitresses used to say when they picked up the change.

On the second, third, and fourth floors of Heaven were dormitories where some fifty or seventy-five Angels slept, five or six in a room. On the top floor was Father Divine's own apartment, where he lived most of the time. Adjoining his rooms were the Heavenly offices. Here his secretary, John Lamb, the white automobile dealer who joined the cult in Sayville, directed a small clerical staff of five or six stenographers and secretaries, some white, some colored. They answered mail from out-of-town followers, took down stenographic records of all of Father Divine's sermons, and performed other clerical tasks. Probably the person closest to Father Divine was Arthur A. Madison, a Negro attorney. He was a pious man who became interested in Father Divine's movement in the early days in Sayville. He was not an Angel, strictly speaking; he had his own home and his own office. He was almost constantly with Father Divine and handled whatever legal matters needed his attention. He was a competent lawyer, a little pretentious in his courtroom manner, and cunning and quick of brain.

Heaven was then the show place of the Father Divine cult. It was the place where visitors were received. In the hall downstairs, which was used both for eating and worship, meetings were held every night. Sometimes Father Divine was present, sometimes he was not. If he was present, he blessed the food, and, during dinner, spoke from a platform. His speeches were a little more understandable that they used to be in the old days in Baltimore, but they were still full of words that nobody else uses. In one speech, transcribed by Angel stenographers, he said to his followers, "You are in a New World. Remember, we are not representing Heaven as a place geographically, but a State of *Consciousness*, wherein all men can arise to, and recognize God's Presence as Real, as Tangibleateable, and as practical as the principles of Mathematics. It is *indeed* wonderful! Not only tangibleated but as tangibleateable. It has been *tangi*bleated, and it can be retangibleated; it can and will continue to materialize, and repersonify, rematerialize, and repersonify, for the great materializing process is going on!"

The followers of Father Divine, sitting at the tables and crowding in from the street to stand and listen, numbered at that time around two or three hundred. There was always a scattering of white people, but the vast majority were colored. A casual observer at one of these meetings noticed immediately the more spectacular of the followers. These were people who writhed and twitched, emitted squeals and incomprehensible bits of gibberish, fell on the floor, and leaped into the air. There was no question but that some of the followers were crazy. In one period of two years, eighteen of Father Divine's Angels turned up in the psychopathic ward at Bellevue Hospital, having been picked up on the streets in states of mind varying from wild exaltation to coma. Only two of these Angels were discharged after observation. The other sixteen were committed to state insane asylums. But most of Father Divine's followers were relatively quiet folk, not given to yelling or twitching. They recited testimonials telling how much better off they were than when they didn't know Father Divine, they sang, and they joined in the rhythmic stomping that went on sometimes for an hour when Father Divine was not preaching. They were for the most part hard-working people, able to hold jobs or to make their services valuable to Father Divine by working directly for him.

Since the beginning of 1933, when Father Divine left Sayville and established his headquarters in Harlem, he became a business-man with many and varied interests, and his responsibilities were crushing. For one thing, he was the outstanding lodging-house keeper of Harlem. He operated, in addition to Heaven, three apartment houses, nine private houses, and between fifteen and twenty flats, all made into dormitories, and three meeting halls with dormitories on the upper floors. All these places were crowded with roomers. The apartment houses, containing from ten to fifteen apartments each, lodged about two hundred and fifty people apiece. The private houses and the dormitories over the meeting halls accommodated about eight hundred more. In the flats were at least three hundred roomers altogether. This meant that Father Divine was providing sleeping quarters in Harlem for more than fifteen hundred persons. The apartment houses, private houses, halls, and flats were called Extension Heavens. It used to be easy to identify them on a tour of Harlem. In the windows were signs that said, "Peace!" and "Father Divine Is God Almighty." The Extension Heavens were all listed, as well, on a bulletin board in the vestibule of Heaven.

Father Divine's followers in Harlem eventually came to be divided into two classes. There were, first of all, the Angels. The Angels, like those of the Sayville period, either worked at outside jobs, mostly in domestic service, and turned over their wages to Father

Divine, or worked directly for Father Divine, donating merely their labor. Some of the wage-earning Angels slept in the houses of their employers and came to Heaven only for the meetings. Other wage-earning Angels slept in one of the Extension Heavens and got their room and board free. Then there were those who were called Children. The Children were people who were impressed by Father Divine, and went to the meetings, but were not faithful to the extent that they were ready to turn over everything to him. About a thousand Children lived in the Extension Heavens and paid from $1 to $2 a week as room rent.

On West 126th Street, between Seventh and Lenox Avenues, were seven four-story buildings in a row, all with signs in the windows which said, "Peace!" and "Father Divine Is God Almighty." This block of buildings was in charge of a colored Angel named Faithful Mary and was known as the Faithful Mary Extension Heaven. It was the largest of the Extension Heavens and the economic plan on which it was run was more or less typical of the others. The main building in the group, wider than the others, was a vast, draughty place that used to be a Turkish bath. What was once a swimming pool in the basement served as a subterranean back yard for drying clothes. A number of the imitation-marble stairways of the labyrinthine upper structure were roped off because they were decayed and crumbling. People going to the dormitories on the upper floors had to use a front flight of steps on one floor, a side flight on another, and a back flight on the next. Plumbers refused to undertake any major repairs because, they said, the pipes were so eaten with rust that a total collapse of the plumbing system was imminent. The place was damp, with mold on some of the walls. On the ground floor was a large hall for eating and worship. Father Divine visited the place occasionally, as he did the other large Extension Heavens. He had an apartment on the top floor but hardly ever used it. Whether he was in the meeting hall of this Extension Heaven or not, the meetings went on all day and into the night. The followers came in and out and talked to him when he wasn't there as if he had been in the room. They gave testimonials of cures and miraculous happenings that had benefited them, they gazed at the chair where he sat when he was with them, and cried, "Thank you, Father!" and "It is *so* wonderful!" Nobody took charge of these meetings; they went along in an informal fashion, with songs and testimonials and an occasional dance—the same rhythmic stomping that could be observed in Heaven, with the men on one side of the room, the women on the other. There was never any sermon except when Father Divine himself was there to deliver it.

Faithful Mary leased the central building of the Faithful Mary Extension Heaven and paid $300 a month rent to the Bruhan Realty Corporation, a white organization. The building didn't show a direct profit. Many of the occupants of the dormitories on the upper floors were Angels who turned their wages over to Father Divine at the headquarters Heaven, or who were working for him directly and earning no wages. But each of the six brownstone houses adjoining the central building showed a profit from room rent. Faithful Mary paid $75 a month apiece for these houses, and in each of them lived about fifty Children, who paid at least $1 a week. That meant that she took in at least $200 a month for each house. Faithful Mary paid a real-estate agent each month with a satchelful of crumpled $1 bills and small change.

In Heaven and in all of the Extension Heavens, the sexes were segregated, as they used to be in Sayville. The Angels and Children slept six and eight in a room. None of them had any regular medical treatment. Father Divine preached against it then as he had done earlier. Records of venereal, tubercular, and cancer clinics in Harlem showed that scores of Negroes who were once receiving periodical medical treatment for these diseases were no longer receiving it, and the superintendents of the clinics convinced themselves by investigation that the cause of this decline was the antidoctor gospel preached by Father Divine. There were never any funeral services at Heaven or at any Extension Heavens. If relatives didn't claim the body of a dead Angel, the chances were it would be buried by the taxpayers of New York City. The case of an Angel named Charles Jenkins is typical. When Jenkins joined the cult of Father Divine he owned a house, which he turned over to the Father, along with all his worldly possessions. Later on, he drove a coal wagon for the Father, and did other odd jobs for him. He slept at night in the furnace-room of Heaven, sharing a bed with Onward Universe, whose real name was Thomas Brown. In September, 1935, Jenkins had a hemorrhage of the lung, was removed to a flat on 129th Street not officially connected with the Father Divine cult, and from there to the Harlem Hospital, where he died on October 7th of the same year. No one claimed the body, and it was buried in the potter's field on Riker's Island.

The accommodations the Children received with their $1 and $2 beds were probably superior to what they could have got elsewhere in Harlem for the same money. In addition to a place to sleep, the Children had the use of a dining room, which was an adjunct of every Extension Heaven. They didn't get free meals, but the fifteen or twenty cents they paid for each meal was slightly less than what they would have had to pay for the same food in a Harlem restaurant. They were simple meals—stew, or a piece of meat with potatoes. Each Extension Heaven had a laundry, and the larger ones had a barbershop and beauty parlor. The prices were cheaper than at comparative places in Harlem.

Each Extension Heaven was in charge of an Angel, who worked directly under the supervision of Father Divine. If an Extension Heaven didn't pay its way, it was abandoned, or a new Angel was placed in charge. Whenever an apartment house, private house, or flat was rented for use as an Extension Heaven, Father Divine himself inspected it and talked to the agent about the rent. If a lease was required, an Angel signed it.

The Extension Heavens, with their rent-paying Children, represented a change of policy on Father Divine's part which took place not long after he settled in Harlem, in 1933. Up to that time he had taken no money from anybody but Angels, and he took no money even from them unless they were willing to give him everything they had. The enormous impetus given to his movement by the publicity attending his trial in Sayville, and by the sudden death of the judge who tried him, made necessary the creation of the class known as Children. He did not have time to devote hours and days of persuasion to each prospective follower as he had done in Sayville, when they were being attracted to him by two's and three's. As soon as he established his Heaven in Harlem, prospective followers began to come to him by the hundreds. Angels were still created every now and then, but save in exceptional cases, and in cases of well-to-do whites, they had to be Children for a while first. In the meantime the Children were contributing something as roomers and boarders.

Father Divine finally began to maintain Extension Heavens on the same general plan in Baltimore, Newark, Jersey City, and Bridgeport. In none of these places, except the New Jersey cities, was his following larger than a few hundred. He visited these out-of-town Extension Heavens regularly and preached to his followers. Usually, when he was going to one of them, two or three busloads of Harlem disciples went along, which added to the popular impression that the nation was teeming at that time with followers of Father Divine. Thousands of people all over the country had been impressed by the newspaper publicity he had received, and the mail at Heaven was bulky. But Father Divine's movement was mostly local.

It was a natural step from the Extension Heavens to the adoption of another new policy, one that took into cognizance the general public of Harlem on a frankly commercial basis. The first undertaking in this direction involved shoe-shine men. Male Angels who were not good cooks, valets, or Pullman porters, and who were not of much help around Heaven or the Extension Heavens as waiters or clothes-pressers, were provided with portable shoe-shining outfits, on which was printed "Peace!" They would go out into the world to shine shoes and return to Heaven at night with a dollar or two. "Father has blessed me with a shoe box," these Angels would tell their customers, "and I'm *so* glad! It's *wonderful!*"

After this came shops and stores, operated by Angels, staffed by Angel clerks, and dealing directly with the Harlem public on a profit-making basis. Father Divine by that time had restaurants, grocery stores, barbershops, cleaning-and-pressing establishments, huckster wagons, a coal business, a sizable holding of farming land, and two weekly newspapers, all operated by Angels.

There were about twenty-five restaurants. They were not big places. None of them had table space for more than twenty persons. The prices were slightly lower than at other Harlem restaurants of the same standard of quality. Father Divine served a fifteen-cent dinner consisting of a piece of meat, potatoes, bread, butter, and coffee, which would probably have cost twenty cents at the same kind of restaurant around the corner. The signs in the windows said, "Peace! It's wonderful! Buy where they give you the most for the least!" The waiters and waitresses murmured, "Peace!" as they set down a plate, and "Thank you, Father!" when the patron paid. There were about a half-dozen Father Divine grocery stores, ten barbershops, ten cleaning-and-pressing establishments, twenty or thirty huckster wagons selling "Peace Father, Clams and Oysters" and "Peace Father, Fresh Vegetables." Father Divine's coal business was a modest affair, operating three trucks between New York and certain coal fields of Pennsylvania where coal could then be bought at $4 a ton. The cashier of a Father Divine Restaurant on Eighth Avenue used to take orders for coal from customers and the trucks made deliveries whenever they came to town, selling the coal for around $7.50 a ton.

On all these commercial undertakings there was a clear profit.

Father Divine didn't have the same labor costs that his competitors had. Occasionally, he did present a hard-working Angel with some gift. The angelic expression, when he did that, was that he had "blessed them." Faithful Mary, for instance, wore a fur coat all that winter, a fur coat she said had come to her direct from God. It was possible now for a clever Angel to carve out a career for himself or herself in the service of Father Divine. There were about forty white Angels living in Heaven, some of whom seemed to be doing this.

Father Divine's two weekly newspapers in those times were the *Spoken Word* and the *New York News.* These publications had joint offices at 36 West 115th Street and were edited by an Angel board headed by Brother Honaeel. Brother Honaeel was a sharp-nosed, bright-eyed white Californian who was famous among the other Angels for having been directed to Father Divine by a spirit who was a proofreader. He said that this spirit came to him in California, told him to drop everything, to go straight to Father Divine, and become an Angel. His angelic name, the spirit said, would be "Honael." The man wrote that down and then heard the spirit say, "No, no. It's spelled with two e's—H-o-n-a-e-e-l." Both papers used to print Father Divine's sermons in full in every issue, sometimes three or four sermons to an issue. There was a sprinkling of news and feature stories, and a few advertisements. The *Spoken Word* sold for five cents a copy, the *News* for three. The *Spoken Word* attributed the death of King George V of England to the fact that His Late Majesty had not replied to a communication about righteous government sent to him by Father Divine. In the *Spoken Word* the date of publication was always printed like this:

"Friday, June 5, 1936 A.D.F.D."

The *News* never did go that far.

Father Divine's farming business was another enterprise. About a thousand acres in Ulster and Orange Counties were purchased at cash prices of around $15 or $25 an acre—an investment of about $150,000 in this project. The deeds to all the farms are held by Angels. Father Divine announced that he intends to go on raising vegetables on these farms, using Angel as workers, and it has turned out very well, to date.

With all these undertakings, Father Divine neither owns nor leases any property in his own name. He has no visible assets. There is no mystery about the source of his income. If you figure conservatively that a thousand Angels are either working for outside employers and turning over wages of $10 a week apiece, or are operating commercial undertakings which show that much profit, you have a gross income of $10,000 a week. Figure—again conservatively—that the profits from the rent-paying Children pay for the living expenses of the Angels who sleep and eat in Heaven and in the Extension Heavens, and you have a net income of $10,000 a week. The mystery is: What does Father Divine do with it all? Worldly, irreligious minds are inclined to think he must have somewhere a substantial treasure of cash. If he does have such a treasure, it is carefully hidden. A painstaking effort to locate it was made by a lawyer some years ago, and his search could not have been more unsuccessful if the treasure had been hidden behind some cloud in the sky.

One day in the winter of 1940, a bus marked "Father Divine (God)" and carrying a delegation of Angels from Harlem to an Extension Heaven in Baltimore collided with a touring car at Aberdeen, Maryland, and the occupants of the touring car were injured. In the spring of the following year, Maryland courts awarded the injured people judgments against Father Divine totaling $6,152, and the judgments were handed over to William W. Lesselbaum, a pale New York attorney, for collection. Mr. Lesselbaum obtained a local court order giving him the right to examine Father Divine in supplementary proceedings, and, accordingly, Father Divine sat in a chair in the lawyer's office. He swore under oath that he owned nothing on which a lien could be placed. The lawyer went into the matter as far as he could, and got nowhere. He found that at a garage on West 144th Street, leased by an Angel and operated by an Angel crew, there were seven buses, nine trucks, and five limousines, all bearing the insignia "Father Divine (God)," but that all these vehicles were registered in the names of Angels. The same indirection was apparent in all the Extension Heavens. The leases were signed by Angels, and therefore the furnishings inside belonged, legally, to the Angels and not to Father Divine. Heaven itself was at that time leased by Lena Brinson, an Angel who used to sell fried chicken from a wagon on the streets of Harlem. Mr. Lesselbaum could discover no bank account in Father Divine's name. He did find out that when Father Divine was buying his farmlands upstate, and embarrassing the neighbors of the Roosevelts, he carried with him a little satchel full of cash. From people who were present at these real-estate transactions, Mr. Lesselbaum obtained depositions stating that at one place Father Divine took $10,000 out of the bag and paid it down for a farm, and that at two other places he paid $7,000 and $1,100 in cash. It is clear that Father Divine was making efforts in those days to invest a considerable amount of cash.

In 1942, Father Divine closed his New York headquarters and moved to Philadelphia, where he has since lived with several hundreds of his followers at a hotel at Broad Street and Fairmount Avenue. Various ex-Angels have won judgments against him in New York courts for money and bonds they say he obtained from them under false pretenses and, according to the New York newspapers, he stays out of New York to keep from being served with papers in connection with these judgments. In 1946, some years after the death of Mother Divine, he married a 21-year-old white girl named Edna Rose Ritchings. In speeches to his followers he said he was married "in name only" and remarked several times that "God is not married." The ceremony was entirely legal, however, and was performed in Washington, D.C. by a colored Baptist clergyman. On the marriage license he gave his name as "Major F. Divine," but he still claims to be God, and only a few months ago took credit for President Truman's decision to go ahead with the construction of the hydrogen bomb. "By intuition and by inspiration," he told his followers, "I led Mr. Truman, our President, to sign for the H-bomb. The H-bomb is being invented and brought out very swiftly and it is going to be out very quickly in the defense of righteousness and peace. It is coming out at my command, at my intuitive and inspirationic command, and I do not do anything *personally*, but my spirit speaketh, and speaketh both psychologically, intuitively, and inspirationally, and guides the destiny of the nations of the earth, whether they believeth or believeth not. It is wonderful! Wonderful! Wonderful!" And his followers at the Philadelphia hotel swayed and jumped up and down and repeated after him, "Wonderful! Wonderful!"

The 1940s

SOME FUN WITH THE F.B.I.

BACK IN 1941, when Harry Bridges was just a militant labor leader and not a convicted perjurer, I had a talk with him one day at the Hotel Piccadilly. I had gathered from newspaper stories that from the point of view of the quarry he was peculiarly familiar with the methods of the F.B.I. For almost a month that summer, the newspapers said, he had lived at the Hotel Edison, on West Forty-seventh Street, knowing that his telephone wire was tapped and that two or more men, whom he identified as F.B.I. agents, were occupying the room next to him. The newspaper *PM* went so far as to name the agents involved and even produced a young lady who made an affidavit to the effect that she had been with the agents in the room next to Bridges for an hour or so, having been invited there by them to listen to the tapped telephone conversation as a sort of lark. Since wire-tapping is a violation of the law, the newspapers were naturally more concerned with what the men in the next room had done to Bridges than with what Bridges had done to the men in the next room. Hardly anything was brought out to indicate how Bridges had discovered that he was being shadowed in the first place or how he had treated the men who were shadowing him and who didn't know he knew they were shadowing him.

"How do you manage to tell when you are being shadowed by the F.B.I.?" I asked him.

"Well," said Mr. Bridges in a matter-of-fact tone which seems to be characteristic of him, "there are various ways to determine that. Should I describe the general ways I use to find out whether they are shadowing me or should I tell you about specific ways I used here in town this summer?"

"Suppose you tell me some of the general ways," I suggested, "and then go into the specific ways you used at the Edison."

He began to talk, slowly and distinctly, and I found it unnecessary to ask questions as he went along. We sat at a table in a corner of the Piccadilly dining room. Bridges, whom the government had for some time even then been trying to deport on the ground that he was a Communist, is an Australian by birth and talked with a strong Australian accent. He was tall, lean, about thirty-five, and had a candid, vigorous, take-it-or-leave-it manner. I did not ask him about the deportation proceedings, or about his political views, and he did not offer to tell me about them.

"In the first place," he said, "the F.B.I. men like to occupy the room next to yours in a hotel, if possible. If they can arrange this in advance, as they usually can, you'll probably be assigned by the management to a room that has a room next to it with a locked door between it and yours. This locked door almost invariably has a space under it, sometimes as much as half an inch; I guess in the old days the F.B.I. men in this other room would look under this door or listen at it, but they've gotten so high-powered that most of them don't bother nowadays. They consider that kid stuff. They usually have a man looking into your room with field glasses from a room in some adjacent building, and usually they have your telephone rigged in such a way that their receiving instruments pick up not only what you say into your telephone but also what you say anywhere in your room. So you look under this connecting door yourself, and you listen. If you see two pairs of men's feet moving around the room and hear no talking except in whispers, you can be fairly certain the room is occupied by F.B.I. men, or at least by men who are not acting like two ordinary men in a hotel room. Of course, you can often see the wire-tapping apparatus— the wires and earphones and so forth—all spread out on the floor of this other room, and then you do not have any further doubts at all.

"Then, too, of course, you get to know how to observe people in the lobby and you look around to see if there are any F.B.I. men there, waiting to follow you around. I usually can spot one or two right away, because I'm suspected, as you know, of being a Communist and I've seen so many F.B.I. men these past years that there are likely to be one or two that I have seen before in the lobby of practically any hotel I am staying at. But if I don't happen to see any F.B.I. men I know, I watch out for men holding newspapers in front of them in a certain peculiar sort of manner. They hold the paper so that it just comes up to the bottom of their eyes, and their eyes are always peering over the top of the paper. They are very easy to pick out because the way their eyes peep over the top of the paper makes them look peculiar. Of course, I don't look at them directly when I am looking for them this way. There are always lots of mirrors in hotel lobbies and I just look in the mirrors and watch them that way—indirectly. Then, if I suddenly start for the door and, just as I'm about to go out, I stop and turn around quickly, one or more of these fellows is likely to have just jumped up to his feet. He will be standing there looking—well, more easygoing like than anybody ever looks who has just gotten up suddenly and stopped in his tracks. If I want to be absolutely sure they are F.B.I. men, of course, I go out and lose anybody that may be following me and then go back and stand in a doorway across the street from the hotel, and when one of the men I've spotted comes out of the hotel, I follow him down to the F.B.I. office when he goes to make his report about what I've been doing. These F.B.I.

men are nearly always tall guys, easy to follow in a crowd, and they never seem to suspect that they are being followed.

"Well, those are what you might call the general ways of finding out whether you are being shadowed by the F.B.I. Suppose I tell you now, as you suggested, the story of the events that occurred at the Edison.

"I checked into the Edison first this summer early in July and I was given an ordinary three-fifty room. That was what I had asked for. This room had a small balcony, a sort of narrow terrace, in front of the windows and there was the customary locked door leading into the adjoining room. I was very busy with union business at the time—I am an officer of the C.I.O., you know, as well as president of the International Longshoremen's and Warehousemen's Union—and I just didn't bother right away to find out whether the F.B.I. was on the job or not. But one night I had a half-hour with nothing to do and I climbed out on the balcony and looked into the window of the adjoining room. A man was in there and I looked at him and he looked at me. I don't know whether he was an F.B.I. man or not. I never heard anything about it, in any case. Then I went away—checked out—for the week-end, and when I came back and asked for the same room or some other three-fifty room, I was told that there were none left but that I could have a fine room on another floor at the three-fifty rate. I was shown to a very large room with twin beds and two big windows, and no balcony. It had the locked door leading into the adjoining room, of course. I was still busy and I didn't bother about the F.B.I. I checked out again for a few days and came back on August 4th. This time I was given this very same big room with the twin beds, and when I said I wanted a regular three-fifty room the desk said I could have this big one at the three-fifty rate for as long as I wanted it. I said this certainly was nice of the hotel, and, of course, I began to look around the lobby for the F.B.I. men.

"I was pretty sure I recognized one whom I had known in San

Francisco, or in some city out there in the West, in connection with the deportation hearing this spring. Then I went through the business I told you about—watching for guys not reading their newspapers, seeing if they got up when I started out, and so on. I was certain I had three of them spotted before lunchtime that day. Would it interest you to know how I remember the face of an F.B.I. man?"

"Yes, indeed," I said.

"Well," said Bridges, "the way I remember the face of an F.B.I. man is like this: I look at him and get his face clearly in my mind and then I try to think of somebody he reminds me of—like a friend or a movie actor or anybody whose face I know very well. This is better than trying to remember a minute description—better than putting your idea of the F.B.I. man's face into words, if you see what I mean. For instance, one of these three guys I had spotted looked like a longshoreman on the Coast, a very old friend of mine I worked with when I was a longshoreman myself. The second of these three F.B.I. guys reminded me of one of the C.I.O. attorneys on the Coast. The third one had a face very much like the face of Gary Cooper, the movie actor. This way I have of remembering the faces of the F.B.I. men seems to sort of place the face in my mind. Something like those tricks they teach you in memory courses, I guess.

"Well, I thought probably my telephone was tapped, of course, so after I had spotted these three guys and knew I could remember their faces anywhere, I went up to my room and made what I call a test call. I called a friend of mine, one of the officers in the C.I.O. here in town, and I said, 'Look, I've got to see the big shot.' This is the kind of talk that the F.B.I. men are always on the lookout for, you see. They're all sort of like college or high-school boys. My friend at the C.I.O. office, of course, didn't know what I was talking about and said as much, and I said, 'Do I have to tell you who I mean? The big shot! The Number One! Listen,' I said, 'meet me at the drugstore here on the corner in fifteen minutes and I'll explain.'

"So then I went downstairs to a telephone booth and called my friend back and told him what it was all about so he wouldn't bother to meet me at the drugstore. Then I walked around for ten minutes or so and went into the drugstore and, sure enough, one of my three guys came in right after me and sat two seats further down the soda fountain while I drank a milk shake. Another one, the Gary Cooper guy, was standing across the street when I went out. I had pretended to be looking for somebody, expecting somebody to come in, because I didn't want to tip them off that I knew they were shadowing me. I went into a movie-theatre entrance as if I was going to a movie and ducked around and looked out at the street from the other side of the change booth, and I saw the first guy start back for the hotel and the other guy, the Gary Cooper guy, go off in another direction by himself. So I followed him and he got into a taxi. I got into a taxi and followed him down to Foley Square, where he got out and went into the F.B.I. office. Am I taking too much time?"

"Oh, no, not at all," I said.

"Well," said Bridges, "then I went back to the hotel and up to my room. I went in my door very fast and dove over to the connecting door, lay down, and looked under it into the next room. Two pairs of feet went by my eye and I could also see some bunched-up telephone wires on the floor—just dumped there and curled up.

"I wanted to see these guys' faces and find out whether they were the two I had spotted downstairs or whether they were different ones. So I waited in my room for a long time, keeping very quiet and with my door into the corridor open just a little. They must have thought I had left the room, which was what I wanted them to think, because finally I heard their door open and I watched them, through the crack in my door, go down the corridor toward the elevator. I then closed my door softly and opened it again in the usual way and started for the elevator myself. I rode down in it with them. They didn't say a word to each other and one of them kept looking at his fingernails. I got a good look at them, of course. The one looking at his fingernails was the guy that resembles my longshoreman friend and the other one was the guy that resembles the C.I.O. attorney on the Coast.

"After tipping off my friends that I was being tapped, I sort of settled down to have some fun with the F.B.I. I wasn't busy and I had some time on my hands. I knew this hotel we're sitting in now, the Piccadilly, overlooks the Edison, so I went over to Sixth Avenue and rented a pair of field glasses. I put up a deposit on them and agreed to pay fifty cents a day rent, but I eventually bought them because I had so much fun with them. I went back to my room and the two guys were in the next room again. Looking under the door, I could see their feet moving around. I called the hotel operator and told her I was expecting an important long-distance call and to put it right on when she got it, that I'd wait for it. Then I left the room very quietly, ducked out of the hotel, and ducked in and out of a couple of stores just in case any of the lobby guys were following me, and came over to the Piccadilly and went up to the roof garden. I had stayed at the Piccadilly before. I spotted my room at the Edison easily enough with the field glasses because I had left some stuff on the window sill which I could recognize. Then I moved the glasses over to the room next to mine and there were the two guys, stretched out on the twin beds with their earphones on, thinking I was still in the room. It seems that most of the time they listen with the earphones while standing up, but I suppose that this time they must have thought it was going to be a long wait, waiting for the long-distance call, so they had lain down on the beds. It was only about a hundred yards from the roof of the Piccadilly to the room in the Edison, and I could see them quite plainly. I'm afraid I'm taking too long with this. Do you want to hear it in this much detail?"

"I certainly do," I said.

"Well," said Bridges, "I decided to rent a room over here at the Piccadilly so I could watch the F.B.I. men at the Edison more comfortably, and I had the idea, too, of having some of my friends up to watch them while I was in my room at the Edison. I had never had such an easy time with F.B.I. men before, although I have always found it comparatively easy to spot them and so forth. Whenever I left the Edison to come over here to the Piccadilly, I would go around a corner, duck into a store, and watch the Gary Cooper fellow go by looking for me, and then I would come over here. They never had any idea what was going on as far as I can tell. Well, I got the room here and I'd get some of my friends, labor people and so on, to stay in my room at the Piccadilly, and I'd go over to my other room in the Edison, usually taking a friend along with me so I could talk to him and keep the F.B.I. men busy. We'd go into my room at the Edison and my friends at the Piccadilly would see the F.B.I. men get up off their beds and pick up the earphones. Then we'd talk all sorts of silly stuff—about how we were planning, for instance, to take over the Gimbel strike so I could use the pretty Gimbel shopgirls to help me take over the New York longshoremen. Stuff like that. Some of it was a bit complicated, too—figured out sort of carefully to mix them up and confuse their various files on people. Some of it, though, was pretty broad. We couldn't help getting to kidding when we thought of them sitting there listening, but the F.B.I. men apparently took it all in and put it all down. As soon as we'd leave the room, one of them would begin typing very fast on a typewriter at a table in front of the window.

"Then I remembered that one of the things F.B.I. men always do is to get hold of any scraps of paper that are left in the room of a man they are shadowing. They get a key to the room, or they fix up a maid, or something. Well, so we would tear up old letters and things and the next morning leave them in my room at the Edison, and then that afternoon we'd see one of the F.B.I. men sitting at the table at the window in their room pasting little pieces of paper together. A couple of times I tore things up in the shape of six-pointed stars, or five-pointed stars, or in the shape of a row of paper dolls—you know that trick of tearing paper, don't you? I used to do it for my kid. Then we'd see this F.B.I. guy holding up the stars and the rows of dolls next day at the window, studying them.

"We also left some well-used carbon paper in the wastebasket, so they could study that, too. The F.B.I. just loves carbon paper, you know. When they get hold of a piece of carbon paper that has been used for the writing of twenty or thirty letters, they really go to town—chemical processes, magnifying glasses, the whole works—and try to decipher what's been written on the carbon paper. I got a lawyer friend of mine to get me some from his office and another friend of mine got a stenographer he goes around with to bring me some from her office, which is a second-hand-furniture concern. We left them five or six sheets to work on. The guys in the room, of course, wouldn't try to decipher carbon paper themselves; they'd take that kind of thing right down to headquarters.

"Well, that's about all except what's appeared in the newspapers. Since I took the microphone out of my telephone box at the Edison and checked out over there, I haven't seen any F.B.I. men. I still have the microphone, though."

"You found a microphone in your telephone box?" I asked.

"Oh," said Mr. Bridges, "I must have forgot to tell you about that. I'm sorry. Except when the F.B.I. men have lots of time and a completely free hand, you see, they usually just put the microphone in the telephone box. It is a special kind that picks up the two-way conversations on the telephone and also anything that is being said by people in the room. I looked in the phone box, of course, and saw it there the day I made the test call and they followed me over to the drugstore, but I didn't disturb it until we had finished having our fun with the F.B.I."

MISTER 880

IN THE LATE summer of 1938, an elderly widower named Edward Mueller found that he was in need of money for the support of his dog and himself. He was a man of simple tastes, and the dog was an undemanding mongrel terrier. Mr. Mueller had for many years been a superintendent in apartment buildings on the upper East Side. Living in the basements of these buildings, he and his wife had raised two children, a boy and a girl. By the time Mrs. Mueller died, in 1937, the children had grown up and gone off to homes of their own. The son had a job and was doing well; the daughter had married. After the death of his wife, Mueller moved out of the basement that had been their last home together and rented a small, sunny flat on the top floor of a brownstone tenement near Broadway and Ninety-sixth Street. He and the dog took possession of it in the spring of 1938. Feeling that he was too old to be a superintendent any longer, Mueller tried for a while to make a living as a junkman. He was sixty-three at that time and was gentle, sweet-tempered, and strongly independent. Only five feet three inches tall, he had a lean, hard-muscled frame, a healthy pink face, bright blue eyes, a shiny bald dome, a fringe of snowy hair over his ears, a wispy white mustache and hardly any teeth. He bought a pushcart secondhand and, accompanied by the dog, roamed the neighborhood when the weather was good, picking up junk in vacant lots and along the river front under the West Side Highway. He went about his work in a leisurely manner and always looked happy. Sometimes he stopped to talk to strangers who wanted to talk, and at other times he carried on fragmentary, one-sided conversations with the dog that trotted at his heels. He was able to sell some of the odds and ends he picked up to wholesale junk dealers, but before many months had gone by, he began to realize that he wasn't making enough to live on, and that if he didn't do better his savings would soon be gone and he would be destitute.

When his son and daughter visited him, and when he went to see them, Mueller said that he was getting along all right and didn't need a thing. For a full half century, he had depended only on himself, and he had the flinty pride of an elderly man who had worked hard since he was a boy of thirteen and had never asked help from anybody. The life he had lived had been a respectable and law-abiding one. Everybody who had ever known Mueller would have said that he was probably the last man in the world to try to make money dishonestly. That was exactly what Mueller did, however. In November, 1938, he became a counterfeiter of one-dollar bills. He continued to look happy and kept on living on a modest scale in the sunny, top-floor flat, cooking his own meals, doing his own laundry, walking his own dog, and making his own money. When he needed cash, he stepped into his kitchen and turned some out on a small, hand-driven printing press he had set up in a corner next to the sink. Then, with his pushcart and his dog, he would go out into the streets, pick up his odds and ends of junk, and pass one or two of his counterfeit bills. For ten years, he passed them at the rate of forty or fifty a month, dividing them equitably among the storekeepers of his own neighborhood and storekeepers in other neighborhoods around New York. During that period, the United States Secret Service conducted a manhunt for Mueller that exceeded in intensity and scope any other manhunt in the chronicles of counterfeiting. The Secret Service called him Mr. Eight Eighty, and then Old Mr. Eight Eighty, after the number of the file kept on him at Secret Service Headquarters, in Washington, for in those years they knew him only by the bills he passed.

At the buildings in which Mueller had worked as a superintendent, he was highly thought of by his employers and by the tenants who occupied the apartments over the basements in which he and his family had lived. He had done his work efficiently, with good-natured gravity, and had given the impression of being thoughtful and occasionally a dryly humorous man. Once a lady tenant asked him to see if he could fix her child's electric train, the toy having stalled late on Christmas Eve. He looked it over, went down to his basement home and got some tools and came back upstairs. Sitting on the floor near the Christmas tree in the tenant's living room, he silently went to work on the train. "Hate to bother you with such a silly thing," the tenant remarked. Mueller looked up at her, grinned, and asked gently, "If it is a silly thing, why did you buy it?" The tenant could think of no answer to that, and she stood there while Mueller went on working. After a moment, he looked up, grinned at her again, and said, "If it is out of order, it should be fixed." He fussed with the toy for a few minutes more and then turned on the current. The train ran around the track satisfactorily. The tenant thanked him and tipped him five dollars. She never forgot the incident. Speaking of it recently, after more than twenty years, she said, "He made you feel that he was thinking serious thoughts all the time and that he was dignified, while you yourself were empty-headed and frivolous, but he was an awfully good superintendent."

Until the summer of 1938, Mueller seems to have made only two noteworthy attempts to become anything more than a good superintendent. In June, 1905, when he was a young man, he sent blueprints for a new kind of camera to the Eastman Kodak Company and received a letter informing him that the company didn't think his invention was commercially practicable but complimenting him on its "extraordinary ingeniousness." Mueller kept the letter and showed it, with diffident satisfaction, to friends and acquaintances. He still had it when he moved into the top-floor flat in 1938. It was frayed and yellowed with age, and he would hold it carefully when he showed it to his new neighbors.

Mueller told these neighbors that he had also invented, when he was a middle-aged man, a Venetian blind that would roll up and down like a window shade. "You didn't have to pull a string this way and that way to make her go up and stay up," he would say. "You'd just give her a twitch, like you do a window shade, and she'd go up and stay up. Or you'd just pull her down, and she'd stay down. It was simple, my Venetian blind." When the neighbors asked him why he hadn't made a fortune out of it, he would explain that the people who manufactured Venetian blinds thought that his wouldn't be profitable. "They told me it was simple and clever, mind you," he would say. "One young fellow who ran a factory over in Jersey nailed her onto the wall of his office when I went to see him, and then he kept pulling her up and down and saying, 'I'll be darned!' but he thought it would cost too much to manufacture it. I remember exactly what he looked like, rolling my Venetian blind up and down, there in his office. He was a fat young fellow and he had on a blue suit and a white shirt. That shirt had a soft collar on it, and the collar had little buttons on it that held the corners of the collar onto the shirt."

Mueller usually interspersed such talk with short silences, during which he grinned at his listeners, as he had grinned at the lady tenant on the Christmas Eve twenty years earlier. Because he had lost most of his teeth by 1938, his grin was striking. "Mr. Mueller had a toothless grin if I ever saw a toothless grin," one of his neighbors remarked recently. "When he grinned, he looked kind of foolish, but when he wasn't grinning, he looked nice, and he looked smart." Another thing that impressed people who knew Mueller at

REPORTING AT WIT'S END

that time was the fact that his mongrel terrier had no name. He was plainly devoted to the dog, and they used to ask him why he didn't name it. The explanation he gave contains another hint of the peculiar mold of his character. He said the dog didn't need a name. He would grin and ask mildly, "What good would a name do the dog? When I talk to him, he knows I'm talking to *him*, don't he? And I know who *he* is without calling him by some made-up name, don't I?" Mueller was delighted when people admitted that although his point of view was unusual, there was certainly some sense in it. When Mueller came to the conclusion that his junk business was a failure and that he needed an additional income, the solution he devised for his economic problem was out of the ordinary for a man of his age, disposition, and background, but the way he conducted himself as a counterfeiter was perhaps characteristic of him as an individual. Although he became in a sense the most successful American counterfeiter of modern times, he put on no airs and he made no change in his standard of living. His son and his daughter, as well as his neighbors, were unaware of what he was up to. The first counterfeit bill he passed on his fellow citizens, in 1938, was a very bad copy of a one-dollar bill. When his career as a counterfeiter came to an end, in 1948, he was still turning out the same crude dollar bills from the same kind of inferior plates, on the same hand-driven printing press in the same corner of the same kitchen of the same top-floor tenement flat, and he never turned out more counterfeit dollars than he needed to support his dog and himself.

COUNTERFEITING IS A prehistoric form of gainful skulduggery. The idea of money was conceived somewhere on the other side of antiquity, and so was the idea of counterfeit money. The idea of money is older than the idea of counterfeit money, but older, perhaps, by no more than a few minutes. There is evidence of the use of both the genuine article and the counterfeit article in the earliest recorded civilizations, and it has been established that primitive tribes had both good money and bad money before there were any civilizations to record. It seems that immediately after certain people realized that they could easily make tokens to represent cumbersome property, such as collections of animal skins and stores of foodstuffs, certain other people awoke to the fact that they could just as easily make tokens to represent the tokens that represented the cumbersome property. The two ideas are so closely related that they are practically twins, and, like the products of the ideas, they are hard to tell apart. If it were not for counterfeit money, the story of money might be simply beautiful. As it is, the pattern formed by the fateful entwinement of money and counterfeit money is intricately grotesque.

Among all the rogues in history, no class has been more persistent than counterfeiters, and only thieves have been more numerous. No penalty for the crime has ever been devised that had any conclusive effect on the obstinacy of counterfeiters or on the popularity of counterfeiting. Civilized people with money they hope is valuable have always possessed a fierce abhorrence of money they know is worthless, and their treatment of counterfeiters has come close to being savage. Until comparatively recent times, by thinking up and carrying out punishments for counterfeiters, civilized people went about as far as they are likely to go in that direction. Some of the earliest counterfeiters laboriously clipped coins around the edges and passed the clipped coins on to their fellow citizens. Then they manufactured counterfeit coins, using the valuable metal they had clipped to make a thin coating for them. To discourage this kind of thing, some of the earliest sound-money men laboriously clipped counterfeiters around the edges, beginning with their ears and going on from there. During the formative period of the Roman Empire, the ears of counterfeiters were cut off and the counterfeiters were also deprived of their citizenship rights. Later on, the noses of Roman counterfeiters were cut off, along with their ears and their citizenship rights. By the time the Roman civilization reached its apex, the hands, feet, noses, ears, and citizenship rights of counterfeiters were clipped away one after another, and the same counterfeiters were then forthrightly castrated. What was left of them was thrown into an arena full of hungry lions. Unclipped and uneaten counterfeiters of that era of civilization do not seem to have been deterred by the threat of these penalties.

As Roman civilization declined, counterfeiting became increasingly popular and was taken up by people in all walks of Roman life. Following a course that had been experimented with in earlier civilizations, counterfeiting was carried on by many respectable individuals and eventually by the State itself. Senators, lawyers, physicians, merchants, and empire builders from the best Roman families were caught counterfeiting. Emperors who believed in a sound currency unhesitatingly fed these leading citizens to the lions, after they had been deprived of their citizenship rights and otherwise clipped. When Nero became emperor, he found the idea of counterfeiting inviting and, in his imperial position, was carried away by the wonderful simplicity of it. The bizarre design formed by the mixture of money and counterfeit money reached a kind of decadent perfection under Nero. Using the government mints, he brought about a synthesis of the two opposing ideas. He turned out worthless leaden replicas of good silver coins in such great quantities that the Roman monetary system collapsed and many civilized Europeans went back to the barter system.

With minor variations, this preposterous cycle has been repeated many times since the fall of the Roman Empire. During the Renaissance, after a counterfeiter had been thoroughly clipped, his eyes were gouged out and he was then drawn, quartered, reassembled, and burned at the stake. Monarchs grew accustomed to having some of their most trusted courtiers and some of their most respected civic and religious leaders brought before them as convicted counterfeiters. On the whole, they punished these fellows

almost as severely as they punished common counterfeiters, showing only occasional flashes of leniency. When, for example, the
Abbot of Messenden was caught making and passing counterfeit
coins, King Edward III stipulated that he be hanged and drawn
but, in view of his calling, not clipped or quartered. Henry VIII,
like Nero, went in for counterfeiting as the head of the state, and so
debased his currency that it collapsed. Various kings of France ruined their currencies in the same way. Through the ages, counterfeit money has caused the downfall of one monetary system after
another, with the result that nations have periodically given up the
idea of money and have gone back to the barter system. Civilized
people have nevertheless been inclined to think of money as a civilized idea and have been amazed whenever they have discovered
that uncivilized people had money. Tacitus records the fact that
the barbarous Goths and even the undeveloped, loose-lipped Franks
had monetary systems, although they lived in wooden huts and
didn't have slaves. Tacitus writes about this in the tone of a dumfounded historian. The Pilgrims who landed in New England
thought money would be something new to the Indians. When
they found that the half-naked, red-skinned aborigines, using their
primitive heads, had conceived and developed the idea of money,
and seemed to be devoted to it, they were flabbergasted and, according to some memoirs, aggrieved.

The tribulations of the early white settlers in New England were
multiplied by the fact that while certain Indians had been engaged
in establishing a monetary system based on wampum, certain other
Indians had been engaged in hacking at that monetary system by
making counterfeit wampum. The Pilgrims were accustomed to
biting coins and ringing them vigorously on cobblestones to make
sure they weren't counterfeit. The Indians were accustomed to spit-
ting on strings of blue wampum and rubbing the shell beads vigorously to make sure that they were the hearts of genuine quahog
clamshells and weren't just pieces of cheap white sea shells that

had been dyed blue with the juice of wild huckleberries by Indian counterfeiters. In the beginning, the Pilgrims didn't know how to detect counterfeit wampum and the Indians didn't know how to detect counterfeit coins. In spite of their privileged upbringing, the Pilgrims were at a disadvantage. Either because they hadn't had much money or because they had thought they wouldn't need it in a place like America, they had brought very little of it with them. There was a shortage of both genuine and counterfeit coins in early Colonial times, whereas there was an abundance of both genuine and counterfeit wampum. Wampum was therefore enthusiastically adopted by the Pilgrims as the medium of exchange. The Pilgrims soon found themselves stuck with fathoms of counterfeit wampum that rascally Indians had passed on them. When the Pilgrims tried to pass it back, even the most ignorant Indian would look at it, spit on it, rub it, drop it on the ground, fold his arms, and shake his head. In time, the Pilgrims and other early colonists learned to spit on wampum and rub it, in order to make sure that it was the real quahog. In a flurry of naïveté, they passed a sheaf of anti-counterfeit-wampum laws.

Following the Roman pattern, the legal penalties for Colonial counterfeiters were at first mild. In 1647, for example, the General Court of Elections in Their Majesties' Colony of Rhode Island and Providence Plantations ordered that "if the Indians shall offer to putt away upon exchange or barter their false peag string beads [wampum] for good, and warrant it to be so, and it be found otherwise, it shall be confiscated to the Public Treasury." This measure appears to have put the savage red men in their place, but it wasn't long before some of the frailer white men began making counterfeit wampum on a scale that Indian counterfeiters had never envisioned. The first glass beads presented to the Indians of New England were designed to look not like glass beads but like wampum, and they were accepted as wampum by both undiscerning Indians and undiscerning palefaces. In the beginning, the white counterfeiters got this counterfeit wampum from England, where it was made in undercover factories. Later, they established undercover glass-wampum factories over here. What penalties were meted out to these counterfeiters is not known, but it is a matter of historical record that the chaos they created caused the collapse of the wampum currency.

By 1690, paper money, in the form of bills of credit, was being used in place of wampum. In the same year, counterfeit bills of credit were being used in place of genuine bills of credit. The use of money and the counterfeiting of it retained most of their traditionally weird aspects. The first recorded trial of counterfeiters on this continent took place in Rhode Island in 1704. Among those convicted of knowingly passing counterfeit bills of credit was Peregrine White, Jr., a son of the Peregrine White who was born aboard the Mayflower on its first trip over and is generally called "the first native white American." Young Peregrine told where he had got the bad paper, pleaded guilty, testified for the prosecution, and got off with a fine and only three months in jail. Of the others, who were found guilty of printing, as well as passing, the fake bills of credit, one was sentenced to "sit in the pillory for one hour on a lecture day, and then and there have one ear cut off [and] to suffer twelve months' imprisonment." Counterfeiting in America had, by these primeval steps, reached the clipping stage. The penalty for it was swiftly raised to two ears per counterfeiter, and heavier prison terms were imposed, along with longer stretches in the pillory. Counterfeiting increased. Soon Colonial counterfeiters were publicly whipped after both ears had been cut off and they were then nailed to the pillory instead of being allowed to shift around while sitting in it. By this time there were many women counterfeiters. Some of them were grandmothers of the Daughters of the American Revolution. They, too, were whipped, but instead of their ears being clipped, their heads were shaved. Still later, Colonial counterfeiters, no matter who or what, were hanged.

Counterfeiting became even more popular. The currency based on bills of credit collapsed.

In 1772, Colonel Philip Schuyler made a speech before the General Assembly of the Province of New York in which he proposed that "paper money be backed with the devices of an all-seeing eye in the clouds, a cart and a coffin, three felons on a gallows, a weeping father and mother and several small children, a burning pit, human figures poured into it by fiends, and a label with the words 'Let the Counterfeiter Rot.'" The Assembly decided that it would be too expensive to put all that on the back of a piece of paper money. It did authorize money with "'Tis Death to the Counterfeit" boldly printed on the back. Counterfeiters found it easy to reproduce this simple phrase, and lightheartedly did so. The new currency soon collapsed. Counterfeiting caused the disintegration of various other paper currencies, both before and after the American Revolution. During the Revolution, the British Government used its own printing presses for counterfeiting and flooded America with spurious Continental dollars. Its intention was to create a financial panic, which, it was hoped, would stop the Revolution. The most memorable result of its effort was the expression "not worth a Continental."

Counterfeiting is still going on in this country, but it is no longer as profitable or as popular as it used to be. It is not widely regarded as a practice that will cause the collapse of the present American monetary system. Contemporary counterfeiters, when they are caught, are usually sent to federal penitentiaries, where only their hair is clipped. One reason for the decline of counterfeiting in the United States is that it is now extremely difficult and fairly expensive to make bad American money that looks and feels anything like good American money. Another reason is that it is just about impossible for an ordinary counterfeiter to stay in business very long without being caught by the United States Secret Service.

The Secret Service is responsible for protecting the nation's Presidents from assassins and the nation's currency from counterfeiters. It is made up of conscientious and overworked men who carry out their duties quietly, anonymously, and with an efficiency that approaches omniscience. Since the Secret Service began taking care of Presidents, in 1901, no President has been assassinated, and in the fiscal year 1948 only $137,318 out of the $27,902,858,000 of American money in circulation was discovered to be counterfeit. The Secret Service is the all-seeing eye in the clouds that Colonel Schuyler wistfully dreamed of in pre-Revolutionary days. In 1948, Secret Service men seized $2,948,437 in counterfeit money before the counterfeiters who made it were able to put it into circulation.

When a man is a counterfeiter, the temptation to make a whole lot of money, and to make it fast, is more nearly irresistible and seemingly more easily gratified than it is in any other line of work, honest or dishonest. Counterfeiters are greedy men when they take up counterfeiting or else become greedy men soon afterward. Old Mr. Eight Eighty's lack of greed was unique and indicated a restraint on his part that bordered on asceticism. When the elderly counterfeiter passed his first counterfeit dollar bill, at a cigar store on Broadway near 102nd Street, in November, 1938, the proprietor—a busy man, who ran the store without assistants—didn't look at the bill or feel it carefully when he accepted it. That afternoon, he took it to the neighborhood bank as part of his day's deposit. A teller detected it. He deducted one dollar from the cigar-store proprietor's deposit slip and told him the law required that the bank turn a bad bill over to the Secret Service. In keeping with the efficiency of this branch of the Treasury Department, a Secret Service man questioned the proprietor of the cigar store the very next day. The proprietor said that he had no idea who had slipped him the counterfeit bill. Although he was frequently interrupted by customers, he received from the Secret Service man a full course of instruction in the detection of counterfeit bills and was told to call the traffic cop on the corner if anybody tried to pass another one on him. Mr. Eight Eighty's dollar bill was sent to the Secret Service Headquarters, where it was given a routine going over by some students of counterfeit money in the Secret Service laboratory in the Treasury Building and then sent on to the technical laboratory at the Bureau of Engraving and Printing for full analysis.

Before it can wear out, all United States currency that is not destroyed or hoarded eventually is turned in to the Treasury. Counterfeit money is usually detected by individuals or banks and turned over to the Secret Service before it reaches that stage. The Secret Service laboratory has a file on every series of counterfeit bills that has ever come to its attention. Most of these files are marked "Closed," which means that the counterfeiter who made the plates from which the bills were printed is in a federal penitentiary, or, having served his sentence, is being checked up on from time to time by the Secret Service, or is known to have stopped making counterfeit money, or is known to be dead. The files marked "Open" contain the products of counterfeiters who are still active and for whom the Secret Service is looking. The men in the laboratory can tell one counterfeiter's work from another's almost as surely as fingerprint experts can tell one fingerprint from another.

Practically all counterfeit paper money these days is produced by a photoengraving process. The counterfeiter takes photographs of both sides of a genuine bill, makes engravings from them, and from the engravings prints his counterfeit money. Genuine money is printed from hand-made steel engravings. These engravings are by first-class artists. There are today only five or six artists in this country who can draw with an engraver's tool on a piece of steel a portrait that is as warm and lifelike as the portrait of George Washington that appears on dollar bills, or the portrait of Abraham Lincoln on five-dollar bills, or those of other great Americans on larger bills. In these portraits, the hair and/or whiskers look real, the faces possess verisimilitude, and the eyes have the highlights and shadows of open, living, human eyes. The artists who draw these portraits and the craftsmen who produce the intricate designs elsewhere on the bills make an honest living working for the Bureau of Engraving and Printing. Counterfeiters' attempts to copy the portraits and decorations on modern United States currency by working freehand with an engraver's tool on a piece of steel have invariably resulted in counterfeit bills that are easier to detect than those made by the photoengraving process.

In the entire period since a national currency was introduced, in 1863, only one counterfeiter has turned up who was a good enough artist to copy a genuine bill with any success by the freehand method, but he didn't try to do it with an engraver's tool. He worked with a camel's-hair brush on paper, drawing a single hundred-dollar bill at a time. His name was Emanuel Ninger. He was known to the Secret Service men as Jim the Penman until he was caught by them in 1896. His method was to place a genuine hundred-dollar bill under a piece of glass and put a strong light beneath it. He would then trace the outlines of the portrait and other designs on a piece of paper of the right size. Then, with magnificent draftsmanship, he would copy the portrait and the designs, using only his camel's-hair brush and his own green and black inks. Like the artists who work for the Bureau of Engraving and Printing, he was a genius in his way, and his counterfeit bills were works of art in their way. They were so nearly perfect that banks accepted them. Jim the Penman's first counterfeit bill went through many hands and was detected as a counterfeit only when it was examined by the Secret Service after it had been turned in at the Sub-Treasury in New Orleans. The Secret Service looked for Jim the Penman for many years and caught up with him, at last, in Jersey City. Secret Service men followed him around for a few days and then arrested him in the act of getting one of his hundred-dollar bills changed in a New York bank. His camel's-hair brush and his paper and ink were confiscated, and he was sent to a federal penitentiary. He made only a modest living by passing his works of art. He could have earned much more than that by helping the Bureau of Engraving and Printing make genuine money, but there was, as he explained, something about counterfeiting that appealed to him.

Counterfeiters have found that the portraits, as well as the subtle shadings of the borders and other features of United States currency, lose much of their clarity and liveness in the photoengraving process. In order to produce even a fair plate, a counterfeiter must first make a photograph of the bill and retouch it by hand, strengthening as best he can the fine lines that would otherwise be lost when the engraving is made. Striving for an unattainable perfection, the counterfeiter then usually tries to etch in on the plate some of the lines and shadings that didn't, in spite of the retouching, come through clearly. This freehand work makes the finished couterfeit bill look a trifle more nearly genuine, but to the men who work in the Secret Service laboratory it also gives each series of counterfeit bills a distinctive quality. This helps them in their efforts to tell counterfeiters apart and, in time, to catch them.

When Mr. Eight Eighty's first counterfeit dollar bill was examined at the Secret Service laboratory, it was found to be unlike any other counterfeit bill, of any denomination, in the files. There was no open file of dollar bills, because in the late nineteen-thirties no counterfeiter besides Mr. Eight Eighty considered it worth while to make a business of turning out dollar bills. Even in the closed files, which go back to the earliest days of counterfeiting in the United States, there weren't many cases of counterfeit dollar bills. A new "open" file was set up. At first, the counterfeiter was known among Secret Service men as Mr. Eight Eighty, but in a few years his case achieved the distinction of being the oldest of the open cases in the Secret Service files, and it was then that they began calling him *Old* Mr. Eight Eighty. During the ten years they looked for Mr. Eight Eighty, they arrested and convicted other persons on counterfeiting charges and seized $3,458,235 in counterfeit money before it got into circulation. The hardest man they ever tried to catch was Old Mr. Eight Eighty.

The lengths to which counterfeiters have gone in trying to outwit the modern American monetary system is exceeded only by the lengths to which the Secret Service has gone in unmasking modern American counterfeiters. In their time, Secret Service men have caught residents of New York's Chinatown who bored tiny holes in the edges of gold pieces, dug out most of the gold inside, and refilled the hollowed coins with cement or mud. They have caught counterfeiters who minted, in portable mints they carried around in their automobiles, fairly good-looking pewter fifty-cent pieces. They have caught counterfeiters who shaved Lincoln's portrait off the fronts of genuine five-dollar bills, replaced it with a conveniently proportioned likeness of a New York judge that had appeared on some campaign leaflets, and, after raising the numerals and lettering, passed the bills in the jurist's own neighborhood as twenty-dollar bills. Secret Service men have posed as counterfeiters and as wholesale buyers of counterfeit money, and have by other hazardous means broken up ring after ring of mass-production counterfeiters with influential underworld connections. They once put two especially persistent counterfeiters behind prison bars and afterward found that they were going right on counterfeiting behind the bars.

Most of the counterfeiters the Secret Service men have caught, or have ever heard of, were extraordinarily clever craftsmen. Old Mr. Eight Eighty was so inept that his counterfeit one-dollar bills were laughable if they were even casually looked at or felt. His clumsily retouched portrait of Washington was murky and deathlike. His border work and his numerals and lettering were botched. The paper he used was an inexpensive bond paper that can be bought at any stationery store. Old Mr. Eight Eighty kept passing the things, though, and he passed them at what the Secret Service considered a hideously humble rate. None of his fellow-citizens ever looked at or felt his dollar bills when he passed them. They were, after all, only dollar bills. When people discovered that they had been stuck with them, they were, it seems, taught a lesson only to the extent that the loss of a dollar ever teaches the average American a lesson. Long before the Secret Service men caught up with Old Eight Eighty, in the spring of 1948, and arrested him in the kitchen of his sunny, top-floor tenement flat near Broadway and Ninety-sixth Street, he was, besides being known to them as Old Mr. Eight Eighty, generally recognized by them as the most exasperating countefeiter of all time, and the least greedy.

THE SECRET SERVICE search for Mr. Eight Eighty began in a modest manner that was in keeping with the denomination of his counterfeits. Within a month after he passed his first bad bill forty more of them had turned up. Most of them were detected by New York banks, and in some cases the banks were able to identify the depositors. They were painstakingly investigated by Secret Service men. None of them seemed to be counterfeiters, and none of them remembered who had given them the bills. A map of the metropolitan area was put up on a wall of the New York office of the Secret Service especially for Mr. Eight Eighty, and every time one of the bills was traced back to a storekeeper or whoever else had presumably received it direct from the counterfeiter, a red thumbtack was stuck into the map to show the location. After a time, the red thumbtacks indicated that most of the bills had been passed on the upper West Side of Manhattan—a section of approximately five square miles, with a population of almost a million.

A duplicate of File No. 880, which had been established at Secret Service Headquarters, was set up in the New York office as a matter of course. The initial entry in this file, which was to become one of the bulkiest in the archives of the Secret Service, was a routine memorandum sent out from Washington to Secret Service offices all over the country after Mr. Eight Eighty's first counterfeit bill had been examined at the Secret Service laboratory. This memorandum, which was witheringly critical of Mr. Eight Eighty's craftsmanship, read as follows:

CIR. #880

12-1-38

This opens your file on this new counterfeit.

New York reports the appearance November 19th of new counterfeit $1 Silver Certificate, 1935 Series; check letter "K"; face plate No. 1371; back plate No. 601; serial No. K70025356A; W. A. Julian, Treasurer of the United States; Henry Morgenthau, Jr., Secretary of the Treasury; portrait of Washington.

This counterfeit is printed on one sheet of cheap quality bond paper from crude photo-etched plates. The portrait is poorly executed against a black background which fails to show any line work. The left eye is represented by a black spot. A heavy line forms the lower lid of the right eye, which is almond-shaped. Washington's right shoulder blends with the oval background and is devoid of any shading. Faulty etching gives a soiled appearance to the lower part of Washington's shirt front. Reproduction of small lettering, particularly the titles, is ineffective, some of the letters being illegible. In the word "Washington," under the portrait, the letters are misshaped and otherwise crudely outlined.

The seal and serial numbers are printed in dull indigo. The design and text of the seal are poorly etched. The figures comprising the serial number are thicker than the genuine and printed more heavily. The highest serial number, printed to date, on genuine notes of this series and denomination is S92,144,000A. The highest face plate number on genuine $1 notes to date is 975, which is 396 less than the face plate number on the counterfeit. The back of this counterfeit, printed in dark green, is of better workmanship than the front. In some places, the vignette has been retouched by hand to obtain depth for weak spots in the design. This is particularly true of the large word "ONE" in the center.

(signed) FRANK J. WILSON
Chief, Secret Service

The New York office was headed by James J. Maloney, whose title was supervising agent. At the end of five years of the search for Mr. Eight Eighty, Mr. Maloney went to Washington as assistant chief of the Secret Service and he became chief in 1947 (before Old Eight Eighty was caught). Toward the end of 1939, when the search for Mr. Eight Eighty had been going on for a year, Mr. Maloney noticed, with a slight sense of irritation, that Mr. Eight Eighty's craftsmanship was growing even worse. On the latest bills that were turning up on Mr. Maloney's desk, the word "Washington" under the portrait of the first President was spelled "Wahsington." The counterfeiter had evidently been dissatisfied with the lettering on the bills and in trying to improve it had transposed two of the letters. This made the bills look more implausible than ever, and Mr. Maloney and his agents began to feel more foolish than ever. They regarded this glaring flaw in Mr. Eight Eighty's bills as one of the most exasperating angles of the case. Secret Service men sometimes grow interested and even excited when they match their wits with those of a clever counterfeiter. The hint of the careless, heavy-handed, flubdubbing personality they received every time they saw one of those "Wahsington" bills made their inability to get anywhere with the search for him almost unbearably provoking.

The more Mr. Maloney and his staff of agents in New York

thought about Mr. Eight Eighty, the more outlandish his character seemed. At the end of the first year, the man had passed only five hundred and eighty-five of his bills, which meant that he was earning less than two dollars a day as a counterfeiter. They had never before heard of such a counterfeiter. Early in the search for him, they had given up the hope that he was a mass-production man, with underworld connections, who might try to make a killing by passing a good-sized wad of his stuff all at once. When Mr. Eight Eighty's bills began to appear, the agents had called in a number of reformed counterfeiters and had them look at the new bills. These experts just laughed at the idea that any experienced member of their profession would try to get by with such a botched bunch of the queer. This confirmed the opinion of the Secret Service men that Mr. Eight Eighty was an odd character—a crank or crackpot who was doing what he was doing as a sort of screwy hobby, or perhaps only to annoy the Secret Service.

The red thumbtacks in Mr. Eight Eighty's map at the Secret Service office continued to indicate that the counterfeiter was passing most of his bills on the upper West Side of Manhattan. The bills turned up in all sorts of other places, though. Some of the horrible "Wahsington" bills were being carelessly accepted by banks and passed along to other banks. The Federal Reserve Bank of Richmond spotted one and was able to determine from its records that a bank in Baltimore had sent it south with a batch of good bills. The Baltimore bank didn't know who had passed the bill on it, and its deposits for that year accordingly sagged in the amount of one dollar. The same thing was happening to other banks. Scores of individuals, as well, had that year casually accepted Old Eight Eighty's bills and gaily passed them along to other individuals without looking at them, and as a result some of the bills were turning up at banks as far away as Atlanta and Denver. One caught the eye of a careful teller in Seattle. The Secret Service dismissed the thought that Mr. Eight Eighty was traveling around the country passing these bills himself. They didn't see how he could afford to do that on his profits.

As a student of counterfeiting, Mr. Maloney was aware of the truism that the interest of the average man in the look and feel of a piece of currency increases in direct ratio to the size of the bill he happens to be looking at or feeling. Even people who know nothing about how to detect counterfeit money usually look twice at a hundred-dollar bill and perhaps rub it between thumb and fingers before accepting it in return for something they know is worth a hundred dollars. Anybody who encounters a thousand-dollar bill looks at it longer and feels it more carefully. Bank clerks and other professional handlers of money are rarely fooled by bad bills, but the smaller a bill is, the more likely they are to fail to look at and feel it. Thousands of circulars describing Mr. Eight Eighty's bills were sent out to banks by the Secret Service during the first year of the search for him. Banks soon stopped accepting them, but individuals kept on taking them and stuffing them in their pockets or pocketbooks without a glance. Toward the end of 1943, when five years had gone by, Mr. Maloney's office had collected twenty-eight hundred and forty of Mr. Eight Eighty's dollar bills. This averaged out to less than two a day. The red thumbtacks on Mr. Eight Eighty's map were by now spread all over New York and its environs. Some of his bills had been passed in Brooklyn, in Jersey City, in Queens, on Staten Island, and in the Bronx, as well as on the upper West Side and in other areas of Manhattan. An inspection of the map indicated that there was a vague suggestion of a concentration of thumbtacks in one particular section of the upper West Side, the center of which was Broadway and Ninety-sixth Street. Those of Mr. Maloney's agents who went to that neighborhood to investigate storekeepers and others who they thought had received the bills direct from the counterfeiter were instructed to visit other storekeepers in the neighborhood and give them circulars describing

Mr. Eight Eighty's bills and a course of instruction in how to tell them from genuine bills. Several thousand storekeepers in the section had been visited by Secret Service men by the end of the fifth year of the search. As a consequence of this extensive trap-setting, about a dozen New Yorkers were caught in the act as they passed Mr. Eight Eighty's bills, but they all successfully established their innocence.

The dismal task of looking for Mr. Eight Eighty did not, of course, exclusively occupy the New York Secret Service men during those first five years, but Mr. Maloney remembers that he used to find himself thinking about Mr. Eight Eighty at all sorts of odd moments, and especially when he was trying to relax. Under his direction, several big professional counterfeiting rings in New York and New Jersey were broken up, a good many hundreds of thousands of dollars in counterfeit money was seized before it got into circulation, and scores of counterfeiters and passers were arrested and convicted. Before Mr. Maloney went to Washington, in November, 1943, he proved that he and his men could catch even a counterfeiter of fifty-cent pieces, provided such a counterfeiter exhibited a touch of human weakness. If Mr. Eight Eighty had tried to make just a small killing—passing, say, five hundred of his bills in one New York neighborhood in a week instead of ranging all over the upper West Side, with numerous excursions to other regions, and passing only one or two a day—Secret Service men think he would have been nabbed with ease. At the time of Mr. Eight Eighty's ascendancy, some fairly good-looking pewter fifty-cent pieces were beginning to appear around the country, and everything about them—the craftsmanship and the accepted method of passing a batch of them in one place in a hurry—indicated a professional ring. One of the makers and passers of these half dollars drove from New York to New Rochelle one day and began going down the main business street buying cheap cigars, shoelaces, and other inexpensive bits of merchandise, unloading his phony half dollars as fast as he could. Somebody detected one and called the Secret Service in New York. The Secret Service called the New Rochelle police. The man was arrested before he got out of New Rochelle. He had fifty-six of the pewter half dollars in his pockets and a thousand more in his car.

This comparatively easygoing counterfeiter was named Edward John Wellman. The Secret Service discovered a lot about him. He was indicted, was released on a twenty-five-hundred-dollar bail, and was shadowed for weeks. Like most professional counterfeiters, he never went anywhere directly. His method of getting somewhere was to cross a street, walk through an apartment house to the back yard, climb a fence, take a subway local, change to an express, ride uptown, ride back downtown, take a taxi to Central Park, walk rapidly through the zoo, row a boat across the lake, ditch it on the other side, take another taxi, duck through another apartment house, and then go to his destination. The Secret Service men stuck with him most of the time and picked him up again whenever they lost him. They hoped that he would lead them to other members of the gang Mr. Maloney was convinced he was a member of. When the day set for his trial came around in August, 1941, it turned out that he had skipped bail and vanished.

Mr. Maloney and his men knew by this time that Mr. Wellman lived a carefree life. Whenever he had money, he went to the horse races, and when he was broke, he went ice skating. He was a personable middle-aged man, an Estonian by birth, an unlucky horseplayer, and an accomplished ice skater. When he began to glide and pirouette, other skaters would slow up, or stop altogether, to watch him. He was known at all the ice-skating places in and around New York. He picked up pocket money at some of them from time to time as a skating instructor. He was jolly with the children and had a courtly manner with the ladies. Descriptions and photographs of him were sent by the Secret Service to all race tracks and all skating rinks, and a little over three months after he skipped bail he was arrested at the Tropical Park race track, in Florida. He had been passing pewter fifty-cent pieces all over Miami and vicinity and betting on the races with his profits. In his car, the Secret Service found seven hundred and eighty-nine phony half dollars, thirty-five pounds of pewter, a bottle of silver chloride, a can of sodium cyanide of potassium, some silver that he used for plating the coins, and the other paraphernalia he required to turn out finished fifty-cent pieces. He could make them without even getting out of his car, a 1941 Buick.

Mr. Wellman was put in jail in Coral Gables to await extradition to New York, but he soon unlocked his cell door with the mainspring of an alarm clock he had brought in with him and was on the loose again. A month later, he was recognized by a New York Secret Service man at the Flushing Meadow Park Skating Rink, where he was dazzling everybody with a whizzing glide to the center of the ice that ended in a triumphant pirouette. As he came out of the pirouette, he was arrested and taken down to Mr. Maloney's office. He realized that he was in for it this time, and he talked freely. The ice-skating counterfeiter was a member of a ring, as Mr. Maloney had thought all along. Three other Estonians, all expert in the use of portable pewter-half-dollar sets, were arrested within a week. Along with Mr. Wellman, they were sent to a federal penitentiary.

When the Wellman case was finished, Mr. Maloney and the Secret Service agents of the New York office felt rather elated for a few days. Then another measly batch of Mr. Eight Eighty's "Wahsington" bills was laid on Mr. Maloney's desk. He knew by then that he was going to the city he had begun to think of as Wahsington, as assistant chief, and he had a talk with John J. McGrath, who was to succeed him here. Mr. McGrath outlined some ideas for stepping up the search for Mr. Eight Eighty. Mr. Maloney promised to help him get all the backing he needed from headquarters. Mr. McGrath did intensify the search to a remarkable degree, but by the time the Secret Service caught up with Mr. Eight Eighty, Mr. McGrath had himself become assistant chief in Washington and Mr. Maloney was the chief. When the teletyped word came from New York that Mr. Eight Eighty had at last been arrested, his plates seized, and his kitchen printing press dismantled, Mr. Maloney sent a teletype message back to New York that, for a Secret Service man, was somewhat emotional. "These developments please me very much," it said.

WHEN THE MOST intensive manhunt in the history of counterfeiting came to an end, early in 1948, it turned out that the object of the manhunt had not been trying to hide. The circumstances of Mr. Eight Eighty's capture proved to be as exasperating to the Secret Service men as everything else about the case had been. Fate, rather than Secret Service men or any other men, interrupted the career of Old Eight Eighty. Fate required some human aid after her initial blow—a fire in Mr. Eight Eighty's apartment—had been struck, and she thereupon chose, in a characteristically frivolous manner, nine gawky boys of the upper West Side, ranging in age from ten to fifteen, to deliver the *coup de grace*. When the Secret Service men at last laid eyes on Mr. Eight Eighty, they found it hard to believe what their eyes told them. The happy-looking little old septuagenarian admitted everything and showed no signs of remorse. He had a provoking habit of answering serious questions with absent-minded and irrelevant loquaciousness. In the course of his rambling replies, he would pause, look at his inquisitors brightly and gaily, and then grin at them toothlessly. Thus the Secret Service men were confronted, on the one hand, by a prisoner who seemed to be on the verge of senility and, on the other, by a group of material witnesses who were rankly pubescent.

The forlorn and painstaking records of the interviews and other encounters of the Secret Service men with the unbearded boys and with the toothless counterfeiter produce in the heart and soul of any red-blooded American an inclination to flip over the pages of the Secret Service files and read about some other case, some episode of the kind for which the Secret Service is justifiably celebrated. This inclination is easily gratified. The solving of counterfeiting cases by the Secret Service is ordinarily like so much clockwork. Even a hasty glance at the other files of the New York office of the Secret Service covering the year in which Mr. Eight Eighty was apprehended fulfills the most romantic expectations. There is, for example, the Soroka case, reassuring in every way, which goes like this:

The New York office learns that an underworld character named Joseph Soroka alias Mousie Joe alias Jersey Joe is trying to dispose of a hundred thousand dollars in first-rate counterfeit money in the respectable denomination of twenty-dollar bills. A teletype message to San Francisco causes a Secret Service man out there (who is not likely to be recognized by any New York counterfeiters) to hop on an eastbound Constellation. Next day, he is instructed by U. E. Baughman, then supervising agent of the New York office and now chief of the whole Secret Service, to pose as a West Coast gangster who is in the market for a good-sized batch of the stuff. The agent seeks out Soroka at an East Side bar and grill, gets into a conversation with him about the West Coast rackets, buys him drinks, flatters him, and eventually confides in him that he has come East to pick up a wad of the queer. Soroka is cautious. No wool can be pulled over his eyes with ease. The agent discovers that Soroka admires but has never seen a certain famous upper-bracket racketeer who hangs out at a luxurious cafe in the East Fifties. Another agent accordingly poses as this racketeer, is introduced to Soroka at the cafe by the undercover agent, and, after the undercover agent has tactfully left them alone together, tells Soroka that the undercover agent is an O.K. guy and can be trusted with anything and everything. Soroka enthusiastically starts negotiations with the first agent for the sale of a hundred thousand dollars in counterfeit twenties. Soroka and the agent become pals. A price is agreed upon—seventy-five hundred dollars in good money for the hundred thousand dollars in bad money. The agent learns who manufactured the twenties and where the counterfeiting plant is. A date is made for turning over the stuff. Soroka brings it in a shoebox to a room in a midtown hotel, where the agent is waiting for him. Another member of the gang comes along with Soroka to be sure he doesn't powder with the pay-off money, which is to be apportioned among the members of the mob. The confederate waits in the lobby while Soroka goes to the room. Soroka is arrested by the undercover agent as he hands over the shoebox full of twenties, and another agent handcuffs the confederate in the lobby. Simultaneously, still other agents raid the plant, which is in Jersey City. Six more of Soroka's confederates are arrested—photoengravers, printers, passers. The printing press is confiscated, but the plates from which the twenties were made are missing. One of the confederates confesses that the plates were thrown into the Passaic River from a bridge near Newark after the money was printed. The plates are recovered the next day by United States Navy divers. The plates check with the twenties in the shoebox. Soroka and his seven confederates are indicted, convicted, and sent to federal penitentiaries. It's just so much clockwork.

There was very little clockwork in the taking of Mr. Eight Eighty. One afternoon in January, 1948, seven of the nine upper West Side boys were fooling around a vacant lot near Broadway and Ninety-sixth Street. There was snow on the ground, and while scuffling in it they came upon an assortment of interesting junk that had not been in the lot the last time they played there. There were old automobile tires, two or three wrecked baby carriages, some sheets of rusty corrugated iron, a beat-up bird cage, and all sorts of odds and ends that an undiscriminating junkman might have picked up in the gutters and areaways of the neighborhood.

The boys' names, later ferreted out and written down by Secret Service men, were Edward Movel, Teddy Sweeney, Gilbert Medina, Paul Ramos, John Melvin, John Hawthorne, and Richard Bealer. Five of them were around fifteen. Hawthorne and Bealer were ten and twelve, respectively. Burrowing into the snow-covered junk, these two found two zinc engraving plates and about thirty funny-looking dollar bills. Although thousands of American adults had accepted the same kind of bills as genuine during the preceding decade, these two American boys, Hawthorne and Bealer, instantly recognized them as arrantly phony. "Look—stage money!" one of them cried, and the older fellows gathered around. Hawthorne and Bealer were generous. They kept the plates but divided up the stage money with the other guys.

This reasonably lively episode was followed by a dull period, during which the boys played innocent and unprofitable practical jokes on other boys with the fake bills. After ten days of this, young Sweeney's father, one afternoon, happened upon his son and some of the other boys playing stud poker in his cellar. They were using some of the funny-looking money. The elder Sweeney examined the bills and decided that they might not be stage money, they might be counterfeit. He took them away from the boys and gave them to a desk sergeant at the West 100th Street Police Station. The desk sergeant turned them over to Detectives North and Behrens, of the same station house. Late that evening, North telephoned the New York office of the Secret Service and told the staff man on duty that they had a small batch of what looked like counterfeit dollar bills. North, who had been understandably bored by the whole business, was flabbergasted by the excited tone in which the Secret Service man replied. "You'd have thought I was Dick Tracy calling in a hot tip to the chief," he said later. The Secret Service man asked him to look at the lettering under the portrait of George Washington on the bills and see how the name "Washington" was spelled. North looked, laughed, and told the Secret Service man that it was, idiotically, spelled "Wahsington." Without waiting to hear any more, the Secret Service man (whose name is not given here because the Secret Service adheres to a policy of anonymity) told North to hold everything, that he or some other agent would be right up. Three Secret Service men arrived a little after midnight. They went at once to see the elder Sweeney at his home, down the street from the police station. He woke up his son, who told the Secret Service men all he knew—that the bills had been found in the vacant lot near Broadway and Ninety-sixth Street, that Hawthorne and Bealer had kept the zinc plates, and that he didn't know their addresses but could point out the apartment houses they lived in. The Secret Service men decided to let that go until morning.

Shortly after nine that morning, young Sweeney showed two Secret Service men the apartment houses in which Hawthorne and Bealer lived, but they had some difficulty in nailing the boys. It was a Saturday, and they had gone off without leaving word as to where they would be. The Secret Service men followed all the tips that young Sweeney was able to give them, and after several hours nabbed Hawthorne in a playground just south of Ninety-sixth Street. Hawthorne came clean. He had given Bealer a used catcher's mitt in return for full possession of the zinc plates and had afterward traded the plates to Robert Boyle, aged eleven, for a Japanese bayonet. He didn't know Boyle's address, but he could point out where Boyle lived. Boyle was out, but the Secret Service men waited until he came home for a rather late lunch. Boyle made no effort to cover up. He had traded the plates to John Canning, aged ten, for a bag of marbles. And he showed the Secret Service men where Canning lived. Canning had finished his lunch and was on the loose on the upper West Side. He returned home around dusk. He, too, was frank and open about the whole thing. He took the Secret Service men to his room and gave them the zinc plates. He also showed them how he had tried to make some more stage money by painting one of the plates green, turning it upside down on a piece of Kleenex, and jumping up and down on it. The Kleenex money John handed over was a mess, but the plates were in fair condition, and they were what the Secret Service men wanted. They were the plates from which Old Eight Eighty had made all his "Wahsington" bills.

While these Secret Service men were immersed in the juvenile aspect of the case, two others were trying to find out how the plates and the money had happened to be in the pile of junk in the vacant lot. Some clockwork appears in this phase of the investigation. After hours of exploratory questioning of people who lived nearby, the Secret Service came upon a piece of information that looked good, and was good. There had been a fire on the top floor of the brownstone tenement at 204 West Ninety-sixth Street a few weeks earlier. The tenement was next door to the vacant lot. The junk in the vacant lot bore evidence of having been scorched. The Secret Service men hurried over to Hook & Ladder Co. No. 22, at Ninety-seventh Street and Amsterdam Avenue, and took Battalion Chief McGowan into a corner of the firehouse for a talk. McGowan had a record of the fire and also remembered it. To use McGowan's phrase, it was of undetermined origin. Actually, of course, it was started by Fate. It had gutted the top-floor flat in the rear of the tenement. The occupant of the flat had not been on the premises, according to McGowan. The flat had been full of junk and McGowan had told his men to expedite their work by throwing it out of the windows into the adjacent vacant lot. There had been no injuries and no deaths, except that an old mongrel terrier in the flat had died of suffocation before the firemen arrived. The superintendent of the building had told McGowan that he thought the dog was twelve or thirteen and probably too decrepit to escape. A curious thing about the dog, McGowan said, was that it had no name. The superintendent's name, he said, was Alexander Flynn.

Flynn received the Secret Service men in his ground-floor room. The tenant of the top-floor rear was up there now, he said. His name was Edward Mueller. He had occupied the flat for ten years. Asked how the tenant had reacted to the fire, Flynn told the Secret Service men that he had been upset most about the death of his dog. He had returned to his apartment after the firemen had left. Flynn had gone upstairs with him, and the old man had been plainly bewildered. When he got over the shock of finding the dog dead and his flat denuded, he had said, "Almost everything that was any good is gone." Flynn remembered distinctly that those were his words. The tenant was an independent junk dealer, Flynn went on to say. Since the fire, he had been living with his married daughter, but he came back practically every day and went up to the flat and stood around. Flynn supposed that he intended to occupy it again after it had been repaired. The insurance was expected to cover the cost of that. There was no possibility, as far as Flynn could see, that the fire might have been started by the tenant. Flynn said that there were sometimes rats in the building and expressed the opinion that one of them had got into a box of kitchen matches or short-circuited an electric wire, or something like that. The Secret Service men told Flynn to come with them. They were going upstairs to talk to the tenant, they said.

Mueller came to the door of the flat when the Secret Service men knocked, and they went in, glanced at the white-haired old man, and turned to Flynn. "Where's the tenant?" they asked. Flynn performed the introductions. "You are the only tenant of this flat?" one of the Secret Service men asked Mueller incredulously. Mueller gave them their first look at his toothless grin and said "Yes." He added that there had been a fire in his flat and that the firemen had let his dog suffocate. They shouldn't have done that, he complained mildly. He talked for some time with one of the Secret Service men while the other took a look around. In the kitchen, near the sink, he spotted a small hand-operated printing press. In a drawer in the kitchen, he found a few of the "Wahsington" bills that had been badly smirched in printing and evidently discarded.

After both Secret Service men had looked at the press and at the bills, they asked Mueller, with studied casualness, how long he had been making these counterfeit dollar bills.

"Oh, nine or ten years—a long time," he said good-humoredly.

"You admit it?" asked one of the Secret Service men.

"Of course I admit it," he replied. "They were only just one-dollar bills." He kept grinning at the Secret Service men. "I never gave more than one of them to any one person, so nobody ever lost more than the one dollar. I gave them all over the city. I went to the Bronx; I went to Staten Island; I went to Queens—the last few years I traveled all around the city, because I never gave more than one of my dollars to any one person."

The Secret Service men asked him if anybody had helped him in his work. He shook his head. They framed many questions on this point, suggesting to him as strongly as they could that some-body must have helped him. The fact was they didn't want to be-lieve that this polite, sweet-tempered old man was the Old Eight Eighty for whom their bureau had searched for nearly ten years. Mueller, still grinning, insisted that he had done the thing all by himself. He told them how he had photographed a real dollar bill with a studio camera he had owned for many years, and he told them how he had made the zinc plates and retouched them by hand. He said he had left the camera at his daughter's house in one of the suburbs after he made the photographs, back in the summer of 1938. It was still there, he said.

Mueller willingly went along with the Secret Service men to their downtown office for further questioning that day, although he said over and over that in his opinion they were going to a lot of trouble about nothing. While other agents went out to his daugh-ter's home, confiscated the camera, and obtained her corroboration of her father's statement that he had left it there in the summer of

1938, Mr. Baughman, the supervising agent of the New York office, listened to a great deal more of Mueller's talk. The better Mr. Baughman and his agents got to know him, the more kindly disposed toward him they felt. They listened to his life history. They heard about the unsuccessful inventions he had worked on during the years when he was an apartment-house superintendent. They took down the addresses of a number of places he had worked, and afterward questioned everybody they could find who had known him. That evening, they told him that he could go home and they would get in touch with him later. When he left, he was followed. All he did was head for his daughter's house and go to bed. He was shadowed from then on, but, as expected, nothing came of that.

By this time, Mr. Baughman and his agents had the whole case well in hand. It was obvious that Mueller had lived a respectable life until, in 1938, he suddenly decided to embark on his restrained career as a counterfeiter. It was obvious that he had had no confederates. It was obvious that his daughter, and his one son as well, had had no idea what he was doing, and that he had gone in for counterfeiting in his senescence only to maintain a modest independence. Mr. Baughman had decided to tell the agents who were shadowing Mueller to bring him in, so that the case could be turned over to the federal prosecuting authorities for disposal, when Mueller, followed by his shadows, took the subway to Manhattan and came to see Mr. Baughman of his own accord.

Mueller sat down in Mr. Baughman's office and, hesitantly at first but with growing conviction, began to tell a different story of his counterfeiting. He said he had had a companion in crime. Mr. Baughman was not unprepared for this. People who are accused of having committed a crime by themselves frequently claim that somebody helped them do it. An agent, sitting in a far corner of the office, unobtrusively made a note of everything Mueller said.

The gist of his story was that in 1938 he had met a man, a man named Reynolds—Henry Reynolds, it was—and that Henry had said he had plates and a printing press for making one-dollar bills, and so Henry had come to live with him in his top-floor flat, and they had made the bills together and passed them together until Henry disappeared, a few weeks before the fire. Mr. Baughman asked Mueller all sorts of questions about Henry, and Mueller gave Mr. Baughman all sorts of answers. After a couple of hours, Mr. Baughman told Mueller that he was glad to have heard this story, and suggested that Mueller go along with one of his agents and see Assistant United States Attorney Thomas F. Murphy, in the Federal Building. It would be necessary for Mueller to be arraigned before a United States Commissioner. Mueller went along good-naturedly. Mr. Murphy was briefed on the case before he got there. When Mueller was arraigned before United States Commissioner Garrett W. Cotter, Mr. Murphy recommended that the prisoner be released on his own recognizance. After hearing a little about the case, the Commissioner agreed that there was no point in sending the old fellow to jail or even in requiring him to put up bail. Mueller's son and daughter were there, and he went away with them. They had already been told by Mr. Murphy that the government would probably ask a federal grand jury to indict Mueller on counterfeiting charges.

Mr. Baughman went to considerable trouble in the next few weeks to check every statement Mueller had made about Henry. The superintendent of Mueller's apartment house was sure that nobody had ever lived with Mueller. His neighbors in the building were just as positive. Mueller had said he'd met Henry in a certain bar and grill around the corner from his flat, where he was drinking beer. The proprietor of the place knew Mueller and was certain that he had never been in his bar and grill. The proprietors and bartenders of other bars in the neighborhood were certain he'd never been in their places, either. It was widely known that Mueller, the old junk dealer, didn't drink. Mueller had said that the camera had belonged to Henry. His daughter had already made a sworn statement that it had belonged to her father for many years before the summer of 1938. Mueller had said that Henry was a hero in the First World War and that he received a small pension from the government. There was no record of such a Henry in the Veterans Administration's files. Mueller had said that Henry was a member of a certain electricians' union. No such Henry belonged to that union.

After his arraignment, Mueller got into the habit of dropping in to see Mr. Baughman and the other agents and chatting with them happily about all kinds of things. They were patient with him, and he felt that they were his friends. On one of these visits, as a final gesture and for the sake of the record, Mr. Baughman suggested to Mueller that he submit to a lie-detector test. He was shown a lie detector, was delighted with the mechanism, and enthusiastically agreed. The test didn't prove much except that Mueller was a very contented old man, with no worries. The operator's report says, in full, "A list of fifteen relevant and irrelevant questions was prepared. When asked these questions, the subject showed no indications of deception in his respiration, and the deviations from his norm in his blood pressure were not significant enough to lead to the opinion that there was deception. Mueller apparently was not suffering from emotional tenseness or physiological or mental abnormalities, but there was an unresponsiveness which subsequent questioning led the examiners to believe was due to the rationalization of the crime to such an extent that lying aroused little or no emotional disturbance. This was evidenced by his statement that he considered himself to be an honest man, that his admitted passing of counterfeit one-dollar bills was a petty matter, as it caused the storekeepers to lose only a few cents."

Mr. Baughman regarded the case of Old Eight Eighty as closed. Mueller had caused the Secret Service more bother and more expense than any other counterfeiter in its history, but neither Mr. Baughman nor any of his agents, even the ones who had laboriously visited the ten thousand storekeepers on the upper West Side, were able to feel anything but sympathy and liking for him. When Assistant United States Attorney Frederick H. Block, who was to prosecute the case against Mueller, asked Mr. Baughman about it, Mr. Baughman gave Mr. Block to understand, as clearly as he could in his position as a supervising agent of the Secret Service, that he thought no useful purpose would be served if Mueller was sent to jail, and that he personally hoped he would get off with a suspended sentence.

It was not until September 3rd, 1948, that the case came up before Judge John W. Clancy, in the United States District Court of the Southern District of New York. Irving Rader, the attorney representing Mueller, had several long talks with him and found him extremely stubborn about one thing. He had been indicted on three counts—possessing the plates, passing the counterfeit bills, and manufacturing the bills. Mr. Rader was almost certain that the Judge would give Mueller a suspended sentence if he pleaded guilty to all three counts and just forgot about his story of Henry. This Mueller gently but flatly refused to do. He said he would plead guilty to the first two counts but not to the third count. There wasn't much point to this balkiness. He could have been sentenced to as much as fifteen years on either of the first two counts and to as much as thirty years on the first two counts combined. Mr. Rader was unable to persuade him. Mueller would just grin and say, "Henry did the manufacturing." There wasn't much point to this, either. Mueller had admitted ever since he told the story about Henry that he had helped Henry with the manufacturing, and he still admitted this to Mr. Rader. He was therefore admitting that he had collaborated with Henry in the manufacture of the bills, and this, in the eyes of the law, made him guilty of the third count of the indictment. Mueller said he wouldn't plead guilty to it, though, and he didn't. When the clerk of the court asked him how he pleaded, he said distinctly, "Guilty to the first count and second count, but not the third." Mr. Block moved that the third count be marked off the calendar, and this was done.

Mr. Block, a youngish man in horn-rimmed glasses, opened the hearing with a review of the salient facts of the case. He proved to be a good friend of Mueller in his way, as Mr. Baughman had been in his. Mr. Block slipped up, however, at one point of his summary. He said, "He (the defendant) had confined himself exclusively to the manufacture of dollar bills."

Judge Clancy looked at the prosecutor grimly and interrupted him. "He has not pleaded guilty to the manufacturing of bills," said the Judge.

"Pardon me," said Mr. Block hurriedly. "I withdraw that. The only kind of bills that are involved in this case are dollar bills, and the apparatus which was at the defendant's place, the similitude of the plates for the manufacture of dollar bills—he admitted passing these bills at the rate of about twelve to fifteen a week for some years." Mr. Block went on for a few moments more, emphasizing the modesty of Mueller's counterfeiting operation.

Then the Judge interrupted him again. "Why is he released without bail?" he asked. "Are there some children or somebody else worrying about him?"

"Well, Your Honor," replied Mr. Block, "after he was arrested—the fact that he is an elderly man, and it was felt that he was just not going to run away."

"What do you recommend?" the Judge asked.

Mr. Rader nodded to Mr. Block and repeated the Judge's question, "What do you recommend?"

"Is that his family—a married daughter?" asked the Judge, indicating Mueller's daughter, who was in the courtroom.

"No, he has two children, as I understand it," said Mr. Block. "He has a married daughter and a son."

"That is right, sir," put in Mr. Rader.

"He is seventy-three years of age," said Mr. Block. "Now, my recommendation, Your Honor, is for a suspension of sentence despite the heinousness of the crime in this case, and the reason I recommend a suspended sentence is almost wholly because of the age of this defendant. There is one other consideration that I have in mind, and that is that he has no prior criminal record."

"I always have dealt rather severely with counterfeiters as a matter of public policy," said Judge Clancy, "and I think I ought to deal the same way with him now." The Judge turned to Mr. Rader and asked, "What have you to say?"

Mr. Rader perhaps made a tactical error at this point. He reviewed the story of Henry and argued that Henry had done the actual manufacturing. Judge Clancy was in possession of, and had presumably read, a probation report that went into the Henry story in detail and that showed that even if there had been a Henry, the defendant had admitted helping him manufacture the bills. Judge Clancy heard Mr. Rader out and then said, "I think everybody who has anything to do with counterfeiting ought to know before he starts in that business that he is going to jail. I am sorry for a man seventy-three years of age, and I would be sorry if he were fifteen years old or so, but I do not think that is any reason why the people should not be protected from receiving bad money. The man has been committing this crime over a period of years and collaborated in the manufacture . . . which does not seem to me to be any basis for keeping him out of jail."

"I want to point out to the court that he is seventy-three years old," said Mr. Rader.

"I am going to send him to jail," said the Judge. "There is no way out of that. I will give him nine months, in consideration of his age, on Counts One and Two, to run concurrently."

All through this, Mueller had stood in the dock. He seemed calm. He grinned, as if to himself, from time to time. He wore a blue shirt and an old, frayed gray suit. He carried a wrinkled felt hat, holding it in both hands and turning it over and over. There were highlights on his pink bald dome, and once, when an attendant opened a window, a puff of fresh air rippled the fringe of snowy hair over his ears. After the Judge pronounced the sentence, Mueller looked at him briefly, and he was grinning toothlessly as he was taken out of the courtroom by a bailiff.

Mr. Block and Mr. Rader then held a whispered conversation with the Judge. They reminded him of the odd legal fact that if the sentence were changed to a year and a day, the prisoner could be paroled after he had served four months of it, but that as the sentence stood now, he would have to serve the whole nine months. Judge Clancy finally nodded and said to a court attendant, "Bring the defendant back!" The attendant hurried out and reappeared in a moment with Mueller. "Tell him, Judge Clancy said, "tell him it has been requested—I understand with his consent—that we make the sentence a year and a day instead of nine months, and (he now addressed the defendant) in that way you may get out in four months. Is that all right with you?"

"Yes," said Mueller, looking at the Judge and still grinning.

"I make the sentence a year and a day," said Judge Clancy, and got up and walked swiftly to his chambers.

There was one more detail to be taken care of, and then Mueller was ready to go along to the Federal Detention Headquarters, on West Street. A sentence of a year and a day must be accompanied by the imposition of a fine. When no specific fine is decreed, the fine automatically becomes a nominal one. It was Fate, rather than Judge Clancy, who by devious means arranged that the fine paid by Mueller to the United States District Court of the Southern District of New York, before he was taken off to jail, was one dollar.

THE CIGAR, THE THREE WINGS,
AND THE LOW-LEVEL ATTACKS

SINCE ASSUMING COMMAND in the middle of January, this year, of the Twenty-first Bomber Command of the Twentieth Air Force, based on Guam, Tinian, and Saipan, in the Marianas, the thirty-nine-year-old Major General Curtis E. LeMay had made training his No. 1 priority for the Command, the bombing of Japan his secondary mission. His predecessor, Brigadier General Haywood S. (Possum) Hansell, Jr., had inaugurated a Lead Crew School soon after the initial operations from Saipan. LeMay had been transferred from China, where he had stepped up the efficiency of his B-29 squadrons by several hundred per cent by the same method (which he is generally credited with having originated in England in the Eighth Air Force), and he employed the system on a big scale in the Marianas. All kinds of training courses were initiated overnight, and special techniques in bombing, pilotage, gunnery, navigation, and so on were introduced. The principle of the Lead Crew School is simply that certain crews are selected for special training, with the idea that these crews will lead the bombing formations over a target. The other airplanes in each formation drop their bombs when their lead airplane drops its bombs. LeMay thought that it would pay off in the end if he cut down on the number of airplanes bombing Japan for a short period and increased the number used in lead-crew training. So for some weeks, while eighty or ninety B-29s bombed Japan every four or five days, other dozens of B-29s bombed Truk, Iwo Jima, Pagan, and other Japanese islands on training missions, and crew members attended special classes day and night. Around March 1st, when LeMay was about ready to start increasing the size of his strikes against Japan, the order came from Washington for a maximum effort beginning around March 10th. Now that the order had come, he had no choice but to put as many airplanes over Japan as he could and to resume lead-crew training, and other training, after the maximum effort had been mounted. This suited him fine, as it happened.

LeMay, whom all of us in the Twenty-first Bomber Command called the Cigar, had been the commander now for about six weeks. He had made few changes in personnel. He had brought with him five or six staff officers from his old outfit in China and India, the Twentieth Bomber Command of the Twentieth Air Force, and they had stepped quietly into important but not top positions on his staff. A Plans Officer had taken over the Plans section under the incumbent deputy chief of staff for Plans, Operations, Training, and Intelligence. An A-2 (Intelligence) had stepped into the position left vacant by Hansell's A-2, who was in Washington for a conference. A young flying colonel, a friend and former tentmate of mine on Saipan, who had told me a little about LeMay (having worked under him in England with the Eighth Air Force) and who had been looking forward to LeMay's coming, had been relieved of his job as A-3 (Operations) and had been given an equally important but less desirable job as deputy commander of the B-29 wing on Tinian, and a new A-3 from China had stepped in at our Bomber Command. All this had happened within a few days after LeMay's arrival. LeMay had selected for the very important post of chief of staff in his new command Brigadier General August W. Kissner, who had worked with him in England. Kissner had flown home from Europe for a week's duty in Washington and a few days' leave, and was with us on Guam by this time. Kissner proved at once to be an ideal chief of staff. Like LeMay, he believes in, and is fond of, people, but his personality enables him to work for the same ends as LeMay by the application of a subtle intellect and by written policies rather than by forthright action and spoken words. LeMay undoubtedly picked him for those reasons. There was between them, also, a high mutual regard. Kissner's assignment had required no shift in personnel, since Brigadier General Roger M. Ramey, who had been Hansell's chief of staff, had been given command of the Twentieth Bomber Command in China, to replace LeMay. Ramey, a hard-bitten, tough, ribald, small-boned Westerner, had returned to the States after the heroic days at Pearl Harbor and the Philippines at the outset of the Pacific war and had been acting commanding general of the Twenty-first Bomber Command throughout its training days at home, until Hansell assumed command just before it moved overseas.

Colonel John B. Montgomery, a brilliant young Southerner, who had been acting chief of staff for Hansell in the early days on Saipan and who had again assumed this post when Ramey left for China, was able to go back to his regular job of assistant chief of staff for Plans, Operations, Training, and Intelligence when Kissner came out to become LeMay's permanent chief of staff. Monty, as this young colonel was known to everybody, had played his guitar in attempted gaiety at a party in Hansell's quarters the night before the retiring General had left for the States, and he had, with equal steadfastness, gone right along working his head off for LeMay. (You somehow never felt that Monty was working for himself.) Many of us, including myself, had wondered whether Monty would outlast the change in command. His was the most important job in the Command next to that of the chief of staff, and he had never met LeMay before LeMay took over. Then, one night toward the end of the first week in March, I had a quick coffee with Monty in the mess hall long after almost everybody else was asleep, and Monty said, "We got some hot stuff coming up. This guy LeMay is a pistol, a real pistol." I looked at Monty carefully. He seemed fine. He was clearly on the beam—a tired, tense, excited, confident colonel of the Air Forces.

Under Hansell, I had achieved a position in which I was in everybody's confidence about plans, even the most secret ones, because Hansell had decided that I could more effectively prevent plans from leaking out to the public (and to the enemy) if I knew what the plans were. I was now in the unpleasant but entirely routine position of being left out of the know in such matters by all concerned until the new boss, LeMay, had indicated to his chief assistants just where I, as the Public Relations Officer and Staff Press Censor, was to fit into the general picture. I had been through this before in other commands and had learned that the only thing to do is to sit tight, do your job, and speak when you are spoken to unless you have something that requires an immediate decision by the commanding general, in which case you put your case briefly, get your decision, and back out fast. My meetings with LeMay had not been the kind that cause anyone to sleep easily. The preservation of self-esteem being the important factor that it is in life, one fears being relieved of a good job in the Army much as one fears being fired from a good job in civilian life, whether or not economics is involved. I had sensed immediately that LeMay was suspicious of the activity called Public Relations, a feeling with which I had the most profound sympathy. But I had found that the generals who first despise Public Relations, and want to bypass or forget it, are the ones who adopt the most reasonable attitude toward it once they understand what it is and what it can be, and once they have confidence in their Public Relations Officer. There are other generals who are greatly impressed by Public Relations and who think they know all about it. These generals hardly ever, in my experience, are able to adopt a sensible attitude toward Public Relations and usually end up with at least one foot in some kind of hot water.

In the weeks that LeMay had been with us on Guam, I had learned, along with other staff officers, how to catch his soft and frequently arresting words, even when, characteristically, he mumbled them through his cigar. It was on March 6th that he said to me, "This outfit has been getting a lot of publicity without having really accomplished a hell of a lot in bombing results." I started, in irritation if not in anger, to tell him of the struggle it had been to keep the publicity down as much as it had been kept down since the first B-29 strike on Tokio from Saipan, three months back, and to tell him how flattering Washington had been about the success, as Washington saw it, of my efforts to persuade the war correspondents not to exaggerate the news of our initial operations. Instead, I looked at him fairly coolly, I think, and said that there was a long story attached to this matter and that I could tell it to him if he wanted but that I thought on the whole I would be wasting his time. He made what looked like a grimace of disgust, stared at the floor, shifted his cigar, and finally said, "Tell Monty to fill you in on everything that's coming up. A lot of it can't be told until we know the Japs know what we're up to, but that's your baby. You see that what we don't want to get out doesn't get out."

"Yes, sir," I said.

He looked at me for a minute more. "This B-29 is a wonderful airplane," he said, and picked up some papers from his desk. "Let me know if you have any troubles I need to know about."

I had learned already that the grimace LeMay frequently made when talking to his people was not intended to express disgust. The grimace is a smile. He had had serious sinus trouble and had neglected it during his tour of duty with the Eighth Air Force in

England. A muscle normally used to lift and spread the corners of the mouth became partially paralyzed, so that it lifts one corner almost imperceptibly and the other corner not at all. I had also learned that he can speak quite clearly and distinctly, with expression and inflection, when he has something important to say, that it is mostly in small talk or on inconsequential matters that he mumbles and tries to stop the trickle of words with the end of a cigar or pipe. I knew, too, that he had humor of a good, sound kind, the kind that is used to illuminate something serious, or semi-serious. Along about this time, a supply officer brought up, in a staff meeting, in a semi-serious manner, the question whether spittoons should be installed in the B-29s for Southern and Middle Western crew members who, according to the supply officer, chewed tobacco all the way to Tokio and back and, after they landed, spat gills of tobacco juice every few seconds for an hour or so. There was some discussion about the matter. In the tenseness, the high excitement of those days when thousands of improvements, in accordance with the perfectionist standards Hansell had introduced on Saipan, were being injected by LeMay everywhere in the sprawling Command, all up and down the line and into every function of every staff position, into all the corresponding staff positions in every wing and group and squadron on Guam and Tinian and Saipan, such a problem as the possible need for spittoons for tobacco-chewing crew members could and did invite a delighted, half-hysterical attention from everybody. This particular problem offered enough comic opportunities to give us all a moment's relaxation but was also sufficiently technical to be allowed to soar for a few minutes to the high status of a matter that had been brought up at a formal staff meeting for an immediate Command decision. LeMay listened to the discussion, cigar in mouth. Then he removed the cigar, smiled his muscle-bound smile, and said, "Tobacco chewers from the South and Middle West spit from pleasure or from satisfaction, not from necessity. You don't need to put spittoons in the airplanes for them. They'll spit when they get home and they won't want to spit until they do get home, where somebody can see them spit."

I T WAS N O T until late in the night of the day I had talked with LeMay, the day he had suggested that I get from Monty the story of what was coming up, that I was able to catch Monty with a few minutes to spare from more important matters. Monty and I were friends. On Saipan, in the sleepless weeks of the initial strikes, we had adopted a deadpan system of allocating a certain priority to my requests for moments of his official time. Monty looked on me as an elderly, rather interesting, somewhat eccentric character with whom, at rare intervals, when both of us had nothing on our minds, he had discussed literature, going into that subject with the same natural, keen, get-to-the-bottom-of-it intelligence and lighthearted concentration that he applied to a problem of air tactics or gasoline consumption.

When I had official business that required Monty's attention, I would say, "Monty, I've got to see you," usually when he was hustling along a hallway, across a coral road, or entering the General's office or quarters.

"Priority?" he would ask. I would show him, in the palm of my left hand, like a baseball catcher, one, two, or three fingers of my right hand. It was understood between us that even a No. 3 priority matter could not be delayed more than twelve hours, or beyond the end of that particular working day or night. This day I found him trotting across the muddy space between the Operations and Intelligence Quonset huts, and I gave him the three-finger sign. "O.K.," he said, looking desperate but resigned and friendly. "If I don't call you this afternoon, come over to the tent about eleven tonight and I'll give you a beer along with whatever it is you want."

"It's top-secret stuff," I said. "The Cigar said for you to fill me in on what's coming up."

"O.K.," said Monty. "The two guys in my tent are in on it, so come on over then if I don't call you."

Monty never called, so I got the dope that night in his tent. Our maximum effort, beginning on March 9th, was to be a series of all-out incendiary raids on the four principal industrial cities of Japan. The cities were to be bombed at night. The B-29s were to carry the new fire bombs, the ones made of a jellied gasoline, a type of incendiary that had not been made public or very much talked about. The airplanes were to carry around six tons of these bombs apiece. There were to be upward of three hundred B-29s on each raid. The raids were to be carried out every other night. The B-29s were to go in at five to six thousand feet instead of the customary twenty-five to thirty thousand feet.

I can convey only rather inadequately what this news must have meant to wing commanders, squadron commanders, airplane commanders, copilots, bombardiers, radio operators, instrument specialists, gunners, crew chiefs, engineers, maintenance men, supply people, mechanics, ordnance people, and others directly concerned with operations in the B-29 outfits on Guam and Tinian and Saipan, and what it would mean to thousands of other officers and men in all kinds of other jobs in the Command, when they learned about it, by saying that although I had worked hard since seven o'clock that morning and was tired and sleepy when I went to see Monty, I could no more sleep than a rabbit when I left him and went to my tent. My tentmate, Lieutenant George C. McGhee (U.S.N.R.), a bright young Texas oil millionaire who was our naval liaison officer and who had, on his own initiative, become our expert on air-sea rescue, was going to bed when I got to my tent. I cagily found out whether he knew of the future plans. He did, and we talked for a half hour or so. Then George went to sleep and I tried to figure things out. I had not wanted to keep Monty up longer than necessary. He had given me the bare facts. The rest I could find out in the morning, with Monty's authority, from the

various people under Monty who would know the details of ordnance, air tactics, bomb loads, and so on. Had I been half as well
indoctrinated then as I am now with the Air Force's (or common-
sense) method of work, play, and sleep, I would have read a detective story for an hour, got to sleep, and found out the rest of what
I wanted to know in the morning. Instead, I read chapter after
chapter of the second volume of "Lee's Lieutenants," which the
long-gone Possum Hansell had swapped me for a collection of humorous essays before he left for the States. I read until six o'clock,
absorbing nothing, had a shower and an early breakfast, and waited
around for the people whom I had to talk with right away.

The four big pieces of news in what Monty had told me were (1)
that the airplanes were going in at low level, at five to six thousand
feet; (2) that they were carrying nothing but incendiary bombs; (3)
that they were carrying around six tons of bombs per airplane instead of the usual four; and (4) that the raids were to be staged
every other night.

The need for maintaining secrecy about such an operation,
even among staff people and other officers and men of the Bomber
Command, was more urgent than might be supposed. The Japs still
held the island of Rota, within sight of Tinian, and on all three
of the main islands of the Marianas, which had been conquered
and converted into B-29 bases, uncaptured Japs still lurked by the
hundreds, some of them conceivably with portable radio transmitters which could reach Rota or Iwo Jima, if not Tokio. Official intelligence had shown in the past that Tokio sometimes seemed
to know just what we were going to do before we did it.

THE FIRST THING I did in the morning was to get filled in on
the background of what was now taking shape. It had been around
March 1st that the maximum effort on the part of the B-29s of the
Twenty-first Bomber Command had been ordered by General of
the Army H. H. Arnold, commanding the Twentieth Air Force (the

over-all B-29 organization) in Washington. This maximum effort
was desired by General Arnold in his capacity as Commanding
General of all United States Army Air Forces and in his capacity as
one of the Joint Chiefs of Staff. The invasion of Iwo Jima had recently begun, and the two other members of the American high
command—General Marshall and Admiral King—knew, of
course, as Arnold did, that the invasion of Okinawa was coming up
on April 1st.

General Arnold's Chief of Staff of the Twentieth Air Force,
Brigadier General Lauris Norstad, had returned to Washington in
January from a trip to Guam, where he had effected, at General
Arnold's request, a change in command whereby LeMay, the big-
time operator, had taken over from Hansell, the big-time planner.
This marked the end of the first phase of the B-29 operations
from the Marianas and the beginning of a new phase. Hansell, who
had got the D.S.M. for having planned and executed the first phase
of B-29 operations, had returned to the States for a new assignment. Norstad knew that LeMay's island-based B-29s could do
something fairly impressive and so did General Arnold.

On Saipan was Brigadier General Emmett (Rosy) O'Donnell's
B-29 wing, which had run the initial strike against Tokio on November 24th (Guam time) and was now at full strength. A new
wing, on Tinian, commanded by Brigadier General John H. Davies,
was almost at full strength and had taken part in the last couple of
missions. A third wing, on Guam, where the Bomber Command
had established its permanent Mariana Islands headquarters, was
getting organized under Brigadier General Thomas S. Power. The
wing on Guam was having quite a time, what with a shortage of
tractors and bulldozers for clearing out the jungle so that the ground
echelons could move in and start building their establishments, but
it was doing all right. One squadron had got tired of waiting for
machinery and had cleared out its own space in the jungle with
axes and trench knives. It was plain enough to all concerned that

by March 10th or thereabouts a maximum effort on the part of all three wings under LeMay could be something pretty good, with a force of perhaps three hundred B-29s over Japan at one time. What it would be, how it would be organized, what tactics would be used, and what particular part of industrial Japan, concentrated in the cities of Tokio, Nagoya, Osaka, and Kobe, would be the target were details that LeMay, as the commander in the field, would have to work out for himself, in accordance with the routine functioning of Army channels of command responsibility. On every clear day since before the first operation, B-29s had flown over Japan on photographic-reconnaissance missions, and LeMay's choice of industrial targets would be based on the pictures they had brought back and on other intelligence.

This was the morning of March 7th, and the raids were to commence on March 9th. I found out that morning that no field order had yet been written. It was being written by the Operations people, giving detailed tactical procedures for the forthcoming maximum effort. How many of the details did Washington know? I needed to find that out because, if Washington knew all about it, whatever wires I had to send it later in the day, or tomorrow, in order that certain matters involving security would be withheld from the press by Twentieth Air Force headquarters there, would make sense; otherwise, they wouldn't. Washington hadn't been informed of the detailed plan as yet, I learned. In fact, hardly anybody knew about it, especially about the unprecedented, daring, almost unbelievable decision to go in at low level instead of at twenty-five to thirty thousand feet. The Cigar had made that decision shortly before I had talked to him yesterday, it seemed. The field order would go out to the wings this afternoon and to Washington at about the same time. General Norstad, the Chief of Staff of the Twentieth Air Force, was already flying out for a conference with LeMay and would arrive on the morning of March 9th, so even Norstad didn't know the details of what was coming up. He knew, of course, that we were putting on a maximum effort, as we had been ordered to do, and he knew that all-out incendiary raids were one of several possibilities open to LeMay if he could see how to make such raids really effective.

The idea of going in at low level had crystallized in LeMay's mind after all sorts of talks he had had with all sorts of people. General Power, boss of the new wing, on Guam, which was just about ready to start operating, had had some ideas about low-level bombing by B-29s, which, when put together with some ideas Monty had been working up with the new Plans officer, had made LeMay see a possibility for a tactical stroke far beyond what Power or Monty or the Plans officer had envisioned. Rosy O'Donnell, up on Saipan, had had some other good ideas. General Davies, the wing commander on Tinian, had contributed some more. Then LeMay had settled down to make a decision of the kind that this war has known only infrequently, a decision like Grant's when he let Sherman try his march through Georgia, and like several other sudden, quick, unprecedented tactical decisions of the Napoleonic and other wars which this war, with its more or less classic alignment of power in Europe and to some extent in Asia, has seldom required of its generals either in the field or in the high command at home.

LeMay wanted to go in at five to six thousand feet, lay a careful pattern of precisely aimed incendiary clusters all over the industrial heart of a ten-square-mile section of Tokio, and burn it to ashes. What would be the effect of flak on our airplanes at five to six thousand feet? He called in all the flak experts from the wings, along with selected airplane commanders who had had experience over both Europe and Tokio. He talked to them. The flak experts, almost to a man, told him he would lose seventy per cent of his airplanes over Tokio if he sent them in at that altitude. They spoke of the effectiveness of flak at twenty-five thousand, at thirty thousand feet. LeMay listened to them and weighed the facts and figures. "If you are right," he said mildly, "we won't have many airplanes left if we go in low." Flak had been heavy, it was true, at twenty-five and thirty thousand feet, but how many airplanes had we lost to enemy flak? Statistical Control had the figures and LeMay looked at them. They were not impressive. What did the airplane commanders with European experience think? He talked to them. Some of them, at least, thought we could pull it off, especially because of the element of surprise. But it would be touch and go, almost everybody felt. At five to six thousand feet, the B-29 is a wonderfully big target for anti-aircraft gunners and for machine-gunners as well. LeMay talked to many other people, all of whom tried to give him their best opinion. Monty was for the precedent-breaking low-level technique. So was Power. So were some others. There wasn't time to ask everybody. There was no time to consult Washington, and anyway this was LeMay's responsibility and nobody else's. LeMay had kept on talking to people for a couple of days and then must have had quite a session with himself.

LeMay, I had begun to learn, was a very tough man, a very tough man indeed. He had the kind of toughness that comes from, or with, innate sensitivity, from, or with, innate goodness and hard, clear honesty, especially when the possessor of such qualities has been faced, in his youth, with reality at its damnedest. I don't know much about LeMay's early years except that he had no advantages, put himself through Ohio State University, and went into the Air Corps for pilot training in 1929, the first year of the depression. He was thirty-five years old when, as a major, he took a group of B-17s to England in 1942. He had trained his air crews relentlessly, and had been so tough with them that they called him Old Iron-pants, and not with affection in those days. He had trained them heartlessly, having a heart that revolted at the idea of what lack of discipline and training would mean to his young crews. He had led

185

them on all their missions and the group, though it had lost three-quarters of its original crews in a few months' time, suffered fewer casualties than any other in the Eighth Air Force in the early days. It also got better bombing results than any other group in the Eighth Air Force.

LeMay stuck to his high standards of discipline and training, led the first mission against Regensburg, became a division commander of the Eighth Air Force, threw his bombers with accuracy and skill at the great strategic targets of Germany when the crews had learned to drop bombs exactly where his intelligence people said to drop them, and became, at thirty-eight, the youngest major general in the Air Forces. He has the capacity to know the complex job of strategic bombardment up and down and in and out and also has, I think, the quality of leadership at its best. Before he had been on Guam a month, there were staff officers all over the headquarters, and other officers in the wings on Saipan, Tinian, and Guam, who, at the mention of his name, would say, as if the phrase were a refrain, "Aw, Jesus, that guy's a pistol, a real pistol." These officers had, as far as I can discover, simply received LeMay's confidence and were breaking their necks to prove that his judgment was sound in trusting them to do their jobs. A few had been jolted by him. There was one rather high officer who was going through what might be called a walking nervous breakdown. He was worrying himself sick every day over a thousand and one matters, seeing ghosts where there were only tough problems, and endangering the efficiency of his part of the B-29 operation and the morale of the men he was trying to help. LeMay heard about the officer from several sources and was advised that he ought to speak to him. "I'll have a talk with him," said LeMay. The talk was brief and miraculous. The Cigar listened to the officer for fifteen minutes and then said to him, "Stop fooling around and get to work." That was all the Cigar said. The officer told me later that it cleared up all his troubles on the spot, made a new man of him, and put him on the beam. "That guy's a pistol, a real pistol," he added, shaking his head from side to side.

LeMay says things to people in a quiet, sometimes distinct, sometimes muffled voice, and always with sincerity. He says things with an effort, a straining to make not just his words but all that is behind his words fully understood. There is in his eyes at such times a tacit admission that he has been frequently disappointed in his wish to be fully understood, but his eyes also intimate that he still has an incurable faith in the ability of people to see things clearly and do a good job if they have half a chance. He keeps treating people this way day in and day out and it isn't long before he has transmitted his own anxiousness to get the job done and the war over to every officer and man in the outfit he is commanding. He has no personal life beyond games of medicine ball to keep fat off a body that tends toward fat, games of poker to relax as best he can a mind that actually never stops thinking about how to do the job better the next day, and a little reading, mostly fairly serious, to improve a mind he considers inadequate. He has a wife and children in Lakewood, outside of Cleveland, and he wants very much to go back to them and stay with them. Except for a couple of weeks at home, he has been overseas since the autumn of 1942. Now and then he grows impatient with some of the niceties, subtleties, and diplomacies that seem to be incumbent upon a major general in dealing with higher authorities in a theatre of operations or in Washington. Not infrequently his staff has to advise him to go easy. "Why?" he usually asks. "All they can do is reduce me to my permanent rank of captain, isn't it?" He will ask this seriously, rather grimly, and, as often as not, he will go right ahead being undiplomatic and unsubtle and not exactly nice and getting results that he otherwise would not have got as quickly, if at all.

In deciding to send his B-29s in over Tokio at five to six thousand feet, LeMay was increasing the risk his crews would run, and he has a deep feeling of personal responsibility for his crews; he was risking the success of the whole B-29 program, which he had pioneered from his China bases before he got his new job in the Marianas and which is dear to him in an emotional as well as an operational way; and he was risking his own future, not only, I think, as an Army officer but as a human being. If he lost seventy per cent of his airplanes by such a decision, or even fifty per cent of them, or even twenty-five per cent of them, he would be through, and I imagine that a man like him would be through in every sense of the word, for he would have lost confidence in himself. He decided that the Jap flak was not really heavy compared to the flak he and his B-17 crews had flown through over Europe. He decided that the Japs would be flabbergasted, that they wouldn't be expecting the great, stratosphere Superfortresses to come in at such an altitude. He decided it was probably not a gamble, that if it was a gamble he was going to take it anyway.

LeMay also decided to take certain unprecedented and even now secret measures to increase the bomb load of his airplanes, to pile on so many incendiaries—some six tons to an airplane—that his three hundred B-29s over Japan would very nearly match the bombing strength of a thousand B-17s over Europe, since the B-17 cannot carry much more than two tons of bombs on a long mission. He decided that it the maintenance crews were asked to do the job, they could get the same force of over three hundred B-29s off every other day for ten days in this maximum effort, although ordinarily it took four or five days to get the B-29s ready to fly again after a mission over Japan. He decided that if several aiming points were carefully selected within the target area of ten square miles in the heart of Tokio, and incendiaries were dropped with precision where they would start fires, that the fires, with the help of the calculable ground wind, would spread and join and become a conflagration that would simply wipe out every industrial target in the area and generally devitalize the city. In deciding all this, he had originated a new technique of strategic bombardment which was unlike the incendiary area bombing employed by the R.A.F. in its night raids over Europe and unlike the pin-point, high-level bombing of the kind generally employed by the Eighth Air Force. It was pin-point, incendiary bombing from a low level, designed not simply to start fires or destroy a single factory but to start one great conflagration whose fury would double and redouble the destructive force of the bombs. He had a highly inflammable city as his target and he decided that the firebreaks and other means of fire control the Japs had devised would be useless if his incendiary clusters landed where he wanted them to land, in such a way that ten square miles of the center of the city would be ablaze within the space of the hour it would take the airplanes in get in and get out.

WE HAD A press conference on the afternoon of March 9th, an hour or so before the airplanes were to take off for Tokio, and fifty-odd correspondents who were primarily covering land and sea operations in the Pacific from Admiral Nimitz's forward headquarters on Guam joined the correspondents already with us and listened to General Norstad and General LeMay tell what was coming up, and what could and couldn't be revealed. Admiral Nimitz's public-relations and press-censorship people had given us every sort of enthusiastic coöperation since the early days on Saipan. The war correspondents would not be allowed to reveal that we were, by design, going in at low level, because the Japs might conceivably think that weather or miscalculation had caused this unexpected innovation and we wanted them to keep on thinking so until we had hit a couple more of their cities. Then we could reveal that we were deliberately going in low. Otherwise, the story could be told in full except for one or two technical matters involving bomb-load figures and air tactics. Then the correspondents went out to North Field, the operational base on Guam, watched the airplanes take off, and wrote their stories. We held them until we got the first bombs-away messages from the airplanes over Tokio, which told us that the raid was on and was going according to plan.

I went to our big operations-control room at about two the next morning to wait for the first reports from the airplanes. Except for the small all-night staff of operations-control officers and clerks, nobody was there but LeMay. He had told the rest of his staff to go to bed if they wanted to, that he was going to sit this one out. Norstad, having flown eighty or ninety hours, on his trip from Washington, with scarcely a rest, was also in the sack, in LeMay's quarters, having been promised a call if anything hot came up. There was really not much anyone could do from now until around nine o'clock in the morning, when the first crews would be coming in to land at Guam and at Tinian and Saipan. However, we could receive the extremely important bombs-away messages that would indicate whether the airplane commanders thought they had started small fires, large fires, or conflagrations and would give some idea of how bad the flak was. LeMay was sitting in the operations-control room, whose walls were covered with charts, maps, graphs, and mission-control boards which told, at a glance, the whole story of the past, present, and future B-29 program. He was sitting on a wooden bench smoking a cigar. He smiled at me and asked me why I didn't go to bed, and I explained that we had to wait to get the first bombs-away messages, to be sure the strike was going off as planned, before releasing the correspondents' stories to the radio transmitters. He ignored my explanation, knowing, I suppose, that my Public Relations staff could and would do that part of the job. "I'm sweating this one out myself," he said. "A lot could go wrong."

This was a time, I decided, when a man in LeMay's position would perhaps get a sort of relief in explaining to a non-technical officer some of the problems of tactics and strategy involved in this operation, or possibly some of his theories about war and so on. "I can't sleep," he remarked. "I usually can, but not tonight." I sat down and we smoked for a while. "If this raid works the way I think it will," he said, "we can shorten this war." He gave this statement all the force of the unusual personality I have tried to describe. He wanted to be fully understood. "In a war," he said, "you've got to try to keep at least one punch ahead of the other guy all the time. A war is a very tough kind of proposition. If you don't get the enemy, he gets you. I think we've figured out a punch he's not expecting this time. I don't think he's got the right flak to combat this kind of raid and I don't think he can keep his cities from being burned down—wiped right off the map. He hasn't moved his industries to Manchuria yet, although he's starting to move them, and if we can destroy them before he can move them, we've got him. I never think anything is going to work until I've seen the pictures after the raid, but if this one works we will shorten this damned war out here."

He looked at his watch. "We won't get a bombs-away for another half hour," he said. "Would you like a Coca-Cola? I can sneak in my quarters without waking up the other guys and get two Coca-Colas and we can drink them in my car. That'll kill most of the half hour."

We drove the hundred yards to his quarters in his staff car and he sneaked in and got the Coca-Colas. We sat in the dark, facing the jungle that surrounds the headquarters and grows thickest between the edge of our clearing and the sea. For some reason, we talked about India, where I had once been stationed. He had got there after I had left, but we had seen the same things and agreed that it was a hell of a place. "The way all those people are in India gets you down," he said. "It makes you feel rotten." We went into this fairly deeply.

LeMay is not the sort of general who makes his rank, purely as rank, very much felt. Here in the dark, drinking Coca-Cola with him in the middle of the night, I was not conscious of the presence of rank at all; I was conscious merely of the presence of a good young guy doing a stupendous job, feeling the right things, keeping his head, and wanting to get the war over with. Here was a representative, I thought, of a great many men in the Army in all ranks who are better men than they have ever been before, better than most men anywhere, and I thought briefly of the much-talked-about problem of readjustment after the war. It may be the people at home, I thought, who will have to readjust themselves to these men, rather than the other way around. The mass effect of LeMay and all his people, all those men on the islands of Guam and Tinian and Saipan, working for a high and common purpose, with leadership based on brains and goodness and faith in human endeavor, was something very nearly tangible, something you felt all around you and inside you when you woke up after a few hours' sleep, those tense days and nights. And this, I thought, is just one outfit, of all the countless outfits in this war, that started something, got going, and did what the men knew could be done. The healthy men of such outfits, it occurred to me, do not want or need to be readjusted and it may well be that they are not readjustable.

LeMay and I got back to the operations-control room a few minutes before the bombs-away message from the first B-29 formation over Tokio came in. It was decoded and shown to him. "Bombing the primary target visually," it told him. "Large fires observed. Flak moderate. Fighter opposition nil." This meant that the weather was clear over Tokio and that as far as weather, flak, and fighters were concerned, we were getting the breaks. Then the bombs away messages from other formations began coming in fast. After the first three, they all reported "Conflagration" and only moderate flak and practically no fighter opposition.

Monty and two or three other Operations officers who either couldn't sleep or had had themselves waked up had come in by now, and they studied the results with satisfaction. "It looks pretty good," LeMay said to them. "But we can't really tell a damn thing about results until we get the pictures tomorrow night. Anyway, there doesn't seem to have been much flak. We don't seem to have lost more than a few airplanes." He shifted his cigar and smiled. Actually, only two were lost, and on the next two low-level strikes none were lost.

THE FOLLOWING NIGHT, around twelve, we had the pictures. They had been taken during the day by B-29 photo-reconnaissance airplanes. They had been rushed through our photo laboratory and five or six staff officers had been alerted when the photo-interpretation officer started in his jeep to LeMay's quarters to wake up LeMay and Norstad and show them the pictures. I was one of the officers alerted, because all the correspondents on Guam were waiting up to get out the news of the results of the raid as soon as our Intelligence people were able to assess the damage after studying the pictures. We had learned, from returning airplane commanders and from General Power, the wing commander on Guam, who himself had flown on the bombing mission and had stayed over the target for an hour studying the results with a map of Tokio in his lap, that the raid had been successful, but it is only by expert examination of post-strike photographs that you can really get the dope on any bombing raid.

The staff officers' five or six jeeps swept up to LeMay's tent like so many cowboys' horses, the officers driving them leaped to the ground, and we all got to the General's bedroom just as the photo-interpretation officer walked in with the pictures under his arm. LeMay and Norstad had been waked up by telephone when the photo-interpretation officer started over. They were in pajamas, rubbing their eyes, and LeMay was lighting a cigar in a dogged manner that seemed to indicate that anybody, or anything, that interfered with his lighting this particular cigar at this particular time would be noiselessly and totally obliterated. The photo-interpretation officer spread the pictures out on a big, well-lighted table and LeMay and Norstad walked up to it and bent over them.

There was about one full minute of silence. "All this is out,"
LeMay then said, running a hand over several square miles of Tokio
which on the enlarged photograph were grayish, almost white, in
contrast to one other large industrial area, through which runs the
Ginza, and the outlying sections of the city, which showed up
black. "This is out—this—this—this." He stood up straight for
a few seconds and looked around at the rest of us. I don't know
what he meant to convey to us as his cigar ranged back and forth
once, slowly, like a turret gun. His face was expressionless. We
crowded in for a better look. "It's all ashes—all that and that and
that," said Norstad, bending over the pictures.

It could be determined at that time (some sections of the city
were still obscured by smoke when the photographs were taken)
that fifteen square miles—all one big whitish-gray swath of the center of the city, without a break anywhere—were burned out, with
hardly a building intact. Some of the few buildings still erect in
the midst of wide acres of rubble and ashes were big factories surrounded by firebreaks and doubtless equipped with fire-fighting
apparatus of their own. Through a microscope you could see that
these buildings were gutted and that the roofs had fallen in. You
could also see that LeMay's plan had worked so well that, in one
hour's time, at least ten square miles of one of the two great industrial and commercial districts of the city were actually in flames
all at once, all in one great fire. Later on, other pictures showed that
the conflagration had spread and burned out a total of 16.8 square
miles, which is something over two-thirds the area of Manhattan
Island. In the great fire following Tokio's earthquake of 1923,
twenty-five square miles of the city were destroyed by a slow fire
that lasted for days. This fire LeMay's B-29s had started had covered two-thirds the area in a few hours.

Since getting back home, a few weeks ago, on leave, I have seen
the newspaper files and I know that the hundreds of thousands of
words I and my public-relations and censorship staff on Guam read

and cleared during the ten-day period covered by our first five great low-level incendiary raids on Tokio, Nagoya, Osaka, and Kobe— Nagoya was hit twice—appeared in newspapers all over the country and were featured above everything else. Yet I don't think people here at home even now understand exactly how great, how devastating these incendiary raids were. I know it took me some days— and I was right there on Guam—to absorb the facts so that I really understood them. I know the war correspondents had the same experience, said so, and wrote so.

Since then, besides tactical bombing of airfields on southern Japan in connection with the invasion of Okinawa, the B-29s in the Marianas have by successive incendiary raids brought the total of destruction in Tokio up to fifty-one square miles. The second large industrial area of Tokio, the one through which the Ginza runs, is now grayish on the post-strike pictures, just as the other big industrial district was after that initial strike. The Industrial and commercial centers of Kobe, Osaka, and Nagoya are also burned out, in varying degrees. The B-29s have struck Yokohama, too, with both high explosives and incendiaries. Our losses on all these strikes have been phenomenally light. Having caught the enemy flatfooted with his first low-level strikes, LeMay seems to have been able to keep him from organizing any kind of effective defenses against the B-29s.

The strikes are still going on. I see by the New York papers that LeMay is throwing his B-29s at the Japs in different ways, with different tactics, every day or so. Sometimes they all go to the same target, sometimes two or three task forces go to different targets on the same day or the same night. Flying low and only at night, specially trained B-29 squadrons have mined the harbors of Japan's main islands, strengthening the naval blockade and preventing the Japs from moving their war industries to Manchuria before they are entirely wiped out on Honshu. Flying these days with the three wings he had when he started the low-level incendiary raids are LeMay's old squadrons and groups from the Twentieth Bomber Command, which have flown the twenty-five hundred miles from China and formed a fourth operational wing, based on Tinian. LeMay and his people on the islands of Guam and Tinian and Saipan are shortening the war.

THE WILY WILBY

O NE SUNNY AFTERNOON in the autumn of 1939, the proprietors of a Chevrolet agency in San Francisco were given
a disheartening shock by an auditor from General Motors who
was making a routine examination of the agency's books. The auditor came out of the accounting department and informed them
that ten thousand of the dollars the proprietors thought they had
were, as a matter of fact, missing. Leaving the proprietors with their
thoughts, the auditor went back into the accounting department
and continued his studies. After several days, in the course of
which he kept uttering sharp cries of amazement and awe, he
came to the proprietors again, with his hands full of bank statements and canceled checks, and with garlands of adding-machine
tape around his neck, and told them that their former secretary and
treasurer, a man known to them as James W. Ralston, had diverted
the ten thousand dollars to his personal bank account and had hidden his defalcations so adroitly and with such originality that it
had been a real pleasure to uncover them. The man known as Ralston had resigned several months before and had left the agency
after shaking hands all around. He had made no secret of the fact
that he was investing his savings in an automobile agency of his
own, in the town of Colton, some five hundred miles south of San
Francisco and not far from San Diego. He had said that he and his

wife were going to settle down there in a little house he had bought. After their conversation with the auditor, the proprietors told an assistant district attorney that Ralston had seemed to them to be a very nice fellow—thirty-five years old, five and a half feet tall, a natty dresser with a gay manner and a sincere way of talking, wavy brown hair graying at the temples, blue eyes, fair complexion. He was picked up the next day in Colton, where he had already come to be regarded as a hard-working, respectable, up-and-coming automobile man. To the officers who took him back to San Francisco, he seemed in no way contrite, and, on the whole, cheerful. Sitting with them on the train, he kept slapping his knee and saying that he'd be damned if he could understand how the General Motors auditor had ever discovered his embezzlement. In jail, he talked shop with the auditor and questioned him closely about that. He paid a lawyer a thousand dollars to handle his case, gave back to his former employers fifteen hundred of the ten thousand dollars he had taken from them, and entered a plea of guilty.

As is customary in such cases, the probation officers tried to find out as much about the prisoner as they could, in order to give the court a report on him before he was sentenced. It turned out that his real name was Ralph Marshall Wilby, that he was a Canadian citizen, and that he had done some embezzling before, both in Canada and in the United States. In his early twenties he had humbugged a Toronto corporation in an unusual fashion while working for it as a bookkeeper. He was employed there under his real name and, using an alias, ingeniously put his other self down on the corporation's books as one of its stockholders. For two years, the corporation faithfully paid him dividends that amounted to several thousand dollars in all. He was cagy enough not to attend stockholders' meetings but, signing his other name, mailed his stock proxies to bona-fide stockholders who he knew belonged to a faction that was in favor of high dividends. After two years of this, Wilby resigned as bookkeeper. As stockholder, however, he continued to receive dividend checks for two more years. Then the corporation discovered what Wilby had been doing to it, and he was arrested, convicted of grand larceny, and sent to a reformatory for a short term. He gave back to the corporation a few hundred of the thousands he had taken from it, but he didn't say he was sorry. He asked many questions about how the corporation had at last come across his defalcations. His behavior at the reformatory was excellent and he was out of it in a year. He then came to this country. Using his real name, he married an American girl, and she lived happily with him until, in 1935, he was caught in the middle of a rather picayune embezzlement in Norfolk, Virginia. The complaint against him there was dropped when the Virginia authorities were assured by the immigration officials that he would be deported to Canada at once. His wife lauded him publicly at the time for his fidelity, generosity, good habits, and sunny disposition. She regretfully obtained an annulment only after he had been sent back to Canada. Wilby then adopted the name Ralston and quickly slipped back over the border, finding a job almost immediately as a bookkeeper at the Chevrolet agency in San Francisco. He was soon made secretary and treasurer, and he then married another American girl. This wife was living happily with him when he was arrested in Colton in 1939. She followed him to San Francisco and, like the first wife, went out of her way to speak highly of him. She had not known he was an embezzler, and when the facts were explained to her, she said, "Well, he's a very fine man except for that one quirk, or whatever it is."

It was discovered while Wilby was awaiting trial in San Francisco that he had played fast and loose with a Buick agency in San Diego a week before his arrest in Colton. The General Motors auditor, who had been impressed by the delicacy of Wilby's methods in San Francisco, was shocked when he found out about Wilby's conduct in San Diego. Wilby had been crude down there. Under the influence of what he later described as a whim, rather than a quirk, Wilby had driven from Colton to San Diego one day and had there dropped into a Buick agency that he knew was occasionally visited by auditors from General Motors. He had introduced himself as Ralston, said he was an auditor from G.M., checked the books and the cash on hand, and simply stuffed eight hundred dollars of the cash on hand into his hip pocket. He had then driven back to his humdrum life in Colton. The two proprietors of the San Diego agency were looking at each other suspiciously when stories and photographs of the San Francisco embezzler came out in the newspapers. They then went arm in arm to the San Diego prosecutor's office. Wilby was taken from San Francisco to San Diego, where he pleaded guilty without bothering to hire a lawyer. The fact that he hadn't yet been sentenced for the more impressive embezzlement in San Francisco seems to have rattled the Southern California judiciary. The San Francisco case was merged with the one in San Diego, and when the case finally came up, early in 1940, the judge was lenient and perhaps naïve. On Wilby's solemn promise never to return to the United States, the judge, instead of giving him a suspended sentence, put him on probation for ten years and turned him over to the immigration officers. He was shipped off to Canada, and his second wife regretfully applied for an annulment. Three months later, he was asking for a job as an accountant in the offices of a New York corporation that had an extraordinarily complex bookkeeping system and had frequently boasted in its brochures that its disbursements amounted to nearly forty million dollars a year. He got the job, and within a few weeks he had married still another American girl and she was living happily with him in Jackson Heights.

Wilby's preparations for his invasion of the New York commercial field were characteristically bold and imaginative. As soon as the immigration officers set him down in Canada, he began to

look around for a new name. What he lived on during this period
is not known, but it is assumed by students of his career that he had
providently deposited some capital in Canadian banks while he was
working and embezzling in California. In any case, he was able to
invest some cash in his search for a new name. This time he didn't
just want to make one up, as he had done when he chose "Ralston";
he wanted a name that meant something. He therefore placed an
advertisement in a number of Canadian and American trade jour-
nals. It declared that there was a wonderful opportunity for a good
certified public accountant in a big firm, not named, with international connections. Applicants were invited to write, stating
qualifications, etc., to Box No. So-and-So. Wilby received many
applications. The one he liked best was from a C.P.A. named
Alexander Douglas Hume. This Mr. Hume furnished impeccable
references; he had worked for a number of New York corporations
and he listed them all, giving in each instance the name of at least
one executive whom he knew personally and who he was sure
would be glad to give him a leg up. Hume was a Canadian citizen
and was at that time working as a chartered accountant in Toronto.
Wilby wrote to him and asked for more details. Hume supplied
them. The two men corresponded for some weeks. Then it began
to look as though there was an obstacle in the way of Hume's taking the job that Wilby seemed to be dangling in front of him.
Hume confessed to Wilby that he had begun to think seriously of
offering his services to the Empire. After all, he said, there was a
war on and he was young and able-bodied. In their correspondence, which continued for a month after this letter, they discussed
the progress of the war. Wilby said he certainly admired Hume's
patriotism, said he wished he were young and fit himself, and so
on. Finally, Wilby received a hurried and somewhat emotional letter from Hume, in which he said he had just accepted a lieutenant's commission in the Canadian Army and that he guessed

Wilby would not be hearing from him again until the Axis powers had been put in their place. Wilby wrote back offering his congratulations and wishing Hume the best of luck.

It was then that Wilby came to New York. He went to an employment agency in downtown Manhattan that specializes in finding jobs for accountants. He filled out a form, giving his name as Alexander Douglas Hume and listing Hume's New York references. When the head of the employment agency saw the form, he sent for him, because he had known Hume slightly when the latter had worked in New York five years earlier. "Glad to see you after all these years, Hume," the agency man said when Wilby walked into his office. The agency man has recalled over and over since then that the man looked at him, grinned, cried, "Why, of course!" and shook hands cordially. "You've lost weight," the agency man remarked, and Wilby explained that he had been on a diet and was in better shape than he had been in for years. Actually, there was no resemblance whatever between Wilby and Hume, but Wilby rose above that. Using his sincere way of talking, he went on to give the agency man some tips on how to avoid the temptation of potatoes and other starches. Then they settled down to the business on hand. The agency man got out a list of corporations that were looking for first-class accountants, and Wilby mulled it over, asking intelligent questions about the volume of business and the accounting methods of the different firms. He finally chose the William T. Knott Company, and the agency man telephoned that corporation. Wilby went to the Knott offices, on West Thirty-first Street, and was shown right in to the private office of the treasurer, a Mr. Casey. The two men talked for quite a while. Casey was impressed by the applicant's knowledge of bookkeeping and also, as he has remembered again and again, by the man's cheerful, modest, and businesslike manner. Casey picked up a telephone, muttering "Just routine, you know," and called one of the corporations Hume had worked for. He spoke to the officer mentioned in Hume's references and, sure enough, the officer said he remembered Hume well, that he was an excellent accountant and a first-class man all around. "Give him my regards," the officer said, and Casey did. As Hume, Wilby was put to work the next day.

The William T. Knott Company is what is known as a management corporation, and is very busy. It manages sixteen department stores in this country and one in Canada for a parent corporation called Mercantile Stores. Among the many things it has to do is pay for the merchandise these stores buy from manufacturers and jobbers. The department stores check the invoices when the goods are delivered and then send the invoices along to the Knott Company, which pays the manufacturers and jobbers by check. Being a trustworthy and successful management corporation, it is careful about the way it disburses this money. It keeps a list of purchase orders, and these are checked against the invoices. A force of accountants, clerks, typists, and business machines then takes the approved invoices and runs them through a labyrinthine bookkeeping system. At the far end of the labyrinth, there emerge in due time a corresponding number of tastefully embossed bank checks, each one made out, in austere black and white, to such-and-such a manufacturer or jobber for a certain number of dollars and one-hundredths thereof. Once the checks have been signed they are clapped into window envelopes and whisked off to the waiting manufacturers and jobbers by United States mail. The human workers and the business machines all get along fine together in the accounting department of the Knott Company. The human workers are male and female, and the business machines are standard. The machines do many of the more tiresome chores. One machine even goes to the bother of signing the checks. This check-signing machine is exceedingly complicated and mechanically above reproach. Only a privileged few of the human workers are allowed to get anywhere near it, and even for them it won't sign so much as small-fry jobbers' checks unless certain secret perforations and hush-hush notches

have been made by various other knowledgeable business machines around the office on certain unmentionable pieces of cardboard, one for each invoice that has been approved for payment.
The check-signing machine takes these pieces of cardboard and, if
the perforations and notches feel all right to it, signs the checks.
When the machine isn't working, some of its most important elements, such as one bearing an engraving of the signature of the
treasurer of the corporation, are removed. These are locked up in
one corner of the office, and the machine itself is locked up in another corner. The system is just about foolproof.

During 1940, Wilby, under his new name, worked for the Knott
Company as a traveling auditor, going from one department store
to another and checking up on their cashiers and bookkeepers.
During 1941, he was an accountant in the New York office. All that
time, the male and female workers and the standard business machines clicked and snuffled along with hardly a mistake and never
a defalcation, and the corporation continued happily to disburse
nearly forty million dollars a year by means of its complicated system. In 1942, Wilby was made chief accountant and put in charge
of that system. His salary, though it had been increased several
times, was only six thousand dollars a year. He nevertheless
thought he was in a position to make a fortune, and he was right.
During 1942, he took $110,936.81. The corporation didn't miss the
money, and the auditors found nothing wrong with the books.
Wilby's work seemed more than satisfactory to his employers.
They not only thought a lot of his efficiency but were delighted at
the way he got along with the people who worked under him. He
was always cheerful and relaxed, even when working at top speed
and under pressure. He was considerate of the human office force
and, even in his high executive position, was not above taking a
personal interest in the business machines. He always had time to
listen to the probems of the accountants, clerks, and typists, and
more than once dazzled a business-machine operator by stepping

up to a recalcitrant machine and diagnosing its inner difficulties after a shrewd glance and some sympathetic fingering. The general feeling at the Knott Company was that the new chief accountant had a truly rare and wonderful personality. At the end of his first year in the job, the corporation gave him the title of assistant treasurer, to add to the title of chief accountant, and also gave him a bonus of five hundred dollars, over and above the six thousand dollars he had earned and the $110,936.81 he had stolen.

Wilby thought he was in a position to do even better in 1943 than he had done in 1942, and he was right again. In 1943, he took $275,984.48. At the end of that year, the Knott Company still was feeling no pain, and it showered another five-hundred-dollar bonus on Wilby. Thus, in the two years, Wilby had got twelve thousand dollars in salary, a thousand dollars in bonuses, and $386,921.29 in stolen funds. He saved some of what he earned and all of what he stole, and he had the money where he could get at it any time he wanted it. He had invested some of it in bonds that were readily negotiable, but most of it was in accounts in New York banks.

While he was accumulating this fortune, Wilby and his third wife lived in an apartment in Jackson Heights, for which he paid sixty-five dollars a month, unfurnished. It was fitted out with maple living-room, dining-room, and bedroom sets from Bloomingdale's. Wilby's wife, named Hazel, had been a salesgirl in the women's-wear department at the Knott department store in Cincinnati. He met her and married her in 1940, while he was a traveling auditor for the Knott Company. A cashier in the Cincinnati store had been suspected of dipping into the till to the extent of several hundred dollars, and the management hadn't been able to prove it. Wilby was sent out there to check up on the fellow. It was a whirlwind trip for Wilby. He trapped the cashier, turned him over to the management, met Hazel, and took her to a justice of the peace. She was just twenty-one, good-natured, extremely good-looking, and a few inches taller than the five-and-a-half-foot Wilby.

While Wilby and Hazel were living in Jackson Heights, she did not know that her husband had at his disposal any funds in addition to his salary and bonuses, and she thought his name was Alexander Douglas Hume. She called him Doug. She was his trusting partner in what their neighbors looked upon as a rather dull existence. For a few months after they were married, they went out fairly regularly to a movie, or to dinner in Manhattan, but after Wilby became chief accountant he seemed to be more closely tied to his work than most of the other husbands in Jackson Heights. He brought home a briefcase stuffed with office records and pored over them until late at night. He went on what he said was a business trip almost every week-end, sometimes rushing all the way to the Middle West and back between Friday night and Monday morning. Hazel never accompanied him. She whiled away the lonely week-ends in a housewifely manner. She had gone to Cincinnati from a small town in Oklahoma, was impressed by New York and thoroughly pleased with her husband, and soberly co-operated with him in his determination to live well within his salary and bonuses. They had a joint checking account in a Jackson Heights bank, and Wilby showed her how to keep it straight and how to detect the trouble if the bank ever made a mistake of a dollar or two in its monthly statement. She read *Vogue* and *Harper's Bazaar* and, on the week-ends he was away, made clothes for herself, keeping track of the fashions of the day and cutting out and sewing up striking ensembles, for which she is still remembered by her former neighbors. Wilby was proud of her good looks and bragged to his friends at the office about how little money she spent on her clothes. On the rare evenings when the husband had no homework, the Humes would go out for a conservative fling at a neighborhood bar and grill, sometimes in the company of a couple who lived nearby and were their particular friends. These friends noted, to their subsequent amusement, how careful Wilby was with his money. He drank moderately, and when the four of them were together he would pay only for himself and Hazel, saying "Dutch, you know," and leaving a dime for the bartender at the end of the evening. "He wasn't stingy in a mean or unpleasant way, but he never threw any of that money around," these neighbors frequently told other neighbors later on. They found Wilby always sociable and agreeable, and usually jolly and lighthearted. A photograph taken at the time shows him holding the neighbors' baby and grinning, his hair slightly tousled and hanging over his forehead. From her greater height, the beautiful Hazel is looking down at him with an affectionate smile.

One Friday morning, toward the middle of January, 1944, when, in addition to whatever Wilby had saved out of his earnings, he had $386,921.29 at his fingertips, he stepped out of his private office at the Knott Company and dropped into the private office of Mr. Casey, the treasurer. He told Casey that he was all tired out. The accounts for 1943 were balanced, everything was under control, and he wanted to know if he could have a short vacation. "Just a long week-end," Wilby said. "I thought I'd run up to Canada for the skiing. Take Mrs. Hume along. I could get away tonight and be back by Tuesday." Casey said, "By all means, Doug," and wished him happy landings. Both men chuckled over the joke, and Wilby thanked Casey warmly. They shook hands. That night, Wilby left for Canada, taking along not only Hazel but also a briefcase, which, as she noted, and joshed him about, he kept under his arm or under his pillow the whole time. Hazel thought they really were going to go skiing in Canada.

On the Tuesday Hume was due back, Casey's secretary brought him a telegram that caused a good deal of concern around the office. The telegram had been sent from a small town near Toronto, and it said, "Douglas has suffered broken leg skiing. Will be confined here several weeks. Letter will follow. Hazel Hume." Casey was distressed. Hazel had not said exactly where her husband was confined, but Casey took steps to find out. He wired the manager of the Knott store in Hamilton, a town near Toronto, to check all hospitals, hotels, and nearby resorts to see if he could locate the company's chief accountant and assistant treasurer, and then find out if poor Hume needed anything. The store manager wrote back in a day or two and said he hadn't been able to find Hume, but that he would keep trying. A week went by and there was no further word either on or from the Humes. Then, one day, Casey began to experience a clutching sensation in the pit of his stomach. He sent somebody out to Jackson Heights to see if the Humes had returned. At the same time, he called in the auditors, told them about the skiing trip, and suggested that they get started right away on the annual audit for the year just ended. The man who went out to Jackson Heights found nobody at home in the Hume apartment. The auditors took the bales of Knott Company canceled checks for 1943, unfastened them, and added up the amounts of the checks on a squadron of adding machines. They compared this total with the total withdrawals from the Knott account, at the Fifth Avenue Branch of the National City Bank. The totals were nowhere near the same; the withdrawals were much higher. This could mean only one thing. Somebody had destroyed some canceled checks, and must have had a shady reason for doing so. The auditors rushed into Casey's office with the bad news. After a little while, Casey telephoned the office of District Attorney Frank S. Hogan. Assistant District Attorney George G. Hunter, Jr., of the Frauds Bureau, was assigned to the case, and Hunter called in Joseph M. Gasarch, a lawyer and a C.P.A. who was then a member of the Bureau of Accounting—he is now its head—of the District Attorney's Office. Hunter and Gasarch went over to the Knott Company and talked to the auditors. The facts the auditors had were very meager. There seemed to be a shortage of $275,984.48 in the 1943 accounts, and some canceled checks were missing. There was no legal evidence that the chief accountant and assistant treasurer had taken the money, but it looked as if he probably had.

Gasarch, who is a chubby, bald, middle-aged man with a plodding manner and a great enthusiasm for his work, nestled down into what he recognized as a delightful situation and did not entirely emerge from it for over a year.

While the Knott Company's auditors devoted themselves to a study of the accounts for 1943, and began to wonder whether the 1942 accounts were as nearly perfect as they had thought they were when they approved them the winter before, Gasarch noted the amounts of some of the missing canceled checks and went to the files of the Fifth Avenue Branch of the National City Bank. This is a careful branch of a cautious institution, and it makes a point of taking a photograph of the face of every check it pays before it cancels it and sends it back to the depositor. Gasarch got hold of the microfilm photograph of one of the missing canceled checks and found that it had been made out—and duly signed by the Knott check-signing machine—to a firm called Avon Mills, presumably a manufacturer whom the Knott Company had paid for goods purchased by one of its department stores. As the bank hadn't made a photograph of the back of the check, Gasarch couldn't tell who had endorsed this one, or even what city the firm did business in. A bookkeeping entry, however, showed that the check had come in for payment from the Trenton Banking Company, of Trenton, New Jersey. Gasarch went over to Trenton and found that the Avon Mills account had been closed some months before, but the bank officials remembered the man who had opened the account, back in March, 1943, and they had his signature on file. It was "A. D. Hume." Nobody else in Trenton had ever heard of a company called Avon Mills. Deposits in the bank account had come to $67,857.90, which had been transferred to another bank. The Trenton bank had a record of that, too. The money had been transferred to the personal account of A. D. Hume in the National City Bank of New York.

Gasarch slid back over to New York and found that the National

City Bank had carried an account for A. D. Hume, in the amount of \$119,050.13, at the same time it was carrying the Knott Company account, and at the same branch. The Hume account had been closed shortly before the chief accountant and assistant treasurer left for Canada. All this was enough evidence on which to base a warrant for the embezzler's arrest, and the police departments of various Canadian cities were, accordingly, asked to start looking for Alexander Douglas Hume. Assistant District Attorney Hunter instructed Gasarch to go ahead with his investigation and see what more he could find out. It was tough going, and Gasarch enjoyed every moment of it. Following the course of Wilby's manipulations, he has said since, was like tracing the ins and outs of a zigzagging mountain brook that sometimes flows underground. For a while, there would be easy stretches of comprehensible book-juggling, and deep, clear pools at the bottom of which he could make out the dim trail of a Knott disbursement leaving the Knott check-signing machine and wriggling into one of Hume's bank accounts. Then all trace of the embezzler and his defalcations would vanish, and there would be a subterranean interlude whose secrets could be explained only by the embezzler himself.

In a short time, Gasarch found that the man known as Hume had stolen the \$275,984.48 between March 20th and July 8th of 1943. Exactly how the Knott Company's machines had been maneuvered into writing and signing the checks couldn't be determined, because the fake invoices and the secret pieces of cardboard the embezzler used had disappeared, along with the canceled checks. Gasarch did, however, discover that those checks had gone to Eastern Mills and York Mills (as well as Avon Mills), which were fictitious firms, operated in Trenton at desk space the embezzler had rented in a broker's office. The operations of these firms consisted entirely of receiving and depositing Knott checks in four Trenton banks. Each of the fictitious firms had had deposits of from sixty-five thousand to seventy-five thousand dollars, and the total of the four accounts corresponded exactly with the shortage in the Knott bank account in New York. All the missing checks for 1943 were thus accounted for. In addition to the large sum deposited in the Fifth Avenue Branch of the National City Bank, the embezzler had put forty-five thousand dollars in another branch of the same bank, and had divided the rest of the money between branches of the Corn Exchange and the Chase National, all in the name of A. D. Hume.

When the embezzler had rented space in Trenton, he bought a beat-up second-hand desk. He did not forget this when, in September of 1943, he closed his mills and transferred to the New York banks the money the Knott Company had unwittingly disbursed. He sent the broker a check for the September rent and, with it, a letter saying he was sorry to have to inform him that he would be "vacating the desk space at the end of this month, as we have decided not to locate permanently in Trenton, at least not at present." He had hired, on a part-time basis, a typist in the broker's office, a Miss Wood, to do the small amount of clerical work he required, and he remembered to speak of her in a complimentary way and to refer, half humorously, half seriously, to his dilapidated desk. "Needless to say," he wrote, "I hate to leave such good company and the excellent work of Miss Wood. And, by the way, if you should learn of anyone desiring the desk—that is, if one should call it that—I certainly would appreciate your arranging an immediate sale for it. Any price will be satisfactory, as it will, of course, be of no use in the future." The broker sold the desk for twelve dollars, sent Wilby a check for that amount, and got another charming note from the man who signed himself A. D. Hume, acknowledging receipt of same.

It wasn't long before the auditors at the Knott Company trooped into the treasurer's office again and told him that the books for 1942 showed a shortage of $110,936.81. They were sure the shortage hadn't been there when they went over the books before, they said. Some canceled checks were missing now, however. Casey told Gasarch about this, and Gasarch, with a nod and a grin, submerged himself in the 1942 situation. The embezzler had made it more difficult for himself, and for Gasarch, that year. He had scattered his fictitious firms all over New England, the Middle West, and the South, instead of establishing them in a convenient industrial center like Trenton, within commuting distance of New York, as he had got around to doing in 1943. In 1942, Wilby had manufacturers and jobbers with palms extended in Boston, Pittsburgh, Cincinnati, Buffalo, Toledo, and Jonesville, South Carolina. Gasarch discovered that the embezzler had rented desk space and had hired part-time secretaries in all those cities, but had not trusted them to do anything except receive his mail and hold it for him, unopened. The only time the embezzler could get around to his desk-space offices was on week-ends, and as Gasarch reconstructed some of those week-end trips during 1942, he was amazed that the man's constitution hadn't cracked under the strain.

The defalcations that year occurred between March 9th and November 13th, and during that time dozens of Knott checks went through the Knott check-signing machine and were mailed to such figments of the embezzler's imagination as Bailey Fabrics, the Edstander Company, Emmons Brothers, Godshall Manufacturing Company, Frederick B. Hecht, the Package Delivery Service, the Qu'Appelle Company, and the Wayland Spread Company. When the embezzler knew that a batch of checks was in the mail, he would write or wire his part-time secretaries, telling them to hold his mail for him until noon on Saturday, and if he hadn't picked it up by that time, to leave it with the doorman or the night elevator operator. Rushing out of New York the moment he could get away from the Knott Company on Friday afternoon, he would pick up the mail in one of the towns before Saturday noon and deposit the checks in the account of one of his various firms, and then move on. He would puff into another city in the late hours of Saturday night or on

Sunday morning, pick up more checks from the elevator operators and doormen, deposit them in the banks' overnight-deposit chutes, and then hurry back to New York in time to be at his desk at the Knott Company on Monday morning. Nobody there ever saw him looking any less fresh than a daisy.

At a bank in Toledo, the fictitious name George B. Towle had been used for an account into which had flowed some of the embezzled money. The Toledo bank wanted to be sure that this Mr. Towle was a proper man to do business with, and went to the trouble of checking his references. There is a notation on Towle's application for an account with this bank that reads, "Expects to become a client of Wm. T. Knott Co. Gives Mr. Hume as reference." Then, later: "Spoke with Mr. Hume of Wm. T. Knott Co., who stated he knew Mr. Towle for many years; knows Towle to be a legitimate businessman (advertising line) and that Towle expects to connect with Wm. T. Knott soon."

To one of his part-time secretaries in the Middle West, the embezzler wrote at the height of the 1942 embezzlements that he couldn't understand why she had not received the ten dollars he owed her for her previous month's services. He had left a check for her in that amount with the night elevator operator, he said. "Kindly check your records again," he wrote, "and if you have not received it, then I shall check with my bank and see if it has been cashed by the night elevator man in question." What had happened, further correspondence shows, was that the elevator man had forgotten to give the check to the secretary, then remembered it a day or two after she got Wilby's letter. "Delighted that your accounts are now in apple-pie order," the embezzler wrote the secretary when he learned this.

Only one person, as far as Gasarch could determine, ever raised any question about what the chief accountant and assistant treasurer of the Knott Company was doing during those two years. This was Dan True, who handled the accounting department of a Knott store in Butte, Montana. This Mr. True didn't like the looks of certain freight charges that had been debited against his store by the Knott Company, and he wrote to the treasurer of the corporation about it. The treasurer turned the letter over to the chief accountant and assistant treasurer, and True was gently put in his place by a home-office memorandum reading as follows:

> Subject: Errors in Control Accounting for Transportation.
> To: Mr. Dan True.
> Copy to: Mr. M. A. Casey—Treasurer, Knott Co.
> From: A. D. Hume.

On the summary attached to your letter of Nov. 19, directed to Mr. Casey, I find one mistake which has apparently been overlooked, and very largely our fault, in New York. On your summary, there is no balance shown as of July 31. However, if you look at our Trial Balance run, you will find that there was a balance of $6,831.63 but this was not shown on the F-I as a separate figure but included with Merchandise-in-Transit. This policy, for the one month of July, was followed with all stores. We had intended, of course, to follow through by actually transferring the freight balance by post-closing entry to Merchandise-in-Transit and then distributing this into purchases in the following month, thereby clearing the freight account at the end of every month, excepting for any distribution that had to be made during the following month, regardless of whether the account was debit or credit. By adding the July balance to your summary, you will find that the freight overdistributed figure does amount to a small balance in favor of the overdistribution, and that is the way your freight account now stands. With best regards,

A. D. HUME

What the embezzler was saying in that memorandum meant something more to Gasarch than it would to most people, and Gasarch grabbed hold of this relatively small example of what the embezzler had done to the Knott Company's accounts after the money was stolen. It led Gasarch to one of the subterranean places he had hoped to get into. He traced the $6,831.63 mentioned by the good man True all the way through the Knott accounting system and was able to see how (or almost how) the embezzler had made the Knott books balance in spite of his defalcations. All the money that had been stolen had been charged to the department stores, and the charges had been so deftly distributed among the stores, in so many different ways, and with such shrewd knowledge of what accounts could stand being raised a bit here and there, that the stores hadn't noticed it. Gasarch could now understand what had happened when the auditors went over the 1942 books. The embezzler had allowed the auditors to add all the bank statements and the canceled checks, including the ones he had himself endorsed, with the result, of course, that the withdrawals from the Knott bank account tallied with the total of the canceled checks. Then he had destroyed the canceled checks he had endorsed and had altered hundreds of entries in the books, so that, in effect, what the Knott Company had lost to him it got back from the stores, in the form of debits against the stores' accounts, such as the freight account. Gasarch couldn't understand, however, why the embezzler had become panicky in the middle of January, 1944, had run off to Canada, and had then disappeared so mysteriously that the treasurer of the Knott Company had eventually got that queasy feeling in his stomach. If the embezzler had waited until the annual audit for that year was over, and had then destroyed the canceled checks, Gasarch believes the embezzlements would never have been discovered.

While Gasarch was rounding out, as best he could without the embezzler's help, the picture of these two years of brilliant

defalcation, the police of Montreal, Toronto, and Ottawa brought
to a conclusion the search for Alexander Douglas Hume. They
traced him to the European Theatre of Operations and found
that, as a major, he was leading a battalion of Canadian troops. The
Toronto police wired New York about this, adding, pointedly, that
Hume had been in the Canadian Army since 1940. They also sent
a photograph of Major Hume, who turned out to be a rather
serious-looking chap with a face not at all like Wilby's. Gasarch
cheerfully went to work to see if he could find out who it was that
had carried out the marvelous Knott Company embezzlements.
He once more visited the Fifth Avenue Branch of the National
City Bank. There, after days of searching through the bank's
records, he found that the man who had called himself Hume had,
in May, 1943, made what to this date seems to have been the only
patently careless mistake that can be scored against him in connection with the Knott Company embezzlements. He had asked the
bank to buy him, with money from his personal account, a draft
for fifteen thousand dollars in Canadian funds. In filling out the
purchase order, he had directed that the Canadian draft be made
out to "Ralph M. Wilby." A bank clerk had written that name
down in the blank space provided for the name of the payee and
Wilby had then changed his mind and asked that the draft be made
out to himself, i.e., to "A. D. Hume." It was the sort of slip any
man with more than one name might easily make.

Newspapers almost invariably refer to an embezzler as a man
who was "a trusted employee" until he juggled his company's
funds. The hackneyed phrase is usually given a moralistic emphasis, evidently with the intention of suggesting that the behavior of
the rascally bookkeeper should be regarded as particularly odious
because the man's employers had never dreamed that he might be
unreliable. When the first news stories appeared in the New York
papers about Ralph Marshall Wilby's embezzlement of $386,921.29
from the Knott Company, he was described as "a trusted em-

ployee" over and over again. All the stories made a point of rubbing that in. In Wilby's case, as in the cases of most embezzlers in
these times, the cliché was inaccurate and its use indicates an old-
fashioned and romantic idea of the relationship between bookkeepers and the people who employ them. The ugly truth is that
the higher a bookkeeper climbs in the accounting department of a
firm, the lower the estimate of his trustworthiness becomes in the
minds and hearts of his employers. Although Wilby had worked
for the Knott corporation for four years, had been given several increases in salary and two bonuses, and had reached the position of
chief accountant and assistant treasurer before he put his stolen
fortune in a briefcase, went to Canada, and disappeared, his employers, it turned out, hadn't trusted him in the first place. One of
Wilby's best friends at the Knott corporation, and seemingly one
of his greatest admirers, was the company's treasurer, Mr. Casey. It
was Casey who had encouraged and aided Wilby's progress from
the position of traveling auditor to that of chief accountant and
assistant treasurer. Yet this same Mr. Casey, acting for the corporation in what a romanticist would have to consider an abominably
gelid manner, had bet the Travelers Insurance Company (which insures all kinds of people besides travelers) that Wilby would someday steal some of the corporation's funds. The Travelers Insurance
Company had bet that Wilby wouldn't. This wager was represented by a bond of three hundred thousand dollars, the terms of
which were that the Knott corporation would pay the Travelers
Insurance Company an annual premium of a good many thousands
of dollars as long as its chief accountant and assistant treasurer
didn't steal any money from the corporation. If he did steal any
money, the Travelers Insurance Company would reimburse the corporation for what he had stolen, up to the sum of three hundred
thousand dollars.

The fact that Wilby's employers had bet against him in this
manner and that the Travelers Insurance Company stood to lose

the three hundred thousand dollars unless Wilby could be hunted down and persuaded to return the larger part of the money he had embezzled from the Knott corporation was one of two circumstances that made his disappearance even briefer than it might have been. The second circumstance was that Wilby's third wife, Hazel, was a very pretty girl. That was one reason Wilby had married her. A New York probation officer wrote of Wilby after he had been brought back to New York, "He is a man who could easily be lost in a crowd, having neither the physique nor the personality to give him distinction." Hazel, on the other hand, had a physique, if not a personality, that gave her distinction. She attracted attention wherever she went, and was totally unable to get lost in a crowd.

The search for the man thought to be Alexander Douglas Hume was put into the hands of Fred Hains, a capable detective attached to the staff of District Attorney Frank S. Hogan. Hains, who has since become a lieutenant, has an easygoing manner, an active brain, and a worldly outlook. Before doing anything else, he wired the police departments of Montreal, Toronto, and Ottawa detailed descriptions of Hume and his pretty wife, and also gave them information about Hume's life as it was summarized on his employment record. It didn't look like much of a case to Hains. He is aware of, and rather entertained by, the fact that there is hardly any place in the world a crook can go now where somebody won't recognize him, provided photographs of him are distributed with sufficient largess. He knew that in this embezzlement case the Travelers Insurance Company would be anxious to put up all the money needed for a wide distribution of photographs. The company, however, had not been able to find a photograph of Hume.

Hains went out to Jackson Heights and talked to the superintendent of the apartment house there in which the Humes had lived. He discovered that Hazel had returned to Jackson Heights on January 19, 1944, the day after Mr. Casey had received the telegram informing him that Hume had broken his leg skiing. She had told the superintendent that she and her husband were going to settle in Canada, and had paid the rent for the two months the lease of the apartment had to run. Then she had packed a couple of trunks and had the furniture crated and moved out. The superintendent said she had seemed to be in a hurry but hadn't looked worried and certainly hadn't acted furtive. Adding this information to what he had been told about the Humes by people at the Knott Company, Hains surmised (correctly) that she wasn't aware that her husband had stolen a fortune. This meant that she probably would be moving around freely, wherever she was, and that her husband probably would be moving around with her. Hains talked to the Humes's best friends, a couple in Jackson Heights. As he had hoped, they had taken a snapshot of the Humes. They found it and gave it to him. The superintendent remembered that the Railway Express had come for the trunks and the furniture. Hains learned from the express company that these had been shipped to Hazel's parents, in Oklahoma. He took down their names and the name of the town in which they lived. He telephoned the sheriff of the town and asked him to arrange to have all mail addressed to Hazel's parents closely watched by the post office.

After a few days, the Toronto police wired that they had a line on Hume. Then, a day or two later, the Toronto police dug up a photograph of the real Alexander Douglas Hume and sent it to Hains. Hains was able to see at a glance that this wasn't the man who had stolen the money from the Knott corporation. Before he had time to let Toronto know about that, Toronto sent him the news that Alexander Douglas Hume had been in the Canadian Army since 1940. Hains laughed, and began to like the looks of the case. He knew now that he was after a man who had somehow been able to obtain the employment record of an honest certified public accountant, had posed as this C.P.A. in New York for four years, and had, in addition, stolen nearly four hundred thousand

dollars while competently holding down the job of chief accountant and assistant treasurer of a big corporation.

It was a week or so later that the embezzler's actual name was
discovered by Gasarch, and Hains then learned very quickly that
Wilby had a record as an embezzler in California and in Ontario.
The Travelers Insurance Company delightedly made thousands of
copies of the snapshot of the Wilbys that Hains had found in Jackson Heights, and began mailing them to police departments, hotels,
railroads, airports, and its branch offices all over the United States
and Canada, along with the information that the man in the photograph was wanted for the Knott embezzlement.

Hains and a fellow-detective, George Salyka, then set out for
Oklahoma. In the town where Hazel's parents lived, they picked up
from the sheriff a letter Hazel had written them after she closed up
the apartment in Jackson Heights. It said that she was returning to
Toronto immediately, that she and her husband were going to stay
in Canada permanently, and that they were thinking of going out
to British Columbia, where he had some relatives. She asked her
parents to keep the furniture for a while, until she and her husband had decided where they were going to settle down. Her
husband had inherited a small fortune from a great-aunt, she said,
and he wanted to look around British Columbia for a good business in which to invest some of this money. Hains communicated the gist of this to Ottawa, Toronto, Montreal, and Vancouver,
and was about to return to New York when his office there relayed to him a wire from the police chief of Victoria, the capital
of British Columbia, that said his men had just missed Wilby at
the Empress Hotel and expected to catch up with him in a day
or two.

As Hazel later testified in court in New York, Wilby had by that
time told her that his real name was Wilby but had not told her
that he was an embezzler. When they reached Toronto, Wilby told
her he had a confession to make. In his youth, he said, he had been

deported from the United States because he had gone over the border without signing the proper papers. He had accordingly found it necessary to adopt an alias when he returned to the United States later. He had inherited a small fortune from a great-aunt who had died in England, and had increased it by playing the stock market, but had not paid any income tax on it. He was afraid to stay in the United States any longer, because he might be sent to jail for violating the income-tax law, and he had therefore brought his fortune with him in his briefcase, in cash and bonds. He asked Hazel to return to Jackson Heights, close up the apartment, store the furniture, and rejoin him in Toronto, after which they would go out to British Columbia, visit his relatives, find a business to invest in, and live comfortably for the rest of their lives. A trusting girl but not a dumb one, Hazel was afraid that her husband night be arrested and taken back to the United States. Wilby reassured her on this point in a characteristically businesslike manner. He took her to a solicitor in Toronto and asked the solicitor's opinion as to whether he could be extradited for not paying an income tax. The solicitor told him he could not. Hazel asked the solicitor a great many questions and soon felt fine about the whole thing. A Canadian citizen, the solicitor told her, could be extradited only for a really serious offense, such as murder or grand larceny. Wilby paid the solicitor a small fee. Hazel came to New York, closed up the apartment, and went back to Toronto. The Wilbys then traveled, in easy stages, across the continent to Victoria. Wilby readopted his real name, and Hazel began to call him Ralph instead of Doug.

By the time the Wilbys reached Victoria, the photographs that were being mailed out by the Travelers Insurance Company had been circulated in eastern Canada, but they had not reached British Columbia. In the meantime, Hazel was noticed in a crowd in the lobby of the Empress Hotel by a photographer on the Victoria *Times* named Flash Strickland. He noticed her simply because she was beautiful. He uttered a low, British Columbian whistle and gaped at her. A girl in the society department of the same newspaper happened to come into the lobby at that instant, in search of news items. She asked the photographer what he was gaping at. He indicated Mrs. Wilby, who was getting into an elevator by then. The reporter went over to the desk, asked who the beautiful girl was, and copied down the name from the register—"Mrs. Ralph M. Wilby, Hamilton." Hamilton, a city near Toronto, was Wilby's home town. An item appeared next day in the Victoria *Times* to the effect that Ralph M. Wilby, of Hamilton, and his attractive young wife were at the Empress Hotel. A few days later, a Toronto paper picked up the item. A stenographer in the Toronto office of the Travelers Insurance Company saw it and recognized the name of the embezzler whose photograph had come in from New York. She told her boss, who told the Toronto police, who told the Victoria police. When the Victoria police got to the Empress Hotel, the Wilbys had checked out. They had gone to visit Wilby's relatives, just outside town. When they returned to Victoria, a few days later, and checked into the Empress Hotel again, Wilby was arrested. That happened on the fifty-eighth day after he had left New York for the long week-end.

Hains received this news without surprise. The Travelers Insurance Company was happy, but only momentarily. The Victoria police wired the following day that when Wilby was searched he had only a few coins in his pockets, and that no money or bonds were found in the Wilbys' baggage, and no bankbooks. Gasarch was glad Wilby had been caught, because he hoped that he would be able to have a talk with him and find out some of the things he wanted to know about the finer points of his embezzling methods. Assistant District Attorney Hunter had obtained an indictment against Wilby by this time for grand larceny, and he went to Victoria to start extradition proceedings. The Canadian law requires that before a prisoner can be extradited, sufficient evidence be presented to convince the presiding judge, for all practical purposes, of his guilt. Gasarch went along with Hunter, as an expert witness for the prosecution. Hains and Salyka went along, too, to bring Wilby back to New York.

It took four months and cost the State of New York at least ten thousand dollars to get Wilby out of Canada. He hired the best solicitors and barristers that money could buy. One of them was a former Attorney General of British Columbia. Wilby had buried some of the stolen money in tin cans in the back yard of a house he had bought on the outskirts of Vancouver, and he had buried some more of it along a highway near Victoria. Hazel later testified, in New York, that she had dug some of this money out of the ground with her own hands and given it to the Canadian attorneys. The Canadian attorneys, still later, asserted that they hadn't dreamed it was stolen money, and nobody was ever able to persuade them to give any of it back, either to the Knott corporation or to the Travelers Insurance Company. Exactly how much they received has never been established. The extraordinary vigor with which they fought for Wilby indicates that they were being well paid or else that their devotion to him was a fine and touching thing. They appeared in court in Wilby's behalf on twenty-three occasions, obtained three writs of habeas corpus for him, appealed when the courts refused to sustain the writs, and were preparing an additional appeal to the Privy Council in London, when Hains and Salyka, taking advantage of a momentary hiatus between writs of habeas corpus, at last managed to grab Wilby and bring him back to Seattle in a small fishing vessel. They had almost got him out of Canada between writs once before that, but Wilby had raised an outcry while he was under their custody in a hotel and had persuaded Canadian police to take him away from the New York detectives. By the time the Canadian police were persuaded that Wilby was not being kidnapped, his attorneys had obtained another writ. Hunter, along with a Canadian barrister the New York District Attorney's office had retained, fought Wilby's lawyers with determination, and even brilliance, but, as Hunter wrote, "such strange things have happened that we cannot count on anything." Wilby conducted himself all this time with the self-righteous dignity of a man of consequence who is being unjustly persecuted. He did not deny having stolen the money, but he was convinced that he shouldn't be extradited for that. He was standoffish with the New York detectives during the short periods they had him in custody between writs. Casey, the Knott treasurer, went to Victoria and talked to Wilby in jail, and Wilby was outraged when Casey asked him please to give up the battle, come back to New York, and straighten out the Knott books. "The books are in a mess, you know," Casey said to Wilby mildly. Wilby told him indignantly that the books were *not* in a mess—that they were in perfect balance, since every penny he had stolen had been carefully charged off to the department stores. On the train back to New York from Seattle, Wilby relaxed somewhat with the detectives and played gin rummy with them for small stakes. "He's a lot of fun to be with, in many ways," Hains said later.

Locked up in the Tombs, Wilby refused for weeks to tell Gasarch what he wanted to know, and also refused to tell the Travelers Insurance Company whether he had any of the stolen money left and, if so, where he had hidden it. He hired an attorney with what the attorney says he hopes was not stolen money, and he finally persuaded Wilby to plead guilty. Before Wilby did so, however, he made a bargain with the Travelers Insurance Company that was as original as his methods of embezzlement. He offered to tell the company where it could find around three hundred thousand dollars of the stolen money if it would give him ten thousand dollars for himself. The company took this up with various surety companies, representing various banks, all of which might have had to assume responsibility for Wilby's fraudulent checks and therefore stood to gain if Wilby returned three hundred thousand dollars of the stolen money. Wilby's argument was that he had had ten thousand dollars of his own money when he went to Canada, in addition to the stolen money. He had, of course, stolen $386,921.29, but, he said, he had given about eighty thousand dollars of it to his Canadian barristers and solicitors. Nobody could find out whether this was true or not, but Wilby was in a strong position to bargain, because he was offering three hundred thousand dollars for ten thousand dollars. The Travelers Insurance Company and the surety companies, all of which were to reduce their losses on a complicated percentage basis through any of the stolen money that was returned, mulled over Wilby's proposition for several weeks and finally accepted it. After Wilby had been given a certified check for ten thousand dollars, he told an attorney for the Travelers Insurance Company where what remained of the stolen money was, and the attorney went to Canada and dug it up. It came to three hundred and three thousand dollars.

IN A CO-OPERATIVE mood now, Wilby not only talked to Gasarch and gave Casey and other Knott people useful tips on how the tangled books of the corporation could be straightened out but also wrote, while in the Tombs awaiting sentence, a ten-thousand-word document that discussed, with the cool detachment of Napoleon's review of the battle of Waterloo, the ups and downs of his two years of embezzling from Knott. The first third of this statement of Wilby's was a masterly explanation of what the Knott accounting system was and how it worked. It told how the department stores managed by Knott sent in their invoices for goods purchased—these invoices are "aprons" in accountancy terminology—and how these aprons were put through the human workers and the business machines so that, at the other end of the system, checks for the manufacturers and jobbers emerged from the Knott check-signing machine. Wilby mentioned by name the various Knott employees who were in charge of sub-departments of the accounting department, and told what their duties were and how well they performed them. Then he quietly started a new paragraph, to explain how he did what he did to the Knott corporation, like this:

As to my defalcations, no fixed course was followed throughout excepting in the year 1943, when they followed a more or less similar routine. During 1942, the methods differed largely from those used in 1943.

In 1943, the course was, to a large extent, as follows: At some time before or after a batch of original aprons had been received from the department stores and distributed by Miss Catala, I would insert a further apron or aprons payable to "my" companies and would correct the accompanying listing by either running a new adding machine tape or making penciled corrections on the original listing that the store had prepared. On other occasions, I took an apron that was payable to some vendor from the originals sent out by the stores and assuming, for example, that this apron was for $235, and payable to John Doe Co., I would add a "6" in front of this amount, thus making the corrected amount "6235" and would erase the name of the original vendor and insert the name of "my own" company. This made changing the store's listing comparatively easy. Then, of course, I would make a further apron just exactly as the store had originally made it and either add it to that day's aprons and listing, or else to a following day's.

So there were several methods by which the aprons payable to "my" companies were supplemented into the various stores' original aprons and listings, but it all adds up to the same thing, that they were included without any difficulties.

As I mentioned before, sometimes they were added before Miss Catala received the mail, which was no trouble, as it was merely a matter of taking an envelope from her desk before her arrival in the morning, or getting it from the mailing department before the distribution was made to Miss Catala's desk on the pretense that I was anxious to get some store's reports. As original aprons were coming in from every store on each day, one just couldn't avoid getting an envelope with some of these original aprons in them. On other occasions I waited until the original aprons were in the course of being mailed before the addition of aprons to "my" companies.

If this act was after the control clerk had noted the original total, I would merely change her figures upon my apron insertion. If my step was taken after the coding, I would have to correct the control figures and would code the apron myself. As I could handle practically the functions of every accounting employee, whatever method followed presented no great difficulties. As soon as the apron was added to a store's listing, "my" apron thereafter followed a normal course, which I naturally permitted, up to a certain point.

The number of settlement checks issued and mailed by Knott averages between 600 and 700 daily. Many more settlement checks, as a rule, are outgoing on Fridays from Knott's than on other days. I had learned from experience that checks mailed by Knott on Friday evenings did not reach "my" offices or post-office boxes by early Saturday mornings, when I went to make bank deposits for "my" companies. But Saturday mornings were practically the only occasions on which I could arrange to be in Trenton, or the other cities, during banking hours, and unless I could actually gain possession of "my" checks on Friday at the Knott office, it meant a delay of one week in "my" deposits. This was contrary to my policy of getting the deposits in the banks just as soon as possible and to withdraw the funds as soon as it appeared to be safe, without arousing suspicion and, of course, always allowing sufficient time for their complete clearance.

227

Therefore, always on Fridays, and generally on every other day also, I would arrange to get those checks payable to "my" companies just before the final functions were completed by the Knott office staff, and would complete these functions myself and then pocket the checks so that I could take them with me for the earliest possible Saturday deposit. There were two or three other reasons why I invariably tried to follow this plan of completing "my" checks myself and gaining possession of them before they left the Knott office.

One of the other reasons was that during the year of 1942, I allowed several of "my" checks to be completely handled by the Knott staff and thereafter my earliest chance to pocket these checks was after they had reached the mailing room. I took these from the mailing room, but they were missed, as their count and the number as per the scratch pad notation was not in agreement. This discrepancy was reported to the audit department head, Miss Murphy, and she, in turn, criticized her clerk, who had inserted the checks in the envelopes and had counted and taken them to the mailing room. Miss Murphy had believed that this clerk was careless and even considered removing her from that capacity. Thereafter, I never resorted to such practice again, because I hated to see the clerk get in trouble through no fault of her own.

There was one method which would have been the easiest course of all—this being to have a notation made on the check, at some point of its preparation, that it was to be given to Mr. Hume upon its completion. But I considered such policy much too risky, just in case some question might be asked or raised about the check during its preparation, and consistently being a sizable amount, this was quite possible, so I did not wish to have my name associated with any of "my" checks whatsoever so far as the Knott office was concerned.

Another reason for my favoring and arranging to complete

the functions of "my" checks, and then pocketing them, was
that, one time early in 1943, I had allowed one or two checks
to be completed in all functions by the accounting staff and to
be mailed out by the company, as was the normal course for all
other checks. But one of these letters bearing a check to "my"
Avon Mills never reached Trenton until one or two Saturdays
following the week it should have been there in the ordinary
course of events. I was literally sick with worrying—naturally
imagining everything. This envelope finally arrived, bearing the
notation that it had been sent to Chicago, Ill., in error by the
post-office department, though it had been correctly addressed.
The mistake troubled me sufficiently that I did not allow any
more checks to be completed and mailed by the office and the
mailing staff of Knott's, though I did mail such checks myself.

Wilby proved to everybody's satisfaction, in his written statement and in conversations with Gasarch and with people from the
Knott Company, that he had worked entirely without confederates. None of the human workers in the Knott accounting department were blamed because Wilby had done what he had done.
Some of the business machines were criticized, however, and were
later taken apart and put together again, after certain newly devised safeguards, which Wilby's methods seemed to make advisable,
had been added. But it was felt by people who know and work with
such machines that if the machines had been able to talk, as well as
think, they would have spoken to somebody about Wilby long before his disappearance caused the corporation to suspect that he had
not been honest with it.

Wilby, it turned out, might have gone on stealing from the
Knott corporation in 1944, and for years afterward, as he had done
in 1943 and 1942, if it had not been for the Federal Bureau of Investigation. The connection of the F.B.I. with the Wilby case has
not been mentioned in the published chronicles of J. Edgar Hoover

and his G-men, but it was the F.B.I. that caused Wilby to leave the Knott corporation when he did. Wilby had covered up his defalcations with such impeccable technique that he would probably never have been suspected of wrongdoing if he had stayed around to steal some more in 1944, or if he had at least waited until the annual audit of the corporation's books was completed, in the winter of 1944, and had then just resigned after shaking hands all around. Instead, he left in a hurry. As he explained in the document he wrote in the Tombs, he had outwitted everybody but he had not been able to foresee the interest of the F.B.I. in his operations. The F.B.I. had no suspicion that he was an embezzler. It thought it was on the trail of a Nazi Fifth Columnist, and had done everything but alert Walter Winchell for a scoop. Wilby had taken no precautions against that kind of thinking. Something of a philosopher, he has possibly reflected, in the years since all these things happened, that the three circumstances that led to his downfall make a crazy pattern, sort of like life. In Hazel's beauty there was truth; the fact that the Knott corporation had mistrusted him all along had about it a flavor of irony; and the F.B.I. contributed a comic ingredient.

In 1942, Wilby related in his confession, he had some Knott checks sent to a fictitious jobber in St. Louis, to whom he had given the name Frederick B. Hecht. It never occurred to him that the fact that it was a German name was going to get him into trouble with anybody. That's what happened, however. In those days, the F.B.I. checked up on all sorts of bank accounts all over the country, and especially those in German names. An F.B.I. man going over the records of Wilby's St. Louis bank came across the Hecht account and asked the bank who Hecht was. The bank knew only that a number of Knott Company checks had been deposited in the account. It sent a man to New York to inquire of the Knott Company about Hecht. He was referred to Wilby, who requested time to look into the matter. "I busied myself towards being able to present the proper invoices for Hecht at my next meeting with the bank's representative," Wilby explained later in the statement. He drew up some new fake invoices, having destroyed the old fake invoices, and thought he had convinced the bank that Hecht was a legitimate jobber who was not engaged in un-American activities, but eighteen months later the F.B.I. still had the Hecht account on its mind. One evening in December, 1943, an earnest young F.B.I. man came out to Jackson Heights to see the Knott corporation's chief accountant and assistant treasurer about it. The F.B.I. man told Wilby frankly that he hadn't been able to find Hecht anywhere. He was positive that Hecht was a Nazi Fifth Columnist, he said, and he asked Wilby if he couldn't think of some clues that might lead to the discovery of Hecht. "I gave some false clues to the F.B.I. man about Hecht," Wilby wrote. "In the next two or three weeks, the F.B.I. man called on me at the Knott office on two further occasions to obtain further information about Hecht. I continued to furnish misleading advice, though I realized that the time for a showdown was rapidly approaching." Wilby did not wait for the showdown.

There was an extended hearing before Judge John A. Mullen, in the Court of General Sessions, when Wilby appeared for sentence, on February 1, 1945. Wilby's New York attorney argued persuasively for leniency, pointing out that the amount of money Wilby had restored represented something of a record. Judge Mullen, however, pointed out that this had been made possible only by the fact that the amount of money Wilby had stolen also represented something of a record.

Hazel testified at length and convinced Judge Mullen, as she convinced everybody else, that until Wilby was arrested she had not known he was an embezzler. "When I married my husband," Hazel said, "I didn't know how much money he had. The reason for that, I asked him one time and very politely he refused to answer my question. I thought perhaps I was being a little too inquisitive, and, therefore, I never asked him again. I knew nothing about his financial affairs."

"I know," Judge Mullen put in. "My probation report indicates that she did not have any reason to believe that her husband had ever taken any money, because it was not spent on her and it wasn't spent on anybody else."

Hazel was asked when it was that her husband had told her he had come into a substantial sum of money, and she said it was on the train going to Canada.

"How did the subject come up on that occasion—do you remember?" the Judge asked.

"Yes, I do," Hazel said. "He was carrying a little brown brief case and out of just one of those questions I said, rather jokingly, 'What have you got in there?' And at the time I don't remember exactly what he said, but, as I recall, he said, 'Well, that consists of our worldly wealth' or some little remark like that."

"And what did you say—anything?"

"Well, I said, 'Don't leave it lying around. You'd better take good care of it.'"

Later on in the hearing, Wilby's attorney made a rambling speech about Wilby's earlier embezzlements and emphasized the fact that Wilby had always lived economically and was highly regarded by all three of his wives. "I am trying at least to indicate what went through Wilby's mind," he concluded.

"That, I am afraid, we will never know," Judge Mullen said.

The Judge had weighed the facts in the case with a good deal of care before this hearing, and he weighed them some more before he pronounced sentence. The facts were not easy to weigh. Wilby's attitude toward embezzlement seems to have been the only flaw in an otherwise perfectly sterling character. He had never been charged with breaking any statutes except those having to do with embezzlement. Embezzlement is a statutory felony both in the United States and in England these days, but Judge Mullen was aware that before the sixteenth century it was not a crime in English law, because it was not regarded as an offense against the people. In those days, it was thought to be laughable rather than criminal and was not to be judged the same way theft was, because the embezzler merely takes money that he has been hired to handle. The only recourse the owner of embezzled funds had, under English law, was to sue the absconding bookkeeper in the civil courts. King Henry VIII, who had himself been humbugged by embezzlers, promulgated the first anti-embezzlement statute in 1592. New York revised its anti-embezzlement statutes as late as 1942 to plug up some loopholes that had offered advantages to certain types of embezzlers. Judge Mullen was also aware that embezzlement is still not generally regarded as a crime against the people, and that courts often give embezzlers suspended sentences or very short prison terms if they make restitution of the funds they have stolen. He was aware that the Knott corporation had lost nothing, because Wilby had restored three hundred and three thousand dollars of the stolen money and the Travelers Insurance Company bond had easily covered the additional $83,921.29. The Travelers Insurance Company had lost something, but, on the other hand, its premium rates allow for just such losses, and it had not suffered any more that year than in any other year, and had shown a handsome profit in spite of Wilby. The same was true of the surety companies and the banks. Wilby, however, had cost the people of the State of New York at least ten thousand dollars just to get him out of Canada, and the fact that firms like the Knott Company must pay for large bonds for employees like Wilby means that this additional expense is passed along to the consumer. Judge Mullen is a jurist who does not believe in punishment except when it can serve as a deterrent. He couldn't help feeling that if Wilby, with the ten thousand dollars in his pocket that he had got from the Travelers Insurance Company, was given a suspended sentence, or even an especially light sentence, he would be a foolish man if he didn't go right on embezzling for the rest of his life. Judge Mullen therefore sentenced him to from five to seven years in Sing Sing. Wilby's behavior there has been good and he will be out soon. Like her two predecessors, Hazel applied for an annulment and got it. She became a model for a while, married again, and is living happily in New York. When Wilby leaves Sing Sing, the immigration officers intend to ship him back to Canada at once.

GOSSIP WRITER

O N SATURDAY, SEPTEMBER 2, 1939, it seemed certain to Walter Winchell, as it did to the rest of us, that Great Britain was about to go to war with Germany. Unlike the rest of us, Winchell did something about this. After turning it over in his mind, he sent a cablegram early the next morning to Prime Minister Chamberlain, as follows:

> May I respectfully offer the suggestion that if Britain declares war the declaration might be worded not as "War Against Germany" but as "War against Adolf Hitler personally and his personal regime," Stressing the fact that Hitler does not really represent the true will of the vast civilian population of Germany. Such declaration might have the astonishing effect of bringing the German people to their senses especially if such declaration can be made known to the German people and inevitably it would via radio and other channels. This is merely a layman's suggestion offered in hopes of a new era of world peace.

The next day Winchell made public the text of this cablegram by printing it in his daily column, "Walter Winchell on Broadway," which appears in the *Daily Mirror* in New York and in a hundred and sixty-five other newspapers in the United States. He printed it without comment, merely making it clear to his readers that it was he who had sent the cablegram.

The day after that, September 5th, Winchell wrote in his column:

> If you read Monday's column, this may interest you. At 2:33 A.M. September 4, the London telegraph agency flashed a dispatch reporting that Prime Minister Chamberlain had just read a proclamation to the German people via a French radio station, in which he stated that Great Britain did not declare war against the German people, but against Adolf Hitler and the Nazi regime . . . The suggestion was sent to the Prime Minister in a cablegram, acknowledgment of which has arrived.

It is significant that in announcing what is to him an extraordinary personal coup, Winchell simply presents the facts unemotionally, setting them down for history's sake, as it were. The inner conviction that he is actually responsible for Chamberlain's proclamation appears to stir him only intellectually. A tone of almost melancholy aloofness is discernible, as if Winchell no longer enjoys as an adventurer the sweet fruits of triumph but is beginning to see himself with sober detachment as an actor on the stage of current events. There is a telling phrase in the text of his cablegram to Chamberlain. He insists that in what he is saying to the British Prime Minister he is speaking merely as a layman. This is the familiar protestation of the man of consequence. Nobody but a distinguished personage whose eminence is unassailable ever tries to palm himself off as an ordinary, run-of-the-mill citizen.

There are probably critics who would say that it is ridiculous for a mere gossip writer to put his nose into serious international affairs, and that for Winchell to presume that his cablegram actually influenced Chamberlain is patently absurd. This is a narrow view. Winchell has no reason to think that gossip writing is dishonorable or undignified, or that, as a gossip writer, he deserves anything but respectful consideration. Calling Winchell a mere gossip writer is like calling Lindbergh a mere aviator or Gene Tunney a mere prizefighter. The writing of gossip, the setting down of items about the private lives of his fellow-citizens, is responsible for Winchell's enormous success in life, but it would be an understatement to sum him up by saying, "He writes gossip," just as it would be to say of Tunney, "He beat Dempsey," or of Lindbergh, "He flew to Paris."

From the beginning of his career as a gossip writer fifteen years ago, people whom Winchell looks up to have encouraged him in his work. Such celebrities as George Bernard Shaw, Theodore Dreiser, Leopold Stokowski, James J. Walker, Faith Baldwin, Gypsy Rose Lee, Rupert Hughes, James Montgomery Flagg, Shirley Temple, and Lowell Thomas have written guest columns for him so he could take vacations in the summer. From the start he has been on friendly and sometimes intimate terms with the members of some of the oldest and most respected families of New York. They call him Walter and give him items for his column. He was the favorite columnist of the leading gangsters of New York when they ruled the town; they took him to prizefights and gave him elaborate parties. One of them once sent him a Stutz. About a year ago he was guest of honor at a luncheon tendered in the Capitol Building in Washington by the Vice-President of the United States, and some months before that the President of the United States, in starting off a forty-five-minute tête-à-tête with Winchell, had slapped him affectionately on the knee and said, "Walter, I've got an item for you." The American Legion has given him a gold medal "in recognition of his contribution to Americanism," and Lakewood, New Jersey, has named a thoroughfare Winchell Street in honor of "the first soldier in our land in the cause of democracy." His patriotic writings have been reprinted at the expense of the government and handed out to the public by the Democratic Party. His valuable life, once zealously protected by bodyguards assigned to him by his friends Owney Madden and Lucky Luciano, has in more recent years been watched over by agents on the payroll of the Federal Bureau of Investigation, assigned to him by his friend J. Edgar Hoover.

To a sympathetic follower of Winchell's career it is clear that his gesture in giving advice to Chamberlain was not that of a busybody trying to mind somebody else's business. It was the thoughtful action of a public figure fulfilling a responsibility which had more or less been thrust upon him. While the idea of conducting the second World War against Hitler rather than against the German people may have occurred to England's best minds before Winchell cabled Chamberlain (the Allies having made the same distinction between the Kaiser and the German people at the beginning of the first World War), it does not seem unreasonable to suppose that Winchell's cablegram was shown to the British Prime Minister, that he read it, and that it was respectfully acknowledged.

AT THE MOMENT Winchell is unquestionably the country's most easily recognized non-layman, with the exception of Father Divine. The major and minor aspects of his existence are distinctive in almost every detail. Success and public acclaim have not made him a stuffed shirt. He has a gift for idiosyncrasy and is not self-conscious about it. He has two children and both are named after him; his son is Walter and his daughter is Walda. He goes to sleep around nine or ten in the morning and gets up in time to have breakfast while his children are having their supper. In the inside pocket of his coat he carries a loose-leaf booklet containing as many as twenty photographs of Walter and Walda, and in another pocket of his coat he carries a loaded automatic. In his overcoat pocket he carries a second loaded automatic. Although he has never been shot at and has been beaten up only twice, he is always expecting to be attacked.

The *Mirror* pays him $1,200 a week and fifty per cent of the money from the syndication of his column, amounting to some $750 a week, and he makes $5,000 a week more for his weekly radio talk. As Winchell has pointed out in his column, he pays around fifty per cent of his earnings to the state and federal governments. This leaves him a net income of approximately $185,000 a year, but he wears shoes until they have holes in the soles. He almost invariably wears a blue suit, a blue shirt, a blue tie, and a snap-brim gray felt hat. He has never played golf or tennis or badminton or ping-pong. He learned to swim only last summer. Until 1932 he had never seen a football game. He took up the rumba a few months ago and is now an enthusiast. Practically the only other form of relaxation his friends have actually seen him engage in is motoring. The New York Police Department has given him special permission to equip his sedan with a short-wave receiving set with which he picks up calls sent from Police Headquarters to police radio patrol cars.

This device forms the centre of Winchell's recreational activities. For hours, late at night, he cruises the streets of Manhattan accompanied by three or four friends and sometimes some celebrity like Brenda Frazier or John Gunther. The radio picks up police messages and Winchell drives hurriedly to the scene of action. The action almost invariably consists of policemen looking for a burglar. Once in a great while the car reaches the scene of a holdup or a murder in time for Winchell to get what he calls "a thrill."

This almost nightly routine is trying to Winchell's friends and the personnel in the sedan is constantly in process of replenishment. The celebrities seldom go more than once. Myrna Loy dropped off to sleep the time she went. It is possible to sleep in Winchell's sedan, for although the Police Department has given him permission to equip it with a siren, he is conscious of the disturbance the siren creates in the early hours of the morning and uses it only when he is going on what looks like a particularly exciting call. One night he was speeding up Central Park West on such a call with the siren on. As he approached the apartment house in which he lives, he shut it off. "I don't want to wake up Walter and Walda," he explained to his friends. He did not turn the siren on again until the car reached 110th Street.

WINCHELL HAS WRITTEN more words on the subject of friendship than any other modern gossip writer, but the people he calls his friends do not number more than seven or eight and most of these are new rather than old. "The best way to get along," he once wrote, "is never to forgive an enemy or forget a friend," but he has made up with at least one man who denounced him publicly and with another who punched him in the nose. Conversely, he has lost many friends by printing objectionable items about them in his column and, in defending this policy, has said, "I never lost a friend I wanted to keep." On several occasions when friends have remonstrated with Winchell for what they considered a betrayal of friendship, he has said, "I know—I'm just a son of a bitch." Some of his friends have accepted this explanation and have continued the friendship; others have regarded it as an inadequate excuse and have broken off with him.

Friends who have not broken off with Winchell are apt to assume a puzzled expression when asked to describe the subject of their attachment. "He's a remarkable guy!" one of them blurted recently, after considerable thought. "He's not a man—he's a column," said another, effusively. Nearly all seven or eight of Winchell's friends will tell you that they have been injured at one time or another by an item about themselves in Winchell's column. One friend had climbed his way up to a position of intimacy with Winchell which allowed him to dandle young Walter, Jr., on his knee. He was doing this when Winchell informed him that an embarrassing item about him would appear in the column the next day. "I'm just an s. o. b.," Winchell explained, using the abbreviated form, while Walter, Jr., innocently played with the friend's vest buttons. The friend started to protest and then nodded acquiescently. He has not broken off with Winchell. Winchell's journalistic integrity is such that his duty to his public almost always vanquishes whatever impulses of sentimentality he may have toward a friend when what he calls "a good item" is involved.

When a friend Winchell wanted to keep was killed in an automobile accident some years ago, Winchell published a eulogy which expresses his faith in the practical side of friendship, if not the sentimental side. "Shucks!" he wrote. "A guy like me cannot afford to lose a friend like Donald Freeman! He was one of the few fellers who liked me—and the second important magazine editor to hold out his hand and lift me into his heaven. When I was on a rag that the whole town belittled [the *Evening Graphic*] away back in 1927—almost a million years ago! Poor Don—he was motoring to see his mother and sister at Mt. Kisco and his car crashed, and now he's no more. I'll miss Donald Freeman. I'll miss that shrewd counsel he always gave me when I needed it . . ." The late Mr. Freeman was managing editor of *Vanity Fair*, which published some articles by Winchell in 1927 and 1928.

Even if no tempting bit of gossip develops to endanger a friendship with Winchell, he is apt to think of something which the friend will find objectionable and then print it. A friendship with Winchell rarely cools off gradually and reaches a condition of mutual indifference. If he feels that the relationship is losing its first flush of passionate admiration on both sides, he is inclined to take the initiative and strike while the friendship is warm. His phrase for what he does is "I let him have it." Winchell was once on friendly terms with Lucius Beebe, a fellow-columnist. Mr. Beebe never has found out what happened, but he thinks Winchell decided that some minor criticism of Winchell in another paper (not the *Herald Tribune*, on which Beebe works) and signed "L.B." was the trouble. Beebe doesn't know who this "L.B." was. In any case, Winchell printed a series of passionately unfriendly items about Beebe. Another time Winchell made up his mind that another very close friend, also a fellow-columnist, had become detached in his attitude toward their relationship. He let the friend have it. The friend happened to possess a thick skin as well as a philosophical attitude toward Winchell. He did not retaliate. Months went by and Winchell was mystified. Finally the two met in a night club and Winchell magnanimously offered to patch things up. "You've been swell," he told his friend. "I like the way you didn't knock me when you were sore at me."

The practical realism of Winchell's slant on friendship is present in his attitude toward casual human relationships as well. In conversation he likes either to talk about himself or to listen to something that will be of use to him in his column. Richard Rodgers, the composer, once had an awesome encounter with Winchell in Palm Beach. Rodgers was telling some companions on the beach about an investment he had made in a manufacturing concern when Winchell happened along and joined the group. Rodgers, who had never known Winchell very well, turned to him politely and began to sum up for Winchell's benefit the subject of the interrupted conversation. When Rodgers was halfway through, Winchell held up a hand with the palm close to Rodgers' face and said, "Never mind, never mind." Rodgers was nonplussed. "How do you mean?" he mumbled uncertainly. "It's no good for the column," Winchell explained, and walked on down the beach. Rodgers finished telling his friends about the investment he had made in the manufacturing concern, but, as he has remarked since, his heart wasn't in it.

When Winchell is talking about himself, he demands the unwavering attention of his listeners. James Cannon, a former sportswriter and one of his closest friends, was in a restaurant one night with his girl and was joined by Winchell. Winchell started to talk about himself. He talked for ten minutes without interruption. Cannon began to wonder if his girl would enjoy the evening more if she had another drink. Keeping his eyes fastened on Winchell's face so as to appear to be attentive, he said to his girl rapidly and out of the side of his mouth, "Honey, you want something?" Winchell stopped in the middle of a sentence and grabbed Cannon's arm. "Jimmy!" he said reproachfully. "You're not listening!"

Winchell believes, with some justification, that practically everybody reads his column everyday. If, in conversation, he wishes to refer to something he has written, he says, for example, "The item on the Brooklyn spy scare. Well, listen. Thursday night I called up Hoover," etc. A friend of Winchell's once admitted he had not seen the column on a certain Tuesday. Winchell wanted to know with sincere concern if the friend had been ill. Another time another friend returned to New York after a trip abroad. "Jeez, Walter," he said, "I sure did miss the column. I didn't see it for two whole weeks." "That's all right," said Winchell. "You can go over to the *Mirror* office tomorrow and look at the files."

A GREAT MANY people, meeting Winchell for the first time in some restaurant or night club, have exclaimed afterward, "Say, he isn't such a bad guy!" This is understandable. Winchell has a peculiarly bewitching personality. He has a lean face, full of alertness, with an expression of questing intelligence like a fox terrier's. His eyes are blue and hard. He is consistently lively and restless; it is impossible to imagine him in repose. He has an enormous nervous energy, and the experience of watching him burn it up extravagantly is stimulating and sometimes touching. What he says may be uninteresting in itself, but his voice and manner are charged with an inner excitement which is communicable. One of his phrase-making friends calls him "a thrilling bore." When he is not talking, he sits forward with his head raised unnaturally in an attitude of intense awareness. His heel is apt to beat quick time on the floor like a swing musician's, his gaze roves ceaselessly over the room, and his hands go on little fruitless expeditions over the tablecloth, up and down the lapels of his coat, in and out of his pockets. In a gathering of ten or twelve at a place like Lindy's or the Stork Club, he appears to listen to the general conversation with only half an ear, but that is enough. If something is mentioned that will make an item for his column, he will say, "I can use that," and will take out a pencil and notebook and write it down. Having responsibilities which far exceed those of the ordinary journalist, he usually carries a notebook instead of a sheaf of copy paper. He is left-handed, and this makes him look especially intense and painstaking when he is writing something down. At all times he gives the impression of being hungry, of being incessantly in want. In a man of such vitality this is an appealing quality. It is possible for a person to have an entirely unselfish impulse to give Winchell something.

Winchell has a certain integrity, as well as a number of codes all his own. He is as magnificently eccentric in thought as he is in action. He is ashamed of nothing he does. He uses his column at times as an instrument of personal revenge, but he does this as straightforwardly as a cave man would swing a club. "I let him have it three days later," he will say evenly, in recalling what he wrote about some person who had slighted or insulted him. He is naturally aggressive and is always on the offensive. There is nothing apologetic or cringing in his nature. He has a childlike pride in his success and he makes no bones about it. He is fully conscious of the damage a casual item in his column can do to persons he has no wish to hurt. He seems to be mellowing. It is a process like the aging of granite and is perceptible to people who have been acquainted with him for years. Lately he has been known to writhe in honest agony when the painful consequences of one of his own items are pointed out to him. To a small degree he literally suffers with those he wounds. His attitude on this curious state of affairs seems to be based on the belief that the appearance of such items in his column is as inexorable as fate. "What could I do?" he will say passionately. "It was a good item, wasn't it?" Thus he continues to print gossip about the marital relations of people who have not applied for divorce, he does not hesitate to hint at homosexual tendencies in local male residents, and he reports from time to time attempted suicides which otherwise would not be made public. He believes that if a thing is true, or even half true, it is material for his column, no matter how private or personal it may be. He makes one exception to this rule. He claims that he never knowingly reports on extra-marital relationships if he knows the marriage is a happy one. This is pointed to with pride by Winchell's greatest admirers as being generous and downright decent.

It is true that Winchell has seen married men and women dallying with persons of the opposite sex in night clubs and has withheld this information from the public. In such cases he has known, or has been told, that the marriage of the person concerned seems to be a happy one. If he knows, or has been told, that the marriage is pretty much on the rocks anyway, he feels justified in printing an item about the dallying. There are times, too, of course, when he just doesn't know, or hasn't been told, that the person concerned is married at all. "I can't be expected to know everything," he has said in defending himself when a harmful item of this sort has appeared in his column. Winchell's reason for suppressing items which he knows might upset a happy marriage seems to be purely personal. "I'm a married man," he says. "Where would I be if somebody printed something about my taking a dame out?"

Winchell makes an effort to check some items with certain more or less fortunate people to find out whether the item will do them any particular harm. These people are usually relatively prominent ones whom Winchell has met and has not taken a dislike to. Sometimes they are called to the telephone by Winchell's secretary, who introduces herself with understandable assurance and says something like "We understand you are sort of crazy about So-and-So. Have you any objection to our printing it?" If the celebrity has what seems to him a legitimate objection, he explains what it is to the secretary and the item is usually not published. This gives the person concerned a feeling of gratitude toward Winchell, coupled with a sensation of general insecurity. Sometimes, even if someone has asked that an item be suppressed, Winchell decides that the request is unreasonable and goes ahead and prints it anyway. Under these circumstances he is apt to accuse the person later of having tried to take advantage of his journalistic ethics. Winchell has been disillusioned many times in thus striving for accuracy and fair play. He cites numerous cases in which both parties to a disintegrating marriage have denied that they were going to separate and have persuaded him to withhold an item saying that they were, and then, without warning, have filed suit for divorce. "You try to play square with people like that," he complains bitterly, "and they lie to you. It burns me up."

Although Winchell prides himself on his accuracy, he fears libel suits and refuses to accept the financial responsibility for libellous items in his column or in his radio program. Some years ago an indignant citizen, a carpenter who, Winchell said in one radio talk, had sat on the end of a tree limb and sawed it off, sued him for libel, claiming injury to his professional reputation. Winchell was asked by his sponsors to share the attorneys' fees, court costs, and a small settlement granted the carpenter. Winchell refused to do this. He demanded that a clause be inserted in his radio contract providing that the sponsors defend and if necessary settle all libel suits which might result from his broadcasts. The sponsors gave in. Then Winchell asked the *Mirror* to put a similar clause in its contract with him. The *Mirror* agreed. Only three or four people since

then have worked themselves up to the point of indignation
achieved by the carpenter.

WINCHELL WRITES HIS column and prepares the script for
his Sunday-night radio broadcast at home. He employs two secretaries, who work in an office at the *Mirror*, which he rarely visits.
He keeps in touch with his secretaries mostly by telephone. His
column goes to press around six in the evening, soon after he wakes
up, and at that time he may make last-minute changes by telephone.
Then he starts on the column which will go to press the next evening. His mail, which is stupendous in size and variety of subject
matter, is sent to him by a messenger around 6 P.M., and he gets a
great part of his material from that. He spends several hours going
through it and selecting items which he will use in the column he
is preparing. He is practically incommunicado during this period
and his secretaries call him only on extremely urgent business. He
scribbles replies on letters he wishes to answer, then they are sent
back to the *Mirror* office and the secretaries work on them the next
day. He does not pay for items.

Winchell does not often go to night clubs any more, except for
the Stork Club. The Stork Club serves as an outside office. He arrives there almost every night around eleven o'clock, having prepared the major part of his column from his mail. He is usually at
the Stork Club until four or five in the morning. After that he drives
around in his car for a while and then goes home, finishes his column, sends it to the *Mirror* office, and goes to sleep around 9 or 10
A.M. While he is asleep, the column is set up in type and proofs are
sent to King Features Syndicate, the Hearst syndicate organization,
where it is edited for out-of-town papers. Most of the changes are
made in possibly libellous items. Winchell accepts this editing without protest. A lawyer employed by the *Mirror* also reads a proof and
makes changes or deletions which he thinks may prevent libel suits.

At the Stork Club, Winchell takes telephone calls from persons he wishes to speak to and receives personally some of the many people who are always wanting to see him, ranging from celebrities and politicians to chorus girls with a complaint about labor conditions. Sometimes he sees them in the Stork Club barbershop and sometimes at a table just inside the entrance. While he is there, the barbershop may be reached only by persons whom Winchell wishes to see. It is in a loft building next door and has two entrances— through the front of the loft building and through a passage from the club. In the club he orders captains of waiters about in a proprietary manner, and although there has been a rumor for years that he has a financial interest in the place, he says he hasn't. His friend Sherman Billingsley, proprietor of the Stork Club, says the same thing, adding that Winchell's frequent mentions of the place in his column have had much to do with its success and that he is grateful to Winchell and friendly with him. "That rat!" Mr. Billingsley exclaimed to some table companions recently when Winchell, in spite of their friendship and the fact that Billingsley is still married, linked his name with that of a musical-comedy star. But he managed to conquer his irritation before he saw Winchell later that evening.

When sitting at his table, surrounded by three or four friends, with perhaps one bodyguard in the offing, Winchell may listen to a reformer from Atlantic City who believes his efforts to clean up the resort will be successful only if he has Winchell's support, or to a hysterical admirer who tiptoes up and says, as if making a speech, "I want to shake your hand, Walter. I think you are a great man and America's most valuable citizen." Winchell shakes the hand. Such tributes are frequent. People sit at the Stork Club bar for hours waiting for Winchell to come in so that they may have the opportunity to compliment him. Many of them are sincere, and have no axes to grind. Occasionally the pleasure Winchell receives from the outbursts of enthusiasm is dulled by an afterthought which the admirer expresses as he bows himself away, such as "I'm a tenor. So-and-So's the name," or "I'm at Loew's State this week. Song and dance. So-and-So's the name." Winchell deplores sycophancy of this sort and never rewards such a person with a mention in his column, even a scandalous one. Then there are the bold ones at the Stork Club, such as the débutante who one night slipped over and grabbed Winchell's bread when he was eating his supper. "A bet," she said demurely, and skipped off. Late at night, a literary relationship between Winchell and Leonard Lyons, gossip man for the *Post*, is apt to be revealed. It is comparable to Conrad's paternal friendship for Stephen Crane. Lyons, who is Winchell's protégé, not a rival, the *Post* being an afternoon paper and his "Lyons Den" gossip column being also syndicated by Hearst, appears unobtrusively from somewhere and says, "Walter, may I check a gag ?" "O.K.," says the veteran. Lyons then recites an anecdote which he intends to pass on to his readers the next day. If it is old or sour, in Winchell's opinion, he advises Lyons to throw it out. If not, he says "O.K." a second time and Lyons goes happily back to his job of hopping from table to table, looking for gossip and gags.

WINCHELL HAS BEEN described in the New York press as "Broadway's Greatest Scribe," "Boyfriend of Broadway," "Little Boy Peep," and "The Bard of Broadway." He prefers the last. His friends sometimes refer to him as The Brain and The King. He is unable to decide which of these is his favorite. He is like a king in many ways but not in others. Edmund Burke once asserted that "kings are naturally lovers of low company." His general argument was that the status of a king is so much higher than that of the next greatest dignitary that the difference between the highest and the lowest non-kings is slight, from a king's point of view. A king, according to Burke, is irritated by the more consequential non-kings because they feel a responsibility for his behavior, frown at his vices, and try to make him go straight. He therefore consorts with lowly folk who flatter and amuse him. Although Winchell is sought after by many prominent people, he usually shakes them off an hour or two after midnight and hobnobs with mediocre newspaper reporters and undistinguished theatrical folk. He feels more at ease with them. On the other hand, kings, throughout history, have made a habit of putting aside their public personalities and going around incognito. Presidents have shown a similar weakness. Both Wilson and Coolidge used to slip away from the Secret Service men and take walks by themselves, revelling in anonymity. If Winchell has ever had such impulses, he has suppressed them resolutely. He seems to have no desire to get away from himself. When he goes to Miami Beach in the winter he always stops at the Roney Plaza, where everybody knows him. For years he spent his summer vacations hanging around night clubs and restaurants in town. Two summers ago, his wife having persuaded him to buy a house in Westchester, he discovered and endorsed the country, but in his summer home he sleeps all day in an air-conditioned room kept dark by lightproof blinds and usually comes to town every night whether he has to do so professionally or not. Occasionally, driving around after midnight with friends, he plays a sort of reverse version of the incognito game, the object being to see how soon he will be recognized in a public place off the beaten track. Almost anywhere in town he is recognized by somebody within a few minutes. If he is not, it is his custom to say to a bartender or waiter, "I'm Walter Winchell." In no time the place is in a hubbub, and Winchell leaves.

Once, not long ago, Winchell and a friend stopped for some coffee at an unpretentious roadside restaurant in lower Westchester. Nobody was in the place but a slatternly girl working behind the counter. She did not recognize Winchell and looked at him sourly, as if he were just a man buying a cup of coffee. Halfway

through his coffee, Winchell winked at his friend and then drew
the girl into conversation.

"Do you read the *Mirror?*" he asked.

"Nah," she said. "I take the *News.*"

"Ever listen to the radio?"

"Sometimes."

"Ever listen to Ben Bernie or Walter Winchell?"

"Nah," said the girl. "What I really like is Hawaiian music."

Winchell and his friend left the place without further talk. As
they got into the car, Winchell said, "Can you imagine that dumb
biddy?" Later, as they drove along, Winchell suddenly said "Huh!"
The friend asked him what he meant by this. "I was just thinking
about that dumb biddy," Winchell said. "Can you imagine it?"

The 1950s

THE BLOWING OF THE TOP OF
PETER ROGER OBOE

THE ARMED SERVICES Committee of the United States Senate digs deeper and deeper into the matter of inter-service rivalry, and I am beginning to feel that eventually it will get all the way down to me. Many people who are still around know what I did in the Second World War and remember it distinctly—people in the Navy, the Air Force, and the Army, and some who were then of Cabinet rank. One or another of them, I feel sure, is bound to let that cat out of that bag at any moment. If this occurs, my fate will once again be in the laps of my superiors. I have had a good many night thoughts about how the thing might go when, having accepted my subpoena, I commence to testify. It might, for example, go like this:

"What is your profession in civilian life?"

"A writer. Mostly journalism, sir."

"Your age?"

"Fifty-three."

"And where were you on the night of May 18, 1945?"

"In the Marianas, on the island of Guam."

"In what capacity?"

"I was Chief Press Censor and Chief Public Relations Officer on the staff of General Curtis E. LeMay, commander of the

Twenty-first Bomber Command of the Twentieth Air Force of the Army Air Forces of the United States. We were bombing the—we were bombing the cities of Japan."

"General LeMay subsequently commanded the Strategic Air Forces and is now Vice Chief of Staff of the Air Force?"

"Yes, sir."

"What was your rank when you were on Guam?"

"Lieutenant Colonel."

"The insigne for that rank is one silver leaf?"

"That is correct."

"Now, to your knowledge, was Admiral Chester W. Nimitz also on Guam at that time?"

"Yes, sir. He lived in a new house, with a flower garden, at one end of the island, and I lived at the other end, in an old tent with six-foot lizards under the floor boards that used to—"

"Never mind that. Now, in what capacity was Admiral Nimitz on Guam?"

"He was Commander-in-Chief of the Pacific Fleet and Commander-in-Chief of the Pacific Ocean Areas."

"In other words, in addition to being commander of the fleet itself he was also the theatre commander in the area in which Guam is situated?"

"Exactly."

"His rank?"

"He was an Admiral of the Fleet, which corresponds to a General of the Army. Like MacArthur and Eisenhower."

"You are referring to the former Supreme Allied Commander in the Southwest Pacific—later also Korea—and to the present Commander-in-Chief of the Armed Forces, the President of the United States?"

"Yes, sir."

"To go back to Admiral Nimitz, what was the insigne of his rank at that time?"

"Five stars."

"Now, on the night in question did you send an official radiogram to the Pentagon in which reference was made to Admiral Nimitz?"

"Yes, sir."

"In fact, you made an accusation against him in that message?"

"Yes, sir."

"Of what did you accuse him?"

"Of high treason."

"Would you please repeat that?"

"I accused him of high treason."

"You understand that you are under oath?"

"I do."

"On what ground did you accuse Admiral Nimitz of high treason?"

"On the ground that he was giving aid and comfort to the enemy."

"By what means?"

"By a course of action which, it seemed to me, would prolong the war against Japan and result in having the Navy, rather than the B-29s of the Twenty-first Bomber Command of the Twentieth Air Force, appear to have been largely responsible for bringing that war to a conclusion."

"Are you still a lieutenant colonel?"

"No, sir."

"Were you court-martialled?"

"No, sir."

"Was Admiral Nimitz?"

"No, sir."

"Were you dishonorably discharged?"

"No, sir."

"Were you discharged on medical grounds, either physical or mental?"

"No, sir."

"Were you reprimanded?"

"No, sir."

"Were you, by any chance, commended?"

"Not for having sent the message about Nimitz—no, sir."

"But you had received a commendation prior to this?"

"Yes, sir."

"For what?"

"For superior performance in conducting the public relations of the Twenty-first Bomber Command and helping it get along with the Navy in the Pacific Ocean Areas."

"By whom were you commended for that?"

"By General H. H. Arnold, C. G., U.S.A.A.F.; C. G., Twentieth A.F.; and member J.C.S."

"Just answer the questions, please."

"Yes, sir."

"Did you receive a decoration?"

"No, sir. I was informed by LeMay some years afterward that he had recommended me for the Legion of Merit two days before the night in question but that the recommendation was disapproved by higher headquarters, on the ground that it might look as if I were being decorated for accusing Nimitz of high treason."

"On the other hand, Admiral Nimitz received a number of decorations for his part in winning the war against Japan, did he not?"

"Yes, sir. The Navy Distinguished Service Medal (four times); the Army Distinguished Service Medal; the Navy Cross; the Philippine Medal of Valor; Knight Grand Cross of the Order of the Bath, from Great Britain; Knight Grand Cross of the Order of Orange-Nassau, from the Netherlands; Grand Officer of the National Order of the Legion of Honor, from France; the Grand Cross of the Order of the Crown and the Croix de Guerre with Palms, from Belgium; and the Grand Cross of the Order of the Liberator, from Argentina."

"After you sent this message, were you required to apologize to Admiral Nimitz, or to retract your accusation?"

"No, sir."

"Did you remain on active duty after you sent this message?"

"Yes, sir."

"Where?"

"In the Pentagon."

"The fact that you had sent this message, then, at least caused you to be relieved and recalled to Washington?"

"I'm afraid not, sir."

"Can you explain that?"

"Yes, sir. Some weeks earlier, you see, Norstad, on a trip to Guam from Washington, had arranged with LeMay for me to return there for temporary duty. He wanted me to work for a while on the public-relations staff of the Twentieth Air Force in the Pentagon, because he thought my overseas experience would be beneficial to the other members of that staff, many of whom had not got beyond Alexandria, Virginia. My replacement had already arrived, my orders had been cut, and I had received a 1-B air priority from the Naval Air Transport Service at Nimitz's headquarters. But LeMay ordered me to stay where I was until the series of fire-bomb raids on the Japanese cities had been completed. We were nearing the end of that particular series on the night in question."

"When you say 'Norstad,' you are referring to the present four-star General Lauris Norstad, now Supreme Allied Commander Europe and Commander-in-Chief, U.S. European Command, or head of the North Atlantic Treaty Organization forces?"

"Yes, sir. You see, I was sort of passed from one Air Forces general to another all through that war; they all called me Mac, and I still think of them on a somewhat familiar basis. I even feel that way about generals I never met, but about whom I had heard a great deal."

"All right. What was General Norstad's status and rank at that time?"

"Chief of Staff of the Twentieth Air Force under Ha—under General Arnold. Norstad wore only one star at that time."

"After the message had been sent, General LeMay no longer wished you to remain on his staff?"

"All he said was, 'So long, Mac,' but I'm sure he wouldn't have wanted me to stay. It would have been awkward all around. I would have had to go on attending press conferences presided over by Nimitz. But anyway the Pentagon had ordered LeMay to put my existing orders into immediate effect. The Pentagon did that soon after my message about Nimitz had been circulated in the Pentagon and on Guam."

"It was circulated on Guam? Did Admiral Nimitz see it?"

"First thing in the morning, sir. It was delivered to his desk. In order to insure close coördination with the Navy, duplicates of all our administrative messages were automatically teletyped into Nimitz's headquarters."

"You would call this an administrative message?"

"Well, sir, it was not an operational message."

"By what priority did you return to Washington, and by what means?"

"I-A, XATS."

"What did you say?"

"The Naval Air Transport Service at Nimitz's headquarters changed my priority from I-B to I-A after I had accused Nimitz of high treason."

"And you worked on General Norstad's staff after your return to the Pentagon?"

"Yes, sir—that is, after the completion of the thirty-day leave an officer returning from extended overseas duty customarily received in those days."

"How long had you been overseas?"

"Seventeen months in India, Burma, and China, and six months in the Marianas."

"Where did you spend your leave?"

"In New York. I got a small suite at the Ritz, and, in the daytime, wrote four long articles for *The New Yorker* under the heading 'A Reporter with the B-29s.'"

"You had been on the staff of that magazine prior to the war?"

"Yes, sir."

"And in these articles you told about having accused Admiral Nimitz of high treason in an official rediogram to the Pentagon?"

"No, sir."

"Why not?"

"Norstad had said when I reported to him after my fast trip home from Guam, 'Now, Mac, as far as we're concerned, this thing never happened. It's forgotten. We have only one request to make of you. That is that you keep the whole matter under your hat. Top secret.'"

"And it has never been made public until now?"

"No, sir. However, the message was not classified as 'Top Secret' by me. I only classified it as 'Secret.'"

"How did you do that?"

"By stamping it 'Secret' with my 'Secret' stamp."

"I see. Now, after your leave was over, how long did you remain on Norstad's staff?"

"Less than two months. Even without Hiroshima, the war was about over, I had enough points to get out, and I asked Norstad if I could apply for separation. He said I could."

"Did he at that time or at any other time discuss with you the message about Nimitz?"

"He never did. When I left for the separation center at Atlantic City, he shook hands with me and said, 'Mac, good luck. You know, Mac, you're a guy who would be willing to die for a principle, but I hope you'll never have to.' I was more sentimental then than I am now, sir, and I wrote that down in a little notebook I used to carry in the breast pocket of my Eisenhower jacket. It also contained notes I had jotted down from time to time on Guam concerning what I had been told were the Navy's efforts to obstruct the B-29 program out there."

"You still have this notebook?"

"No, sir. I finally threw it away."

"I see. Now, is this message of yours on file in the Pentagon?"

"It should be, sir. I saw a copy of it after my return to Washington."

"You do not possess a copy of it now?"

"No, sir. I wanted one, for sentiment's sake, but it had been reclassified as 'Top Secret,' and I was told recently that all copies of it are now sealed and labelled 'Not to be opened except by express permission and in the presence of the Chief of Staff of the Air Force.'"

"Now, did any individual collaborate with you in the composition of this message?"

"No, sir. I typed it out myself in my public-relations tent, and my two sergeants simply delivered it to the message center in takes, or short installments. Actually, I didn't let it start going until a little after 2 A.M. Guam time."

"Was there some special reason for its being sent at that hour?"

"Yes, sir. That meant it would begin to come snuffling out of the teletype machines in the Pentagon around 8 A.M. Eastern Daylight time, when the generals and admirals were coming in for the day's work."

"Did any officer besides yourself approve the message for transmission before it was sent?"

"No, sir."

"Approximately how long was the message?"

"I believe it was a little over three thousand words."

"Now, can you explain to us exactly how you came to make

this accusation against Admiral Nimitz, on what you based your accusation, and how you managed to send a message of such inordinate length by official radiogram to the Pentagon from Guam without anybody's having seen it except your two sergeants and the teletype operators in the message center?"

"It's a long story, sir, and somewhat complicated."

"Suppose you try to tell it in your own words."

"I have tried to do that on a number of occasions, sir, but have never been able to get the whole story out of my mouth or down on paper. I have here in my hand now, sir, the beginning of a manuscript for a book I started to write on the subject. Perhaps I might be permitted to read this to you? I'm afraid it is largely about me, however."

"Do you regard it as pertinent to this inquiry?"

"Yes, sir. Because I don't think anybody but me would have accused Admiral Nimitz of high treason, and in order to understand how that came about, I feel that you have to understand me."

"Well, we only have a week or so set aside for your testimony, but we'll see how this manuscript of yours goes. Proceed."

"Thank you, sir. This is how it goes:

"'IT ALL COMES back so clear. If it hadn't been for the existence of Peter Roger Oboe, I suppose I would find it embarrassing, and perhaps even painful, to attempt to explain in pitiless detail the climax of my unusual career as an officer in the Army Air Forces in the Second World War, and what led up to it. Peter Roger Oboe was what I was called all through that war by higher headquarters. It was, of course, Army alphabetical code for P.R.O. or Public Relations Officer. To me, though, it was more of a pseudonym or an alias—a label for a new and weird identity that, more or less against my inclinations, I had been persuaded to assume. "Yount from Arnold for Peter Roger Oboe," said the teletype messages that came in 1942 to the headquarters of the Flying Training Command, in

Fort Worth, Texas, in command of Major General Barton K. Yount. They were immediately brought to my desk. They were for me. I was a captain at that time. "Alexander from George for Peter Roger Oboe," said the ones that came in 1943 to General Edward H. Alexander at the headquarters of the India-China Wing of the Air Transport Command, in Assam, from the headquarters of General Harold L. George, in Washington. In New Delhi and Calcutta, they said, "Stratemeyer from Arnold for Peter Roger Oboe," and sometimes, when I was Acting Chief Public Relations Officer at General Stilwell's Rear Echelon Headquarters, they said, "Stilwell from Marshall for Peter Roger Oboe." By that time, I was a major, but more bewildered than I had been when I was a captain. In Ceylon, they said, "Mountbatten from C.C.S."—that is, Combined Chiefs of Staff—"for Wedemeyer info Stratemeyer for Peter Roger Oboe." And, finally, in the Marianas, when I was a lieutenant colonel, they said, "Arnold to LeMay from Norstad for Peter Roger Oboe info Nimitz." As the war progressed, I felt less and less like myself and more and more like Peter Roger Oboe. To this day, when I think of all that happened it is as if these things had befallen not me but Peter Roger Oboe. This story is more Peter Roger Oboe's story than mine. In a sense, I am doing it for him.

"'I would never have become an officer in the Army Air Forces in the first place if a flying major general I had never heard of hadn't read and agreed with some paragraphs I wrote in 1942 for *The New Yorker,* on whose staff I had been peacefully working with a noiseless typewriter since 1933. They appeared on the first page of the magazine, under the general heading "The Talk of the Town" and the subheading "Notes and Comment," and this general, sitting in a fresh headquarters in Fort Worth, Texas, read them. He sent emissaries to ask me to accept a commission as a captain and help the Air Forces with its public-relations problems. Unable to think how to refuse, I accepted. It probably goes to show that a writer ought to be careful of what he writes, especially in wartime.

" 'The paragraphs that got me into the Army Air Forces are more readily understood if one returns in one's memory, or in history, to those first five or six months after the Japanese bombed Pearl Harbor, on December 7, 1941—specifically, to a day in May of 1942 when the whole country and the people in it were uplifted and made to feel that we were getting somewhere in the war against Japan. That was the day the news at last came out that Brigadier General James H. Doolittle and a handful of Army fliers, taking off from naval carriers, had bombed Tokyo. For weeks there had been rumors about it, and the Japanese radio had broadcast its version of what had happened, but nothing conclusive had been released by the government in Washington. Reading the papers that day, I was elated by the news, like everybody else, but I resented the manner in which that news had been given out. It was apparent that the release of the news had been held up for a while for security reasons, but it was also apparent that it had been held up a while longer for reasons that had nothing to do with security. I wrote and rewrote my reflections on the subject (using the editorial "we") until I had composed the following paragraphs—the ones the flying major general in Texas read:

" 'We were interested, as was everybody else, we imagine, to read in the newspapers last week that it was Jimmy Doolittle, the old speed flier, who led the air raid on Japan last month and that there he was, right in the White House, receiving a medal for it at what the newspapers called "a surprise ceremony." Even Mrs. Doolittle didn't know why she had been summoned to Washington, according to the *Times*. She thought her husband was in the battle zone until the moment she walked into the White House, after having been flown from the Coast in an Army plane, and saw him standing there, well and safe. Then came the decoration of the hero, then the newspaper photographers and the newsreel men, and finally the release of the news that everybody wanted desperately to hear. As a student of the drama, we found the whole performance somewhat weird and overdrawn, and as a citizen of a democracy at war, we were not grateful for having been informed in this particular manner that the bombing of Japan had been a military success and that none of our fliers had lost their lives. [It was much later on that the public was told that many of the fliers were lost in the Doolittle raid, some of them who made forced landings in Japanese-occupied China having been put to death after being tortured as far as torturing can go.] We felt enthusiastic, but groggy—as if, on coming into a theatre to see a new play, we had been asked to applaud the actors vigorously and then to sit ourself down and find out what they had done to deserve our adulation. We suspect the rest of the public felt pretty much the same way. Hooray, however, for Doolittle.

" 'To go right on with this subject, it is our guess that the aforementioned element of weirdness at that ceremony had its origin in an activity (or state of mind) known as public relations. This is a profession (or viewpoint) which has in relatively recent years come to occupy a position directly between the individual or institution it represents and the press. In other words, if you have something to say to the public through the press, you employ a public-relations man (or a public-relations viewpoint) to tell you *how* you should say what you have to say. The public-relations principle may be used both as a means of minimizing what you have to say and as a means of magnifying, or exploiting, it. In the present instance we are concerned with the latter use.

" 'The usual public-relations method of magnifying or exploiting news is based on the more or less well-meant assumption that the public will appreciate a fact more fully if the fact is somehow dramatized, or dressed up, preferably with photographs. Since the drama of the fact or event itself is not always tangible, or may lie in the distant or recent past, the public-relations principle is to set some kind of stage, arrange some kind of stunt or spectacle, or at least to persuade somebody to do something in front of a camera which is not necessarily logical or attractive but is flashy. Recent examples of public-relations activity in the government were the newspaper photographs and newsreels of Leon Henderson riding a bicycle with his secretary on the handlebars. The object of this stunt was to get the idea across to the public that riding bicycles would save automobile tires. As you can see, public relations, on the whole, is a strange and awesome profession (or point of view) because, while it seeks to woo or hypnotize the public, it frequently succeeds only in arousing suspicion or resentment in the public mind. When you come right down to it, the public-relations profession is not as realistic or as practical as it thinks it is. It is a good deal like the profession of the circus press agent or of the old-fashioned medicine man and is therefore likely to be either cynical or romantic in its attitude toward the public.

" 'Now, as a student of public relations (we can also ice-skate), it is our opinion that the "surprise ceremony" at the White House was an expression of the romantic phase of the public-relations principle as it appears in the activities of the government today. The drama of the bombing of Japan was the bombing of Japan, just as the drama of the rubber shortage was, and is, the rubber shortage. Yet the public-relations principle demanded some kind of setting for the presentation of the news of the drama of the bombing of Japan because (1) the bombing had occurred a month ago, and (2) there were, as yet, no photographs of it. The logical (or non-public-relations) thing to do would have been for the government to announce in a straightforward manner the news that General Doolittle had brought, or had radioed ahead, and then decorate him appropriately when he got to Washington. This the public would have understood and appreciated. But the public-relations principle demanded the manufacturing of some drama and the setting of a stage, with the result, we think, that the public appreciation of General Doolittle's achievement was minimized rather than magnified. We make this assertion on two counts: (1) The public resented the fact that the news of the bombing of Japan was withheld for even one moment after military censorship had been lifted, and (2) the public considered it incongruous that a hero should have been awarded the Congressional Medal of Honor *before* the people had been told what it was he had done to deserve that particular medal. For all these and a good many other reasons, it seems to us that it would be a delightful thing if the government would make up its mind to quit using such methods in its relations with the public and simply outlaw the public-relations principle as an instrument of national policy.

" 'One evening, a few days after those paragraphs on Army public relations were published, I dropped in backstage at the Shubert Theatre to see Burgess Meredith, who was playing Marchbanks in Katharine Cornell's revival of Shaw's "Candida." ' "

"Now, just a minute! Do we have to know what shows you went to see? And is it necessary to bring stage people into this?"

"Well, sir, it was Burgess Meredith who was instrumental in getting me into the Army Air Forces, and if I hadn't got into the Army Air Forces, I would never have accused Nimitz of high treason."

"Very well, but we can't go on like this forever. Only a few more days, and we must get back to Admiral Nimitz. Proceed."

" 'The play "Candida" was being put on for the benefit of the Army Emergency Fund and the Navy Relief Society. Meredith, who had shortly before been drafted, was a private in the Air

Forces and was assigned to the public-relations section of the headquarters of the Flying Training Command, newly set up in Fort Worth, Texas. For the benefit performances, the Air Forces had ordered him to play Marchbanks. I had enjoyed the show, and I went backstage to say hello to Meredith, who was an old friend and a fellow-habitué of the Artists & Writers Restaurant, "21," Tim Costello's saloon, on Third Avenue, and other dives, high and low. "Stick around," he said after shaking hands with me in the crowded dressing room. "I've got to talk to you." His manner was oddly brisk. When the dressing room cleared out, he said, "Say, Mac, who wrote that editorial in *The New Yorker* about Army public relations?"

" " "Why?" I asked.

" " "General Yount wants whoever wrote it," he said. "He called me up about it yesterday."

" " "Who the hell is General Yount?"

" " "My God, he's Major General Barton K. Yount, commanding the Army Air Forces Flying Training Command! Don't you know anything?"

" " "I know what he can do," I said belligerently, "if he thinks he can stop us saying what we please, war or no war. What is a Flying Training Command, anyway? Is it always on the go, or what? Furthermore—"

" " "Listen! Yount *likes* the piece about Army public relations. He *agrees* with it. Did you write it? Old Yount reads *The New Yorker* all the time, and he's aware of the fact that I know you guys. He called up and asked me to find out about it."

" " "I wrote it."

" " "Well, you're a captain, then, or maybe a major. He isn't sure he can get another major on a direct commission right now, because of his table of organization, but you can go in as a captain and it won't be long before you're a major."

" 'I could think of nothing to say to this.

" ' "He believes," Meredith continued, "that somebody who feels the way you do about public relations is just the man he wants in his public-relations section down there."

" ' "Down where?"

" ' "In Fort Worth, Texas, for the love of God! That's where the headquarters of the Flying Training Command is! I'll call him tomorrow morning. There'll probably be a guy—a major—who'll be in touch with you. He's up here to get a staff together for Yount's P.R.O. section. Let's go have a drink.'

" 'I said I was tired and was going straight home, and I did. I wanted to try to do some constructive thinking, and although my home was unaccustomed to having me do that in it, I couldn't think of anywhere else to go. As a grass widower, I lived in the former drawing room of what had been a handsome mansion, at No. 8 East Eighty-third Street, just off Fifth Avenue. It had a kitchen and bath—was an apartment, actually—but what I admired about it was the enormous room, panelled in dark mahogany, richly furnished with pieces bought at antique shops or charged at Lord & Taylor: a double-size studio bed at one end and a desk at the other; a big, deep divan and some large, comfortable chintz-covered chairs; a bar in a corner; a great open fireplace; long, wide louver-shuttered windows across the front, facing the street. The rent was eighty-five dollars a month. I was extravagant in those days. I had a cheerful full-time Negro cook-butler-valet, who seemed contented with his salary of fifteen dollars a week and who slept in a room in the basement when he wasn't busy cooking or handing around cocktails and canapés or taking care of my clothes.

" 'Before I entered the Army, my way of life was so different in every respect from my way of life afterward, and now, that I find the facts hard to believe, even though I can remember every moment of those prewar years with clarity and accuracy whenever I want to. Most of the time I don't want to. I was thirty-seven years old in 1942, and acted, I'm afraid, as if I were still in my late teens.

I have been told that I also looked younger than I was; if that is so, it suggests that the climate of the primrose path is salubrious as far as the human exterior is concerned. I'm not positive that the explanation of the over-all nature of my prewar existence could be set down as a shifty disinclination to grow up, but I wouldn't be surprised if it could. Besides my apartment and my cook-butler-valet. I had an olive-green 1931 Pierce-Arrow convertible touring car, eight cylinders, with headlights on the fenders. No other make of car had headlights on the fenders in those days. It had cost five hundred dollars in 1938 and looked as if it had cost five thousand and had been in the family for years. It drank two quarts of heavy oil and slupped up ten gallons of gas before it even began to get into its stride. It was magnificent in every way. So was I—or at least in some ways. I charged my suits and topcoats and overcoats and shirts and hats and gloves and shorts and shoes and socks and neckties at Brooks Brothers and De Pinna. I had the suits custom-made at one or the other, because, with the unerring sense of style of a Scotch-Irishman born in Charlotte, North Carolina, the son of an impecunious Presbyterian preacher, I felt that Brooks's ready-made suits needed more padding in the shoulders and De Pinna's less. In addition to other things for my wardrobe, the Brooks tailors had been successful in putting together a Norfolk jacket for me to wear on country weekends or at "21" for Sunday supper. That's the way things were going with me in 1941 and the first part of 1942.

"'Reflecting on what Meredith had said to me in his dressing room, I told myself that I was not likely to be drafted, because of my age and the fact that I had two dependents. I also realized that the only uniform I'd ever worn was the uniform of the Boy Scouts of America. In that organization, I had never been able to get farther than second class and had earned only one merit badge. That was for proficiency in taxidermy, and had entailed the skinning, stuffing, and mounting of one chipmunk, trapped in Rock

Creek Park, in Washington, in the winter of 1917. I also took stock of my physical and mental attributes. My formerly active ulcer was precariously dormant in a stomach whose normal functioning was marred by a constitutional mix-up called a hiatal hernia. A medical dictionary had told me that this ugly medical term meant there was a protrusion in the upper part of the digestive organ—a condition that tends to form two stomachs where there should be only one—and my symptoms had suggested over and over again that the one stomach hardly ever knew what the other was doing. In spite of all that, I was extraordinarily healthy most of the time, and usually ate and drank what appealed to me. I had, to be sure, gone through what in those frivolous days was called a nervous breakdown. I had spent three months at the Austen Riggs Center, in Stockbridge, Massachusetts (which a surprising number of friends of mine, including my employer, H. W. Ross, had also visited, for shorter or longer periods), and I had frequently found it necessary, both before and after that, to creep away from New York for long weekends at a mildly therapeutic resthouse in the Catskills called Dr. Ford's. At Dr. Ford's, as at Riggs, it was the policy not to take in alcoholics or deeply disturbed people but only tired, nervous people.

" 'Before I went to Riggs, I was trying to get started on an ambitious writing project, had been unable to put anything on paper, was not sleeping, and was drinking too much, and Ross suggested I try Riggs. I did, and had a pleasant interlude, writing some thirty thousand publishable words in two months and learning a fair amount, at the same time, about myself. The psychiatrists there felt that my effort to stay detached about my subject had been the immediate cause of my breakdown, but they left no doubt in my mind that I (like a number of my friends in New York) had an unstable disposition, and that this was aggravated by my habit of trying to be both highly moral and lowly libertine, tightly repressed and loosely rambunctious. I was privately convinced by the time I returned to New York that the trouble in my head was along the lines of the trouble in my stomach—two heads instead of one, with one of them Presbyterian and the other King Henry VIII— and that I wouldn't get any better than I then felt (and I then felt fine) unless I became a Presbyterian clergyman, as most of my male ancestors had done. I thought it would be impractical for me to go back and finish high school at my age, then go through college, and then go through a seminary and into a pulpit. Even if I did, and got into the pulpit, it would be unrewarding in every way, I thought, because I was incapable of making a public speech. I had keeled over backward in a dead faint the one time I had tried to, at a small banquet at the Waldorf. I was inclined to stick with journalism. Ross said I wasn't cut out to be a preacher; he claimed the only trouble with me was that I was under the impression that all money had to be spent before dawn or it would be called in, and that I believed all women had to be courted as a result of pretty much the same fallacious reasoning. Thinking about all these things, I fell asleep long after I got home that night.

" "The major that Meredith had mentioned telephoned me in the afternoon and asked me to lunch with him at "21" the following day—one way or another, everything in my life seemed to be settled at "21" in that era—and a few days afterward I took my physical and mental examinations down at Whitehall. I had confessed the facts about my disabilities to the major, and he had said, grandly, that it would be best not to mention them to the doctors. Consequently, when the medical military man asked me about stomach trouble, I said I had a certain amount of it occasionally, and he solemnly thumped me along my way. The Army psychiatrist, on learning I had been married and divorced three times, asked if I was capable of learning by experience, and I coldly told him that I was. He O.K.'d me. A few weeks later, I received my War Department telegram, took it to Brooks Brothers, got into the ready-made uniform they sold me, and walked out onto Madison

Avenue on a sunny afternoon looking, I hoped, like a captain in the Army Air Forces.'"

"WELL?"

"Well what, sir?"

"What happened then?"

"That's as far as I got in writing this book, sir."

"Good. Perhaps we can now proceed to Guam?"

"Well, sir, I didn't get to Guam until a long time after the day I put on my captain's uniform at Brooks. There were the six months in Texas and then the seventeen months in India, Burma, and China."

"Do we need to go into all that here?"

"I don't think so, sir, except—"

"What?"

"Perhaps I would lay myself open to a charge of covering up evidence if I failed to tell you about the time I nearly got all the generals killed."

"What generals? Where?"

"Generals Stilwell, Stratemeyer, George, Hardin, Alexander, and two others, whose names have slipped my mind. In India."

"And you tried to kill them?"

"Well, I told the Japs they were flying over the Hump to China, all in one airplane, and the Japs thus had every opportunity to send fighters up from their fields in Burma—which were directly under the air route we used—and shoot the plane down with all the generals in it."

"Were you court-martialled for this offense?"

"No, sir."

"Were you—Oh, never mind! Since this incident appears to indicate a tendency on your part to show little respect for rank—generals as well as admirals—perhaps you'd better tell us about it."

"I was then a captain, sir, and was on the staff of General

Alexander, commander of the India-China Wing of the Air Transport Command. Our headquarters was in Chabua, in Assam, in the northernmost part of eastern India, where our planes took off for the flights over the Hump to China. The heat was on, the tonnage flown to China was going to be increased ten times over in order to help Chiang Kai-shek fight the Japs, and all the generals had turned up for a conference—a conference that started in Chabua and was to be continued in Kunming and Chung-king. I was supposed to fly over to Kunming that day in a B-24 with the generals, and so were Eric Sevareid and a couple of other war correspondents, but when we were about to step into the plane after the generals, Alec—I mean General Alexander—decided it would be too crowded, so he turned to me and said, 'Mac, call Jorhat'—that was one of our other airfields—and tell them you are speaking for me. Tell them to get another B-24 here at once. You and the boys can come over in that.' Although I'd never used it, I knew that the communications shack at the Chabua airfield had a telephone on which Jorhat could be communicated with, so I went in there and told the sergeant I was speaking for General Alexander and wanted to get in touch with the operations officer at Jorhat. He twiddled some dials and handed me the phone, and I told the operations officer at Jorhat that I was speaking for General Alexander and that I had to have a B-24 right away to fly the Hump. When he seemed to hesitate, I said we were supposed to have flown over with Stilwell and Stratemeyer and the other generals, but Alexander had decided we needed a second plane, and we had to have it right away, because the generals were just taking off. The operations officer kind of whispered 'Wilco,' and I handed the phone back to the sergeant, whose mouth was wide open. Then I learned from the sergeant that this wasn't an ordinary telephone but a radiotelephone, and that one was supposed to speak in code when talking over it, because the Japs monitored it all the time. Only then did it dawn on me that I had told the Japs the generals had just taken off, and that the Japs had plenty of time to send up fighters and shoot them down. For some reason, the Japs did nothing about it, and nobody but the sergeant and the operations officer at Jorhat knew of my sin, and neither of them ever told anybody. After the conference was over, it was decided that General Stratemeyer would take over command of all the Army Air Forces in India, Burma, and China, and he arranged with General Alexander for me to become his Chief Public Relations Officer, and I was then promoted to major."

"I see. Now, what did you do to earn your promotion to lieutenant colonel and your assignment to the job in the Marianas?"

"Well, I had malaria four times and lost forty pounds, and General Stratemeyer thought I ought to go home on temporary duty. He also thought that if I went to Washington, I could explain to the top Air Forces people there some of the public-relations problems in India, such as the problem of British censorship. The British, you see, were responsible for what was called 'the security of the area,' and therefore were able to censor or delay, presumably for security reasons, all news that went out of India. In those early days out there, whenever our Air Forces did anything—such as dropping supplies to British-Indian troops that had got themselves cut off by the Japs in Burma—the British would censor it or delay it, because, they said, it would endanger the security of the area. Actually, of course, the ones who did that didn't want the American forces to get any credit. We blamed No One Hundredths for this situation, because he seemed to be anti-American, and—"

"Wait! Who?"

"I beg your pardon, sir. I was referring to Mountbatten's public-relations man, who came from an old Anglo-Norman family—Air Vice Marshal Sir Philip Joubert de la Ferté. We used to call him Air Vice Marshal Sir Philip Joubert de la Ferté and No One Hundredths."

"Kindly complete your explanation of your promotion from major to lieutenant colonel."

"Stratemeyer thought somebody in the Pentagon might be able to do something about the British censorship in India if I explained the situation personally. He said that he would like to promote me before I left but that his table of organization wouldn't hold another lieutenant colonel—especially a lieutenant colonel of public relations. He said, however, that if I could get Hq. A.A.F.—Headquarters Army Air Forces, in Washington—to let me come home, he thought he could put the promotion through while I was there on temporary duty, because that wouldn't interfere with his table of organization in India, Burma, and China. So I wired my chief in Washington—Colonel Rex Smith, Arnold's public-relations man—suggesting that I return for conferences having to do with public-relations matters in India, and this was approved, and I flew to Washington. There, Colonel Smith said that I wouldn't be returning to India—that something hot was coming up in the Pacific, and that I would be sent there after I got my health back. Before I was formally transferred from Stratemeyer's command to the Headquarters Staff of the Army Air Forces, in the Pentagon, Stratemeyer put my promotion through. I found an efficient officer—a former public-relations man in an industrial concern—to take the job in India. On learning that I was going out to the Pacific with the B-29s, Stratemeyer wrote me a personal note saying, 'Mac, out here you had the Chinese, the Indians, and the British, and out there you'll have the Navy, the Navy, and the Navy.' This turned out to be true. The Navy, you see, was responsible for the security of the area out there."

"Just what was it that was coming up in the Pacific?"

"Well, sir, this was the summer of 1944, and the Navy, the Marines, and the Army in the Pacific Ocean Areas—all under Nimitz—were taking the Marianas, which meant that B-29s could be based there. From the Marianas, the B-29s could bomb Tokyo, for the first time since the Doolittle raid. The first raid on Tokyo by B-29s was to be made from bases on Saipan, and the fact that B-29s were to be based in the Marianas was to be top secret until the first raid on Tokyo had been accomplished."

"Admiral Nimitz, then, was to direct these air operations, as the over-all commander in the Pacific Ocean Areas?"

"No, sir. That may have been what made the Navy sore about the B-29 operation. The B-29s were to be based in areas under Nimitz's command, but they were to be commanded direct from Washington by Arnold. It was the beginning of a separate Air Force. The B-29 was a new airplane, twice as big as the B-17s that had bombed Germany, and was capable of flying thirty-five hundred miles with a four-ton bomb load—a sixteen-hour mission, without refuelling. In September, 1943, the Army Air Forces had managed to convince the Joint Chiefs and the President that the B-29s were potentially 'a global air force' and therefore should not be placed operationally under any particular theatre commander. For this purpose, the Twentieth Air Force was created, in April of 1944, and Arnold became its commander, in addition to his other duties as Commanding General of the Army Air Forces and member of the Joint Chiefs. Norstad became his Chief of Staff. Under the Twentieth Air Force, with headquarters in the Pentagon, would be Bomber Commands stationed in areas that were under theatre commanders, but these Bomber Commands would be under the theatre commanders only administratively and logistically—not operationally. The Twentieth Bomber Command had already been operating from Stilwell's theatre in China and from Mountbatten's theatre in India, bombing certain targets from China, and having a go or two at Rangoon from India, to make Mountbatten happy. But this more or less experimental force of B-29s couldn't reach Tokyo or the other big Japanese cities from the bases in non-Japanese-occupied China. They could reach those cities, though, from the islands of Saipan, Tinian, and Guam, in the Marianas, as soon as they had been taken away from the Japs. So the Twenty-first Bomber Command was going to be based initially on Saipan, with other wings to be based on Tinian and Guam later. And the Twenty-first Bomber Command Headquarters would eventually be moved from Saipan to Guam, where Nimitz also was to establish his headquarters."

"Now, in what way did all this concern you?"

"I was sent to Honolulu, to Pearl Harbor—Nimitz's headquarters at that time—before the Marianas had been completely taken, with instructions from the Pentagon to arrange for the news of the first B-29 raid on Tokyo to be released to the public as soon as the B-29s had dropped their bombs. Tokyo had not been bombed since the Doolittle raid in 1942. The plan was that once the base had been built on Saipan and the force of B-29s was there, ready to stage the first raid on Tokyo, I was to call in the war correspondents, reveal to them what was going to happen, let them write their 'advance' stories, which the Navy would censor in case they said anything that might endanger the security of the area, and which I would censor in case they violated B-29 security regulations. Then I would hold the stories until we received the 'bombs-away' message from the flight leader over Tokyo—General Emmett (Rosy) O'Donnell—at which time I was supposed to see to it that the stories got out to the world by means of whatever communications I had been able to line up."

"That seems sensible enough. Isn't that what you suggested should have been done in connection with the Doolittle raid?"

"Yes, sir. But I hadn't intended in 1942 that this would be my responsibility in 1944. All I said in that little editorial was that—"

"We have heard what was said in the editorial, in full. Now, did you encounter any difficulty in making these arrangements?"

"Quite a lot, sir, at first. At Nimitz's headquarters at Pearl Harbor, I was told by his public-relations people—but not by Nimitz himself—that since the raid would be carried out from Saipan and since the correspondents would report it from Saipan, the Island Commander on Saipan would have to approve the censorship and public-relations arrangements, because he was responsible for the security of the area. As soon as Saipan was definitely taken and I was able to get air transportation there, I went to see the Island Commander about my problem. Later on, the Island Commander of Saipan was an Army man under Nimitz, but at this time it was a Navy man under Nimitz. He was a rear admiral. I forget his name. He had an entirely different plan for the release of the news of the first B-29 raid on Tokyo."

"What was his plan?"

"Well, he said that, in the first place, the correspondents couldn't be told anything at all until the raid had actually been carried out and the planes had returned to the base on Saipan, because to tell them earlier than that would, in his opinion, endanger the security of the area. However, he said that once the planes were back on Saipan, he would gladly consent to my calling in the correspondents and telling them that B-29s were now based on Saipan and had bombed Tokyo eight hours earlier. Then the correspondents could write their stories, and I could bring the stories by jeep and boat from our headquarters to his flagship, which was anchored off the other side of the island from where our headquarters was to be. On the flagship, they would be censored by a naval censor and then given back to me, after which I could return by boat and jeep to our headquarters and could then airmail them to Pearl Harbor, where, if the Navy press radio was able to accommodate them, in addition to news stories of what the Navy was doing, the dispatches would be radioed to their destinations—the Associated Press, the United Press, the International News Service, the *New York Times*, and so on. This would mean that with good luck all around—nobody falling into the water on the way to or from the Island Commander's flagship—these dispatches about the first B-29 raid on Tokyo would reach the public about a week or ten days after the event. I thanked the Island Commander and flew back to Honolulu."

"How was the thing finally accomplished?"

"Thanks to Admiral Nimitz, I was able to brief the correspondents—about twenty of them—several days before the date set for the first B-29 raid on Tokyo, and they wrote their 'advance' stories at our headquarters on Saipan. A naval censor was assigned to duty at our headquarters, and he censored the stories there. Copies of all these dispatches were airmailed to the Pentagon for release when the 'bombs-away' message was relayed from our headquarters to the Pentagon. Pending receipt of that message, the stories were classified 'Top Secret.' In case the copies of these dispatches didn't get to the Pentagon in time, the originals were filed with naval communications centers on Saipan and Guam and with our own communications centers on the same two islands, to be radioed to their destinations when we got the 'bombs-away' message. When the planes returned to Saipan, of course, there were follow-up stories—including those written by a number of correspondents who had gone along on the raid—and these were also censored at our headquarters and radioed to their destinations."

"You say this was accomplished thanks to Admiral Nimitz?"

"Yes, sir."

"Will you explain how that came about?"

"Through staff work on our part and what I believe was a sincere willingness on Admiral Nimitz's part to coöperate with us."

"What did this staff work consist of?"

"The Twenty-first Bomber Command, which was still in training in Colorado, was represented in Honolulu by an advance echelon of five or six supply officers, one Wac, and myself, but it had the status of a headquarters. I wrote and delivered a top-secret memorandum to Nimitz's headquarters—everything having any reference to the fact that B-29s were to be based in the Marianas was top secret at that time—and in this memorandum, in military language, I explained that the Joint Chiefs of Staff had directed the Twentieth Air Force to direct the Twenty-first Bomber Command to move a force of B-29s to Saipan by way of Honolulu as soon as the base on Saipan was ready and to stage a raid on certain targets in Tokyo on or about November 24th of that year of 1944, and that our headquarters requested the coöperation of Nimitz's headquarters in making it possible to release the news of this event in accordance with the Presidential directive of September 1, 1943. Then the memorandum suggested that a broad top-secret directive along the lines of the one attached to the memorandum be approved by Nimitz's headquarters and sent to all naval commanders in the Marianas who might in future be concerned. The attached directive directed the naval commanders concerned to, in general, assist our headquarters in accomplishing the release of the news of the first B-29 raid on Tokyo in accordance with aforementioned Presidential directive and, specifically, to assign the necessary censorship personnel to our headquarters on Saipan when the headquarters was established there and to furnish all available means of radio communication for the correspondents' stories; in other words, this directive directed the naval commanders concerned to coöperate in every way in the carrying out of our original plan for the release of the news."

"What was the Presidential directive you referred to?"

"In that directive the Secretary of War stated that the President had directed him to direct all commands of the Army and the Army Air Forces to see to it that news of their combat operations was released to the American public without delay as soon as security regulations had been met. I presume the Secretary of the Navy had been similarly directed by the President, but I never checked up on that."

"In any event, Admiral Nimitz approved your memorandum and signed the suggested directive?"

"Yes, sir. I had one brief and altogether pleasant conversation with him after he received the memorandum and the suggested directive. He said that it was a good directive and he would be happy to sign it, and then he asked me a lot of questions about *The New Yorker* and the people on it. It seems that, like the general in Texas, he was a regular reader."

"So your initial relations with Admiral Nimitz were cordial in every way?"

"Yes, sir."

"Did you see him often prior to the night on which you accused him of high treason in the radiogram to the Pentagon?"

"Only a few times, at press conferences. He always spoke to me in a friendly way and shook hands with me."

"Have you met him since the night in question?"

"Only once, at a cocktail party given in New York a few years ago by the Overseas Press Club."

"What did he do?"

"He nodded to me in a friendly way and shook hands with me. I've never been certain whether or not he knew just who I was on that occasion."

"You did not remind him?"

"No, sir."

"Now let's proceed to the circumstances leading up to the night on which you accused him of high treason. Had you personally got along well with the Navy out there?"

"Extremely well, sir, as far as public-relations and censorship matters went. The censors assigned to us were all good guys, and many of them became friends of mine. The new Chief Public Relations Officer on Nimitz's staff, Admiral H. B. (Min) Miller, was also a good guy and a friend of mine."

"Well, what about as far as other matters went?"

"From my fellow staff officers of the Twenty-first Bomber Command and from our personnel in the various wings and groups of our forces in the Marianas, I kept hearing a great deal during the winter and spring of 1945 about what they considered deliberate efforts on the part of members of Nimitz's staff to obstruct the B-29 program. Supply officers, for example, were sore about what they considered unnecessary delays in getting supplies—and we were dependent on the Navy for logistical support. Supply, of course, affected everybody in the entire outfit. It encompassed everything from bombs for the combat groups on Saipan, Tinian, and Guam to food, beer, and liquor for all concerned. Even our chaplains were sore. They claimed the naval chaplain service held up delivery of Bibles and prayer books."

"Did you think these complaints were justified?"

"From what I heard, yes, sir. But until the night in question I put it all down to inevitable and more or less harmless inter-service rivalry. Ever since I had found myself in the Air Forces, I had noticed that lower echelons invariably resented and complained about higher headquarters—no matter what branch of the service it happened to be—and I had come to think of this as a normal condition of war. Stilwell was sore at Marshall, at Chiang Kai-shek, and at Mountbatten. Mountbatten was sore at the Combined Chiefs of Staff and at the Viceroy of India. Stratemeyer was sore at Stilwell and Arnold, Chennault was sore at Stratemeyer and Stilwell, and so on. There was not only inter-service resentment all over the place but intra-service resentment as well. Army engineers were sore at the Signal Corps. The combat Air Forces were sore at the Air Service Command and at the Air Transport Command. It was the same thing inside the Navy. The Seabees were sore at Nimitz's headquarters, the submariners were sore at the destroyer people, and vice versa. But the Navy seemed to be united in its resentment toward the Twenty-first Bomber Command and the Twentieth Air Force. I persuaded myself to try to understand the Navy's feelings about the B-29 program. The Navy had been fighting out there in the Pacific against overwhelming odds ever since the disaster at Pearl Harbor, and it was just beginning to get somewhere when the Joint Chiefs ordered it to take the Marianas for the express purpose of basing our B-29s there. And now—in May of 1945—the B-29s were burning up city after city in Japan, bringing the war to a close, and the Navy couldn't reach the Japanese islands with anything except occasional inconsequential fighter-bomber strikes from carriers. These carrier strikes represented no more than a drop in the bucket compared to what the B-29s of LeMay's Twenty-first Bomber Command were doing. I could understand how—unconsciously and sometimes quite consciously—naval men out there resented the presence of the B-29s, even though everybody admitted the B-29s were shortening the war against Japan and saving the lives of a great many naval personnel. It was the natural resentment of men who had seen other men called in to finish a job they had started. I used to try to make my fellow staff officers at the Twenty-first Bomber Command understand this, but without much success. No doubt one reason I argued in favor of getting along with the Navy was that it had been drummed into me again and again in the Pentagon, and by Norstad on his visits to the Marianas, that our getting along with Nimitz was going to have a lot to do with the realization of the Air Forces' goal of becoming a separate service after the war. If I had any resentment against Nimitz at this time, I suspect that I put it aside more or less automatically."

"You seem to use 'Navy' and 'Nimitz' as if they were synonymous. Were they?"

"Well, sir, they had pretty much become so in my mind and in the minds of most of our B-29 people out there. Not many of us had met Nimitz or even seen him, but we spoke of him as if we had—'Nimitz has just done such-and-such' or 'What's Nimitz up to now?' and so on. He was an institutional symbol to most of us, rather than an individual, and although I knew him and liked him and had never had any trouble with him, he was a symbol to me, too. He was the Navy and he was higher authority."

"Now, about this message accusing Nimitz of high treason?"

"Sir, I beg your indulgence, but before we get to that, could I ask permission to read one excerpt from the pieces I wrote about the B-29s as soon as I returned to this country after the sending of the message?"

"Is this digression necessary?"

"I honestly believe it will give the senators a feeling of what was going on at that time in the Marianas and what the general atmosphere was like at the time I sent my message."

"How long were these articles?"

"I should say, sir, in the neighborhood of twenty thousand words."

"Good God!"

"But the excerpt I ask you to hear is roughly a thousand words—about a third the length of the Nimitz message."

"All right. Proceed."

"If this excerpt strikes you, sir, as being somewhat romantic—even downright emotional—I ask you to put that down to the spirit of the times."

"Get on with it, please."

"Yes, sir. This is the excerpt from the articles published in June of that summer of 1945:

"'IN THE ARMY Air Forces, and especially in the Air Forces overseas, the officers and men of an outfit are often called, simply, "the people." Official papers frequently use the phrase in place of "all personnel" or "officers and men," and air commanders are likely to say, "I've got two thousand people to worry about" or "What I want more than anything else is some decent rations for my people." The term minimizes the disparity between officers and enlisted personnel and encourages the impression that an outfit fighting a war is an entity, almost a personality, made up not of ranks and grades and ratings but of human beings doing different jobs with a common end in view.

" 'When toward the middle of March this year the first series of great, low-level, night incendiary strikes against Tokyo, Nagoya, Osaka, and Kobe were being carried out by the B-29s based in the Marianas, the Twenty-first Bomber Command of the Twentieth Air Force, and all its people on the islands of Guam and Tinian and Saipan, were like a good golfer at the top of his form or Babe Ruth all set for a long one. The B-29 crews and the people on the ground, the whole bunch that composed the Twenty-first Bomber Command, had achieved their highest point of efficiency. There had been the early days, when the first B-29s were arriving on Saipan; the first pioneering strikes against Japanese aircraft factories by daylight from twenty-five and thirty thousand feet. There had been the organizing of the new wings on Tinian and Guam, a rapid gathering of strength, and a striving for perfection. And in January of this year, there had been the change in command which replaced Brigadier General Haywood S. (Possum) Hansell, Jr., the brilliant planner, with Major General Curtis E. LeMay, the tough, shy, soft-voiced bigtime operator whom everyone called the Cigar. "Now we're in business," the B-29 people said to one another after the first of the low-level incendiary strikes, which burned out about seventeen square miles of one of Tokyo's most congested industrial areas. The people of the Twenty-first Bomber Command had reached a state in which there were certain ingredients that I find indefinable but in which I do know there was a certain kind of fatigue brought on by sleeplessness, undereating, and hard, uninterrupted concentration on the performance of a task. There was a calmness, almost a lassitude, which was not laxness or laziness. There was also a tenseness, a quickening of tempo, that was neither youthful nor nervous nor feverish. The mind, the body, the spirit, the whole being seemed free and ready for anything and confident of success. It was not elation so much as it was a knowl-edgeable acceptance of maturity.

" 'Whatever their jobs were, officers and men did not want, and seemed unable, to sleep more than three or four hours at a time. They ate irregularly, sparingly, and hurriedly. They worked almost incessantly and, when they felt like it, played or relaxed completely, knowing they had it coming to them. Even airplane commanders and their crews, back from a fifteen-hour mission to Japan, usually hit the sack for not more than five or six hours and were up and around again, attending classes, studying tactics, bombardment, nav-igation, and ordnance, and forming little groups in Quonset huts, talking flying, talking fighting, using their hands as airplanes, the way fliers do, flying the latest mission over again, perfecting it, and flying the next mission once or twice in advance, before the take-off. Good men were better. Men who had seemed mediocre be-came good.

" 'At the headquarters of our Twenty-first Bomber Command, on Guam, and in the B-29 wings and groups and squadrons on all three islands, staff people who had felt uncertain about how to do their jobs and had been inclined to stick to the book, to take the safest course, became confident, aggressive, eager to think of short cuts, eager to show that they could take them. Assistant adjutants and their clerks, in military sections devoted to red tape, suddenly broke through the system they had themselves created, got out com-plex orders and directives by new, swift methods, and performed a thousand other worrisome and necessary drudgeries with an undreamed-of simplicity and speed. Messengers walked faster and took an interest in seeing that the right message got to the right man at the right time. Jeep drivers took care of their jeeps and never ran out of gas. A supply officer at headquarters, after all sorts of wangling both in and out of channels before he left the States, received an icebox for his tent and never got around to opening the crate and installing the precious mechanism until it had sat in a corner of his tent for five weeks. This unused icebox just sat there, like an unopened Christmas present in a child's room. As a symbol of tantalizing self-denial, it got on everybody's nerves. Finally, the supply officer's boss took him aside during one of the inspired moments of those delicious, smooth-running days and nights and said to him, "Listen, son, you go fix up your goddam icebox in your tent right now, and don't come back here until your beer and your friends' beer is cooling in it, see?"

" 'Everybody seemed to realize that everybody else was working his head off. Requests were made, commands were given, in quiet voices. Everybody seemed almost miraculously full of tolerance and understanding.

" 'Ground crews, who had the stupendous task of getting the B-29s ready to fly on all-out strikes in less than half the time they had always had before, leaped on the big airplanes like hounds on a stag the second the returning pilots switched off the engines after the long trip to Japan and back. I saw a mechanic one day get his stepladder all set against one of the engine nacelles of a B-29, waiting for the pilot to switch off the engines so he could start getting at the insides to tune them up for the next trip. The pilot finally switched off the engines and the propellers coasted round and round, slower and slower. This mechanic couldn't seem to wait. He put out a determined gloved hand and eased the enormous blade of his engine to a stop; then he went to work with his wrenches. Mechanics worked through the nights and days, for twenty-four and sometimes thirty-six hours at a stretch, without a rest and with only some gulped coffee and Spam sandwiches for nourishment, until the airplanes took off again. Major General LeMay, commanding the Twenty-first Bomber Command and working at the same high pitch as his men, issued a significant order after two of the incendiary missions had been run. He directed all airplane commanders to

examine personally the exteriors of their airplanes two minutes before takeoff time and make sure that no mechanics were still cling-
ing to the undercarriage, working on something.'"

"Is that, by any chance, the end of this excerpt?"

"Yes, sir, it is."

"Fine. Now I shall ask you a digressive question. Can you give
us some idea of what, exactly, the B-29s accomplished in their air
war against Japan before Hiroshima?"

"I happen to have the facts here in my briefcase, sir, taken from
an official War Department study made public after the war. Before Hiroshima, the B-29s flew 32,612 sorties and had 100,000,000
miles of combat flying. In the last six months of operations, they
dropped 160,000 tons of bombs, laid 12,049 mines around the harbors of Japan, destroyed 2,285 Japanese fighters, burned down 65
of Japan's most important cities and 158 square miles of urban industrial areas, destroyed 581 vital war factories, cut steel productive
capacity 15 per cent and aircraft productive capacity 60 per cent,
killed outright 310,000 Japanese, injured 412,000 more, and rendered
9,200,000 homeless.'

"Thank you. And what were the casualties in the Twenty-first
Bomber Command?"

"Before Hiroshima, we lost 437 B-29s and 297 crews, or about
3,267 officers and men."

"And what was the direct cause, or causes, of your deciding to
accuse Admiral Nimitz of high treason on the night in question?"

"Nimitz's combined sea, air, and land forces had recently taken
Iwo Jima, a very small island between the Marianas and Japan, at a
cost of 4,900 American lives, mostly Marines. Iwo Jima was close
enough to Japan for the new long-range Army Air Forces fighters
(the P-51s) to give the B-29s fighter cover on their raids over Japan,
and it was decided in the Pentagon to base a group of these fighters
there. There had been a dispute between the Army Air Forces and

the Navy over who should command these fighters, and the decision of the Joint Chiefs of Staff—a compromise—had been to place them under the operational command of Admiral Nimitz, as a part of the Seventh Air Force, for assault and defense operations at Iwo Jima and Okinawa, and under LeMay when they served as fighter cover for his B-29s. The Seventh Air Force was a regular Army Air Forces outfit that had been under Nimitz's command throughout most of the war in the Pacific. When I heard about this decision of the Joint Chiefs, I thought it sounded absurd—dividing the command of the fighters that way—but I put it down to relatively harmless inter-service rivalry and thought no more about it."

"Well, what happened then?"

"I was leaving Nimitz's headquarters on the afternoon of the night in question, after briefing the war correspondents about the next fire-bomb raid by B-29s—on Kobe, I think it was—when the chief Navy press censor, a friend of mine, stopped me and handed me a naval publicity release that was to be issued the next day. He said maybe I'd better glance at it, since it was indirectly connected with B-29 operations. It simply said that a group of Admiral Nimitz's long-range fighters, based on Iwo Jima, would furnish fighter cover for the B-29s in future raids against Japan. I asked the naval censor to let me show it to our Chief of Staff, General August W. Kissner, to make sure he didn't think it affected the security of B-29 operations. He said sure, show it to Kissner, but added that the publicity release had already been approved and was being released to the correspondents on Guam and the newspapermen in Washington on the following day."

"And then?"

"I showed it to Kissner when I got back to our headquarters. He was a mild-mannered sort of officer, a kind of intellectual, who was a crackerjack at all kinds of staff work. He said he didn't think Nimitz ought to make public this information about the new fighters' being used in the B-29 raids on Japan. In the first place, the fighters were not under Nimitz when they were doing that, and, in the second place, it might be dangerous to advertise the fact that they were being used as fighter cover for B-29s. As things stood at that time, the Japs were not bombing Iwo Jima, because we were using that little island only as a landing place for three or four crippled B-29s at a time, and consequently it was not a worth-while target for the Japanese heavy bombers or for fighter-bombers from Japanese aircraft carriers. He said he'd ask LeMay, and he did. After he'd talked to LeMay, he called me into LeMay's office, which was in a Quonset hut. LeMay said he thought we ought to protest about the publicity release, because it might easily stir the Japs up into bombing Iwo Jima. Neither LeMay nor Kissner appeared to me to be particularly concerned about the fact that the Navy evidently wished to call these fighters 'Admiral Nimitz's fighters' whether they were actually operating under his command or not. And I knew that Kissner was anxious to avoid relatively unimportant protests from LeMay about naval doings, because of the more important protests our headquarters had to make about naval doings from time to time—both to Nimitz's headquarters and to the Pentagon. Kissner said there was an old War Department regulation that authorized a press censor—which I was, of course—to protest directly to the War Department on his own responsibility if he believed that some action by another unit or headquarters was endangering, or was about to endanger, the security of the area in which his own unit was operating. So Kissner suggested that I send a message to the Pentagon citing this old regulation (he looked up its number and gave it to me) and protesting in a polite, official fashion about the impending release by Nimitz's headquarters of the information about the fighters' being used to support the B-29 operations. He said he wouldn't need to see or O.K. my message, because it was being sent on my own responsibility as a press censor. I suggested that I might send it around two o'clock in the morning, so that it would get Norstad's attention the moment he reported for duty the next day. Kissner agreed to this and gave me a slip of paper authorizing me to communicate with the Pentagon at that hour on my own responsibility as a press censor. I then went by my public-relations tent and asked one of my sergeants to wake me at midnight. Going along to my quarters—a tent I shared with a naval lieutenant who had been as-signed to our staff as naval liaison officer—I went to sleep."

"Do you mean to say that you sent this message accusing Admiral Nimitz of high treason in your sleep?"

"Oh, no, sir. Not at all. I went to sleep, but I was awakened af-ter a couple of hours—around eleven o'clock that night—by my tentmate's coming in to grab some sleep himself. He was a rich young Texan named George C. McGhee, who later became a spe-cial assistant to the Under-Secretary of State and, still later, our Ambassador to Turkey, during the Truman Administration. He was burned up about something he said Nimitz—that is to say, the Navy people—had done the day before. He hadn't been back to our headquarters or had any sleep since then. After we had talked for a while, I was burned up, too."

"What did he say the Navy had done?"

"Well, the Navy had been putting pressure on us from every di-rection to coördinate some of our raids on Japan with strikes from naval carriers. This enabled the Navy to issue press releases brag-ging about the part the Navy was playing in the bombing of Japan that was bringing the war to a conclusion. It was not unlike the situation that had developed over the long-range fighters based on Iwo Jima, only it was far more serious, it seemed to me. According to McGhee—and later I heard exactly the same story from other officers who were present, some of them of high rank—LeMay had gone to a conference with some of Nimitz's air-operations people, accompanied by McGhee and four or five of our staff of-ficers, and the Navy people had indicated some targets—factories, as I remember—that they thought Nimitz's carrier planes might attack in conjunction with the next B-29 raid. The targets were near the east coast of the main Japanese island, Honshu, whereas the B-29 targets for the raid the Navy wanted to take part in were too far inland for the carrier planes to reach. At the conference, LeMay had pointed out that the targets the Navy wanted to attack had already been destroyed in previous B-29 raids, and showed them photographs to support his statement. In fact, there appeared to be no undestroyed targets that could be reached by this particular carrier force. The Navy men, however, said that the carrier force would attack the targets anyway. LeMay pointed out that some of the pilots from the carriers would inevitably be lost, but the Navy men said, in effect, that that was not LeMay's concern. LeMay then folded up his maps and photographs and walked out of the conference without saying good afternoon. McGhee, although a naval officer then (he later got transferred to the Air Forces), was so angry while he was telling me about it that he was purple in the face. Finally, he went to bed and went to sleep.

"I tried to go back to sleep, but couldn't, so I went on over to my public-relations tent. I wrote the polite protest concerning the long-range fighters on Iwo Jima. It was very brief, and merely stated that I understood that, in the opinion of the commander of the B-29s in the Pacific, the naval announcement would endanger the security of the B-29 operations, in that it would invite enemy attacks on Iwo Jima. Then I worked on something else—I forget just what—until close to 2 A.M., at which time I gave one of my sergeants the message to deliver to our communications center around the corner, along with the note of authorization from Kissner, which I told him to bring back to me after he had shown it to whoever was in charge of the communications center at that hour. The communications center was in the charge of another sergeant at the time, my authorization from Kissner was explicit, and my sergeant brought back the authorization and said the message was on its way. That was all there was to that."

"But what about the message accusing Nimitz of high treason?"

"That was coming right up, sir—in my mind. While the sergeant was gone, I began to get sorer and sorer about inter-service rivalry. All the things I had heard and tried to ignore concerning the alleged instances of the Navy's obstruction of the B-29 program seemed to line themselves up in my head in an orderly fashion, and I asked myself if these things, taken in a bunch, didn't represent something worse than inter-service rivalry. A thing like the projected carrier strikes on targets that had already been destroyed, for example, was going to cost lives, and the fact that—as I thought—the war had been prolonged because the B-29 program had been obstructed had cost a great many lives, too. If any attempt to make it appear that the Navy was doing more than it actually was would result in further prolonging the war, this was giving aid and comfort to the enemy and represented treason—high treason. And Nimitz, I told myself, had to accept the responsibility for everything that went on in his command, whether he—personally, as an individual—was or wasn't aware of what was going on. It all seemed very logical to me. I slipped a piece of paper into my typewriter and began to write very fast, starting off, as I remember, with something like 'I hereby accuse Fleet Admiral Chester W. Nimitz, Commander-in-Chief of the Pacific Fleet and of the Pacific Ocean Areas, of high treason.' And so on. I felt very calm and clearheaded, and when I read the message over in the Pentagon not long afterward, it seemed calm and clearheaded, too—at least, the first three-quarters of it. It mentioned specific instances that I thought represented evidence in support of my charge—things I had heard about and made notes of in that notebook I later threw away. It pointed out that everybody knew that this sort of thing went on in every theatre of war, and that the Air Forces and the Army were quite capable of doing the same thing to the Navy, or to each other, but it said that it was time somebody put a stop to it, once and for all."

"In your opinion, the last quarter of the message was not calm or clearheaded?"

"I'm afraid not, sir. I got more and more worked up as I wrote, and toward the end the things I said seemed to me muddleheaded if not hysterical when I read them over in the Pentagon. The sergeant who had been transmitting the message in takes evidently thought so, too, because he had the colonel in charge of communications waked up, and the colonel came to my public-relations tent and asked me what was going on. I showed him the memorandum from Kissner; it seemed to satisfy him, and he went away. I kept on writing. After I had begun to use some profanity and obscenity about the Navy and its ways, I myself realized that I must have run out of ideas, so I ended the message, and one of my sergeants took the last of it over to the communications center and passed along the information that that would be all for that night."

"How did you feel at this time about what you had done?"

"I regretted having run out of ideas and fallen back on expletives, but I thought the message as a whole was good enough to make an impression and attract some attention around the Pentagon and at Nimitz's headquarters. I figured I would be courtmartialled, and perhaps shot, though I thought the latter unlikely. And if I was court-martialled, I thought that a great deal of evidence about inter-service rivalry would be brought out and made public, and that this couldn't help being a good thing all around. I was looking forward with pleasure to the court-martial, and pungent things I would say to the prosecutor kept running through my head. I was extremely tired, but relaxed and unworried. I suspected I might be out of my mind, but I didn't really believe I was. I remember that it was a windy, rainy night, and that about this time a gust of wind blew the sign that said 'Public Relations, Twenty-first Bomber Command' off the front of the tent, and it clattered to the ground. I remember that I picked it up, looked up at the sky, and said, 'We'll have no miracles, thanks,' and, laughing to myself, returned to my typewriter."

"Hadn't you finished writing?"

"Oh, no, sir. I felt there was still a lot to be done. I was by that time not very logical in my thoughts, I'm afraid, but I didn't realize this at the time. I was under the impression that nobody but me would know how to proceed after the message had achieved its initial effect. First of all, I thought, Nimitz would, of course, be placed under arrest—confined to his quarters—pending disposition of my charges against him. I was sorry about that, because I had become rather fond of the old gentleman, but I felt I had to face the fact that he was, after all, responsible for everything that went on in his command. I would be confined to my quarters, too, I thought, and for that reason I was anxious to write a memorandum for Kissner and LeMay, advising them how to proceed both administratively and operationally while Nimitz was confined to his quarters. I regret to say that I didn't see this memorandum afterward, and I doubt if it still exists; I have no clear recollection of what procedures it suggested to my commanding general and his chief of staff. At any rate, it was not completed."

"Why not?"

"I was still working on it when Kissner, a flight surgeon, and two armed sergeants came into my tent. This was around eight in the morning. Kissner spoke to me, and I waved at him, indicating I'd be with him as soon as I finished what I was doing. He must have decided I was harmless, for he dismissed the armed sergeants and they went away. Then he said he thought I had done enough for one night, or something like that—he was very gentle—and the flight surgeon handed me two Nembutal pills and a cup of water and said if I would take the pills I'd get a good, long sleep. I swallowed them, and vaguely remember riding, half asleep, in the flight surgeon's jeep to the Army hospital on the other side of the island."

"We would be interested to know what was done to you all along the line, now that we know what *you* had done. What was done to you at the hospital?"

"Nothing, sir. I woke up in about four hours and remembered everything very distinctly. My first thought was that at the court-martial that was to come it might be claimed by the Navy that I was insane when I wrote the message, and that unless I could prove otherwise, the effect of my message would be nullified. I thought I'd better go and tell Kissner and LeMay about this, so I started to dress. I was in the medical ward of the hospital. A medical sergeant came over and told me that he was sorry, sir, but I couldn't leave unless I was signed out by my flight surgeon, and the flight surgeon had gone back to our headquarters. I argued with him in a patient, good-natured fashion, but he was firm. Those were the regulations, he said. Then I asked him what would happen if I insisted on leaving. He said he would have to place me under arrest and take me to the locked ward—the mental ward. I asked him if that would mean I would have to undergo an examination for mental fitness. He said that it would, and that until that was over, I would have to stay in a locked cell by myself, because I was an officer. 'You mean a room of my own?' I remember asking him, and he answered, 'Yes, sir.' That settled it."

"Settled what?"

"In the first place, I thought that if I was examined for mental fitness at that time, and was declared sane, the Navy wouldn't have a leg to stand on in its effort to claim that my message was irrational, and, in the second place, the idea of being in a room of my own, locked or unlocked, appealed to me more than I can say. I hadn't had a room of my own in a long time."

"So you were removed to the locked ward and the locked room?"

"Yes, sir. It was a very comfortable little room, with bars on the windows and on the door. An orderly brought me some breakfast, and I asked him if I could have a typewriter and some paper, explaining that I had some important work to do, but he shook his head. Then I asked him if I could have a pencil and a writing pad, and he grinned and said, 'Oh, sure, Colonel. Everybody in here writes all the time.' He brought me a long, thick pad of lined yellow paper and a pencil. He also brought me a sedative. I started writing very rapidly and then fell asleep."

"What were you writing?"

"I had decided that I had failed to indicate clearly enough, in my message about Nimitz, that the Seventh Air Force and the Army ground forces, both of which were under Nimitz but were commanded from separate headquarters in Honolulu, were exactly as guilty as Nimitz, and I had started off on a memorandum about them when I fell asleep. After I woke up, I went right on with it, and it was going fine when Kissner and the flight surgeon came to see me. Kissner, as usual, was very gentle, and when I asked him what was going on in connection with my message, he said that nothing was going on—that everything was fixed up, and I was going home on my existing orders as soon as I had had a few days' rest. I asked him what had happened, and he said, in effect, 'The message was simply withdrawn, Mac, because you were suffering from operational fatigue at the time.' I was afraid this might mean that it had never got to the Pentagon, or to Nimitz's headquarters, but he said, 'Oh, no, it got to both places all right, and I'm sure it has been widely read. The only thing was, Mac, that LeMay had to go and apologize in person to Nimitz, and he didn't like that at all—not at all.' I was getting drowsy again and they left."

"Did you undergo a mental examination?"

"Oh, yes. The psychiatrist in charge of the locked ward, a major, talked to me a long time—or, rather, listened to me—and gave me various tests. Then he said I would be discharged in forty-eight hours. I asked him if I was insane, and he said, 'Oh, no. Just a case of operational fatigue, Colonel.' So I had a good rest and was discharged after a couple more days."

"Were you in contact with other inmates of the mental ward during this period?"

"Only to try to say hello to them, sir, on my way to and from the washroom. As was the custom there, I was accompanied on these trips by an armed guard, but he let me hang around in the enlisted men's ward for a while on the way back to my private room. Most of the inmates were writing, and I hesitated to disturb them, but two were not, and I got interested in them and tried to talk to them."

"About what?"

"Oh, anything at all. But neither of them could speak. One was a Negro who resembled the servant I used to have at my apartment on East Eighty-third Street. I was, I think, in full possession of all my faculties by this time, and I really thought he might be a brother or a relative. The psychiatrist told me later that he was suffering from dementia praecox and had an attitudinal fixation. He sat all day and all night straight up in his cot without leaning against anything, and with his right arm held up over his head—curved like half an arch. The psychiatrist told me he had been working in the galley of a battle cruiser ever since Pearl Harbor, and had suddenly gone off his rocker—or at least had adopted this rigid posture and had ceased to speak—and that nobody had been able to do anything with him. I used to offer him cigarettes, but he evidently had no use for them. The last day I was there, I sat at the foot of his cot and told him he looked as if he might be the brother of this servant I used to have back home, and he began to weep—silently and without changing his attitude or moving a muscle of his face.

The only movement was that of the tears rolling down his cheeks. The psychiatrist told me afterward that this could be interpreted as a sign of progress—that maybe he would snap out of his attitudinal fixation, if not out of his dementia praecox, since at least he had been able to weep."

"There was a second one who couldn't speak?"

"Yes, sir. He was an extremely happy-looking young Marine—pale, with red hair. He had dementia praecox, too, the psychiatrist told me, but he hadn't the attitudinal fixation. He sat or lay around, and whenever anybody spoke to him or looked at him, he would smile and utter a pleasant-sounding singsong that was always the same—a kind of 'Whee-oo, whee-oo, whee-oo' that was not exclamatory but sounded a little like the voice of a dove in a treetop. He had been in four Marine beachhead landings, the last on Iwo Jima. The psychiatrist told me there wasn't much hope for him but that at least he didn't seem to be suffering."

"When you left the hospital, what did you do?"

"I got my luggage together and had dinner, as usual, with LeMay and his staff, and everybody there seemed extraordinarily cordial—some of them even deferential—but no mention was made of my message about Nimitz. Next morning, I took off for home in the NATS plane."

"Were you under arrest at this time?"

"For a while, sir, I thought maybe I was. A colonel, a group commander returning home for reassignment, was introduced to me by Kissner at the airfield—Kissner had taken me there in his jeep—and Kissner said this colonel was going to report to Norstad, too, and would be with me on the trip home. But at Honolulu, where I thought I would probably have to stick with the colonel during the four-hour layover, he said he had some friends he wanted to look up, and would see me later. I looked up some friends myself, had a fine time, and rejoined him at the plane for the flight to Washington. We got to Washington late in the afternoon and went directly to the Statler, where we shared a room, and we started out to-gether that evening for drinks and dinner, but we returned to the hotel separately. I figured I wasn't under arrest, after all. Next morn-ing, the colonel called Norstad's office, told them we had arrived, and was told by Norstad's executive officer to come right on over, that Norstad would see us at once. My superior, Colonel Rex Smith, appeared to be waiting for me, because he joined the other colonel and me when we came down the corridor on the way to Norstad's office. He went into Norstad's office with us. There, Norstad shook hands with us, told the colonel where his new assignment was go-ing to be, and wished him luck, and the colonel left. Then, as I've told you, sir, Norstad just said that this whole thing had been forgotten—that it had never happened, and so on. After that, I was given the thirty-day leave and went to New York and wrote the four articles on the B-29 operations."

"Didn't you discuss what had happened with anybody at all at the Pentagon?"

"Yes, sir, I did. Colonel Smith seemed disinclined to talk about it, just grinning at me and winking, but I had lunch the same day with a friend of mine, a lieutenant colonel, who was one of Smith's assistants, and he filled me in on what had happened. It seems that there was a great deal of running up and down the corridors of the Pentagon by high officers of the Air Forces and the Navy, and even the Army, and that for a while General Arnold, wanted me brought home and court-martialled, or court-martialled out there. Arnold was fit to be tied, my friend said, because he'd had to try to explain to his fellow-members of the Joint Chiefs that same afternoon—Admirals Ernest J. King and William D. Leahy and General Marshall—how it could happen that a lieutenant colonel in the Army Air Forces could send such a message. He was respon-sible for me, you see, both as Commanding General of the Army Air Forces and as Commanding General of the Twentieth Air Force. But when our headquarters sent the message saying my message was withdrawn, everybody realized that nothing more needed to be done, and Lovett calmed Arnold down."

"You are referring to Robert A. Lovett, then Assistant Secretary of War for Air, later Under-Secretary of State, and later Secretary of Defense?"

"Yes, sir."

"Did he call you Mac, too?"

"Yes, sir. As a matter of fact, I knew him better than I did any of the generals, having been acquainted with him in New York before the war and having been to dinner parties at his home a number of times."

"Did you discuss your message about Nimitz with him?"

"Yes, sir. Since I had been told that Lovett had perhaps prevented Arnold from having me court-martialled, I went around to thank him that same afternoon."

"Then you were no longer looking forward with pleasure to being court-martialled?"

"It's hard to describe, sir, but, as a matter of fact, I think—half of the time, at least—I was somewhat disappointed that things had turned out the way they had. I felt as Zola might have felt if nothing had happened after he wrote 'J'Accuse' except that everybody kept shaking hands with him. The other half of the time I was glad it would not be necessary for me to devote the rest of my life to being a martyr—a sort of Billy Mitchell who was called Peter Roger Oboe and who couldn't pilot an airplane."

"So you went around to thank Mr. Lovett, in any case?"

"Yes, sir. His secretary said to go right in, and I went right in, and Lovett shook hands with me and laughed. I said I hoped I hadn't been the cause of any embarrassment to him, and he said by no means. He said that the Navy had come to him in considerable ferment and had asked what was going to be done about my message, and that he had said nothing could be done about it, because it had been withdrawn, that it no longer existed as an official document, and that the Air Forces were interested only in finding out if any of the things I had said in the message—things that had been noted before the message was withdrawn—had any basis in fact. 'They went away, I remember his saying, 'and they never brought the subject up again.' "

"Did he indicate that he believed what you had said in that message?"

"Certainly not that Nimitz was guilty of high treason, or even ordinary treason, sir."

"Did you also at this time go around to see General Arnold?"

"No, sir. I had never met him. But as I left Lovett's office that afternoon, Arnold was waiting in the reception room outside, and Lovett introduced me to him."

"Now, suppose you tell us exactly what was said on this occasion."

"Lovett said, 'General Arnold, I don't believe you have met Colonel McKelway. He's just back from Guam.' "

"And what did General Arnold say?"

"He didn't say a word. He grinned and looked at me keenly and then shook hands with me."

"Did you say anything?"

"I said, 'Pleased to meet you, sir.' "

"Well, then, did Mr. Lovett say anything else?"

"No, sir."

"I see. Now, I have a question to put to you. Don't you think inter-service rivalry is, on the whole, a good thing?"

"No, sir."

"I believe that is all."

"Thank you, sir."

THE COCKATOO

THIS IS A factual story about childhood and death, but I will try to make it salient, which, the dictionary says, is from the Latin *saliens* and clearly means "moving by leaps and springs." And what is thinking? Well, it is "mental concentration on ideas as distinguished from sense perceptions or emotions." It's a word from Middle English, which is sometimes cloudy. The point I want to make is that in the short period of my life with which we are dealing here—the child from thirteen to seventeen—I didn't think about death. I was aware of it, but I didn't give it thought. Not in the dictionary sense. Not, at least, until after the incident that has to do with a cockatoo at the zoo in Washington, D.C., in the summer of 1922. That comes toward the end of the story.

I suppose some young people start thinking about a number of things, if not about death, long before they are seventeen, but I'm not sure of this. The young are receivers. In order to have something to give, they must take, and in order to give what they have taken—even if it is only to give it to themselves—they must think. In the dictionary sense. I know only about myself, of course, but about myself I know everything. I know the things I heard and saw in those years, the things I felt and smelled, and I know on what smooth-running reels my imagination turned to show me things that weren't there. And I know what I did. I have forgotten nothing.

If I had had any thoughts, I would remember them. I haven't iso-
lated every conceivable subject on which I might have had thoughts
(in the dictionary sense) and dipped them one by one into memory
to test and make sure beyond all doubt that no thinking went on in
connection with them; I don't think that is necessary. If I wasn't able
to think about death in this thirteen-to-seventeen period, it must be
that I wasn't able to think about anything. I experienced the sense
perceptions, the ripples and breakers of the emotions, the excursions of the imagination, and the goings on that occur in dreams and
nightmares, and I acted this way and that way.

My father reached the age of fifty-two before he died. I
was thirteen then, and was getting over a case of scarlet fever. When
I first came down with it, my mother decided it would be easier to
take care of me if I occupied the second-floor bedroom in which
she and my father customarily slept. Accordingly, I was tucked into
their double bed, and my father was moved into a bedroom on the
third floor. My mother nursed me and slept on a couch in her
sewing room, which was next to their former bedroom. When I
was still in bed but getting better, my father brought me my first
Meccano set, No. 1-A. He had left his office early and gone to buy
it at the toy department of Woodward & Lothrop's. And he was a
very busy man. He was a Doctor of Divinity, like practically
everybody else we knew, but had given up preaching to Presbyterians in order to become secretary of the National Child Labor
Committee. He was trying to get Congress to take the first steps
toward adoption of an amendment to the Constitution that would
keep children from being put to work in the cotton mills of the
South, many of which were owned and operated by Presbyterians.
Because of the danger of catching my infection or carrying some
of my germs with him when he left the house to go to his office,
he wasn't allowed to enter his former bedroom, where I was, but
could only stand at the door while I lifted up what I had made

with No. 1-A and showed it to him. The house was quarantined. My mother, who was in constant contact with me and my germs, wasn't allowed to leave the house. My two older brothers were away at training camps, getting ready to fight in the World War, and my sister had been sent to stay with some cousins in Maryland until the quarantine was lifted. The only other person at home was our Scotch-Irish housekeeper, Miss Annabelle, who had become a member of the family before I was born. Since she dealt with the tradesmen who came to the house, she couldn't come into the sickroom, either. The doctor didn't need to tell me about the contagiousness of my infection. My mother had already told me. She knew all about sickness, and in many ways was at her best when confronted with it. She had a great deal of love for those close to her but also a strong sense of responsibility to God for their shortcomings. When they were hale and active, they sometimes felt oppressed by the relentlessness of her critical faculty, but when they were ailing and stationary, she eased up and put her whole self into ministrations of devotion.

My father brought me No. 1-B, No. 2-A, No. 2-B, and No. 3-A Meccano sets in the weeks of my convalescence, and would have brought me No. 3-B if he hadn't come down with an infection himself. My mother told me he absolutely had not caught my infection. What he had was a bad case of bronchitis, she said. Then she told me he had confessed to her that he also had heart trouble. A doctor he'd gone to see, about the time I first got sick with the scarlet fever, had told him so, but he hadn't wanted to worry her. My mother said this meant he would have to take things easier after he got over the bronchitis. He would have to walk very slowly the six blocks up the hill to the streetcar line, and, of course, after I got well, he wouldn't have to climb the three flights of stairs to the room she had put him in. In the meantime, she could nurse him as well as me, because he wouldn't be going out of the house until after the quarantine for my scarlet fever had been lifted.

Then, one morning about a week after my father got the bronchitis, my mother came in to see me and, as usual, I asked her how
he was.

"He's gone away from us," she said. "God has taken him. He
went very peacefully. It was late last night after you went to sleep,
son. I took him some warm milk and crackers, and I was just helping him sit up in bed while I fluffed up the pillows for him. He
sighed and sank back and was gone."

"He's dead?" I asked.

"Yes," she said. "Go ahead and cry, son."

She waited until I pretended to cry and then left the room. The
doctor said the six-week quarantine was almost over, that my skin
had stopped peeling, that in his opinion I was no longer contagious, and that consequently he would take a chance, in view of
the circumstances, and just go ahead and lift the quarantine. Two
days later, I was allowed to dress and go downstairs to the parlor,
where everything was ready for the funeral, which was to be held
the day after that. From the parlor I went into the kitchen, where
Miss Annabelle kissed me on the cheek and then made out that she
was busy with something she was cooking. I knew she was crying
and that she wasn't crying because of my father; she was crying because I was a fatherless child. In the back yard was my Boston terrier, Bessie. My father had brought her to me from a pet store on
K Street almost six months back, at Christmastime. She jumped on
me and began to race around in circles, because she hadn't seen me
since I got sick. I cried then, but I didn't cry at the funeral or afterward at the Rock Creek Cemetery.

THIS WAS BEFORE the invention of the talking pictures that
were later to come to the movie houses in Washington and elsewhere, but talking pictures were showing in my head just the same.
Some of them were entirely from the memory, some were from the
imagination, some were from the emotions, and some were from

wherever it is that nightmares come from. At times the memory, the imagination, and the emotions became merged with one another into a continuous series of overlapping pictures, with accompanying dialogues. But in the nightmares it was the same scene over and over, and all nightmare. I would find my father after hunting for him in banks of clouds, and I would upbraid him, shaking my finger at him and sometimes screaming at him. I would tell him he ought to be ashamed of himself for going away from us. I would tell him he had to come back to us right then or I would tell my mother. I would tell my mother our secret about the partridges he let me shoot that time on Sunday when just the two of us went on the hunting trip to his birthplace, in Charlotte Courthouse, Virginia. I tried to stamp my foot to show him how angry I was and to show him I meant every word I said—that I would tell my mother he had lied when he said it was on a Saturday that he let me shoot the partridges—but my foot would only go through the cloud I was standing on, and my stamping made no noise, and my father would just look at me and put on the imitation painful-face he had teased me with the time I pretended to have the stomach ache at our first house in Washington—the house in Georgetown, not the house in Mt. Pleasant, where he had died—when I was just starting grade school. Then he would grin at me and wink at me, and I would wake up. My memory would thereupon quickly show me some talking pictures connected with the nightmare. For example, it would show me the stomach-ache scene—my mother putting me to bed and saying I needn't go to school that day, and my father coming in before he left for his office and seeing me make my painful-face and then making his imitation painful-face at me, indicating he knew I was malingering. My mother took my side that time and told him he shouldn't tease the sick child, and he winked at me and went off chuckling, and I was mad at him because he had made fun of me. But I felt conspiratorial with him at the same time, because he had winked at me, indicating he knew I was putting on a show to keep from going to school but that he wouldn't tell.

Then my memory, as likely as not, would bring out the pictures of Siegfried dying in the back yard of the Mt. Pleasant house right after we moved there from Georgetown. Siegfried was my brother Zan's Great Dane. We all loved him as if he were a member of the family, like Miss Annabelle. When he was a puppy, he was so big and heavy that his forelegs buckled under him, and the veterinarian said there was nothing to do with a Great Dane when that happened but chloroform him. My mother said that was perfectly ridiculous; all the puppy needed was some splints. So we made some splints out of pine kindling wood and sandpapered them until they were as smooth as the piece of Chinese jade my mother's missionary cousins had given her on her thirtieth birthday. My mother fixed them on Sieg's legs with sticking plaster, and as he grew bigger and stronger, we made new splints, and when she finally took them off for good, Sieg's legs were perfectly straight and didn't buckle, and my mother said, "So much for veterinarians!" But then, a long time afterward, Sieg caught distemper, because we had the vanity to show him in the dog show when we should have just been proud and happy to have such a nice Great Dane as a member of the family. My mother said it was vanity, and that all of us, including herself, were guilty of it. Sieg won blue ribbons but he got distemper and died. Only, he didn't die, exactly. The veterinarian had said he was surely going to die and ought to be put out of his misery, and everybody had said we couldn't let him be put out of his misery, and Sieg lay in the back yard in a tent Zan put up for him, and barked and bayed and howled and whimpered in his delirium, and my father said he was having ancestral dreams of the chase, hundreds of years before in Denmark. But Sieg barked and bayed and howled and whimpered day and night for a week, and everybody was going around very melancholy, and nobody could eat, no matter what Miss Annabelle cooked, and finally my

mother—on her own responsibility, she said it was—told the veterinarian to put him out of his misery, and the veterinarian did
when we were all at school. He put a cloth over Sieg's face, with
chloroform on it. When my brother Zan got home from his high
school, where he played left half back on the football team, he said
Sieg had been killed, murdered, and he shouted at my mother, "I'll
never forgive you as long as you live!" She burst into tears, and so
did my sister and I and Miss Annabelle.

My imagination would then show me pictures of my mother
putting a chloroform cloth over Sieg's face, and then pictures of
her putting a chloroform cloth over my father's face while she told
me he was in misery and had to be put out of his misery and that
this would have to be our secret. But then I would see other pictures of my germs flying up the third-floor stairs and killing my father, murdering him, and still other pictures of God coming down
to see him in the third-floor bedroom where my mother had put
him, and God saying, "McKelway, I need you up here; you've got
to come," and my father saying, "I'm willing, God," and going
away from us. God called him by his whole last name that way, the
same as President Woodrow Wilson did. The President was strongly
in favor of the child-labor amendment to the Constitution. My
mother said there had to be an amendment, because the federal
child-labor bill my father had worked on so hard and got Congress
to pass had been declared unconstitutional after the President
signed it. There was a real picture, a photograph, of the President
signing that bill, and in the photograph, from left to right, were my
father, my mother, my sister, the President, and me. It was framed,
and it was in my father's study, standing on the mantelpiece. In that
photograph my father was looking very solemn, and my memory
gave me a picture of him in his coffin on the day of the funeral,
and he looked the same way he looked in the photograph except
that his eyes were closed.

There were some pictures I kept making my memory show me

over and over, because I liked them best and they didn't make me nervous. They were about the day when I was nine years old and was going to be punished by my father with a razorstrop, which was something he had never in his life used on anybody—not even my brothers. Through carelessness and bad judgment, I had dropped a milk bottle filled with live grasshoppers from quite a height, intending for it to break on some rocks near where a congressman's son was playing in Rock Creek Park, and it had hit that boy on the head and made him bleed, and the doctor had had to take twelve stitches. The pictures showed my father coming home from his office while I was waiting for him in my room, to which my mother had sent me, and coming straight upstairs with the razorstrop and saying, "I'm very sorry, son, but this is mighty serious." It seemed the congressman had walked into his office without knocking and had told him to stop bothering Congress about the children in the cotton mills of the South and start looking after his own children in the District of Columbia. The congressman had said I ought to be sent to the reform school. The talking pictures showed my father asking me to tell him all the circumstances before he punished me severely, and me telling him all the circumstances, and him dangling the razorstrop and beginning to moan and sputter. I thought he was crying, but he was laughing, and when he recovered, he couldn't bring himself to whip me with the razorstrop, or even spank me, but could only say, "Oh, son, it makes me laugh because at least it was a congressman's son and not a *senator's* son." And the only punishment I got for the whole thing was that I had to pay that boy's doctor's bill and go and apologize to him and his father, the congressman. I paid it out of money I had made raking leaves at the zoo during the summer.

THINGS WERE MOVING very fast all around me as well as in my head. My brothers came home on leave for the funeral, and went away again. It was the first time I had seen them in their uniforms. At the funeral, which was held in the parlor and was attended by many prominent Washingtonians and some congressmen and two senators, my mother and my sister and my brothers and Miss Annabelle and I sat in chairs on the second-floor landing, where we could hear everything but couldn't be seen by the people downstairs. My mother cried with a handkerchief held over almost her whole face, and my sister cried the same way. Miss Annabelle didn't cry, because it would have attracted attention to herself, and that was something she never did, but her face was all screwed up as if she were in agony. My brother Zan, in his uniform of a naval flier, cried and used his handkerchief, and my biggest brother, Bo, in his uniform of a second lieutenant in the infantry, cried and didn't use his handkerchief, and the tears rolled down and dropped off the end of his nose. I tried to cry but I couldn't, so I pretended to cry and used my handkerchief. Then, soon after the funeral, my mother rented the house and all its furniture to a wartime official of the Interior Department, on a year's lease. My sister was sent away to normal school to start learning how to be a schoolteacher. Miss Annabelle was given a leave of absence and sent to visit some of her relatives in North Carolina. My mother and I went to visit one of her sisters in Virginia. My mother knew that her sister's husband didn't approve of dogs, and she said she wouldn't want to impose Bessie on him, so Bessie was sent to some friends of Mother's in Georgetown, who said they'd give Bessie a good home. My mother said they would let us have her back again after we got settled, unless the children in that family got too attached to her, in which case she would find me another dog somewhere. All during those first days after my father died, whenever my mother looked at me I would avert my eyes. I couldn't help it.

Toward the end of that summer, my mother and I returned to Washington and boarded with the Hobarts, a family who lived up the block from our rented house. The Hobarts' boy, Phil, was a close friend of mine, but my mother didn't care much for the Hobarts. They were what she called common. My mother said she didn't want to obligate us to the Hobarts by asking them to let Bessie stay there. I had the influenza at the Hobarts', and it left me depressed, exactly as my mother said it would. Influenza germs did something to the metabolism, she said. When I got over the influenza, we went to board with the Whitmans, in Georgetown. My mother and Mrs. Whitman were bosom friends, as they said, but my mother didn't think much of Mr. Whitman. She said he was an autocrat. They had a daughter, Justina, who was my age. I ignored her. I was starting my first year at Western High School, I frequently smoked cigarettes in secret, and I had fallen in with some freshmen who not only smoked but knew all about everything. What they said seemed incredible, but after a while I believed it. Although there were girls in my head, I had no use for them in the flesh. I was unnecessarily mean to Justina. If one of the pleasant pictures about my father was going on in my head, the girls there sometimes broke right in and started running off a reel about themselves when I didn't want them to, but if some of the bad pictures about him were going on, I couldn't make them stop even if I deliberately tried to get the girls started up. I kept having the same old nightmare almost every night.

I was still in short pants, and my mother said I couldn't wear long pants until I was fifteen. I joined the Western High cadets in order to get one of their long-pants uniforms, and when I got it, I wore it whether it was a drill day or not, and also on Saturdays and Sundays. I was almost six feet tall, and many people thought I was at least sixteen. My mother gave in and bought me a long-pants civilian suit, a single-breasted blue flannel, at Woodward & Lothrop's. My uncles and my aunts and my first cousins and my mother's friends would say, "So this is the man of the family!" when we went to see them or when we ran into them after church on Sundays, and my mother would say "Yes, indeed, he's the man of the family now." They would smile at me, and I would look serious. My mother talked to me a great deal when we were alone together, and told me all her worries. I couldn't look straight into her eyes, and I couldn't ask her if she had a secret she wanted to share with me. Still, I felt as if I really was the man of the family. I cut down on cigarettes, broke off relations with the carefree gang of freshmen I had first taken up with at Western, made new friends among sophomores, juniors, and even seniors, and started going to dances with real girls, some of whom I hugged and kissed on the lips in the back seats of automobiles on the way home. Then the war ended abruptly, and my mother and I moved back into the Mt. Pleasant house. Miss Annabelle returned to active duty. My brothers came home, took off their uniforms, and joined the family circle. I was sure they didn't like me any more because I was so grown up. I began to smoke even more than I used to, and, for the first time, to steal and to skip school.

When my mother decided to take two or three of what she called paying guests into the house, I resented them as intruders but, at the same time, welcomed them because of the stealing I was going in for. In the daytime, with some of my best friends as accomplices, I stole all kinds of stuff from ten-cent stores. Once in a while, at night, we stole somebody's automobile that had been left on the street with the ignition key in it. We would drive the car around for an hour or so and park it in some other neighborhood. Singlehanded I occasionally stole quarters and half dollars from my mother's handbag. She always missed the money and questioned me about it, without, of course, accusing me. When the boarders came, I stopped stealing from her and stole only from the boarders. One of them, a Mr. Gireaux, was a gold mine. He was a bachelor, a clerk in the Treasury Department, who tittered shyly at my mother's dinner-table conversation, raising his napkin to his mouth and ducking his head. My mother liked him. She said he came from good French Huguenot stock—the Gireauxes.

She thought he might be related to the Huguenots on her father's mother's side of the family—the Micheauxes. In any case, Mr. Gireaux fell in love at first sight with one of the lady boarders. When he went down the hall to take a bath and comb his hair down slick, I would step into his room and steal some of the loose change he always left on top of his bureau. He never seemed to miss it. I began looking into his billfold and taking, sometimes, as much as three dollars. Not a word or a sign came from him. He was befuddled with love.

I used the money I stole to supplement my allowance of two dollars a week, which barely covered the cost of carfare and lunch. Miss Annabelle made me an excellent lunch every day of chicken or roast-beef or Virginia-ham sandwiches and fresh fruit, wrapped it in a paper bag, and tied it up with string, but I tossed it every day into the sewer at the corner of Klingle Road, on the way to the streetcar, because the older crowd I was going with ate lunches of hot dogs or baloney sandwiches, and no fresh fruit, at the delicatessen across the street from the high school. I had forty-five dollars in a savings account at the National Savings & Trust on Pennsylvania Avenue—money I'd earned during the Christmas holidays delivering flowers for a florist—but I wasn't supposed to touch that, and I didn't. I depended on Mr. Gireaux. Finally, I took a ten-dollar bill out of his billfold, and this time he did miss the money. He told my mother he couldn't be sure, but he thought a ten-dollar bill had disappeared from his billfold. She questioned me about it, without, of course, accusing me. That blew over. Mr. Gireaux and the lady boarder became engaged to be married, and seemed happy, although my mother was inclined to think she was too young for him and was close to being common.

I PROBABLY WOULD have gone back to Mr. Gireaux and his billfold again if I hadn't run away from home about that time. I had been skipping school for days at a stretch and persuading a girl, a senior, to write excuses for me, to which she forged my mother's name. On the whole, skipping school was a tiresome and worrisome business. The free time hung heavy on my hands. It was too cold to go swimming or fishing. About the only thing I could think of to do was to go to the movies. But the movies didn't open until eleven o'clock, and in order to pretend to be going to school I had to leave the house at half past eight. From then until eleven, I was at a loose end. I spent most of those mornings at the Smithsonian Institution, a museum which, along with other museums, I loathed at that time, owing to its educational values. It was warm inside the Smithsonian, though, and as good a place as any to hang around in at that hour of the morning. Sometimes I went to the zoo, which was not far from our house, but I had worked there in past summers raking leaves, I knew all there was to know about it, and it interested me even less than the Smithsonian. I couldn't smoke in the Smithsonian, but, once inside a movie theatre, I could sit down in a deep leather chair in the gentlemen's lounge in the basement and smoke. But if I smoked a whole cigarette when I went in, I would miss some of the picture. I usually smoked half a cigarette and didn't really settle down to smoking until the program was over. Then I would go back to the smoking room and smoke for a long time, and afterward would see some of the program over again if I felt like it. Unless I wanted to spend the rest of the day alone, I had to leave the theatre before the end of the second showing and catch a streetcar over to Georgetown, in order to be outside the high school when the classes were dismissed at three o'clock. Then I could join up with some of my friends and find something to do until time to go home to supper.

At last, things came to a head. I went back to school one February morning with a forged excuse, handed it in, and, after an hour or so, was summoned by the principal. He told me he had found out my excuse was a forgery, that he had been in communication with my mother, that I was suspended indefinitely, and that I could

go home. It was around half past eleven. I got on a streetcar, expecting to change at Dupont Circle and get on another one for
Mt. Pleasant and go home, but before I got to Dupont Circle I had
a picture showing me running away. The streetcar was going downtown, and I stayed on it. I went to the National Savings & Trust
and drew out my savings. Things still seemed to be moving very
fast. I realized I couldn't get far on forty-five dollars, and it also occurred to me that I would need some clothes and a suitcase to carry
them in. I took a blank check from the desk in the bank lobby on
my way out.

I then went to Woodward & Lothrop's. My mother had a charge
account there. I had occasionally bought things for her in the past,
at her direction, and charged them. But before charging anything
this time I went to the cashier's window in the bookkeeping department, filled in the blank check for forty-five dollars, signed it,
and gave it to the cashier, a Mr. Maltby. I told him I had a checking
account at that bank, which was a lie, and added that my mother
had one there, which was the truth. He knew me and he knew my
mother. He cashed the check without hesitation.

I then went to the gentlemen's-clothing department and asked
to see some lightweight suits. I didn't know where I was going to
run away to, but I pictured a place that gave me a feeling of being
a long way off, probably somewhere south of Washington, where
it was warmer. The clerk said he didn't have any lightweight-wool
suits, and added laughingly that it was a little too early for Palm
Beach suits. I said that as a matter of fact I was going to Florida—
that a cousin of mine had been taken ill down there—and a Palm
Beach suit might be exactly what I was looking for. He said their
summer supply had come in a few days before and wasn't on the
racks yet but that he would be glad to show me some. I tried on
several and chose one—they were all the same cream-colored
shade—and charged it to my mother. It fit perfectly except that the
trousers were a little long. The clerk wanted to have them altered,

but I said my train was leaving in a couple of hours and that I would get my sick cousin's wife to shorten the trousers when I got to Florida.

I went to the haberdashery department and charged two white shirts and two semi-stiff collars with long points, two suits of B.V.D.s, two pairs of black lisle socks, and two cotton handkerchiefs. I couldn't think of anything else I wanted. I decided the shoes I had on were all right and that I would buy a straw hat with a red-and-black striped band when I arrived in Florida. I was wearing my single-breasted blue flannel, a dark green-and-crimson plaid mackinaw, and a woollen snow cap with ear flaps. I carried my bundles to the luggage department, charged a medium-priced imitation-leather suitcase, had my initials, which were rather long and complicated, stamped in gilt letters on the top of it, and put my bundles into it. I can't understand to this day why somebody in that department store didn't suspect something crooked was going on. I can only presume that it was because I had an honest face.

By the time I left the store, I had made up my mind to go to Key West. It was the only place in Florida I had ever heard of except Palm Beach, and it was as far away from Washington as I could get in a southerly direction and still stay in the country. I had a notion I might wind up somewhere in South America later on, like an O. Henry character, but I didn't want to go there first off. At Union Station, I inquired about trains, bought a through ticket, and engaged an upper berth on a Pullman. The total price was outrageous. While waiting for my train to be called, I bought a cheap edition of O. Henry short stories at the newsstand and put it in a pocket of my mackinaw. I also bought some plain stationery. I found a desk in the waiting room and sat down and wrote a short letter to my mother—the kind of letter, I suppose, that a runaway fifteen-year-old customarily writes. It expressed regret for the worry I was causing her and for the failure I had made of my opportunities. It gave assurances that I would let the family know from time to time that I was in good health, but said that I wouldn't reveal my whereabouts until I had made good. It promised to pay back the National Savings & Trust the forty-five dollars I had drawn by means of the blank check and also to pay for the items I had charged at Woodward & Lothrop's—as soon as I had made good.

I DIDN'T BEGIN to make good until after I returned to Washington, five months later, and got a job as a messenger boy in the advertising department of the *Herald*. In Key West I lived for a few days at a commercial hotel, and then in a boarding house, which was less expensive, until my money ran out. The only work I was able to find was soliciting subscriptions for a Miami newspaper— Key West had no newspaper—and there was obviously no future in it, Key West was not a resort in those days, very little of anything was going on except fishing and cigar manufacturing, and the last thing any resident of Key West wanted was a subscription to a Miami newspaper. When I had no more money, I packed my suitcase and walked down to the wharves, carrying it. I was, of course, wearing my Palm Beach suit and the straw hat with the red-and-black band that I had bought on arrival. I had found that turning up the cuffs of the trousers made them the right length without my spending money on having them altered. I pictured a tramp steamer leaving for South America, but there were nothing but fishing boats, and the captains of these spoke only Spanish. I knew some Latin but no Spanish. Finally, when I got hungry, I went into a lunchroom and asked the man behind the counter if I could do some kind of work in exchange for a meal. He seemed surprised. I suppose I looked rather well dressed. He gave me a meal without requiring me to do any work, and advised me to go to Miami or Jacksonville if I was looking for a job.

I got on the train for Miami and told the conductor when he came around that I had no money but would send him the price of the fare from Key West to Miami if he would tell me the amount and give me his name and address. He seemed dumfounded. When I pressed him for his name and address, he said "Ah, the hell with it," and went to the end of the car and read a copy of the *Saturday Evening Post*, which he slapped every now and then.

After a while he came back and said, "If you want to bum around the country, you can't bum around in those clothes with that hat and that suitcase. You won't get away with it on this railroad or any other railroad. It just happens I'm a softhearted man. Why don't you go back wherever you came from? What do you want to run away from home for anyhow?"

When I told him I was going back home as soon as I had made good, he said "Oh, my God!" and went back to the end of the car and picked up his magazine again.

As I was stepping down from his train in Miami, he said, "Jacksonville's the best place around here to find work. Miami'll be as dead as a doornail until next winter. But you'll have to hop a freight, you understand? You can't get away with this."

I asked him where I should go to hop a freight.

"Oh, my God!" he said. "They slow down at that bend there, going out of the yards," he went on, pointing. "They're mostly empties."

I had established contact with my family by telephoning the house, collect, about a week after I arrived in Key West. I persuaded myself to make the call on the ground that it would relieve my mother's worries if she heard my voice, but I didn't care for the way she talked to me, or for the way my brothers and one of my uncles talked to me, after I had let it be known that I was in good health. They demanded that I return home immediately, and said they would wire the money for the railroad fare. All their sentences ended with the interrogation "you hear?" I replied that I wasn't ready to come home, that I had just got a good job as a reporter on a newspaper in another city, in another state, that I was leaving Key

West for that city and state right away, that it would do no good to put the police on my trail but would only bring disgrace on the family name, and that I would let them know from time to time that I was in good health. As a matter of fact, I wanted to be a newspaper reporter, but I knew that newspapers paid cub reporters only five or ten dollars a week and sometimes asked them to work for nothing while they were getting experience.

I hopped a freight to Jacksonville without difficulty, and learned from some of the other passengers in the empty freight car that there was always work on the Jacksonville docks, at seventy cents an hour. In Jacksonville, I got a room in a first-class rooming house in a good neighborhood without having to pay anything in advance to the landlady. For many weeks, I worked as a stevedore on the docks. I figured that eight hours a day, six days a week, at seventy cents an hour would be thirty-three-sixty a week, on which I could live handsomely and save money, but I usually gave up working after about five hours, drew my pay, had something to eat, and went to the rooming house and lay in bed. Most of the time, I didn't feel lonely, because my head was full of optimistic daydreams of the future. They ran along in my head in between the regular showings of the pictures about my father, and about the girls.

In time, my landlady took an interest in me. She discovered how I was earning the money for my room. She said her brother-in-law was in charge of the Union News restaurants at all the railroad stations in Florida and Georgia, and offered to ask him if he had a respectable job for me. He had one for me in a railroad restaurant at Saint Augustine, not far from Jacksonville. I was to be the all-night counterman, and the hours were to be from seven in the evening until seven in the morning. I could have all the food I wanted to eat, and would receive twelve dollars a week in salary. All I had to pay for was my room, which would be in the house where the restaurant manager and his family lived. I accepted the job. I had written several notes to my mother, saying I was getting along fine but not giving her any address where she could reach me, and now I decided to let the family know where I was. Soon I began to receive letters requesting, not demanding, that I come home. I needn't go back to high school, they said, if I didn't want to. I could go to work in Washington, if that was what I wanted to do, and make good there while living in comfort at the house in Mt. Pleasant. All I had to do to get the money for the railroad fare home was to ask for it, they said. Miss Annabelle sent me three dollars of her own money in cash and said she hoped I would buy something I needed with it. I wrote to my mother and said I was getting some valuable experience at the restaurant, that it was a great place to study human nature, and that I would come home as soon as I had finished an article I was doing for the *Atlantic Monthly* on what it was like to be an all-night counterman in a railroad restaurant in Saint Augustine, Florida. I typed out the article on the manager's typewriter between trains in the early-morning hours and sent it to the *Atlantic*, but they rejected it. Then I typed out and sent to *Judge* an anecdote I had heard my mother tell at the dinner table. It seems that Mr. Burleson, the Postmaster General, had told Alice Roosevelt Longworth that he was opposed to woman's suffrage because woman's place was in the home. "Ah, Mr. Burleson," she told him, "I see that you know as little about the female as you do about the mail (male)." *Judge* liked it and sent me a check for five dollars.

I hadn't been able to save anything out of my salary as an all-night counterman, because the rent for the room in the manager's home was nine dollars a week and that left me only three dollars for cigarettes, toothpaste, soap, stationery, and other incidentals. This was only a dollar more than the allowance I used to get when I was in high school. After I received the check from *Judge* and the manager had cashed it for me, I told him I would like to quit as soon as he got a replacement. He said, in a bored tone, that there had been complaints from customers that I was always either asleep behind the counter or writing on the typewriter in his office, and that I could consider myself fired as soon as I packed my suitcase. I glared at him, and ignored him when he wished me good luck.

I had learned all about railroads from the train crews that stopped at the restaurant. Carrying my suitcase, I climbed on the next train for the North, and stood up in the small space between the locked door at the front end of the baggage car and the rear end of the coal car, behind the engine. The journey was uneventful, but by the time I got to Washington, my Palm Beach suit, my straw hat, and my face and hands were black with coal dust and soot, so I jumped off the train when it slowed down in the yards before it reached Union Station, made my way toward Mt. Pleasant through out-of-the-way neighborhoods, and was able to approach the house from the woods at the edge of Rock Creek Park, instead of coming down the block, where everybody could see me.

I had often pictured what my reception would be like. I had guessed it would be like the return of the Prodigal Son, and it was, except that Miss Annabelle cooked a chicken pie, my favorite dish, instead of roast veal, which I liked only moderately. My brothers treated me as if I were almost as old as they were, and seemed genuinely interested in the narrative I gave them, covering the highlights of my experiences in Florida. My mother held family prayers after supper and thanked God for allowing me to get home safe and sound, but she didn't go on about it, and when she talked to me alone before I went up to bed, she only said she wished she hadn't rented the house after my father went away from us, because she was afraid that year had been hard on me. I told her it was just that I was tired of school and wanted to earn my own living and make good, and she said I could do anything I wanted to, that she wouldn't interfere. I still couldn't look her in the eye.

IT WAS ONLY after I had got the job as messenger boy on the *Herald* and had been promoted to mail clerk, then to stockroom clerk, then to assistant bookkeeper, and finally to payroll clerk and was making thirty dollars a week and studying to become a certified public accountant that I began to feel I still wanted to be a newspaper reporter. As payroll clerk, I was well acquainted with all the department heads, including the managing editor. I knew what everybody's salary was, and the department heads knew I did, which made them treat me with a kind of hollow cordiality when I came around each Friday, the day before payday, to get their signatures on the payroll sheets I had made out. The managing editor was a kindly, patient man named Mike Flynn (who inherited a share of the paper years afterward, when Cissy Patterson died), and I used to ask him about the chances of getting a job as a reporter. I was full-grown by this time and was saving up to buy a Ford coupé, and my seventeenth birthday was behind me. I was interested in girls, motorcars, and the wide variety of Arrow collars on display in the haberdasheries. I was troubled by the talking pictures about my father only once a month or so.

Mike Flynn and I always came to what seemed to be a dead end on the subject of my becoming a reporter. I said I couldn't afford to take a reduction in salary, because I was saving up to buy the Ford coupé, and he said he couldn't pay an inexperienced reporter anything like thirty dollars a week. Some of his best local men, he said, pointing at the payroll sheet in front of him, weren't making that much. Flynn seemed to like me, though, and, besides, the impasse made him angry. Like all newspaper editors in those days, he detested the business office, and felt it was an affront to the editorial department when a likely young man could be worth so much money in the business office that he couldn't afford to become a reporter.

"If you're really keen on this," he said one Friday afternoon that summer of 1922, "you could try doing some feature stories in your spare time. I couldn't pay you anything for them, but if you wrote some that we could print, maybe I could argue that you weren't a cub—that you were an experienced man—and get you the thirty a week. Take a run out to the zoo on Sunday, why don't you? There's always a feature story at the zoo."

"What kind of thing did you have in mind?" I inquired.

"Oh, a piece about some animal. Some animal gets born or dies, or something like that. You know—human interest."

He signed the payroll sheet, and I thanked him.

On the following Sunday afternoon, I wandered around the zoo, talking to the keepers. I knew most of them having met them when I was a leaf-raker. I found that the elephants were all in good health and had produced no offspring. It was the same with the lions, tigers, and pumas, the bears, monkeys, buffaloes, wolves, and foxes, the camels and giraffes, and the seals and sea lions. I was finally reduced to the birdhouse. There, though, I learned from Wally, the birdhouse keeper, that a cockatoo had died of old age on the floor of its cage that morning. It was a white male cockatoo from Malaya. It had been there for more than twenty-five years, and had lived all that time in a cage with its mate, a white female cockatoo, also from Malaya. Their names were on the signs on the cage. The dead cockatoo's name was Jack, and his mate was named Jill.

I pumped Wally from every angle. "I'm a reporter on the *Herald* now, you know," I told him. Like all keepers in all the zoos of the world, he was anxious to coöperate with the press. He racked his brains. He began to bring out, bit by bit, a small store of anecdotal material having to do with Jack and Jill. I took him across the road to the refreshment stand, bought him a sarsaparilla, and urged him to sit down comfortably on a bench and relax. "Just keep thinking of Jack and Jill," I suggested, "and say whatever comes into your mind." He recalled a number of little characteristics that served to differentiate the one cockatoo from the other. He cited their preferences in grain and seed, he described the billing and cooing they did at certain seasons of the year, he told how Jack liked to hang upside down using only one claw and how Jill customarily perched in her corner in a dignified fashion. He remembered that Jack and Jill sometimes had their squabbles and pecked at each other, their wings outspread and flapping.

I began to picture a kind of true O. Henry story of a long, happy marriage of two cockatoos from Malaya that had ended tragically in the death of the husband, by which circumstance the bereft widow was left alone in her cage with only a few of his feathers to remind her of him. When Wally wanted to know if the *Herald* was going to take a photograph of Jill, and said he'd be glad to pose with her, I went to a telephone booth, called up Mike Flynn, and told him the gist of the story, with the idea of finding out if he thought it would be worth sending a photographer out to take Jill's picture.

"It's worth a picture on a dull Monday morning," he said, "but it doesn't sound like much of a story. She didn't kill her mate, by any chance, did she?"

I hesitated, and a strange emotion took hold of me. The emotion of a very young person who is anxious to write something? I don't know. What I do know is that I told Mike Flynn that the birdhouse keeper had, as a matter of fact, said Jack and Jill used to fight, flying at each other with their wings outspread and flapping.

"That might do it," he said. "She loses her temper and pecks him to death, and now she's in solitary confinement for life. Anyway, it's worth a picture. Come on in after you get through, and you can take a shot at doing a story."

MY STORY APPEARED in the *Herald* the next morning, under a three-column headline on page 3, and my name was on it in a byline. Although some unknown copyreader in the *Herald* city room was put to the trouble of correcting the spelling and the syntax, I had no difficulty in writing it. It had poured out of me. The headline composed by the copyreader was:

COCKATOO AT ZOO KILLS MATE; KEEPER PUTS HER IN "SOLITARY"

And there was a two-column picture of Jill in her cage and Wally frowning up at her.

I showed the paper to my mother, in the dining room after breakfast, and she read it through, pausing only to reconstruct one of my sentences so it wouldn't end in a preposition. I listened to her and watched her. She read my story aloud to Miss Annabelle—not because Miss Annabelle couldn't read it herself but because my mother enjoyed reading aloud. Then she told me she'd always known perfectly well I wasn't cut out to be a certified public accountant, and added that as a journalist I would have almost as much opportunity for doing good as I would have had if I'd gone into the pulpit, like my father and my forefathers before me. I looked at the glowing, adored face, and into the blue eyes that had never been averted from me. She started to smile and stopped, and said, "You know, son, you haven't looked at me like that since your father went away from us," and I left the dining room quickly, because I felt I was about to cry. But it was only that I was about to think. (In the dictionary sense.) Creatures and people could die from death, I thought. I concentrated on the idea. I thought of death, of the death of my father. He'd been killed by death, my germs hadn't killed him, my mother hadn't killed him, he didn't want to die, he hadn't agreed to die because God needed him, there was no secret, nothing hidden, he had died of death, in this house he died, where I loved him he is dead, my father is dead.

By leaps and springs, the father's dead, the child's dead, the child's a man. And what is man?

A CASE OF FELONY MURDER

O F ALL THE burglars and safe-crackers in New York who are watched over by the detectives of the Safe and Loft Squad, Morris Shapiro and Jacob Weiss were for many years the favorites. The Safe and Loft Squad operates out of Police Headquarters in Manhattan and is mainly concerned with keeping track of known specialists in the breaking-and-entering field of crime. The detectives follow them around when they seem to be getting ready to pull something off and try to catch them before, rather than after, they have done it. Shapiro was a tall man with a bulbous head, scrambled, irregular features that made his face look like a child's drawing, and an immense, oval body. He weighed more than three hundred pounds. Weiss had startlingly large brown eyes in a pinched, sad face and was about the size of a jockey. The Safe and Loft men had a feeling for Shapiro and Weiss that was almost affectionate. Like most people who knew Weiss, they called him Little Jake, but in speaking of Shapiro, who was commonly referred to by his acquaintances as the Ape Man, the detectives called him Moishe, which is what some mothers call a child whose first name is Morris. Because Moishe was so tall and fat and Little Jake so short and thin, it was delightfully easy for the detectives to follow them around. The pair looked and acted a good deal like Sydney Greenstreet and Peter Lorre in some movie melodrama. The gigantic

Moishe waddled when he walked, and chuckled frequently in a sinister fashion. The tiny Jake had to hop and skip to keep up with Moishe, and he had an unforgettable way of simultaneously licking his thin lips and rolling his enormous eyes when he looked up at his partner. Through the years, Moishe and Little Jake were caught red-handed time after time just as they were about to finish picking a difficult lock or blowing a burglar-proof safe in a jewelry store or some other business establishment. The terms they served in Sing Sing and other penitentiaries were usually brief, because they could rarely be convicted of anything more than an attempt. They hardly ever actually committed a burglary, but they kept trying to until they grew old and tired. In the summer of 1951, Moishe was seventy years old and Little Jake was sixty-seven. Little Jake was the operator of an unprofitable bar-and-grill on Clarkson Avenue, in Brooklyn. Moishe did legitimate odd jobs around the same neighborhood and hung out in Little Jake's place a good part of the time. They seemed to have retired from their lifelong profession of attempted burglary, but nevertheless the Safe and Loft men still kept track of them.

Around the middle of August that summer, word came to the Safe and Loft Squad from a stool pigeon that Moishe and Little Jake were acting as if they were about to pull something off. They had been doing a lot of whispering in one of the back booths of the bar-and-grill, and several times when a stranger in a new Chrysler had parked outside the place and tooted his horn, Moishe and Little Jake had gone out, got into the back of the car, and talked to him. Little Jake had an old Dodge sedan with New Jersey license plates (he couldn't get license plates in New York State because of his record), and he seemed to be going out in it with Moishe more often than usual, both in the daytime and at night.

Detectives Howard J. Phelan, Francis Shannon, and James L. Daggett were assigned to keep watch on Moishe and Little Jake, and they did, sometimes working together and sometimes in shifts, depending on the press of other Safe and Loft work. For a couple of weeks, the detectives didn't see them do anything that looked suspicious. Then, on the morning of August 31st, Moishe and Little Jake went in the Dodge to the corner of Sutter Avenue and Thatford Street, in Brooklyn, where truck drivers and their helpers hang around looking for jobs with trucking companies in the neighborhood. The drivers congregate in one group on the sidewalk and the helpers in another. Moishe and Little Jake parked their car, and after a while Moishe called to a spry, shabby-looking old fellow who was standing with the helpers and appeared to be one of them. The man came over and talked to them for a while, and the detectives got the impression that he was accepting some kind of proposition. He kept nodding enthusiastically, and then he grinned, bowed, waved, and walked off.

That afternoon, Moishe and Little Jake drove the Dodge to a public garage on Rockaway Avenue, in Brooklyn, and put the car inside. Little Jake stayed in the garage, and Moishe walked outside and sat down on a bench. Pretty soon, the man the detectives had taken to be a truck driver's helper got off a bus and joined Moishe. They sat and talked briefly and then went inside the garage. There, Moishe, Little Jake, and the helper removed from the Dodge ten brown corrugated-cardboard cartons tied with heavy twine and put them in a locker. After that, the three men drove to Manhattan and drew up in front of a loft building at 9 West Eighteenth Street, in the garment district. Leaving Moishe and the helper in the car, Little Jake walked around the corner and presently reappeared with a well-dressed, respectable-looking middle-aged man. They stopped to speak to Moishe and the helper, and one of the detectives managed to hear Little Jake address the middle-aged man as "Mr. Keshner." The middle-aged man then unlocked the street door of the loft building, and he and Little Jake went inside. A sign on the building listed the various tenants, one of which was Abraham Keshner, Inc., manufacturers of sports jackets and lounging garments. The Keshner factory occupied the fifth floor.

In about fifteen minutes, Little Jake and Keshner came out. Little Jake got back in the car with Moishe and the helper, and Keshner walked over to Fifth Avenue and up to Nineteenth Street, where he waited at a bus stop. Little Jake and his companions picked him up there in a few minutes, and the four men drove up and down and back and forth around the district, finally parking the car on Sixth Avenue near Fourteenth Street. Moishe, Little Jake, and Keshner stood on the sidewalk and talked for about a quarter of an hour, while the helper sat in the car, and then Moishe, Little Jake, and the helper drove off. Keshner walked back to a parking lot near the loft building and drove off in a new Chrysler.

The detectives assumed that Keshner had hired Little Jake and Moishe to bring the cartons to his factory, steal some of his merchandise, and carry the loot out in them. This is a not uncommon practice among businessmen who are in financial difficulties and want to collect burglary insurance. The detectives figured Moishe and Little Jake had come to look the place over, and would do the job soon. They stuck with Moishe and Little Jake day after day and night after night. One evening, Moishe, Little Jake, and the helper got together at the Brooklyn garage, put the cartons into the Dodge, and met Keshner on West Eighteenth Street. Another night, Keshner met the three men at the garage and they all drove over to the loft building in his Chrysler, with six of the cartons in the luggage compartment and four on the rear seat; upon returning to the garage, they moved the four cartons on the rear seat into Little Jake's Dodge. On neither of these trips did they take the cartons into the building; both times, the men just waited around outside for a while and then drove away. On both visits, Moishe carried a long, flat package.

Then, around seven o'clock on the evening of Monday, September 10th, three days after the trip in the Chrysler, Moishe, Little Jake, and the helper drove in the Dodge to a cafeteria at Broadway and Eighth Street. Leaving the helper outside in the car, Moishe and Little Jake went inside, and were joined almost at once by Keshner. The three men sat together over coffee and talked for twenty minutes. When they came out, Keshner walked down the street to his car and drove it up alongside Little Jake's car. The four cartons that had been put in the Dodge after the previous expedition were now moved back to the rear seat of the Chrysler. The two cars were then driven to the loft building and parked in front of it, and Moishe got out, carrying the long, flat package. Keshner opened the luggage compartment of his car, and he and Little Jake and the helper took the six cartons in there and the four on the rear seat into the building, accompanied by Moishe. Detectives Phelan and Daggett had parked their car across the street, far enough down the block to watch the men but not close enough to attract their attention, and Detective Shannon had parked on the corner of Fifth Avenue.

In half an hour or so, Keshner and the helper came out of the building carrying a couple of cartons apiece, put them on the rear seat of the Chrysler, and went back and got more. When they had put all ten cartons on the rear seat, they got in and drove toward Fifth Avenue. Detective Daggett stayed to keep a watch on the building, and Phelan and Shannon went after the Chrysler in their cars. At Fourth Avenue, Phelan forced the Chrysler to the curb and Shannon, who was right behind him, jumped out of his car, drew his gun, and covered Keshner and the helper. When Phelan opened the door of the Chrysler to take a look at the cartons, he smelled gasoline. The top of one of the cartons hadn't been properly tied, and Phelan saw a tin container inside. He took it out and looked at it. It was a five-gallon gasoline can, and it was empty. He ripped off the tops of the other cartons and found that all of them contained empty five-gallon gasoline cans. Until that moment,

Phelan and the other detectives had assumed that the cartons had been carried into the loft building empty and carried out filled with some kind of loot. Now Phelan realized that what the men had in mind was arson.

KESHNER, WHO WAS known to his friends as Al, has been described by a psychiatrist as "a short and stocky, mild-spoken, middle-aged individual, without psychosis, of average intelligence, aggressive, abstemious in his personal habits, a good husband and father, but a man who possessed a rather deep acceptance of the questionable ethical standards with which he was evidently familiar in his every-day dealings in the garment district of Manhattan." Around 1943, he had borrowed seven thousand dollars from friends and relatives in Brooklyn, where he was brought up, and had gone into business for himself, manufacturing sports jackets and bathrobes. He paid off his debts in three years. When business was good, he employed about forty workers in his factory, had a weekly payroll of four or five thousand dollars, drew a salary of a hundred and fifty dollars a week for himself, and most years made a profit of eight or ten thousand dollars. He had a married daughter, an eighteen-year-old son at college, and another son four years old. He lived in a comfortable apartment in Brooklyn, and in the spring of 1951 he had bought the new Chrysler, paying cash for it out of his savings, which amounted to something over seven thousand dollars. He went to lunch nearly every day at the Longchamps at Fifth Avenue and Twelfth Street, a favorite place among successful businessmen in that district. He spent his evenings quietly with his family.

While Phelan looked over the cartons and Shannon kept the two men in the front seat covered, Keshner said nothing and neither did the helper. Finally, Phelan spoke to Keshner, and the following eerie dialogue, later introduced in court as evidence, occurred:

"What's this going to be, a fire?" asked Phelan.

"Yes," said Keshner. "What's this all about? I am a businessman. I have a place of business on Eighteenth Street."

Phelan frisked him and found no weapons. Then Keshner reached in his vest pocket, handed him one of his business cards, and repeated, in an injured tone, "I am a businessman."

"What time is the fire going to take place?" Phelan asked.

"About five o'clock in the morning."

"Is Jake and Moishe going to stay in the building?"

"Yes, but—my God! Do you know them?"

"Yes, I know them a long time."

"How did you get on to this?"

"Well, I know Jake and Moishe a long time. What happened last Friday night?"

"My God! Were you around then? There was somebody in the building and we couldn't make it. I have been trying to make this damned fire for a month, and I was going to make it myself. Can't we straighten this thing out? Can't we talk this thing over? Can't we let this thing go off?"

"Are you crazy? If you let this thing go off, there might be a hundred firemen killed. Ten five-gallon cans of gas is fifty gallons of gas."

"Can't you let it go off? I need the money. I'm in a desperate way."

Phelan put an end to the conversation by telling Keshner to hand over the keys to the building and ordering him to drive back there in a hurry. Shannon took the helper in his car and followed Phelan. Then Shannon stood guard over both men while Phelan joined Daggett, who had been watching the front door. They let themselves into the building and climbed up four dark flights of stairs to Keshner's factory. Inside, Moishe and Little Jake had finished systematically sloshing gasoline around, pouring it on the floor, on the desks, in the filing cabinets and wardrobes, and under the sewing machines. Moishe had his coat and shirt off and was sweating. He was evidently ready to set the fuse, which was in the long, flat package. The usual method used by professional firebugs is to play out the fuse down a couple of flights of stairs and light the end of it on their way out of the building. After the detectives had arrested Moishe and Little Jake, Phelan, who was almost overpowered by the gasoline fumes, said, "We better get out of here. This place is loaded." They started downstairs. Then, at Phelan's suggestion, they all went back into the factory to let Moishe get his shirt and coat, which he had hung on an office chair.

A minute or two after Moishe, Little Jake, and the two detectives went back into the factory, something set off the gasoline. There was an explosion that was heard for blocks, and flames shot out and upward from the fifth-floor windows to a height of thirty or forty feet. Detective Shannon, sitting in the car with Keshner and the helper, later said the sight reminded him of a flame-thrower. A moment earlier, Keshner had asked Shannon, "Can't we please go up there and dump the gasoline down the toilet and clean the place up before my employees come to work in the morning?"

Moishe and Detective Daggett were burned to death inside the factory. Little Jake was taken to St. Vincent's Hospital, where he died. Detective Phelan was knocked unconscious. He came to shortly, crawled out of the office, and fell halfway down a flight of stairs. "I kept yelling for Daggett, and I could hear two voices screaming inside the loft," Phelan said afterward. "My clothes were afire, and I managed to get my coat off and part of my shirt, and there were several bits of stuff all around the floor—part of the wall, which had collapsed onto the stairway—and I managed to get down the stairway to between the first and second floor, at which time I observed the form of a man hanging in the elevator shaft. I thought it was Daggett, and I called his name several times, and then I saw it was Little Jake. There was a lot of other debris and burning material that came down in through the elevator shaft, and it forced me out through the front door." Phelan was also taken to St. Vincent's Hospital, and he remained there for two months, being treated for third-degree burns of the face, back, and hands. He was later retired on a disability pension. He has never fully recovered, but he is now able to do some work as a private investigator.

Keshner was taken to the Tenth Precinct station house while firemen were still trying to put out the fire. There he talked freely to detectives and to Assistant District Attorney James L. Daly, of the Homicide Bureau. He made no attempt to deny he had hired Weiss and Shapiro to set the fire and had helped them with their preparations for it. His motive, he said, was to collect fire insurance. He knew he was in trouble and evidently thought he would be sent to jail for second-degree arson. When Assistant District Attorney Alexander Herman, chief of the Homicide Bureau, had absorbed the main facts of the case, he conferred with District Attorney Frank S. Hogan, and it was decided that Keshner should be, and possibly could be, convicted of first-degree murder under a New York statute that covers what is known as a felony murder. Holdup men who kill somebody without premeditation, or even by accident, in the course of committing the felony of armed robbery have frequently been sent to the electric chair in this state, but there was no precedent that exactly covered Keshner's case. However, the definition of murder in the first degree, which includes the so-called felony murder, appeared to Hogan and Herman to encompass Keshner's act. The definition is: "The killing of a human being is murder in the first degree when committed, first, from a deliberate and premeditated design to effect the death of the person killed; and, two, when committed without a design to effect death by a person engaged in the commission of, or in an attempt to commit a felony, either upon or affecting the person killed, or otherwise." If it could be proved beyond a reasonable doubt that Keshner had hired Weiss and Shapiro and had helped them prepare for the fire, Keshner would be guilty of attempting to commit arson in the second degree, even though he wasn't in the building when the fire broke out, and an attempt to commit arson in the second degree is a felony. Keshner was indicted for the murder of Detective Daggett. The truck driver's helper, whose name was Jacob Mayron, insisted he hadn't known about the arson plot, but he was nevertheless indicted on the same charge. Keshner and Mayron were held in the Tombs without bail and went on trial together before Judge Francis L. Valente and a jury in the Court of General Sessions in April, 1952, seven months after the fire.

BEFORE THE TRIAL, Assistant District Attorney Herman had talked over the case at great length with Assistant District Attorney Richard G. Denzer, chief of the Appeals Bureau, and had tried to prepare it as carefully as possible. Herman and Denzer had sounded out many of their friends in the legal profession, and almost all these lawyers were certain that under the circumstances outlined, a conviction for first degree murder couldn't be obtained, and that even if it were, the Court of Appeals wouldn't sustain the conviction. Herman and Denzer, supported by Hogan, believed that Keshner and Mayron were as guilty of murder in the first degree as they would have been if a death had resulted from an armed robbery they had conspired to commit, and they based their case on that belief. As chief of the Homicide Bureau, Herman ordinarily leaves prosecutions to his assistants, but he decided to handle this one himself, with the help of Daly, who had taken Keshner's statement a few hours after the fire and had done most of the leg work in the preparation of the case. Keshner hired James D.C. Murray, one of the best criminal lawyers in New York, to defend him, and Mayron had Abraham J. Gellinoff, Morris Dickman, and LeRoy Campbell, who were appointed by the court.

Herman's opening statement to the jury was brief, factual, and unemotional. A police detective had been killed, he said, in a fire that had resulted from an arson plot in which the defendants were conspirators, and, under the law, that constituted a felony murder. "Gentlemen of the jury," he said in conclusion, "we will prove to you that these two defendants, Keshner and Mayron, with two associates, Weiss and Shapiro, who are now dead, caused the death of Detective James Daggett by committing this criminal fire, this arson which all four of them perpetrated in Keshner's loft at his request and at his direction, so that he might collect the fire insurance. Listen well and carefully to the evidence, gentlemen. See where the truth lies. Apply the laws of this State to the facts as you find them to be, apply the laws as you get them from His Honor without mental reservation, and exactly as you get them, and do justice not only by these defendants but by the People of the State of New York."

Murray said, in part, "This defendant, Al Keshner, is a man in his early forties. All his life there was no taint or criminality connected with him. We will prove that he worked all his life honestly, trying to earn a living, and that he never in all his life committed a criminal act. And I shall call character witnesses to show you his reputation in the business world and in his social contacts. Gentlemen, I say to you, and we shall prove, that the defendant Keshner may have been ill advised, he may have done things he should not have done, he may have been guilty of some dereliction, but murder—never. It was the farthest thought from his mind that any human being should ever be harmed. It is true that business was bad. It is true that he had insurance. . . . It is true that he set about to have a fire made. This being a felony murder, this being one of the charges, one of the harsh features of the law, we will prove to you that he tried to stop anything that would hurt anybody in this case. And I say to you again, without going into details, that he may not have done what was right, but murder—never."

The attorneys for Mayron told the jury that his defense would be that he knew nothing of the arson plot, that he had been paid fifteen dollars to help carry the cartons, and that he had not been allowed to carry them all the way to the fifth floor of the building, where he might have seen what Weiss and Shapiro were doing with what was inside the cartons.

The first witness for the prosecution was Dr. Milton Helpern, Deputy Chief Medical Examiner. Daggett's body had been found inside the factory, with all his clothes burned off and his detective's shield resting on his chest. The body had been identified at the morgue, in Dr. Helpern's presence, by a brother, a friend, a first cousin, three firemen, and a patrolman.

"Will you describe the body as you found it, and give us your findings?" asked Herman. "And give us the cause of death, if you can?"

"The body was that of a white man appearing to be about the stated age of thirty-seven years," said Dr. Helpern. "It was five feet eight inches tall, and weighed a hundred and forty pounds, and was rather slender but otherwise well developed and well nourished. At the time of the autopsy, it was noticed that the body was extensively burned. A section of the head and chest, abdomen, back, the extremities, were burned so that the tissues were actually charred by flame, but despite the extensive burning it was possible to demonstrate a scar on the left side of the scalp, and also a scar on the abdomen, on the lower right side. That scar was really a double one. One was the scar of an operation and the other was the scar of a drainage operation. It was a pair of scars, old surgical scars, and I emphasize this because they were described to me by the relatives of the deceased."

"You recognized them as identifying marks?"

"Yes."

"Go ahead, Doctor."

"Now, the autopsy indicated that the deceased had been burned to death. The burns were very extensive, and there was definite indication that the deceased had been alive before the burning had taken place, and that evidence was found by the presence of soot which had been inhaled into the air passages, and also by the presence of carbon monoxide in the blood. When anyone dies in a fire, the smoke which is inhaled contains carbon monoxide, and that accumulates in the blood and shows up on chemical examination. So the inhalation of the soot and the presence of the carbon monoxide in the blood indicated that this man was alive when the burning occurred, and also confirms the fact that he burned to death. The autopsy otherwise was essentially negative, except for the burns."

"And what was the cause of death in this particular case?"

"The cause of death, in my opinion, was the extensive burns of the body."

"That is all."

Murray made no attempt to dispute this testimony when he cross-examined Dr. Helpern, and merely brought out the fact that Dr. Helpern had performed autopsies on Weiss and Shapiro after the fire and that both these men had also died as a result of burns.

Firemen then testified that the explosion blew out all the windows in the building and also in buildings across the street. The building was gutted from top to bottom, they said, and it took several hours to get the fire under control. No firemen were killed. They told of finding the bodies and about the shield on Daggett's chest.

A man who hung around the garage where the conspirators had met testified that he had seen them several times in and near the garage, had known that the cartons contained gasoline because he had smelled it, and had been told by Shapiro that they were taking the gasoline to Montauk for a fishing boat they owned. Detective Shannon then took the stand and told of the various meetings between the conspirators, and of what Keshner had said when he and Phelan stopped him at Fourth Avenue before the fire. The next witness was Samuel Tabor, a chemist who works at the Police Laboratory. He testified that he had obtained enough of the contents of the cans to identify it as gasoline. He had tested it by smelling it, by chemical analysis, and by lighting it to determine its flash point—the temperature at which a vapor explodes. The flash point proved to be that of gasoline. Then an insurance broker testified that Keshner had two policies, one for twenty thousand dollars and one for twenty-five thousand, against loss by fire. Detective Phelan testified about the meetings he had observed between the conspirators and repeated his conversation with Keshner just before the fire. Detective Shannon corroborated his testimony. Two fire marshals and a detective who had questioned Keshner testified that he had told them, in more detail, the same story he had told Phelan. Keshner's statement to Assistant District Attorney Daly was introduced in evidence, and it, too, was substantially the same.

In the cross-examinations of all these witnesses, nothing of much benefit to Keshner's defense was brought out, but Mayron's attorneys established several times that, as far as the witnesses knew, Mayron had had no knowledge of the arson plot.

The question of what had set off the fire was taken up next. Detective Phelan had testified that both he and Daggett had put their guns in their holsters when they realized how strong the gasoline fumes were in the factory, because they knew that an accidental shot might cause the fumes to explode. Daggett's gun had been found near his body. An expert from the Ballistics Squad testified that the gun had contained four undischarged shells and two discharged shells. However, he said, the primers of the discharged shells showed no indentation of the sort made by the firing pin of a gun. This witness and other ballistics experts testified that in their opinion the discharged shells could not have been fired by pulling the trigger but were set off by the heat of the fire. The defense did not dispute this testimony.

The last witness for the prosecution was William G. McKenna, Chief Chemist for the Bureau of Explosives of the Association of American Railroads. He is a member of the American Chemical

Society, the National Research Institute, the National Academy of Sciences, and the National Fire Protection Society. He qualified as an expert on inflammables, and especially on gasoline. He testified that gasoline vaporizes when poured over a flat surface, but that it will not ignite of its own accord.

"In other words," asked Herman, "can gasoline vapor when mixed with air ignite spontaneously?"

"No, sir, it does not," replied the witness.

"You say it has to have a source of ignition?"

"That is correct."

"What do you mean by that?"

"Well, a match flame, some sort of a spark, such as in your automobile the sparking of the two electrodes of your sparkplug, or some source of, any source of flame—spark."

"An electric spark?"

"Yes, sir."

"How about static electricity?"

"That would do it, sir."

Under cross-examination, Murray brought out that gasoline fumes could be set off by the firing of a gun, by lighting an electric light, by the ringing of an electric bell, by a shoe nail scraping on concrete, and by a spark of static electricity caused by a man walking across a carpet and touching another man. The defense lawyers took pains to have the witness reiterate the fact that gasoline fumes could not be set off without some kind of igniting agency.

The prosecution rested, the jury was asked to leave the courtroom, and the defense attorneys argued long and hard in support of motions for the Judge to dismiss the indictment. Keshner's attorney had an exchange with Judge Valente that brought out the difficulties of obtaining a conviction in such a case, and also made fairly clear the views of the Judge in the matter.

"Your Honor is inclined to believe, to be more precise about it," said Murray at one point, "that the mere fact that the arsonists [Shapiro and Weiss] spread gasoline about in the loft on the fifth floor of this building at 9 West Eighteenth Street, without any further effort on the part of the arsonists, constitutes murder in the first degree, a felony murder, because Officer Daggett died, without any proof of any further overt act on the part of the arsonists—is that your view, Your Honor?"

"Yes," said Judge Valente. "On the theory, of course, as I have indicated, that at least there was an attempt to commit the crime of arson in the second degree, and that their activity at the time of the commission of the act in furtherance of the attempt is what controls. Even if they were in custody at the time this place was ignited, I say it is not their status at that time that controls. It is their conduct in spreading that gasoline that fixes, that attaches that responsibility."

"I see Your Honor's reasoning, but what intrigues me is this: They are both under arrest and they are outside of the loft premises and they can do nothing in furtherance of igniting the gasoline. I think that is conceded."

"Yes."

"They are taken back by the police. They don't go back themselves. And my view of it, Your Honor, is even though we concede spreading the gasoline was an attempt to commit arson, that there must be some overt act on the part of the arsonists to cause the fire and the consequent explosion. You have nothing like that in this case."

"But you have the attempt, which consists in the spreading of the gasoline, and if it had not been for the fact that they were taken in custody it is a fair assumption they would have gone on to ignite it. It would have made the completed crime of arson in the second degree."

"But, Your Honor, they could not have caused the death without some overt act beyond what they had done, isn't that so? I mean from the evidence in the case?"

"Yes, but it was that overt act which was the primary cause of the fire that in turn resulted in Daggett's death."

"But, Your Honor, that was not a competent cause for igniting. Anything they did did not ignite this gasoline, according to the evidence in this case."

"That is true."

"Absolutely nothing."

"But if they had not spread it, there would not have been any igniting."

Murray argued a little while longer, and then the Judge asked Herman if he had anything to say.

"I don't think it is particularly necessary to take up Your Honor's time," said Herman. "Confining my consideration only for a moment to the last point of argument of both counsel, it seems to me that the question before Your Honor to answer is whether an attempt to commit the crime of arson was present, and as the result of that attempt was there a fire which was touched off or sparked off by an unknown agency, was that attempt followed by a fire which was caused through the attempt, and if that is so, was Daggett killed as the result of that fire? If that were so, why, then, Daggett was killed as the result of this attempt, and that is the underlying felony of attempted arson."

After the jury was brought back in, a number of character witnesses called by Keshner's attorney testified that Keshner was an honest businessman and a good family man, and the prosecution did not try to controvert what they said. Then Keshner took the stand in his own defense. Murray led him through a summary of his early life in Brooklyn, where he grew up as the youngest of five children in a comfortably situated middle-class family. He told how his garment business, which was owned by him and his wife, started losing money in the summer of 1951. He told how he had met Weiss casually in a Brooklyn restaurant, had learned that Weiss might be willing to "take care of anybody who had enough fire insurance," had looked Weiss up at his bar-and-grill, and had started the negotiations that had led to the fire. He had agreed to pay Weiss and Shapiro fifteen hundred dollars to set the fire and had given them two hundred dollars as a starter and eleven hundred and fifty dollars more on the night of the fire. He said he didn't know the cans in the cartons contained gasoline but had thought it was something that would have to be mixed with something else before it could be used to start a fire. He said he had postponed the fire on the two earlier times they had taken the cartons to the loft building because he had found other people in the building and hadn't wanted anybody to get hurt. He said it had never occurred to him that firemen might be hurt or killed fighting the fire, and that when Detective Phelan had brought this possibility to his attention he had wanted to go into the building and call the thing off. He didn't deny the testimony of the detectives, the fire marshals, and Assistant District Attorney Daly as to what he had said to them before and after the fire, but he did say he couldn't remember all he had said, because he had been under an emotional strain. He said that, as far as he knew, Mayron hadn't been aware of the plot and hadn't been allowed to go up to the fifth floor. He himself went up, he said, and had seen Weiss and Shapiro pour the contents of the cans into a large metal trash barrel and then put the cans hack into the cartons. He said he was supposed to dump the cartons at a junk yard in Brooklyn that Weiss had told him about.

Under cross-examination, Keshner stood up fairly well, but even before the cross-examination he had testified that he had hired Weiss and Shapiro to set fire to his factory and had helped them in their preparations for it. Undisputed evidence presented earlier had established that Daggett had met his death as a result of a fire that would not have occurred if these preparations had not been made. After summations by Herman and the defense lawyers and the Judge's charge had been delivered, the jury retired at one o'clock in the afternoon. It returned to the courtroom two and a half hours later.

"The jurors, please rise," said the court clerk. "The defendants, please rise. Jurors, look upon the defendants. The defendants, look upon the jurors. Gentlemen of the jury, have you agreed upon a verdict?"

"We have asked for some information from the Court," said the foreman.

"You have not agreed?"

"We have not agreed."

"Please be seated," said the clerk.

"I am in receipt of a communication from the jurors, which reads as follows," said Judge Valente. " 'Will you please read that portion of the charge which has to do with the definition of conspiracy, and does the guilt or innocence of a defendant depend upon his full and specific knowledge of the nature and extent of the conspiracy to commit an arson?'

"Now, I will read to you the law defining a principal and then go into conspiracy. The law defining a participant, a principal, or an accomplice in a crime is as follows, and I quote: 'A person concerned in the commission of a crime, whether he directly commits the act constituting the offense, or aids and abets in its commission, and whether present or absent, is a principal, as is also a person who directly counsels, commands, induces, or procures another to commit a crime.' You can see from this definition that you are a principal in the commission of a crime and guilty of the commission of that crime if you do it yourself, help someone else do it, or procure someone else to do it. . . . Now, answering your question: 'Does the guilt or innocence of a defendant depend upon his full and specific knowledge of the nature and extent of the conspiracy to commit an arson?' In order for a defendant to be considered a member of the conspiracy, you would have to be satisfied beyond a reasonable doubt that whatever he did was done by him with knowledge of the purpose; namely, in this instance, to commit an arson in Keshner's loft so as to collect on the insurance. Is that clear now?"

"Yes, sir," said the foreman, and the jurors retired to deliberate for another three-quarters of an hour. Then they returned to the courtroom and said they had found Mayron not guilty and that they had found Keshner guilty of murder in the first degree, without a recommendation. When there is no recommendation in a case of first-degree murder, the judge has no course but to sentence the convicted man to death. Ten days after the verdict, Keshner was brought back before Judge Valente to be sentenced.

"Al Keshner," said the court clerk, "have you any legal cause to show why judgment of death should not now be pronounced against you according to law?"

Keshner said nothing. His attorney did the talking.

"Well, there is nothing I can say, Your Honor; I wish I could," said Murray. "Your Honor's hands are tied and the judgment is mandatory."

"There is nothing that the Court has to add to what has already been said. It is an unfortunate situation," said the Judge. "This man, in his desire for money, literally pulled his own house down on his head."

Murray remarked, in effect, that Keshner had saved Mayron's life by his testimony concerning him. "There is no question in my mind about that whatever, Your Honor," Murray added, "and I think it was a pretty decent thing on the part of this defendant."

"I agree with you," said the Judge, "and whatever satisfaction it is to him, he can find some solace in that."

"Of course, Your Honor," Murray went on, "it was more or less a grievous blow to me that the jury didn't recommend life, and perhaps it was some failing on my part that brought about that situation."

"I do not think it was any failing on your part at all, Mr. Murray," the Judge said. "It was one of those situations that developed here in this court. Certainly you had a very difficult case, and I think you used all your years of experience to good advantage and did everything you possibly could do for this defendant. It is just one of those situations where the jury saw fit to do as they did, and certainly it is in no wise due to any lack of effort or lack of ability on your part. I think everyone in this courtroom is in agreement as to that, and you shouldn't take the verdict as a reflection on yourself personally or on your ability as an attorney."

While Keshner stood waiting to be sentenced, Murray continued for some moments to discuss the case with the Judge and seemed to find some solace in what the Judge said. "Your Honor," he said finally, "to me, in certain instances, the felony-murder theory, I think, is proper and just, but I think in this case the felony theory that makes this man guilty of murder in the first degree is barbarous. That's what I think about it."

"Well," said the Judge, "if it reaches the point where it will come to the hands of the Governor, I am sure you will be able to make a very good argument."

"That's about all I could do," said Murray, "and I haven't got the remotest doubt that it will fall on deaf ears."

Judge Valente then turned to Keshner and sentenced him to die in the electric chair at Sing Sing during the week beginning Monday, June 23, 1952.

THE DATE OF execution was postponed when Keshner filed an appeal. His son had to leave college and go to work, and his wife spent the remainder of the family savings on the attorneys' fees and other legal expenses in connection with the appeal. Murray dropped out of the case, and the law firm of Wegman, Epstein & Burke represented Keshner from then on. As chief of the Appeals Bureau, Assistant District Attorney Denzer spent most of that summer doing research and preparing his brief in support of the conviction.

The Court of Appeals upheld the conviction by a vote of six to one. Justice Edmund H. Lewis, in a dissenting opinion, dwelt on the fact that, according to the evidence, neither the defendant nor his accomplices actually set the fire and that therefore the defendant could not be held responsible for the death of Detective Daggett. There was no majority opinion; the six other justices simply voted to sustain the conviction.

Keshner's execution was set for Thursday, March 12, 1953. His attorneys petitioned Governor Dewey to exercise executive clemency and, although the District Attorney's Office had fought hard to get a conviction and to have the conviction sustained, after many conferences Hogan, Herman, and Denzer decided to support the petition by recommending clemency.

"Mr. Herman and I spent, literally, many hours in analytical discussion of the moralities and philosophies of the problem, both with each other and with other members of the office," Denzer wrote at the time in summing up the case. "During this period, I made it a point to harass both legal and lay acquaintances by posing the factual situation and requesting personal opinions as to whether or not Keshner should suffer the death penalty. I must have waylaid from fifty to seventy-five persons in this fashion, and in the vast majority of instances I received the answer that Keshner should not go to the chair. When asked the reason for that opinion, the person interrogated would cite one or more of the following factors: that while the crime was a most unsavory one, the actual consequences resulted from a most extraordinary and unforeseeable series of incidents; that Keshner unquestionably would never have entered upon the venture had he had any inkling of the outcome; that he cannot be classified with the armed robber who kills during a holdup; that he was not a criminal by trade but a legitimate businessman with a previously clean record; and that while he deserves very severe punishment, this is not a case for the extreme penalty.

"Far from satisfied with such offhand expressions of opinion, or by our own inconclusive discussions of the matter, Mr. Herman and I delved into the feelings of those more closely affected by the tragedy. Mr. Herman sought the opinions of the father of the deceased detective, of the injured detective, and of their commanding officer. I spoke to Police Commissioner George Monaghan. Each of these men volunteered that he had no opposition to the exercise of clemency.

"Despite all this, and despite continued discussion of the matter with Mr. Hogan and among several members of the office, we never reached any clear-cut conclusion concerning the merits of the application. In one respect, however, we were unanimous. In everyone's mind, doubts appeared from all directions. In this troubled state of our feelings, it was the opinion of Mr. Hogan and all who had wrestled with the problem that we should extend the defendant the benefit of those doubts in a situation where his life was at stake, and for that reason we recommended clemency."

On March 10th, the warden of Sing Sing sent out the customary invitations to those officials, including a representative of the District Attorney's Office, who by law were supposed to attend the execution of Keshner on March 12th Governor Dewey commuted his sentence to life imprisonment on the day the invitations were sent out.

"Keshner's crime was a heinous one," said the Governor in commuting the sentence. "He hired persons to set a fire in the midst of a populous city and caused the death of three men. The nature of his confessions to the detectives after his arrest discloses a total failure to apprehend the tragic consequences that might and did result from his acts." The Governor said he had decided to commute Keshner's sentence largely in view of the recommendation made by the District Attorney's Office and of the fact that the father of the dead detective, as well as the injured detective, were not opposed to it.

After the death of Moishe and Little Jake, the Safe and Loft men made some inquiries in the neighborhood of Little Jake's bar-and-grill in Brooklyn. They are convinced by what they learned that the tall fat man and the short thin man took up arson more or less as a whim, and that the job on Eighteenth Street was undoubtedly their first attempt in this new field of crime.

THIS IS IT, HONEY

W HEN ASSISTANT DISTRICT Attorney Vincent J. Dermody, of the Homicide Bureau, finished talking to Dr. Milton Helpern, of the Medical Examiner's Office, on a morning in
January some years back, he put down the telephone and got out the
file on a man named Jerome Roberts, who was being held without
bail in the Tombs on a charge of murder. He found the stenographic
record of a statement Roberts had made to him a couple of weeks
earlier and read it once more from beginning to end. He remembered how Roberts had sat across the desk from him that day after
he was brought in by two detectives from the Tenth Precinct, on
the lower West Side, and how Roberts had answered the questions
promptly and politely as if he were anxious to please. Dermody is in
the habit of making quick judgments of defendants and putting
them into words in a journal he keeps. "Roberts' tweed sports jacket
and gray flannel slacks were rumpled and he needed a shave," he
wrote in his journal after the interview. "But there was something
inescapably impressive about the expression on his face that seemed
to suggest that he was, in one way or another, a distinguished man,
with some kind of uncommon ability."

DERMODY'S QUESTIONS AND Roberts' answers at the interview went like this:

"Before we start, I want to explain something to you. This gentleman seated on your left, who is operating a machine, is a stenographer attached to the District Attorney's Office. He is going to take down every word that is spoken in this room, every question I ask you, and every answer you make. Do you understand that?"

"Yes."

"Your name is Jerome Roberts?"

"That is correct."

"How old are you?"

"Thirty-nine."

"Are you married or single?"

"Single."

"Before we go any further, I want to introduce myself to you. My name is Dermody. I am an Assistant District Attorney and I am going to question you now about the killing of a woman named Madeline Barry. This killing occurred approximately at 3:30 A.M. on December 18th. That would be yesterday, Thursday morning. It took place in the basement apartment, rear, of a building on West Fourteenth Street. Do you want to tell me everything you know about the events that occurred in the apartment at the time? Answer yes or no."

"Of course I want to."

"Before we go any further, I must warn you—you don't have to say anything."

"There is nothing to hide."

"Anything you say now can be used against you later on. Do you understand that?"

"Yes."

"Knowing what I just told you, do you want to tell the truth?"

"Absolutely."

"Did you know the deceased, Madeline Barry?"

"Know her? Mr. Dermody, I have been living with her for nearly two years."

"What time did you go to bed that night?"

"Pretty early. Around twelve o'clock."

"Did you have anything to drink before you went to bed?"

"We had two drinks before we went to bed."

"What did you drink?"

"Scotch whiskey and beer."

"You were sober?"

"Yes."

"What about Madeline?"

"She was sober, too."

"What happened then?"

"We went to bed."

"Undressed or wearing pajamas?"

"No, we never wore anything in bed. We just curled up and went to sleep."

"Did there come a time when you woke up?"

"Yes. It must have been around three o'clock. It happened right after that."

"What happened?"

"I woke her up. I don't know—I just said, 'This is it, honey.' "

"Now, what do you mean by you said, 'This is it, honey'?"

"Well, I started to choke her to death."

"How did you wake her up before that?"

"She was lying on her stomach and I just shook her shoulder a little bit."

"Did she then turn around?"

"No, she put her face up and around, that's all, and I kissed her."

"When you said, 'This is it, honey,' what did she say?"

"She said, 'O.K.' "

"Well, before, what did you mean by saying, 'This is it, honey'?"

"She knew what I meant."

"There had been some discussion about you killing her before?"

"Not that night. About a week ago. We had talked it over and settled it and we were waiting for the moment."

"What moment?"

"Well, the right moment."

"What did the discussion consist of?"

"Well, we just thought we and this particular life—We weren't attuned to it. We're not—This isn't our type of life."

"What led you to believe this wasn't your type of life?"

"Well, it's one of those things."

"Had you been having difficulties with the deceased—with Madeline?"

"No."

"Was there anything happened that made you feel you wanted to kill her?"

"Well, the idea was we were both supposed to go together."

"Had you discussed this with Madeline?"

"Yes."

"And what plans had you made about taking your own lives?"

"We had tried it once before—last spring, in April. We cut our wrists, but it didn't work, so we went to Bellevue."

"For observation?"

"Something like that."

"At any time during the discussion a week ago did you tell her you were going to kill her?"

"Yes."

"I ask you again, when was the last time before you strangled this girl that you talked about doing away with yourselves?"

"It was a week ago."

"And you told her you were going to kill her?"

"Yes."

"Did she agree to that?"

"Yes."

"How were you supposed to do it?"

"I thought the way I wanted to do it was to turn on the gas and let it go."

"And then?"

"And then on Thursday morning, gosh, I don't know—it just came into my mind and I did it."

"Well, you say you woke her up and told her, 'This is it, honey'?"

"Yes, sir."

"By that you meant you were going to kill her?"

"Yes, sir."

"And she said 'O.K.'?"

"Yes."

"Why didn't you turn on the gas?"

"I did that the next day."

"I mean why didn't you turn on the gas before you woke her up if you wanted to do away with yourself and her?"

"That's kind of hard to explain. I just said, 'This is it, honey' and took her life."

"How long were you awake before you decided to strangle her? Can you tell me?"

"I just woke up and shook her a little and woke her up and said, 'This is it, honey.'"

"And then what did you do?"

"I strangled her."

"How did you go about it?"

"I put my hands around her neck."

"Did she offer any resistance?"

"No."

"Are you sure of that? Are you telling the truth?"

"Absolutely the truth."

"She didn't fight you off at all?"

"No."

"How long did you hold your hands pressed against her throat?"

"That's hard to say."

"Can you try to tell us?"

"Well, it was at least ten minutes."

"What happened after you released the pressure?"

"Then I knew she was dead. I felt her pulse and heartbeat."

"What happened then?"

"I turned her over and closed her eyes and kissed her."

"Did you notice anything about her face, her physical appearance, when you turned her over?"

"It had a kind of peculiar look."

"What did you do then?"

"Well, I just lay there beside her."

"Did you go to sleep?"

"No."

"How long did you lie there?"

"I guess a couple of hours."

"How did you feel?"

"I felt peaceful. She had gone and I was going to be with her pretty soon."

"What did you do after those two hours?"

"I dressed and went to the White Rose Bar down the street. We always went there. It was kind of a home to us. I had a drink to her and went back."

"And what did you do when you got back?"

"Oh, just drank some beer and said hello to my baby."

"What do you mean by 'my baby'? Madeline?"

"Yes."

"What was the next thing that happened?"

"I stayed in the room all day. I fell asleep and sometime later I got up. The radio was playing and there was a news broadcast that said something about eleven o'clock. It was night. I went out and bought a fifth of Scotch at a liquor store and six beers at the delicatessen. Then I went back and drank a lot."

"Then what happened?"

"It was dawn again and I turned on the gas. All the burners on the stove. Then I lay down again beside Madeline."

"What is the next thing you remember?"

"The next thing I remember, the police were there."

"Now, you say there was no argument or quarrel before you strangled this girl?"

"No, we never quarrelled."

"No argument or fight?"

"We never argued or fought."

"Roberts, have you made this statement of your own free will?"

"Yes."

"Has anybody forced you to make this statement?"

"No."

"Have you ever been convicted of a crime?"

"No."

A tenant of the four-story brownstone house in which Roberts and Madeline had a one-room basement apartment smelled gas when he came downstairs around nine o'clock that Friday morning and called the superintendent, a Mrs. Larsen. She is a cheerful, deaf, ailing widow in her sixties. She lives in a basement room with a large white cat and a small brown dog and takes care of the whole building singlehanded—cleaning the corridors every day with a mop and pail, putting out the trash and garbage, collecting the weekly rents. Mrs. Larsen unlocked Roberts' door and she and the tenant went inside, turned off the gas, opened the one window, and called the police. A patrolman from the Tenth Precinct saw that Madeline was dead and thought that Roberts was dead, too. He called the station house, and a detective came over in about ten minutes. As the detective walked in, Roberts woke up. He looked

359

around and, putting his hands over his face, said, "Oh, no! Oh, no!" The detective asked him what had happened. He got up, put on a bathrobe, coughed for a spell, and then sat down in a chair near the open window.

"He didn't seem drunk," the detective said later. "He seemed calm and sad, but he didn't cry or anything like that. He told me he had this suicide pact with his girl and that he had strangled her and turned on the gas to kill himself. He seemed like a refined sort of guy, but dissipated. He was keyed up, of course, but he talked in a refined way. He said, 'This seems sordid but it was beautiful, what we had. It was a meeting of minds and bodies, but we couldn't make a decent living, and things weren't going well.'

"I called Homicide, of course, and while we were waiting for them, Roberts said, 'Before they come, could I say goodbye to my baby?' I said sure, and he went over to the bed again and knelt down and kissed her on the lips. I've got it in my notes here. He said, 'I'm sorry I had to do it, honey, but we had our agreement. Oh, my baby, my baby, I wish I had gone with you!'

"We let him freshen up and rest over at the station house before we took him down to the lineup at Headquarters and then on to the D.A.'s office. He didn't give us any trouble at all. He seems to have been a kind of black sheep of a fairly good New York family. He kept saying in a matter-of-fact way—you know, not hysterical or anything—that he wished he had gone with his girl, but he didn't make any attempts on himself or anything like that. I kind of got to like the guy. I thought it was too bad Madeline and him couldn't make out some way. She was a pretty girl, that Madeline. She was very small and delicate-looking and pale, and she had long black hair. Of course, we had to leave her where she was—couldn't touch anything until Homicide arrived. She looked wonderful, lying there, and she seemed to be smiling, or almost smiling."

After their first attempt at suicide, on April 9th, of the year be-

fore, Roberts and Madeline had gone voluntarily to the Psychopathic Ward at Bellevue and, after their wrists had been treated and
bandaged, they were interviewed separately by psychiatrists. A stenographer sat behind a screen and took down what each of them
said.

"Ill try to make this as short as possible," said Madeline. "I've
led an artistic life, but I've never done a really stupid thing like this.
I've been living with this chap for over a year. I'm technically married to another man. I only saw my husband for two weeks after
we were married six years ago. It wasn't a marriage at all, really.
Afterward, I lost track of him I've never obtained a divorce, but I
want one, and I want to marry this fellow. We want to make it legal. We're very compatible. I've never really known a man before,
and this may seem strange to you, because I'm thirty-one years old,
but it's true. I've been living with my mother all my life. Not that
she is a domineering woman—she is a wonderful artist, a landscape painter. But lately she began interfering a little too much in
our lives. We had our own home, of course, but it was in the same
town she lived in—in Connecticut—so about three weeks ago we
decided to lead our own lives in New York. I've been a music
teacher since I left college—my father was a concert pianist—but
I had caught the measles from one of my child pupils a couple of
months before this and I hadn't been giving any lessons since then.
We sold our car for a couple of hundred dollars and planned to
start all over, but instead of looking for work when we got to New
York we stayed in a hotel and visited friends and drank every single day. Finally, we were running out of money and desperate and
depressed from all the drinking and we decided to cut our wrists.
I knew I was only playing or acting. We realized it was all the consequence of so much drinking and not eating and just all so much
foolishness, so we thought the best thing to do was to go to a hospital and rest a few days, pull ourselves together, and start all afresh.
As we couldn't afford a private one, we thought of Bellevue, but I

never dreamed it would be anything like this. I've been drinking a good deal for the last few years and he's been drinking since he was in his twenties, but neither of us is really an alcoholic. My family always had wine at the table, but I didn't really start drinking until a few years ago, after that two weeks with my husband. I was a virgin and he was horrible. It wasn't really a marriage at all. These last three weeks I've had more to drink than I ever had before. We were terribly happy and free and compatible and we just couldn't seem to stop, and then everything suddenly seemed hopeless, and we wanted to die together and end everything. We wanted to end all the pain."

The psychiatrist's notes on Madeline read, "This patient is very high intellectual level. Father was concert pianist, mother a landscape painter. She is alert, coöperative, neatly dressed, fine appearance, speaks in friendly manner. Feels rather silly about her attempt at suicide. She's a dramatic girl with histrionic behavior pattern." After nine days of medication and observation, the psychiatrist added, "No delusions or hallucinations, no acute or prolonged anxiety or depressions, no paranoid trends or psychotic tendencies. Character neurosis, possibly chronic alcoholism with reactive depression. Discharged to custody of her common-law husband."

Roberts said to his psychiatrist, "When I first met this girl, I wanted no part of her, because of her drinking, but we couldn't get along without each other. It was a meeting of minds and bodies. We were getting along pretty well in Connecticut, but her mother interfered with her all the time, so we gave up the house we had rented, and sold the car, and then, after we had finally spent all our money, we just decided to give up life. We had come to New York and stayed at a hotel near Times Square for a week, drinking every day and very happy but knowing it had to end. We couldn't pay our bill, so we went out without our baggage and checked into another hotel, just down the block. We had dinner and went to the movies. Then we bought a single-edge razor. We went to bed, and when we woke up, she slashed her wrists and I slashed mine. There was very little pain from the razor. We lay in bed bleeding and then we went back to sleep in each other's arms and we thought we wouldn't ever wake up again, but when we woke up we had stopped bleeding, and we didn't feel so depressed—we felt sort of exhilarated—and we decided to come here. I was here once before. My wife put me in for drinking. I was married when I was twenty-one and divorced some years later. I have a son of seventeen. He's in the Marines. My wife was an actress and still is. She wanted a career and I wanted a home. I left school after two years of high school and worked as a clerk and a messenger for law firms for five years. Then I was a professional photographer for four years and did pretty well, but I got to drinking and everything went to pieces. After that, I worked as a timekeeper for a trucking company for a year and a half and then I really began to go downhill. I worked as a bellhop in hotels in New York, Miami, Savannah, and New Orleans. For a few years, I was a common seaman on merchant ships. I'm one of ten children—the oldest. Mother died of cancer of the breast. She was one of the most wonderful people in the world. I guess I was the apple of her eye. Because I was the oldest, she pampered me. I always had good clothes. Grandmother gave us presents all the time. When I was older, I used to take Mother to the theatre and things like that. Father remarried less than a year after Mother's death. I haven't seen him or any of my brothers or sisters for about three years."

"This patient does not appear anxious," the psychiatrist wrote in his report. "He repeats again and again that the suicidal attempt was all foolishness and feels it was the influence of alcohol that made him do this. He does not appear to blame anyone else for his troubles. He is well oriented in all spheres. His fund of knowledge, for his education, is good. Memory is intact, ability to concentrate is poor, insight and judgment poor. Patient is relevant, coherent, does not fabricate. Impression: Neurotic character disorder, with chronic alcoholism and reactive depression." Before discharging Roberts, the psychiatrist noted, "No evidence of psychosis. Does not appear to be seriously suicidal. Patient is quiet and friendly and follows ward routine."

What Dr. Helpern had told Assistant District Attorney Dermody on the telephone that morning of January 7th, before Dermody got out the Roberts file, was that, in the final and official opinion of the Medical Examiner's Office, Madeline had not been strangled but had died of a heart attack. Dermody received a written report dealing with this half an hour after he had spoken to Dr. Helpern. Most of the report had already been prepared. Dr. Helpern had been waiting only for the results of some conclusive tests, having to do with Madeline's brain, before completing it and sending it over to Dermody.

"There is absolutely no question about it," Dr. Helpern said to Dermody. "This girl wasn't strangled. There isn't any evidence at all that anybody even attempted to strangle her. She died of occlusive coronary arteriosclerosis and acute alcoholism. There was three-plus ethyl alcohol in the brain. No barbiturates and no other soluble poisons. I guess the poor guy just had been planning all those days to kill her and himself one way or another, and maybe had been planning to strangle her without telling her he was going to do it that way, and when he saw she was dead, he thought he *had* strangled her."

In his official report, Dr. Helpern dictated to a secretary as he was performing the autopsy, "The body is that of an adult white woman, scale weight ninety-five pounds, five feet and one inch tall, slender frame, slight build. Black hair, few gray hairs. Black eyebrows and brown eyes. The breasts are small. The hands are small. The fingers are slender. The ears are small. The lobes are punctured for earrings. No hemorrhages in the conjunctivae.

"There are no evidences of traumatic injury on the surface of the neck. The lungs are rather large and heavy. The heart lies free in the pericardial sac. The aorta is narrow in calibre.

"The neck organs are removed and dissected. No hemorrhages found in any of the soft tissues of the neck or in any of the muscular structures. The tongue is normal, tip is dry. The larynx is small. No hemorrhages noted in any of the intrinsic muscles of the neck or any fracture of the components of the laryngeal or hyoid bone. No injuries to the spine, ribs or to the bones of the extremities.

"The heart is dissected and removed. The heart is small. Arteriosclerosis. Occlusion. Anatomical diagnosis: Segmental occlusive coronary arteriosclerosis.

"No anatomical evidence of traumatic asphyxia.

"Cause of death: Occlusive coronary arteriosclerosis and acute alcoholism."

Dermody had been preparing a first-degree murder case against Roberts, for presentation to the grand jury. Instead, he had Roberts brought from the Tombs to Felony Court that afternoon and, after conferring with a lawyer from the Legal Aid Society who was representing Roberts, recommended that Roberts be committed to Bellevue for observation. The Legal Aid lawyer agreed with Dermody that it would be best not to tell Roberts about the Medical Examiner's report until after the psychiatrists had examined him. Dermody's idea was that the psychiatrists might find out something from Roberts that wasn't already known.

At Bellevue, Roberts told the psychiatrists what he had told them before. He also talked to a psychologist. Being a prisoner charged with murder, he was given a more thorough examination this time. It included various oral and written tests. One of these was the word-association test, and a psychiatrist noted, "For 'lonely' he says 'frightened,' and for 'woman' he says 'Madeline.'" He told the same story of Madeline's death that he had told to the detective and to Mr. Dermody. He said that he had been working as a counterman in a cafeteria for the past several months and that he hadn't been able to earn enough to give Madeline a decent life. "I was in love with the girl," he said at one point. "We couldn't get along in the world and we wanted to escape, that's all."

The psychologist's report tended to corroborate Dermody's original impression that Roberts had elements of distinction. "His score is superior," the psychologist wrote. "Some slight obsessive doubting about his ability hampers his functioning, or otherwise he would score within the very superior range. Dynamically, there are suggestions that his relationship to his father is a relatively healthy one, while that toward his mother shows some fear reaction, some feelings of hostility combined with guilt over these feelings. It is possible that his relationship with the girl he strangled was, in a sense, a rebellion against a threatening mother figure while at the same time his 'standing by her' when she continually went off on drinking bouts was an attempt to make restitution for his hostility."

The psychiatric report said, "No delusions, hallucinations, or other psychotic trends. Superior intelligence. His may be classified as an inadequate, immature, unstable, and schizoid type of personality, with a rather deep-seated character neurosis, an individual subject to alcoholic excesses and depressions. In summary, there is no evidence of a psychosis or mental deficiency at the present time. He is not in such a state of idiocy, imbecility, or insanity as to be incapable of understanding the charge of murder that is against him, or understanding the proceedings, or making his defense."

Roberts was under observation for three weeks, and was then discharged and sent back to the Tombs.

When Dermody got the report from Bellevue, he conferred with District Attorney Frank S. Hogan and Assistant District Attorney Alexander Herman, chief of the Homicide Bureau and it was decided between them that Roberts ought to be a free man. Dermody called up the Legal Aid lawyer and told him of their decision, and it was arranged to have Roberts brought to Felony Court immediately. It had been about six weeks since Madeline's death. In the Tombs, Roberts had given no trouble, and his file there says he was "friendly, quiet, coöperative, and cheerful, in spite of the fact that he expects to go to the electric chair." He had written no letters and had not asked to be allowed to use the telephone. The Legal Aid lawyer hadn't been to see him, because the usual procedure is to commence the preparation of a defense in such a case only after the prisoner has been indicted by the grand jury.

From the Tombs, Roberts was taken over to the detention pen adjoining Felony Court where prisoners wait for their cases to be called. There the Legal Aid lawyer said to him, "Roberts, you're going to get the surprise of your life. You're a free man. In a minute, the D.A. will make a motion to dismiss the charge against you, and that will be that."

"But I'm guilty of first-degree murder," said Roberts. "I don't understand. What do you mean?"

"You didn't strangle Madeline," the lawyer said. "You just thought you did. Probably some kind of hallucination, or a dream. The Medical Examiner's Office has made a thorough study of Madeline's remains and there is absolutely no evidence of strangulation or attempted strangulation. Madeline died of a heart attack. That is the official diagnosis of the cause of death."

Roberts was sitting on a bench with other prisoners. He got up and walked a few steps toward the far end of the corridor, and the lawyer followed him and put a hand on his shoulder. Then Roberts began to cry. "He didn't make any noise," the lawyer said later. "He just cried silently, the tears streaming down his face. He couldn't talk, and I didn't try to make him talk. Then the case was called and we started into the courtroom. He'd more or less got control of himself by the time we got there."

In the courtroom, Dermody gave the judge a summary of

Roberts' confession and of the Medical Examiner's report, and then made the motion to dismiss the charge against Roberts. Without further discussion, the judge did so. Both Dermody and the Legal Aid lawyer shook hands with Roberts afterward, and Roberts asked Dermody if Madeline's mother had arranged for the funeral. He was told that she had not, and that Madeline had been buried in Potter's Field, on Hart Island, off Pelham Bay. The lawyer rode down in the elevator with Roberts and asked him how he felt. Roberts hesitated and then said, "I really don't know." The lawyer went with him to the entrance of the Criminal Courts Building, shook hands with him again, and wished him luck. "It was hard to tell whether he was happy or not about getting off," the lawyer had said. "He just thanked me and said goodbye and walked out into the world."

That same afternoon, Roberts went to the house on West Fourteenth Street and saw Mrs. Larsen. She had rented the basement room to another couple but had saved Roberts' small store of belongings. She had sent Madeline's things to her mother by parcel post; first, though, she had written to Madeline's mother, telling her she would send them as soon as she could, but that she was having an attack of arthritis and might not be able to get to the post office for a few days. She showed Roberts two letters from Madeline's mother.

"You need not try to send Madeline's things until you are feeling better—if it will make it easier for you," the first letter read. "It may be easier for me to get them a little later, too—right now I am not up to meeting much more. Time can only soften the ache, but never heal it. Thank you for your kindness. It helps." The second letter read, "The box came yesterday. Thank you so much. I do appreciate your kindness and the time and effort that I know went into sending me the things. I am so sorry you had to know Madeline as she was while at your place, for that was not the real

Madeline. When not drinking, she was fine and lovely, but this terrible affliction which got hold of her made her a changed person. I have tried so much and when she was with me it was all so different. I consented to her relationship with Mr. Roberts because I hoped it would make her happier and perhaps keep her from giving in to her affliction. Thank you again, and I do hope this finds you feeling better. I will be so grateful when I can feel that I want to go on. Enclosed is one dollar for the expenses of mailing the box. Please let me know if it does not cover all that you have spent."

Roberts read the letters and handed them back to Mrs. Larsen without comment. After a moment, he asked, "Is there anything at all of Madeline's left?"

Mrs. Larsen said there wasn't. Then she remembered a note Madeline had sent her on Thanksgiving Day after she had brought them a platter of turkey as a good-will gift. She gave it to Roberts, who read it and put it in his pocket. "Thank you not only for the turkey but also for the beautiful thought of offering it," the note read. It was signed, "The Robertses."

"I asked him where he was going to live," said Mrs. Larsen later, "and he smiled—he had a nice smile—and then he said, 'I really don't know,' and left."

The bartender at the White Rose Bar still remembers Roberts and Madeline, but he hasn't seen Roberts since he stopped in there on the morning of Madeline's death. "They were hard drinkers and sad drinkers, but they weren't mean drinkers," he said recently. "They just sat close together at the end of the bar and looked at each other all the time and didn't talk much. Madeline drank more than he did, and sometimes she would cry and he would put his arm around her and take her home. He sure seemed to be in love with Madeline."

Two weeks after this, Roberts turned on all the burners in a basement room he had rented in Manhattan and was dead when the police arrived. He was buried in Potter's Field—a long distance from Madeline's grave. The plots fill up fast in Potter's Field and nobody can reserve one in advance.

THE PERILS OF PEARL AND OLGA

O N THE MORNING of December 31st, some years back, two young women, among many other people, got on a subway train separately at the Fifty-fifth Street B.-M.T. station in Brooklyn, and sat down across from each other in a car as the train moved off toward Manhattan. They had never met, had never spoken, but their lives had been drawn together and the entwinement was a sinister one. They were both working girls and more than ordinarily attractive. One of them was tall, with pale, clear skin and large, dark eyes and shining black hair; she was twenty-eight years old, and her face, besides being beautiful, had an interesting, troubled look about it. She had noticed that the other girl was carrying a gift-wrapped package about the size of a large shoe box. It had an aperture at one end, from which protruded what looked like the lens of a camera. Without thinking much about it, this first girl wondered idly what kind of gift was inside the package. The second girl was barely nineteen and was small and blond. Her name was Pearl Lusk. Only a week earlier, on the day before Christmas, Pearl had found herself disillusioned with New York and its ways, but the mood hadn't lasted long. Now, as the subway train jounced and clattered along, she felt excited and happy. She held her gift-wrapped package carefully on her lap with both hands. Every now and then, she glanced briefly at the tall, dark girl across the aisle, as if to make sure she was still sitting there.

Except for two things that happened to her on Christmas Eve, Pearl Lusk had been pleased with New York ever since she came to the city to seek her fortune, and she told everybody so. She had arrived in the autumn of that same year, some months after graduating from high school in Quakertown, not far from Philadelphia. For a while, she lived with her mother and her stepfather in Brooklyn, but as soon as she got a job—as a salesgirl in a department store—she moved to a furnished room all her own on the upper West Side of Manhattan. She did over both herself and the room almost at once. She began using mascara for the first time, and she settled on a darker shade of lipstick than the girls at Quakertown High had gone in for. On the advice of an expensive hairdresser on West End Avenue, she abandoned her blond bangs and thenceforth lifted to her new world a head of carefully tousled blond curls. She hung pink curtains at the one window of her room and bought a lavender coverlet for the studio couch. She made friends quickly with many of the salesgirls at the store and lunched at a soda fountain every day and dined in a cafeteria almost every night with large groups of them. Her favorite lunch was African-lobster-tail salad and Coca-Cola, followed by a junior banana split. Her favorite dinner was chicken potpie with mushrooms, pecan pie with whipped cream, and coffee. She was healthy and cheerful, and grinned and laughed a great deal, often for no particular reason. Soon she began having dates with young men who worked at the store. As the holiday season approached, her landlady more and more frequently called her to the telephone in the downstairs hall. On evenings when the telephone didn't ring for her, she read twenty-five-cent editions of popular novels and and detective stories, one after another, lying at ease on the lavender coverlet of her studio couch.

Pearl was a well-brought-up girl and never went out with

young men to whom she had not been introduced, no matter how handsome they might be. On Thanksgiving Day, a man, whom she considered the handsomest she had ever seen, except for certain movie stars, tried to pick her up on the subway in Brooklyn when she was going to see her mother. Although she talked to him in her amiable way, she refused to have a drink with him or to give him her name and address. He told her his name was Allen La Rue. Afterward, from time to time, she thought somewhat regret-fully about his good looks and romantic name, but on the whole she was glad she hadn't consented to go out with a stranger. What with the crowded lunches and dinners with the chattering gangs of salesgirls, the occasional dates with the fellows she had met at the store, and the twenty-five-cent books, she was contented and occupied. Then, on Christmas Eve, after only three months of her new life had been lived, the department store laid her off, along with batches of other salesgirls, because the Christmas rush was over. On top of that, her landlady told her that same day that she was getting tired of calling her to the telephone and in the future would call her only if her mother wanted to speak to her.

By thus eliminating Pearl's salary and obliterating her social life, the department store and the landlady were unwittingly preparing Pearl for her next encounter with the handsome stranger she had once fended off. She ran into him the second time in a subway train in Brooklyn on the evening of the day after Christmas, when she was on her way back from her mother's, and this time she agreed to get off with him at Times Square and have a drink. She ordered her favorite, which was Scotch whiskey and a 7-Up. She told him about losing her job, and about the landlady, and he was sympa-thetic. Later on, she remembered that his manner had seemed to change subtly as they chatted over their drinks that evening. "He seemed interested in me like any other man at first," she told an As-sistant District Attorney, "but the more I talked the more I felt like he had some different kind of interest in me." At any rate, after she had talked awhile, the man said he had a job for her if she wanted it. He told her about the work, and she was enchanted. It reminded her of the sort of thing Perry Mason, the lawyer, was always asking his secretary, Della Street, to do in those absorbing novels by Erle Stanley Gardner that she had been reading. Besides being the handsomest man she had ever seen off the screen, she thought Allen La Rue was by far the best-dressed. He had on a double-breasted gray suit with widely spaced pencil stripes and sharply pointed lapels, and the coat had padding that emphasized his broad shoulders and made the cloth drape smartly down to his narrow hips. His white-on-white shirt had a collar with extra-long points, and he wore a striking blue tie with a flowered design in ivory and gold. Before the evening was over, Pearl had enthusiastically accepted the job, her employer was calling her Pearl, and she was calling him Allen.

Pearl jumped out of bed early the next morning and, after doing her face carefully and brushing her blond curls, put on her best daytime dress. Over it she wore a coat of imitation Persian lamb that she was buying from the store on the installment plan. She had three hats; the one she liked best was a gray one with a large white bow on top, and she put that on. She was to meet Allen around the corner from a building at 42 West Thirty-ninth Street at half past nine. She was anxious to get started on her new job, not only because it was a job but because it sounded so exciting. Allen had told her he was a private detective working for an insurance company that specialized in insuring jewelry and, consequently, in recovering jewelry when it had been stolen from its clients. He had reason to suspect, he said, that a young woman named Olga, who was private secretary to the owner of the Croyden Hat Company, with offices in the building on West Thirty-ninth Street, had stolen some valuable jewelry from one of their clients and was carrying it pinned inside her clothes. The woman knew Allen by sight, and for that reason, Allen said, he couldn't risk being seen by her, because then she might think he suspected what she was up to, and stash the jewels somewhere or dump them with a fence. He couldn't ask the police to arrest her until he could prove that she actually had the jewels. Pearl was going to help him prove that, and he was going to tell her how when she met him that morning.

Allen was waiting for her when she got there. As she later reported the conversation, he said, "Here's what I want you to do first. Go up to the offices of the hat company and ask the receptionist if Miss Sadie White is working there. There isn't any Sadie White, of course, but while you're talking to the receptionist you'll get a chance to take a good look at Olga, so you'll know her when you see her again. She sits just outside the door that leads into the private office of the owner. Here's a photograph of her," he went on, taking one out of his inside coat pocket, "but I want you to see her in person so you'll be sure to recognize her, even in a crowd— like in a subway crowd. I'm going to get you to follow her around when she leaves this afternoon. Now, go up there, and then meet me here afterward and tell me if you think you can recognize her good enough to tail her wherever she goes when she leaves."

Pearl carried out this mission competently and rejoined Allen. She told him that she would now know Olga anywhere and that she had memorized not only the clothes she was wearing but also her street coat and hat, which were hanging near her desk. "That's great," said Allen. "Now I'll tell you how we're going to work this, and don't forget there's going to be a big reward in it for you when we get those jewels back. You take most of the day off—go to the movies or something—but don't tell anybody about this, because there are leaks all over in this racket and it might get back to Olga. She leaves here every afternoon at five. You meet me at my apartment, at 204 East Seventeenth Street, at half past three and I'll show you exactly how we're going to prove she's carrying those jewels."

Pearl went to a double feature, called on some of her friends who were still working at the store, and met Allen at his apartment on the dot. There he showed her an interesting object that he said was an X-ray camera. It looked like a shoe box with a hole in one end and was done up in brown wrapping paper, like an ordinary parcel. A short piece of wire with a loop on the end of it hung out of the bottom of the box. "All you do is point this at her and pull this wire," he explained. "The X-ray picture will show us if she has the jewels. But don't snap the picture where she can see you do it. Take it when she gets off the train in Brooklyn—that's where she lives. You want to be right behind her when you follow her out of the train, so you can take it at close range. You want to be only two or three feet away from her when you snap the picture. After you take it, meet me where we had the drinks last night and I'll take the camera and get the picture developed."

Enthralled, Pearl went back to Thirty-ninth Street, spotted Olga as she left the building, followed her to the Times Square subway station, sat near her until the train reached the Fifty-fifth Street station in Brooklyn, followed close behind her as she got out, pointed the box at her, and pulled the wire. Hoping she had got a good picture, she caught a train back to Times Square. Allen was waiting for her in the bar-and-grill. He questioned her carefully as to just how she had taken the picture, how close she had been to Olga when she took it, and whether Olga had noticed anything. Pearl told him that she wasn't more than two and a half feet from Olga when she pulled the wire, and that Olga hadn't noticed anything, because her back was turned and she was hurrying out of the station. Allen said he would get the picture developed that night, and if she would come to his apartment in the morning, he would tell her how it had turned out. When Pearl saw him the next morning, he said the picture hadn't turned out well at all. "I think the camera is the trouble," he said. "I'll have to get a better one, and it may take a couple of days. You call me here in three days and I'll let you know how things stand."

When Pearl telephoned Allen, he told her that he had the new camera and that he wanted her to meet him in an Automat near Union Square at eight o'clock the next morning—the morning of December 31st. Pearl was punctual. She found that the new camera was bigger and heavier than the other one and that it had the same sort of looped wire hanging out of the bottom. It was wrapped like a gift, in paper with "Merry Christmas," in red, and "Happy New Year," in green, printed over and over. Allen said he wanted her to ride over to Olga's station in Brooklyn and pick her up when she got on the train to go to work. Then she was to sit near her in the subway and, when she got out of the train at Times Square, take the picture exactly as she had taken the one with the other camera. "Remember to aim it low, at her waist," he said. "That's probably where she's carrying the jewels—pinned inside her dress at her waist."

Pearl did as she was told; when the train reached Times Square, she followed Olga through the door, pointed the parcel at her, and pulled the wire. There was a roaring explosion and the parcel nearly jumped out of her hands. Olga screamed and fell on her back, holding her left leg, which seemed to have been nearly blown off. A subway guard rushed up, asking "What happened? What happened?" and Pearl, who had been so close to Olga that she was splattered with blood, said to him, "I just took a woman's picture and somebody shot her." A man in the crowd put a tourniquet on Olga's leg, and a policeman appeared and grabbed Pearl, ripped open her parcel, and quickly saw that what was inside was a sawed-off shotgun. Then Pearl, at last, put two and two together. She began to cry. With the patrolman holding her arm, she leaned over Olga and said, "I'm awfully sorry I shot you. There was this new job, you see, and I thought I was taking your picture with an

X-ray camera." Olga looked up at her and quickly looked away, as if she considered Pearl's role in this drama unworthy of her attention. Speaking to nobody in particular, she said, in what seemed to those who heard her a tone of resignation, "Well, he got me this time. Now if he wants me he can take me. I'm crippled. I wonder what happened to the police? He must have been too smart for them."

During the last two months of that year, it turned out, Olga had told her story to the police a good many times, and she was to tell it again and again later on, occasionally in the presence of stenographers. The transcript of one of Olga's statements (all of them were the same in substance) goes like this:

"When were you married, Olga, and what was the name of your husband?"

"His name was Alphonse Rocco and we were married about a year and a half ago."

"Did you separate from your husband?"

"Yes."

"About when was it that you separated?"

"About April of the following year."

"And where did you live at that time?"

"I lived at 1434 Fifty-seventh Street, in Brooklyn."

"Who did you live there with?"

"With my parents and a married sister and her husband and daughter."

"Now, how far is your home from the subway station?"

"I would say it is about four or five blocks."

"Now, sometime in the early part of October—after you were separated—did you meet your husband?"

"Yes."

"Where were you when you met him?"

"I was on the West End express, going to work."

"And where were you employed at that time?"

"At the Croyden Hat Company, at 42 West Thirty-ninth Street, in Manhattan."

"In order to get to your place of business, what station did you get off at?"

"The Times Square station."

"So that you would get on at the Fifty-fifth Street station in Brooklyn and get off at the Times Square station?"

"Yes."

"Now, you say, then, that in the early part of October, you were on one of these trains bound for Manhattan and it was there—it was on that train—that you met your husband?"

"Yes."

"Did you have a talk with your husband?"

"Yes."

"Were you feeling well on that occasion?"

"No."

"And after you talked to your husband, what, if anything, did you do?"

"We got off at Ninth Avenue and crossed over and rode back to Fifty-fifth Street, because his car was parked at the exit of the station. He offered to drive me home so that I wouldn't have to walk when I wasn't feeling well."

"Did you get into his automobile?"

"Yes, I did."

"Did he drive you home?"

"No, he did not."

"Where did he go?"

"He drove to Manhattan."

"What, if anything, did he do in the automobile?"

'Well, he had a knife and it had a little button on it and he pressed that button and a big blade shot out of it and he pressed it up against my throat."

"Did you try to get out of the automobile?"

"I asked him to stop the car so I could get out."

"Did he stop the automobile?"

"No, he would not."

"What did he do with this knife, if anything?"

"He held it up against my throat and said that he would kill me if I screamed or if I cried too loudly in the car."

"Now, where did he drive to?"

"He drove toward the Manhattan Bridge and we went over that, and then on the highway near Riverside Drive and then toward the country places—Poughkeepsie."

"What happened up at Poughkeepsie? What did he do up at Poughkeepsie?"

"He stopped at one of the tourist cabins and he rented a cabin."

"Did you want to go into the cabin?"

"No."

"What, if anything, did he do?"

"He had this knife in his pocket and he told me that if I would scream out or anything to the lady who was renting us the room, he would kill me."

"How long did you stay up at Poughkeepsie?"

"Two days."

"Did you stay there of your own free will?"

"No, I did not."

"Did he have any other weapons up there?"

"Yes. He had a shotgun and he had a revolver, and the little knife he carried with him."

"Now, then, did he drive you back to New York after those two days?"

"Yes."

"Where did he go when he drove back to New York?"

"He made me go to this place on Canal Street."

"What kind of place was it?"

"It looked to me like a place that sells guns and shotguns."

"Now, did he get—did he get anything there?"

"Yes."

"What did he get there?"

"I saw the man hand him something, and he put it in his pocket."

"What was it?"

"It was a revolver."

"All right. Now, after he got the revolver did he do anything with that revolver insofar as you are concerned?"

"Yes, he did."

"What did he do?"

"We got in the car and he held it up to my temple."

"Now, then, did he drive—where did he drive after that?"

"We went back the same way again, back to Poughkeepsie to a different tourist cabin."

"Did you go of your own free will?"

"No, I did not."

"All right, now, how long did you stay up there?"

"Five days altogether."

"All right, now, after five days where did you go?"

"We drove back to Brooklyn."

"And where did you go?"

"I went to my niece's home."

"And what happened at your niece's home?"

"I collapsed on the steps there."

"Did you ever go out with your husband after that?"

"No."

"Something happened on the first of November?"

"Yes."

"Where were you when something happened?"

"I was in my home in the kitchen."

"What happened?"

"I was helping Mother set the dinner table."

"Keep your voice up, Olga."

"I was helping Mother set the dinner table and the window was open and all of a sudden I felt a very sharp sting in my right leg and when I bent down to touch it, it was bleeding."

"What else did you observe about your leg at that time? Did you observe any hole?"

"Well, I could not see because it was bleeding so much. I could not see."

"Some time after that did you notice a hole?"

"Yes, I did. Yes."

"And where was the hole?"

"It was in my thigh. There were two separate holes in my thigh. On the right side and in the back of my thigh."

"Was an ambulance summoned?"

"Yes, we called the police."

"You were confined in the hospital for a period of time?"

"I was there for ten days."

"And during that time did you see any detectives?"

"Yes, I saw Detective O'Brien and I saw—I believe he was an Assistant District Attorney, and a stenographer."

"You told them about your—about the trips to Poughkeepsie and the five days you were with your husband?"

"Yes, I did."

"And about the shooting in your home?"

"Yes, I said that I was positive it was my husband, that it couldn't have been anybody else."

"Now, you went back to work on December 9th?"

"Yes."

"Did someone go with you?"

"My sister did. She was employed on Thirty-seventh Street in Manhattan and she went with me."

"What, if anything, did you observe the first day you went back to work?"

"As we were walking toward the station—there are Elevated pillars on New Utrecht Avenue—I saw my husband in back of one of them, and my sister did, too."

"What, if anything, happened after you got to work?"

"When I got to work I called up the police at the Sixty-sixth Precinct station in Brooklyn and I told them that I had seen him and that I was very frightened that he would do something to me. And I spoke to one of the detectives there at the precinct and he told me not to worry."

"Now, did you get a telephone call from your husband on December 9th at your place of business?"

"Yes, he called that very morning."

"What did he say to you?"

"He said he was watching me, he knew everything, he knew when I went to work, and that he did not aim right the first time but that when he would aim again he would kill me."

"Did you tell the police about that?"

"I usually spoke to Lieutenant Giddings. He always answered the telephone there. I told him please to send somebody, to please have somebody escort me home, that I was afraid, that I knew something terrible was going to happen to me, and he said that I should not worry."

"And when was the next time you saw your husband?"

"Well, maybe a few days later. I used to see him on Thirty-ninth Street lurking in hallways and behind cars, and I also saw him at the Times Square station one night when I was going home."

"Now, how often did your husband telephone you at your place of business?"

"He called every single day."

"And after he telephoned you, what did you do?"

"I always called the Sixty-sixth Precinct and spoke to some detective there, and I used to repeat everything that he would say

REPORTING AT WIT'S END

to me, and I would ask them to please send somebody to escort me home and take me to work. And they said they would, that I should not worry."

"Now, you said that on one occasion you saw him in the Times Square subway station. Just about when was that?"

"I believe it was between the Christmas and New Year's holiday, one of those days that come between those holidays."

"What did you do when you saw him?"

"I flew down the steps and I paid my fare, and there is another flight of steps that you have to go down to go to the trains, and during the rush hour there is a guard there that stands there all the time, and I went and stood right next to him, and he saw that I was very frightened."

"What did you say to him?"

"I told him, 'I am so frightened, my husband is following me. I know he is going to do something terrible to me. Please, could I stand next to you?' And he said that I could not stay there because of the people that were going down the steps at that time."

"Was this the rush hour?"

"Yes. He pointed to a pillar that was very close by and said that I should stand there until my train came in and that he would watch me from where he was, and then the West End express pulled in and I got into the train and I went home."

"Was there any occasion about that time when you saw your husband on the platform at the Fifty-fifth Street station in Brooklyn?"

"Yes, I saw him. Yes. About a week and a half after I went back to work, it must have been around December 20th, around that time."

"Did you tell the police about that?"

"It was Lieutenant Giddings. He promised me he would send two detectives to the office, that I should wait for them after work, and that they would be there and I should not go home until they arrived."

"Who waited with you until the detectives arrived?"

"My sister. She came every evening and escorted me home."

"Did the detectives drive you home?"

"Yes. I told them about all the threatening calls, I told them what he had said to me on the telephone, that he was going to kill me, that I had better start saying my prayers, and I told them about the five days that I had been away from home that he had kidnapped me, and I related all the times that I used to see him on Fifty-fifth Street, and the times that I saw him on Thirty-ninth Street, and I related almost every little incident to them, because the ride is rather long to Brooklyn from Thirty-ninth Street."

"All right. Now, on December 30th did you go anywhere?"

"Yes, I did. I went to see Police Inspector Reynolds at the Bergen Street headquarters."

"Who did you go there with?"

"My brother-in-law."

"What did you say to Mr. Reynolds?"

"I told him that I had to go to work and that my husband called me every day and he had shot me and that I knew that he was going to do something terrible to me and that he called me every day and I—"

"Just take your time."

"I cannot catch my breath."

"Take your time. There is no hurry."

"I told him that I had to go to work because I had old parents, and I was very afraid to ride on a train and that there was nobody to help me, that I came to him, to please help me and do something for me."

"All right. What did Inspector Reynolds do or say?"

"He asked me for the precinct, I told him it was the Sixty-sixth Precinct, and he asked somebody to get them on the telephone and he spoke to Lieutenant Giddings. He asked for him."

"What did you hear him say to Lieutenant Giddings?"

"I heard him say, 'There is a young lady here, Olga Trapani Rocco, she is in a hysterical condition. She is crying and she is pleading with me to please help her. She told me that she has reported that she was shot on November 1st and that her husband calls her and he threatens her daily, and that she has seen him many times'—and he repeated the story and the threats I had told him about, how he said he was going to aim right, and then he [Reynolds] said, 'What are you doing? Waiting for a homicide?' Then he told them to have some detectives at my home, and then he hung up and he told me that I would find the detectives there when I got home."

"Did the detectives come to your home that evening?"

"Yes."

"What detectives were they? What were their names?"

"I believe they were Detectives Cooperman and Kahn and McNally, and there was Detective O'Brien there, too."

"What did the detectives say to you at your home that evening?"

"They told me that I should not be frightened, that they were going to protect me and that they would guard me when I went to work and that nothing was going to happen to me."

"Well, now, the next day, December 31st, did you leave your home with someone at the usual time in the morning?"

"Yes. With my sister."

"Did you see any detectives that morning?"

"No."

"Now, on the subway train, did you notice the girl that you now know to be Pearl Lusk?"

"Yes, I did."

"Where was that girl when you first noticed her?"

"She was on the platform, waiting for the train to come in."

"What did you notice about her?"

"She was carrying a box, a rather large box, and it was wrapped,

Christmas wrappings, and it had something that protruded at one end of the box."

"About what size was the box?"

"A little larger than a shoe box."

"At that time, did you have any recollection that you had ever seen her before?"

"No."

"Did you speak to her?"

"No."

"Did she speak to you?"

"No."

"Did you notice her at any time in the car?"

"Yes."

"Where did she sit?"

"It was across from me but with her back toward the front of the train."

"Now, did your sister continue to Times Square?"

"No."

"Where did she get off?"

"She got off at Thirty-fourth Street."

"All right. Now, when the doors opened at Times Square station, just what happened?"

"Well, I took about three or four steps, walking toward the Fortieth Street exit, and all of a sudden—"

"On the platform?"

"On the platform. And all of a sudden I heard a very loud blast and I felt a very sharp pain in my left leg, and I bent down to sort of hold it and I reeled over and fell down on my back, and then I remember people running toward me and I remember a gentleman bending over, and I remember a girl, and the girl was Pearl Lusk."

"You say you—"

"The girl who had been sitting in the train. She bent over me and she said—"

"Now, get control of yourself. What did you notice about your-self?"

"I did not feel my leg—it just didn't feel like it was there—and I was practically swimming in blood."

"From what part of your body were you swimming in blood?"

"All under me, all of me, and I remember talking to a subway guard. He asked me for my name, and he asked me for my tele-phone number, and I gave it to him, and then I remember being put on a stretcher and being carried up the steps, and I also remember being in the ambulance when they took me to the hospital, and I was in the emergency room there, and I remember they cut off my clothes, and the next morning they cut off my leg six inches above my knee."

After the shooting, Pearl Lusk was taken to the West Thirtieth Street station house, where she told her story and was shown a pho-tograph of Olga and Rocco that had been snapped in a night club before their marriage. In the photograph, Rocco was grinning ex-pansively, and, dressed in a pencil-striped suit, a white shirt, and a flowered tie, he looked happy and prosperous. "That's the man," said Pearl. "He even has the same clothes on." While the police were looking for Rocco, they tried to find out what they could about him. Neither Olga nor her parents could tell them much. All they knew was that he had met Olga at a dance in Brooklyn in 1944 and had married her after a brief courtship. He would disap-pear sometimes for weeks and return with lots of spending money—and, as often as not, a new car. He was fond of hunting and camping, and once or twice went away by himself for a week-end in the Catskills, taking along a shotgun and a sleeping bag. He had never talked about his background, and was vague about how he made his living. He was very jealous of Olga. After some vio-lent quarrels, she left him, and it was then that he began telling her that he would kill her if she didn't come back to him.

The police discovered that some eight years earlier Rocco had been in the business of stealing automobiles in Manhattan and selling them in the Bronx. He had been arrested for that and had served a term in Bronx County. He had no other criminal record. The probation report made on him at that time noted that his parents had died when he was a child and that he had been brought up in orphanages and foster homes. "He denies the use of narcotics and does not drink to excess," the report went on. "He admits sexual promiscuity. He is not a member of any organized social group and states that he has few friends. He is inclined to be self-condemnatory and thinks he received a poor 'break' in life. He attributes his actions to the lack of helpful guidance from his elders. He was pleasant and agreeable and showed no unusual reactions or ideas. He appeared to be of dull, normal intelligence." The report quoted a statement from the psychiatric ward at Bellevue Hospital, which said that Rocco "was not insane and not mentally defective, average intelligence, no delusions or hallucinations, emotionally cheerful."

Six days after the shooting in the subway, Rocco's trail was picked up in the Catskills, where, riding in a stolen car, he forced a number of farmers at the point of a gun to give him food. Fifty state police and two New York detectives found his car parked on the side of a mountain road, and soon afterward discovered Rocco in a sleeping bag under a spruce tree. It was night, and there was snow ten inches deep. The police called to Rocco to surrender, and one of them fired a warning shot into the air. Rocco fired four times in the direction of the flash and then was killed when the police opened up. Among the things taken from his pockets was a print of the photograph of Olga and himself in the night club.

Pearl and Olga afterward became friends, and they still see each other occasionally. Pearl has married and is raising a family. Olga barely manages to earn a living selling costume jewelry. For years, she had hopes of obtaining some compensation for the loss of her leg, because she and her lawyers believed that the police had been negligent in not protecting her from Rocco. Eventually, the case came up in the New York County Supreme Court in the form of a suit for $200,000 damages brought by Olga, as plaintiff, against the City of New York, as defendant. The trial lasted for five days and was presided over by Justice Joseph A. Cox. Olga hobbled to the witness stand on crutches, and told her story once more. Various detectives corroborated those portions of it that had to do with her efforts to have them protect her from Rocco. Pearl, too, told her story again. The City of New York, represented by Assistant Corporation Counsel William F. Miller, made no effort to deny, or obscure, the facts of the case, and Justice Cox, after hearing all of them, dismissed Olga's claim. It was the facts of the case that were against Olga. Nobody denied that the Police Department had been informed that Rocco was trying to kill Olga. If Rocco himself had followed her into the subway and shot her, Olga might conceivably have had a case against the city on the ground of police negligence, but, as Mr. Miller argued, that was not what had occurred. He seemed to find it difficult to settle on an adjective that adequately described the scheme that Rocco, in his jealousy, had thought up. "The facts in this case," Mr. Miller said at one point, "indicate that this plaintiff was shot by another passenger on the subway system, a woman unknown and unsuspected—by the name of Pearl Lusk—under the most unsuspicious and unanticipated, bizarre and fantastic circumstances." Almost as if he regretted having to rub this in, he added, "There was absolutely no legal duty on the part of the city to this plaintiff to afford her any protection from Pearl Lusk, an unidentified, unknown individual, concerning whom no one knew anything, concerning whom it is not even attempted to be claimed here by the plaintiff that the Police Department had any notice. She was unknown even to this plaintiff. The only person, apparently, that she was known to was Rocco himself, under an assumed name. She did not even know the relationship between Rocco and this plaintiff. There was absolutely no duty upon the part of the city to provide protection to this plaintiff against any such unknown and unsuspected individual."

Olga's attorney argued as best he could, but it was soon evident that no amount of circumlocution could get around the facts. When Justice Cox rendered his decision, he found it necessary to recite those same facts once more. "The proof is clear," he said in a level tone, "that a woman unknown to the plaintiff was duped into carrying an ordinary-appearing package containing a gun with which she shot the plaintiff, believing she was photographing her. In the absence of any proof showing that the defendant [the city] foresaw, or could reasonably have foreseen, such an occurrence and took no effective action to avoid the same, there can be no recovery from injuries received from such an assault." When, after some little time, Justice Cox got around to announcing his decision, he made it clear that although the case was dismissed, it was not necessarily resolved. "In closing," he said, "the Court is constrained to observe that this has been a shocking occurrence, the deed of a criminally diseased mind, and it is most unfortunate that some redress cannot be afforded the plaintiff."

THE RICH RECLUSE OF
HERALD SQUARE

AROUND HALF PAST two o'clock on the morning of March 6, 1931, during the great depression, a middle-aged attorney named Morgan J. O'Brien, Jr., who lived with his elderly parents at 729 Park Avenue, was awakened by the ringing of his bedside telephone. He was afraid that it was a personal call and that it might be bringing him bad news. His father and mother, both of them in their late seventies, had gone South for their health a few days earlier, and he had been worrying about the strain the trip might have imposed on them. The call, however, was a business one and although it was from an undertaker, it did not turn out to be bad news. The undertaker gave his name, which was P. B. McDonnell, and said he was calling from the Herald Square Hotel, on West Thirty-fourth Street. He had been asked by the manager to arrange for the burial of an aged lady, Miss Mary E. Mayfield, who had died there the day before. Miss Mayfield, the undertaker went on, had lived with her sister and the two of them had occupied the same two-room suite in the hotel for the past twenty-five years. Miss Mayfield was ninety-one years old and the sister was ninety-three. The sister had identified herself as Mrs. Benjamin Wood and, upon being asked by the undertaker for a reference, had said that Judge Morgan J. O'Brien used to be her attorney. The undertaker indicated to Mr. O'Brien that he thought she was some kind of crazy recluse.

Mr. O'Brien explained impatiently that he was not Judge O'Brien, that the Judge was his father, that the Judge had more or less retired and would be out of town for at least a month. The undertaker was persistent, though circumspect. He said that Mrs. Wood didn't look to him as if she had much money, and that while he would be willing to attend to her sister if Judge O'Brien really was a friend of the family's, he just couldn't afford to risk the expense otherwise. After all, he concluded, the times were hard for everybody. Although he was in a hurry to get back to sleep, Mr. O'Brien, in an orderly way, made a note of Mrs. Wood's name, of the undertaker's name, and of the gist of the conversation, and promised to get in touch with the undertaker when he reached his office, in his father's law firm, the next morning. Later on, Mr. O'Brien had reason to be glad he had made those notes, for Mrs. Wood was in need of somebody to help her take care of a hoard of what many people lacked that year. Tucked in her clothes, in an old shoe box, and in various other hiding places she had $752,200 in cash, $175,000 in securities that were, even in those times, sound, and jewelry worth $75,000.

Judge O'Brien's law firm was one of the most distinguished and influential ones in the city, and it had a magnitude of nomenclature second to none. Its name was O'Brien, Boardman, Conboy, Memhard & Early. It occupied 9000 square feet of floor space at 39 Broadway, and besides eleven active senior members and two inactive ones, it had on its staff fifteen associates, four law clerks, eighteen secretaries and stenographers, two file clerks, a cashier-bookkeeper, two telephone operators, a receptionist, and five office boys. Judge O'Brien had sat on the New York State Supreme Court bench from 1887 to 1915 and had served in the Appellate Division of that court for ten of those years. He had been a faithful Tammany man for more than half a century, and still was.

When the younger O'Brien reached the offices of the firm that morning, he mentioned the telephone conversation with the undertaker to his father's secretary, an elderly man named J. C. Walsh. Mr. Walsh told him that Mrs. Benjamin Wood might easily be the widow of the Benjamin Wood who had been a rich man in the seventies and eighties and had owned the New York *Daily News* until around 1900, when it was sold to Frank A. Munsey. When Mr. O'Brien heard this, he grew impatient again, but not to get back to sleep. In those wretched days of 1931, when so many people were idle, even a law firm like O'Brien, Boardman, Conboy, Memhard & Early was not as busy as it felt it ought to be. The firm held a conference forthwith, and the decision was that the younger O'Brien should telephone the elder O'Brien for information and advice. The younger O'Brien did so, and the elder O'Brien told his son that when he was a lawyer, in the 1880s he had known Mrs. Wood quite well, both professionally and socially. She had been one of the beauties of New York in those days, he said, and, in addition to that, a smart businesswoman. Nobody had heard of her for many years now. The gossip around town was, he believed, that she had converted her fortune into cash shortly before the panic of 1907 and had then disappeared.

The younger O'Brien found himself thinking more and more about Mrs. Wood's plight. He hoped she could be considered a client of the firm, because if she was it would be easier to help her, and he wanted to help her. He asked his father if, in his opinion, Mrs. Wood could be considered a client. The elder O'Brien said in a regretful tone that he hardly thought she could be but that he felt it was his son's duty to call on her, because she so obviously needed help and her mention of the O'Brien name to the undertaker might well have been a call for help; also, the elder O'Brien said, it might be a good idea, when he went to see Mrs. Wood, to take along a member of the firm's staff named Harold G. Wentworth, who specialized in the handling of estates. Mr. O'Brien still remembers that his father said to him, "Of course, she may be destitute. If so, I think the firm should underwrite the cost of the funeral of her sister, Miss Mayfield, just for old times' sake. After all, your mother and I often entertained Mrs. Wood and her sister at our home. But it does not appear to me to be likely that Mrs. Wood is destitute."

Before O'Brien and Wentworth took a taxi to Mrs. Wood's hotel, O'Brien telephoned the undertaker and told him the firm would see that the burial of Miss Mayfield was paid for one way or another. When the two lawyers reached the hotel, they first talked to the manager and some of the employees, and found out a few things about the sisters. The manager had been at the hotel for six or seven years and had never seen either Miss Mayfield or Mrs. Wood. To the best of his knowledge, they hadn't been out of their suite in all that time. They had paid their bills in cash ever since he had been at the hotel. His records showed that they had moved into two adjoining rooms on the fifth floor in 1907, along with Mrs. Wood's daughter, Miss Emma, who had died in a hospital, in 1928, at the age of seventy-one. A Negro elevator operator, who had been with the hotel for nineteen years, vaguely remembered having seen all three ladies at rare intervals when he first went to work there, but he didn't know anything much about them and had never known which was which. An Irish maid took care of the fifth floor; she had been there only a couple of months and hadn't got into the sisters' rooms at all, she told the lawyers. Twice, she said, she had persuaded the ladies to hand over soiled sheets and towels and accept clean ones, but they hadn't let her past the door. A Negro bell captain said it had been his custom for a number of years to knock on the door once a day and ask the ladies if they wanted anything. Usually, they would send him out for one thing or another and pay him in cash, tipping him a dime. They seemed to live on evaporated milk, coffee, crackers, bacon, eggs, and an occasional fish, he said. Once in a while, he had been inside the parlor of the suite, but never in the bedroom. He said they had fixed up a makeshift kitchenette in the bathroom, where they made the coffee and cooked the bacon and eggs, but not the fish. They ate the fish raw. Miss Mayfield slept on a couch in the parlor and Mrs. Wood presumably slept in the bedroom. From time to time, Mrs. Wood asked the bell captain to buy Copenhagen snuff, Havana cigars, and jars of petroleum jelly. Both ladies smoked the cigars and used the snuff, he said, and he had the impression that Mrs. Wood spent hours every day massaging her face with the petroleum jelly. On the afternoon of the day of Miss Mayfield's death, the bell captain had seen Miss Mayfield stretched out on the couch in the parlor, had heard her moaning, and had asked Mrs. Wood if she wanted him to get a doctor. In a meandering way, Mrs. Wood had said that her sister was sick but that there was no use getting a doctor—that she had called a doctor when her daughter Emma was sick a few years before and he had taken her to a hospital and she had died, and that consequently there was no use getting a doctor now for poor Mary. Nevertheless, the manager, upon being informed of this by the bell captain, had asked the house physician of the nearby Hotel McAlpin to stop in to see Miss Mayfield that afternoon. The doctor was soon convinced that she was suffering from cancer of the stomach, and she had died while he was there. A medical examiner from downtown had released the body to the undertaker for burial.

Their heads swirling with snuff, cigars, stocks, bonds, and petroleum jelly, the two lawyers went up to the fifth floor of the hotel and knocked at the door. The undertaker let them in. The body of Miss Mayfield, covered with a sheet, was still on the couch. The undertaker said Mrs. Wood had locked herself in the bedroom and wouldn't come out. Neither of the two lawyers ever forgot their first encounter with Mrs. Wood. "Perhaps after five or ten minutes of hammering," Wentworth later testified in court, "the door opened, and the figure of an aged woman appeared. Her hair was very much dishevelled and she had a pronounced stoop. She was perhaps five feet tall, with the stoop—very feeble. She had a dirty old hotel towel pinned around the upper part of her body, which was apparently the only covering that she had on, and the lower portion of her body was covered with material that enclosed it and was held together with pins or something. It was not a dress, as we know it. She had considerable difficulty in walking. She walked very, very slowly, and she came over to a chair and invited Mr. O'Brien, Jr., and myself to sit down. . . . She appeared to be unable to read anything, and the way that came up was this: Certain papers—she was desirous of giving certain papers to Mr. O'Brien, Jr., and myself, and she brought out an old shoe box in which these papers were kept, and she asked Mr. O'Brien, Jr., and myself to look over various of the papers in order to find out what papers she wished to give us, and she said at the time that she could not see. She also was extremely deaf. It was almost necessary to shout into her ear to make her hear. . . . She referred at one time to ten hundred shares, and at another time to eleven hundred shares, of stock in the Union Pacific Railroad Company, stating that she owned it. She also referred to a ten-thousand-dollar bond of the Union Pacific Railroad Company and, in answer to a question as to where this property was, she pointed to the inner room and said that she kept it locked up in there."

"The parlor was unbelievably dirty and dusty," O'Brien has since said in recalling the same scene. "The undertaker was working on the body of Miss Mayfield while Wentworth and I kept hammering on the bedroom door. The parlor was crammed with an accumulation of old newspapers, cracker boxes, balls of used string, stacks of old wrapping paper, and several large trunks. When Mrs. Wood came out, I told her my name. She sat down in a rocking chair and started massaging her face with this petroleum jelly we had heard about, and I realized she was rather deaf. I kept shouting my name at her, and finally she seemed to understand what

I was saying and she got up and came over to me. She was very little and was bent over like a question mark, but you could see she
had once been a pretty woman, and her complexion was smooth
and unwrinkled. She couldn't see very well, apparently. She came
up to me and felt my face all over with her hands, and then she
drew back and exclaimed, 'You're not Judge O'Brien at all!' I tried
to tell her I was Judge O'Brien's son, and she finally seemed to understand that. She sat down again and lighted a long, thin cigar.
She talked fairly sensibly and amiably for a while, although in a
rather wandering fashion. She showed us some Union Pacific bonds
and some uncashed dividend checks. She said her daughter and her
sister had both had money in their own right and had willed it to
her. She hinted that she had a good deal of cash in the bedroom. I
asked her if she had a bank account, and she said that she didn't
have one now but that she used to have one at the Morton Trust
Company. She told me she had no relatives and no friends. But
then, all at once, she sort of switched, and became very irate and
hysterical. She called me an impostor and a crook, said I was just
after her money, like everybody else, said she didn't like my voice
or my looks, and didn't want a lawyer anyway. She told me to get
out. Then she snatched up the shoe box and the bonds and papers,
and hobbled with startling speed into the bedroom and closed and
locked the door. Wentworth and I hung around for a while, bang-
ing on the door and trying to get her to come out, but she wouldn't,
so we finally went back to the office. Frankly, we didn't know
what to do."

The firm of O'Brien, Boardman, Conboy, Memhard & Early
spent a good part of the rest of that day deciding what to do. It
was able to find out from the Union Pacific Railroad Company
that Miss Mayfield and Mrs. Wood owned stocks and bonds in that
company worth around a hundred and seventy-five thousand dollars and that they had not cashed their dividend checks for ten or
twelve years. From other sources, the firm learned that Mrs. Wood

herself, rather than her husband, had sold the *Daily News* to Mr. Munsey; her husband had died in 1900 and had willed the paper and whatever else he possessed to her. As nearly as the firm could figure out, Mr. Munsey had paid her almost a quarter of a million dollars for the newspaper. People who seemed to know about the deal remembered that she had demanded, and received, spot cash from Munsey. At the Guaranty Trust Company, a senescent teller remembered Mrs. Wood from her Morton Trust days and remembered, too, that in 1907 she had drawn out all her money, amounting to nearly a million dollars, in cash, had put it into a large string shopping bag, and had never come back to the bank again after that.

In the beginning, the law firm had been warmheartedly willing to help Mrs. Wood even if she was poor. It was now warmheartedly willing to help her even if she was rich. Yet after revealing to O'Brien in a tantalizing way that she had a fortune in securities, and hinting that she might have a large store of cash—and, on top of that, indicating in all sorts of ways that she was incapable of handling her financial affairs herself—she had unaccountably accused him of being an impostor and a crook, had stated that she didn't want a lawyer, had ordered him out, and had locked herself in her bedroom. Consequently, she was not a client but only a prospective client.

Perplexed, but still willing to help Mrs. Wood, the firm put all its heads together and decided that it could be tragic indeed if Mrs. Wood, needing help so badly, did not avail herself of the firm's willingness to help her. If a lawyer goes around barefacedly proposing to prospective clients that they become his, he is violating the lawyers' code of ethics. Under this code, he is not required to sit in his office and wait for prospective clients to offer themselves to him, but when he runs across a prospective client, he is permitted, under the code, only to ingratiate himself with the prospective client and impress upon the prospective client the extent of his talents. The behavior of ethical lawyers at such times resembles in many ways the behavior of inhibited males toward prospective mates; courtship among living organisms, all the way from human beings down to crustaceans and insects, is marked by a bizarre and pathetic indirection, and so are the ways of ethical lawyers with prospective clients. The *Encyclopædia Britannica* lists a host of living organisms whose behavior in courtship is pathetic but only a few whose behavior is as bizarre as a large and ethical law firm's has to be when it is ingratiating itself with a rich nonagenarian lady who is badly in need of help but fitfully inclined to think she can get along without it. When the firm of O'Brien, Boardman, Conboy Memhard & Early undertook to convice Mrs. Wood of its concern for her welfare, it may, with some embarrassment have felt a little like the male of the insect called the empis and at other times like a male fiddler crab. According to the *Britannica*, the male empis, approaching the female empis, manufactures a glistening balloon, blowing it up until it is bigger than he is, and putting into it tiny bright objects—"which renders him and his gift very conspicuous." The male fiddler crab has one enormous and gaudy claw, and when in the presence of a female fiddler crab, says the *Britannica*, "he stands on tiptoe and brandishes his claw in the air, frequently for long periods of time."

The younger O'Brien could see that he might not be the man for Mrs. Wood, because she seemed to have taken a distinct dislike to him. The firm agreed with O'Brien but felt that Wentworth might stand a chance with her, because Mrs. Wood had volunteered no estimate of her regard for him. The firm decided to send Wentworth back to see her again that day, and off he went, encumbered by a glistening briefcase and a bunch of bright red roses. At the same time, Martin Conboy, who was then the active head of the firm and two years later became United States Attorney for the Southern District of New York, made a decision that, if it did not serve to ingratiate the firm with Mrs. Wood, may well have impressed her with its talents. He telephoned a private detective agency and asked that two good men be instructed to hire a room next to Mrs. Wood's and keep a twenty-four-hour watch on her until further notice. The fact that these private detectives ran up a bill of more than seven thousand dollars just for watching is an indication of the thoroughness with which the firm protected Mrs. Wood.

Wentworth called on Mrs. Wood, and after that he found himself drawn to her again and again by a desire to help her. Within a few weeks, she became the firm's client not once but several times. A kindly man with a gentle approach, Wentworth was a faithful suitor. But Mrs. Wood was fickle. She was never a client for more than twenty-four hours, and sometimes she was a client for only a few minutes. She appeared to appreciate the first bunch of red roses he brought her. She grabbed up an empty coffee tin and, after filling it with water in the bathroom, stuck the roses in it and set it on one of the trunks in her parlor. Wentworth took her a bunch of red roses almost every time he went to see her, which was almost every day. Sometimes she seemed pleased with them, and stuck them in the coffee tin, and sometimes she snapped their heads off and threw them over her shoulder. Wentworth never knew what to expect, but he kept going back to see her. He sat with her for hours at a time. They were an odd-looking and odd-acting couple. Anybody watching them through the transom—as the private detectives were—would have found it hard to tell what they saw in each other. While Wentworth talked at the top of his voice, Mrs. Wood would sit in her rocking chair smoking one of the long, thin cigars and, with her free hand, massaging her face with petroleum jelly, a jar of which she kept handy on top of a splintery old orange crate. Sometimes she would stop the smoking and massaging and munch crackers and sip evaporated milk out of the can, and every few days she would eat a raw fish in front of Wentworth's eyes. He went on shouting at her about uncashed dividend checks, hoarded cash, the likelihood of robbery, the security of safe-deposit boxes, and the concern that was felt for her at O'Brien, Boardman, Conboy, Memhard & Early. Wentworth tried to persuade her to let the maid clean the rooms, and in time she agreed to having the parlor done, but she wouldn't let the maid or anybody else into the bedroom. When he suggested to her with elaborate circumlocution that it might be wise for her to have her stocks and bonds and cash put in a safe place, she would shake her head from side to side and languidly puff on her cigar.

One day while Wentworth was yelling at Mrs. Wood about the wills of her daughter and her sister and about the regrettable fact that they had never been submitted to the Surrogate's Court for probate, she abruptly handed them over to him and asked him to take care of them. Wentworth took this to be the answer to the question that ethics had kept him from popping, but as he held the wills in his hands and started to express his and the firm's pleasure at having her as a client, she changed her mind, grabbed the wills back, hobbled into her bedroom, and locked the door. Other days followed in which Mrs. Wood would simply bring out the wills and allow Wentworth to hold them for a while and then snatch them back. She dallied around with interesting batches of bonds in the same fashion. A day came when she let him put the wills in his briefcase and go off with them, but early the next morning, before the Surrogate's Court opened, he got a telephone call from the hotel maid, who said Mrs. Wood had asked her to tell him that if he didn't bring the wills back to her immediately she would have him arrested for robbery. He took the wills back and Mrs. Wood resumed her role of non-client. By this time, it was the middle of June. The Wentworth-Wood affair had been going on for more than three months and the firm owed the private detectives thirty-five hundred dollars when a fortuitous circumstance led the firm to give up the effort to help Mrs. Wood in the way it had been trying to help her. It found itself able to help her just as effectively as it had wished to from the beginning, but in a different way.

The firm had not told the newspapers that there was a ninety-three-year-old rich recluse, a former belle of New York, living in squalor at the Herald Square Hotel, eating odd bits of food and smoking cigars while private detectives watched over her. Word of it got around nevertheless, with the result that an elderly man named Otis Wood turned up at the offices of the firm one day, identified himself as a nephew of Mrs. Wood, and said that he desired to help her. He was told that the firm would be glad to help him help her but unfortunately could consent to do so only if he desired to become a client of the firm. Mr. Wood became a client.

Otis Wood was a son of Fernando Wood, who had been Mayor of New York in the fifties and sixties, and was a brother of Mrs. Wood's husband. As far as the firm could determine at that time, he and his relatives were Mrs. Wood's closest kin. Besides Otis, there were three other sons of Fernando in New York, all of them substantial businessmen, and several grandchildren, and before long the firm was representing a cozy bevy of ten Woods. Then it turned out that Mrs. Wood's husband had had a son by an earlier marriage and that *he* had had some children, who were thus stepgrandchildren of Mrs. Wood. This group of relatives numbered five and was headed by a Mrs. Blanche Wood Shields. The Shields relatives hired a law firm of their own named Talley & Lamb. It was possible that these two sets of relatives would fight over Mrs. Wood's money someday, but during the initial effort to assist Mrs. Wood they stood together, because they and their lawyers had agreed that the only way to give Mrs. Wood real help was to have her declared an incompetent, so that somebody could be appointed who would be legally empowered to take care of Mrs. Wood's money, and, in order to do so, to take it away from her—if need be, by force.

The firm of O'Brien, Boardman, Conboy, Memhard & Early, representing Otis and the other Woods, filed the necessary petitions in the New York State Supreme Court, and on August 4th, Justice John F. Carew ordered that a sheriff's jury be impanelled to decide whether or not Mrs. Wood was an incompetent. A week earlier, at the request of the firm, Justice William Harmon Black had appointed a special guardian for Mrs. Wood. The special guardian was empowered to try to persuade her to let him help her but was not empowered to help her by force, pending the outcome of the incompetency proceedings. He was a lawyer named Edward T. Corcoran, and although he got along better with Mrs. Wood than anybody else had up to that time, he was able to persuade her to turn over to him no more than $50,000 in securities and a measly $50,000 in cash. Early in September, she was declared an incompetent by the sheriff's jury, and Otis Wood was named "committee of her person and property," which meant looking after her physical welfare and, if necessary, forcing her to allow him to take the rest of her money away from her and handle it for her. In spite of everything, she managed to hang on to it for a month after she had been declared an incompetent. She was under the care of a doctor and two nurses, was feeling better, and was growing increasingly alert and suspicious. Finally, on October 6th, after repeated failures to persuade her to be sensible, a suite of rooms was rented for her directly below the ones she had occupied for so many years. With the help of the two nurses and in the presence of three or four relatives from both factions, and their attorneys, she was moved downstairs. Then her former bedroom was searched and $247,200 in cash, mostly in $1,000 and $5,000 bills, was found in a shoe box she kept there. None of the people who counted and re-counted the shoe-box money thought they would ever see so much cash again, but two days later the same people watched the nurses slip an oilcloth packet out from under Mrs. Wood's dress when she was asleep, and when they counted what was in the packet it came to $500,000 in $10,000 bills. The rest of her stocks and bonds turned up here and there around the vacated rooms during succeeding days as the search went on.

As soon as all the cash had been securely deposited in various banks, some of it began to circulate. The first disbursement went, appropriately, to the firm of O'Brien, Boardman, Conboy, Memhard & Early. The firm applied to Supreme Court Justice Untermyer for a fee of $10,000 for helping Mrs. Wood, this sum to come out of Mrs. Wood's money. Justice Untermyer reduced the claim to $8000. Talley & Lamb asked for $1500 and got half of that. A psychiatrist who had testified before the sheriff's jury that Mrs. Wood was incompetent asked for $2200 and got $1150, and another psychiatrist, who had testified to the same thing, asked for $1525 and got $810. The medical man who had attended to Mrs. Wood's physical needs asked for $535 and got all of it. James G. Donovan, the commissioner who had presided over the incompetency proceedings, asked for $1000 and got $300. Corcoran, the special guardian, asked for $5000 and got $3500. The detective agency that had been watching over Mrs. Wood at the request of Mr. Conboy asked for $7755.69 and got $6323.69. There were a few other relatively small miscellaneous disbursements. All in all, in the six months after the undertaker telephoned O'Brien, the fortunes of Mrs. Wood were diminished by the sum of $22,268.59 over and above what she had had to spend during that period for evaporated milk, coffee, eggs, bacon, fish, crackers, rent, cigars, and petroleum jelly. However, Justice Untermyer had, in a way, saved her $8239 by cutting down the claims.

There was now nothing much for the two sets of relatives and their lawyers to do but wait. Mrs. Wood lived on in her new suite of rooms at the hotel under the care of the two nurses. The whole city had heard of her by this time, and hundreds of non-relatives tried to see her in order to ask her for some of the money she no longer had with her, but they were turned away by the nurses. The newspapers reported that "her tantrums are sometimes heard along the corridors" and that "she glowers through old spectacles at strange people who flit in and out of her rooms." Otis Wood said of her, "She is small, you know, and can move very quickly when she wants to. She has an amazing strength. She is very courteous, you know, very precise in etiquette. To talk with her is like going back into another age when people were more careful about little things than they are now. She is a curious mixture of sentiment and hard sense. She wanted two things today, her photograph folio of old pictures taken in the fifties and sixties and a sight of her bankbook. We are, of course, letting her have both."

Mrs. Wood's mental and physical health continued to improve as the last months of 1931 went by. In November, a *Times* reporter went to see her and she talked lucidly about the past. She told him she had made a lot of money in the stock market before the panic of 1907. "My broker was named Frank Work, and he was a very handsome man," she said. "I sold out everything before the panic struck. I did quite well, you know, and it seems very strange they should call me incompetent. I made money and I kept it. So many people whom everyone considers quite competent can't do that." She said that she and her daughter and sister were "tired of everything" when they moved into the hotel in 1907, and that, except for going out occasionally to shop during the first few years, they saw nobody but the bellboys and maids. Her nurses reported that "she's like a willful child and is at times difficult to handle." She continued to smoke the long, thin cigars and to massage her face with petroleum jelly.

While waiting, the relatives and their lawyers conducted a search to make sure Mrs. Wood hadn't hidden some more money somewhere. It was about as thorough as a search can be. After going through the five trunks that were in her rooms, they took apart every piece of furniture and burrowed into the plaster of the walls in places where it sounded hollow when they rapped on it with their knuckles. Then they went through the fourteen trunks she kept in the basement of the hotel and the forty trunks she had stored in an uptown warehouse. Then it occurred to one of them that Mrs. Wood might have hidden some money in her sister's coffin before it was closed and taken away for interment in Calvary Cemetery. This evidently struck O'Brien, Boardman, Conboy, Memhard & Early as a reasonable possibility. In the presence of the long-suffering Wentworth and a lawyer representing the Shields set of relatives, the coffin was dug up and the same undertaker who had attended to the funeral opened it. A few minutes later, he reported to the lawyers that there was nothing in it but the body.

After that, little happened until a day in January, 1932, when one of Mrs. Wood's nurses decided to throw away three boxes of moldy crackers Mrs. Wood had brought with her when they moved her out of her old rooms, and had insisted on keeping close at hand ever since. The nurse put them in the garbage can while Mrs. Wood was asleep. Then, having a second thought, she took them out and looked under the stale crackers in each box. In one of them she found a beautiful diamond necklace, which, when appraised the next day, was said to be worth around $40,000. The nurse told her about the necklace and spoke to her reproachfully about hiding things. She had a minor tantrum and then said, "Please take good care of that necklace. It cost Mr. Wood a great deal of money when he bought it for me." It was turned over to the lawyers and afterward sold to the jeweller who offered more for it than anybody else. Mrs. Wood lived on for another two months. Early in March, she caught a cold that developed into pneumonia. She seemed to be stubbornly recovering from the pneumonia, but on the morning of March 12th she had a heart attack. She died that afternoon. Among the people who came to look at her as she lay in her coffin in the hotel suite was the younger O'Brien. The memory of that visit still has the power to make him speak of her in a silver-tongued fashion. "You could see what an extraordinarily pretty woman she once was when you saw her lying there at peace with all the world," he said recently. "Her complexion, in spite of her age, was as creamy and pink and as unwrinkled as any I have ever seen. It was like tinted ivory. Her profile was like a lovely cameo." One of the many disbursements that were made out of her estate before it was at last divided up among her closest kin covered the cost of the funeral. It was a moderately priced one. She was buried in Calvary Cemetery, not far from the recently opened grave of her sister.

The firm of O'Brien, Boardman, Conboy, Memhard & Early had for some time before Mrs. Wood's death been facing with stiff upper lips the melancholy fact that their clients, the Woods, stood little or no chance of inheriting any of the estate. The other set of relatives—the descendants of Benjamin Wood, by his first marriage—obviously had a sounder claim than Otis Wood and the other descendants of Benjamin's brother Fernando. The relationship between the firm of Talley & Lamb, representing the descendants of Benjamin Wood, and O'Brien, Boardman, Conboy, Memhard & Early turned out to be a friendly one because the two firms shared a solicitude for Mrs. Wood. Otis Wood's status as committee of Mrs. Wood's person and property was not interfered with until after her death. At that time, Talley & Lamb moved in court to have one of its clients appointed to take Otis's place, on the ground that its candidate was closer kin to her than Otis. The motion was granted without much argument. The new administrator, represented by Talley & Lamb, had to have an accounting of the handling of the estate up to then by the committee, represented by O'B., etc. The accounting proceedings were heard by Francis J. Sullivan, a referee appointed by Justice Black, and the transcript of the record came to 1,708 pages. Among the claims on the estate that Talley & Lamb questioned, but not convincingly enough, in the opinion of the referee, was one for $30,000 to be paid to O'B., etc., for representing Otis Wood during the period of his administration of the estate. When the hearing was over, O'B., etc., was paid the $30,000 and, in addition, $750 for representing Otis during the hearing itself, which had consisted mostly of arguments between the two sets of counsel as to whether or not Otis had administered the estate competently. Talley & Lamb also received $7500 for representing the new administrator during the hearing. Otis himself was paid $5000 for his services as committee. Sullivan, the referee, was paid $12,000 for being the referee. Later on, when, owing to an unforeseen development in the squabble over the estate, the courts appointed the Public Administrator to supplant Talley & Lamb's client, Talley & Lamb and their client were paid $17,500 for their services during the client's administration and during the accounting that the Public Administrator had to have before *he* could take over.

The unforeseen development grew out of the revelation of a secret Mrs. Wood had carefully and successfully kept since her girlhood. When she was in her teens, around the eighteen-fifties, she adopted the name of Mayfield, because she liked the sound of it. When she was married to Benjamin Wood, in 1867, the stories of the marriage in the New York newspapers said she was "the former Ida E. Mayfield, daughter of Judge Thomas Henry Mayfield, of Louisiana," and that she had been a New Orleans belle before she became a New York belle. She not only changed her own name to Mayfield but also changed her mother's and sister's names to Mayfield. In 1883, when her mother died, she was buried in Calvary Cemetery as "Ann Mary Crawford, widow of Thomas Henry Mayfield." Actually, Mrs. Wood was born plain Ellen Walsh, and her father was an immigrant peddler from Ireland who, after a stopover in Malden, Massachusetts, died in California in 1864.

Mrs. Wood's secret was publicly revealed some six months after her death by Edward T. Corcoran, the lawyer who had served for a brief time as her special guardian before she was declared incompetent. He had got some hint of the truth from his conversations with Mrs. Wood and from some of the family records she had shown him, had kept mum about it, and had gone to Ireland a few days after she died and hunted up two brothers named Kennedy—Hugh and Michael—who operated the well-known Kennedy's

Bakery in Dublin. He convinced them that they were cousins of Mrs. Wood and possibly her closest kin, and they became his clients, along with a cousin he found in Bridgeport, Connecticut. Then he returned to New York and put in their claims for the estate. More than a hundred other claims had been filed with the Surrogate by that time, most of them by Mayfields from the Deep South who said they remembered Mrs. Wood when she was a New Orleans belle and they were just little tiny chillun. At about the time Corcoran was hunting down the Kennedys in Dublin, O'Brien, Boardman, Conboy, Memhard & Early, in making an independent investigation of Mrs. Wood's ancestry, discovered her true name and began trying diligently to find some cousins in Salem, Massachusetts, where she was brought up. Mr. Conboy himself went up to Salem and came back with five Salem cousins as clients. A few days later, he went over to Elizabeth, New Jersey, and came back with two more cousins as clients. The legalistically delightful case was at last closed in 1939 when these seven cousins and the three represented by Corcoran inherited the entire estate of Mrs. Wood, amounting to $84,490.92 apiece, minus lawyers' fees of approximately twenty-five percent to Corcoran, and to O'Brien, etc. As the younger O'Brien remarked to another member of the firm when the whole thing was over, "It just goes to show that it is a good thing for a lawyer to answer his telephone no matter what time of night it rings."

The 1960s

THE EDINBURGH CAPER

O N THE WHOLE, I haven't greatly minded, these past couple of years, the fact that the Central Intelligence Agency, in Washington, knows something of what I did during my vacation in Scotland in the summer of 1959. I've simply tried to rise above it. Some months ago, however, I did have on my mind the likelihood that General Maxwell D. Taylor, who was investigating the C.I.A. for President Kennedy, would come across the file I'm sure they have on me down there. General Taylor is a thorough officer. He never misses anything, and nobody can pull any wool over his eyes. And in my night thoughts I became pretty well convinced that the General was going to send a couple of his special staff officers up to see me in New York, where I live alone except for a young Scottish terrier named Jock. These two officers were going to interrogate me at length about that vacation trip, and I was going to have to tell them the truth about it. But General Taylor completed his investigation and reported to President Kennedy, and it looked to me as if I weren't going to be interrogated after all. Then, one night quite recently, the thing I'd been preparing myself for suddenly took complete charge of my night thoughts.

TWO OFFICERS HAVE come in. They've brought a tape recorder with them, of course. It snuffles along unobtrusively on my

413

coffee table, which is a beat-up, unfashionable-looking antique that I bought for four dollars in a junk shop in Greenwich Village in the nineteen-twenties, when I was a nineteen-year-old reporter on the old New York *World* and was supporting my bob-haired, fun-loving first wife in what seemed to us magnificent style on a salary of fifty dollars a week. Now that Jock has stopped growling at the tape recorder and has also got through sniffing it, he has settled down at my feet, where he likes to lie. It's long past Jock's bedtime.

Jock took to the first of the two officers at once. This one is an Air Force brigadier general, whose wings are those of a command pilot. He is doing most of the interrogating. Jock seems a trifle suspicious of the other chap—an Air Force major, whose insignia show that he is a flight surgeon. Both men are young—years younger than I am—and both are relaxed, casual, and at the same time extremely businesslike. They didn't telephone me and ask when it would be convenient for me to talk to them. They simply rode up to the eighteenth floor of the apartment hotel in which I live, and rang my bell. It was after midnight. Jock woke up and barked, and I got out of bed, where I had been reading a book. When the bell rang, I slipped on the handsome MacGregor-tartan bathrobe I bought that summer of 1959 at a fine shop on Princes Street, in Edinburgh on a wonderful, cool, sunshiny afternoon in July before all that hell broke loose over there. The brigadier general and the major barged right in, introducing themselves perfunctorily and showing me the official identification cards in their billfolds. Both of them were in uniform. I'd been expecting them, as I say, so I showed them into my cozy living room, with its view of the Central Park reservoir, and its deep, chintz-covered chairs and sofa, which, like the rest of the furniture, belong to me. I offered the two officers drinks.

"No drinks, thanks," said the general. "Perhaps some coffee later, if you'd like to make some or have some sent up from downstairs. This is going to take hours, you know."

"And if coffee won't keep you going, Colonel, I can give you something," said the major. "Are you in pretty good shape these days, Colonel?"

"Not bad," I said. "But there's one thing, Major. I'd much prefer not to be addressed as 'Colonel.' It's courteous of you, of course, and I appreciate that. In the first place, in the Second World War I was only a *lieutenant* colonel, and, in the second place, that's all over and done with now. Just call me 'Mister,' Major. I'm not a lieutenant colonel any more."

"Oh, but you are," said the general. "Technically, you see, you are simply an *inactive* lieutenant colonel in the Air Force. Any time the Air Force wished to, it could issue an order and you'd be an *active* lieutenant colonel. This is an official inquiry, Colonel, and while you're not under oath, you are expected to tell the truth, the whole truth, and nothing but the truth about this caper in Edinburgh in the summer of 1959."

I was glad to hear the general say this. There was hardly anything I wanted to do more than get this story off my chest, and I certainly intended (as I now intend) to tell the truth, the whole truth, and nothing but the truth. I smiled encouragingly at my visitors, and the general went on.

"Now," he said, "your file at the C.I.A. discloses, for example, that on two occasions in July and August of that year you alerted a unit of the United States Security Force, under the command of Colonel Scott and, later on, Colonel Gragg, based at Kirknewton, on the outskirts of Edinburgh, concerning a plot by the Russians to kidnap President Eisenhower during the visit he was soon to make to Scotland. At that time, too, you had alerted the Air Intelligence officer at the American base at Prestwick about the same plot. The file on you is voluminous, but General Taylor doesn't feel that it tells the whole story, and he recommended that you be interrogated. This was, of course, only one of a great many recommendations he made to the President. We have come to get the whole story."

"My God, is it thought to be as important as all that?"

"General Taylor considers everything connected with the C.I.A. as important as all that, as you put it. Did you know the General during the war?"

"No. He's one of the few generals—or so it seems to me—on whose staff I *didn't* serve as a public-relations officer and press censor during that war, but I have enormous respect for him. Almost as much as I have for the last of my Air Force bosses, General Curtis E. LeMay."

"You were on General Curtis E. LeMay's staff toward the end of the war, of course."

"Yes. That was my last job in the Air Force. After that, or not long after, I became what you call an inactive lieutenant colonel."

"It was while the Colonel was on General LeMay's staff," put in the major, "that he accused Admiral Chester W. Nimitz, at that time Commander-in-Chief of the Pacific Fleet and Theatre Commander of the Pacific Ocean Areas, of high treason, in an official teletype message to the War Department from General LeMay's headquarters on the island of Guam. The Colonel described that incident at length in an article published in *The New Yorker*, in the issue dated June 14, 1958."

"I know that, Major," said the general. "The article in question is in the C.I.A. file on him, and I have read it, although I haven't read *everything* in his file. It was indeed a very long article. Incidentally, Colonel, what was Admiral Nimitz's reaction to that article?"

"I sent him an advance copy of the magazine and he wrote me a very friendly letter. He said he remembered the incident and thought my account of it was, on the whole, funnier than a book about naval public relations called 'Don't Go Near the Water.'"

"I talked," said the major, "to General LeMay about all this yesterday, General, but you and I had so much else to discuss

about the case on our way up here from Washington this evening
that I didn't get a chance to fill you in. General LeMay, sir, seems
to have a high regard for the Colonel, both professionally and
personally. In spite of the fact that the Colonel accused Admiral
Nimitz of high treason in an official teletype message to the Pentagon, General LeMay suggested, some years later on, when the
General was commanding the Strategic Air Command out in
Omaha, that the Colonel might like to come back into active
service as a public-relations adviser. The Colonel didn't take the
General's suggestion, on the ground that he wasn't at that time
sufficiently recovered—emotionally—from his wartime experiences and his peacetime experiences to be of much use to the Air
Force. The Colonel was undergoing some intensive psychoanalytically oriented psychotherapy at that time, you see, and didn't
wish to interrupt it."

"I see. Are you still undergoing intensive psychotherapy, Colonel?"

"Oh, no, General. It's simmered down to deep psychoanalysis
now—with Dr. Hubert F. Carter, of 1163 Fifth Avenue, one of the
top younger analysts of the high-muck-a-muck group. I'm in my
third year of that, and I have hopes of completing the analysis before I go plunging into my sixties, at the beginning of the year 1965.
If I do, I expect to live to be a tranquil old man. Is the Major by any
chance a psychiatrist as well as a medical man?"

"Yes, sir."

"Now, Colonel," said the general, "I want you to understand
the precise nature of this interrogation. We want everything. No
detail of what we'll call Operation Edinburgh is too small or too
trivial to be of interest to us. Have you told anybody else about
Operation Edinburgh?"

"My analyst, of course. But I haven't told even him about it in
exhaustive detail. We've had more fruitful stuff to work on. I've

told nobody else since that summer. A dear friend of mine—a lady—turned up in Edinburgh while the thing was going on, and she knew a little bit about it but by no means *all* about it. I've hinted here and there to a couple of other friends that I had a damn weird experience on that Scottish vacation, but I've never attempted to try to tell them the whole story. For one thing, I don't know if I'm *capable* of telling the whole story. It's as intricate as a long nightmare—or as one of those early 'entertainment' novels by Graham Greene about international intrigue. But perhaps—if you've got the time and patience—I can manage to tell it to you and the Major."

"There's no 'perhaps' about it, Colonel. You're *going* to tell it. We've got all the time in the world, and we're both very patient. The Major has been in touch with your analyst—who, incidentally, is an inactive captain—and he gave the Major a rundown on your present condition, which is, on the whole, O.K. The Captain feels that you have every chance of coming through this interrogation with flying colors."

"To change the subject, Colonel, what's the longest you've ever gone without sleep?" asked the major.

"Oh, I guess four days without *any* sleep. During the war. During the high, hot times on Guam when LeMay's B-29s were bombing the Japanese cities from our bases in the Marianas and shortening the war out there. Or when I'm writing a long piece here in these rooms. After four days, I'm apt to get exhausted—start sneezing a lot. And if I want to get to sleep then, and can't, I'm likely to begin calling up old friends long distance just for something to do. Old friends in the Air Force, among others. They're scattered all over, and that makes it damned expensive. But it's relaxing. You probably know about me and barbiturates, Major, if you've talked to the Captain. And about me and Benzedrine."

"The Colonel is the comparatively rare type that is stimulated and elated by barbiturates, rather than sedated," the major explained to the general. "And Benzedrine is apt to put him to sleep instead of keeping him awake."

"That's very interesting," said the general.

"Same over-all type, sir, as some of the most valuable operatives in the C.I.A.," the major said. "Hypersensitive. High-strung. More or less creative. Mild manic-depressive tendencies. Blessed—or cursed—with total recall. Affable when drinking, and sometimes overgenial. Not incapable of minimal fantasies of a faintly paranoid character. But on the whole, controlled. Quite sane."

"Thanks," I said.

"Well, Colonel, we're in no hurry, of course, but did you by any chance keep any notes during Operation Edinburgh, and have you still got them?"

"I did, General, and I have. In the file—*my* file, I mean, over by the desk there in the corner. I not only kept my notes, which were meagre. I kept every damn scrap of paper connected with the thing, and all the newspapers—the Edinburgh and London newspapers. Everything's there in the file, and it's labelled 'My Vacation in Scotland.' It's arranged in more or less chronological order— my own notes on what you call Operation Edinburgh and on everything else that occurred during that trip. I look it over every now and then. I spread it all out on the big divan over there by the west window—the visiting cards, the chits and memoranda, the reminders of lunch dates and dinner dates, my cables to my of-fice and my editor's replies, copies of the magazine pieces I wrote during that trip, the newspapers, the road maps, everything. When I spread them out on the divan, little Jock knows enough now not to jump up on that divan. Would you fellows like some coffee?"

"I would, as a matter of fact," said the general.

"So would I, thanks," said the major.

"I'll put the kettle on. I hope you like *espresso*."

"I prefer it to any other," said the general. "But what effect, Major, does *espresso* have on the Colonel?"

"Oh, coffee's O.K. for him," said the major. "It acts on him just as if he were an ordinary individual."

I PUT ON the kettle, and, after a while, brought in the eight-cup *espresso* pot.

"Delicious," said the general when he had taken a sip. "Look, Colonel, instead of asking you to try to tell us the whole story from start to finish, I think the Major and I will ask you questions as we go along. It'll be easier that way. Easier for you, I mean."

"Go right ahead, General," I said. "I'll just spread the stuff out on the divan, here, and you and the Major can get cracking, as some of the Scots and Englishmen say."

"When was the very first instant that you found yourself believing that what you were on wasn't an ordinary vacation trip to Scotland?"

"The answer to that is: When I discovered that somebody had gone through my briefcase in the living room of my hotel suite in Glasgow while I was asleep in the bedroom. That wasn't something I merely suspected. There was no question about it. Manuscripts disarranged—you know."

"There's no doubt in our minds that your baggage was gone through by somebody," said the general.

"Really? Well, anyway, I don't ordinarily live in two-room suites when I'm travelling—certainly not when I'm travelling alone—but this was my first trip to Scotland, where my McKelway ancestors came from a long way back, and in the two or three days I was planning to spend in Glasgow before going on to Edinburgh I thought I'd do myself proud. So when I got to Dublin—where I spent a pleasurable week at the Dolphin, down by the Liffey—I wrote to the manager of the St. Enoch Hotel, in Glasgow, telling him I expected to do some things for *The New Yorker* when I got there. I asked him to reserve a small suite for me, if possible. I sent him a check on my New York bank for fifty dollars as a deposit.

And when I was shown into the suite after flying over from Dublin, I couldn't believe my eyes. It was the biggest place you ever saw. And it only cost twenty dollars a day. The living room—or drawing room, as they call it—had a marble mantelpiece and an open grate, and enormous French windows overlooking St. Enoch's Square. There were overstuffed couches and chairs—enough of them to seat twelve or fourteen people. There was one of the grandest desks I've ever seen in my life, set between two of the French windows. It was very old, and had a leather top burnished and mellowed by time and polishing, and it was about the size of one of our enormous American executive-type desks, with an old Windsor chair to sit in when you were using it. The bedroom was equally magnificent. It also had an open grate in it. I'm wild about open fires. Even in midsummer, in Scotland, an open fire is comfortable in the evening and in the early morning—as well as cheerful to look at—whether or not the building has central heating. There was kindling wood and coal for the two open grates of my hotel suite—standing in great brass scuttles on the hearths—and when I asked the bellboy if the fireplaces worked, he said, 'Why, yes, sir. That's their purpose. Would the gentleman wish to have a fire lit in the drawing room now? I'll send the maid in, sir.' I had dinner in front of the fire in the drawing room—served by a happily talkative Irish room waitress—and I felt so relaxed and contented I thought I might just settle down right there and write something lengthy and significant. Something along the lines of Tolstoy's 'War and Peace.' "

"And did you write anything?"

"Not a syllable."

"Why was that?"

"Well, chiefly, I think, because I felt *too* good. I wasn't elated or manic; I just felt too fine to work. Once, Freud had an experience like that. Freud would be technically classified as a mild manic-depressive today—like me. Isn't that so, Major?"

"Absolutely, Colonel. And possibly not necessarily mild."

"Why was your mood so good at that particular time, Colonel?"

"Oh, the magnificence of the suite, the way I took to Scotland straight off—as if I had been there before and had come back home to a place I'd always loved—the exhilaration I felt from the effects of a motor trip through the lovely countryside to the village of Dollar. All those things."

"Why did you go to the village of Dollar?"

"I happened to see it on a map in the classic guidebook—'Muirhead's Scotland'—before I left New York, and I thought a visit to a place in Scotland named Dollar might produce a little piece for the magazine. You see, I didn't really expect to do much work on that trip—it was mostly a vacation—but before I left New York I'd written a short piece for the Talk of the Town department, called 'Hall En Route,' in which an imaginary character I long ago invented, a crotchety old codger named Hall who lives on Murray Hill, with a manservant, tells of his plans for his summer vacation in Europe, and so on, and I hoped to do a few pieces of the same kind in the course of the trip. Except for the character named Hall, these pieces are factual, and they are supposed to be humorous. I have here a cable I sent from Glasgow to the editor who handles my stuff at *The New Yorker*, and the reply I received from him about these Hall pieces."

"Read them," said the general.

"I didn't keep a copy of the first cable I sent, but that was from Dublin. The second one is right here on the top of this little pile. It goes like this:

WIRED YOU WEDNESDAY OUTLINING ANOTHER POSSIBLE HALL PIECE ON DUBLIN ON STRIKE AT SHELBOURNE HOTEL THERE, BUT NO REPLY RECEIVED. AM AT HOTEL ST. ENOCH, GLASGOW, FOR PRESENT. SINCE CABLING YOU, RAN INTO JIM FARLEY IN DUBLIN AND HERE, AND HIS COCA-COLA TRAVELS COULD BE INCLUDED IN

SHELBOURNE PIECE OR MIGHT BE SEPARATE PIECE IF STRIKE STORY
NOT WANTED. ADVISE AND REGARDS.

"The answer I received to that said,

ENJOYED YOUR FIRST DUBLIN PIECE. DOLLAR STILL SOUNDS FINE
AND YES ON SHELBOURNE PIECE. SORRY THAT OWING TO MY BE-
ING OUT OF OFFICE PART OF LAST WEEK I DID NOT REPLY TO
YOUR EARLIER CABLE. WE PLAN TO RUN HALL EN ROUTE PIECE IN
ISSUE GOING TO PRESS MONDAY, JULY 27TH, AND YES FARLEY
MIGHT MAKE A FOURTH. REGARDS.

"Interesting," said the general.

"You see, when I discovered that somebody had gone through
my briefcase but that nothing had been taken—and I had a small
batch of traveller's checks in there for emergency purposes, in addition to some I was carrying in my wallet—I figured it might
have been the British Intelligence people or Secret Service people,
or something like that, who went through it. After all, it was a very
sensitive time in the world—the Queen was touring Canada and
was soon coming back home, and Eisenhower was coming over to
England and Scotland before long—and I thought it might easily
be that the British were checking up on all travellers just to be on
the safe side. Then it occurred to me that my general behavior and
my incoming and outgoing cables would look rather suspicious
from the point of view of a British secret agent."

"Why?"

"Well, it seems to me that the cables kind of sound like something in code when you read them from that point of view. Don't
you think so? As for my general behavior, it occurred to me that it
would look as if I were somebody *posing* as a writer, rather than
somebody who was a real writer. I was going around in such a
daze of happiness—talking to strangers, laughing a lot, listening to

long stories of all sorts in the Glasgow pubs—that, from the point of view I've mentioned, it might easily look as if I were playing some kind of role. I would seem too happy-go-lucky to be real, looked at from the point of view of a C.I.D. man or a secret agent. And my visit to Dollar, I thought, would seem extraordinarily mysterious to them."

"What measures did you take to see if you were being followed?"

"I didn't do much about it, actually. I was amused by the idea that the Secret Service might be tailing me, but I did take a second look at anybody I saw who I thought might be a British secret agent. However, when you start doing *that* sort of thing, you soon discover that there are a great many gentlemen in Glasgow who might be in that line of work. They wear tweeds and carry raincoats and smoke pipes and swing sticks and have easygoing ways and bright, intelligent eyes, and they seem to have plenty of time for lounging around in pubs and hotel lobbies talking to people like me. I decided to stop being suspicious. It tended to spoil my fun. I spent a few more delightful days in Glasgow and moved on by train to Edinburgh, where I'd reserved a room at the Roxburghe Hotel—a marvellous old-fashioned place overlooking Charlotte Square, at the end of George Street and just a block from Princes Street. I liked Edinburgh even better than Glasgow, and although I'd originally planned to go on to Paris, I decided to stay in Edinburgh until the end of my vacation. I was taking about six weeks off all told. I cashed all my traveller's checks at the Bank of Scotland branch on Princes Street—I'm always afraid of losing those damn things—and opened a checking account there. I made friends all over. Mostly at the Press Club, to which I was given a visitor's card by one of the journalists on the *Scotsman*, and at a particularly superior pub, named Scott's, on Rose Street, around the corner from the Roxburghe. I'd been told by a friend in New

York who travels a lot that Scott's was sort of like what '21' used to be back in the early nineteen-thirties, and it was—except that Scott's has no restaurant, only snacks and drinks. I met lawyers and doctors and wool merchants and sheep farmers there, and other interesting people, some of whom became my friends and are still my friends. I correspond with a couple of them to this day."

"If the General doesn't mind," said the major. "Look, Colonel, I know it's an imposition, but—well, I'm starving! And it's too late for room service. You wouldn't have something in your kitchenette there, would you? I'll get it myself, if you'll let me. Any old thing at all."

"I guess I'll nibble at something, too, Colonel, if you've got anything in there," the general said.

"How would some Stilton cheese, pumpernickel, sweet butter, and homogenized milk all around strike the two of you?"

"Thank the good Lord for all his blessings!"

"Stilton and pumpernickel!"

"COLONEL," SAID THE general after a while, "had you pretty much stopped suspecting that you were being followed or checked up on by the British Secret Service by the time you left Glasgow and went on to Edinburgh?"

"Completely. By then I was simply having a wonderful time, and if—as I told myself—I was close to the edge of euphoria at the beginning of my stay in Glasgow, I had levelled out nicely by the time I went to Edinburgh. I was just feeling good, not *too* good. Still, I hadn't really done any work."

"At what moment of what day after your arrival in Edinburgh did you again begin to think that you were being followed?"

"Not until the morning after the night I got hit on the head. That was on Saturday, July 25, 1959."

"Who hit you?"

"I think I'd better tell you first about meeting Mr. and Mrs. Cameron. I was with them when I got hit on the head."

"Go right ahead, Colonel."

"You see, I had been in Edinburgh for two days and I was keeping more or less to the same schedule I had laid down for myself in Glasgow. I met Mr. and Mrs. Cameron—"

"Suppose you tell us about the schedule and then about Mr. and Mrs. Cameron."

"O.K. At the Roxburghe, in Edinburgh, I would wake up shortly before 7 A.M., which was the earliest I could get breakfast. I would call the night porter and ask for a pot of morning tea. I would be bathed and shaved and dressed—or anyway half dressed—by the time the porter got there with the tea. There would usually be a few biscuits on the tray. I would eat one or two of these and drink three or four cups of tea—with milk and sugar—and have a cigarette. Do you really want all this?"

"Yes."

"By that time, the Edinburgh and London newspapers would be outside my door, along with my freshly shined shoes. I would finish dressing, put on the shoes, and call room service, which would just be opening up for breakfast. In New York, I eat all sorts of different and dreary things for breakfast, when I eat anything— I frequently don't have breakfast at all—but in Scotland I was always hungry in the morning and yet, at the same time, I had no wish to try anything except the fruit and porridge and the haddock and eggs poached in milk, which were just as delicious at the Roxburghe as they had been at the St. Enoch. So while I was gobbling up this breakfast, I would glance at the headlines, and then I would get down to *really* reading the papers. I had a single room at the Roxburghe—not much bigger than a drawing room on a Pullman car—and liked it fine. The bath was just down the hall, and I always seemed to be the first one up on that floor. The one window of my room, which was on the third floor, looked out on

Charlotte Square. And Charlotte Square is just as beautiful today, I guess, as it was in the eighteenth century. I would sit there reading the papers and looking down at Charlotte Square for an hour or so. Then I would perhaps take a gander at my notes for the piece I intended to do on the village of Dollar. Then I would decide to do that piece the next morning. Then—"

"By the way, did you ever write the piece on Dollar?"

"No, General, I didn't."

"Now, to get back to the schedule you had laid out for yourself, what did you usually do after reading the papers for an hour or so in your room at the Roxburghe?"

"Having by that time decided not to do the Dollar piece until the next day, I would take the London *Times* and the *Scotsman*—my two favorite newspapers of all the ones I had delivered to my room every morning—and set out for a walk with the two papers under my arm. I would stroll all around Edinburgh without any particular objective in mind, drinking in the atmosphere I found so stimulating and at the same time so soothing. The gray stones out of which so many old Edinburgh houses and other buildings were built, in the sixteenth, seventeenth, and eighteenth centuries, have been turned almost black by time and the thin but incessant vapors from all the open grates in which coal is burned, and from the comparatively small number of industrial plants in and around Edinburgh, which also burn coal. I found the sight of the buildings strangely beautiful, and at the same time evocative, almost familiar—as if I had known them in some earlier existence. I also enjoyed looking at the tweeds in the men's shops on George Street. In short, I enjoyed everything about Edinburgh. By eleven o'clock in the morning, I was ready for a pint of ale, and I usually had it at Scott's, the pub I mentioned a while back. There I would continue to read my *Times* and *Scotsman*, and perhaps talk to the bartenders and to Miss Scott, the proprietress, or to customers I'd already got to know. Miss Scott's father started the place in 1899.

She has kept it exactly as it was then. When lunchtime approached, I would feel like having a pink gin, but instead of having it at Scott's I would have it at the bar at the Roxburghe, or at the North British Station Hotel or at the George Hotel, on George Street. It was in the cocktail bar at the George that I met the Camerons. Do you want me to go ahead and tell you about the Camerons now, General, or do you want me to tell you what my afternoon schedule was?"

"Whichever you like, Colonel. But if you have no preference, perhaps it might be just as well to tell us about the Camerons now."

"Right. I breezed into the George at a quarter to one on the afternoon of July 25th. It was that night that I got hit on the head. I sat down on a stool in the cocktail bar at the George—there are three or four different bars in the George, but this was the cocktail bar, at the left as you go in the front door from George Street—and ordered a pink gin. There was a couple sitting there on stools some distance from the one I selected for myself. I had finished my *Times,* but I hadn't quite got through the *Scotsman.* I was reading a column called 'A Scotsman's Log,' by Wilfred Taylor—an entertaining piece that day, in which Taylor described how he was writing his column while trying to cure himself of an acute common cold. So I took my first sip of the pink gin and went on reading Taylor's column. The man and woman at the bar were chatting with the bartender, and I didn't pay any attention to what they were saying. By the time I'd finished the pink gin, I had also finished Taylor's column, and I put my folded papers on the bar beside me, and ordered another pink gin as soon as I could do so without interrupting the conversation going on between the two other people and the bartender. I glanced over at the couple and saw that they were an attractive woman, whom I guessed to be somewhere in her forties, and a nice-looking chap who looked as if he might be about my age or a bit older.

"The woman smiled at me and said, 'Where did you get that shirt?'

" 'At Brooks Brothers, in New York,' I said, smiling back at her.

" 'Then my husband would have to go a long way to get one like it, wouldn't he? Unless you could have some made here, Ian,' she went on, turning to her husband. 'With those little buttons that hold down the corners.'

" 'I like the looks of that shirt, too,' the man said to her, 'but why do you want me to wear a shirt with those little buttons on it?'

" 'Because the collars of your shirts always begin to turn up at the corners by midafternoon, if not before.'

" 'Tommy,' said the man to the bartender, 'something similar, I think. And,' he went on, speaking to me, 'won't you join us?'

" 'Thank you very much,' I said.

"Well, General, it turned out to be one of those happy occasions that are not unusual in bars all over the world but that, in my opinion, are likely to occur more frequently in Scotland than anywhere else. At least, they did in my case. Before we said goodbye to go our separate ways for our two-o'clock lunches, Mrs. Cameron had invited me to come over to their flat, at No. 12 Glencairn Crescent, at seven o'clock, have a drink with them, and then have dinner with them at some country inn in the environs of Edinburgh. By that time, I knew a good deal about them and they knew even more about me. I had been told, for example, in the course of our casual, gay, and wide-ranging conversation, that Mrs. Cameron was recuperating from a very serious operation, which had kept her 'in hospital' for some weeks; I had been told that Mr. Cameron never had to worry about sleep, because, as a British Intelligence officer in London during the Second World War, he had worked pretty much around the clock, and, as Mrs. Cameron put it, 'Ian can drop off to sleep absolutely at any time he chooses, just like a dog'; I had been told that until recently Mrs. Cameron had been

REPORTING AT WIT'S END

the owner of an old Scottish castle—she didn't say exactly where it was, and I didn't ask—but that, like so many people over there who inherit property of that sort these days, she'd had to sell it to pay the death duties; and so on. I had no idea whether they were rich or poor or somewhere in the middle, but my impression was that they were at least comfortably off. It was after we had chatted for about half an hour that Mr. Cameron said, 'By the way, my name's Cameron, and this, of course, is my wife.' I then told him my name and gave him one of my business cards. He got out his wallet and searched around in it, evidently looking for one of his own business cards, and finally fished one out and handed it to me. From it I learned that he was named Ian E. Cameron and that the firm he worked for—or owned—was 'Ian Cameron, Ltd., Firearms and Fishing Gear, Glasgow, Estd. 1778.' Later on, when Mrs. Cameron asked me to have dinner with them, Mr. Cameron asked me to give his card back to him, and he then scribbled on the back of it their home address in Edinburgh and their Edinburgh telephone number—Caledonia 5269. He said that it was a new number and wasn't in the Edinburgh telephone directory. They had told me they had only recently moved into the flat on Glencairn Crescent. I got there a few minutes after seven o'clock, and—"

"I hate to interrupt the continuity of what you're saying, Colonel, but I think perhaps it would be best at this point if you told us what you did the rest of that afternoon. Perhaps that would also give us an idea of what your typical afternoon schedule in Edinburgh was."

"As you say, General. Let me see, now—I kept a sort of date diary in the calendar part of my pocket address book during that vacation. Where the hell is it? Oh, yes, here we are. I had lunch at the Press Club that day. I went there quite a lot. Ladies were let in after six in the evening but not in the daytime. The club was in what used to be a modest three-story private residence—one of a row

430

of old houses—with a fireplace in practically every room. Drinks and food were paid for cash on the nail—a system that eliminated both bookkeeping and delinquent accounts. On that day, being rather late for lunch, and having had several pink gins, I went straight into the dining room, and didn't stop at the bar. I sat alone and didn't talk to anybody—probably because there was hardly anybody there at that hour. I strolled around the streets for a bit after lunch, and bought a knitted waistcoat—a sweater vest—at the Stewart Christie & Co. shop, on George Street. Then I went along back to the Roxburghe and took a nap. I woke up in time to bathe and dress and go down at five o'clock to the lobby—which, incidentally, has deep black leather chairs and leather couches in it, and French windows looking out on Charlotte Square. There I had a high tea. Little, thin sandwiches, hot scones, and butter and jam and so on, and one soft-boiled egg. I read the latest European edition of *Time* magazine for a few minutes, and then put it in the wastepaper basket. I didn't talk to anybody during this. I took a stroll in the direction of the Old Town of Edinburgh, and got back to the Roxburghe again about six-thirty. I had asked Mrs. Cameron how to get to Glencairn Crescent, and she had told me to simply ask Mr. Ross, the head porter, to give me directions when I was ready to start over there. She said that they'd stayed at the Roxburghe many times and that Mr. Ross was a great fellow. I had already made his acquaintance, and he was indeed. He was about fifty years old, six feet, and solidly built, and he could carry six or eight suitcases as easily as I might carry six or eight books. He was a semi-professional Scottish ballad singer, and often wrote his own words and music. His knowledge of Edinburgh was encyclopedic. Just as I came up to the entrance of the Roxburghe, a Rolls-Royce touring car with a trailer attached to it was pulling up in front of the hotel. On the trailer was a large rowboat. Two gentlemen in tweed fishing clothes and hats stepped out of the Rolls and marched into the hotel, while Mr. Ross, without having been given any instructions by them, began unloading their luggage—fishing rods, wicker hampers, and so on. I drifted into the hotel in their wake and saw them registering. The pretty Irish girl behind the desk handed each of them a key, so evidently they had separate rooms. It occurred to me that they had perfect 'cover' if they were secret agents, but I hardly gave this a second thought.

"Mrs. Cameron had advised me not to waste money on a taxi but to get Mr. Ross to tell me which bus to take, because, she said, I could get the one I wanted right at the corner of George Street, ten yards from the hotel. When Mr. Ross was through with the fishermen's gear, I told him I was going to No. 12 Glencairn Crescent to see his friends Mr. and Mrs. Cameron. 'Aye, they are splendid people,' he said heartily, and then gave me explicit instructions about taking such-and-such a bus at the corner and getting off at Palmerston Place. He said he could tell me how to get to Glencairn Crescent from where I got off the bus but that I might be better off if I simply asked some pedestrian when I got to Palmerston Place.

"I thanked him, and caught the right bus, and got off at Palmerston Place in about five minutes. I don't know how they do it, but the buses in Edinburgh manage to go like hell. I asked a nice-looking middle-aged pedestrian—a man—how to get to Glencairn Crescent, and he told me, and said it was just a five-minute walk. I got there at exactly five minutes after seven.

"I rang the push-button bell of No. 12, and nothing happened. I tried the door and it was off the latch, and since they'd told me they lived in a 'flat,' I thought there might be some other kind of push button inside the vestibule. I couldn't find any, but at that point Mr. Cameron appeared at the top of a flight of curving stairs. 'Come on up, McKelway,' he said, and I went on up.

"Mr. Cameron led me into their 'flat' and told me that Mrs. Cameron would be down soon.

" 'My God, what a marvellous place!' I said, looking around the drawing room, which fronted on a tidy little park of green grass, with full-grown trees in it.

" 'We were very fortunate,' he said. 'It's an Adam house.' He took me over to one of the tall windows. From there I could see all the way to the end of the little park. The park was oblong, and the houses on both sides of it had been built along two crescent-shaped streets, which, of course, had been laid out expressly for these houses, late in the eighteenth century. This house I was in was at one end of its crescent, so that as you looked straight down the park from the Camerons' drawing room you could see how the two crescents bulged, so to speak, and then almost came together again at the far end of the park.

" 'My God!' I said again to Mr. Cameron.

" 'Yes,' he said. 'I thought I might have a Scotch-and-soda. What will you have?'

" 'Something similar,' I said, quoting his words to Tommy, the bartender at the George, that afternoon.

" 'Ah, but you miss the point,' he said. 'It's when you've already *had* a drink that you say "something similar." The plot is that in saying this you avoid saying "another," or "one more." '

" 'It's a wonderful expression,' I said. 'I can't wait to try it on the bartender at a saloon called Costello's, on Third Avenue, in Manhattan.'

" 'You know, I've never been to New York,' he said. 'And I want very much to go. So does my wife.'

"I figured out that when the Camerons called this place of theirs a flat they were simply avoiding calling it a house, probably because they felt that calling it that might in some way be verging on the vulgar. As a matter of fact, they had the whole house, which was three stories high. On the ground floor was a separate apartment, in which lived an old lady who performed the duties of what we would call a superintendent over here. Mrs. Cameron came down, and there was some discussion as to whether we should drive out of the city in his car or her car. It appeared that she wouldn't let him drive her car and he wouldn't let her drive his. She had a Hillman and he had a Mercedes. It had become clear to me by this time that Mr. Cameron was determined to let his wife do just about anything that came into her head—because, it was my guess, she was still a little tensed up after her operation. I found Mrs. Cameron to be an altogether charming lady, every bit as loquacious as I am, and the friendship of the three of us had grown so fast that she and I were already contending with each other conversationally, in a joking way, and each of us was accusing the other of talking too much. She was as unaffected, and had a manner as simple and as full of individuality and quality, as one of those young duchesses one occasionally runs into at parties in London. Mr. Cameron was a big man, a little taller than I am—and I'm six feet tall—and his eyes were his outstanding feature. They were extra large and dark brown, and when he said something to you, he looked at you with them in a truly penetrating fashion. This didn't seem to be an affectation on his part but simply something he was born with. Mrs. Cameron was perhaps the more humorous of the two; Mr. Cameron laughed when she said anything witty or comical, but when he himself had the floor—and it wasn't easy to get the floor in that threesome—he was more likely to use his conversational gifts to explain something to me about Scotland: its customs, its history, or its people. Even before Mrs. Cameron had happened to remark to me earlier in the day that her husband had worked under great stress as an intelligence officer during the Second World War, I'd sensed that he was or had been some kind of military man of the highest type. A general, say."

"While I think of it, Colonel," my general said, "I notice that you are talking without making any reference to those notes you have over there on the divan. Did you make any notes on these conversations with the Camerons?"

"No. You see, many years ago, as a young newspaper reporter, I found out I didn't have to make notes, except for specific things like names, street addresses, and so on."

"And the Colonel is blessed—or cursed—with total recall, General," the major said.

"Thank you, Major. Shoot, Colonel."

"Mr. Cameron and I finished our long drinks while Mrs. Cameron had what they call over there 'a wee Scotch.' It's a one-ounce drink, taken as it comes. They discussed where the three of us might go for dinner, having finally settled the question of which car to take. Mrs. Cameron was to drive us in her car. After talking over the good qualities and minor faults of various inns in the environs of Edinburgh, they agreed that we should drive to a little village called Gifford, where there were two inns.

" 'One of them has a nice little bar, so arranged that when you stand at it or sit at it you look through the bottles—set in wide windows—into a nice little garden,' Mrs. Cameron said. 'The food at the other one is a bit better, we think, than it is at that one.'

" 'Yes,' said Mr. Cameron.

"So we started out for Gifford. I had no idea how far away it was or where it was, and I didn't care. At the moment, I felt relaxed and calm and happy at the prospect of being in such good hands. Mrs. Cameron, it soon turned out, was a fast driver. I'm not ordinarily nervous in automobiles, but I found myself pressing my right foot against the floorboard quite frequently as we sped in and out of the traffic on Princes Street toward one of the main exits from Edinburgh. Mr. and Mrs. Cameron sat in the front seat, and I sat in the back seat. I decided that the trouble with me was that I hadn't yet got used to the cars approaching us on the wrong side of the road, but I still found myself a bit tense, for it soon developed that Mrs. Cameron not only liked to talk while she drove but felt that when she was addressing me she ought to turn around and look at me.

" 'Tell McKelway about the lock and the police, Ian,' said Mrs. Cameron as we raced along.

" 'You tell him,' said Mr. Cameron.

" 'But I must turn around and look at him at least part of the time when I'm talking,' said Mrs. Cameron, 'and once or twice I noticed he was looking a little pale.'

" 'Tell me about the police, Mrs. Cameron,' I said. 'I feel as cool as a cucumber.'

"Mrs. Cameron then told me a very long story involving an Adam door, an Adam lock, and an Edinburgh bobby. It ended with the bobby's telling the Camerons that if anything at all out of the way ever happened to them, to be sure to call the police.

" 'Call the police!' said Mr. Cameron, laughing.

" 'Call the police!' said Mrs. Cameron.

"We drove on gaily, and frequently in the course of the delightful long evening one or another of us would find an opportunity to say 'Call the police!' when something somebody else said seemed to give us an opening. And running along as a minor refrain beneath the animated three-way conversation during this first part of the evening was an intermittent sort of sub-conversation between Mr. and Mrs. Cameron about how to get to Gifford. The pretty little lanes we were barrelling along were of the sort that had been there for centuries, and they followed the contours of the hilly Scottish terrain. Except that I could see the sun beginning to go down in the west—it goes down very late in summertime in Scotland—I wouldn't have had any idea by this time what direction we were travelling in. Actually, the way the lanes wound around, we were going in all directions. It soon developed that Mr. and Mrs. Cameron were hopelessly lost, but at that point Mrs. Cameron seemed to come upon a lane that was familiar to her—although it didn't go to Gifford—and she made a quick left turn into it without slowing down.

" 'Where are you going?' asked Mr. Cameron.

" 'This leads to the palace. I think he'll like it, don't you, Ian?'

" 'Yes,' said Mr. Cameron.

"Our new destination turned out to be a medium-sized palace that, according to Mrs. Cameron, the future King Edward VII had built for himself when he was Prince of Wales. As Mr. Cameron explained to me, it is now a hotel run by a commission of the Scottish government. Anybody can stay there and eat there and drink there, and the prices are only slightly higher than they are at an ordinary country inn. The exterior of King Edward's modest palace—he used it for comparatively brief visits during the summer and autumn, Mr. Cameron told me—was not up to the standard of the more ancient castles and palaces in Scotland. It looked too modern to me. It was built of stone, and it had hardly had time to get properly mellowed. But the setting was lovely. The palace was right on the sea, and it had its own golf links, of course. It was surrounded on three sides by formal gardens of the kind King Edward had a fancy for, and in the midst of all that wild Scottish scenery their stiffness gave their beauty a startling quality. We walked in at what must originally have been a side entrance, and turned to the right, off a comfortable-looking great hall, into a cozy room with a fireplace and a small bar. The bar seemed at home there, although it had been put in long after King Edward's time. French windows opened out onto one of the formal gardens. There were a few comfortable leather chairs and one or two small tables, and in the corner opposite the bar was a leather banquette, at which there was a larger table. Nobody was in the room except the bartender.

" 'Mr. Cameron, Mrs. Cameron,' said the bartender, with evident pleasure, when we came in.

"The Camerons asked him whether he had been 'in again,' and this seemed to be a big joke—which I did not understand until they explained later that he'd once been threatened with a short stretch for being drunk and disorderly on his day off, and that

Mr. Cameron had gone to bat for him. While I was taking in the view of the formal garden, Mr. Cameron beckoned to me conspiratorially. I followed him out of the room and down a small hallway leading off the great hall and through a door and onto a flagstone terrace—and there was the sea! Some geese were lounging around on the terrace, and they began to clatter noisily. Mr. Cameron gave them half a handful of cocktail biscuits he had picked up in the bar. Without saying anything to me, he waved an arm, indicating the sea, and we both stood and looked at it. I was disgusted with the poverty of my vocabulary, so I just grinned at him, and we walked up and down the terrace for a few minutes while he told me about the golf courses that stretched for miles, one after another, along this coastline. He told me that the courses were all public now, and we saw one family of golfers moving along a nearby fairway in the growing dusk. There was a father, a mother, a teen-age boy and girl, and two or three other children, the smallest being a boy five or six years old. He was carrying a putter, and one of the older boys and the father were carrying bags of clubs.

"'That's the way the Scots often play golf,' said Mr. Cameron. 'They make a family outing of it. It's just a pleasant way of taking a long walk along the grass beside the sea.'

"We reached the end of the terrace, and he indicated with another wave of his arm the great, wide expanse of the long string of golf courses, reaching as far down the coast as the eye could see.

"'What a place for a paratroop drop!' he said, surprisingly, and, I thought, rather grimly.

"We strolled back in and joined Mrs. Cameron, who was talking with three big young Scots in dark-blue business suits and a pretty Scots lass who was with them. Mrs. Cameron had a delightful way of striking up conversations with strangers, and this was an example of it. The young people seemed to have accepted her as one of themselves, and, without actually appearing to question them, she soon found out that the young men were an assistant engineer on a merchant ship, a postman, and a coal miner who had risen to a sub-executive position in a mine near the village in which all three of them and the girl had been raised. The girl was a student nurse at a hospital in Glasgow, and the four of them were on a weekend lark. Mr. Cameron ordered drinks, including the four young people in the round by making an unobtrusive circular gesture to the bartender with his forefinger. Soon the seven of us were talking about all sorts of things, and when the engineer, at some point, asked me if I was from England, I found myself feeling mysteriously flattered. But I told him I was from New York.

"I managed to buy a round, with considerable difficulty; the postman wanted to buy and insisted it was his turn, but Mrs. Cameron told him that he simply must acquiesce in the wishes of an American visitor. After one more round, which the postman did buy, Mrs. Cameron got explicit directions from the bartender as to how to get to Gifford, and the three of us were once more bowling along the twisting lanes.

" 'Are you very hungry?' Mrs. Cameron asked me.

" 'I'm completely happy, and I'm not a bit hungry,' I said. 'I had a big tea at the Roxburghe.'

" 'Good,' said Mr. Cameron, looking at his watch. 'We shall be sitting down to dinner in Gifford in thirty minutes.'

" 'Unless I get lost again,' said Mrs. Cameron.

" 'Yes,' said Mr. Cameron.

"Gifford was supposed to be ten or fifteen miles inland. We were soon lost again, in a maze of charming little lanes.

" 'Gifford doesn't seem to want to see us tonight,' said Mrs. Cameron, drawing up at the side of a lane while Mr. Cameron lit a cigarette for her.

" 'I have maps in my car,' said Mr. Cameron, 'but we're not in my car.'

" 'If I have a map, I *never* get to my destination,' said Mrs. Cameron. 'I invariably see some place with a tantalizing name and I veer off and go there.'

" 'We just went through the village of Duns.'

" 'Duns. Oh, *Duns!* Then we're only a few miles from a place somebody told me about only the other day, at Long-something. Longwich? Long-mackie?'

" 'I don't know.'

" 'It's a house-hotel and it's something-Burne.'

"A very aged countryman came hobbling toward us along the lane at this point, and when he got abreast of us, Mrs. Cameron hailed him politely, and the two of them had an animated chat about crops and sheep, but he was unable to tell her where the something-burne hotel in Long-something was.

" 'Oh, blast it!' she said, after he had hobbled on. 'It's exactly where we ought to go tonight. It's owned by a painter, who lives there with his family, and it's up in the Lammermuirs. There's a very small village, I was told, and from the inn there is not another house in sight in any direction. It attracts artists and writers, and there's quite a library, these people said. It's quite high in the hills, and they said that on a clear day you could look down all the way to the sea, twenty miles away. Oh, damn it! And this is a clear evening and the sun is just going down.'

" 'We must find out where it is from our friends and take Mc-Kelway there on another day,' said Mr. Cameron.

" 'Now we haven't any destination,' said Mrs. Cameron.

" 'I've just thought of something,' said Mr. Cameron. He turned to me and asked, 'Do you like Danish food?'

" 'I sure do,' I said.

" 'Oh, Ian, you *are* a dear!' Mrs. Cameron said, and then, to me, 'Duns is only ten or fifteen miles from Melrose, and there is a splendid little inn quite near there, where they have a very superior *smörgåsbord* and exceptional soup, which the proprietress makes herself. It's just what we want, after those drinks.' She whipped the car around and presumably headed for Duns.

"It turned out to be a comparatively straight course from Duns to Melrose and thence to Peebles and thence—after one or two pauses for directions in another tangle of little lanes—to the inn they were talking about. It was on the village street, and was, in fact, the village pub. We were greeted as we went in by the proprietor and his wife, who seemed to know the Camerons quite well. The working people in such places usually patronize the public bar, although they can go into the private bar if they want to. In the private bar, our host brought us little open-faced Danish sandwiches on buttered pumpernickel as hors d'oeuvres while each of us had an akvavit poured out of a bottle encased in ice, the way the Danes serve it in Copenhagen. The place was fairly crowded, but he said we could have a table in a few minutes. He brought us menus, and while Mr. and Mrs. Cameron were chatting with some strangers, he told me that he and his wife had bought the place some years before and, by means of a semi-official arrangement with the Danish Consul General in Edinburgh, had had their chef and three waitresses trained in Copenhagen, at the expense of the Danish government, while they themselves were restoring—and remodelling, to a small extent—the ancient village pub. Mrs. Cameron ordered some smoked eels, smoked salmon, a salad, and the fish soup, and Mr. Cameron and I both ordered the Danish-style steak tartare, as well as the eels and salmon, the salad, and the soup. We all decided against having any wine and agreed that we would go along with just the akvavit and the Carlsberg beer on draught, which was one of the specialties of the house. We sat at a corner table overlooking a garden, which was surrounded by a low stone wall, and in which a small, fluffy white bitch of Tibetan ancestry was playing with her two three-month-old puppies. We were all feeling very gay but not in the least drunk. To be exact, I'd say that Mrs. Cameron and I were a good way this side of being tipsy, and that Mr. Cameron was just the same as he'd been when we started out."

"This is a good place to ask you, Colonel, about you and alcohol. Can you drink a good deal without getting drunk?"

"When I'm in good form, as the Irish say," I told the general, "my tolerance for alcohol is considerable; in fact, I have sometimes found it frightening. But if I'm feeling low, my tolerance for it decreases, depending on how low I'm feeling. I can drink a good deal under certain conditions, but it's very likely to creep up on me if I'm not careful, even when I'm at my best. I don't know what my capacity would be right now, however, because, except for the drinking I did in Edinburgh and one or two subsequent and more or less inadvertent lapses, I don't drink. The Captain has convinced me that drinking in the course of my analysis tends to anesthetize my emotions, and thus short-circuit everything, and that my drinking would only prolong the analysis, which, naturally, I'm in a hurry to complete. So on the whole I don't drink."

"Did the Colonel and the Camerons stay at the Danish food place very late that night?" asked the major.

"No, Major. You can't stay very late at a pub in Scotland. The pubs shut up tight at ten o'clock, and then, as they say over there, you've had it. We got there a little after nine, and were having coffee and brandy when the 'Time, gentlemen, time' time came around. You can finish what you're drinking when that hour arrives, but you can't get any more, no matter who you are, unless you are staying at the inn, and are thus a 'traveller,' in which case, according to Scottish law, you can drink your head off until breakfast time and right on through the day, if you want to, as long as you don't behave in an intoxicated manner. Hasn't either of you been over to Britain yet?"

"No, sir. The General was in the Korean War, and I had a tour of duty in Japan. But since then we've both been stuck in or near

Washington with the Research and Development Command of the Air Force."

"But I thought you were with the Central Intelligence Agency!"

"Oh, no," said the general. "We're on temporary duty with the C.I.A. We were on General Taylor's small personal staff during his investigation of the C.I.A. for the President, and we're still doing odd jobs there as they come along."

"Oh, I see. Well, the only thing the Camerons talked about during dinner that bothered me later was about the Tory Scots. And the Highlanders. They said some of the extreme Tories—landowners—in Scotland were close to being Fascist. That they still hated England as their ancestors had, and they hated the Labour Party, and even Macmillan's Conservative Party wasn't conservative enough for them. And that they were quite capable of working up a movement of force against England if they thought they could put it over and make Britain a Fascist country. And, the Camerons said, since the Soviet Union was so similar to a Fascist regime, in spite of its being Socialistic, many people feared that someday, if exactly the right circumstances arose, the extreme Tories in Scotland and England might try to make some kind of deal with the Russians that would tie in with their plans for a totalitarian Britain. And, they said, the true Highlanders were so wild and savage, at heart, that they were capable of joining in just about anything if it meant a fight against England. The Camerons spoke of this mostly in a humorous and speculative vein, but it stuck in my mind.

"Well, anyway, the Camerons and I left the Danish place at a few minutes after eleven and started back to Edinburgh. In those few minutes before we left, we were chatting with the proprietor and his wife and sort of kidding around, and I teased Mrs. Cameron about how hard it was to get a word in edgewise when one was surrounded by taciturn Scots, and she said, 'We call McKelway, here, the Noisy American,' and then she said, 'Shall we just throw him in a ditch on the way back to Edinburgh, Ian?' and Mr. Cameron said, 'Yes, and then we'll call the police,' and I said 'Call the police!' and we all laughed at our private joke. And then, on our way back to Edinburgh, we got lost again. I'd had a marvellous time, but my nerves were a little jumpy, what with all the fast driving, the cars coming at me on the wrong side of the road, and the lickety-split speed of our wide-ranging conversation, and when we got lost in still another cluster of small lanes, and I saw a signpost at a crossroads, I volunteered to jump out of the car and see if the signpost would tell us how to get back to Edinburgh. So Mrs. Cameron stopped the car. It was pitch dark by now, and cloudy—no moon, no stars. Mrs. Cameron turned up the headlights and shifted the car so they were focussed on the signpost, which was on the other side of the lane from us, about ten yards off. I got out and went loping cheerfully in the direction of the signpost, looking up at it as I trotted along, and the next thing I knew I'd been hit on the head and was coming back to consciousness after what seemed a long time. There was blood all over my face, and I was at the bottom of what I at first thought was my unfilled grave. What had apparently happened was that, not then being acquainted with the fact that all such lanes in Scotland have deep ditches on both sides of them, whereas we would expect in this country to find only soft shoulders at the sides of a road, I'd fallen into the ditch. And the signposts in Scotland are made of iron. As I groped my way back into this world, I figured out that this was a ditch I was in and that I had fallen feet first into it as I trotted toward the signpost, and that my momentum had carried my head bang into the base of the signpost, knocking me out cold, so that I then sank into the ditch full length on my back. I crawled out of the ditch, mopping my bleeding forehead with my handkerchief, and discovered that the headlights were still turned on the signpost—and on me—and that two helmeted motorcycle policemen, having dismounted from their motorcycles, were talking to Mr. and Mrs. Cameron, who still sat in the front seat of their car. I tottered over to them, and there were exclamations all around. It seems that as I approached the signpost, and before I fell into the ditch, Mrs. Cameron had flagged down the two policemen, who were going in the opposite direction, with the idea of asking *them* how to get back to Edinburgh. Since neither Mr. nor Mrs. Cameron's eyes were on me when I disappeared from view, they thought I had walked on past the signpost. In any case, Mr. Cameron all at once assumed the role of a British Army officer confronted with a wounded trooper. He sprang out of the car and took a look at the front of my head, and asked me how long I thought I had been unconscious, and when I told him that I had no idea, but that it couldn't have been very long, he said he thought that to be on the safe side I'd better let them take me to the Royal Infirmary, in Edinburgh, because I probably had a concussion, if not a fracture. He said the cut on my forehead was about an inch long and looked rather deep. The cut was still bleeding to beat hell, and he made a tight bandage for it with a clean handkerchief that he took from his jacket pocket, so that I looked and felt just like the soldier in the threesome playing 'Yankee Doodle.' My head didn't hurt much, and I was laughing about the whole silly business, although actually I was damn well shaken up, but before Mrs. Cameron, on the drive back to Edinburgh, said something about the coincidence—the fact that they had said they might throw me into a ditch and call the police, and so on—I had already thought of it myself."

"Did you at that time believe it possible that somebody *had* hit you on the head, rather than that you had hit it on the base of the signpost?"

"Not for an instant—at that time. I was preoccupied with being a brave soldier and was cursing myself out over the fact that I would now be going around Edinburgh for at least a week with

445

some kind of bandage on my forehead, making me look as if I had been in a drunken brawl, or something."

"Have you ever been in a drunken brawl?" asked the major.

"Well, I've never been injured in one."

"Then why did you think other people would think that was where you suffered this injury?"

"You've got me, Major. I suppose because, in my youth, I frequently woke up in the morning surprised to find that nobody had hit me on the head or on the nose the night before. But nobody ever did. Anyway, I'm as vain as the next man, I guess, and I was annoyed about being even temporarily disfigured. In short, I felt like a fool."

"Did Mrs. Cameron drive straight back to Edinburgh then?"

"As straight as she could. On the way, I told Mr. Cameron I didn't think I needed to go to the Infirmary, and he said we'd stop at the North British Hotel, where, in the gentlemen's room, I could wash my face and let him take a closer look at the cut. We did that, while Mrs. Cameron sat waiting in the lobby. When I took a look at my head in the mirror, I agreed with Mr. Cameron that I had better get the hell on to the Infirmary. There was a lump the size of a small egg on my forehead, halfway between my right eyebrow and my receding hair, and the cut looked ugly. Also, I was beginning to feel kind of weak—as if I might faint, or something. They took me to the Infirmary—Mrs. Cameron driving as safely and as competently as one of those lady Red Cross ambulance drivers in the war—and they turned me over to the nurses. I was taken straight into the emergency ward. The Camerons came along with me."

"Now, exactly what did they do to you in the Infirmary? Don't leave anything out, Colonel."

"Nobody else was waiting in the emergency ward, and a young doctor came along in a couple of minutes. There were two pretty young nurses, and each of them had held me by an arm when they brought me into the ward—evidently thinking that I might be about to black out. They had eased me into a chair, and I was sitting there when the doctor came up. Mr. Cameron explained briefly to him what had happened—that is, that I had fallen against the base of an iron signpost in the environs of Edinburgh—and the doctor asked me to get up on what looked like an operating table, and I did, lying on my back. The doctor examined the cut under a bright light and said something I didn't catch to one of the nurses. She went away and reappeared in a couple of minutes carrying a hypodermic needle and stood waiting to give me a shot of something in the arm after the doctor had rolled up my sleeve. I asked the doctor what that was, and he said it was an anti-tetanus shot. When the nurse had given me the shot, he said that it didn't look as if I had a fracture but that I probably did have a concussion and that in any case he wanted to have my head X-rayed right there and then. Mr. Cameron had told him that I was an American journalist, and so on, but I'm sure that had nothing to do with the efficiency and thoughtfulness with which I was treated. When the doctor said he wanted to X-ray me, I told the Camerons not to wait, because it would probably take a while. With what seemed like some reluctance, they said good night, and told me to be sure to call them the next day and let them know how I was getting along. Before they left, Mr. Cameron said it would be wise for me to drink a lot of milk the next day. The doctor said that unless I had a fracture it would not be necessary for me to stay at the Infirmary that night. In due course, I was X-rayed from every possible angle, and after I'd waited quite a long time in the waiting room—until the X-rays were developed and the doctor had studied them, evidently along with an X-ray specialist—the doctor told me the story."

"And what was that?"

"In the first place, he said that I had no fracture, and that I should take it easy for a day or two and shouldn't have any strong drink for forty-eight hours at least, on account of the mild concussion I had probably suffered. He said it would be a good idea if I stayed in bed the next day, but that if I felt all right in the morning it wouldn't do me any harm to move around as long as I took it easy and didn't overexert myself. He was a very solemn, serious-minded young doctor, and was extraordinarily thorough. His name was MacLean. He was writing out a long passage in longhand on some kind of hospital form, and as he did that, he would pause and go on telling me about my injury."

"But what else was there to tell you?"

"Well, although my head didn't hurt, I had begun to feel a good deal of pain at the bottom of the back of my neck—at the top of my spine—and when I'd mentioned this to the doctor, before being X-rayed, he'd nodded as if he knew all about that. Now he said that in falling I had apparently wrenched the back of my neck, and that I already had what he called an 'arthritic pocket' in that particular area. He said that this wrenching of the top of my spine might activate the incipient arthritis, and that he would advise me to come to the Infirmary every day for about ten days and undergo a series of orthopedic treatments and exercises, which he said might serve not only to relieve me of the discomfort at the back of my neck but to prevent an onset of acute arthritis in that area later on in my life. He said that I really ought to have these orthopedic treatments and exercises—even if I had not been injured—and that I ought to continue them after I got back to New York. He said good night to me, and shook hands and wished me luck, and left me in the care of one of the nurses. One of them went out with him and soon returned with one of those complicated braces of the sort that people wear when they have broken their neck. My neck wasn't really bothering me much by this time, and I told the nurse that I simply couldn't go around in that brace, that I had a lot of work to do and a lot of people to see, and that I wouldn't wear it unless I was absolutely ordered to do so by the doctor. She said that the doctor hadn't ordered me to wear it but that he had advised it, and that I didn't have to wear it unless I wished to. The doctor had taken three stitches in my forehead, and had told me that the swelling would go down if I applied hot and cold towels to it as often as I could after I got back to the hotel, and again on the following morning. He hadn't put a bandage on it, and he'd painted it with colorless iodine. The threads he'd used to stitch it up with, however, were black, and when I got back to the hotel, by taxi, and saw myself in the mirror, I certainly looked a mess. Before I climbed into bed and sank into a deep sleep, I made a firm resolution to rest up on Sunday and get to work the next day in earnest."

"So you got to work in earnest on Monday morning, I take it."

"Well, not exactly, General. I wrote six lines—the beginning of the piece on Dollar—very fast on my portable typewriter while I was waiting for my breakfast, around seven o'clock, having had my usual early-morning tea and biscuits. Then I—"

"Do you have a copy of what you wrote?"

"Why, yes. Let's see, that would be in this pile over here. In fact, it's right at the bottom of the pile, under the copies of the *Dollar Magazine*, a school publication. I must explain, General, that these little pieces I write for the Talk of the Town department, using my imaginary character Mr. Hall, are written in the form of a letter to the editors of that department, and are in the first person singular. Now, this beginning of the Dollar piece says, ' "It occurred to me this morning," says an airmail dispatch from our old-timey operative Mr. Hall, "that some of your more materialistic readers might be interested in a small Scottish village some twenty miles northwest of Edinburgh, the name of which for several centuries has been Dollar." ' That's all I wrote that morning, and I never got back to that piece again."

"It seems to me you had a good start there, Colonel, although

I don't pretend to know anything about this writing game," said the general. "Why didn't you go on with it?"

"I was feeling extremely restless. I felt as happy as ever, but I wanted to get into action. Limiting my action to finishing that inconsequential little piece on Dollar didn't seem like enough. I wanted to do some kind of piece that would include a whole lot of my impressions and feelings about Scotland in general and Edinburgh in particular. I don't mean that I wanted to do a travel piece. I wanted to do what I suppose would be called an impressionistic, if not Surrealistic, piece, over my own signature, that would show what it was like to be an American in a lonely hotel room in Edinburgh, an American who was nuts about Scotland and the Scots, and at the same time was bewildered and confused by them—by the subtle differences in the style of the English in the newspapers, by the labored and long-winded inscriptions on the plaques to be found on old castles and new monuments, by the kind of things he found himself reading and rereading, such as hotel menus and hotel guest booklets, and customs and immigration regulations on the forms they give you when you arrive in Scotland. Then, I also wanted to get on with my ancestor search. I had been neglecting that, along with neglecting the piece on Dollar, in favor of simply drifting around and having a wonderful time. And then, too—"

"Colonel, suppose you tell us about the ancestor search and then go back to the 'piece' you were now thinking about writing."

"Ancestor search. That's over here. A whole big envelope full of it. Do you want all of it or some of it, or what, General?"

"Just go ahead with it in your own way and see how it turns out."

"Well, it starts with a cable I sent from Edinburgh to my elder brother, in Washington, which says—"

"I think the General ought to know who that is, Colonel. The Colonel's elder brother is Benjamin Mosby McKelway, editor of the Washington *Evening Star* and president of the Associated Press. He is also a member of the board of trustees of the Rockefeller Foundation."

"Hmm. Thanks, Major. Shoot, Colonel."

"My cable to him says,

DEAR BEN WHAT WAS NAME OF ORIGINAL DOCTOR MCKELWAY WHO WENT TO U.S. FROM GLASGOW AND WHEN DID HE GO STOP ALSO WAS HE OUR GREAT OR GREAT GREAT GRANDFATHER OR WHAT STOP WE MAY HAVE SOME COUSINS IN THIS WONDERFUL CITY STOP PLEASE REPLY COLLECT LOVE TO ALL,

and it's signed 'SAINT,' which is what the family calls me. Then under that in this pile is the reply from my brother, which says,

DOCTOR JOHN MCKELWAY BORN GLASGOW 1788 CAME TO TRENTON 1817 AND WAS SON OF ALEXANDER JEFFREY STOP DOCTOR JOHN'S SON ALSO NAMED ALEXANDER JEFFREY STOP BORN GLASGOW 1813 STOP WAS FATHER OF UNCLE ST. CLAIR AND OF OUR GRANDFATHER JOHN STOP WE HAVE ENOUGH COUSINS AS IS.

You see, I had been told by one of the lawyers I met in Scott's pub that—"

"What was the lawyer's name?"

"I must move over to the Scott's pile for that. Here it is. He wrote his last name and address and telephone number on the back of one of *my* cards. Doesn't give his first name. His last name is McConnachie, and his office is at 32 Charlotte Square and his telephone number is Caledonia 5554. He had told me that the place to initiate an ancestor search was at the Registrar General's Office of the Scottish government, in an old public building on an alley in back of Princes Street, not far from the North British Hotel. McConnachie told me that if I had any trouble there I should call him, and he would drop everything and run right over and, as he put it, 'start them off on the right foot.' He said that the Registrar General's Office would give me for nothing anything they had on my ancestors, but that for a few shillings I could hire one of the clerks there to make a special search for records not in the possession of the Registrar General's Office. I wanted to get this search under way, because in recent years I've become more and more interested in who the hell I am and where I came from, and my brother and I have always wondered whether this original Dr. McKelway was Scots or Irish. We've never heard of any McKelway in the United States who was not a direct descendant of this same ancestor, and both of us have made a practice of looking for McKelways in the telephone book of whatever city we may happen to be in, either in the United States or abroad. I had looked in the telephone books of both Glasgow and Edinburgh, and had found none. In spite of the fact that I had to cable my brother to set me straight on the paternal ancestral line, I carry around in my head a great many facts and names relating to my maternal forebears—most of whom were definitely Scots or English. I wanted to write a memorandum for the Registrar General's Office giving them what dope I had on both ancestral lines, and as soon as I started writing this that morning—having put aside the piece on Dollar—I realized that it could also be the basis of a speech."

"A what?"

"A speech. I had made friends with a young doctor at Scott's named Bignold, and he was a member of the Liberal Club at Edinburgh. He'd said that he would like to persuade me to make a speech at the Liberal Club, at some kind of annual stag get-together they have in the summer, at which foreign visitors who they hope are interesting are asked to give little talks. I'd never made a public speech in my life, but I'd always been aware of the reputation of both my Great-Uncle St. Clair and my brother Ben as after-dinner speakers, and I was feeling so optimistic and so full of self-confidence at this time that I thought I would accept the invitation of the Liberal Club if Dr. Bignold extended it to me officially. I wanted to get this memorandum-and-speech done, in addition to the Surrealistic piece on the lonely American in his hotel room, and the Dollar piece, and I now decided I would need a secretary, because all three projects were of the kind that I can do faster by dictating a first draft to a secretary and then polishing it up by running it through my typewriter. So I got a secretary. However, she couldn't come over until the next morning, so I decided not to get to work on any of these projects until I could start dictating, and after breakfast I went by taxicab to the Registrar General's Office, where I could get somebody started on the comparatively simple job of finding out whether the McKelway name was originally Scottish or Irish. A good many Americans turn up at the Registrar General's Office, also searching for their ancestors, but it is seldom crowded, because the great majority of Americans who engage in ancestor worship prefer to go to the private genealogical setups in Edinburgh, where some of them not only do a quick job of running down your ancestors but also sell you a coat of arms, whether you really deserve one or not. The Registrar General's Office is a thoroughly efficient and serious government bureau. I climbed three or four flights of stairs in the old public building in which the Registrar General's Office is situated, and waited at a long counter until one of the clerks was free to talk to me. The clerk who finally got around to me was a jolly, roly-poly little middle-aged lady, whose card I have right here. Her name is Miss E. Winifred Binning, her home address is 224 Bruntsfield Place, Edinburgh 10, and her telephone number is Fountain-bridge 7145. I told her I wanted some special research done as soon as I had finished writing a memorandum about it, and she said she would be available for this special work—which she does in her spare time—and that the charge would be ten shillings an hour, plus a small government tax, which goes to the Registrar General's Office of Scotland. I told her I would try to mail her the memorandum on the following day, and asked her if, in the meantime, she had any sort of Scottish-name book, which might throw some light on the origins of the McKelway name. She briskly said, 'Of course,' and took down an enormous volume from one of the bookshelves. In no time at all, I was reading what it had to say about the origins of the name McKelway. But before I read those short paragraphs, I flipped the pages to the beginning of the book, in order to see what the title was and who had written it. To my astonishment, I found that the book had been published in 1946 by the New York Public Library, which is exactly a block and a half from my office in New York. The author of this big volume was George F. Black, Ph.D., who, Miss Binning told me, was the leading Scottish authority on Scottish names, and who had had the book published by the New York Public Library instead of by a British publisher because in 1946 Britain was, as she put it, 'in a state of considerable disarray,' as a result of the Second World War. I thanked Miss Binning, and she left me with Dr. Black's book. I then read the following paragraphs under the heading 'Mackelvie, Mackelvey, Mackelvy, Mackilvie.' I'm giving them to you in full, General, because all this seemed later on to have a direct bearing on my involvement in the plot to kidnap President Eisenhower. The paragraphs went like this:

"MACKELVIE, MACKELVEY, MACKELVY, MACKILVIE, G. *Mac Shealbhaigh,* 'Selbach's son,' Sealbach mac Shealbhaich is the hero in the tale of the Balieveolan Glassrig (Macdougall, *Folk Tales and Fairy Lore,* 1910, p. 216). Morice Macsalny of Dumfriesshire rendered homage. 1296. His seal bears a hunting horn stringed *S'Morici f' salni* (*Bain,* II, p. 210, 557). In 1300 we have record of an allowance to Mathew, son of Maurice Make Salui, a Galloway hostage (ibid., 1179; *Hist. Docs.,* II, p. 426). Robert M'Kelvie in officecroft in Tongueland 1736 (*Kirkcud-*

bright). and Andrew M'Kelvie was barn-officer of the Earl of Stair, 1744 (*Wigtown*). In 1684 the name appears (*Parish*) as McKelvie. McIlvey, Mclwie, McKelway, Kelvie (Kelvy).

"SELBACH, or Sealbach, an old Gaelic personal name, meaning 'rich in possessions' (*Watson* 1, p. 239). The Annals of Ulster under 701 mentions the destruction of Dunollie, near Oban, the principal stronghold of the tribe of Loarn, by Selbach: 'distructio Duin Onlaigh apud Sealbach;' and in 714 its reconstruction by him: 'Dun Ollaigh construiturapud Selbacum.' Selbach claimed the chiefship of the tribe of Loarn (719) and also the kingship of Argyll (723). In 723 he relinquished his kingdom and entered the monastic life."

"That's the end of the reference I read in that big book."

"Very interesting indeed."

"I found it so, General, but for some reason it left me jumpy with anxiety. As I stood there in that ancient office, inhaling that peculiar odor that old records have and watching Miss Binning as she scooted around fulfilling the requests of other ancestor worshippers, I felt as if I were playing a small but essential part in some kind of thriller—something along the lines of that fine old movie called 'The 39 Steps,' one of Hitchcock's first pictures. Miss Binning herself looked like a character actress, and so did all the other clerks; they all looked to me like people playing parts, rather than real people. Then, the fact that what she had pulled out of the shelves to show me was a book purporting to have been published by the New York Public Library—Well, General, the whole setup seemed somehow eerie to me, and at the same time I was stimulated by the poetic images that that scholarly passage by Dr. Black created in the back of my battered head. I had told Miss Binning briefly what had happened to my head—making an anecdote of it—and she had given me a small, bright smile that I found as heart-warming as a burst of laughter would have been from somebody else."

"And what did you do the rest of that day and evening?"

"After leaving the Registrar General's Office, I walked slowly half a block to the Café Royal. I was feeling O.K.; the flash of elation and anxiety had quickly dissipated itself. I no longer felt that there was anything peculiar about the Registrar General's Office or about the Public Library book, or about the passage about my ancestral name, or about Miss Binning. I had copied the passage in longhand, and I had it in my pocket. I ate a quiet lunch on the second floor of the Café Royal, at a table by a window, and didn't have anything to drink. After lunch, I stopped at a flower shop and sent a basket of wild flowers and heather to Mrs. Cameron. I got a taxi back to the Roxburghe and went to sleep, waking up in time for my usual high tea in the lobby. While I was having it, the bellboy said there was a call for me. It was Mrs. Cameron. She thanked me for the flowers and asked me how I was. I told her that I was fine and that I would like to take her and her husband to dinner the following evening, if they weren't doing anything. She said that they'd be delighted, and that they would pick me up at the Roxburghe at seven-thirty, if that suited me. I said that would be just right for me, and we said goodbye. Following the doctor's advice, I had dinner quietly in my room, but I gave myself half a bottle of Niersteiner to drink with the grilled salmon. After dinner, I read 'Muirhead's Scotland' in bed for an hour or so, and dropped off to sleep quite early."

"Good. And the secretary came the next morning?"

"Yes. At nine o'clock."

"Who was she, and how did you get hold of her?"

"Her name was Ann Dirleton, it says here on the bill for £2.4.6, and I got her by asking the pretty Irish girl behind the Roxburghe desk if she knew of a public stenographer who was accustomed to working with journalists. She said she knew of one who did a lot of work for music critics who came to the Festival every year in August, and she gave me this secretary's name and telephone number.

When Miss Dirleton came in, she told me she could work for me for only three days, because she was flying off to Copenhagen for her vacation, and I said I thought I might clean up what I had for her in that length of time. But when I told her I wanted to dictate some articles and other matter rather fast, she confessed that her shorthand was not up to snuff. However, she said that she was very good at typing from a record made by a tape recorder. I said I had no tape recorder, and she said that she had one at her office and could get it in ten minutes. She said that there would be a slight charge for the use of the tape recorder but that since her rate for typing was below what a secretary who could take fast dictation would charge me, it might work out to our mutual advantage. I liked her—a busy little Scottish lass, she was, with steel-rimmed glasses and a practical air. I told her to go ahead and get the tape recorder, and she charged off and was back in nine minutes; I timed it. With her was some kind of electrical technician from her office, and he saw to it that the tape recorder was in working order. He had to change the plug, because some of the electrical fixtures at the Roxburghe are practically antediluvian. However, knowing this, he had brought an old-fashioned plug with him that fitted the Roxburghe outlet. He was gone in five or ten minutes, and Miss Dirleton followed on his heels, having told me what time she would pick up the reel of tape with my words on it and what time the next morning she would deliver the finished typescript, two carbon copies, and her bill for services rendered up to that point. I don't have any copies of the early drafts of this piece on Scotland, or any of the many revisions, but I do have a copy of the finished draft, which I cabled to New York collect three days later, using my Western Union press card. By that time, I had developed in my head—while I moved around and while I was reading—my original idea of the lonely man in the hotel room. In my fancy, the lonely man had turned into a woman. She was a sort of combination of Ethel Merman and Mary Martin—that is to say, a

combination of the characters those two stars play in musical come-
dies. The idea of the piece was that this character of my own—
whom I might as well call Ethel Merman, for convenience' sake—is
alone in her hotel room in Edinburgh, and enjoying her visit. At
the same time, she is confused by the Scottish manners and customs, and she is homesick. She feels a need to communicate with
her 'daddy'—her businessman friend in the United States. She
picks up her phone to send him a cable, and is, of course, referred
to the Scottish Post Office, which handles the cable business of
Scotland. She is soon talking to a typical Scots postal clerk, of the
kind I myself had talked to on the phone when I sent my short cables. In a nutshell, she likes the clerk and he likes her, and eventually he comes to her hotel room, and at the climax of my
Surrealistic piece the two of them are singing a duet of the sort
that might have been written by Irving Berlin or Cole Porter or
Rodgers and Hammerstein. It was a good enough idea, but I was
too full of myself to write it properly. It was rejected."

"Now, when did you cable the complete article to New York?"

"On July 31st, six days after I got hit on the head. But a hell of
a lot had happened in those six days besides my finishing that and
getting it off."

"I'm sure that's true. But before we get to that—did you also
dictate the memorandum for the Registrar General's Office? And
do you have a copy of it?"

"Yes. It makes sense, as it happens. And some of it could have
been the basis of the speech to the Liberal Club, except that I
never got around to that."

"Would you say that it has any connection at all with the plot to
kidnap President Eisenhower?"

"Absolutely not. It's just a lot of dope on my Presbyterian-
clergyman forebears on both my mother's side and my father's side
of the family."

"Now, Colonel—quite seriously—did you think at that time that you were being followed? Or being led?"

"Yes, General, I was beginning to think so. And I felt it much more surely than I ever did in Glasgow, when it seemed to me like some kind of lark. As I was waking up from a deep sleep on that morning when the secretary first came to work for me, a jumble of disturbing thoughts flashed through my head with great rapidity. But I'm sure you two are not interested in what thoughts I had."

"On the contrary, Colonel, in this particular case we are. Don't you agree, General?"

"Yes, I do. I'm not sure I understand why, but that's neither here nor there. The Major's right. Please go right ahead, Colonel."

"I was not dreaming when these thoughts went through my head. I was awake and was trying to go back to sleep. The gist of what I thought was that there was something funny going on and that the Camerons were somehow at the bottom of it. Now, you must understand that I considered the Camerons—and still do—to be among the nicest couples I've ever met in my life. In fact, in the language you use in your line of work, Major, it could be said that I loved them. Like a brother and sister, or like a father and mother. I remember being particularly touched by something Mrs. Cameron said in the course of that evening in the environs of Edinburgh, which I have neglected to tell you. At some point, I had said something that I suppose seemed charming, and she said to Cameron, 'Oh, I think we'll have to adopt him! Don't you think we'll have to adopt him, Ian?' And I said facetiously that I would first have to be convinced that they were stable enough, both economically and emotionally, to adopt a fifty-four-year-old child. But in those waking thoughts that morning in the hotel room at the Roxburghe I thought of the Camerons as being somehow menacing. In short, I hated them. It is only to those we love that we turn at unexpected times the gnarled and ugly face of hatred. And in that realm suspicion readily moves into the space close to our hearts that we thought could be occupied only by trust. These thoughts of mine, you understand, came into my head with terrific speed and were gone again in a few seconds, but in those few seconds I saw Cameron as a Soviet agent of the highest type, and Mrs. Cameron as a co-agent. If that was what they were, they would be charming and likable, just as they had seemed to me to be. They'd only recently moved into their flat in Edinburgh. There was the business about the lock on the door. They weren't in the telephone book. There was his remark about 'What a place for a paratroop drop!' There was the information that he had been in British Intelligence in the Second World War. There was their talk about the implacable independence of certain types of Tory Highlanders— the lower classes as well as the upper classes—and these people's conscious and unconscious hatred of the English, and their regret over the failure of Scotland to become an independent country, like Ireland, instead of a part of the United Kingdom. And almost concurrently with these flashes were other flashes, in which I saw Cameron as a *British* secret agent and Mrs. Cameron as a co-agent, and in this series of flashes I saw how this setup was equally plausible. If that was what they were, it seemed to me, they were most likely engaged in testing me for some kind of intelligence job they wanted me to do for them. In that case, I figured, they would be in cahoots with the American Central Intelligence Agency or with the American Air Intelligence people. My thoughts, of course, went back to the fact that my briefcase had been gone through by somebody in Glasgow. And to the fact that I might have been intentionally hit on the head, and been given a shot of something that wasn't anti-tetanus at the Infirmary. But after giving all these fragmentary thoughts a quick run for their money, so to speak, I dismissed them from my mind as ridiculous, and jumped out of bed and rang for my early tea, as usual. However, from that day on I was seriously on the lookout for anything that might be rationally interpreted as support for those two offhand theories—if they can be *called* theories—that the Camerons were Russian agents or that they were British agents. Otherwise, I went on about my business."

"Did you keep your engagement to have dinner with the Camerons that same night?"

"Yes, General, I did. They picked me up at seven-thirty at the hotel, and we went directly to a country house-hotel the Camerons were fond of, called Prestonfield House, where I had reserved a table for three. We had a fine time. They brought me back to the Roxburghe before midnight."

"I think you'd better tell about that dinner in detail, Colonel. We want just about everything the Camerons said and just about everything you said, and also what other people said—if you met any other people that night."

"It will be a pleasure, General. It was one of the most delightful evenings I've ever spent in my life. I was standing near the desk of the Roxburghe at seven-thirty, chatting with the pretty Irish girl, when Mr. Cameron came in on the dot.

" 'My wife is driving again,' he said. 'I'm glad that swelling on your forehead has gone down. That might have been a nasty business. How are you feeling?'

" 'I feel splendid,' I said as we walked toward the street. 'I don't think I had even a *mild* concussion.'

" 'Did they treat you all right at the Infirmary?'

" 'All right? They were terrific! I never saw such a hospital— and I've seen a great many.'

"As I climbed into the back of the car, Mrs. Cameron greeted me cordially; as a matter of fact, I think I could say she greeted me affectionately. 'Let me look at you, McKelway. Why, it's quite a dis- tinguished scar! If you were a German, you could say you got it fencing!'

" 'Oh, I've got a better story than that,' I said as we whipped into the traffic on Princes Street and turned left. 'I tell people that my great-great-grandmother was a MacGregor, which is a fact. But it seems that I was in a pub a couple of nights ago, and I let this fact slip out in the course of a chat with the barmaid. Three Campbells—enormous chaps—overheard me say this, and when I left they cornered me in the alley outside. I hated to do it, one of them being the father of four children, but it was more or less in self-defense, and after all, you know, I was a Commando in the last war, and so—'

" 'That's quite enough,' said Mrs. Cameron. 'I hate these gory stories.'

"It was as if the three of us had picked up our mood where we had left it before I got hit on the head. We drove directly to Prestonfield House. Inside the house, a young woman came scurrying down the stairs and was going on quickly toward the back of the house when Cameron called, 'Oh, Mrs. Oliver!'

"The young woman stopped and came back to us. She was an attractive woman whom I guessed to be in her thirties. Her mother also lived in the house-hotel, and I met her later on. The Camerons introduced me to Mrs. Oliver, and she said that our table was ready for us any time but that perhaps we'd like to have a drink in the bar first.

" 'We sure would,' I said.

" 'I hope I'll see you later on,' Mrs. Oliver said to the three of us. 'Frightfully busy just now, don't you know—and the chef is sulking. We've got three busloads of French tourists coming for supper on the lawn.'

" 'Ah!' said Mrs. Cameron. 'Then there'll be a piper.'

" 'The same one we had the last time you were here,' said Mrs. Oliver. 'I must be off.'

"Mrs. Oliver trotted toward the back of the house, and we climbed up the worn stone stairs to what is called the Leather Room. A red-coated butler was behind the bar, and nobody else was there, or in a long drawing room that opened off the Leather Room. A fire was burning in a grate.

" 'I'll have a wee Scotch,' I said. 'What will you all have?'

" 'I'm going to be hungry by the time we sit down to dinner, and I think I'd like a cold dry Martini,' said Mr. Cameron. 'Would you care for one, my dear?' he asked his wife.

" 'That's exactly what I want,' said Mrs. Cameron.

" 'As a matter of fact, so do I,' I said, and the butler began to make the cocktails without any instructions from me.

"Now, look, General, I can reproduce just about our whole damn conversation from that time until midnight that night, but, good God, it's getting on for ten o'clock in the morning right here and now, and I'm ready for a big breakfast. You two must he ready for one, too. I've got a menu here somewhere, so what do you say we order breakfast and I'll summarize the conversation of that evening for you while we eat. Then, if you want to ask me further questions about it, you can. What about it, General?"

"That suits me fine, Colonel. If you let us pay for our breakfasts."

"By the way, how are you feeling, Colonel?" asked the major.

"Tiptop. Jolly good. Swell."

We ordered breakfast, and it was wheeled in fairly promptly by the room-service waiter.

"To GET BACK to Scotland," I said to my visitors, "Mr. and Mrs. Cameron and I were drinking more temperately than we did on our first evening together, and we passed what you might term a quiet evening—except for the piper. We talked about all sorts of things during dinner. In the Leather Room, we had studied the menu and discussed it and the wine list, and I had ordered a hell of a meal, because it was clear that all three of us were hungry. We had hot consommé and grilled salmon and a roast duck with orange sauce, and that duck had no meat left on its bones when it was taken away from the table. We were waited on at dinner by Martha, another character actress out of 'The 39 Steps'—a cheerful, solemn-seeming little middle-aged woman with an appalling nervous tic. But at the same time, her tic was somehow endearing—when you got used to it. It caused her to shake her head from side to side, at more or less regular intervals, as if she were giving an impatient and negative response to whatever it was you were saying. There were only a few other people in the dining room, but it was obvious that she was nevertheless mighty busy—probably helping out with the French tourists between our courses. However, she somehow managed to serve us efficiently, and she forgot only one thing. That was when she served the strawberry fool, which we had for dessert. She had forgotten to give me a dessert plate, and so I pretended, when she served me the strawberry fool, to be about to put my large helping on the linen doily. This made her shriek in alarm, then laugh uproariously, with her free hand over her mouth, when she realized I was teasing her. As was the case with all the people of her class we ran into, Mrs. Cameron found out all about Martha's origins and family, past and present, without appearing to question her. And so it went. I've gone over that dinner conversation again and again in my mind, General, and there isn't anywhere in it anything that was what I would call a 'clue.' It was just a very pleasant dinner, and, as I said, it was a quiet evening, except for the piper."

"I'll accept that for the time being," said the general. "But what about the piper? Do you mean the bagpiper?"

"Yes," I said. "We heard him playing for the French tourists in the distance during dinner, and when we went back to the Leather Room for coffee and a liqueur, Mrs. Cameron asked the butler if he could ask the piper to come up and play for us when he had finished playing for the French tourists. And after a while the piper appeared, his music having grown louder and louder as he marched from the back lawn through the house and up to the Leather Room, piping as he came. He finished the piece he was playing, and Mr. and Mrs. Cameron shook hands with him and introduced him to me. As is the custom in bagpiping circles, the piper accepted a drink when Mrs. Cameron offered him one, and what he accepted was a tumbler half filled with straight Scotch, which he downed, as far as I could see, in one gulp. Then he began to march around again, as is the custom, while he played his pipes. He would march at a military pace to the end of the long drawing room, make his two half turns to the right, and march back through the Leather Room again, and sometimes he would pause when he reached a point in the ancient air he was playing that needed all his strength. I'd never heard bagpipe music except at a distance during such things as the St. Patrick's Day parade on Fifth Avenue, and at one meeting of the St. Andrew's Society, in New York, which I'd attended as a young reporter back in the twenties. I found the music deafening at first, but I got the hang of it as Mrs. Cameron asked for this tune and that tune, and told me the history of some of the tunes before the piper played them. I don't think I can describe to you how the music made me feel after I'd got over thinking that it was too loud. I felt as if it reached something in my bones, and as if it weren't really very long ago that I had heard this same sad, wild music while going into battle with the MacGregor clan— against the Campbells, or some other bloodthirsty adversary. In short, I was carried away by the music, General. And the Montrachet we had had with dinner was heady stuff. After the brandy we had with coffee, we took nothing to drink until the piper joined us, at which time we each had a Scotch. Then the three of us sat and stood around and had a last Scotch for the road.

" 'I'm a Lowlander myself,' said Mr. Cameron. 'Glasgow and its environs. My wife, here, is pure Highlander. They're a wild, wonderful, and somewhat mysterious race. You know, some of the most recent ethnic and archeological studies suggest that what we call the Highlanders came originally from somewhere in the vicinity of Abyssinia. Then the Norsemen, of course, put some new blood in their veins, and so did the Normans, one way or another, much later on. And, of course, the aboriginal Picts.'

" 'All those popular notions about the strait-laced, repressed Highlanders.' Mrs. Cameron. said, 'neglect to take into account the fact that we need—or think we need—to keep our feelings under lock and key, because our feelings are extremely savage, and we are simply boiling with primitive instincts. Are you going up to the Highlands, McKelway?'

" 'I'm not sure,' I said. 'I feel about the Highlands sort of the way I feel about France—where, curiously enough, I've never been. I don't want to go there unless I can spend two or three months there, at least. I think I'll probably just stick around Edinburgh and its environs and come back next summer or the summer after, when I can afford to rent a car and wander all over the Highlands to my heart's content.'

" 'Oh, but you must at least go up to the Orkneys for a week-end,' said Mrs. Cameron. 'It's a day's drive, and, of course, there's a train, and there are planes as well, and buses. I'd like to send you up there and see to it that you meet the right people.'

" 'I see what McKelway means, my dear,' said Cameron. 'He wishes to have a long look at the Highlands, and not just a glimpse.'

" 'That's exactly it,' I said.

" 'It seems such a shame,' said Mrs. Cameron. 'But I suppose you're right.'

"This short conversation, General, was the only thing that bothered me later on. And, as I said before, the Camerons dropped me off at the Roxburghe before midnight."

"And did you go to the Infirmary for the orthopedic treatments and exercises?"

"No. An appointment had been set up for me, but I went over there and told the head nurse of that department that I couldn't possibly keep it—that something had come up and I'd be too busy.

She seemed rather put out, but when I told her that it simply couldn't be helped, she smiled and said, 'Very well, sir. Good luck to you.' "

"Right. Now, what did you do Wednesday morning?"

"I got up a bit later than usual, and I think I had just a trace of a hangover. This surprised me, because I really hadn't had very much to drink. Maybe it was the excitement, or the duck, or the Scotch on top of the wine—I don't know. However, I had my tea and biscuits, and went out for a brisk walk, and then had breakfast downstairs in the dining room. I read my papers, and they were full of international news. Nixon was in Moscow, talking it up with Khrushchev. Here's the pile of papers right here. The Queen was in Canada, and there was some concern over the fact that she was cancelling several of her state engagements over there and was going to fly back to England sooner than she had planned. In the tabloids and other sensational English papers, there were rumors that the Queen was ill. In the same papers, there were rumors that some important crisis in the British government made it necessary for the Queen and the Duke of Edinburgh to come back home in a hurry. There were also rumors—but nothing authoritative as yet—that President Eisenhower was planning a private summit conference with Khrushchev, and one paper said that the two leaders might meet in Scotland, which would be convenient for both of them, because Eisenhower was soon to fly to Paris, and he expected to have a talk with Prime Minister Macmillan in London after that. And he had that private apartment of his in Culzean Castle in Ayr. There was another crisis brewing over Berlin. A few days earlier, Khrushchev had cancelled his 'grand tour of Denmark, Sweden, Norway, and Finland,' because of the 'unfavorable reactions' of the people of Scandinavia to his proposed visit. The United States and Russia had signed an agreement under which scientists would be exchanged over a period of two years. The Devlin Report rejected the idea that there was a 'murder plot' in

Nyasaland. A widespread strike of printers had disrupted British book publishing and, in some cases, newspaper publishing. Thirty-five people had been killed in a panic in the French Congo. The Scottish Council of Development and Industry was initiating 'a thorough inquiry into the root causes of Scotland's unemployment and general industrial problem'—or, as another newspaper put it, in a headline, 'Scottish Council to Find Out Why Scotland Doesn't Tick.' Uranium had been discovered by a group of geologists in the Kinloch Bervie area of Sutherland—up in the Highlands—but Professor C. F. Davidson, of St. Andrews University (where the golf course is), who was the former head of the Atomic Energy Division of the Geological Survey, wasn't sure that the discovery would have any economic importance.

"I went back up to my room and worked on the Surrealistic piece about my imaginary Ethel Merman and the postal clerk with whom she was carrying on a flirtation by telephone. I was steamed up about it, and I really thought I had something. Then I dictated the thing into the tape recorder and played it back to myself, and I didn't like it. However, I finished dictating a first draft of the piece, and it was ready for Miss Dirleton when she whizzed in at one o'clock and whizzed out again with the reel of tape, so that she could take it back to her office and type it. I then walked over a few blocks to a little hotel where somebody had told me they had a very good Danish snack bar, and I was having some akvavit and smoked eels and steak tartare at the crowded snack bar and chatting with the Scots barmaid when a couple of United States Air Force cadets in blue uniforms sat down beside me. They could tell I was an American, of course, and we were soon talking about the Air Force. I told them that I had once been a lieutenant colonel, and they gasped. I urged them not to give it a second thought—told them that I had been a *civilian* lieutenant colonel and only a public-relations officer at that. I told them what I did for a living now. They were nice boys. They said they would like to bring me a couple of quarts of American bourbon and leave it for me at the Roxburghe; they could get it for practically nothing at the Officers' Club out at Kirknewton, they said. I thanked them, but told them that I was doing all right on the spirits of the country, and that I was a Scotch drinker anyway. I told them to call me up any time they were in Edinburgh and I would buy them a drink at the Roxburghe, and they said they would. I left them drinking Carlsberg and wolfing down Danish snacks. I drifted back to the Roxburghe, bought some picture postcards, and sat down at a desk in the writing room. I addressed them to a number of friends, in New York and elsewhere, with routine postcard messages on them, and I sent one to General LeMay, at the Pentagon, telling him that I had just run into two of his cadets and that they certainly looked like the type that could take care of anything, if anything ever came up. I bought airmail stamps at the desk and dropped the picture postcards into the letter box just inside the entrance. I was loitering at the desk, chatting with the pretty Irish girl, when, about three minutes after I'd dropped the postcards in the box, a postman came in and collected the contents of the box. I had a disturbing flurry of anxiety. Could it be that the British Secret Service—or somebody else—was keeping track of what I was sending by mail? I was aware, of course, that the Scottish postal authorities were in close touch with what I was sending and receiving by cable. But now I was half convinced that something really was going on— simply on account of the prompt postman. I told myself to say the hell with it, and I walked over to Scott's. There I encountered Mr. McConnachie, who was having a half pint. He asked me to join him, and I did, and then he asked me how my ancestor search was going. I told him about the New York Public Library book— making an anecdote out of it—and I showed him the cable from my brother, the last line of which also made him laugh. Another Scotsman, whose name I never heard, joined in our conversation about Americans and their Scots ancestors. He seemed a bit tight and was very emphatic in telling me that I must get in touch with a man named McNab, who, though an amateur, was a great authority on Scottish genealogy, he said. He insisted on writing down McNab's address and telephone number, but he had no paper or pencil with him, so I gave him Miss Binning's card, and he wrote on the back, 'J. M. McNab, 68 Cameron Lane, Edinburgh 10, Edinburgh 5238.' This Scot who'd joined us had an enormous R.A.F. mustache and was attired very much in the fashion of Sherlock Holmes. He had on a Norfolk jacket, he carried an Inverness cape over his arm, and on his head was a deerstalker cap—all of tweed, of course. He went on to say that there was an interesting graveyard in a little village called Gifford, and that it would be worth my while to drive down there someday and see the graveyard. 'The names on the ancient tombstones are fascinating,' he said, and then he finished his half pint and stalked off. Another new-found friend of mine came in—a wool man named W. Ogilvie Pentland. We chatted for a while, in the way you do at Scott's, until the 3 P.M. closing time, when I went back to the Roxburghe for a nap.

"But I didn't take a nap. I felt that the Sherlock Holmes character was trying to tell me something and that he had some role or other, on one side or the other, in what had now begun to form in my mind as some kind of plot involving either the Queen or President Eisenhower, or both. I put in a call for McNab, but there was no answer. I then told myself that I was being silly, but at the same time I decided to go to Gifford. It was a lovely afternoon—it hardly rained a drop the whole time I was in Scotland—and I figured I could have a nice drive and have a drink down there at the inn Mrs. Cameron had mentioned, where they had the bottles in the windows overlooking the garden, and dinner at the place where she had said the food was superior. You see, General, I only believed with one of my heads that there was really anything strange going on. With all my other heads, I was just having a nice time. I—"

"I don't understand. How do you mean 'heads,' Colonel?"

"Well, General, the Captain and I have pretty much come to the conclusion that I have a great many heads. I've counted and identified twelve separate heads, or identities, that I know I possess."

"Briefly, General," said the major, "the Colonel has what in simple terms might be called a multiple personality. He assumes many different roles inside his head, but hardly anybody who knows him is aware of this. He doesn't act out these roles, or if he does, it is in such an inconspicuous fashion that few people would ever notice it."

"Well, Colonel, did you drive down to Gifford that afternoon?" the General asked.

"Yes, I took a taxi down there. It's only twenty miles from Edinburgh, and those Edinburgh taxis are like the London taxis, you know—comfortable and compact—and they have reasonable rates. The city drivers love to get out in the country, and half the time they don't want to charge you for the time they are waiting outside or inside the country pub you are in. I found that they would usually make for the public bar of a country inn as willingly as I made for the private bar, and that was the case on the first afternoon I went down to Gifford. This was on the afternoon of July 29th, and, as I said, it was the beginning of what we are calling Operation Edinburgh. I didn't take down the driver's name. He was an intelligent middle-aged family man, and we chatted about this and that as we bowled along. But while we were bowling along I was looking with pleased eyes at the lovely countryside, and with sharp eyes, so to speak, at the cars behind us, the cars coming toward us, and the cars that passed us. In other words, with one or two of my heads I was alert for anything out of the way, but with most of myself I was simply enjoying the ride. Now, the cars in Scotland have two or three capital letters on the license plates, as well as numerals, and I found myself reading the letters on the license plates of the cars that were behind and in front, coming toward me

471

and passing me. There is just about every alphabetical combination in these license plates that you can think of, and most of them
didn't mean anything to me, but some of them meant a great deal
to me. For example, 'KSW' was directly behind me, and 'EBW'
passed me and went scooting on ahead. And then 'WG' came hell-
bent down the highway in the opposite direction, and others that
I saw going in one direction or another were 'CA,' 'JB,' 'GB,'
'MB,' 'RMC,' 'PDV,' 'JF,' 'JG,' 'BG,' 'MG,' 'TH,' 'EJK,' 'EFK,'
'AJL,' 'LL,' 'WN,' 'FB,' 'MDR,' 'WS,' 'DET,' 'JT,' 'SV,' 'HGW,'
and 'REW,' to mention just a few. And it happens that all those
combinations are the initials of editors and writers and artists on
the staff of the magazine I work for, most of whom I've known
for nearly thirty years. Then there was one license plate that said
'JB3-something' and another that said 'HT-something' and another that said, 'CF-something.' And those happen to be the initials of three old friends of mine, two of whom work for the
Central Intelligence Agency. The third one goes back into the Air
Force for active duty every now and then, and I think—although I
don't know—that he also works for the C.I.A. some of the time, if
not all the time.

"Now, the first of these three old friends has written many articles for the *Saturday Evening Post,* both serious and humorous. After the war, in which he served in the Navy, he went into an
executive position in the C.I.A., and there was no secret about it.
All his friends and many other people knew he had the job. For
one thing, he was recruiting college seniors for jobs in the C.I.A.,
so the colleges knew who he was. The second old friend was on
General LeMay's Intelligence staff on Guam. He is an artist, and
before the war he achieved considerable fame in New York as a
practical joker of a truly extraordinary sort. His practical jokes
never did anybody any harm. I could tell you a hundred of them,
but a typical one was that he once bought a bench of the sort you
see in Central Park from a second-hand-furniture dealer on Third

Avenue, and got a bill of sale for it. He had it delivered to his apartment, on the upper East Side, and after midnight one night he and one of his friends carried it into Central Park and left it there beside one of the walks, where other benches are to be found. Sometime before noon the same day, he and the friend returned to Central Park and sat on the bench until they saw a policeman approaching, whereupon they picked up the bench and started out of the park with it. The policeman shrieked, of course, and ran after them, and my friend showed him the bill of sale. The policeman arrested them anyway, for disorderly conduct, but a city magistrate let them off, after he stopped laughing. This lark of my friend's got into the papers. In fact, he was frequently written up in the papers in those days, as New York's leading practical joker. When he turned up on Guam as a first lieutenant of Intelligence, it made me a bit jumpy at first, but I soon realized that he was a crackerjack at piecing together our information on Japanese targets, and also at presenting the day-to-day operational picture to LeMay and his staff, which he made more vivid by expertly drawn graphs and charts. He never played any practical jokes on anybody out there, but he almost succeeded in taking in the *Reader's Digest* around that time. Under the title 'The Most Unforgettable Character I Ever Met,' he wrote a plausible article for them that told of a little old lady who lived in a Victorian house on the edge of one of our Guam runways and who served tea to the pilots when they got back from bombing Japan. The *Reader's Digest* not only nibbled at this but swallowed the story whole, and editors in Pleasantville were corresponding with him, asking for additional details and more anecdotes about the little old lady and the B-29 forces, preparatory to sending him a check. Then it dawned on one of the sub-editors there that the author had the same name as the famous New York practical joker, and the jig was up. This friend also went into Central Intelligence after the war, and it was no secret. He's since resigned, and is writing and painting on his own. Hell of a nice guy. The third member of this threesome is a professional humorist, who was a lieutenant colonel in the Air Force when I saw him on Guam, and later became a full colonel. I'd known him for years. Well, it occurred to several of my heads that these three jokers might easily be in Scotland in connection with the forth-coming visit of President Eisenhower, that they might have dis-covered I was in Edinburgh, and that they might have rigged up the license plates with all those initials and might be leading me on a sort of paper chase that would end in a happy reunion and a bar-rel of laughs. At the same time, I told myself that since the Scots used all the letters of the alphabet on their license plates, I could find any imaginable combination of them if I looked, as I was do-ing, at every automobile in sight. While this was going on in my head, you understand, I was chatting with the driver and taking in the scenery.

"The driver had only a little difficulty in finding Gifford, and we got there a long time before the pubs were to open, at five o'clock. I told the driver I'd find him later on, either in his taxi or at the public bar of one or the other of the two inns, and I went to look at the old burial ground. It was beautiful and still—gray tombstones in green grass—and I found many of the names fasci-nating, as the Sherlock Holmes character had told me I would. I found it only mildly disturbing that many of the names were the names of people I'd known at one time or another—many of them in the Air Force. You could throw a dart at an Edinburgh tele-phone book and wherever it hit you would see a bunch of names that were the same as those of many of your friends, and I realized that. Nevertheless, I came across the name of Tommy Power, the present Commander-in-Chief of the Strategic Air Command; of John Montgomery, who was the hotshot Deputy Chief of Staff for Operations on LeMay's staff on Guam and later in Omaha, and is now president of Daystrom, Inc.; and of an O'Donnell, which of course brought to mind Rosy O'Donnell, the young general who led our first strike at Tokyo from the island of Saipan. In flashes here and there, the burial ground and the entire tiny village seemed so nearly perfect in their way that they looked as if they might have been constructed on the Paramount lot in Hollywood. They almost seemed *too* nearly perfect. There was the one little street of old stone cottages with thatched roofs, a brook running under a stone bridge on the one street, old gentlemen walking old terriers on leashes, and all that. It went through my mind that this place might be some kind of undercover headquarters for some special American Air Force outfit, and that the Sherlock Holmes character in Scott's had intended to put me on to it for some reason connected with *our* side of the plot—or, rather, with a counterplot we were working on to outwit the Russians who were planning to kidnap Eisenhower. However, I also told myself that this was nonsense. And I walked around for an hour, absorbing the atmosphere with my eyes and ears and through my pores, and when it got to be five o'clock I went into the bar of the first of the two inns I came to, and found that it was the one with the bottles in the window looking out on the garden.

"I had a Scotch and chatted with the proprietor, whose name I didn't ask, and then I walked around some more, and went into the private bar of the other inn, which was called the Tweeddale Arms Hotel. There I got into quite a conversation with the proprietor, a youngish chap named E. A. R. Mackay, who ran the bar, and his wife, who ran the kitchen. I told them that Mr. and Mrs. Cameron had recommended their restaurant, and they grinned with pleasure. Mrs. Mackay went off to the kitchen, and Mr. Mackay and I went on talking about this and that. I mentioned at some point that I had been in the American Air Forces in the last war, and he said that he had had many American Air Force people, both during the war and afterward. I gave him one of my cards. He looked at it and then said that, as a matter of fact, he had just had an airmail letter from the wife of a former Air Force officer named Phillips, who had told him that a friend of theirs, and of his, named Celène Hobbs had bought a charming place in the Virgin Islands, and thought it was the sort of place Mackay and his wife ought to buy and turn into an inn like the one they had in Gifford. Mackay got out the letter and asked me if I would read it while he went to wait on the people in the public bar, because there was something in it relating to life in the United States that he didn't understand and that I could perhaps explain to him. It was a long airmail letter in single-spaced typewriting, as you can see, General (this is a true copy of it), on the kind of stationery they sell in Paris with 'Air Letter—Aerogramme' and 'Par Avion' printed on it, and that you fold up into the size of a regular letter before you mail it. I read it carefully, and the fact that the salutation was 'Dear Mac' didn't help me to keep my feet on the ground. I will turn it over to you, of course, and you can read the whole thing at your leisure, if you want to, General, but I will quote you just one excerpt of the kind that made my spine tingle when I read it, because it seemed to at least a part of me that this letter was meant for *me*, and that it was trying to tell me something. In fact, I decided momentarily that it had been written by LeMay himself. In the second paragraph it says:

I was so delighted to hear that you were settled for a time in Scotland and if my trip abroad had given me more time, I was anxious to check on you. But I flew to Madrid for ten days and then to Florence for eighteen days, and then back to Paris, where I arrived just before de Gaulle got in, and so was a bit disturbed at my *cool* reception by the French.

"It goes on and on, and, as you will see when you read the whole thing, it could be a chatty letter from the wife of a former Air Force officer or it could be some kind of cloak-and-dagger method of communicating to me the troubled state of Europe as it was seen by an active officer of the Air Force who had flown all over hell recently and had put it all down in a kind of code for my enlightenment. When Mackay came back, I told him I'd like to take the letter with me, because I thought I knew somebody in Edinburgh who knew Phillips and would enjoy hearing about what the Phillipses were up to these days. I explained the point about life in the United States that had mystified Mackay, and he said by all means take the letter along with me and mail it back to him if I didn't get down to Gifford again. I put the letter in my pocket and went on chatting with Mackay, and after a while I had an early dinner, found my driver in the public bar of the other inn, and drove back to Edinburgh, getting to the Roxburghe about half past seven.

"There I had a bath and put on my pajamas and bathrobe, thinking I might stay in and read or work, but I found myself refreshed by the bath and decided to drop over to the Press Club and see my friends there. Before this, I had been in the Press Club only for lunch and at the early cocktail hour of five o'clock, and I was astonished to find that at eight o'clock the joint was really jumping. The little bar and the dining room were jammed with journalists, their wives and girls, and other members of the club and *their* wives and girls, and I was told that this was what went on there every evening. In the bar, I was welcomed by two or three of my journalistic friends, who urged Scotch on me, and I bought rounds of drinks in return. I found myself getting close to tipsy, but I didn't care. I was having a good time and I felt very much at home. I was more than tipsy an hour or so later, when I found myself in a spirited argument with a wild-seeming Highlander about the land of my birth, which he had never visited, but concerning which he had extreme and adverse opinions. For some reason, I was feeling extraordinarily calm, and I argued with him in a calm fashion that he evidently found irritating. It must have been, I figured out later, that he took my serenity for smugness. At any rate, he became so incensed that although he was in his middle thirties, and much younger than I was, he flipped my four-in-hand necktie out of my newly bought Scotch waistcoat by way of emphasizing one of the points of his argument. I usually lose my temper completely under such circumstances, and am apt to take a wild swing with my fist, although I'm utterly incapable of delivering an efficient blow, knowing very little about boxing. This time, however, I elected to stand on my dignity, and I said something—which must have been even more infuriating—about my opponent's having forfeited the prize for the debate by violating the established rules of gentlemanly conduct. This unpremeditated remark of mine brought a roar of approval from quite a few Scotsmen who seemed to be listening, and there were also cries of 'Hear! Hear!' My opponent apologized to me in a disarming way. The battle was over, and I had made a new friend. I soon realized that I was getting drunk, and I wended my way out about eleven o'clock. Before I did that, a young man had handed me this small card I have in my hand here, and I had read it during the lull in the Press Club goings on. It says:

PRESS CLUB   EDINBURGH
                                               29 JULY 1959
SIR:

　　As a Saxon, probably an Anglo-Saxon, may I apologize for the behavior of the moron in the trousers whom you were so unlucky to meet. I am not a member here but a guest, and recalling that the first lesson I had in life was to be hospitable, I feel ashamed. I *write* this because it is politic, but my sentiments are shared by the Scots folk present.

                                       Yours sincerely,
                                       J. GEORGE KIGHT
                                   Edinburgh International House

"As I walked out of the front door of the Press Club, I was joined by two young fellows, who asked me which way I was going, and I said I was walking back to the Roxburghe, where I was staying. It was only a few blocks, you see. One of the young men seemed to think I knew him. He talked indirectly about how embarrassed he had been at the behavior of the Highlander, and I realized that this chap must be the one who had given me the card with the note on it. The two of them walked along with me to the Roxburghe, and although I was walking straight enough, I felt that perhaps they had thought I ought to be accompanied. It occurred to me that I might be drunker than I thought. However, I felt quite in possession of my faculties, and my locomotion was O.K., and when we got to the hotel I invited them in to have a nightcap. As a pukka traveller registered in the hotel, you see, I could order drinks there any time of the day or night. They declined a drink, but they sat and chatted for a few minutes in the writing room, which was just inside the door of the hotel, and I don't remember much of what they said except that it was clear to me that they were liberal or radical, rather than conservative, in their politics, and, in fact, that they might be farther to the left than, for example, the most stalwart members of the Labour Party. I can't remember what the second young man looked like, but I still have a clear image of the first one—the one who sent me the note—partly because I saw him on the evening, two days later, when I was on my way to Prestwick in a fast limousine to see the Air Force Intelligence officer there, because I had what seemed to me by then some plausible evidence that there *was* a plot to kidnap President Eisenhower when he got to Scotland. Any questions, either of you?"

"No," said the general. "Just go right ahead with what happened the next day. You, Major?"

"No," said the major.

"Well, actually, nothing happened the next day, which was a

Thursday. When I was saying good night to the Camerons when they brought me back to the hotel after our dinner at Prestonfield House on Tuesday, I had been told that Mr. Cameron went to Glasgow nearly every day and was seldom free for lunch, and I had asked Mrs. Cameron, as I got out of the car, if she would like to have lunch with me one day soon. She said that they were going to London at the end of the week but that she would love to have lunch with me that Friday if I was free. I said fine, and that I would call her on Friday morning and we would decide where to go. So on Thursday, following my late evening at the Press Club, I worked with the tape recorder, and with Miss Dirleton, stopping only for lunch, which I had in my room. I got a final draft of the Ethel Merman piece completed in time for Miss Dirleton to take it away and retype it as a long cable. She said she would deliver it at ten o'clock the next day. When she left, at six o'clock on Thursday, I took a bath and changed my clothes and drifted over to Scott's. I had a few whiskeys with my friends there, but nothing came up that is of any interest to us here, as far as I know. I had an early dinner sent up to my room, read for a while in bed afterward, and had a long sleep. I had been in touch by telephone with the American representative of Western Union in Edinburgh, and I called him again at nine o'clock the next morning and told him that I had a long and rather peculiar cable I wanted to send to my office, and that I'd like to bring it over to him sometime after ten o'clock and explain how important to me its complicated punctuation was. He said he'd be glad to come to the hotel and pick it up, to save me the trouble of going to his office, and he arrived after Miss Dirleton had delivered the finished draft and I'd gone over it once again and made one or two changes. I explained to him that the message might seem like gibberish to the cable operators, and told him the idea behind it. He laughed, and said that he fully understood and that he would see to it that it went off with the punctuation exactly as it was in the typed draft. He went away with the piece in his briefcase, and I decided to take the rest of the day off. I was a bit jumpy, partly because I had had another of those series of flash thoughts right after I woke up, in which I seemed to see quite clearly that something strange was going on in Edinburgh and that I might be involved in one of four ways.

"First. I figured that Cameron was a Soviet agent, and Mrs. Cameron was a co-agent.

"Second. I figured that Cameron was a British secret agent and that Mrs. Cameron was simply his wife. But I felt that both of them had been trying to tell me—by the indirect methods so familiar to me from my reading of suspense novels about international intrigue—that some extreme Tories, or Fascists, in Scotland were going to try to make some kind of deal with Khrushchev, and were going to kidnap Eisenhower, and possibly the Queen and the Duke of Edinburgh, when Khrushchev came over to Scotland to meet Eisenhower for their private summit conference. Why Cameron didn't just convey what he knew to the American Intelligence people was a question I asked myself, but I had no answer to it. However, I felt that in any case this strange business might be approaching a point at which I ought to turn over my suspicions to somebody in my own country's Intelligence setup who would know what to do with it.

"Third. I thought that Cameron, in cahoots with my own country's Intelligence people, was deliberately giving me some leads that were supposed to excite my suspicions that something was going on, and that my own country's Intelligence people were watching everything I did with the idea of asking me to undertake some kind of special job for them if I acted on my suspicions in a fashion that satisfied them.

"Fourth. I still thought that the whole thing could easily be a practical joke engineered by my C.I.A. pals, and that if I followed the trail in the paper chase they had laid out for me I would find them eventually and we would have that reunion and the barrel of laughs to which I've already referred. But by that time I didn't think there was anything funny about all this, and I had firmly resolved to surprise my old pals, if this reunion occurred, by boxing them smartly on the ears for fooling around and being a little *too* funny about something that might be extremely serious.

"However, as the morning went on, I told myself that when I came right down to it I had no real facts to communicate to the Intelligence people of my own country, and that the sensible thing for me to do was to go on about my business, not drink too much, keep a cool head, and have some fun. You see, in spite of these sub-surface anxieties about the plot to kidnap President Eisenhower, and possibly the Queen, I was still enjoying myself. In fact, I think I could almost say that up to this point my speculations about the possible plot, and the possibility that I might be somehow involved in the outer fringes of it, along with the third alternative that the whole thing might be a practical joke engineered by my C.I.A. pals, *added* to the good time I was having. It was as if I were listening to a symphony, the main theme of which was my vacation, and as if the main theme were rendered more exciting by three minor themes having to do with these three theories. In any case, it was now eleven o'clock, and I called up Mrs. Cameron and suggested that we go to Prestonfield House for lunch. She said fine, and offered to pick me up in her car at the hotel, but on an impulse I told her that I was going to be moving around, and that I would rather meet her there, if that would suit her. She agreed, and said she would meet me there at one o'clock. The truth is that I had suddenly realized while I was speaking to her that I was jumpier than I thought, and that I didn't much want to go through another ride with her in her car, in spite of the fact that I was by then convinced that she was an excellent driver and as safe as houses.

"Soon after I hung up the phone, I put the morning *Scotsman* and the London *Times* under my arm, went over to Scott's, and had a half pint while reading them, until it was time to take a taxi to Prestonfield House. Mrs. Cameron was on time, and we had a pink gin in the Leather Room and ordered lunch. During our drink and the lunch, I told her a lot about myself, and she reciprocated. Among other things, she told me that she was Mr. Cameron's second wife, and that she had brought up his two daughters but that they had no children of their own. She said both her stepdaughters were married now, and she mentioned that one of them was married to an Englishman who had an important post in the British Atomic Energy Commission. She didn't go into detail about this, and I didn't question her about it. We enjoyed talking to each other, and when our main course came and I was looking at the wine list, I was feeling very gay and relaxed, and I suggested that we have a bottle of champagne, explaining that I had just finished a piece of work and felt like celebrating.

"'Oh, I wouldn't dare,' she said. 'But then again, perhaps I would. Let's compromise and have a half bottle between us.'

"I ordered a half bottle. And then Mrs. Cameron said something that disturbed me at the time and disturbed me even more later on. She said, 'You know, you have a really remarkable resemblance to the male members of the British Royal Family. You look amazingly like the Duke of Gloucester, and I'll wager that when you were younger you looked very much like the Duke of Windsor when he was Prince of Wales.'

"I laughed, and said that, as a matter of fact, many people had told me in my youth that I did resemble the then Prince of Wales, but that I thought it was mostly because of my small, short nose.

"However, Mrs. Cameron said again that I could easily pass for the Duke of Gloucester, and, as she put it, 'with a bit of makeup and by shaving off your mustache, you could even pass for the Duke of Edinburgh.' When she said this, I tingled all over with some kind of intense anxiety or perception, and it flashed through my head that the plot I'd been brooding about and trying to dismiss from my mind included some complex maneuver, either by our side or by the other side, in which I was to be used as a stand-in of some sort for the Queen's husband, and that Mrs. Cameron was indicating this to me to see how I would react to it.

"'My favorite in the Royal Family,' said Mrs. Cameron, 'is the Princess Royal—Mary. The Queen's aunt, you know. She's highly intelligent and well read and perfectly charming. I feel I'm lucky to know her. I wish I could arrange for you to meet her, and perhaps I can if she comes up here with the Queen after we get back from London. The Queen usually comes in August, you know.'

"This stuck in my mind, too, for more reasons than one, but otherwise, in every respect, we finished lunch much as we'd begun it. Mrs. Cameron said she and her husband were leaving for London the next day but were coming back in four or five days. I told her that an old friend of mine—a lady—was flying over from Paris in a few days to visit Edinburgh for the first time, and that I hoped the four of us could get together. I told her who the lady was and that she was coming by way of Dublin. Mrs. Cameron said that she and her husband would love to get together with us, and I said I would telephone her sometime the following week. I told her I had half a notion to move from the Roxburghe to a room at Prestonfield House, if there was a vacancy, and that I was going to talk to Mrs. Oliver about it later on. Mrs. Cameron said she had a lot of shopping to do, and packing besides, and I saw her out to her car. I kissed her on the cheek, she waved goodbye, and that was the last I ever saw of her.

"I went back into the hotel and found Mrs. Oliver, and it turned out that she would have two rooms available the day after my friend expected to arrive. I told Mrs. Oliver who my friend was, and she said we could have the two rooms for as long as we liked. One room was on the ground floor and the other was on the third floor. The occupants of both rooms were out, and Mrs. Oliver showed them to me. Both of them were large, square, comfortable double bedrooms, and both of them had open grates in them. I told

Mrs. Oliver that I was sure my friend would like this place as much as I did, and that for a stay of a couple of weeks or more I thought we would both like it better than the Roxburghe—fond as I was of the Roxburghe. So I made the reservations definite, and that was that. I asked Mrs. Oliver what was the best way to get a taxi, and she said that she would call for one for me—that there was an outfit named Radiocabs, Ltd., which she had found first class, and that they usually managed to get a car there within a few minutes, because all the cabs were equipped with shortwave radios and the drivers kept in constant communication with the dispatcher in Edinburgh. The taxi got there promptly."

"Would you go ahead now with what happened the rest of that day, please?"

"Sure. The driver of this taxi was by far the most accomplished character actor I had met in Scotland up to that time. His name was MacKaye, the same as that of the Tweeddale Arms proprietor but spelled differently. He had a speech impediment that would have made the late Arnold Bennett consider himself a smooth talker. This driver couldn't have been more than five feet tall, his face looked sort of like a composite of the faces of Disney's seven dwarfs, and he had a chipper and sunny disposition. I took a liking to him straight off, and, on an impulse, told him to drive me out to Kirknewton, which was the American airbase in the near environs of Edinburgh. I just thought I would see what kind of base it was. And perhaps see some Air Force people for the fun of it. But as soon as I told him to drive there, my anxiety began to increase, and by the time we got there—it was a fifteen-minute ride—I had decided to ask to see the intelligence officer at the base and get this whole load of cloak-and-dagger material off my chest.

"At the entrance to the base proper was a gate guarded by two American Air Force sentries, and I told them that I was an American journalist and a former lieutenant colonel in the Air Force, and that I would like to see the intelligence officer. The sentries called a sergeant, who was in a sort of gatehouse there, and the sergeant told me that there wasn't any intelligence officer at this base. I asked to see the Officer of the Day, and the sergeant made a telephone call and pretty soon a major appeared. I told the major the same thing I'd told the sentries, and he said that the nearest Air Force Intelligence officer was at Prestwick, which is some seventy miles away from Edinburgh, on the west coast. I asked him who was commanding the Kirknewton base, and he said that Colonel Scott was the commander but that Colonel Scott was going back to the United States almost immediately and was being replaced by Colonel Gragg. He said that if I badly wanted to see Colonel Scott I would probably find him at Price's Hotel, in Edinburgh, where most of the officers stayed unless they had permanent quarters with their families. I told him I didn't know whether I would need to see Colonel Scott or not, and thanked him and got back into my taxi. By this time, I was telling myself again that I was being foolish. I felt like having a drink somewhere in the countryside, but all the pubs and all the bars of the inns were closed between three and five, and it was now exactly three. So we went back to the Roxburghe, and by the time I got there I didn't feel the need of a drink any more, and I went up to my room and had my usual nap. When I'd paid the driver, I had told him I would like to be able to call him again when I wanted to ride around the environs of Edinburgh, and he gave me a Radiocab card with his name written on it. This is the card.

"After my nap, I decided to go to Price's Hotel, see what it was like, and talk to Colonel Scott if I felt like doing so when I got there. Price's turned out to be a small hotel in a converted house on Abercrombie Place, and although it had been pretty much taken over by officers of our Air Force, it was open to the public, like any other hotel. When I got there, nobody was in the little bar, but sitting on the bar was a bell of the kind you bang on and a sign that said 'For Service, Sound the Bell,' so I sounded the bell and a Scotswoman appeared. She went behind the bar and said good afternoon and asked me what I would have. I asked for a wee Scotch, and while she was serving it a couple of young officers came in, with women who were evidently their wives, and in a couple of minutes another officer came in, who had the eagles on his shoulders. I felt a little as if I were a civilian intruder in a military establishment, but they were chatting among themselves about the Edinburgh shops and the lovely weather, and—just as the Scots do in pubs—they seemed to include me in their conversation. Soon I was chatting with them and telling them that I used to be an Air Force officer myself. 'As a matter of fact,' I said at one point, 'I was thinking of looking up Colonel Scott. I had a notion I might have known him during the last war.'

" 'Well,' said the colonel, grinning at me, 'have you ever seen me before?'

" 'I guess not,' I said. 'I must have been thinking about another officer named Scott.'

" 'There are a good many of us in the Air Force,' he said. 'Anyway, my name's Scott,' he went on, and offered me his hand, and then introduced me to the two young officers and their wives. I told them my name and I also told them I was an American journalist. He said he was leaving for the States in a day or so, and we went on chatting like any other Americans who run into each other abroad. I told him about being on LeMay's staff on Guam, and, of course, the Colonel and I discovered that we had many mutual friends in the Air Force. At the time I was on Guam, Colonel Scott was a captain, it turned out. I decided to curb my garrulousness and my pleasure at talking with these Air Force people, but when I told them goodbye I asked the Colonel if he would mind stepping outside with me for a second, because I had something I wanted to ask him. He came outside with me, and I told him very briefly that I might easily be out of my mind but that I'd run across some stuff that made me suspicious and I thought I ought to tell an Air Intelligence officer about it, just in case. He said—as the Officer of the Day at Kirknewton had said—that the nearest Air Intelligence officer was at Prestwick. I asked him if he could tell me the simplest way to get there, in case I decided to go, and he said he thought the best thing to do was to ask the porter at my hotel to get me a good car, rather than a taxicab— unless I wanted to go by train. I thanked him, and he shook hands with me again and wished me luck. And again, as I set off on foot for the Roxburghe, I felt I was being foolish. Nevertheless, I de- cided to have a quick dinner at the counter at the Café Royal and then to go back to the Roxburghe, order a good car, and go to Prestwick to see the intelligence officer there, a Lieutenant Cooper. When I got to the Café Royal and was checking my top- coat and hat, I ran into Dr. Bignold, who greeted me cordially, and whose invitation to have a Martini with him at the bar (where, he said, they really knew how to make a good Martini) was so sincere that I accepted, in spite of my determination to stay cold sober and get the hell over to Prestwick. So instead of having one Martini, of course, I had two. Chatting along, Dr. Bignold let drop the fact that he serves as the Queen's physician when she is in Scotland. After a while, I told the doctor goodbye and had my quick meal at the counter in one of the other rooms of the café. Then I went by taxi to the Roxburghe and told Mr. Ross that I wanted a good car to take me to Prestwick and back, and the car was waiting for me when I came down from my room, ten minutes later. In my room, I put in a call to the American base at Prestwick, got Lieutenant Cooper, and told him I was driving over there and wanted to see him. He said he'd be there all night. I had stuffed in my inside jacket pocket all the notes and chits and memoranda containing names and addresses, and so on, that I thought were pertinent, and I found myself calmed down after having made the decision to go to Prestwick. I was by no means drunk, or even tipsy, but the two Martinis had certainly had a stimulating effect. And all my antennae, so to speak, seemed to have reached a high point of sensitivity. The note from the young fellow named J. George Kight and the radical views he'd expressed that Wednesday night after I left the Press Club seemed to be particularly on my mind, and when I got in the car I told the driver I wanted to stop for five or ten minutes at the Edinburgh International House, which Kight had given as his address. I'm not sure exactly what I had in mind, but I wanted to see what the International House was like, and I probably had a notion that I might run into Kight there and be able to make up my mind whether he was just a nice young fellow who had, in a way, befriended me, or whether he was still another part of this damn cloak-and-dagger business.

"The International House turned out to be on the upper floors of a large old building at the lower end of Princes Street, and I knew nothing about it except that it was a club of some sort to which almost anybody could belong who was visiting Edinburgh from another country and was not an ordinary tourist. After climbing three flights of stairs, I introduced myself to the Scotswoman at the reception desk, gave her one of my cards, and told her that I was interested in seeing what the club was like. She told me that she would be happy to have one of the club officers show me around, and she also said that I could join the club for a few shillings if I knew of one member who could vouch for me. I told her I knew Mr. Kight, and she said that he hadn't come in yet but that she knew where she could get hold of him at once by telephone and that she would be glad to do so. In the meantime, she introduced me to a gentleman whose name I didn't take down, and he showed me through several crowded rooms, in which men and women of every conceivable nationality, race, and color were to be seen. When we returned to the reception desk, Kight had arrived, breathless from running up the stairs, and he shook my hand warmly, after which I paid the few shillings and got my membership card. He asked me to come into the bar with him and have a drink, and I followed him, and ordered a bottle of Heineken's Dutch beer after he had shown me the long list of alcoholic and soft drinks, from just about every country in the world, which were one of the features of the club. He introduced me to three or four young men and women, from China, Africa, France, and so on, and soon I was knee-deep in a spirited conversation about the much talked-about forthcoming summit conference between Eisenhower and Khrushchev, and was being asked a lot of questions as to what I thought might come of it and whether it would be good or bad for the free world. This was not a round-buying group, I was glad to find; everybody seemed to go Dutch at the International House. I finished my beer and offered another to Kight, explaining that I had to be on my way, because I had an appointment, but he declined, saying that the one he'd bought me was the traditional welcome to International House. And then he said—surprisingly, I thought—'Perhaps you'd care for a glass of milk.' He went on to say, 'Milk is splendid stuff. Milk-drinking is an American custom that we are adopting more and more over here in Scotland. You'll find a great many of the young people over here drinking milk, just the way I understand they do in America.' I said goodbye to them all, and as I left, Kight said, 'Be sure to try the Scotch milk, sir. It's awfully good milk.'

"I got back into my car, and found that I felt highly excited but not anxious. I determined to try to calm down completely on the drive to Prestwick and not to stop at a pub on the way there, which I certainly would have done under ordinary circumstances on such a drive. It was a honey of a car, a Mercedes, apparently brand-new, and upholstered in real leather of a dark maroon shade. It was a limousine, though a small one, and it was as comfortable as a Rolls. The chauffeur was a tall, gaunt Scot about my age, dressed in a chauffeur's cap and a long, dark overcoat. I'd already found out that his name was Hunter. When he saw me coming out of the International House, he jumped out and saluted and held the door open for me. I had told him when we started out that I wanted to go to the American Air Force base at Prestwick, and as we got under way, and he was about to close the glass between his seat and mine, I asked him if he had served in the British armed forces during the last war. He said that he had—that he had been a noncommissioned officer in the Royal Scots Regiment. I asked him why he had saluted me, and he said that he took me to be an American officer. I then told him to get to Prestwick as fast as he could without violating any speed laws, and added that I thought I might take a nap on the way there. Without saying anything, he instantly drew up at the curb, jumped out, opened the back door of the car, and showed me how to raise the armrest that divided the back seat in two. Then he put up one of the jump seats, so that I could rest my feet on it, and called my attention to a leather pillow on which I could put my head. He jumped back in the car again and closed his window, and I was soon stretched out smoking a cigarette and feeling very relaxed indeed. Before I dropped off to sleep, I had a clear idea in the back of some of my heads that this was an American Air Force staff car and that Colonel Scott had told Mr. Ross to ask for it for me if I said I wanted a car to go to Prestwick. I slept off and on during the fast, smooth ride to Prestwick.

"When we got to Prestwick, the driver opened his window and asked me if I wanted to go to the Operations Building at the American Air Force base or to some other building. I told him to see if he could find out where the Officers' Club was, having decided that that would be a good place from which to call the intelligence officer and tell him I had arrived. The base didn't seem to be guarded by sentries but was more like a public airport, and the driver got directions from a couple of passing American officers in uniform and drove along a number of side roads and then drew up at what seemed to be the back entrance of a long, low building. He jumped out and opened the door for me and said that the Officers' Club was inside. I have never been sure whether this was actually an officers' club or not. It was crowded with officers and men in uniform, some of them with parachutes on their backs, and there were also a good many men in civilian clothes who were obviously air travellers. Except behind the various counters, there were no women in the room. There were counters at which beer and snacks and coffee and milk and other soft drinks could be had. Nobody seemed to pay any attention to me or asked for credentials of any kind, but I couldn't tell whether this was because I had come in the back door or whether it was a place that was open to the public anyway. There were slate bulletin boards showing incoming and outgoing flights of military transports, and at one counter, presided over by an American girl in a Waf uniform, there was a telephone instrument. I told the Waf I wanted to get in touch with the base intelligence officer, and she indicated the phone and said just to ask for him. I did, and Lieutenant Cooper came on. He asked me where I was, and I told him that I didn't know but that I would put the Waf on and she could tell him. I handed the phone to her and asked her if she would tell the Lieutenant where he could find me, and after a short conversation with the Lieutenant she hung up the phone and said that he would he over in about ten minutes.

"I went to one of the refreshment counters and ordered a glass of milk. At this point, I found myself suddenly overwhelmed by a distinct conviction that 'milk' was a code word of some sort, and I felt under what I now recognize as an inescapable compulsion not only to order the glass of milk and drink it but to circulate among the military and civilian personnel, who, I could tell from the operations board, were waiting to resume a flight to Paris that had started at New York, and to keep bringing the word 'milk' into my conversations with them. I felt surely and definitely that Cameron, who advised me to drink milk after the accident, intended for me to do this, or else that Kight had somehow put this bug in my ear. It seemed to me that my carrying of this milk message to Garcia, so to speak, was intended either to bring about the cancellation of some kind of secret air operation involving Paris or to speed it on its way. Then, in a shorter time than it takes to tell it, I got over the feeling of inescapable compulsion and told myself that this milk business was idiotic, but I nevertheless circulated and made such remarks as 'They certainly have good milk here,' and 'I just had a glass of milk and I think I'll have another.' I was no longer in the least panicky but was falling into this cloak-and-dagger role of mine in a sort of deadpan, humorous way, which I figured was harmless if my message meant nothing but would get the message over if by some chance it did mean something. And I would soon be telling the Lieutenant all about it. In any case, I had another glass of milk and went back to the Waf's counter, where, in a few more minutes, Lieutenant Cooper found me and introduced himself.

" 'It took you long enough to get here,' said the Lieutenant, and I sensed that while he intended to remain openminded about me and my mission, he was a trifle irritated at having been got out of bed by me at such a late hour. He took me into a small office in the same building, which was obviously his own office, and there I got out my memoranda and told him my story, making it as clear to him as I could that I had every reason to think I had simply run into a series of perfectly innocent people and circumstances in which there was nothing out of the ordinary, but that I felt I ought to tell him about it just on the long chance that I had stumbled on something that might fit in with other things known to him or to the Central Intelligence Agency people, with whom I presumed he was in touch. When I had finished, I told him that I thought he ought to know that I had blown my top once during the Second World War, when I was on General LeMay's staff on Guam, and that the form this top-blowing had taken was that I had accused Admiral Nimitz of high treason in an official teletype message to the Pentagon from LeMay's headquarters. His manner changed when I told him about that, but, to my surprise, it changed for the better. He said that he'd heard that story—that, in fact, it was a 'legend' in the Air Force, and that it was a pleasure to meet me. I told him that, of course, this idea of mine that something strange was going on in and around Edinburgh might have no basis at all except my hypersensitivity, but that it certainly was a relief to me to get it all off my chest. And I asked him what he would do with what I had told him. He said it would go forward from him through channels, and I asked him if that meant that the Air Force and the C.I.A. in Washington would be on the other end of one of those channels, and he said they would indeed. I thanked him, and told him I hoped I hadn't kept him up too late on what was probably a wild-goose chase, and he said not to give it a second thought—that I had done exactly what I should have done under the circumstances, and that, for all he knew, what I had told him might be of real importance. He shook hands with me, and I started back to Edinburgh, feeling that whether or not the young Lieutenant was simply humoring an old, somewhat unstable Air Force man, the whole thing was now out of my lap and in his, and I could resume my vacation and my enjoyment of it."

"And did you enjoy yourself, Colonel?" asked the general.

"Not exactly, General—at least, not all the time."

"Did you go on with your writing work?"

"No. I couldn't expect a very quick response from my office after cabling them the piece on Ethel Merman—since it was not the kind of piece an editor could make up his mind about in a hurry—yet I was anxious to know. I read it over the next morning and I saw that it was too wild—that while it had been a good enough idea, what I had sent them really represented a rough draft, rather than a finished, polished, acceptable piece. By this time, it seemed that months had gone by since I visited the village of Dollar, and for one reason or another I kept putting off writing that piece. Anyway, I was also aware that my mood had been pretty damned high, and I decided to take things easy, forget about the cloak-and-dagger business and the possibility that my C.I.A. pals had been playing a practical joke on me, and otherwise try to get back on a steady beam. I got this four-page single-spaced memorandum from Miss Binning that I have in my hand here. To summarize, it says that she'd been unable to find any certain records pertaining to that medical ancestor of mine in the birth and marriage records of Glasgow that were easily available to her, but that she had turned up a good many other McKelways around Glasgow, Wigtown, and Kirkcudbright about 1780, who may or may not have been ancestors or cousins, or something. I paid her small bill and decided not to engage her to make a further and more costly search, partly because I was running low on cash. My friend from Paris was arriving in a few days."

"Colonel, I gather that you don't wish to talk about your friend from Paris, but you must realize that a thorough check was made on her, and, in fact, on all the people you told the Lieutenant at Prestwick about in connection with this Edinburgh caper, and that all the data is in your C.I.A. file in Washington."

"I see. Well, I'm still not going to call her by her true name. I'll call her Susie. But I will tell you about her connection with this thing—an innocent connection, needless to say—because it *is* part of the story, after all. I realize now, of course, that you already know that she is the daughter of a French diplomat who at present has a position of considerable importance in the French government and who was deeply involved in the underground movement in France during the war."

"Yes, Colonel. The C.I.A. would have known all that whether she had ever come to spend part of her vacation in Edinburgh at the time you were there or not. That goes without saying. But before we go into what happened after she arrived, perhaps you'd better fill us in on what happened *before* she arrived. That is, what happened during the next couple of days, after you got back from Prestwick."

"O.K., General. I went around much as before, and nothing

happened out of the ordinary until I decided one morning, on an impulse, to call up that nice Radiocab driver I'd had before—the short one, with the speech impediment—and go down to Gifford again for lunch. I liked that village. I had made two copies of Mackay's letter from the Air Force wife and had given one to the Lieutenant at Prestwick, and I wanted to return the original to Mackay. And I also wanted to enjoy the peacefulness of Gifford without any cloak-and-dagger stuff on my mind. We set out in time to get there for lunch. On the way down, I again noticed that I was surrounded by license plates bearing the initials of dozens of people I knew in New York and in the Air Force, but I ignored them and revelled in the beauty of the scenery. At Gifford, I returned Mackay's letter to him, had a couple of drinks at his bar, and was eating my lunch peacefully and reading 'Sinister Street,' by Sir Compton Mackenzie, when I looked up and saw a woman sitting with another woman and a man at another table in the dining room. The woman had on a gold pin of a distinctive design—it was a gold pin made in the form of a tiny French horn—that happened to be exactly like a pin I had bought at Tiffany's the year before and given Susie for her birthday. I was at once overwhelmed by anxiety—this time, anxiety over Susie I thought that she might have been kidnapped and that this might be the other side's way of showing me they had her. At the same time, of course, I told myself I was being absurd. Nevertheless, I left my table without waiting for the check and went outside to see what kind of car the threesome had come to Gifford in. There was a small limousine that looked like an exact replica of the one that had driven me to Prestwick, and I asked a villager if three people had just arrived in it. The villager said, 'Aye, it was two women and a man,' and added that they had gone into the dining room of the Tweeddale Arms, which I had just come out of. I asked where the driver was, and the villager said he was in the public bar. I tried the doors of the limousine. They were locked. I looked into the public bar and there was the driver I'd had—the one named Hunter—having a half pint. I then went into a panic, but it was what I suppose would be called a *controlled* panic. I walked quickly to the other inn, and went into its pub and told the proprietor that I wanted to call the police and asked him how to do it. He wanted to know what was wrong. I told him that it was too complicated to explain but that I wanted them in a hurry and that it was serious. He seemed impressed, and said he would call them—that there was a road-patrol headquarters a few miles away. I found MacKaye, my driver, and told him to stand by in his car and to be ready to go. Then I saw the two women and the man come out of the Tweeddale Arms dining room, and I joined them, making a casual remark about what a fine day it was for travellers. They said it certainly was. They were obviously American or Canadian. I asked them if they were tourists, and the man said that they were and that he was a doctor from Canada who was attending some medical conferences in Edinburgh. We chatted, as fellow-tourists do. The woman's pin hypnotized me, as it were. I introduced myself to them and got out a card, and the doctor got out one of *his* cards, and we agreed to have a drink together one day while he and his friends were still in Edinburgh. He said they were at the North British. I decided I'd have no trouble finding them again if I wanted them and if my suspicions turned out to be right, but I also decided to maintain my deadpan-American-journalist role and let them think that I wasn't suspicious—that I either hadn't noticed the distinctive pin or attached no significance to it.

"You see, General, I was by this time enveloped in suspicion and panic except for perhaps just one of my heads. This head kept telling me I was being absurd, and it managed to maintain a certain amount of control over the other heads. But the other heads were nevertheless pretty much in charge of me. I suddenly decided that the somewhat mysterious place Mrs. Cameron had mentioned that first evening—the one up in the Lammermuirs—was where I was now supposed to go, either to find my practical-joker friends or to find the leaders of the plot to kidnap President Eisenhower and the people who had captured Susie and were holding her as a hostage in order to make me do whatever it was they wanted me to do. Or my own Air Force people might be there. I told the doctor and the two women goodbye as Hunter drove them off in the limousine, and then I told my driver to see if he could find out where a small inn up in the hills near here was—a place that attracted artists and writers, that had a large library, and so on. He consulted various villagers, and came back and told me that it was the Rathburne Hotel, at Longformacus, and that he knew how to get there—that it was about ten miles up in the hills, in a very secluded spot. I said O.K., for him to get me there as fast as he could. At this point, the proprietor of the other inn joined us, and as I started to get into the taxi, he said, 'But the police are on their way here, sir. What shall I tell them?'

" 'Give them this card,' I said, handing him one of my cards, 'and say that I have a jewelry theft to report, but that I've had to leave here in a hurry and that I'll be in touch with them later. Tell them I've gone up to the Rathburne Hotel, at Longformacus.'

" 'They are not going to be pleased about this,' said the proprietor.

" 'Then tell them to go jump in the lake,' I said, and I myself jumped into the taxi and we were off.

" 'I canna do that!' the proprietor called out in a helpless tone, and he stood there watching us and all but wringing his hands as we scooted toward the road that led up into the hills.

"If, before this, I had been reminded of that old motion picture 'The 39 Steps,' I felt on this wild ride up into the hills in the taxicab that I was a starring member of the cast of that melodrama. The road became a dirt one after a mile or two, and the moors on either side of it were absolutely unpopulated, desolate, scary, and beautiful. The taxicab followed the single-track, narrow, winding road, gaining altitude all the time, and on the entire drive to Longformacus we saw only one human being—a character actor dressed like a sheepherder, who stood motionless under a tree, gazing toward the sea, and who didn't turn his head as we passed along the road fifteen feet away from him. It took us twenty-five minutes by my wristwatch to get to Longformacus. This was a slate-roofed village consisting of five or six houses and one tiny general store. We stopped at the store and I asked the way to the Rathburne Hotel. We then drove through the village, across a stone bridge over a roaring brook, and turned in at a driveway about half a mile from the village, and there was the Rathburne. It was a three-story stone building with several chimneys and a gabled roof. There was a good-sized parking space with some other cars there, and I got out. I told the driver to turn his car, so that he could get away fast, and I also told him that if I should come out by the front door and wave to him, that would mean for him to get the hell back to Gifford and bring the police up here with him, unless he found that he could telephone them from the village of Longformacus. I felt quite sober, and, in fact, I hadn't felt the few drinks I'd had. But I was still in a panic. The driver seemed impressed with what I said and ready to do whatever I told him. As I went in at the front door, I saw him park the taxi so that he could shoot right out of the driveway at a moment's notice.

"Inside the front door, I looked around for the bar and found none, but I heard a soft clatter of dishes coming from the rear of the large hallway, so I went to the end of it and found a waitress and asked her where the bar was. She was telling me where it was when a middle-aged chap in a beret, gray flannel trousers, and a velvet jacket came up and asked me if he could help me. He introduced himself as the proprietor and said his name was Graham. I told him my name and what magazine I worked for, and he seemed suddenly very flustered. He led me down a short corridor, which ran crosswise at the back of the house, and into a small bar that had a back door into a second parking lot. Three or four men who looked like countrymen were sitting at the bar, and there were also three men who looked like English or Scots gentlemen who might be travelling about the country. I ordered a wee Scotch and asked Graham if he would join me, and he said he would be happy to. He said that he had been a subscriber to *The New Yorker* for many years, and I realized that it could be he was flustered not because I had discovered the headquarters of the ringleaders of the plot to kidnap President Eisenhower but simply because he hadn't expected a member of the editorial staff of *The New Yorker* to come walking into his lonely hotel up in the Lammermuir hills thirty-two miles from Edinburgh."

"Colonel, what was going on in the back of your heads at this point?" asked the major.

"By this time, Major, all except one or two of my heads were in thorough agreement with my main head that all this cloak-and-dagger stuff was nonsense. Still, this small part of me was on the lookout for anything out of the way. Graham asked me if I was staying for dinner, and I said that I wasn't sure—that I was wandering around the countryside seeing the sights, and that if it was all right with him, I would let him know in a little while whether I would want dinner or not. He told me to make myself at home and to look over his large library and the exhibition of paintings—which were to be seen everywhere on the walls of the hotel—and to send for him if I wanted anything. He left, and I had another wee Scotch and struck up a conversation with some of the men in the bar about fishing and grouse shooting. All these chaps in the bar were character actors out of one melodrama or another, of course. The countrymen were made up for the parts of countrymen, and the gentlemen were made up for the parts of gentlemen. They told me that in some forthcoming field trials for hunting dogs there would be Labradors, setters, pointers, golden retrievers, and Weimaraners.

" 'The Labradors will go in on Monday, the tenth, if the good weather continues,' said one of the countrymen, speaking with a heavy Scotch burr but in perfect English. 'Then the setters and pointers will go in, and on Wednesday, the Glorious Twelfth, the Weimaraners will finish the thing off.'

" 'Time, gentlemen, time!' the bartender called out, and I realized that it was three o'clock.

"The countrymen finished what they were drinking in a leisurely way, goodbyes were said, and they left by the back door. The gentlemen stayed right on, paying no attention to the time, which proved that they were travellers. The bartender, who was an aged Scot and one of the first taciturn Scots I had run into in Scotland, said good afternoon to the rest of us, and disappeared. He was immediately replaced by Mr. Graham, who evidently took care of the bar during the hours when it was closed to all but travellers. I asked him whether I could pass for a traveller or not, and he said, 'Oh, positively, positively! Let's regard you as a traveller, and you may have anything you wish at any time of the day or night. It is the same for these gentlemen here, because they are guests of the hotel. It is only the local people, who can find no way of claiming to be travellers, who must observe the closing hours between three o'clock and five.'

"Graham then introduced me to the three chaps in the bar and made a round of drinks, which he said was on him. I didn't take down their names and I don't remember what they were. One of the men was about my age, and the two others were probably in their forties, and all three of them could have been Russian secret agents or simply English or Scots gentlemen on vacation. I decided with all but perhaps one of my heads that they were the latter. I now felt relaxed and happy, and I determined to bring Susie to this unique inn for lunch or dinner after she arrived. I told myself that although the pin I had bought for Susie at Tiffany's was distinctive it certainly wasn't the only one of its kind in the world, and that my panic in Gifford had been as baseless as all my other imaginings in the cloak-and-dagger category. I offered to buy a round of drinks, and the three gentlemen and Graham accepted. We chatted about all sorts of things, and as we did so I was gripped by a sudden small wave of anxiety, centering on the Princess Royal and my resemblance to the British Royal Family, which Mrs. Cameron had talked about at such length when she had lunch with me at Prestonfield House, and on the same old plot."

" 'Is the Princess still here?' I found myself suddenly asking Graham in a casual fashion.

" 'The Princess?' said Graham. 'Ah, so you've heard about our guest! Why, yes, of course she's still here. Do you know her, Mr. McKelway?'

" 'No, I don't,' I said, 'but I certainly would like to meet her.'

" 'You would?' said Graham. 'I think I might arrange it. I'll tell you what. I'll have tea served for her, as usual, in the room just to the left as you come in the front door of the hotel, and if you happened to drop in there in about an hour or so—let's say at five o'clock—I wouldn't be at all surprised if she asked you to join her in a cup of tea.'

" 'Fine!' I said.

"I didn't know what the hell this was all about, but every one of my heads was now convinced that I had stumbled right into the middle of something very eerie indeed. And, of course, I was thinking of the Princess Royal. One of the gentlemen bought another round, and after we had finished that one, the chap who was about my age asked if I wouldn't like to stroll around the garden. The four of us went out at the back door together, and as I left, Graham gave me an unmistakable wink. I nodded and grinned at him, and went along after the others. The two younger gentlemen said they were going for a walk over the moors, and I found myself alone with the other chap, who showed me around the garden and then took me to a long slab of closely cut lawn that I recognized as a lawn-bowls court. He asked me if I played, and I told him that I hadn't played lawn bowls since I was in Bangkok in 1931 but that I would like very much to try it, if he could put up with my play-ing. My companion said that he was no expert at lawn bowls and that he would be delighted if I would have a game with him. Al-though I don't remember his name, he was a very nice chap, and before we started to play, I said to him, 'Sir, if by any chance you are in British Intelligence, I wish you'd pass the word along that I've had enough of this monkey business, and that I want to be ei-ther let in on this thing or left alone, but if you're not an Intelli-gence man, I hope you'll disregard what I've just said, and we'll see what twenty-eight years have done to my skill at this game of bowls.'

" 'I'm in the tobacco business in London,' said my companion. 'But tell me, sir, are you being bothered by our cloak-and-dagger chaps?'

" 'I'll be damned if I know,' I said. 'But don't give it a second thought.'

"We played a couple of games, and I found I wasn't as rusty as I'd thought I might be. He won the first game and I won the sec-ond, and as we were playing the rubber, Graham and a teen-age boy, whom he introduced as his son, joined us, and looked on while my companion defeated me by a close margin. I looked at my watch and saw that it was just five o'clock, so I thanked my companion, said I would go along and see if the Princess would offer me a cup of tea, and left them.

"A tall, gaunt elderly lady was pouring tea in the room to the left when I went back into the hotel, and when I bowed slightly to her, she smiled, and said, 'Ah, so you're the American journalist! Won't you join me in a cup of tea?' We had tea with muffins and jam and cake, and chatted about any number of things. She looked a good deal like the Princess Royal, but I didn't think she *was* the Princess Royal. I didn't know who the hell she was. At some point in our conversation, she told an anecdote in which one of the maids at the hotel said to her, 'Why, Miss Carter, I thought you were out in the garden!' So I presumed that she not only wasn't the Princess Royal but wasn't any kind of princess, and that Graham and perhaps the guests of the hotel called her 'the Princess' behind her back. Having figured this out, I laughed at myself once again, and when Miss Carter finished her tea, rose from her chair, and gave me her hand—very much as a princess might have done—I took it and bowed over it and told her how much I had enjoyed our conversation. I followed her into the hall, and she disappeared up the stairs. I fooled around for a while, looking at the books in the library and at the paintings on the downstairs walls, and then Graham came along and said he'd like me to meet his wife. He took me into what seemed to be his office, and introduced me to Mrs. Graham, who was very pleasant and cordial. We started to chat, and, for some reason I have still not been able to fathom, I found that I was again being clutched by deep anxiety. The whole experience seemed extremely unreal and eerie. Graham said that he and his wife always had a whiskey-and-soda at this time of day, after tea, and asked me to join them. I said I would be glad to, and he called a waitress and gave her the order. As the three of us sat chatting and having our drinks, I tried to overcome my increasing tension. When we finished the drinks, Mrs. Graham said she had to supervise the oncoming dinner, and Graham wanted to know whether I wished to dine there, and, if so, whether I would consider it an imposition if he asked me to dine with him and his family in their private dining room, off the kitchen. I said I'd be delighted, although I didn't feel delighted at all, and then I said I thought I'd go into the bar and chat with my new acquaintances until dinnertime. He said that he'd let me know when the family dinner was ready—that they usually had it about half an hour before dinner was served to the guests. He went off somewhere, and I walked out at the front door and told my driver to relax. I suggested that he find his way back to the kitchen and see if they wouldn't give him a bite to eat, if he was hungry. He said that he wasn't hungry but that he might slip into the bar and have a half pint, if I had no objection. I said of course, and went into the bar with him. I asked him to let me buy him the half pint, and he consented, although when he got his half pint, he took it to a table in a corner of the room and joined some countrymen who were sitting there. I stayed at the bar, and was telling my bowling companion about the impending visit of my friend from Paris, and how much I was looking forward to it, when Graham came along again and, overhearing what I was saying, said that I must bring her up for a visit one day after she arrived. I turned on Graham in a sudden fury, and said, 'I know you've got her already, you unspeakable monster, and if you so much as touch a hair of her—' And then, before I finished this strange outburst, I recovered myself and grinned at him. His pipe had dropped out of his mouth and clattered to the floor, and as he stood gaping at me, all the blood gone from his face, I explained cheerfully that I was just pulling his leg and was pretending that we were all actors in a melodrama about international intrigue. He smiled in a rather sickly fashion, picked up his pipe from the floor, and rather hoarsely ordered a round on the house.

"I soon found myself completely calm again, and in a little while I joined Graham and his family and ate a delicious dinner. There were the teen-age boy and two or three smaller children, along with Mr. and Mrs. Graham and me, in the small private dining room off the kitchen. Graham told them about the joke I'd played on him, they all laughed, and he got out a bottle of good white wine and poured it out for his wife and me and himself when the grilled salmon was served, followed by roast chicken. After coffee and brandy at the end of the meal, I knew I was tipsy, and while I was no longer anxious or tense, I began to act in what the Major, here, would call a compulsive fashion. I thanked the

Grahams for the wonderful meal, and having been turned down rather peremptorily by Graham when I asked him in private if he wouldn't let me pay for my dinner, because I had intended to have dinner in the main dining room anyway, I strolled around outside for a while in an effort to clear my head, or heads. However, I didn't clear them. I discovered that in the back parking lot was a small motor van of the kind you see all over Scotland and never in the United States any more. It was black, with an open front seat, and the rest of it was closed, with doors that opened at the back. In short, it looked like a small ambulance or a small patrol wagon of the kind used by the American police twenty years ago. I took it into all my heads that the plot had now definitely become a counterplot and that a sort of dry run was going on in which I was supposed to play a part. The intricate details of this counterplot have vanished from my mind—if, indeed, they were ever in my mind in a clear way. In any case, I felt compelled to start taking handfuls of books and papers, and so on, out of Graham's office and carrying them through a second back door, which led directly from the office into the back parking lot, and putting them in the black van, the doors of which I found were not locked. Nobody paid any attention to me as I acted out this mysterious mission, and I went on with it, half serious and half chuckling to myself, until I did not feel compelled to put any more books and papers in the back of the van. I still don't know whether anybody observed me while I was doing this. When the compulsion dissipated itself and I was left free to do as I pleased, I joined my new acquaintances in the bar once again, had one for the road, told everybody goodbye, and got into my taxicab.

"As we started off down the lonely road toward the village of Longformacus, my driver turned on his shortwave radio and told his dispatcher in Edinburgh that he was leaving Longformacus and was heading back to the city. On account of his speech impediment, this took him quite a few minutes. He then turned his radio off and asked me whether I wanted to go back by way of Gifford or take the route that led through the town of Duns. I told him to take the latter route. I then got it into my heads that this was no regular radio taxicab but that my own Air Intelligence people could listen to everything I said to the driver as long as his radio was turned on, instead of off. I also reached the conclusion in a fast flash that this counterplot that was now going through the dry run had to do with a small airplane piloted by an old friend of mine in the Air Force named Dick Kight, who, the last time I saw him, in 1944, was second-in-command of the India-China Wing of the United States Air Transport Command, with headquarters at Chabua, Assam, far up in the northeastern corner of India, from which our planes flew over the Hump to China. Kight was then a lieutenant colonel, and a couple of years before that he had piloted the plane in which Wendell Willkie made his tour of the world, including Russia. I was now quite convinced that Kight was going to lead a squadron of fighter planes in for a landing on the moors around Duns as a part of the counterplot, and that, in my taxi, I was supposed to talk into the radio as I drove from Longformacus to Duns, and describe in detail everything I saw on that route—as if the fighter planes were actually flying to Duns in accordance with my directions. So I asked the driver to flip on his radio again, and as the muffled voices from cabs in and around Edinburgh came over, along with the occasional voice of the dispatcher, I began to describe in ringing tones such things as telephone wires and poles, cattle, flocks of sheep, houses, and churches—on the right and on the left—until we whizzed into the outskirts of the town of Duns, seven miles from Longformacus. There I told the driver he could turn his radio off, if he wanted, and I relaxed, feeling that I had done my job for the night. The late sun was just beginning to go down, and we drove along peacefully, while I dozed from time to time, until we drew up in front of the Roxburghe, in Edinburgh, about half past ten o'clock. I was by now feeling quite sober again and was pretty well on to the fact that I'd been acting like a drunken American. My driver, however, seemed to think that the whole thing was a pleasant lark, and he grinned and tipped his cap when I paid him, and said that it had been an enjoyable outing for him, and that he hoped I wouldn't have any difficulties the next day with the police of Gifford.

"I went into the Roxburghe and up to my room, where I took off my clothes, had a cold bath, and almost immediately went to sleep. I awoke with a start after what seemed to be a very short time, and I was heavy with anxiety again. I felt that it was absolutely necessary for me to find the newly arrived Colonel Gragg, who had just taken Colonel Scott's place as commander of the base at Kirknewton, and tell him what had gone on with me that day at Gifford and at Longformacus and on the taxicab ride to Duns. I dressed hurriedly, put all my memoranda and notes and chits, and so on, in the inside pocket of my jacket, grabbed up my topcoat and tweed hat and my portable typewriter, and went straight out of the hotel and flagged a taxi. I told the driver to go to Price's Hotel, and I was there in five minutes. I found the hotel locked, but there were lighted windows on the upper floor, so I was then convinced that Colonel Gragg and his fellow-officers were prisoners inside the hotel, and I banged on the door and rang the bell until the Scotswoman I had seen before came to the door and told me rather sharply that it was long past the closing hour and that I couldn't come in. When I protested that I had to see Colonel Gragg, she told me I would have to see him in the morning. And she shut and locked the door more or less in my face. I then stood outside for a few seconds, thinking hard, and decided that I was supposed to communicate with the officers inside the hotel by singing them excerpts from the song I had written in that Ethel Merman piece—the one I had cabled to New York. I can't sing very well, but I nevertheless gave it a try. Windows flew up, and I could see that some of the officers inside the hotel were looking down at me and that people in the adjoining houses and apartment buildings were also looking down at me and, presumably, listening to my efforts to sing the Ethel Merman song. I heard several cries of 'Call the police!' and a pedestrian who looked like one of the usual character actors in 'The 39 Steps'—tweeds, pipe, umbrella, and so on—came up to me and very courteously told me that unless I stopped singing I was almost certain to be arrested. I thanked him and went right on singing. It seemed to me that the fact that the police were being called was exactly as it should be, and that they would come and take me away to safety and also rescue the imprisoned officers in the hotel. The private joke I'd had with the Camerons about calling the police occurred to me again and again. Pretty soon a police van came hurrying up, and three or four enormous policemen took charge of me and my typewriter in a gentle but firm fashion. I was helped into the patrol wagon, and in a few minutes I was being booked at an Edinburgh jail for being drunk and disorderly. I took all this as a matter of course and was still quite convinced that I had saved my country and my Air Force from a nasty situation. The police clerk took all my belongings, including my memoranda and other papers, and I was glad of this because the proper authorities would, of course, need these memoranda to go by. I was escorted into a rather large cell, of which I was the only occupant. It had a dirt floor and no bunk or any other furniture. I was now in the grip of clear and, on the whole, rather pleasant hallucinations in which I figured that the Strategic Air Command, having got word from the rescued officers that all hell was breaking loose in Edinburgh, and that it was a question of whether the Russians would strike us first or we would strike them first, was alerted and was on its way to either bomb Russia or threaten that country with total destruction unless they agreed to our terms, whatever those terms were. At the same time, I was troubled by faint notions that I had simply got drunk and had been arrested for it, and that I was going to find it hard to explain my escapade to my Edinburgh friends when, or if, I got out of the cell I was in. However, most of the time and with almost all my heads, I still thought I was a hero. I remember beating on the wall lightly with my fist, not as a protest against my incarceration but in order to beat time as I sang under my breath the same old Ethel Merman song, to which I ad-libbed such phrases as 'Now the Labradors! And now the setters and pointers! And here come the Weimaraners!' These seemed to me to represent different types of Strategic Air Command bombers that were on their way to the rendezvous over Russia. Pretty soon I got tired of this. I also found that the clerk had taken my cigarettes and matches along with my other belongings. I was thinking of calling out to see if I could get some cigarettes when a guard in uniform appeared, unlocked my door, and escorted me into a much larger cell, in which twenty or more drunks in all stages of intoxication and post-intoxication were sitting, standing, and leaping around. I instantly realized that I was not being treated as a hero, and that the powers that be had decided I was just another drunk. I resented this, but I felt too forlorn to express my resentment. I simply sat down on the floor in a corner of this large cell and put my hat over my eyes. I felt absolutely desolate. I felt that I had ruined my whole vacation by this escapade, that it would probably be written up in the sensational press, if not in the conservative papers, and that I would be made to look like a drunken fool, both at home and abroad. It was the damnedest roomful of unfortunate men that I ever expect to see. They were mostly bums and sailors, and while no fights were going on, I expected one to break out at any moment, and I fully expected to become involved in it, whether I continued to sit in my corner with my hat over my eyes or not. Some of the men were sleeping, some were being sick on the floor, some were jumping around and hollering and singing, and one young chap, who seemed somewhat better dressed than the others, was performing flabbergasting feats of acrobatics. I could tell at a glance that he was in a manic state and that he was not trying to control it. He would let out a whoop and run the length of the crowded room and halfway up the wall, and then throw himself backward in a somersault and land on his feet. I sat there and shuddered, while a cold sweat broke out all over me, and I was entirely convinced that some kind of riot was going to start at any moment and that I would either be killed or get badly injured. Nevertheless, I drifted off into a short doze. I suddenly felt something poke me hard in the ribs. I jumped up, and found that the acrobat was standing in front of me with a tin cup of tea in his hand. 'Tea, old gentleman!' he said, and handed me the tin cup. Then he flexed his muscles and dug out a cigarette butt from somewhere inside his clothes and handed that to me, along with a match. I smoked the cigarette butt gratefully and drank the tea. The acrobat let out a whoop and began his wall-climbing exercises again, and I began to think that perhaps I was in no danger after all. A pitiful old Irishman who must have been close to eighty was shoved through the door by the guard, and the door was again locked from the outside. The old man was weeping and muttering, and I heard him say, 'I killed him, I killed him.' A middle-aged sailor who seemed to be sobering up gave the old man a cigarette butt and his unfinished cup of tea, and asked the old man who it was he had killed. 'The landlord, the landlord,' said the old man. 'I shot him as he rode along between the hedges.' 'When?' asked the sailor. 'Last night, last night,' moaned the old man. 'Where?' asked the sailor. 'In Galway, in Galway,' moaned the old man. More drunks were shown in from time to time, and a couple of them had a hair-raising fight, which ended up with bloody noses.

"After what turned out to be a couple of hours of this, I began to get desperately jumpy and I was afraid I would grow hysterical. I wasn't quite sure what would be done with me by the prison guards if this happened. Half of me was telling myself that I'd got drunk and behaved like a drunk, and the other half of me was telling myself that my compulsive behavior—going to Prestwick and talking about milk, for example, and singing the code song to the officers in the hotel, along with my trip to Longformacus and my strange behavior there, which was only partly induced by alcohol, and especially my notions about Colonel Kight and the Air Force fighters—might mean that I had been doped somewhere along the way. I also got a notion in some of my heads that somebody might have rigged Miss Dirleton's rented tape recorder so that when I was asleep under the influence of some drug—sodium amytal, for example—it told me things I had to do later. But mostly I was afraid of going to pieces in that communal cell and being taken to a bughouse. So finally I beat on the door with one of my shoes until a guard appeared. I told him quietly that I wanted him to get me out of there and put me in a cell to myself, because I was afraid I might lose my mind and get hysterical if I was left in there any longer. I also said I thought I needed to see a doctor. The guard gazed at me for a minute and then took me by the arm and led me outside and on to the desk where I had originally been received. There I told the sergeant what I had told the guard, and without hesitation the sergeant gave orders for me to be taken under guard to the Royal Infirmary. It was only a short ride in a Black Maria. There I was shown into the same emergency ward in which my injured head had been treated. One of the same nurses asked me what was the matter, and I told her politely that I couldn't discuss it with her but would like to see a doctor. In due course, the same Dr. MacLean appeared, and after taking one look at me, and the two policemen who were guarding me, he asked the nurse to get me a cup of coffee. She did that, and as I drank it, I told him that I had been drunk and disorderly but that I had a notion I might have been given some kind of drug somewhere along the way on the evening before, because I had been behaving in a compulsive fashion that at times was beyond my control, and that the whole thing had to do with some kind of cloak-and-dagger business, part

of which I had already reported to the American Intelligence officer at Prestwick. The doctor asked me if I thought I had been
doped there in the hospital when he was treating my head, and I
said I was sure I hadn't been. He wrote on a report form for some
time and at some length, and then he said, 'You need to see a psychiatrist.'

" 'I see one all the time at home,' I said, 'but what I'm afraid of
right now is that I might go into a panic and perhaps into a psychotic break of some sort if I have to stay in that communal cell
any longer.' I told him that I realized I fully deserved to be treated
like any other drunk but that I didn't think it would be of any use
to the kindly Edinburgh police if I was driven out of my mind.

"He said he thought the sergeant on the desk would probably
let me have a cell of my own, under the circumstances, and he shook
hands with me once again, said goodbye and wished me luck, and
turned to take care of his next patient, a drunk who had been badly
beaten up.

"While I was on my way back to the jail, it occurred to me that
the thing for me to do was to ask to see the American consul. I
no longer cared how much publicity I got—I simply wanted to
preserve my sanity. The sergeant was very kind and said he would
telephone for the consul right away. It was now getting on toward
nine o'clock, and the sergeant told me that all of us would be
charged and arraigned before a judge at around ten o'clock. He let
me sit in a small vacant office while he was telephoning. The consul appeared in about half an hour and said his name was McClary.
I told him that I was sorry I had had to disturb him, and that I was
being treated fine by the Edinburgh police and the prison guards,
but that I had found myself getting panicky in the communal cell
and I was afraid I might go out of my mind if I had to go back in
there. He said I wouldn't have to go back in there, and he went
away and presently returned with a begowned and bewigged attorney of some kind, who seemed to be the public prosecutor. They

explained to me that I would be charged with being drunk and disorderly, and that if I pleaded guilty, it would all be over in two minutes after I went before the judge, and that I would probably be fined one pound, which I could pay within ten days. They said that the newspapers probably wouldn't publish anything except a short paragraph saying I had been fined one pound for being drunk and disorderly. But if I pleaded *not* guilty, I would have to raise bail and stand trial, and so on. I said I was guilty, there was no question about that, and I would so plead. Mr. McClary said that he would wait around for me and would take me back to his office in his car, in case there was anything I wanted to tell him, and that he would send me back to my hotel afterward in the same car.

"After a while, the guards took me into a courtroom, where a clerk read out the charge and asked whether I pleaded guilty or not guilty. 'Guilty,' I said. A begowned and bewigged judge accepted the plea and fined me one pound, pointing out that I could bring the pound or mail it within ten days, and that was the end of the matter. I was a free man again, and wasn't feeling too bad. In fact, I felt rather well except that I was hungry and badly wanted some more coffee. Mr. McClary took me out to his car, which was driven by a chauffeur, and we rode to the Consulate, where we went into his office. It was a large, comfortable one, and I sat in an easy chair while he sat at his desk. I told him that I had suspected I was mixed up in some kind of cloak-and-dagger business, and that I had told the intelligence officer at Prestwick all about it. I told him I really didn't know whether there was any basis for my suspicions or whether I had simply dreamed them up. And he said that when one got into that sort of thing, it was extremely hard even for seasoned secret agents to know for sure whether they were imagining things or whether they were being confronted with something that required action. I nodded, and said that there was no use my wasting his time in telling him my story but that I thought I would go to see the intelligence officer at Prestwick again and bring him up to date on what had happened to me, or else I might see Colonel Gragg at Kirknewton and tell *him* the whole story, if he wanted to listen to it. I told Mr. McClary that I also had a notion that the whole thing was some kind of practical joke being played on me by three humorous friends of mine in the C.I.A., but that, again, I had no proof of this. However, I said, if that was what it was, and if he, Mr. McClary, was in touch with them, he might want to tell them for me that I had a surprise ending up my sleeve for them. Mr. McClary seemed a little concerned when I said this, but I laughed and told him that my surprise ending would do nobody any harm. (I was only thinking of boxing their ears.) I then told him that I had been worrying about Susie, who was supposed to arrive that morning from Paris. She was coming by way of Dublin, where she had expected to stop over for a few days, I told him, and I hadn't heard anything from her since she had wired me saying she was leaving for Dublin, some days back. I asked him if he would let me telephone the Roxburghe and find out whether she had arrived, and said that if she had, I wouldn't take any more of his time. He put in a call to the Roxburghe desk and handed the phone to me, and I ascertained that Susie had just arrived and was waiting in the lobby until her room, which had been vacated only a few minutes before, was ready. So that was that. She hadn't been kidnapped; nobody had stolen the pin I'd given her, she wasn't being held as a hostage in order to make me do something or other. She just hadn't thought it necessary to tell me she had arrived in Dublin safely and was having a good time there. I apologized again to Mr. McClary for having caused him so much trouble, and he said that that was what he was for. He said he was leaving Edinburgh the next day for a new assignment and was being replaced by a Mr. MacLaren, and that if I needed any help of any kind not to hesitate to get in touch with his successor—that he'd tell Mr. MacLaren about me, so he'd know who I was if I called him. Then Mr. McClary took me down to his car and dropped me off at the Roxburghe.

"Susie was sitting in the lobby, in front of a window, happily having a cup of coffee. I discovered that I felt fine, and was surprised to discover, further, that I had no hangover. This again made me think I might have been doped somewhere or other, but I dismissed the whole matter from my mind as I greeted Susie, and began to concentrate on having a happy time with her in Edinburgh and its environs."

"And did you?"

"Yes and no. After Susie arrived, I drank less, partly because I didn't want to run any risk of getting put in that jail again, and partly because when I'm with Susie I usually drink what she drinks, and she likes wine and mild apéritifs, and abhors cocktails and whiskey; in other words, her drinking customs are more French than American or Anglo-Saxon or Celtic. And yet I was, if anything, even more anxious than before about the plot to kidnap President Eisenhower and perhaps the Queen and her husband, and I was also afraid that something might happen to Susie while she was in my company. The morning after the day I got out of jail, I went to see Mr. MacLaren, while Susie was shopping. I told him pretty much the bare facts of what had happened to me and also what I thought might be going on around Edinburgh, and then I told him that there was nothing I could see that he or anybody else could do about it, except to tell me where I might obtain a car and a driver that he knew would be absolutely safe for Susie and me to use. I also told him I intended to go and see Colonel Gragg that day or the next and tell him everything I knew and everything I had imagined. Mr. MacLaren gave me the number of a firm that had chauffeur-driven cars, and said that the Consulate had used them for years and had every confidence in them, and that he would call them after I left and make sure that they gave me a driver who had been with them a long time. Then he said he'd also call Colonel Gragg and tell him I was coming to see him, and so on. He said that he couldn't pretend to know, or guess, whether there was anything in what I sensed was going on, but that one never could be sure in these cloak-and-dagger matters, and that I was doing the right thing in keeping in touch with the American military authorities.

"Later on that day, I asked for a car and driver from the firm whose number he'd given me, and they sent an enormous limousine not unlike a Rolls-Royce. Susie and I both felt self-conscious in it as we went breezing down to the Danish-food place for dinner that night, and Susie wanted to know why I didn't just take a taxi, or at least an ordinary-looking car. I explained to her that I was afraid I was mixed up in some kind of cloak-and-dagger business, and that, whatever might be going on, I'd wanted to be sure we had a safe car and a driver who was dependable. 'Oh dear!' she said. 'That's the story of my life!' She meant, of course, that during her girlhood her father had always been on the run, with a price set on his head by the Nazis. I decided to tell her nothing more about the plot and the counterplot, and we had a nice time at the Danish place and at several places we stopped at on the way there, and on the drive back to Edinburgh afterward. Next day, I got the same driver and a less conspicuous car. Nothing happened to increase my anxiety, and I had no more panics until four or five days later. By that time, I was taking ordinary taxicabs again. I still thought it quite possible that the plot and the counterplot were entirely of my own imagining, but when I stopped and put all the stray circumstances together, they were quite impressive."

"How did you put them together, Colonel?"

"Like this: I dismissed as unimportant the notion that the whole thing was a practical joke engineered by my pals in the C.I.A. If it was, it didn't matter. What did matter, it seemed to me, was that I might have been hit on the head that night at the edge of the road not by falling against the signpost but by some person or persons unknown, that I might have been doped at the Infirmary, that the tape recorder might have been used to put ideas into my head that it later seemed necessary for me to carry out, that I was to be made use of, either by my own people or by the other side, to in some way act as a stand-in for Prince Philip or some other member of the Royal Family, that the extreme Tories in Scotland might be on the verge of making some kind of deal with Khrushchev, and that this deal involved kidnapping the President, the Queen, and a collection of other prominent Britons and Americans and holding them as hostages in connection with a takeover of the United Kingdom. And that our counterplot was, roughly, that we would let the other side think they were getting away with this, but that actually the people they kidnapped would be stand-ins and that at the proper moment we would grab Khrushchev and *his* bunch and do to the other side exactly what they'd planned to do to us. And that I was involved in one way or another. I told myself all the reasons *not* to believe this, but at the same time I pointed out to myself that the plot and the counterplot were quite plausible.

"Susie and I had moved to the rooms at Prestonfield House the day after I got out of jail, and Susie loved the place as much as I did. We made friends with all the regular guests there—people who lived there the year round—and with many of the travellers who were staying there for a few days. I was bothered intermittently by flurries of suspicion, about the plot to kidnap President Eisenhower and the Queen—what the Major, here, would call 'minimal delusions of a faintly paranoid character'—but, except for one rather fantastic interlude, nothing happened either inside my head or heads or outside it or them. We made particular friends with a Professor Pearl and his wife. He was a retired science professor from Dartmouth. An English writer named David Keir, whose wife is prominent in British politics, came to Prestonfield House from London for a visit; we made friends with him, and he took us to see Sir Compton Mackenzie at his Edinburgh house, where we spent most of one night chatting with Sir Compton. We had a delightful evening at Mr. Pentland's house in the country—he was the wool man I'd met in Scott's—and we later had Pentland and his wife and their three grown children to dinner at Prestonfield House.

"I was having such a good time that I kept putting off the visit to Colonel Gragg at Kirknewton that I'd told Mr. MacLaren I would make. I figured that MacLaren would pass on to Gragg what I'd told him, if Gragg wanted to know about it, and that if, as I still half suspected, the whole business was simply something I'd dreamed up, I wouldn't have to risk making a bigger fool of myself by paying the call on Colonel Gragg. Then the fantastic episode occurred.

"You will remember that the black van at the Rathburne Hotel, in Longformacus, had appeared to me to have some special significance. Well, one evening about nine o'clock, when I returned to Prestonfield House after dinner at the Press Club—Susie was having a quiet dinner with Mrs. Oliver—I saw, as my taxi drove into the Prestonfield grounds, a black van standing near the gate. It wasn't parked in the parking lot but was on the driveway, headed out. After I'd paid off the taxi, I strolled over to it and tried the back doors. They were locked. I went on up to the Leather Room, and there a nice young Scots couple named Colling were talking to Susie and Mrs. Oliver. It seemed the Collings had an estate on which they raised sheep. It was in the vicinity of Gifford. They'd started in to Edinburgh to have dinner, they said, having left their five children with a housekeeper, and their car had broken down on the outskirts of Edinburgh, near a garage owned by a friend of Colling's. The friend was out, however, so they left their car there to be repaired and took his van and drove on to Prestonfield House, where they'd just had dinner Colling was a likable chap, though uneducated, like many men and women of old families and of the old nobility—or so he seemed to me—and he expressed many re-actionary opinions of the kind traditional with some of the old-family Scots lairds and landowners.

"I chose to think the story about the van an unlikely one. I'd had in one or two of my heads for days the notion that a black van, or several black vans, was to figure in both the plot and the counterplot, and I decided that this one the Collings said they'd borrowed might be a part of the plot—not the counterplot. I tele-phoned MacKaye at the taxi company and asked him to bring his cab out to Prestonfield House. When he got there, I told him to stand by—that I wanted to follow the lorry when it left. We fol-lowed it and soon lost it. I decided I was being silly, and returned to Prestonfield House. It was then rather late, and Susie had gone to bed. I took it into my head to see if any of the hotel guests were missing. I looked into the room the Professor and his wife had been occupying—on the ground floor, next to my room—opening the door noiselessly. The moon was out, and I could see quite clearly that the beds were rumpled but that nobody was in the room. I decided that the plot was being carried out that night and that the Professor and his wife had been taken away in the black van by the Collings. I went into my room and telephoned the base and asked for Colonel Gragg, but he was out. I got his executive officer and told him to tell Colonel Gragg that whatever it was that was going on in Edinburgh had just started, and that 'they' had the Professor and his wife. I explained who the Professor was. I then called Prest-wick and told Lieutenant Cooper the same thing. Then I went up to the Leather Room to see if I could find a drink, and discovered that some Americans were playing bridge in the drawing room. I had never seen any of them before. They said they'd just arrived that evening. One of them said he was an Air Force officer on leave. There was a short-wave radio in the Leather Room, and I decided to turn it on and see what news was being announced in the various capitals of the world. I couldn't get anything. I asked the American who said he was an Air Force officer—he was a young man—to see if he could work the radio. He tried, but he couldn't get anything, either. He said that the radio was working all right but that there didn't seem to be anything on in Moscow, London, New York, or Paris. I took this to mean that all hell had broken loose and that silence was being observed everywhere except in Edinburgh. Still, I wasn't sure, so I said nothing to the Americans. The Americans went to bed, but I stayed up. The liquor in the Leather Room was locked up, so I wasn't able to get the drink I very much wanted. I tried to call MacLaren, but I couldn't reach him. I could think of nothing further to do. I couldn't sleep, so, as quietly as possible, I took a bath to calm my nerves, and then I put on clean clothes and read a book, and, at last, it was dawn. About an hour after the sun rose, I heard sounds in the kitchen and managed to get some tea and biscuits. Then I started up to the second-floor bathroom—there was no bathroom on the ground floor—and there I met the Professor, in a dressing gown, on *his* way to the bathroom. I said good morning and asked him if he had moved to a different room. 'Yes,' he said. 'Mrs. Oliver thought we'd be more comfortable on the top floor, in a larger room than the one we had downstairs.' I laughed inordinately, and the Professor looked as if he thought I'd lost my mind. Then I looked into the Leather Room. A man was there, hard at work repairing the radio.

"So now the mystery of the radio was cleared up. And from then on I had no more anxiety and no more panics. MacLaren, however, *did* have some anxiety—or at least he was very much concerned about me. He called me the next day and told me that Colonel Gragg had said he'd like to see me out at Kirknewton and show me around the base, and had suggested that I bring Susie along, if I liked. Susie and I went, and on the way Susie asked me to stop the taxi at a flower shop. I did, and she bought a potted plant for Mrs. Oliver's mother. I figured the sentries at Kirknewton would surely think the wrapped-up potted plant was a bomb, but they paid no attention to it. They took us in to see Colonel Gragg, who greeted us cordially and introduced us to a young officer, Captain David Faris, whose insignia showed he was a flight surgeon. Faris said he'd like to show Susie around the base while I talked to Colonel Gragg. I told Gragg the bare bones of my story and assured him that last night's episode had finally convinced me that the whole thing was just something going on inside my head. He said, in almost the same words MacLaren and McClary had used, that once one began to think or act along cloak-and-dagger lines, one found it extremely difficult to tell fact from fancy. We chatted about people we both knew in the Air Force. Susie and Faris returned. I asked Faris if he was a psychiatrist as well as an aviation-medicine man, and he said that he wasn't but that he was 'psychoanalytically oriented.' He asked me if I thought I needed to see a psychiatrist or needed to get into a nursing home. I said that I didn't think so, that last night's business had cleared up the whole thing, and that I now felt quite free from anxiety. He gave me his phone numbers—at both his office and his home—and told me not to hesitate to call him if I decided I needed anything. 'You'd be surprised how many intelligence officers and C.I.A. people have to have psychiatric advice from time to time,' he said. Both Gragg and Faris told me they'd known about me and my Guam caper for years, and Gragg said in an offhand way that he knew General LeMay thought very highly of me. I figured that he had been in touch with the Air Force in Washington and had been told by LeMay or by one of his staff people that I was a friend of LeMay's, and that LeMay had indicated to Gragg that he should be kind to me but at the same time should be prepared to throw a net over me if I showed signs of wishing to get to an official teletype channel that led into the Pentagon. I was feeling entirely normal and happy and relaxed, and Susie and I left the airbase after a while and returned to Prestonfield House. That was the end of Operation Edinburgh. I had a few more days there with Susie—days and evenings that came and went without any more flurries of suspicion or anxiety—and then we went to Dublin, where we were to fly our separate ways back to New York and Paris. The day before we left Edinburgh, I had a note from Mrs. Cameron saying that she and Ian had been delayed in London and that they hoped I'd still be at Prestonfield House when they returned, but I wasn't, and I haven't seen them again, although we've corresponded from time to time. I certainly intend to look them up, along with all my other friends over there, when I go to Scotland on another vacation, which I hope will be soon. On our last evening in Edinburgh, I took Susie to dinner at the Rathburne Hotel at Longformacus and we had a splendid time viewing the paintings and having tea with the Princess and dinner afterward with the Grahams, and from the garden we watched the late sun go down in the ocean beyond the purple Lammermuirs. And Susie pretended—as I did—to enjoy no end Mr. Graham's account of the joke I'd played on him that other evening in his bar when I'd called him an unspeakable monster. I didn't tell Graham I thought I'd been involved in a plot—or a counterplot—having to do with Eisenhower and the Queen. In fact, I've never again told anybody about that until tonight."

"Well, Colonel, we've found out everything we wanted to know," the general said, "and that's that."

AND IT WAS.

THE BIG LITTLE MAN
FROM BROOKLYN

O N NOVEMBER 25, 1890, in one of a long row of red brick
two-story houses in Brooklyn that had five gray stone steps
leading up to the front doors, coal stoves for heat, and toilets in the
back yards—each house exactly like the other houses in the row,
and also exactly like the ones on the opposite side of the street—a
boy was born who was named by his parents Stephen Jacob Weinberg. He wasn't entirely satisfied with his name or with himself.
Soon after he reached the age of twenty-one, he started tinkering
with his name and being people other than himself. Except for
swift, recurrent periods during which he was Royal St. Cyr, he
stayed fairly close to the essentials of the name he had started out
with. He was Royal St. Cyr only when he wished to drum home
to himself and other people the notion that he was a lieutenant in
the French Navy, which he wasn't. Otherwise, he was, more or less
successively, S. Clifford Weinberg, Ethan Allen Weinberg, Rodney
S. Wyman, Sterling C. Wyman, Stanley Clifford Weyman, Allen
Stanley Weyman, and C. Sterling Weinberg, and he went back to S.
Clifford Weinberg and Ethan Allan Weinberg for second and third
tries. In middle age, he settled firmly on Stanley Clifford Weyman.
From then on, he used only that name, but under it he continued
to carry out impostures of great artistic merit. For the sake of sim-

THE BIG LITTLE MAN FROM BROOKLYN

plicity in a chronicle that cannot be other than compound, and in deference to the man himself, he will generally be called here by the name he seemed to like best—Stanley Clifford Weyman.

Weyman was a dedicated impostor. He was a man who, unwilling or unable to remain an obscure citizen of Brooklyn, became many men in the course of a long career of being people other than himself. The men he became were never obscure, and in time he himself ceased to be obscure. For him, it was not enough simply to have a dream of glory and then put it aside and go about his business. He acted it out. Only when it had been fulfilled did he put that particular dream of glory aside, as a painter puts aside a finished painting. Then he would find a fresh role to play and would perform another piece of impeccable imposture. And more than once he actually tasted glory.

No matter what imposture Weyman was engaged in, he never altered his face—not even by so much as shaving off a thin, spruce mustache, which, along with expressive, bright brown eyes, an aquiline nose, a strong, solemn mouth, a shapely head, and a trim figure, gave him an air of distinction that he carried with disarmingly modest grace. Although Weyman was unaware of it, he bore a rather remarkable resemblance to the comic character with the wispy mustache and the shuffling gait created by Charles Chaplin on the silent motion-picture screen. Weyman, however, was not a conscious comedian, and it is doubtful if he possessed a trace of a sense of humor until the declining years of his long and changeable life. It was his destiny most of the time not to be funny to himself but to make other people look funny to still other people.

"Be yourself" is a common command. Sometimes it is addressed to a friend, a lover, a husband, a wife, or somebody else who the person uttering it has cause to think is not being himself or herself. At other times, an individual issues this command to the soul that exists at his very center. In any case, it is an edict that is infrequently carried out. Few people are entirely satisfied with being themselves. The urge to be somebody other than oneself is so universal and so deep-seated that it may well be an elemental instinct of the human species. Many people—and creative people in particular—admittedly spend the better part of their lives trying to find themselves; the inference is that the self they are making do with in the meantime is not their own but somebody else's. Children as young as three years of age, or even two, enjoy not being themselves. It is only a pathologically unimaginative child who doesn't try to palm himself off as an Indian or a cowboy as soon as he is big enough to make a horse out of a stick and ride it. And the chances are that long before that, by barking, mewing, or roaring, the ordinary child has endeavored to be a dog, a cat, or a lion instead of himself.

It would seem that human beings find, accept, and retain a single, permanent identity only with the greatest reluctance. Clearly, they would rather be two or more people than just one person. The wish often leads to lunacy. But in the world of art—and especially in literary art—sane grown people are able freely to indulge their tendencies toward dual or multiple personalities. Except for mental hospitals and the world of art, the only world in which these gratifications and satisfactions can be fully realized is the world of dedicated imposture. Everybody, of course, no matter who he or she is, engages in minor impostures to at least a small degree at one time or another, if not all the time. When we temporarily or permanently assume a facial expression or a posture that conveys something we are not feeling inside, we are imposturing. It goes without saying that actors and actresses engage in imposture on the stage—and, not infrequently, off the stage as well. And in the world of politics, of course, a rather inferior variety of imposture is as rampant as a dizzy billy goat in a field of nanny goats. But few of us are dedicated impostors.

Dedicated impostors are, in a sense, artists. Their creations are the selves they successfully impose upon those with whom they come in contact while they are engaged in an imposture. And the relation of the impostor to the artist is a close one. It is also a somewhat mysterious one. Many great artists feel that they are impostors. Especially in their early years, men of genius often find it difficult, if not impossible, to believe that the extraordinary gifts they possess are really theirs. They are sometimes inclined to feel that they stole these gifts. In time, the artist usually becomes at least two people—his private self and his creative self. This division is frequently recognized by painters, sculptors, composers, and, especially, writers in their use of both a true name and a pseudonym. Novelists, poets, composers, sculptors, and painters are often curiously preoccupied with a tendency to tinker with their true name, even if they don't actually use a pseudonym. They insert or delete an initial, or drop a first name in favor of a middle name, or the reverse. And artists of all sorts through the ages have been peculiarly fascinated by impostors and by the ramifying subject of imposture. The switching of identities and other imposturous episodes are ever-recurrent themes of ancient myths and fairy tales and of all religions, and in literature, from its earliest beginnings, the same themes abound.

Dr. Samuel Johnson was not entirely happy with being himself. Several times, he remarked that he would rather be George Psalmanazar than himself. Psalmanazar was the assumed name of an impostor who presented himself to the eighteenth-century world as a Japanese. He invented a false history, geography, alphabet, and language of the island of Formosa, where he said he came from. He was so successful in his masquerade that his true name and the facts of his birth have never been definitely known, though it was later fairly well established that he had never travelled outside Europe.

Goethe became so deeply interested in the background of Count Cagliostro (who wasn't a count and wasn't named Cagliostro) that he sought out the impostor's humble Sicilian family. He travelled to

Sicily to do this, and while doing it he became an impostor himself; he used a false name and false credentials, and made a pretense of bringing the impostor's mother a letter from her son, which he himself had written, in disguised handwriting.

Fritz Kreisler is an example of a genius who as a young man either didn't believe that his gifts belonged to him or wished to convince other people that they didn't. At the age of eighteen, he publicly launched a series of imposturous compositions—a fact that he didn't reveal directly until the occasion of his sixtieth birthday. In those early years, he composed a number of entirely original pieces and attributed them to then little-known composers of the past, such as Vivaldi, Pugnani, Francœur, and Couperin. He proceeded to perform these works at his concerts, listing himself on the concert programs as their editor and stating that his editing was a free treatment of the originals (which, of course, didn't exist); at the same time, being as vain as the next genius, he stipulated that if these impostured works were played in public his name must be mentioned in connection with them. Later, he began presenting other original compositions under his own name, and didn't like to be questioned about those earlier works; he would evade such questions, or else he would falsely state that he had found the manuscripts of the compositions in old libraries. This explanation was similar to that given by the Scottish impostor James Macpherson in connection with the great eighteenth-century hoax of the Ossianic poetry, which he himself had written, and it was also similar to that given by Thomas Chatterton, in the same full-flowering century, in connection with the poems he attributed to a fictitious Thomas Rowley—poems that Chatterton had in fact written himself.

In a manner of speaking, all dedicated artists are dedicated impostors in that the self they impose upon their public is not their true self. It is their creative self. And that they create at all impresses other people as being magical. Conversely, the performances of impostors impress other people as having the marvellous quality of artistic achievement. This is especially true of dedicated impostors, for whom works of imposture are like the creations of dedicated artists in that they form the core of the creators' existence. In fact, the careers of dedicated impostors seem miraculous and inspired, like works of art. The impostor's ability to put on convincing acts of impersonation, including excellent reproductions of special skills—such as those of the impostured doctor, lawyer, or prince—is very similar to the artist's ability to create something out of nothing.

Dr. Phyllis Greenacre, a New York psychoanalyst, is the leading contemporory authority on the ins and outs of this odd entwinement of the impostor and the artist. "In both the creative artist on the brink of a new surge of creativity and in the impostor, between periods of imposture," she has written, "there is a sense of ego hunger and a need for completion—in the one, of the artistic self; in the other, of a satisfying identity in the world." Having spent many years studying both the world of art and the world of imposture, Dr. Greenacre speaks solemnly in one of her best-known works, "The Relation of the Impostor to the Artist," of "the dark, imposturous character which accompanies, like a shadow, the tread of genius." It might be said—less solemnly—that genius accompanies, like a shadow, the tread of the dark, imposturous character of the dedicated impostor.

Although the rich variety of Weyman's creations is not what establishes his superlative standing in the world's gallery of impostors, it is surely as impressive as that achieved by any other impostor in history. Some gifted impostors, like some gifted authors, composers, sculptors, and painters, have tended to settle into a rut. This is true of one of the most authentically talented impostors of the twentieth century, Prince Michael Romanoff. Like Weyman, he is a native of Brooklyn. At an early age, he decided that he wasn't Harry Gerguson of Brooklyn but was Prince Michael Romanoff of Russia. Even people who knew that he wasn't Prince Michael Romanoff of Russia liked to feel that he was when they rubbed shoulders with him, and they still do. He was until lately a successful restaurateur, and although he was a charming host, an intelligent, perceptive, and cultivated gentleman, it is undoubtedly a fact that one reason his Beverly Hills restaurant, called Romanoff's, was so popular in its golden years was that the people who used to go there were under the impression—even though they knew it to be a false impression—that they were being catered to by a member of the vanished nobility of Russia, a man who might have been a czar if it hadn't been for Marx and Lenin.

Another Johnny-one-note in the world's gallery of impostors was Dr. Johnson's idol, George Psalmanazar. He kept on and on with the Formosan imposture, and never attempted any other. James Macpherson was tiresomely devoted to being the poet Ossian. And it is understandable that he stayed in that rut. Macpherson's imposturous works, which he attributed to the third-century poet named Ossian, received much acclaim, were imitated by Goethe, Byron, and other great poets, and are generally credited with having deeply influenced the romantic movement in literature. Thomas Chatterton, a really talented poet, also perpetrated only one imposture. It was so much admired and he himself was so gratified with it that he may have felt that life under one name could hold no further satisfactions for him; in any event, he poisoned himself before he came of age.

There have not been as many female impostors as there have been male impostors, but one of them was in some ways the greatest of all impostors. This was Joan, or Joanna, who had her fling in the ninth century. The story of Joan has been handed down through the ages, and it was skillfully and delicately retold in 1886 by a Greek writer named Emmanuel Royidis, who because of it was excommunicated from the Greek Orthodox Church several decades before his book was engagingly translated into English, by Lawrence Durrell, in 1954. Although the very existence of Joan is generally questioned by Roman Catholic laymen, most of whom haven't heard of her, and by Roman Catholic churchmen, most of whom have, the fact remains that she is included in the "Lives of the Popes" written by Platina, the faithful and serious fifteen-century church historian, who was a secretary to a pope and a librarian to the Vatican, and who was not excommunicated. In any event, Joan, after a period of experimentation, also got in a rut and stayed in it, but it was an extraordinarily high rut. She pretended to be a male monk and eventually became pope, under the name of John VIII. After being elevated to the papacy, and reigning as pontiff for more than two years, she inadvertently let the cat out of the bag in a motherly fashion by prematurely giving birth to a baby girl while riding in a papal procession in her imposturous role as the Holy Father.

Our modern hero, Stanley Clifford Weyman, never allowed himself to get in an imposturous rut. He performed throughout his long life one imposture after another, and once he had achieved a solid imposturous creation, he quit and left it alone. Then, after a contemplative period, he went on to perform a fresh piece of imposture. In addition to being a lieutenant in the French Navy, several doctors of medicine, and two psychiatrists, he was a number of officers in the United States Navy—ranging in rank from lieutenant to admiral—five or six United States Army officers, a couple of lawyers, the State Department Naval Liaison Officer, an aviator, a sanitation expert, many consuls-general, and a United Nations expert on Balkan and Asian affairs.

Weyman was frequently satisfied with fooling only some of the people some of the time. Unlike Pope Joan, he avoided placing himself in predicaments that would inevitably result in the exposure, and thereby the failure and discontinuance, of the imposture on which he had embarked. Like all great artists, he exercised a certain amount of restraint. For example, in his series of naval impostures he only once made the tactical error of going aboard a ship, and when he was being an Army officer he did not even once make the mistake of mingling with troops. As an aviator, he never attempted to fly an airplane; he was nevertheless cheered by New York street crowds for feats of aeronautics he hadn't performed either above the ground or on it. As the State Department Naval Liaison Officer, to be sure, he mingled with both State Department people and United States Navy people, but he sensed that the ambiguity of his assumed title was confusing, and he was right; the Navy people presumed he was a State Department person, and the State Department people presumed he was a Navy person. Except for the time he went aboard a naval vessel while posing as a naval officer, Weyman was not once in his entire career unmasked because he was improperly or unconvincingly playing the role he had assumed. He was exposed only when somebody recognized him who had seen him before in one role or another. The people who exposed Weyman were usually either newspaper reporters or photographers or officers of the law.

Weyman was sent to state and federal penitentiaries on thirteen recorded occasions after his twenty-first birthday, and spent more than a third of his adult life inside them. But on six of the thirteen occasions he was sent behind bars simply for violation of parole. When he was engaged in imposturous activities of a lofty nature, he understandably found it beyond endurance to go to lower Manhattan at regular intervals to report to a parole officer, as he was supposed to do, and when he failed to do that he was sent back to prison. Actually, for a man who dedicated his life to being people he wasn't, Weyman's criminal record was a modest one. He pleaded guilty to or was convicted of grand larceny only once, forgery only once, impersonating an attorney only once, impersonating a naval officer only twice, disorderly conduct only once, running a school for draft dodgers only once, and embezzlement only once. For some of his most successful impostures, Weyman wasn't arrested at all. For example, he wasn't arrested for posing as Pola Negri's personal physician during the funeral of her loved one, Rudolph Valentino, in New York, in 1926, or for assuming, and acting out, the role of public-relations adviser to Valentino's manager, in which role he pretty much ran the whole, fantastic funeral of the famous movie star. One reason he wasn't prosecuted for posing as a doctor that time was that Miss Negri steadfastly refused to bring a complaint against him. She informed the American Medical Association several times that Weyman was the best doctor she had ever had or ever expected to have; another reason that neither the A.M.A. nor the District Attorney's Office could make a case against Weyman for this imposture was that he not only asked for no fee but refused to accept one when Miss Negri offered to pay him for his services.

Above all else, it is Weyman's firm disregard for the importance of money and fame, his dedication to imposture for imposture's sake, that sets him apart from most other impostors in history. Many of these failed to rise to the great heights of imposturous expression because, like mediocre practitioners in all the other arts, they were more interested in material things and in fame than they were in the private satisfactions of creative accomplishment. Weyman, it is true, made efforts to earn both honest and dishonest money at various times in his long career, but almost invariably his integrity as an impostor got in the way of his impure ambition to be a rich man. And when he did, on rare occasions, amass large sums of honest money, he quickly spent them. Time and time again, his imagination, his creative impulses, and his faithfulness to his desire to be somebody other than himself prevented him from cleaning up in situations, both honest and dishonest, in which a greedier man, or a man without artistic ideals, might have made a fortune. Very often, Weyman embarked on impostures in which there was clearly no money to be made and from which he couldn't expect any fame, and some of these stand out as superior works of imposturous genius.

Prince Michael Romanoff was capable of going hungry in

preference to dropping his princely pose, though it was never recorded that he was unwilling to accept ready cash when he had none. Years ago, before Romanoff became a successful restaurant man, some of his friends found him on a New York City street, destitute and suffering from malnutrition. As his biographers have recorded, these friends took him to somebody's apartment, put him to bed, and called a doctor. Before the doctor arrived, they brought him an empty tumbler and a pint bottle of milk. In those days, two grades of milk were sold in New York—Grade A and Grade B. The Prince read the label on the pint that had been offered him. Then he struggled into a sitting position and hurled the bottle against the wall. "Grade B milk for a Romanoff!" he croaked indignantly as he sank back on the pillows.

A similar set of circumstances never confronted Weyman, but there is no doubt that he would have met them as triumphantly as Romanoff did. In some respects, Romanoff was fortunate, for without marring his princely imposture he could appear to be poor when he actually was poor. An impoverished prince is in every way artistically and imposturously acceptable, whereas a physician, a psychiatrist, a lawyer, an officer in the armed forces, or the State Department Naval Liaison Officer, like the other men Weyman pretended to be, had to seem, for the sake of authenticity, to be solvent, if not wealthy. Weyman was stone broke when he turned down Pola Negri's offer of a fee; the fact that, as a doctor, he felt above accepting that fee can be explained only by the assumption that he thought of himself at the time as being such a rich and successful physician that he couldn't stoop to take a hundred dollars or so from a charming motion-picture actress whose fits of nerves he had soothed with avuncular advice and a few aspirin tablets; he evidently felt that it would have been as if one of the heads of the Mayo Clinic had shown a willingness to accept a fee for treating somebody who had a fainting fit in a theatre.

Perhaps the most nearly perfect example of Weyman's work

that constituted imposture for imposture's sake was an occasion on which he posed as a member of the New York State lunacy commission. This was in 1925. By that time, he had been in and out of penitentiaries in New York State and in and out of the Federal Penitentiary in Atlanta, and had spent much time in the psychiatric wards of the prison hospitals. He had what he considered some constructive ideas concerning the inferior psychiatric treatment that prisoners with neurotic or psychotic personalities and manic-depressive tendencies received in those institutions. One morning, he was lounging around his home in Brooklyn in a state of depression, full of ego hunger, when he read in a newspaper that in a few days' time there was to be a meeting of every known variety of medical man, including mental medical men, at the Middlesex College of Medicine and Surgery, in Cambridge, Massachusetts. When he read that item in the newspaper, he perked up. He shaved and took a shower. From his extensive wardrobe he selected a dark-blue suit that he had bought at Brooks Brothers during one of the periods when he had made some honest money. To go with the suit he selected a Brooks Brothers shirt of the button-down-collar sort, which was then coming into vogue. Low in funds that day, he took the precaution of making himself a couple of bologna sandwiches, and he put these into a small black bag of the kind carried by general practitioners. He had often used this bag before when hanging around various hospitals, dressed in a long white coat of the sort worn by doctors on a hospital's staff, and gratifying his wish to be taken for a physician by people he chatted with. The only things he ordinarily carried in the bag, in addition to a sandwich or two, were a few bottles of tablets of a harmless kind, such as aspirin and soda mints. These he would occasionally dispense to would-be patients who got him in a corner. He was a gentle and decent man at heart, and never undertook to treat anybody who was seriously ill.

That day in 1925, he put into the bag, along with the bologna sandwiches, the aspirin, and the soda mints, a blank notebook such as he had used in high school for composition work. He also put into the bag the newspaper containing the item about the meeting at the Middlesex College of Medicine and Surgery. Around that item he had drawn a circle.

At Grand Central, Weyman caught the next train for Boston and occupied a seat in a day coach for the five hours it took to get there. From Boston, he rode the subway to Cambridge. He reached Cambridge in time to mingle with the physicians, surgeons, and psychiatrists who had come from all over. He introduced himself to them as Dr. Allen Stanley Weyman and told them he was a member of the New York State lunacy commission. To several of the psychiatrists who were attending the meeting he mentioned some of his ideas having to do with the improvement of psychiatric treatment in prison institutions, and they were so impressed by what he said and by the way he said it that they asked him to be one of the speakers at a banquet that was taking place that evening in an assembly hall of the college. He had put down some notes for just such a speech in his composition book during the train ride to Boston. According to several psychiatrists who were there, and who are still alive, his speech was vigorously applauded by one and all. Weyman left Cambridge late that evening, after being clapped on the back by many a new-found learned acquaintance, with whom he promised to keep in touch. He didn't keep in touch, and many of the psychiatrists didn't learn until years afterward that he was an impostor. Weyman asked for and got nothing out of this escapade except perhaps a sense of satisfaction at having given a leg up to a movement in which he was interested—the reformation of psychiatric services in the nation's penitentiaries. In time, these services did improve, and, to some extent, he was able to take advantage of the improvements.

This quietly magnificent piece of Weyman's imposturous work would probably never have become known to those who have studied his career if it had not been for the fact that a short time after his trip to Cambridge he was picked up in Manhattan on the humdrum charge of impersonating a lawyer. Somebody had recognized him and turned him in. Still short of funds at that time, he had pawned the briefcase he usually carried while impersonating a lawyer, and was making do with the little black bag of the medical practitioner. In this bag detectives found the newspaper with the circled item about the Middlesex meeting. They asked Weyman about it. He told them that he had attended the meeting, posing as a member of the New York State lunacy commission, but that he hadn't done so with larcenous or other criminal intentions. And when the detectives questioned the learned acquaintances Weyman had made at the medical get-together they found that what he said was true.

The name Stanley Clifford Weyman and the other names that this big little man from Brooklyn gave to and took away from himself were aliases, but they were aliases in an unusual sense. He would think them up and adopt them not so much to conceal an old identity as to adorn a new one, and he switched them around as offhandedly as he changed his hats, shoes, shirts, collars, neckties, jackets, vests, trousers, topcoats, overcoats, and military, naval, and diplomatic getups. As in the case of names, he had more clothes than any of his fellow-citizens of Brooklyn, who, on the whole, seemed to find the rituals of conformity more attractive than he did. When he was in funds, he bought all kinds of wearing apparel, and he never pawned any of it. And although from the age of twenty-one on he was frequently wanted by the police, and sometimes by the federal authorities, he never tried to hide behind a new name or an old one. As a matter of fact, he never tried to hide at all. He always made his home in the same neighborhood in Brooklyn—the one in which he was born and brought up and first arrested, and in which he was based when he carried out his first imposture. He might enter his home as Lieutenant Royal St. Cyr of

REPORTING AT WIT'S END

the French Navy and emerge from it later on as S. Clifford Weinberg, the top-hatted, striped-trousered, morning-coated Special
Deputy Attorney General of the State of New York, but he never
sneaked or ran in or out of his house, even when he knew there
was a warrant out for his arrest. At one time, he happened actually
to be—there are no two ways about it—a bona-fide Special
Deputy Attorney General of the State of New York, and on both
of two entirely tangible motorcars he owned at the time he had
placed tags of his own design that said in plain English that he was.
In the feathery galaxy of comprehensible fabrications that represented almost the entire firmament of Weyman's existence, there
occurred from time to time mundane truths such as that he *was* for
a period a Special Deputy Attorney General of the State of New
York. Standing out, as they did, in what was otherwise an orna-
mental cloudland of pure imposture, these verities tended to increase the befuddlement of men who had been instructed to find
Weyman and handcuff him, and also of men who, having no wish
to know Weyman, discovered that Weyman wished to know them,
or to *be* them.

The law-enforcement officers were further rattled by Weyman's
trait of being open and aboveboard. His neighbors in Brooklyn
grew accustomed to seeing him go in and out of his house in broad
daylight, one time as one man, another time as another man, and
soon ceased to give the matter a second thought. But the police
seem at first to have been incapable of grasping the fact that Weyman's life was an open book. They persisted in the belief that the
fellow they were after was a shamefaced scapegrace whose tactics
would be studiedly underhanded, and that he was bent on pulling
the wool over their eyes. Because they were sure he would be too
sly to go home when the heat was on, they almost never made an
effort to find him there. He was practically always there except
when he was out on some imposturous jaunt or other, yet he was
usually recognized and picked up by the police while he was

jaunting around, rather than tracked down by them to his home in Brooklyn.

All of Weyman's getups, like Weyman himself, had a Chaplinesque quality. With striped trousers and morning coat, for example, it was not unusual for him to wear a pair of tan shoes. He occasionally put on a white tie with dinner clothes or a black tie with tails. And his military and naval uniforms were never exactly right—a brass button might be missing, an epaulet might be askew, there might be too many gold stripes on one sleeve and too few on the other. Yet nobody ever seemed to notice these imperfections when face to face with Weyman and listening to Weyman talk. When Weyman was well perked up, full of self-confidence over not being himself, and his ego was fattened with success, he spoke to, and frequently barked at, people, and seemed to have a hypnotic effect on them. In any case, they almost always did exactly what he told them to do, and they usually believed everything he said to them. It was only after he had left them and their heads had begun to clear that they were able to remember that he looked quite a lot like Charlie Chaplin—or, to be more precise, like Charlie Chaplin posing as a millionaire, an admiral, an Army officer, a physician, the State Department Naval Liaison Officer, or whatever. It was sometimes not until years afterward, though, that these people found themselves able to laugh, for it was Weyman's contribution to the gaiety of nations that in one way or another he made people look funny to everybody but themselves and himself.

As things turned out, picking up Weyman without going to his Brooklyn home became comparatively easy for the New York police to accomplish. After a few years of being perplexed into a state bordering on numbness by Weyman's undeceitful ways, they appear to have put their heads together and figured out that what Weyman would probably do was try to outwit them by making himself conspicuous. Once they had evolved this theory, police detectives would nonchalantly haunt the most noteworthy event that was enlivening metropolitan life on a particular day, and, sure enough, they would usually find Weyman mixed up in it some-where, and possibly in charge of it. They would recognize him by his face and pick him up.

An example of what came to be the standard police method of capturing Weyman occurred on April 23, 1917, when he was twenty-six years old. On that day, nothing much was going on in Manhattan, but there was a military shindig in progress at an ar-mory in Brooklyn. Police Detective Francis X. Sullivan, of the Delancey Street station, in Manhattan, wanted Weyman, because a while earlier Weyman had forged the name of United States Senator William M. Calder to a letter of recommendation that had landed Weyman a job as a cashier at a downtown branch of the Bank of United States. Weyman hadn't run off with any of the bank's funds, and wasn't trying to, but Senator Calder, the bank, and the District Attorney's Office felt that Weyman's procedure in getting the job had been felonious. Detective Sullivan went over to the armory in Brooklyn and hung around. Weyman showed up after a short time, and Sullivan recognized his face, if not the rest of him. On the one occasion that Sullivan had seen him before, Weyman had been wearing the top hat, morning coat, and striped trousers of his identity as the Consul General of Rumania. Now he was in the dress uniform of a rear admiral of the United States Navy—a striking outfit, with a high-crowned cap, epaulets, flotil-las of brass buttons, and garlands of gold braid. It was the sort of naval uniform that is never seen anymore except in movies or on the covers of historical novels. After returning the salute that the Army sentries at the entrance to the armory gave him, Weyman sailed inside, received and returned a salute from the major general in charge, and told the general that, as a gesture of interservice cour-tesy, he had come to inspect the troops. Sullivan, like most human beings, took pleasure in delaying a foreseeable climax, and he drifted along unobtrusively in the admiral's wake. The general was about to start inspecting the troops with the admiral when Sullivan lunged, put the handcuffs on the admiral, and took him to the Delancey Street station house.

Sullivan could have had Weyman earlier that day if he had simply gone to Weyman's home in Brooklyn and waited for him to come out, or had walked into the house and pounced on him while he was taking off the uniform of the French Navy in order to put on the uniform of the United States Navy. Weyman had been St. Cyr that morning. Newspaper clippings and a railway stub that were taken from his wallet when he was booked at the Delancey Street station house showed that he had just come back in a lower berth of a Pullman car from a visit to Washington, D.C., where, as Lieutenant St. Cyr of the French Navy, he had been, as the society editor of the Washington *Evening Star* put it, "among the more colorful guests" at a succession of dinner parties. One of these dinners was a stag affair given for a group of men of consequence by Vice-President Thomas R. Marshall, who was celebrated in those days as a conscious humorist rather than an unconscious one, and was the man who said, among other witty things, that what this country needed was a good five-cent cigar.

Weyman didn't get to the White House on that 1917 trip to Washington. The Chief Executive at that time was, of course, Woodrow Wilson. When Weyman was searched at the Delancey Street station house, there was a letter in his pocket from Mrs. Wilson's social secretary, which was addressed to "My dear Lieutenant St. Cyr," and which said, "In reply to your letter of recent date, permit me to say that the President and Mrs. Wilson have so many engagements in the near future that it would be impossible to arrange a time when they could conveniently receive Mme. St. Cyr and yourself." At that time, Weyman wasn't any more married than he was an officer in the French Navy or in the United States Navy. In spite of a contrary impression he gave many people who were casually acquainted with him, or who cursorily studied his career, Weyman was married only once, and he stayed married to the woman of his choice. Both his courtship and his marriage were as tempestuous—and perhaps as happy—as those of the hero of *The Taming of the Shrew*. However, one of his foibles, both before and after his marriage, was to offer rare treats, such as prearranged visits to the White House, to ladies of his acquaintance. He nearly always came through with what he offered, too. Four years after the 1917 visit to Washington, he promised to take a different lady to call on President and Mrs. Warren G. Harding, and he came through with that in grand style. That he was not received at the White House until the summer of 1921 should not be taken as an indication that he wouldn't have got in there sooner if he had been able to try again after his initial failure with the Wilsons. He didn't have a good chance to try the Wilsons a second time because he was in prison almost continuously from the day Detective Sullivan picked him up in April, 1917, until March, 1920, and by that time the Wilsons were in their last year in the White House and the President was recovering from his illness. And Weyman probably could and would have called on the Hardings on one pretext or another soon after Harding's inauguration, in March, 1921, if he had not been away on a foreign mission. In late 1920 and for a part of 1921, Weyman was working as a physician and sanitation expert for an American engineering company in Lima, Peru.

There were many things that might have furrowed the deceptively noble brow of President Harding in the summer of 1921, but that he was worried about the newly independent country of Afghanistan is not indicated in any of the studies of his troubled Administration that have been made—by his admirers or by his detractors. On the whole, the international scene in the summer of 1921 was similar to the international scene in the summer of 1968. Everybody was talking about disarmament, and President Harding was inviting the principal powers to a summit conference.

There was a strong objection in some quarters to United States foreign policy in the Far East. China, which had not been invited to the conference, was trying to get itself invited. The collapse of the Communist government of Russia was being prophesied in the West, and the Russian Chairman, Nikolai Lenin, was advocating peaceful coexistence with the capitalist countries until such time as the wave of worldwide Communism enveloped them. Anti-American sentiments were discernible in the Caribbean, and Cuba was complaining about the United States policy there. As for the domestic scene, an editorial in the *Times* stated that the country was "groaning under taxes." Almost everybody in Congress was complaining that the United States was giving too much money away to foreign countries. The Secretary of Labor felt so passionately about the necessity for a balanced federal budget that he had just announced that his department was going to save fifty thousand dollars a year by using pencils without erasers. The Washington baseball team was playing miserable baseball. Forward-looking citizens in all sections of the country were urging that more playgrounds be built for underprivileged children. By this means, they asserted, juvenile delinquency would be eliminated. Bills had been introduced in Congress to make Lincoln's birthday a legal holiday in the District of Columbia, but the Southern Democrats were dubious about it. They threatened a filibuster. On the day that Weyman was to take a lady to the White House, President Harding had just returned from a camping trip in Maryland with Henry Ford, Thomas Edison, and Harvey S. Firestone, and he was looking forward to playing eighteen holes of golf that afternoon.

It is doubtful if Weyman cared any more or knew any more about Afghanistan at the beginning of that summer of 1921 than President Harding himself did. Prince Amanullah Khan had become Amir of Afghanistan in 1919, displacing his uncle, Nasrullah Khan, and in May of that year Amanullah had sent troops into India against the armies of Great Britain, which, with her allies, had at last succeeded in defeating Germany in the First World War. After a few weeks of sporadic fighting in the deserts and mountains of the Gunga Din terrain—the terrain that had set Kipling atingle and that later spawned so many motion pictures—Amanullah sued for peace. A temporary treaty with Great Britain was signed at Rawalpindi on August 8, 1919, whereby Amanullah lost the annual subsidy that Britain had been granting the country but obtained— or so he thought—freedom from British control over his relations with other foreign powers. His envoys signed a treaty with Russia in February of 1921 and with Turkey the following month. In July of that year, Amanullah sent a diplomatic mission to Washington, headed by Prince Mohammed Wall Khan, perhaps with the idea of signing a treaty with the United States. Prince Mohammed and his mission arrived in Washington but got very little attention in the newspapers; in fact, nobody, including Secretary of State Charles Evans Hughes and President Harding, seemed to be very much interested in him or his mission.

However, there arrived in New York that same month a princess from Afghanistan, and she got a great deal of attention in the New York newspapers. Her name was Princess Fatima. She wore long robes "like nightgowns," according to one reporter, and in her left nostril she wore a large sapphire. She was a comfortably stout, mahogany-colored lady of middle age. She had come to New York by train from San Francisco, having taken ship from Karachi and sailed through the Indian Ocean and across the Pacific to California. She was accompanied by her three teen-age sons, whose names were Ashin, Azic, and Akber, and she and her sons were ceremonially received at City Hall by Mayor John F. Hylan and given keys to the city. To the New York newspaper reporters on that day, Princess Fatima said that she was going to England by way of America for two reasons—she wished to be introduced to "that handsome man"

President Warren G. Harding, at the White House, and she hoped to dispose of an enormous diamond she had brought with her from India. This diamond, the newspapers noted, was called the Durya-i-Moor and was a jewel of great worth that had been in her branch of the Afghan royal family since the time of Alexander the Great. The newspapers said that the name of the diamond meant, in English, River of Glory. With the proceeds she expected from the sale of the diamond, Princess Fatima told the newspapers, she intended, after meeting the President in Washington, to go on to England and send her sons to Eton and Oxford.

The day after these revelations, which were accompanied in the newspapers by photographs of the Princess in her robes and with the sapphire in her nose, Associated Press dispatches from Washington indicated that she might encounter some difficulty in getting an introduction to President Harding. It was pointed out in these dispatches that Prince Mohammed Wall Khan of Afghanistan was in Washington as the head of a mission from the Amir, and that he had been unable to arrange a meeting with Secretary of State Hughes, let alone President Harding. It appeared that the British Ambassador, Lord Hardinge of Penshurst, had asked the State Department to hold off on establishing formal diplomatic relations with Afghanistan until Great Britain had signed a permanent treaty with the newly independent kingdom. The Associated Press noted that Prince Mohammed was annoyed about the whole situation. Its dispatches from Washington said that he had spoken unchivalrously of Princess Fatima when asked about her, and that he had said she was a distant cousin of his ruler, the Amir, and "a member of the tribe of Mohammed Zaie." History tells us that it was not until November of that year that Great Britain signed its permanent treaty with Afghanistan, and it was not until fifteen years later that formal diplomatic relations were established between the United States and Afghanistan. Whether Prince Mohammed waited around for this event, or went away and came back, or went away and was replaced by some other diplomat, history doesn't tell us. In any event, he didn't get to meet President Harding in 1921.

But Princess Fatima did. After expressing her wish to meet President Harding, she settled down in a suite at the Waldorf with her three sons and began negotiating with some jewellers for the sale of her diamond. And, of all the hundreds of thousands of New Yorkers who read in the newspapers that week in July of 1921 about Princess Fatima's chagrin at not being able to go to Washington and meet President Harding, only one person did anything about it. This one person was Weyman. Before the month of July was out, Weyman had taken the Princess and her three sons to Washington on the Congressional Limited—after telling everybody in an entirely convincing fashion that he was "the State Department Naval Liaison Officer" and telephoning the White House to make an appointment—to meet President Harding. He had then simply led the Princess and her three sons into the White House. There he performed the introductions, and later he posed on the White House lawn for a group photograph that included the President, Mrs. Harding, the military and naval aides at the White House, and the Princess and her three sons. Only a little over a month after he had first read about Princess Fatima in the newspapers, he returned to his home in Brooklyn, having washed his hands of the whole affair. His work of art had been accomplished, and he was done with it.

It was a long time, though, before the State Department in Washington was able to wash *its* hands of the whole affair, and when it did wash them, it turned the whole affair over to the Department of Justice. By then, the State Department file on Weyman weighed about five and a half pounds. Its file on Afghanistan up to the time of the beginning of its file on Weyman was so skimpy that the Afghanistan file was simply stuffed into the Weyman file. The combined file covering that period opened with a letter from the British Embassy to the State Department. It was addressed to Secretary of State Hughes and was signed by Lord Hardinge, and it said, "My government do not look with favor on the activities of this [the Afghanistan] mission or their endeavors to conclude agreements with other countries. . . . We consider Afghanistan, though ostensibly independent, as still within our sphere of political influence, and are anxious to discourage any proceedings which imply that we are not concerned in the foreign relations of that country." On July 9th—before the arrival of Princess Fatima in New York—Mr. Warren D. Robbins, the acting head of the State Department's Division of Near Eastern Affairs, wrote a memorandum to Secretary Hughes that said, "I trust it will not be necessary to take up the President's or your valuable time with this [the Afghanistan] mission. We have, to my knowledge, no particular interest in Afghanistan, and in view of the British attitude toward the object of this mission, it would seem to me that we might accede to the desires and pay as little attention to the mission as we can with propriety do."

This was the entire file on Afghanistan when Weyman, lying in bed late one morning at his home in Brooklyn, read in the New York newspapers about Princess Fatima's desire to meet President Harding, and about the standoffish attitude that the State Department had adopted toward the Afghanistan mission in Washington and, by extension, toward the Princess in New York. Weyman had been feeling depressed for weeks, and his ego was ravenous. He had simply been lounging around the house, spending much of his time in bed. But when he read about Princess Fatima and her dilemma he began to perk up. He decided he was the man to take her and her sons to Washington and introduce them to President and Mrs. Harding.

For Weyman, perking up constituted a rather extraordinary physiological and emotional process. In later life, he described this process time and time again to any number of psychiatrists, both in prison and on the outside, and, in addition to that, a number of the prison psychiatrists were able to observe him in the act of perking up. From all the available evidence, it seems that what happened to Weyman when he read about Princess Fatima in the newspapers was that he pictured himself introducing her to President and Mrs. Harding at the White House. Then, in a flash, he asked himself why *he* would be introducing Princess Fatima to President and Mrs. Harding at the White House, and he quickly answered himself that he would be doing this because he was the State Department Naval Liaison Officer. In a jiffy, he had shaved his jowls—but not his Charlie Chaplin mustache—taken a bath, and put on a uniform that made him look something like a commander in the United States Navy. The fact that there was no such thing as the State Department Naval Liaison Officer didn't bother him, any more than the fact that his uniform was actually that of an officer in the United States Junior Naval Reserves, a non-governmental organization that was a kind of seagoing Boy Scout affair.

Well perked up, Weyman rushed out of his Brooklyn house on that July morning in 1921 and boarded an I.R.T. subway train. He got off at Seventh Avenue and Thirty-fourth Street, walked the two blocks to the old Waldorf-Astoria, and blew into the lobby at around eleven o'clock. He was soon talking with Princess Fatima and her three sons. The turbulent cascade of words that issued from the lips under the wispy mustache included a question about whether she would be ready to go to Washington within a week or ten days. She delightedly said that she and her sons could go any day at all. A few days later, Mr. Robert Woods Bliss, Third Assistant Secretary of State, got a long-distance telephone call from New York in the course of which he was told that Rodney S. Wyman, the State Department Naval Liaison Officer, wished to report to him that Princess Fatima was agreeable to seeing President and Mrs. Harding on or about July 25th, and that he, Wyman, would make arrangements for the visit by communicating directly with the

White House. Bliss took this to mean that one of his superiors in the State Department—possibly Secretary of State Hughes—had decided that Princess Fatima ought to meet President and Mrs. Harding, and so he told the State Department Naval Liaison Officer "Uh-huh," or syllables to that effect. After hanging up the telephone, Bliss read over to himself a memorandum from the acting head of Near Eastern Affairs, addressed to Secretary of State Hughes and dated July 14th, that said:

1. The Department was not notified by any diplomatic or consular office that Princess Fatima intended to visit the U.S. She arrived as an individual and without any credentials or recommendations.

2. Newspaper clippings indicate that her relations are not cordial with the Afghanistan mission.

3. There is no need for the President or Secretary of State to receive the mission. If mission is not received, there is no need for the Princess to be received. Moreover, unpleasant feeling may be created between the Mission and the Princess if the latter should be received while the former is not.

4. If, on the other hand, it should be deemed advisable to receive the Mission, the importance of its being received might be somewhat diminished should the Princess also be received. Such a course, if it should meet with the Secretary's approval, would probably please the British.

Bliss was a very rich and charming fellow whose residence was a huge Georgetown estate called Dumbarton Oaks. He was accustomed to thinking hard about international affairs late in the morning after garden parties, dinner parties, supper dances, and balls. When Bliss had looked at the Afghan affair every which way over some black coffee around half past eleven (and looked forward to lunch), it seemed obvious to him that if the State Department

Naval Liaison Officer was arranging for Princess Fatima to be received by President and Mrs. Harding on July 25th, it might be a good thing for the Secretary of State to acquaint the President with at least some of the facts about the complex Afghan situation before the Princess arrived. According to the State Department file on Weyman and Afghanistan, Secretary Hughes briefed the President on Afghanistan on July 18th.

The meeting of Princess Fatima with President Harding was described at length in the Washington *Post* of July 26th. On the afternoon of the same day, the Washington *Evening Star* published a photograph of Princess Fatima, her three sons, President and Mrs. Harding, and "Commander Rodney Sterling Wyman of the United States Naval Reserve, the State Department Naval Liaison Officer." The *Star*'s write-up was rather matter-of-fact, but the *Post*'s story was all that its readers could ask for.

> Royalty touched hands with Democracy at the White House yesterday [the *Post* said] when Princess Fatima, Sultana of Afghanistan, and her three sons were received by President Harding in special audience. They were accompanied by Prince Zerdecheno, Crown Prince of Egypt. The President received the party in the Red Room.
>
> Seldom has the President received a more picturesque group. The brilliant hues of the Princess' garments and jewels were contrasted with the sombre hues of the conventional clothes worn by the men of the party, to which their turbans added a striking touch.
>
> The costume of the princess was of deep pink satin heavily embroided in Egyptian designs in gold and black. The coatlike bodice was high at the neck and had loose sleeves, which revealed many bracelets when she moved her arms. Her skirt was narrow and ankle length, bearing a close resemblance to the present harem boudoir gowns.

The pièce de résistance was the large sapphire worn like an earring in the left nostril. A huge 50-carat diamond, enormous diamond pendant earrings, many chains of pearls and other jewels, a jewelled girdle about her waist, and a long veil caught about her head by a close fitting bandeau of green ostrich feathers and twined about her waist completed the costume. She wore American-made sandals of black kid and a glimpse of conventional black silk stockings could be seen as she walked.

The Princess brought gifts of cashmere shawls, veils, Kermanshah rugs, table cloths, and turbans to the President. One veil was a counterpart of the one worn by the Princess and is woven of finest wool. Its gossamer quality was suggestive of the softest, silkiest chiffon and was shot through with stripes and embroidered in 14-carat gold thread.

Princess Fatima told the President through an interpreter [Weyman] that she was in this country as a traveller and to obtain an education for her sons and to acquire an understanding of the United States.

"I admire your civic ideals and institutions," the Princess said, "and the glorious history of your land. It is God's chosen land."

It is understood she asked for the quasi-protection of the government usually accorded to royal travellers who are not the official guests of the nation. The President welcomed her cordially and expressed interest in her mission.

In her apartment in the Willard, the princess sat in state and talked through an interpreter [Weyman] with the Washington *Post* reporter. She said she had been in most of the countries in the old world, but was so impressed by America [by that time] she might decide to make her future home here instead of staying only four years while her sons obtained an American education.

"When I first arrived in New York," the Princess

exclaimed, "I thought it the most symmetrical city in the world, but it cannot compare with Washington. Your men and your women are so interesting, too. I want to learn what I can from them so I may help my own people."

Princess Fatima is unique among the women of her race as an advocate of women's suffrage and is the only woman of her family who does not wear a veil over her face. For a number of years she has been living in India.

The princess and her party were escorted around the Capitol by Senator Medill McCormick of Illinois. They listened, with the aid of an interpreter [Weyman], with great interest to the discussions in both chambers.

Secretary Hughes will receive the party this morning. Prince Akber Khan, one of the sons, expressed a desire to see the great seal of the United States and the original Declaration of Independence. The princess wanted to see the little red trunk in the library of the State Department in which Dolly Madison carried the Articles of Confederation in her flight across Chain Bridge to Virginia when the British burned Washington in 1814.

A visit to the tomb of Washington to place a tribute at the shrine of the great American whose fame has also reached to their native land is also a part of the program planned by the royal visitors.

Comdr. Rodney Sterling Wyman, U.S. Naval Militia, is acting as personal adviser and physician to the princess [as well as her interpreter].

The princess, it was learned, takes out her nose jewel when she goes to bed at night, as other women remove their earrings. Unlike American women, she is not afraid of rats, mice, or bats. The reason for this immunity from those customary feminine fears is that in the Mohammed religion, which she professes, not only cats but all animals are sacred.

Readers of this chronicle will have noted that the *Post* story said Princess Fatima's party was "accompanied by Prince Zerdecheno, Crown Prince of Egypt." Here the *Post* was not quite accurate. Prince Zerdecheno hadn't gone into the White House with the Princess's party—or Weyman's party—but had only come out of it with that party. The Prince was an impostor himself. He had talked his way into the Executive Mansion somehow and had made his exit with the Princess on or near his right arm. More will be said about the obtrusive Crown Prince of Egypt in due course.

The fact that Weyman (or Wyman) was described in the *Post* as "acting as personal adviser and physician to the Princess" should be put down not to careless journalism but to the excessively rapid and seemingly whimsical changeableness that Weyman displayed in telling people just who he was. What appears to have happened in this instance is that Weyman decided that his usefulness as the State Department Naval Liaison Officer had run out when he walked into the White House and introduced Princess Fatima and her sons to President Harding. He therefore told Princess Fatima after the White House ceremony that the State Department had given him a leave of absence in order to let him act as her personal adviser and interpreter, and he threw in as an afterthought the statement that he was a doctor of medicine, in case she needed a doctor of medicine. Whatever he was, he was able on that trip to Washington to chalk up a meeting with Woodrow Wilson and Mrs. Wilson against his failure to meet them in 1917. While he was returning from a quick visit to Mount Vernon in a hired limousine with Princess Fatima and her sons, the limousine had a blowout. Woodrow Wilson and his wife happened to be passing by in another limousine, and saw the predicament of the Princess and her party, stranded at the side of the road. The former President told his chauffeur to stop. Weyman performed the introductions while the Wilsons' chauffeur helped the Princess's chauffeur fix the tire.

A good time having been had in Washington by all, Weyman

returned to New York with Princess Fatima and her sons. Prince Zerdecheno had tried to stay close to the party, but Weyman had given him the cold shoulder and some heated words, and the Crown Prince had sloped off to other pursuits, only to turn up later in New York, as will be seen. Somewhere along the line, and somewhere in Weyman's head, a grandiose plan had been formulated under which Weyman hoped to persuade the Princess to persuade the United States government to give her some land and an annual stipend. A few days later, Mr. Henry Fletcher, Under Secretary of State, received a letter about this from New York, signed by Princess Fatima. The Princess could speak and write English perfectly well, having been educated at English schools both in England and in India, and the fact that she spoke to President Harding through an interpreter must be put down to a desire on her part to make that meeting appear to be more highfalutin than it was by pretending that she knew no English. In this sense, she was engaging in imposture herself, along with Weyman and the so-called Crown Prince of Egypt. In any case, students of Weyman's mind and of Weyman's prose have reason to believe that the letter to Mr. Fletcher from Princess Fatima was written by Weyman; in fact, it could hardly have been written by anybody else. Here are some excerpts from this letter:

> We sincerely feel that this country is the haven of all who aspire to live under a rational system of government. Your political system is the Utopia of all forms of government, autocratic and otherwise. For precisely this reason, it is the desire of my children and self, to reside in this country permanently with the avowed intention of becoming citizens thereof . . . In order that we may carry our plans into execution, it is requested that this government may grant us requisite lands in any part of the territorial domains and stipend. We wish to be

treated as members of foreign royalty and not as citizens. We are the only members of royalty that have come from such a far distance to visit this country. It has come to our information that, by enactment of a federal statute, lands are granted only to those who have exercised the prerogatives of citizenship. In the event of this information being accurate, we ask this government to waive said restrictions so as to enable us to procure requisite acreage for our sustenance and well-being. . . . By reason of circumstances which cannot be divulged in this communication, we would elect to make this country our permanent residence . . .

There is no record of a reply from Mr. Fletcher. It may be that he was mulling over the nice question of whether, in order to receive territorial domains and an annual stipend, Princess Fatima would have to relinquish her Afghan citizenship and become a citizen of the United States or whether it would be simpler for the government just to go ahead and waive these restrictions. In any event, Fletcher seems to have had no keen desire to dwell on the matter, for he quickly turned the letter over to the already quivering Third Assistant Secretary of State, Mr. Bliss.

For weeks afterward there seemed to be no means by which Bliss could return to his gay, carefree ways. On August 14th, for example, he received a wire from Weyman that said,

PRINCESS FATIMA SULTANA WISHES TO MAKE APPOINTMENT WITH YOU AFTER 20TH REGARDING PERSONAL MATTER WILL IT BE ALL RIGHT FOR ME TO COME ALONG ARMED WITH ALL NECESSARY DOCUMENTS AND DATA IN HER BEHALF ADVISE DATE AND INFORMATION.

The telegram was from "RODNEY S. WYMAN, HOTEL MARSEILLES, NEW YORK." By that time, the Princess and her party, including

Weyman, had moved from the Waldorf to the Marseilles, because the Princess, who hadn't sold her diamond, was running out of cash. Bliss wired Weyman the same day,

PREFER YOU WOULD WRITE ME DETAILS OF MATTER TO WHICH YOUR TELEGRAM ASKING FOR AN APPOINTMENT REFERS.

Frustrated by this telegram, Weyman went through one of his swift changes of attitude. He decided that the request for a territorial grant and an annual stipend, which he had persuaded Princess Fatima to make, was not a good idea, and that the Princess was to blame for the fact that it was not a good idea. In the grip of this new attitude, Weyman telephoned Bliss and then whipped off the following letter to him:

MY DEAR MR. BLISS:

Supplementing conversation with you this afternoon regarding letter sent you by Princess Fatima, wish to state that same was sent to you, although the letter itself was addressed to Mr. Fletcher. Inasmuch as I have taken this matter up with you, I would ask that you make reply to same, in the event that it has gone to Mr. Fletcher.

Personally, I wish to make it clear that I realize the fallacy of her request, but she has insisted that same go forward, and has even advised that I go to Washington to see you.

I suggest that the entire situation be made clear to her, citing that part of the law which deals with grants of land to citizens only, and that if she proposes to make this country her permanent place of abode, she will receive that which is usually accorded to all citizens.

You may state therein that you have discussed the matter with me and in this manner I will be in a more secure position to deal with her and impress her as needs be.

Inasmuch as she will carry with her on her return to India certain impressions, it is advised that your letter be made as conciliatory as possible under the circumstances.

Trusting you will pardon my seeming presumption, I beg to remain, my dear Secretary,

Sincerely,

RODNEY S. WYMAN

Faithfully following Weyman's advice, Bliss wrote, on August 20th, a rather long letter to Princess Fatima explaining, in conciliatory terms, that it was utterly impossible for the United States government to award her any grant of land or any annual stipend, and that there would be even less chance of its being done if she became a citizen of the United States than if she remained a member of the royal family of Afghanistan. Bliss's prose had for some reason begun to sound like Weyman's prose. At one point in his letter he said, "Captain Wyman had previously discussed this matter with me from New York by telephone, and I beg to confirm the information which I then communicated to him to the following effect . . ."

If Bliss thought that after writing this letter he was through with Princess Fatima and Weyman, he was mistaken. On September 11th, he received the following wire from Weyman, which had been dispatched from New York at five-twenty that morning:

AM TAKING THIS OPPORTUNITY OF ADVISING YOU FINANCIAL AF-FAIRS PRINCESS FATIMA ABSOLUTELY PENNILESS AND I HAVE AD-VANCED HER 700 TO SEPT FIRST STOP SHE HAS CONTRACTED VARIOUS OBLIGATIONS IN THIS CITY AND ELSEWHERE CLAIMS SHE HAS FUNDS IN INDIA STOP I HAVE CABLED FOR SAME JULY 28 NONE FORTHCOMING STOP UNPRINCIPLED IN HER DEALINGS WITH ME AND IN GENERAL IS ASSOCIATING WITH FAKE CROWN PRINCE EGYPT RECENTLY EXPOSED BY NEW YORK WORLD STOP SONS IMMORAL

AND BECOMING RECOGNIZED CHARACTERS STOP SHE HAS PLEDGED
JEWELRY AT NEW WILLARD AND IN THIS CITY STOP SITUATION
SUCH THAT I BELIEVE SHOULD BE BROUGHT TO YOUR ATTENTION
STOP SHE IS SURROUNDED BY NUMEROUS PSEUDO ADVISORS STOP
INDIANS STUDYING AT COLUMBIA WHO AGITATE AGAINST BRITISH
GOVERNMENT PROPAGANDA FROM THIS CITY STOP WILL TRANSMIT
DETAILED REPORT UPON REPLY STOP ADVISE FULLY.

Just what was going on in Bliss's throbbing brain by this time is
not made clear in the State Department file. Some authorities on
Weyman's career believe that it had begun to dawn on the State
Department that there was no State Department Naval Liaison Officer, and that the dapper, charming man with the thin mustache
who had arranged for Princess Fatima to meet President Harding
and had convinced both the White House and the State Department that in doing so he was acting for the State Department
was an impostor. It is claimed by the followers of this school of
thought that Lord Hardinge, the British Ambassador, huffed and
puffed with rage when he read in the newspapers that Princess Fatima had been introduced to President Harding and was carrying
on generally as if she were a citizen of a free country. He is then
supposed to have gone to the State Department and protested the
uncompliant attitude that it was showing in respect to Great Britain's
desire to go right on controlling Afghanistan and all Afghans as it
had been doing ever since Disraeli presented India to Queen Victoria as another jewel for her crown. It is at this point that the State
Department is supposed to have initiated an intra-departmental inquiry as to just who it was who had made the commitment under
which the cornerstone of the State Department's policy toward
Afghanistan seemed to be that President Harding ought to shake
hands with Princess Fatima. However, in the light of all the available evidence, it now seems more likely that the State Department
had forgotten—or, at least, had wished to forget—that the intro-

duction of Princess Fatima to President Harding was not an act of God but something that had been initiated by the State Department itself or by somebody (Weyman) *acting for* the State Department. At any rate, there is no evidence that the State Department was in a mood to find fault with itself in relation to the Princess Fatima episode until September 13th—seven weeks after the introduction had been performed. On that day, Princess Fatima herself wrote to Secretary of State Hughes. This letter was obviously not composed by Weyman (who, incidentally, had promoted himself from commander to captain by this time), or by anybody but Princess Fatima. It went as follows:

The Honorable Charles Evans Hughes,
Secretary of State,
State Department,
Washington, D.C.
Dear Sir:

About two weeks ago I gave Capt. Wyman, who was sent by the State Department to help me, some four articles as presents from me to Mrs. Hughes. He had promised me to present them to you at once, but I very much doubt whether he ever did so. While here, and with me, he behaved in a very objectionable manner, and did great disservice to me, instead of being helpful to me, for which purpose I understand the State Department had sent him here. His hostile activities have compelled me to dispense with his help, and I have nothing to do with him any longer.

But in spite of my several requests he has failed to respond to me re the presents I had given him to carry to Mrs. Hughes.

I do not know whether he has presented these to you or Mrs. Hughes either. I shall feel very thankful to you if you would let me know they have been received there. In case you have not received them, would you ask Capt. Wyman to make them over to you right away.

With best wishes and kind regards to you and Mrs. Hughes, I am,

Yours sincerely,
PRINCESS FATIMA

Though it might be supposed that this letter would stir up the State Department, there is nothing in its Wyman-Afghanistan file to indicate that it did. Three days after writing it, Princess Fatima—clearly having received no reply from the State Department—wrote a second letter to Secretary Hughes, in which she had this to say:

It is a sad thing that the purpose of my addressing you on this occasion is an unhappy one. But the circumstances force me to write to you things which I have hitherto hesitated to even touch upon.

Captain Wyman came to me one day, when I was staying at the Hotel Waldorf-Astoria, and told me that he was detailed by the State Department to be helpful to the Afghanistan Royal Party. A few days later he brought some letters addressed to me from the State Department stating that Captain Wyman was a thoroughly reliable man, that the State Department guaranteed his honesty, and that I could safely place my affairs in his hands. This appeared to me to be quite sufficient testimony and I trusted him with many of my personal affairs. One of the first things which was managed by Captain Wyman was my trip to Washington to see Mr. Harding. The story of this trip is long in its details, but it would be enough to mention here that he spent the better part of the $600 I had placed in his hands, without my permission or knowledge. When I learned of the expenses he had done, I was astonished, but the bills having been drawn up in my name, I had to pay them all just to avoid unpleasantness. But that did not end the trouble. Captain Wyman so manipulated my affairs in New York that all my money was spent, and I was left in a fix. He then tried to fool me into something like auctioning the diamond I possessed. I refused to do that, but I was persuaded to give him the power of attorney for the sale of the stone, at my price. This document was duly signed by me, countersigned by a notary public. Now more than two months passed and he failed to arrange for the sale of the diamond. Then I asked him to return the papers, which he flatly refused to do.

On August 13, I was informed on the telephone by one of your staff that if I went over to Washington in person I would know better after conversation with Mr. Bliss the situation regarding my application dated August 9. I decided to go to Washington on the 18th. But one morning Captain Wyman came to me and said that the State Department had instructed him to tell me that I should not go to Washington and that I should send Wyman alone with my family papers. Believing his words to be true, I gave the family papers to him. Then after a few days absence he returned and told me that the State Department had examined the papers and is going to address me a letter regarding the matter shortly. But the letter never came, and he charged me about forty-two dollars for this trip which I doubt whether he ever took.

In many cases it has been proven that he actually incited the people to file suits against me for debts of whose existence I had no knowledge. And all this time, he posed as my secretary.

The instances of his improper behavior were legion, but I always thought of the recommendations of the State Department and of his character as your representative with me.

But my latest discovery of his misdemeanor is simply astounding. It so happened that I owed a sum of $339 to the New Willard Hotel of Washington. I gave $200 to Wyman to be paid to this hotel as a part payment. He brought to me a paper which he called a receipt by the New Willard Hotel for $200. Then came the representative of the New Willard Hotel to collect the bill. I showed him the receipt for $200 and offered to pay the balance of $139. But he informed me that the receipt was false and that the New Willard had not received any part of the $200. On closer examination and further investigation, I am convinced that Captain Wyman has cheated me for this amount of money too. I have been trying for the last ten days to get in touch with him, but he has successfully evaded coming in contact with me. I therefore naturally feel inclined to start legal proceedings against him. But since he was your representative, I deem it advisable first to inform you of the whole affair and request you to tell me as soon as possible if you could do something to help me recover from him the money I have been robbed of. It would save me a great deal of trouble and expense in this foreign land if you could take steps to have my grievance redressed.

Very truly yours,
PRINCESS FATIMA SULTANA

It appears from the State Department file that upon receiving this letter the State Department was at last stirred up. Secretary of State Hughes and his various assistants turned the matter over to one of the State Department's special agents, R. C. Bannerman, to investigate and, if possible, interview the man who had introduced Princess Fatima to President Harding.

The State Department had asked the New York police to try to find Rodney Sterling Wyman—the only name the State Department had for our man—and place him under arrest for having impersonated a naval officer, since the impersonation had occurred in New York as well as in Washington. The police had reported to the State Department that they had been unable to find Rodney

Sterling Wyman, and it is evident that they did not recognize the name as merely another name for the impostor they had been well acquainted with since 1911 and had arrested three times (for grand larceny in 1911, for forgery in 1917, and for impersonating a naval officer in 1920), besides having been concerned in picking him up for violation of parole four times. Bannerman, the State Department special agent in Washington, was sent to New York with instructions to report to R. S. Sharp, the State Department special agent in New York. This was a matter of State Department protocol, Sharp being superior in rank to Bannerman. Sharp turned Bannerman loose on the case, and Bannerman soon found that in a number of letters to Princess Fatima the impostor had given his address as 71 Maujer Street, Brooklyn, and his telephone number as Stagg 3060.

I called at 71 Maujer Street in an endeavor to locate Wyman and found a lady there who disclaimed any knowledge of Wyman but stated I might be able to find him in one of the other houses [Bannerman noted in a report to Sharp]. In the one she suggested, I found a man named Weinberg, an elderly man, who emphatically stated that he knew nothing of Wyman. Later, in checking up the telephone number, I found that Stagg 3060 was in a drugstore at 292 Leonard Street. The druggist, on being questioned as to Wyman's home address, said, "Oh, he lives across the street—perhaps at 617." I proceeded to 617 Metropolitan Avenue, which was the place referred to, and searched the building completely. I found no trace of Wyman. I returned once more to the drugstore and was informed by a clerk there that Wyman did live at 617 Metropolitan Avenue but that he was known there by his real name, which was Weinberg. There, after diligent research, I found Wyman's wife, a frail little girl, with a baby three or four months old, and her mother, a Mrs. Sheer. They told me that the lady I had spoken to at 71 Maujer Street was his mother, Mrs. Weinberg. They also stated that the elderly man I had spoken to was his father. They said his father would have nothing to do with him but that his mother at all times protected him as far as possible.

Having ascertained where Weyman could be found, Bannerman took up with the Naval Intelligence people in New York the matter of bringing about the impostor's arrest for impersonating a naval officer. He found that the Naval Intelligence people did not wish to have anything to do with the case. In his report to Sharp, he implied that the reason for this was that, the year before the Princess Fatima incident, the impostor had been hobnobbing with Admiral Henry Braid Wilson, who was Commander-in-Chief of the Atlantic Fleet. He had been a guest of the Admiral's at dinner on several occasions. It was the Admiral's fear of notoriety that caused the intelligence people to adopt their hands-off policy, Bannerman indicated. In looking further into the case of this 1920 impersonation by the impostor, Bannerman found that Weyman had merely been brought before a Brooklyn judge, fined ten dollars, and released, even though he was on parole from another conviction at the time. With this information Bannerman concluded his report to Sharp, and Sharp then sent to Washington a rather pointed memorandum addressed to Mr. Bliss, which gave the gist of Bannerman's report and said, among other things, "I call your special attention to the fact that the officials of the State Department made no preliminary inquiries as to the rights of this criminal to represent Princess Fatima. It is apparent that if any preliminary inquiry had been made regarding the status of this man it would have developed the entire situation at once. I therefore close the case out without further instructions to Special Agent Bannerman as to the prosecution of this criminal and refer it to your office for such further action as the Department deems necessary."

Bliss was evidently unable to persuade the Navy Department to prosecute the impostor, but he did think of one constructive thing that the State Department could do in the matter. Bannerman had discovered in the course of his investigation that the impostor possessed a passport issued to "Clifford Grete Weston Wyman," so if Bliss could not do anything about the fact that the impostor remained free to move around the United States, he could at least see to it that he was not free to move around the world. Accordingly, Bliss instructed Sharp to instruct Bannerman to pick up the impostor's passport, and on October 4th Bannerman reported to Sharp as follows:

Pursuant to instructions received from the Chief Special Agent to take up Passport No. 104155, issued to Clifford Grete Weston Wyman.

Realizing that it would be impossible to secure this passport other than through subterfuge, I enlisted the services of R. J. West & Company, Incorporated, 130 West 42nd Street, New York City. This company is an employment agency. On September 25, Wyman had written them a letter applying for a position.

Mr. West signed the letter which I wrote to Wyman on the suggestion of the agency to the effect that there was a position there open for a man of his ability and if he would be in their office Saturday morning, October 1, at 10 A.M., the client of the agency would be there at that time. On Friday, September 30, Wyman telephoned them stating that it would be impossible for him to keep that engagement, inasmuch as he had to meet a friend coming from Europe and proceed to Washington the following morning. However, he would return to New York on Monday morning and set the hour at 10 o'clock.

At the appointed hour, I was in the office of R. J. West and

Company, and Wyman elaborated on his experience in audit-
ing and his experience as a foreign trade adviser for large concerns and spoke nonchalantly of his acquaintance with men of
affairs in this country and others. Stated that he was the personal, confidential agent of Harold McCormick of Chicago.
Stated further that he had been called in to rearrange the system of handling goods through the Custom House—in fact,
felt that he would install an entirely new system so as to expedite matters going through the Appraiser's Stores. This sort of
talk continued for some time until I, as his prospective employer, asked Wyman for his references.

He produced one from the Comsr. of Immigration.

One from Senator Pat Harrison.

One from Earle S. Kinsley, Director, Republican National
Committee from Vermont.

One from H. E. Higginson, Consul General of Peru in
New York.

One from Southern Pacific Company signed by Chester
Reddy.

Notation, typewritten, showing his service record in the
Treasury Department.

One from David R. Francis.

After listening to his tale of experiences during the last few
years, and noting numerous places where his period of service
with different concerns or individuals overlapped, and noticing
a certain similarity of signatures on his references, I put his references in my pocket, informed him as to my real identity, and
demanded that he appear in our office at 4 o'clock in the afternoon with his passport, the articles of handiwork which
Princess Fatima had given him to present to Mrs. Hughes, and
also his power of attorney—all of which I submit with this report, including copies of his references and newspaper articles
showing his recent activity in the Harold McCormick case.

I am positive this man could not tell the truth in any instance and therefore can place no reliability on anything he would say. If the Department wishes to prosecute him, I feel that he can always be located directly or indirectly through his wife.

Regardless of the repudiation by Mr. McCormick of any connection with Wyman in the articles appearing in the newspapers, Wyman called me on the phone to ask if I had noticed these articles. On being assured that I had, he stated that no doubt Mr. McCormick felt justified in doing this inasmuch as Wyman had probably talked too much with the press, but he assured me that his connection with Mr. McCormick was bona-fide, inasmuch as at the moment in which he was talking to me, he was in possession of Mr. McCormick's Rolls-Royce car, which I could confirm by calling on Mr. Brooks of the Plaza Hotel, who had furnished him the money from Mr. McCormick with which to pay the customs duty on it.

Having received this memorandum and, with it, the passport, Sharp now did manage to close the case for good as far as the State Department was concerned. He sent the passport to Bliss, along with this final memorandum:

. . . You will note that Special Agent Bannerman has succeeded in procuring this passport and I herewith enclose the same for your disposition. . . .

You will also note from the Special Agent's report that Wyman has turned in a number of the articles which it is alleged the Princess Fatima delivered to him with instructions to turn over to Mrs. Hughes, the wife of the Secretary of State. Three of these table covers are now in our possession, and we will await your further instructions with reference thereto. One of these covers is still in the possession of

Wyman's wife and can be recovered, and the other two making up the entire six articles which Princess Fatima claims to have sent by Wyman to Mrs. Hughes, Wyman claims were sent by him to the White House by way of a telegraph messenger boy picked up by him on the street. Wyman is such an inveterate liar, however, that this story is not believed by us and on the contrary, we are of the opinion that he has sold these articles or otherwise disposed of them and kept the proceeds.

In his personal conversation with us, Wyman is very positive that he has worked for both the Republican and Democratic National Committees. . . .

My personal observation of this man confirms me in the belief that his mind is not right, and he admits that he has served a term in an insane asylum. He frankly says that he cannot see any objection to telling these lies in order to secure a position. His mind is positively brilliant, and his memory for dates and details is wonderful. I am positive that any admonition which might be given him will be of no avail and that he will continue to do in the future what he has done in the past.

You will note from Agent Bannerman's report herewith, his very latest escapade was to ingratiate himself into the good wishes of Mrs. Harold McCormick, the daughter of John D. Rockefeller, and at the same time we have positive evidence in our possession that this statement to the effect that he was also working in connection with Mr. Harold McCormick, Mrs. Edith McCormick's husband, is true. In other words, he was doing to the McCormicks in their domestic entanglements exactly what he was doing to the Republican and Democratic National Committees, working things at both ends and in the middle.

You will note the evidences of his insanity in the interview which he gives out to the New York *News*, a daily illustrated publication in New York City, who are so completely duped by this man that they do him the honor of publishing his picture.

In April of 1922—eight months after he had introduced Princess Fatima to President Harding—Weyman was tried and convicted in the Federal Court in Brooklyn on a charge of wearing the uniform of a United States naval officer. Judge Thomas I. Chatfield presided over the trial, Weyman's attorney was Herman C. Pollack, and the prosecution was conducted by Assistant United States Attorney Guy O. Walser, acting for the Department of Justice. Weyman's defense was that when he introduced Princess Fatima to President Harding he was wearing the uniform not of the United States Navy but of the United States Junior Naval Reserves, to which he did in fact belong. He was nevertheless found guilty.

Before Judge Chatfield pronounced sentence, his lawyer began a plea for light punishment, but he didn't get very far. "His record," said Pollack, "has been against him, but a careful scrutiny of it will prove that he has never done anything which shows moral viciousness. He—"

"He has done many things," Judge Chatfield interrupted. "I think that he is a dangerous man to be at large until he learns that playing tricks on people while trying to keep within the letter of the law is not the way to live."

Mr. Pollack then pointed out that the charge was almost a year old and that his client had "a good explanation as to why he had arranged to introduce Princess Fatima to President Harding."

"His ability to satisfy you on that score only shows that his skill in making explanations is considerable," Judge Chatfield said.

Weyman's father then appealed to the Judge to suspend sentence, and promised to support his son, his daughter-in-law, and his grandchild, and to pay for psychiatric treatment for his son. After that, Weyman's wife began an appeal on behalf of her husband but burst into tears and had to be removed from the courtroom. Next, Weyman himself addressed the court. "I do not wish to discuss the insanity theory, on which you seem to have made up your mind," he said to the Judge. "In none of my acts has there ever been intentional turpitude. All were committed in a phase or cycle or period of recurrent manic depression, to which the doctors found I was subject."

Judge Chatfield then sentenced Weyman to serve two years in the Atlanta Federal Penitentiary and to pay a fine of one dollar, remarking that the maximum sentence for Weyman's offense was three years in the penitentiary and a fine of one thousand dollars. Seemingly as an afterthought, the Judge said he was convinced that Weyman had succeeded in fooling the doctors into thinking he was crazy.

As for Princess Fatima, she had for some time been receiving from the British Government, through the British Consul General in New York, enough money for herself and her sons to live on. Her diamond, which she had said was worth half a million dollars, had finally been sold for four thousand dollars, of which two thousand went to a Fifth Avenue jeweller who had advanced her that amount some weeks earlier. The British Consul General persuaded her to agree to leave the United States for India on the steamship *Lahore*, sailing from New York on March 16, 1922, but neither the Princess nor her sons were on board when the ship left, and no further intelligence concerning Princess Fatima is available in the newspaper files or in the files of the State Department of the United States.

LOOKED AT FROM the outside, the party that celebrated Stanley Clifford Weyman's twentieth birthday, in 1910, was an ordinary sort of birthday party. It was attended by his mother and father and his five younger brothers. His mother had baked a chocolate cake

and decorated it with twenty candles, and there was the bringing
in of the cake to the dining room and the presentation of gifts to
the eldest son. It was inside the young man's head that extraordinary things were going on during that party. He had graduated
with high marks from Eastern District High School, in Brooklyn,
in 1909, and the plans he then had—the same plans he still had on
his twentieth birthday—could be called grandiose if it were not
for the fact that he can be said to have carried all of them out later
on. What he wanted to do was to go to Princeton, take a B.A., apply for an appointment in the Foreign Service, pass the State Department examinations, and do some consular and diplomatic work,
then study medicine at Johns Hopkins University, in Baltimore,
and take an M.D., and, after that, study law at the Harvard Law
School and take a law degree. His father had never acquired a degree of any kind but had managed to establish himself in Brooklyn
as a moderately successful real-estate broker. He was in favor of his
eldest son's going to college, but he thought that the boy ought to
make up his mind to become either a diplomat or a doctor or a
lawyer, not all three, and that until he did make up his mind it
might be a good idea for him to go to work and get some practical experience at something.

The father and the other members of the family were sure that
the eldest son would go a long way once he had started off in some
single direction. He was good-looking, had charming manners,
and talked slowly, eloquently, and with great persistence in a soft
voice. In his senior year in high school, he had taken the affirma-
tive in a debate on the desirability of woman suffrage, which was,
in those days, a controversial subject. There were some people
who were under the impression that women wanted to vote, that
they ought to be allowed to vote, and that if an amendment to
the Constitution of the United States should be adopted allowing them to vote, the internal and external affairs of the country
would be improved beyond belief. And there were others who

held that woman's place was in the home, that she shouldn't be allowed to vote even if she wanted to, that for her to attempt to assume the responsibilities of the voting citizen would make her more masculine than she had any right or, deep in her heart, any desire to be, and that woman suffrage could lead only to a serious mixup in the relations between men and women and to the nation's adoption of foreign and domestic policies that would end in confusion, if not disaster. When the eldest son of the Weinberg family delivered his oration on behalf of woman suffrage in the assembly hall of Eastern District High School, some of the woman-suffragists who heard it were so entranced, both with what he said and with the way he said it, that he was invited to attend that year's meeting of the National American Woman Suffrage Association in Washington, D.C. He accepted the invitation, attended the meeting, made a prepared speech, and was given a gold medal, which he afterward carried around with him in his vest pocket, or in the watch pocket of his trousers if he didn't happen to be wearing a vest. After his graduation from high school, and after weeks of discussion with his father, he was persuaded to take a job as a clerk in a small real-estate firm in Brooklyn whose owners were friends of the family. He did well there for about six months. Then he made a speech to the owners in which he outlined plans for an expansion of the firm, assuring them that if they followed these, the business could be converted from a small one to a gigantic one. The owners were fascinated, as almost everybody seems to have been whenever the young man talked, but after several days' consideration they decided that his plans were too ambitious and they told him so. He then quit the job. His father and mother and his younger brothers later recalled that he stayed in bed most of the time for about a month afterward, and that for the next half a year he did nothing much but lounge around the house, moody and listless.

Then, inexplicably, he began to perk up. Soon he was once again urging his father, softly and persuasively, to send him to Princeton and let him get started on his careers as diplomat, doctor, and lawyer. When his father found himself still unable to agree that these three-way plans were sound, the boy announced to the family that he would get a job entirely on his own hook and make the money to send himself to Princeton. Encouraged by his father to do that, he found a job as a sort of apprentice to a man named Harry Pincus, who had a camera store in lower Manhattan, near City Hall. It turned out to be a job with a future that neither he nor Pincus nor the Weinbergs had envisioned.

In addition to owning and operating the camera store in lower Manhattan, Pincus was a professional photographer and a Tammany worker, and Weyman had been attracted to the job in the camera shop because Pincus knew a good many important people. These were mostly lawyers and politicians. Pincus frequently went out with his camera, tripod, and black cloth hood and took photographs of these people on noteworthy occasions in their lives. He would drop their names when he talked to his apprentice, and Weyman would pick the names up and drop them, in his turn, around his home in Brooklyn. At the end of the first month, Weyman asked Pincus politely if he wouldn't give him his wages, so that he could start building up the fund that was to send him to Princeton, but Pincus told him that up to that point his services had not been worth anything. Weyman, who was then and afterward mostly mild-mannered, lost his temper when he found he was working for nothing, and accused Pincus of taking unfair advantage of him. Pincus then told him he was fired.

An ordinary young man would probably have been glad to see the end of this wageless job, but Weyman was not an ordinary young man. His dismissal infuriated him further. He stalked out of the store in a huff, but before he did he picked up one of Pincus's most expensive cameras when Pincus was not looking, and when he left the store the camera was hidden under his topcoat.

He told nobody about the theft, and didn't try to sell or pawn the camera. He kept it in his room in his father's house in Brooklyn, out of sight under his shirts in a bureau drawer. Weyman's employment at the camera store having been the loose arrangement that it was, Pincus didn't know Weyman's home address, and consequently he never came after the camera, although, as things turned out, it is clear that he correctly guessed, when he missed the camera, that his unpaid apprentice had stolen it.

After this experience, Weyman didn't sink into one of his periodic low moods but went on talking optimistically to his father and others about his plans, saying that he still intended to join the Foreign Service after he graduated from Princeton, and then, in due course, become both a doctor and a lawyer. Like many a young man of those days who had not been to college, he earned money doing various odd jobs—as a messenger boy in the garment district of Manhattan, as a soda jerk in Brooklyn, as an office boy on a newspaper. He quit these jobs because he got tired of them or because they didn't pay enough. When he realized that it would take him years to save enough money to go to Princeton, he had a quarrel with his father because his father still refused to put up the money to send him there. The boy then ran away from home, got a job selling newspapers, and stayed for a while at the home of a fellow-newsboy. While his father was at his office, he would go home to see his mother, who would feed him and give him money. For a few weeks, he slept in the vestibule of his parents' house, and his mother somehow kept his father from knowing he was there. He spent a good deal of time in the public library near Borough Hall, reading in the omnivorous and unsystematic fashion of young men of his age. All this time, he was dreaming of the future and of his plans, and soon he began to carry out his plans in a hurry.

He selected a post that he thought he would like as a starter in the Foreign Service of the United States, and, in a way, assumed it.

This made it unnecessary for him to go to Princeton and take a B.A. or to pass the State Department examinations. The post he picked out was that of United States Consul General to Algiers. He told a Fulton Street stationer who he now was, and, instructing the stationer to send the bill to his father, ordered a stack of engraved invitations and suitable envelopes to mail them in. He mailed them to nobody in his family and to none of his friends but only to notable strangers whose names he had seen in the newspapers or heard in Pincus's camera store. The invitations asked the recipients to be present at a banquet at the Hotel St. George, in Brooklyn Heights, at eight o'clock on a Tuesday evening. Formal dress was suggested. The occasion, the invitations said, was a bonvoyage party in honor of S. Clifford Weinberg, the newly appointed United States Consul General to Algiers. They were mailed to about a hundred people, more than seventy-five of whom turned up on the dot at the St. George, the men in white tie and tails, and their wives in evening dresses. The men were mostly lawyers, doctors, and politicians, but there was at least one justice of the New York State Supreme Court.

Weyman's banquet in honor of himself went off without a hitch. In a dress suit he had bought at a Brooklyn department store and charged to his father, he made a graceful speech, thanking friends he didn't name for having arranged the banquet for him, and afterward called on a number of the guests to say a few words. All of them started out to do that and all of them said more than a few words. The justice was one of those who spoke at length. As the banquet was breaking up, late in the evening, the justice buttonholed the new Consul General to Algiers and invited him to come to his court, in the County Court House in lower Manhattan, the next day and sit on the bench with him to witness the disposition of equal justice under law. This was an honor that Weyman was happy to accept.

The bill for the banquet at the St. George included charges for food, wine, and flowers, and amounted to around four hundred dollars. It was brought to Weyman's father the next morning at his real-estate office, near Borough Hall, by a messenger who had instructions from the hotel management to wait for and bring back the real-estate man's check. The bills from the stationer and the department store had already been mailed to Mr. Weinberg, and he was staring at them when the messenger from the St. George arrived. The bills gave the father his first hint of what his son had been up to. While the messenger from the hotel waited, he telephoned the banquet department of the hotel, the credit manager of the department store, and the stationer, and learned further details from them. In later life, he told many people exactly how he felt that morning and what he did. The first thing he felt was a wish that his son had invited him to the banquet, but then he said to himself that his not being invited probably served him right for having put obstacles in the lad's way when all the time the lad had been secretly boning up for and passing the State Department examinations for the diplomatic service—without having gone to Princeton or any other college—and was now ready to embark on what might easily turn out to be a brilliant diplomatic career, whether or not it was followed by the careers in medicine and the law he had so often talked about.

Mr. Weinberg cheerfully paid the bills, and then he closed up his office, caught a streetcar on the run, and went home to congratulate his son. But his son wasn't at home. His son was sitting on the bench of the New York State Supreme Court in the New York County Court House, with the justice on his left. It wasn't a busy morning in court, and the justice chatted amiably with the new Consul General to Algiers while he disposed of such routine matters as accepting pleas of guilty or not guilty from a batch of accused prisoners and sentencing some convicted felons to terms of hard labor at Sing Sing. Then the justice had an idea. He chuckled mysteriously, told the Consul General he was going to have a surprise for him in a few minutes, and whispered something to the clerk of the court. The justice had decided that what he wanted—as a souvenir, and as something the press might possibly be interested in—was a photograph of himself and the new Consul General to Algiers sitting together on the bench. Having been summoned on the telephone by the clerk, Pincus soon stepped into the courtroom unobtrusively; as he had learned to do in the past when the justice wanted a photograph taken. He silently set up his tripod and camera, and disappeared under his black cloth hood. Under the hood, he brought the features of the justice and the Consul General to Algiers into sharp focus. Then he flung back the hood and created an unseemly uproar in the courtroom. He shouted out that the young man sitting on the bench with the justice was the young man who had stolen one of his most expensive cameras. The young man instantly and smoothly confessed to the theft of the camera and began to explain about it at some length to the justice. Weyman said he had taken the camera for no other reason than to show Pincus that a young American of his potentialities shouldn't be asked to work for nothing. He went on confessing and explaining for several minutes, in a cheerful, easygoing fashion. He talked softly, slowly, and eloquently, and seemed unable to stop. Taking the justice deeper and deeper into a labyrinth that the justice had no desire to enter, he confessed that he had given himself the banquet at the St. George simply in order to place his father in such a position that he would be forced to send him to Princeton, where, in due course, he would take a B.A., preparatory to passing the State Department examinations and spending a few years in the Foreign Service, most probably as Consul General to Algiers. After that, he went on, he would start working for an M.D. at Johns Hopkins, because he thought it wiser to get the M.D. there before going to Harvard to get a law degree. While Weyman was still talking, the justice turned to the clerk and told him to tell Pincus to get a policeman and have the policeman take Weyman away. The elderly justice then retired groggily to his chambers. According to eyewitnesses, he stumbled twice along the route from the bench to the door leading to his chambers.

Pincus and the policeman accompanied Weyman to his home in Brooklyn, where the camera was returned to Pincus. Then Weyman's father accompanied the policeman and his eldest son to a magistrate's court in Manhattan, where he put up bail so that his son wouldn't have to spend the night in the Tombs, the famous prison next door to the old Criminal Courts Building. A few weeks later, Weyman, after pleading guilty to a charge of grand larceny, was given a suspended sentence and was placed on probation. By then, his mood was low again, and he was staying in bed much of the time and lounging around the house in a bathrobe the rest of the time. On the advice of the family physician, his father took him to the River Crest Sanitarium, a private institution in Astoria, Queens, for diagnosis and treatment.

Weyman was to look back on the six months he spent at River Crest Sanitarium as one of the happiest periods of his life. The psychiatrists there took an interest in the hypersensitive, highly intelligent, and charming lad with the soft, persuasive voice, the gentle manners, and the large, liquid brown eyes, and gave him as much psychotherapy as it was thought advisable in those years to give a patient. At the beginning of the second decade of the twentieth century, the discoveries and recommendations of Dr. Sigmund Freud were, on the whole, still being taken with more than a grain of salt at all mental hospitals in this country, as in those in the rest of the world. Freud's major work, *The Interpretation of Dreams,* was not translated into English until 1913. However, the gist of Freud's investigation of his own unconscious, which formed the basis for his theory of psychoanalysis, was widely known both here and abroad. Some people were inclined to agree with the Freudian theory, and others were not. Those who disagreed with it were rather emotional about the matter, as some people still are today. In 1910, Professor H. Oppenheim, a famous neurologist and the author of what was then the leading textbook on his subject, proposed in a speech before a neurological congress in Berlin that any institution in which Freud's views were tolerated be boycotted by members of the congress. According to Dr. Ernest Jones, Freud's biographer, "all the directors [of mental institutions] present stood up to declare their innocence." That year, too, at a meeting of German neurologists and psychiatrists in Hamburg, Professor Wilhelm Weygandt, a leading medical man of his time, banged on the table with his fist when a delegate started to read a paper outlining Freud's theories of sexuality, and shouted, "This is not a topic for discussion at a scientific meeting; it is a matter for the police!" In Australia, at about the same time, a Presbyterian clergyman had to leave the ministry because he had expressed sympathy with Freud's work. Dr. Jones himself had been forced to resign a neurological appointment in London in 1908 because it was discovered that he had made inquiries into the sexual life of his patients Dr. Jones moved over to Canada, and before long the government of Ontario ordered a publication called the *Asylum Bulletin* to cease publication because Dr. Jones and his staff were contributing articles to it that the government of Ontario found "unfit for publication even in a medical periodical." And in Berlin, in the same period, Dr. M. Wulff, a world-famous psychiatrist, was dismissed from the staff of a mental institution because he displayed interest in Freud's theories; he continued his career in Russia, which at the time was freer in such matters than Germany. At a meeting of the American Neurological Association in Washington, D.C., in May, 1910, Dr. Joseph Collins, a leading New York neurologist, who, according to Jones, had a proclivity for telling indecent jokes in mixed company, attacked Dr. James J. Putnam, another leading neurologist, for reading a paper on Freud's theories in connection with female hysterics. He claimed that the paper was made up of "pornographic stories about pure virgins," and declared that "it is time the Association took a stand against transcendentalism and supernaturalism and definitely crushed out Christian Science, Freudism, and all that bosh, rot, and nonsense."

Even those medical men who were inclined to think there might be something in the Freudian theories concerning sex and the unconscious were cautious about following any of Freud's therapeutic procedures, possibly because the medical profession in general hadn't entirely recovered from an earlier discovery of Freud's—the discovery that a new and untried drug called cocaine was useful in the treatment of patients suffering from depression. Like Weyman, Freud in his younger days was a neurotic personality, and was subject to, among other things, manic-depressive trends. Freud had discovered that cocaine, swallowed or sniffed or taken by intravenous injection, caused him to perk up when he was feeling low. He was on familiar terms with the drug in 1884, when, at the age of twenty-eight, he wrote to his fiancée, Martha Bernays, who had lost her appetite, "Woe to you, my Princess, when I come. I will kiss you quite red and feed you till you are plump. And if you are froward you shall see who is the stronger, a gentle little girl who doesn't eat enough or a big wild man who has cocaine in his body. In my last severe depression, I took coca again and a small dose lifted me to the heights in a wonderful fashion. I am just now busy collecting the literature for a song of praise to this magical substance." The song of praise that Freud subsequently sang in honor of cocaine was widely and more or less uncritically accepted for quite a while by the medical profession both in Europe and in this country, with the result that as late as 1911 a great many patients and a great many physicians all over the world were still trying to get off the stuff. (Freud himself had long since ceased to recommend its use except as a nerve anesthetic in dental and surgical work.) Dr. W. H. Halsted, for example, who was one of the founders of modern surgery and was regarded as America's greatest surgeon, had learned Freud's song of praise to cocaine and had begun to sing it himself, and it took him several painful years to rid himself of his addiction so that he could go on founding modern surgery.

Freud, as it happened, was not an addict type, and neither was his fiancée; both of them could take cocaine or leave it alone, as many other patients and physicians before the turn of the century could and did. Freud's discovery that there was such a thing as an addict type—persons whose inner makeup caused them to have an intense craving for anything that might relieve the strong tensions and depressions that they had, and other people didn't have—eventually helped to lead him toward the investigation of the unconscious and on to the theory of psychoanalysis. It wasn't until years after 1911, however, that he and his followers ceased to believe that the ups and downs in human moods—the extreme manifestation of which is now called the manic-depressive psychosis—were incurable, and that the moods themselves were by forces other than those to be found in the human unconscious. For this and many other reasons, it seems accurate to state that if Freud himself had been on the staff of River Crest Sanitarium in Queens in 1911, he couldn't have done much more for Weyman in six months than was accomplished by the psychiatrists who did treat Weyman there.

The doctors at River Crest felt that in Weyman they had a promising patient. Weyman had never taken anything stronger than a morning newspaper to make himself perk up when he was depressed. He neither drank nor smoked nor sniffed, whereas Freud, until he finally gave up cocaine, did all three, and also freely administerd cocaine to himself, his fiancée, and his patients, by mouth and by intravenous injection as well as by nose. For a long time after Freud reached the conclusion that the prescription of cocaine for himself and others had had some evil results, he clung to the notion that it was not the cocaine itself that was so harmful but the fact that he had injected it into people's bloodstreams instead of encouraging them to swallow it. In time, he discovered the cause of this notion in his own unconscious, and dealt with it, and with other and less complex notions he found there, such as a virulent hatred of his father, whom he thought he had only loved, and what he called "an unruly homosexual feeling," which conflicted with his desire to continue kissing Martha. River Crest was accustomed to alcoholics, dope addicts, and compulsive neurotics such as women who had fits of hysteria if everything wasn't tidy, men who were incapable of entering or riding in elevators, women who thought they were Joan of Arc, men who thought they were Napoleon, and people of either sex who were under the impression that they were floating in the air or were under water. Compared to most of the other patients, Weyman was the rock of Gibraltar. He had no phobias, delusions, or compulsive neuroses, and was tractable and anxious to please. The only thing that appeared to be the matter with him when he entered the sanitarium was that he was suffering from severe depression and was entertaining thoughts of suicide, though he hadn't made any attempt to kill himself. His doctors did not inquire into his sex life or investigate his unconscious. Years later, one of the doctors remembered that he first saw Weyman after the new patient had been settled in a private room and been served dinner on a tray, and found him sitting up in bed but not trying to eat the steak that was on the tray on his lap. The doctor asked why he was not eating his steak, and Weyman replied lugubriously that he couldn't cut it up. The doctor then cut Weyman's steak into small pieces, as a mother might do for a child, and Weyman ate it all. And he immediately began to perk up. The doctor chatted with him for a while in a friendly way and, by the time he left him, suggesting that Weyman try to get a good night's sleep, was convinced that he wouldn't have much trouble with this patient. He was right.

Weyman was put on a strict schedule, which gave him something to do at all times and relieved him of the necessity of making any decisions, and he talked with one of the doctors for an hour or so six days a week. He rose at seven, bathed, dressed, and had breakfast with those of his fellow-patients who were well enough to come down to the dining room and could be trusted not to make a disturbance. From eight until nine, he walked in the open air, rain or shine. From nine until ten, he talked to and listened to his doctor. From ten until noon, he engaged in occupational therapy, such as carpentry work, weaving, modelling, or painting in oils or watercolors. From noon until one, he rested in his room. From one until two, he lunched, and from two until three he again walked in the open air. From three until five, he did more occupational therapy, and from five until seven he played whist, or battledore and shuttlecock, or chess with fellow-patients who could do so. At seven, he dined, and from eight until ten he played more whist or other games. At ten, he went to his room and read a book, and at eleven the lights were turned out all over River Crest and those patients who were able to went to sleep until seven o'clock the next morning. In his sessions with his doctor, Weyman was encouraged to talk about himself, and he did so with ease and volubility, and the doctor who listened to him took many notes. Information about the lad was also obtained from his parents. When Weyman's case was discussed by the members of the staff at one of the customary staff conferences, it was agreed that Weyman had had a common, ordinary, normal American conception, birth, and babyhood.

In other words: A short time after Weyman was born, his mother took him in her arms, fondled him all over with her hands, and introduced him to her bare breasts. He quickly learned to suck one breast and then the other until he had had enough milk, after which he went to sleep. At intervals, he was stripped naked, bathed with warm water and soap, wiped dry with a fluffy towel, powdered and patted all over, and dressed again. Almost from the start, he seemed to be aware of pleasurable sensations in the area of his genitals—a reaction that in 1911 had hardly ever been mentioned out loud by anybody but Dr. Freud.

Having been born into an orthodox Jewish family, Weyman was taken to a synagogue on the eighth day after his birth and was circumcised, by a mohel, or ritual circumcisor. The operation consisted of three stages, known as *milah*, *periah*, and *mezizah*. It was an operation that in 1911 in this country was performed on Gentiles only of the upper-middle classes, and then only by surgeons. (It is generally available for all infants now and is a one-stage affair.) If Weyman had been a Persian Muslim, the operation would have been performed in his third or fourth year, and if he had been a Christian Copt, a Fijian, or a Samoan it would have been performed in his sixth or seventh year. Even in his eighth day, it was a painful and generally upsetting operation, and it took him a week or more to recover just from the physical effects of it. His feeding and bathing routine was continued, with minor variations, until he was about eight months old. By that time, his diet had been supplemented by baby foods of various kinds, which he had learned to eat from a spoon, although he still depended heavily on his mother's milk. Then his mother suddenly ceased to nurse him, and after a while she had another baby, who, in his presence, took possession of the breasts he had been so fond of. When Weyman bawled at this and other indications that he had ceased to be the primary object of his mother's attention, she would pick him up and cover him with kisses and pat him all over until he stopped bawling. Then she would give him something to play with while she fed the new baby.

Weyman's relationship with his father was similarly run-of-the-mill, and the father's attitude toward him was apparently above reproach. Like any other father, the elder Weyman was inordinately fond of and proud of his eldest son at the same time that he looked down his nose at the way the eldest son became for a while the center of the wifely and motherly attentions that had previously been his own. When, as a small baby, Weyman was happily in possession of his mother's breasts and lay beneath them sucking, gurgling, and squirming, the father would stand by and observe him with wonderment and love in which impatience, envy, and jealousy were mixed in healthy quantities. It was the father who encouraged the mother to wean Weyman at a reasonable time instead of allowing him to go on feeding at her breast until he was seven or eight years old—a custom that was still generally adhered to in certain unspoiled mountain regions of the United States, where the culture and bloodlines were pure Anglo-Saxon. After Weyman had been weaned, the father was in favor of moving the baby's crib out of the parents' bedroom. This was eventually accomplished, although Weyman wailed bitterly at bedtime and at other times even after he had had an opportunity to grow used to the new arrangement.

By the time Weyman reached puberty, around the age of fourteen, he had a total of five younger brothers. Both his mother and his father believed him to be the cleverest of the lot, and, from what he told the doctors at River Crest, it is evident that he did everything in his power to support them in this belief. Almost from the time he could walk around and talk, there was a great deal of discussion among the adults of the family—including a number of uncles and aunts as well as the mother and father—as to what he would be when he grew up. Weyman came to relish these discussions no end. When such talk petered out, he would revive it himself, perhaps with recitations indicating that he was fit to be a lawyer. Sometimes he would say he intended to be a doctor, and he would cause flurries of applause and amazement in the family by taking the temperatures of all the other boys, reporting accurately which one was slightly above normal, diagnosing the ailment as a cold, and prescribing and administering gargles and nose douches of hot salt water. After he discovered pink spots on the skin of the youngest boy and solemnly told his mother that the child had chicken pox and it was found that the child did, his mother was convinced—and so was his father—that he would become a doctor rather than a lawyer when he grew up.

As far as the River Crest doctors could determine, it had looked like clear sailing ahead for Weyman in every way until his frustration over not being able to pursue his plans for a higher education led to his frustration over the wageless job with Pincus and to the theft of Pincus's camera and from there to the prank he played on his father when he pretended he had become the new Consul General to Algiers. Weyman's explanation of this last episode encouraged the doctors to consider it nothing more than a prank. He told them convincingly that he had simply wished to demonstrate to his father how well equipped he was to be a Consul General, and thereby persuade his father that the sensible thing to do would be to send him to Princeton, where he could get the necessary education and pass the State Department examinations he had pretended he'd already passed. The doctors could understand that the double disillusionment Weyman faced when he was unmasked by Pincus in the courtroom would be enough to send any young man into a fit of deep depression; sitting on the bench with the justice, Weyman had been, to all intents and purposes, the new Consul General to Algiers, and a moment later he not only had not been the new Consul General to Algiers but had been a delinquent adolescent who had stolen a camera and hidden it under his shirts in a bureau drawer in his room. However, from the moment, on the first night of his stay at River Crest, that his kindly doctor cut up his steak so he could eat it, Weyman had ceased to be depressed, and he suffered no further depression during the whole six months of his stay. Even Dr. Freud and his followers knew very little about what was then called "manic-depressive insanity," and the River Crest doctors knew even less. Still, Weyman's behavior gave them no reason to believe that he would ever have a deep depression again, or would ever again go into a state of elation that might encourage him to engage in an imposturous episode. At the end of those six months, Weyman, after shaking hands all around, left River Crest feeling splendid and full of plans for the future.

At first, Weyman's plans were not grandiose. He had talked over his future with the doctors at River Crest and had told them he now realized that his past ambitions to become both a doctor and a lawyer after a Foreign Service career were absurd. Moreover, he said, he realized how much money his father was spending for his stay at the sanitarium, and understood that his father could hardly afford to send him to either Princeton or Harvard, let alone both. With the doctors' help, he had finally decided that working as a newspaper reporter was a thing he would both enjoy and be good at, and had concluded that, since newspaper employment didn't require a college degree, he could probably find such a job in either Brooklyn or Manhattan and would be able to live at home until he was making enough money to get married and have a home of his own. He had no particular girl in mind, but he wanted a wife and children when the time came, he said. His doctors were pleased—and so was his father—at his apparent steadiness of purpose. After his discharge from River Crest, he got a job as a cub reporter on the Brooklyn *Daily Eagle* and was soon made a district man, at a salary of fifteen dollars a week. A district man mostly telephoned in the facts of whatever story he had covered, the story then being written by a rewrite man, but Weyman also managed to write some Sunday feature stories on his own, and was paid for them at the prevailing space rates, which added five or ten dollars a week to his income. The judge who had given him a suspended sentence had instructed him and his father that as long as the young man remained in a sanitarium, he need not report to the probation authorities, but that once he left the sanitarium, he would have to report to them regularly, for his status remained that of a person under suspended sentence and on probation. Weyman did report regularly to the probation authorities for more than a year after

leaving River Crest, but gradually his appreciation of his rising status as a district man and a writer of feature stories got in the way
of his realization that he was also a person on probation, and this
led him to ignore the facts of his situation to such an extent that
he stopped reporting to the probation authorities for a month or
so. Then he was arrested, brought before the same judge, and given
an indeterminate sentence to the Elmira Reformatory, where he
sank into such a deep depression that he was transferred to the reformatory hospital at Napanoch. Once he was back in a hospital
routine, and talking to doctors who were sympathetic, and who
got in touch with the River Crest doctors to check on his case,
he recovered from his depression. He was then returned to Elmira,
where he spent a few more weeks, and on June 20, 1913, he was
paroled. Altogether, he had been at the reformatory and the Napanoch hospital for eight months.

The Brooklyn *Daily Eagle* didn't rehire Weyman upon his release, possibly because its court reporter had given the city editor
the facts about his criminal record—grand larceny, for the theft of
Pincus's camera. Weyman earned a little money by writing feature
stories for other papers in the city, but after six months he violated
parole and was sent back to Elmira. The reformatory again transferred him to the Napanoch hospital, and again he was released
on parole after a few months, only to violate parole once more, in
May of 1915. When he got out this time, he managed to stay out
until April 2, 1917, on which date he was sent to prison for a year,
first to Blackwell's Island prison and then to the prison hospital at
Dannemora, on a new charge—that of forging United States Senator William M. Calder's name to his application for a job at the
Bank of United States. Three months after he was paroled this
time, he was sent back yet again for violation of parole, and stayed
in prison for two years and seven months. By then, he was twenty-
nine years old. And he had become addicted to imposture. The
most glowing memories of his life were those connected with the

banquet he had given himself as the new Consul General to Algiers, and he tried to duplicate the feelings he had had on that occasion by buying a uniform so as to pose as an American naval officer and, with some alterations to the uniform, as Lieutenant Royal St. Cyr of the French Navy. In June of 1920, three months after he had finished serving his term of two years and seven months, he was picked up by officers from the Brooklyn Navy Yard for impersonating a naval officer. A Kings County judge fined him ten dollars for this, although impersonating a member of the armed forces is a federal offense. While he was carrying out this imposture, he met a girl in Prospect Park and, after exciting her interest with his seagoing talk, suddenly confessed to her that the whole thing was an imposture and that he was nothing more than a young man from Brooklyn who had no steady employment. But, he added, he wanted her to marry him if she had faith in him. When he was freed, after paying his ten-dollar fine, she did marry him, and they remained married for the rest of his life. They had one child, a daughter, who, after Weyman became a notorious character because of his repeated impostures, changed *her* name and led an independent life, seeing her father and mother only on rare occasions.

Weyman's marriage took place in 1920, and afterward he got a steady job and reported to the parole authorities regularly for two years. He managed in this period, though, to collect the beginnings of his famous wardrobe and to engage in several more or less innocent impostures—for the fun of the thing, as far as anybody knew, and sometimes accompanied by his young wife. He would take her to dinner at some fine restaurant in Manhattan, for example, both of them in formal dress, and would let it be known that he was the new Consul General *from* Algiers, rather than to it; then, having obtained very good service, he would pay his bill and go back to his home in Brooklyn with his wife. On one rather special occasion, he posed, in an unidentifiable but impressive uniform, as the new Consul General from Rumania. While so doing, he rented a launch and visited the flagship of a United States naval fleet anchored temporarily in the Hudson. He so charmed the admiral on the flagship that the admiral ordered a twenty-one-gun salute to be fired for him, and, after a pleasant visit all round, he shook hands heartily with the admiral and the other naval officers on the flagship and took his launch back to Manhattan and the subway back to Brooklyn. By that time, his wife was expecting their child, so she did not accompany him, but she was enthralled by his offhand and (as always) serious report of how he had spent the afternoon. He began to feel the need of a better job than the one he had, and after studying the help wanted ads for a few days he came across one that looked promising. It was through this ad that Weyman embarked on his first major and extended imposture, which led to his becoming a sanitation expert with an American company in Peru. This imposture did not get into the newspapers until long afterward, but the facts of it were discovered by R. C. Bannerman, the State Department special agent, in the course of an investigation of Weyman's career that he undertook in 1921, following Weyman's imposture as the State Department Naval Liaison Officer, assigned to Princess Fatima.

The ad that stirred Weyman up said that the Foundation Company, of 120 Liberty Street, Manhattan, wished to employ a young doctor to go to Peru and take charge of certain sanitation work that the company was under contract to perform for the Peruvian government. Some twenty applicants for this position turned up at the offices of the company, and one of them was Weyman. The firm's employment officer was instructed by a Mr. Whelan, its manager, to interview the applicants, weed out the ones who did not make a good impression, and retain the five who seemed most likely to succeed. Weyman was one of the five. Mr. Whelan then met these five in his own office. The one he was most impressed with was in the uniform of a medical officer in the United States Navy with the rank of Lieutenant. This, of course, was Weyman. He gave his name as Clifford Grete Weston Wyman and his residence as 71 Maujer Street, Brooklyn, and the credentials he produced seemed to show that he had had eighteen months' service as a naval medical officer overseas. Mr. Whelan said later that he was inclined to pick this young man at once but that since he was not a doctor himself he told the five applicants he was going to ask the assistance of a Dr. Fletcher, who was a professor of medicine at the Columbia University medical school. He told them that they would have to go to see Dr. Fletcher and talk with him, and that on Dr. Fletcher's final recommendation would rest the appointment to the post in Peru. When the five applicants appeared in Dr. Fletcher's office the next day, Weyman stepped out of the group, walked up to the Doctor, shook hands with him warmly, and said that he was a great admirer of the Doctor's work and had several times attended the clinics that the Doctor was conducting at Columbia. Dr. Fletcher recalled subsequently that he had the immediate impression that the young naval doctor had been one of his students. He was sure, in any case, that he had seen the young man before, and he was right. Weyman, although he had never been a student of Dr. Fletcher's, had hung around the Columbia medical school several years before, posing as a medical student. Bannerman noted in his report, "There, either out of sheer curiosity or with some ulterior motive, he had attended the clinics and, being naturally bright and apt, he picked up numerous medical expressions and terms and was well acquainted with the routine in vogue at these clinics. With his unlimited nerve, and ability to talk himself into the good graces of people he met, the impostor, before any of the other applicants had had a chance to open their mouths, said that with his eighteen months' service overseas as a naval medical officer he was ideally suited for the job with the Foundation Company." Dr. Fletcher, according to Bannerman, exchanged a few words with each of the other applicants, and when the five had departed, he telephoned

Mr. Whelan and told him that the naval doctor called Clifford Grete Weston Wyman was the one he recommended.

That afternoon, Mr. Whelan telephoned the young naval doctor at his home in Brooklyn, told him that he had been picked for the job, and instructed him to apply for a passport at once, so that he could proceed to Lima, Peru, as soon as possible. How Weyman was able to obtain a passport under a name he did not receive at birth neither the State Department nor anybody else knows; nevertheless, such a passport was issued to him, on October 26, 1920. Weyman proceeded at once to Lima, in the company of an attractive young woman who was not his wife. Weyman's wife stayed at home and regularly received money from her husband for her support. Neither Bannerman nor anybody else was ever able to find out who the young woman was who made the journey to Lima with Weyman and lived with him while he was there. On his arrival in Lima, Weyman rented a luxuriously furnished marble residence. He bought a limousine on credit and hired a chauffeur to drive it. He appears to have carried out his duties as a sanitation expert satisfactorily. He and his young woman companion began giving parties for Peruvian society in the marble house, and they became very popular and were invited out a great deal. After about six weeks, the young woman became ill, and, following the usual custom of upper-class Peruvians, Weyman took her to the American hospital in the Panama Canal Zone. From Panama he wrote a letter to one of the Naval Intelligence men—his name was Sheehan—who had declined to prosecute him on the charge of impersonating a naval officer in New York earlier that year. It was a friendly, chatty letter, in which Weyman told of his success as a sanitation expert with the Foundation Company in Lima and mentioned that he was giving a tea for a number of naval officers then resident in the Canal Zone who had entertained him while his companion was in the hospital. Sheehan decided that he ought to tell the Foundation Company in New York that the man who was working for them in Lima was an impostor, and he did. By the time Weyman and his companion returned to Lima, the company officials there had received instructions from Mr. Whelan to tell Weyman to report at the New York office at once. But when Weyman arrived in New York and went to see Mr. Whelan, the Foundation Company decided not to prosecute him, because of the notoriety that would result. Having presumably bidden his companion goodbye, Weyman returned to his home in Brooklyn.

On February 11, 1921, the *Times* carried a short item under the heading "Leaves Peru to Fly Here—Son of President Leguia Starts Seaplane Trip Today." The story did not come from Peru. It was a local New York story, and it went as follows:

> Commander Juan Leguia, head of the Peruvian Naval Air Service and son of the President of that republic, will leave Callao, Peru, today on the first leg of a seaplane flight to New York, it was announced here yesterday by Captain Sterling C. Wyman, United States Navy.
>
> Captain Wyman, who is a personal friend of the South American aviator, said he had received a cable message from Commander Leguia stating that he hoped to make the long trip in two weeks.
>
> Commander Leguia is on his way to England, where he is to be married, according to Captain Wyman.

Weyman's ego had evidently been well fed by the Peruvian escapade. He was living quietly in Brooklyn, reporting regularly to the probation authorities, and making money at various honest jobs, one of which was that of auditor for a firm called the Goldberger Manufacturing Company. Following a fire in which the firm's books had been destroyed, Benjamin Goldberger, the head of this company, had advertised in the New York papers for an auditor. Weyman answered the ad at the end of February, gave the

impression of knowing all about accountancy, and said that he had
been employed by Will Hays, then chairman of the Republican
National Committee, and that he was a good friend of United
States Senator William M. Calder. He worked for Mr. Goldberger
for about six weeks and then, one day, failed to show up at the office. Mr. Goldberger tried without success to reach him at his
home in Brooklyn, and, when four or five days had passed and
Weyman had still not come back to work, hired another auditor to
go over the books that Weyman had been keeping. The auditor
found nothing wrong with the books, and Mr. Goldberger stopped
worrying. Then a bill for several hundred dollars was mailed to
Mr. Goldberger from Goldfarb's, the florist. Mr. Goldberger had
not been buying any flowers, so he called up the florist and told
him there must have been a mistake. The florist said that the flowers had been ordered from time to time by Captain Sterling C.
Wyman, of the United States Navy, and that the Captain had instructed him to send the bill to Mr. Goldberger. Mr. Goldberger
told the florist he wouldn't pay this bill, and he and the florist
argued about the matter from time to time until December of
1921. In that month, Weyman's photograph appeared on the front
pages of all the New York newspapers because he had become private secretary to Dr. Adolf Lorenz, a Viennese physician who was
world-famous at the time as "the bloodless surgeon." When Dr.
Lorenz arrived in New York from Europe, Weyman went aboard
ship to meet him and introduced himself as Dr. Clifford Weyman.
He told Dr. Lorenz that he had been asked by the New York
Health Commissioner, Dr. Royal S. Copeland, to welcome him to
New York and to offer his services as Dr. Lorenz's private secre-
tary. Dr. Lorenz was to conduct a clinic at the Hospital for Joint
Diseases, the head of which was Dr. Henry W. Frauenthal. The
New York newspapers gave a great deal of publicity to Dr. Lorenz's
arrival, and when Dr. Lorenz introduced his new secretary, Dr.
Clifford Weyman, to the photographers who met the ship, the

photographers took a picture of Dr. Weyman. Dr. Lorenz was pleased in every way with his secretary, and Weyman worked with him satisfactorily for one week and would no doubt have continued to work for him indefinitely if Dr. Frauenthal had not received a telephone call from one of Princess Fatima's sons, who had recognized Weyman's photograph, and who told Dr. Frauenthal who Weyman was. Dr. Frauenthal called the New York Police Department, which sent a detective over to interview Weyman. Weyman readily confessed that he not only had posed as the State Department Naval Liaison Officer but while doing so had introduced Princess Fatima to President Harding, that he was not a physician, and so on. Both Dr. Lorenz and Dr. Frauenthal were present at the interview, and Dr. Lorenz said that he nevertheless wished to retain Weyman as his private secretary, because his work had been most efficient. Dr. Frauenthal took the matter up with the New York Health Commissioner, Dr. Copeland, and Dr. Copeland said Weyman must go, because he was not a doctor, and also because he had represented himself as the Health Department's representative. Dr. Copeland then called the newspapers and told them that Weyman had been exposed and was being fired, and the newspapers again had front-page stories accompanied by photographs of Weyman—plus, this time, summaries of his career as an impostor. Princess Fatima's son also telephoned the State Department in Washington, and the State Department alerted the Department of Justice. A federal agent named Lamb came to New York to pick him up, and Weyman was at last arrested and arraigned in the Federal Court in Brooklyn on the charge of impersonating a naval officer. Dr. Lorenz, who had agreed to pay Weyman two hundred dollars a week and had thought him worth every penny of it, said publicly that he was sorry to lose Weyman's services. Dr. Copeland sent Dr. Lorenz a new secretary, Dr. Walter Galland, and Dr. Lorenz made do with him for the rest of his stay in New York.

At the Atlanta penitentiary, Weyman studied law under the auspices of the warden, and before he left, having got time off for good behavior, he passed a bar examination and became an accredited attorney under the laws of the State of Georgia, which apparently did not then provide that a man convicted of a felony could not become a lawyer. Or it may have been that the authorities in Atlanta did not think that impersonating a diplomat in order to introduce Princess Fatima to President Harding *was* a felony. In any event, Weyman returned to New York in fine shape and, within a few months, was working, under the name of Stanley Wyman, as a clerk in the office of the New York Title & Mortgage Co., on lower Broadway. His job, for which a legal training was necessary, had to do with real-estate transactions, and by working closely with his father, who was still in the real-estate business, he made a great deal more money than just his salary as a clerk. Before any action was taken to foreclose mortgages on real estate whose owners were in trouble, Weyman would learn what was in the wind and would pass the tip on, enabling his father to acquire the real estate at low prices. Weyman made enough money to buy, for cash, an olive-green Pierce-Arrow limousine and a crimson Daimler roadster.

During this period, Weyman made the acquaintance of Samuel J. Siegel, who is at present a well-known New York criminal lawyer with offices in the Times Square district, and who at that time had recently obtained his law degree and was also working as a law clerk at the New York Title & Mortgage Co. Siegel remained Weyman's friend and lawyer for the rest of Weyman's career. He remembers vividly, as any man would, the day on which their friendship began. It was a hot Saturday morning in the summer of 1924, and Siegel happened to remark to some fellow-employees standing around the water cooler that he was going to spend Sunday with his parents, in Lakewood, New Jersey, and that he wasn't looking forward to the trip, which in those days citizens of New York usually made by crosstown streetcar, ferryboat, and railroad train.

"My wife and I are driving down there tomorrow, my dear chap," said one member of the water-cooler group. "I'll be glad to give you a lift."

Siegel knew the man who had made this offer only slightly; he knew him as Stanley Wyman, and knew that although he was liked well enough around the office, where he was called Stan, he was commonly thought of as being—a phrase Siegel later came to consider inadequate—"a kind of a nut." Weyman was capable of eccentricities that would flabbergast students of abnormal psychology again and again in the years ahead, but his behavior in the offices of the New York Title & Mortgage Co. in 1924 was out of the ordinary only in that he dressed excessively well, spoke in an accent that vaguely suggested a Continental background, and was in the habit of showering newly hired stenographers with rich gifts, such as orchids and imported bonbons, and asking nothing of them in return except their astonished gasps. Siegel accepted the offer of the lift to Lakewood, and Weyman said he would pick him up the next morning in front of the Hotel Commodore, on Forty-second Street.

When Weyman picked up Siegel that Sunday morning, he was not just in a car but in what Siegel remembers as something amounting to a motorcade. First, there drew up in front of the Commodore a Pierce-Arrow limousine driven by a chauffeur in livery and escorted by two uniformed policemen on motorcycles. There was no passenger in the limousine, and Siegel did not at first identify it with Weyman. Behind the limousine, however, another car drew up—a crimson Daimler roadster with a right-hand drive. Its top was down, and Siegel could see Weyman at the wheel and, beside him, an attractive young lady. Weyman hopped out, shook hands with Siegel, and introduced the young lady as his wife. "You

ride in the limo, dear," he said to her breezily, helping her out of
the Daimler and into the back seat of the Pierce-Arrow while she
nodded and smiled acquiescence. A moment later, having given an
authoritative signal to the motorcycle cops, Weyman indicated that
he and Siegel would ride in the Daimler. Siegel remembers that
Weyman politely escorted him around the front of the Daimler
and opened the door for him. Then Weyman got behind the
wheel and waved to the chauffeur of the limousine and to the police escort for the procession to start. The limousine proceeded
west on Forty-second Street at a fast pace, and when the motorcycle cops turned on their sirens the pace became even faster.
Siegel asked Weyman how he happened to be able to provide the
police escort, and Weyman shrugged and said, in an offhand fashion, "I have considerable political influence. I'm a Special Deputy
Attorney General of the State of New York, you know. Also, I slip
the boys a ten-spot each for their trouble." In a very short time, the
two cars arrived at the ferry landing at Forty-second Street and the
Hudson River, and were driven onto a ferry. After the two motorcycle cops had seen them safely aboard, they grinned and waved to
Weyman and cycled away, their sirens going.

"Weyman talked a blue streak as we crossed the Hudson on the
ferry," Siegel recalled in later years. "Among other things, he told
me that in the past he had worked for both the Republican and
the Democratic State Committees, and also for the local political
parties—Tammany Hall and the Republican organization. Lately,
he said, he had been able to contribute considerable sums to both
parties. He told me about the Princess Fatima incident and about
how unjust it was that he had been sent to Atlanta for impersonating a naval officer when it had been proved in court that the uniform he wore during that escapade was that of a sort of seagoing
Boy Scout organization and was perfectly genuine. We got out of
the car and walked around during the ferry trip, and at one point,
while Weyman was chatting gaily with the good-looking girl in

the limousine, I noticed that on the front of each car there was a plate, like a license plate, that said 'Special Deputy Attorney General—New York.' I asked Weyman about these plates, and he said that he had had them made himself but that he really was a Special Deputy Attorney General of the State of New York, and when we got back into the Daimler he pulled from his coat pocket a handsomely printed document with a red seal on it that certified that he had been appointed as a Special Deputy Attorney General. Some weeks after that, I had occasion to check the list of Special Deputy Attorney Generals, and found that Weyman was on the list, which consisted of a number of prominent citizens of New York, most of whose names I recognized, and all of whom were presumably lawyers. On the way to Lakewood, Weyman told me a good deal about his life, both in prison and out. What he told me I later found was true. He talked with the charm of a child and did not seem to want to hide anything. When we got to Lakewood, it was getting on toward lunchtime, and Weyman invited me to join the young lady and himself for lunch at one of the posh hotels there. I later found out that the young lady was not his wife but just one of the many good-looking girls whom Weyman was in the habit of taking along on outings of this sort but with whom, as far as I have ever been able to determine, he was on casual, rather than intimate, terms. Led by Weyman—who, incidentally, was dressed in a morning coat, striped trousers, and a top hat of the kind that folds up—the three of us swept into the hotel, where the bell-boys, the bell captain, and the clerk behind the desk seemed to leap to attention, greeting Weyman cordially and with great deference. Bellboys had followed us into the hotel with five or six handsome pieces of luggage. The desk clerk handed Weyman two keys, and Weyman gave one to the young lady, remarking that she would no doubt wish to go to her room and freshen up. A bellboy took the key from her, and when she indicated one rather small suitcase, he picked it up and preceded her to the elevator. 'I must change for luncheon,' Weyman said to me as a couple of other bellboys picked up the four or five pieces of luggage remaining. 'Why don't you come along up to my suite while I change?' I went along with him to a handsomely furnished two-room suite upstairs. The bellboys put all the luggage in the bedroom, and Weyman, after they had gone, talked for a few minutes in a charming way and then left me alone in the living room, saying that he would change his clothes now but that it would take him only a few minutes. I sat there and thought about Weyman and felt as if I were taking part in a pleasant dream of some kind. He reappeared in a short time dressed in a very natty outfit, which I guess he felt was more suitable for the country than his morning coat and striped trousers. He had on a pair of expensive looking tan Oxfords, beige stockings, heather-colored tweed plus fours and a matching Norfolk jacket, a white shirt, and a brightly striped tie of British regimental design, which clashed somewhat with the tweed of his Norfolk jacket and plus fours. We went down to the lobby, where the young lady was waiting for us. She had on the same attractive but ordinary street dress that she had had on before. With Weyman in the lead, we went into the ornate dining room and were obsequiously shown to a table in a bay window by the headwaiter. And so it went. Weyman remarked that they were staying overnight and that after lunch he was going to show the young lady around the golf course. 'She has never seen a golf links,' he explained gravely. 'I have not played golf myself since I went to Atlanta.' To the young lady, he said, 'We'll just walk around the eighteen holes, and when we get back you can have a little rest in your room while I change for tea.' I explained to Weyman that my parents lived only a short distance from the hotel, and said I would walk to their house after lunch. He offered to drive me back to New York on Monday morning, but I told him I must return that night. I never did find out what kind of clothes he wore that afternoon for tea or what kind he wore for dinner, but I am sure that they were spectacular." Weyman continued to work for the New York Title & Mortgage Co. for a good many months, but Siegel left in order to go into private practice as a criminal attorney in Manhattan. Weyman kept in touch with Siegel. They had a meal together once in a while, and Siegel represented him several times in minor cases.

It was in August and September of 1926 that Weyman engaged in one of his greatest impostures—in fact, in a double imposture—not only posing as Pola Negri's physician during the New York portion of the sensational funeral of Rudolph Valentino but also posing as a public-relations man representing George Ullman, who had been Valentino's manager in Hollywood. As the latter, Weyman pretty much ran the funeral, handing out statements every day to the newspapers, which the newspapers solemnly printed. Not until the final day of the extended lying-in-state at Campbell's Funeral Church, on Broadway at Sixty-sixth Street, did the newspapers—it was never made clear just how—discover that the man they had publicized as Pola Negri's physician and as the public-relations man in charge of the funeral was the same old Stephen Jacob Weinberg whom they had so frequently exposed as an impostor in past years.

Just as he had blown into the old Waldorf-Astoria Hotel a few years earlier to give succor to Princess Fatima of Afghanistan, Weyman blew into the Hotel Ambassador, carrying his little black bag, to give succor to Miss Negri soon after she had established herself there in a four-room suite. In Hollywood she had told reporters that she was "out of her mind with grief" over the death of Valentino, to whom, she said, she was "formally though secretly" engaged. To her personal maid, who answered the door of the suite when Weyman knocked, he introduced himself as Dr. Sterling Wyman, a New York physician who had been a close friend of Valentino's. The maid showed him into the parlor, disappeared for a few moments, and then escorted him into one of the three bedrooms, where Miss Negri was sitting up under the counterpane and dabbing her lovely Polish eyes with a lace handkerchief.

"Rudy would have wanted me to take care of you, my dear," said the big little man from Brooklyn, as Miss Negri related years afterward. "You are very thoughtful," she told him, and moved over a little so Weyman could perch on the edge of her bed. Star gazed at star, and after he'd taken her pulse and given her some aspirin out of his little black bag, he talked to her soothingly. He told her he would devote all his time to watching over her during her dreadful ordeal, and, since he'd had some experience in public-relations matters, he would be glad to handle her press relations for her and to issue frequent bulletins on the state of her health. "I shall be at your service at all times, day or night," he assured her, and she recalled later that she was so impressed by him, and felt such confidence in him, that she suggested without hesitation that he make himself at home in the extra bedroom (the maid being the occupant of the other). Weyman bowed his head in gratitude and accepted the suggestion. Valentino's manager, Mr. Ullman, called on Miss Negri soon after that, was introduced to Weyman, and before he left Weyman had offered his services as public-relations man to *him*, and they had been gratefully accepted.

When the lying-in-state began the next day, Weyman not only attended Miss Negri in her suite and in a private room at the funeral parlors but also attended dozens of the tens of thousands of other mourners who surged through the streets and into Campbell's that day and for many days afterward, most of them women and adolescent girls who blubbered and occasionally swooned or became hysterical. He set up a kind of first-aid clinic in still another room at Campbell's and there dispensed comforting words and aspirin to the more aggravated cases of bereavement. He performed these services free of charge. He was busier on Broadway than any surgeon ever had been on the banks of the Marne in the preceding decade, for besides handing out bulletins on Miss Negri's health, and statements quoting Mr. Ullman on this and that, he was also giving advice and sometimes aspirin to the harried police officials and to the officials of the funeral parlors, who were feverishly trying to formulate improved methods of handling what soon became an obstreperous though grieving mob.

"Many of the strange, typical celebrities of the day," recalled Beverly Smith, later on in the *Saturday Evening Post* for which he subsequently served many years as its Washington editor, and has since retired, "got into the act with lavish manifestations of grief." Among them were Mrs. Francis Peaches Browning, whose marital adventures with "Daddy" Browning had provided a field day for the artists of the *Evening Graphic*. Also Mrs. Richard R. Whittemore, still mourning for her husband, the bandit hanged for murder after a sensational trial. Strangest of all was an earnest-looking man who, introducing himself as Dr. Sterling Wyman, Miss Negri's New York physician, bustled into the headlines as impresario of the complex funeral arrangements. He was gracious and accessible to the press. He discoursed learnedly on the details of Valentino's fatal illness. The authoritative *Times* identified him as "the author of *Wyman on Medico-legal Jurisprudence.*"

The *Times* was extremely reticent at first about making known the fact that the man whose public-relations announcements it had been printing was an impostor, and so were the other newspapers. Then, after a couple of days, the New York *World* overcame its embarrassment and decided that the double imposture was a good story. The *World* printed several articles about Weyman's past impostures and also printed an interview with him. The reason it was able to interview Weyman was that after he had been exposed, and had been repudiated by Mr. Ullman, he continued to act as Pola Negri's physician, because Miss Negri said he was the best doctor she had ever had, no matter what else he may have been. The *World* said of Weyman, "To reporters he reiterated his claims to be both a lawyer and a doctor as well as a lecturer on medical jurisprudence, but when pinned down as to where he got his degrees he would change the subject—or would wave at the reporters what he said were his rolled-up diplomas, saying that he was too busy to unroll them. He said that he was an M.D., an L.L.D., a Ph.D., and a J.D., the latter a degree that he said stood for Doctor of Jurisprudence, and that he had studied law in the afternoon and medicine at night in the early 1920's." The *World* told about the Princess Fatima imposture and about Weyman's having delivered a lecture at the Middlesex College of Medicine and Surgery, in Cambridge, Massachusetts, in 1925, posing as a member of the New York State lunacy commission. The *World* also revealed that Weyman was the owner of a Daimler, a Mercedes, and a Chandler (he had apparently shucked the Pierce-Arrow), and that each of the three cars had a siren on it and carried, in addition to its regular license plates, a Police Department plate (No. 212) that had been issued to him when Mayor John F. Hylan was the chief executive of the City of New York. By this time, Weyman must have ceased to decorate his cars with the plates stating that he was a Special Deputy Attorney General, perhaps because the Police Department licence plates were more impressive. The *World* revealed that on June 27, 1926, an eleven-year-old girl named Emily Malley, of 115 Charles Street, Manhattan, was run down by one of Weyman's cars, which was being driven at the time by Elliott Johnson, of 57 Baltic Street, Brooklyn, and that Johnson told the police he was the chauffeur for Sterling C. Weyman, the lawyer, and was let go. The *World* said that it was established at the time that the accident was not the fault of the chauffeur, and it said that Weyman sent flowers and dolls to the little girl and made such a hit with her parents that they almost appeared to be pleased that the accident had occurred.

A few days after the *World* story came out, the New York *American* printed accounts of some incidents in Weyman's past career and also noted that Warden Lewis E. Lawes, of Sing Sing, recalled that when he was warden of Elmira Reformatory he had known Weyman as an inmate. Lawes said that he had next met Weyman at Sing Sing in 1925, when Weyman was not an inmate of any institution. Weyman had called on the warden at Sing Sing and introduced himself as an advocate of prison reform, and had made an eleventh-hour attempt to save the life of one Frank Minnick, a Buffalo bandit convicted of murder, who was subsequently electrocuted on schedule. The *American* also told about the adventures of Warden Henry O. Schleth, of the Blackwell's Island prison, when Weyman was an inmate. Schleth said that while Weyman was there he had managed to obtain a writ against the warden that accused Schleth of, among other things, corruption and bad conduct. Schleth had denied the accusations, and the writ had been dismissed. Schleth also told the *American* that while Weyman was on Blackwell's Island he had managed to send out of the prison uncensored letters soliciting funds for prison reform, identifying himself in them as Lieutenant Commander Ethan Allen Weinberg, of 600 East Fifty-fifth Street. This was the address of the prison on Blackwell's Island, but to many of the recipients of the letters it apparently seemed like a fashionable address in the neighborhood of Beekman Place. Schleth said that Weyman received several hundred dollars in checks, money orders, and cash, and that he spent the cash lavishly on food and entertainment for the other inmates. According to Schleth, Weyman also somehow got hold of one of Schleth's personal checks and made it out for fifteen hundred dollars, forging the warden's name. Weyman sent the check to a young lady in Brooklyn, so that she could make a part payment on a house she wanted to buy, but Schleth's bank recognized the signature as a forgery and Schleth didn't lose any money. Schleth didn't press charges against Weyman, but he had him removed to the hospital for the criminally insane at Dannemora. "That man is a pathological liar," Schleth told the *American*. "He's dangerous to society and should receive continued custodial treatment. He possesses a splendid brain—of that there is no doubt—only it works along the wrong channels." Schleth said that at the time of his experiences with Weyman the man "looked like a sheik and was very good-looking, always dignified and affable, and always a very snappy dresser."

Next, the *Daily News* ran a series of articles by its reporter Grace Robinson about Weyman's career. Miss Robinson dug up some new facts about the big little man from Brooklyn. She discovered that it was Attorney General Albert Ottinger who had appointed Weyman a Special Deputy Attorney General, and that the appointment had been made in 1924. She also found out that during Mayor Hylan's campaign in 1921 Weyman had become acquainted with Bird S. Coler, the city's Commissioner of Public Charities, and had later told Coler that he was private secretary to Frederick A. Wallis, the city's Commissioner of Correction. Coler had been much impressed by the man, and, with Coler's approval and endorsement, Weyman had pitched in and—so Coler told Miss Robinson—done a great amount of campaigning and speechmaking and worked in other ways to elect Hylan, who was not a mayor of distinction. By September 8, 1926, Miss Robinson's articles about Weyman were being given more prominence in the *Daily News* than the Valentino story. On that day, when Valentino's body was at last laid to rest in a borrowed crypt in the Hollywood Cemetery, the *Daily News* ran its dispatch from California about this as a follow-up to Miss Robinson's final article in her series about Weyman; the Hollywood dispatch occupied a quarter of a column, compared to a column and a half for the Weyman story.

When Siegel saw the first of the photographs of Weyman in the newspapers after the Valentino imposture, he called Weyman up at his home in Brooklyn to see if he needed any help. Weyman didn't. In posing as Mr. Ullman's public-relations man, he hadn't committed any crime that the police could charge him with, and since Miss Negri refused to bring a complaint against him and had paid him no fee, the American Medical Association found that he could not be prosecuted for impersonating a physician. The newspapers continued to write about Weyman for more than a month after the entombment of Valentino. On October 30, 1926, the New York *Journal* ran the last of the year's Weyman stories. That paper persuaded Dr. A. A. Brill, a well-known psychiatrist of the era, to study all that had been revealed about Weyman's past career and to give his opinion of the man. The *Journal* quoted Dr. Brill as saying, "No man living has gotten away with the grand gesture more often than he has. In his way he is an artist. It is impossible to study his career and not take off one's hat to his persistent cleverness, audacity, and aplomb." The *Journal* also elicited an opinion of Weyman from Bernard Sandler, a prominent New York attorney who had had him as a client for a short time some years earlier. "I personally think he is suffering from a form of mild insanity," Sandler said. "He always wants to play to the grandstand and his mind is full of grandiose ideas. He's really a likable fellow with excellent manners, from a good family, and he has a wife and child." Finally, the *Journal* interviewed Weyman himself, at his home in Brooklyn, and quoted him as having said, "What is the sense in all these exposés? I wish you would let me alone. I am not doing anything wrong. Get this straight, and you may be able to understand me and my position better. I am an American boy, one hundred percent, born in Brooklyn. From my earliest days as a kid, I have been imbued with the go-gettem spirit. Now one of the first things that an ambitious lad learns is that every opportunity for increasing his fame must be taken advantage of. Take off your coat, jump right in when you see the advantageous gulf at your feet. And if the opportunities don't materialize spontaneously there is just one thing to be done and that is to create them. That's been my motto all along, and people who have made up their minds that

I'm cracked or have some sinister motive are simply deluding themselves."

In April of 1928, the newspapers again had a great deal to say about Weyman. It was in that month that the famous aviators known as the Bremen Fliers—Baron Gunther von Huenefeld, Major James Fitzmaurice, and Captain Hermann Koehl—flew the Atlantic, taking off from Ireland, and landing, a day and a half later, at Greenly Island, a barren spot off the coast of Canada. In the course of the landing, their plane was damaged, and they were stranded. The newspapers played up the flight almost as hysterically as they had played up Lindbergh's flight from New York to Paris eleven months earlier. Two famous American fliers, Floyd Bennett and Bernt Balchen, flew from Detroit to Canada with a planeload of relief supplies for the heroes. But Bennett contracted pneumonia and died on the journey. His body was returned to the United States and given a hero's funeral at Arlington National Cemetery. Soon afterward, the Bremen Fliers announced by short-wave radio from Greenly Island that they were intent upon proceeding to Washington, D.C., by whatever means of transportation they could get, in order to lay a wreath on Floyd Bennett's grave. Balchen finally brought the Bremen Fliers as far as Curtiss Field, on Long Island, where a huge crowd had gathered to meet them. To the intense disappointment of Grover Whalen, New York's eternal official greeter, the heroes announced that they were going straight to Pennsylvania Station to take a train for Washington and would not participate in the ticker-tape parade up Broadway that Mr. Whalen had arranged. "We don't want a reception now," said Baron Gunther von Huenefeld. "Before we do anything else or accept any official greeting, we shall go to Washington and bow our heads at the grave of that brave and noble gentleman, Floyd Bennett." Mr. Whalen, who had planned an official welcome for the fliers at City Hall, had to content himself with meeting them in Pennsylvania Station in the company of only a handful of local dignitaries and newspaper reporters and photographers, and even in this modest ceremony of greeting, which was held in the office of the stationmaster, William Eagan, Mr. Whalen found himself interrupted in the middle of his speech of welcome and literally shoved aside. He was interrupted and shoved aside by Weyman, who had rushed into the crowded office of the stationmaster, announced that he was Captain Stanley Wyman, of the United States Volunteer Air Service, and said that Major James J. Walker had personally assigned him the mission of welcoming the Bremen Fliers to New York. Weyman was dressed in cavalry boots, light-colored whipcord breeches, and a darker Army jacket with a captain's bars on the shoulders and with embroidered silver wings on the breast. After shouldering Mr. Whalen aside, the Captain shook hands with the fliers and made an eloquent speech of welcome while Mr. Whalen stood tongue-tied. The Captain gave the fliers various pieces of advice, and then announced that all unauthorized persons must leave the room. There were three policemen there, and they were so hypnotized by the Captain's words and manner that they helped him shoo the people he said were unauthorized from the room, among them most of the dignitaries Mr. Whalen had brought with him and all the newspaper reporters and photographers. With the help of the policemen, the Captain then escorted the fliers to their train and put them aboard. The afternoon newspapers printed photographs of the Captain—taken before the press had been banished from the stationmaster's office—along with stories of the unusual ceremonies at the station. The reporters from the afternoon newspapers had had to hurry back to their offices to write these stories, but the reporters from the morning newspapers had hung around until after the Captain put the heroes aboard the train. Some of these reporters found themselves haunted by vague memories, and when the Captain reappeared, they forthrightly accused him of being the impostor who had run the funeral of Rudolph Valentino. Weyman muttered indignantly that such accusations were irrelevant, and stalked off—evidently to a subway that would take him back to Brooklyn. In the city rooms of the morning newspapers, the photographs of Captain Stanley Wyman were compared with photographs of Dr. Sterling C. Wyman, Pola Negri's physician, and the next morning the newspapers once again exposed an imposture after it had been successfully carried out. Grover Whalen was asked to comment on the matter but declined to do so. Siegel was in touch with Weyman after this escapade, and learned that the police were ignoring the whole matter, perhaps because three of them had been instrumental in making the imposture at Pennsylvania Station the success it was. The newspapers discovered that Weyman actually was a member of the United States Volunteer Air Service—though not a captain—and that he had joined it two months before he welcomed the Bremen Fliers at Pennsylvania Station. Lowell Limpus, a reporter for the *Daily News*, then joined the organization in order to investigate it from the inside, and he found that few of the members were pilots, and that even the head of the organization, a man named Glenn Elliott, had never flown an airplane.

Weyman was by now thirty-seven years old. He had been working at legitimate jobs of various kinds and reporting regularly to the parole authorities, and continued to do so after this imposture until February of 1930. He then failed to report to the parole officers, was arrested for violation of parole, and was sent back to Sing Sing, where he stayed for a year and five months. The same thing happened in February of 1932, except that this time he spent only ten months in Sing Sing. Siegel, who had kept in touch with him, found that after serving this sentence Weyman seemed much steadier than ever before, and Weyman told him that the psychiatrist at Sing Sing had helped him a great deal. Weyman said that his manic-depressive cycles had diminished in intensity, and that although he still had high moods and low moods, he didn't seem to have the compulsion any longer to get in on great events or to pull off impostures. He managed to support himself and his wife in the early years of the Depression, and in December of 1933 he was employed by the City Home Relief Bureau, working as a private secretary to Travis H. Whitney, the Civil Works Administrator. Newspapermen recognized him as the famous impostor, and all the newspapers carried first-page stories in which his past career was summarized once more. Weyman was quoted at this time as saying, "I was not sailing under false pretenses. I used my own name. I never pretended to be anything but what I am. I got along as well as I have on my own merit." Mr. Whitney himself was quoted as having said that he was "astonished" to learn who his private secretary was, that Weyman had been most efficient and helpful, and that, whatever he had been in the past, his job with the Home Relief Bureau was not in danger. The day after this exposure, Weyman resigned from his job. Mr. Whitney accepted his resignation without comment but made public Weyman's brief letter of resignation, which read, "My association with you has been a pleasant one. It was indeed a pleasure to have worked with you. It is with regret that I take this step, but I would rather suffer and sacrifice than embarrass you in the least." In January of 1935, Weyman was picked up by police on the Bowery and charged with vagrancy. Brief paragraphs about this in the newspapers at the time described him as "penniless and very bedraggled." A city magistrate sentenced him to four months in the workhouse. After he had served his sentence, he evidently pulled himself together somehow, for Siegel found later on that he was holding various legitimate jobs and was supporting his wife and daughter. For eight years, Weyman was not arrested for violation of parole or for anything else, and nothing appeared about him in the newspapers.

Then, in the summer of 1943, when the country was at war with the Axis powers, Weyman was arrested in a midtown hotel in Manhattan by the F.B.I., on the most serious charge that had ever been brought against him. The F.B.I. announced that Weyman had been operating a school for would-be draft dodgers, and that he was "the most flagrant violator of the Selective Service law yet to turn up here." Weyman engaged Siegel to defend him, and pleaded guilty to the charge before Judge Samuel Mandlebaum in the Federal Court in Manhattan. The F.B.I. had got wind of what Weyman was doing when a man named John P. Mataritondo, of East Eighteenth Street, in Manhattan, who had been drafted and assigned to Fort Dix, New Jersey, complained to his commanding officer that he had paid Weyman several hundred dollars because Weyman had promised to teach him how to pretend to be insane, so that he would not be drafted. In time, the F.B.I. rounded up six other men of draft age who admitted that they had paid Weyman to teach them how to evade the draft by faking symptoms of insanity. After being investigated thoroughly by the probation bureau of the Federal Court, and being examined by psychiatrists at Bellevue Hospital and declared sane, Weyman appeared in court to hear his sentence. He was now fifty-three years old, and he faced possible imprisonment of thirty-five years and possible fines of seventy thousand dollars. Before he was sentenced, he was asked if he had anything to say in his own behalf. He made a plea for "one more chance" to devote his "remaining years to some good." He had admitted freely in the course of the investigation that what he had done in running the draft-dodgers' school was wrong, but he pointed out that he had taken money only from men who could not pass the Army physical examinations and therefore would not have been drafted anyway. This proved to be true. All the men rounded up by the F.B.I. had been examined by the Army and turned down on physical grounds. Mataritondo, the one man who had been drafted, was discharged from the Army a short time later on the same grounds. Weyman was sentenced to seven years' imprisonment and fined seventeen thousand five hundred dollars. The men who had paid him pleaded guilty at a separate hearing and received sentences ranging from one year to five years, the most severe sentence being handed out to a man whom the judge denounced because he had in the past received assistance from ten different city, state, and federal welfare agencies. Mataritondo, who had put the F.B.I. on Weyman's trail, was given a suspended sentence. When Weyman was sentenced, he was wearing black shoes and gray spats, a dark business suit, and a black-and-white cheeked silk necktie, and was carrying a good-looking topcoat. He was able to pay a few thousand dollars of the fine but by no means all of it. He served five years of the seven-year sentence, being released early because of good behavior, and was paroled on November 10, 1948.

It wasn't long after Weyman was free again that he began looking around for the biggest thing going on in New York. The biggest thing going on was the United Nations. Using the name that he had now been using for many years past—Stanley Clifford Weyman—he got a job with the Erwin News Service, which had an office in Washington and also an office at the U.N. For two years, Weyman worked as a reporter for the news agency and, for the same agency, acted as the master of ceremonies for a weekly radio program on Balkan and Far Eastern Affairs for Station WFDR-FM, on which he conducted interviews with dozens of diplomats from various countries who were working at the U.N., and who, as far as anybody knows, were at least as genuinely diplomats as Weyman was genuinely an expert on Balkan and Far Eastern affairs. Nobody recognized him as the famous impostor from Brooklyn. He got several raises in salary from the agency and was highly thought of by its head, Robert A. Erwin, a Washington journalist. He was also highly thought of by the diplomats he interviewed on the radio program. One of these, the U.N. representative from Thailand, was so impressed by Weyman that he recommended to his embassy in Washington that it hire him as its press officer. The offer was duly made to Weyman, and Weyman wrote a letter to the State Department asking that he be allowed to accept this job with a foreign nation. The State Department, as a matter of routine, turned the letter over to the F.B.I., requesting that the bureau determine whether the applicant was eligible to become a registered agent of a foreign government. The F.B.I. took one look in its files and told the State Department who Weyman was. The F.B.I. also told the Erwin News Service in Washington who Weyman was, and Robert Erwin wired his New York office to discharge Weyman at once. Erwin said later that he had hated to do this but could hardly have done anything else. He said Weyman had done a splendid job in every way, and had never shown any sign of being anything except a competent journalist and a talented master of ceremonies on the radio program and a knowledgeable expert on Balkan and Far Eastern affairs. Weyman again hit the front pages of the New York newspapers, and of the Washington ones as well. Siegel saw him at this time, and recalled subsequently that, as far as he could see, Weyman had entirely overcome whatever mental trouble he had suffered from in the past, and seemed to accept what had happened philosophically and without rancor. He was sixty-one years old then, and was still living with his wife in Brooklyn. He had violated no law, and was not arrested.

Weyman's final appearance in court as a defendant occurred in May of 1954, when he was sentenced in the Federal Court in Brooklyn after being found guilty on a four-count indictment charging him with making false statements to obtain loans from the Federal Housing Administration. The indictment charged that he had obtained twenty-one hundred dollars from the Nassau County National Bank of Rockville Center and six thousand dollars from the Franklin National Bank of Franklin Square, both on Long Island. In his application for the F.H.A. loans, he had said he owned property on Pacific Street, Brooklyn, and on Van Buren Avenue, East Meadow, Long Island. He was represented by Siegel, and when the trial came up, before Judge Leo F. Rayfiel, he pleaded not guilty. In the course of the trial, Siegel established that Weyman actually did own the two pieces of property, for the deeds were in his name. The prosecution, however, brought out that the only buildings on the lots were dilapidated wooden shacks, and that actually Weyman had no equity in the pieces of property, because of liens against them. Weyman was convicted and sentenced to eighteen months in the Federal Penitentiary in Atlanta. Before he was sentenced, he was asked if he had anything to say in his behalf, and he shook his head. He was dressed in a neat gray business suit. He stood with his head up, and there was an unmistakable air of dignity about him. As he was being taken out of the courtroom by two guards, he evidently said something amusing to them, for just before the door closed behind them one of them chuckled and the other smiled. Weyman himself had a thin smile on his lips, beneath his trim mustache. Before being tried, Weyman had been examined by psychiatrists appointed by the court, and they had certified that he not only was legally sane but, as far as they could tell, was without symptoms of any kind of mental illness or emotional instability. In the years that had gone by since Weyman had described himself in another court as a manic-depressive, that particular mental illness had ceased to be regarded as incurable. At the time of his last appearance in court, it was being classified as a psychotic condition that could be cured by psychoanalysis, and there had been some case histories of manic-depressives who, like Weyman, had been able, with a small amount of help from psychiatrists, to achieve sufficient insight into their condition to cure themselves.

When Weyman emerged from his last stay behind prison bars, he was in even better shape, physically and emotionally, than when he was sentenced. Siegel saw him several times. Weyman's younger brothers were all doing well, and some of them had contributed to the support of his wife while he was in prison. They continued to help him along for a while after he returned to Brooklyn from Atlanta. Weyman used some of the cash they supplied him with to go several times to Dinty Moore's, the famous New York restaurant on Forty-sixth Street just west of Broadway. He dined there alone. He told Siegel later on that he had gone to this restaurant simply because he wanted to eat some superior food after his long stay in prison. He still had good clothes to wear and still possessed his great charm, and he got well acquainted with the waiters and the captains, and one day he introduced himself—as Stanley Clifford Weyman—to Dinty Moore's daughter, who had inherited the place and was actively engaged in its operation. He told Miss Moore that he thought he could make himself useful in her restaurant as a sort of informal greeter and host, and told her he would ask for only a small salary and his meals in return for his services. Miss Moore was impressed by him, as so many other people had been over the years. She told him she would give him a trial, and he soon became a favorite of many of the regular customers, who included numerous celebrities of one kind or another, and also quite a few lawyers and judges. As far as is known, none of the judges who had sentenced him to prison in the past happened to eat at Dinty Moore's. After a few weeks, Miss Moore raised Weyman's salary. When that happened, Weyman told her in a disarming fashion that he had been in prison many times and that he was the famous impostor from Brooklyn, of whom she had probably heard. She was astonished, but told him that what he had been in the past didn't make any difference to her. She told him not to reveal his true identity to the customers, because it might tend to alarm them. As Weyman went about his duties, he didn't carry a menu in his hand, nor did he take orders for food or drinks. He would say a few words to customers at the entrance and chat with them pleasantly until they were taken in charge by the headwaiter or one of the captains. He put on no airs, and he never forced himself on old customers or new ones. Frequently, customers would beckon him over to their tables after they had sat down, and engage him in conversation, because they found him modest and enjoyable to talk with and well informed on a vast variety of subjects. One of the regular customers was the editor-in-chief of a well-known national magazine, who often had lunch or dinner alone at the restaurant. He came to know Weyman well—or, at least, he came to know the Weyman of this particular phase—and used to have long conversations with him about all kinds of things. This customer said later that Weyman showed immense sensitivity and tact, seeming always to know exactly when he felt like talking and when he wished to be left to himself. People who had known Weyman in his youth and middle age and who saw him during this period noticed that he seemed to have a sense of humor— something he had never displayed before. He had not become a phrasemaker or a gagman, they explained later, but he appeared to have developed a different way of looking at life and at himself, which led him to say amusing things. In other words, it seemed that he looked at himself and at life with humor, and that he had learned that humor illuminates the truth. The editor later remarked that Weyman's sense of humor was one of the most attractive things about him. Weyman had probably always had a sense of humor, but it had been dormant for most of his adult life, because of the pressures of unresolved interior conflicts and the effects of his particular psychosis. As he freed himself from compulsions and conflicts, he also managed to set loose his sense of humor. In any event, he was clearly content, and perhaps even happy, in his senescence.

To Miss Moore's surprise, Weyman told her before opening time one morning that he wanted to give up the job at which he was obviously such a great success. He told her he had found that there was a job open as the night manager at the Dunwoodie Motel, one of several modern motels on Yonkers Avenue, in Yonkers, and that he wished to take the job, because it would be an easy one, with adequate pay. Miss Moore offered him a higher salary than he was getting, but he told her that it wasn't money he was interested in—that, actually, his salary as night manager of the motel would be less than the one she was already paying him. Miss Moore said later that Weyman had told her he enjoyed his job at the restaurant. "Then why do you want to leave?" Miss Moore said she had asked him. "I seem to require a certain amount of solitude," he replied. "I want more time to think, and with this all-night job in the motel I can sleep in the mornings and have all afternoon to take short walks around town and sit in the sun in Central Park on nice days."

Late at night on August 27, 1960, about a year after Weyman went to work at the motel, a pair of gunmen walked in and came up to the reception desk. Weyman was alone behind the desk, and the occupants of the motel were all asleep in their rooms. They were awakened by the sound of gunfire. One of them called the police, and a squad car with two patrolmen arrived in a few minutes. The patrolmen found Weyman dead. His body was not behind the reception desk but on the floor of the reception room itself; the cashbox, still locked, was on the floor behind the counter. Detectives were eventually able to reconstruct what had happened. The cashbox was normally kept on a shelf under the counter. "What the man did, evidently, was to take the cashbox from the shelf as if he were going to hand it to the holdup men," one of the detectives said later. "Then he must have thrown the cashbox over his head and onto the floor to distract them and leaped over the counter, going after the armed men barehanded. It took the agility of a young man to leap over that counter. But he must have leaped over it after he threw the cashbox over his head, because if he had simply *climbed* slowly over it, they would have shot him while he was doing it. As it was, they must have shot him just before he got to them, because his body was about seven feet beyond the counter. I've known about the man's past record for years. He did a lot of things in the course of his life, but what he did this time was brave."

A NOTE ON THE AUTHOR

ST. CLAIR MCKELWAY was born in Charlotte, NC, in 1905, and grew up in Washington, D.C. A high school dropout, he worked as an office boy at the old *Washington Times-Herald* and went on to report and edit for the *New York World*, the *New York Herald Tribune*, the *Chicago Tribune*, and the *Bangkok Daily Mail*. He eventually became a staff writer at *The New Yorker*, where he worked for over thirty years, serving as managing editor from 1936 to 1939 and leaving an indelible mark on the magazine's style. In his lifetime, his writings for *The New Yorker* were collected and expanded in four books, *Gossip: The Life and Times of Walter Winchell*, *True Tales from the Annals of Crime and Rascality*, *The Edinburgh Caper*, and *The Big Little Man from Brooklyn*. McKelway died in 1980 at the age of seventy-four.